WRISTWATCH ANNUAL 2008

THE CATALOG

of

PRODUCERS, PRICES, MODELS,

and

SPECIFICATIONS

by

PETER BRAUN

ABBEVILLE PRESS PUBLISHERS

New York   London

Hand-engraving of the butterfly bridge for the Caliber 90

The art of craft.
The craft of art.

The PanoMaticLunar XL.
Delicate filigree details, hand-engraved with artistic precision give this u
its unmistakable character. Its Caliber 90 automatic movement boas
mechanics, hand-crafted in Glashütte Original's time honored watchm
Find out more about us at www.glashuette-original.com or telephon

RGM
WATCH COMPANY

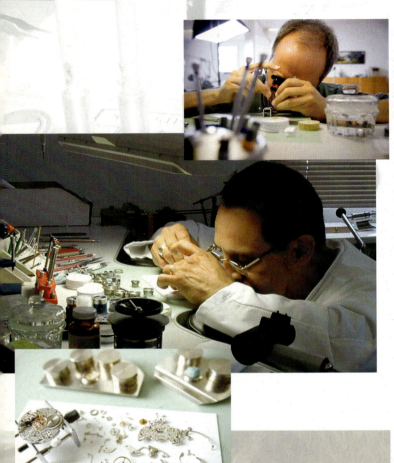

EXPERIENCED PROFESSIONALS IN WATCH REPAIR & RESTORATION.

www.RGMwatches.com
tel. 717-653-9799

Letter to Readers

Dear Readers,

The mechanical renaissance can be proclaimed officially over. After the quartz crisis almost finished off the world of non-battery-driven timepieces for good in the 1970s, mechanical watches began a surprising comeback in the mid-1980s. By the end of that decade, the mechanical renaissance was in full swing.

Now, twenty years later, there is no question in anyone's mind that mechanical watches are here to stay. However, an interesting development has begun to make itself known: technicians practicing the traditional art of watchmaking have started to search for ever more practical solutions to the age-old problems of making the mechanical watch more accurate and in need of less maintenance. Thus, it may well be said that the mechanical renaissance is over, for the era of new technologies has begun.

Some brands featured in this book have played pioneering roles in both these movements. Ulysse Nardin is widely acknowledged as helping to bring the mechanical watch back to the public eye and being one of the front-runners in the quest for new technologies and materials. And a joint venture with Sigatec, a new supplier for silicon components, will now make the industry's most talked-about technology available to any company that desires to use it. This fact alone could conceivably make the 2009 edition of *Wristwatch Annual* much different from previous issues—including this one.

As always, we need to bring the subject of retail prices to your attention. Please remember that at the time *Wristwatch Annual* goes to press, the prices we show underneath each watch—thoroughly checked and double-checked with each brand—are 100 percent correct. Because watch companies generally adjust their figures again during the year—thanks to the ever-changing price of precious metals and fluctuations in foreign currencies—the numbers we show may at some time no longer be "right on the money." Please use these numbers only as ballpark figures and make sure to talk to your local retailer for more precise pricing information.

We wish you many wonderful hours perusing these pages, which contain all the excitement inherent to the world of high-quality watchmaking.

The Blu-Tourbillon MT3 is featured on the cover of Wristwatch Annual 2008 (photo: Ralf Baumgarten).

Contents

Alpina	92
Angular Momentum	94
Anonimo	96
Arnold & Son	98
Askania	95
Audemars Piguet	100
Aviator	106
Azimuth	108
Backes & Strauss	110
Ball Watch Company	112
Baume & Mercier	114
Bell & Ross	118
Ernst Benz	120
Jochen Benzinger	124
Blancpain	126
blu-source du temps	132
Rainer Brand	125
Martin Braun	134
Breguet	136
Breitling	140
Brior	144
B.R.M	146
Carl F. Bucherer	148
Bulgari	152
Buti	156
Cartier	158
Chase-Durer	162
Chopard	164
Chronoswiss	168
Frédérique Constant	174
Corum	176
Cuervo y Sobrinos	178
Cvstos	180
Cyclos	181
De Bethune	182
De Grisogono	184
Pierre de Roche	188
DeWitt	186
Dornblüth & Sohn	189
Doxa	190
Du Bois & Fils	192
Dubey & Schaldenbrand	194
Roger Dubuis	196
Ebel	200
Eberhard & Co.	202
Edox	206
Epos	208
Louis Erard	210
Jacques Etoile	212
Fabergé	214
Ferrari	216
Fortis	218
Gérald Genta	222
Girard-Perregaux	224
Glashütte Original	230
Glycine	236
Graham	238
Greubel Forsey	240
Hamilton	242
Hanhart	244
Hautlence	241
Hermès	243
Hublot	246
IWC	250
Jacob & Co	260
Jaeger-LeCoultre	254
Jaquet Droz	262
JeanRichard	264
F.-P. Journe	266
Kobold	268
Pierre Kunz	270
Maurice Lacroix	272
Lang & Heyne	290
A. Lange & Söhne	276
Jacques Lemans	282
Limes	284
Longines	286
Giuliano Mazzuoli	291
MeisterSinger	292
Richard Mille	294
Milus	296
Montblanc	298
H. Moser & Cie	297
Mühle Glashütte	300
Franck Muller	302
Ulysse Nardin	306
Rainer Nienaber	310
Nivrel	311
Nomos	312
Omega	314
Oris	320
Panerai	324
Parmigiani	328
Patek Philippe	332
Perrelet	340
Piaget	342
Paul Picot	346
Poljot International	341
Porsche Design	350
Rado	352
RGM	354
Rolex	356
Daniel Roth	362
Scalfaro	364
Jörg Schauer	366
Schaumburg Watch	368
Alexander Shorokhoff	369
Alain Silberstein	370
Sinn	374
Sothis	378
Stowa	380
Swiss Watch International	382
TAG Heuer	384
Temption	388
Tissot	390
Tutima	392
Urwerk	404
Vacheron Constantin	396
Ventura	405
Villemont	402
Vogard	407
George J von Burg	406
Vostok-Europe	408
Wempe	410
Harry Winston	412
Dino Zei	414
Zenith	416
ETA Movements	422
Glossary	16
Cellini	38
MB&F	44
Thomas Prescher	50
HD3	56
Rodolphe	62
Romain Jerome	66
U-Boat	70
Bozeman Watch Company	76
Michel Jordi	80
Rob's Report	221
Pronunciation Guide	319
Addresses	427
Masthead	432

MASTER TOURBILLON. A reference complication merging precision and reliability. Large balance with an inertia of 11.5 mg x cm², grade 5 titanium carriage, second time-zone, bidirectional jumping date display. Mechanical automatic movement 978, made in-house (details exposed for photo).
Manufacture Jaeger-LeCoultre, Vallée de Joux, Switzerland, since 1833.
For information 1-800-JLC-TIME - www.jaeger-lecoultre.com

INTRODUCING THE RICHARD MILLE RM016
RICHARD MILLE

A RACING MACHINE ON THE WRIST

CALIBER RM 016
AUTOMATIC
DOUBLE BARREL TORQUE STABILITY
DATE DISPLAY
55 HOUR RESERVE
TRIPARTITE CASE, 30 METERS
AVAILABLE IN TITANIUM, WHITE GOLD, & RED GOLD

BEVERLY HILLS 310.271.0000
LOS ANGELES 310.470.1388
www.westimewatches.com

Limited edition 47.5mm World Timer Tourbillon
Understated sophistication embraces 13 cities. A world first.

Jacob & Co. Watches
48 East 57th Street, 4th Floor • New York, NY 10022 • US
Tel +1 212 888 2330 • Fax +1 212 719 0074

www.jacobandco.com

World Firsts
The World GMT (top) and the H24 Five Time Zone Automatic (bottom). Limited editions merging time zone technology with sophisticated movements.

JACOB & CO.

URWERK presents
The 201 AND
ITS REVOLVING SATELLITE
COMPLICATION

A NEW PATH
IN HAUTE HORLOGERIE

URWERK has its origins in the town of Ur of the Chaldees, Abraham's city in Mesopotamia. In 6000 BC, its inhabitants, the Sumerians, first observed the concurrence of the heavenly bodies with the seasons, and developed the first measurements of time. Our work is a tribute to this past so much linked up with our present. We invite you to enter with us the circle of time.

*also available in platinum and white gold

URWERK®
GENEVE

WWW.URWERK.COM

Westime
BEVERLY HILLS 310.271.0000
LOS ANGELES 310.470.1388
www.westimewatches.com

HAUTLENCE HL^{S}08
Ti2 Sandblasted base with DLC treatment
Screws: Ti5
Jumping hours
Retrograde minutes
Waterproof 5 atm

Glossary

Annual calendar

The automatic allowances for the different lengths of each month of a year in the calendar module of a watch. This type of watch usually shows the month and date, and sometimes the day of the week (like this one by Patek Philippe) and the phases of the moon.

Antimagnetic

Mechanical movements are easily influenced by the magnetic fields often found in common everyday places. This problem is generally solved by the use of anti- or nonmagnetic components in the movement. Some companies, such as Sinn, IWC, and Bell & Ross, take things a step further and encase movements in antimagnetic cores such as the one shown here from Sinn's Model 756, the Duograph. Here the inner core is easily recognizable, as are the dial, movement holder ring, and second case back. These precautions make the watch antimagnetic to 80,000 a/M—far exceeding the norms demanded by DIN and ISO.

Antireflection

A film created by steaming the crystal to eliminate light reflection and improve legibility. Antireflection functions best when applied to both sides of the crystal, but because it scratches, some manufacturers prefer to have it only on the interior of the crystal. It is mainly used on synthetic sapphire crystals. Dubey & Schaldenbrand applies antireflection on both sides for all of the company's wristwatches such as this Aquadyn model.

Automatic winding

A rotating weight, set into motion by moving the wrist, winds the spring barrel via the gear train of a mechanical watch movement. Automatic winding was invented during the pocket watch era in 1770 by Abraham-Louis Perrelet, who created a watch with a weight swinging back and forth (that of a pocket watch usually makes vertical movements contrary to a wristwatch). The first automatic-winding wristwatches, invented by John Harwood in the 1920s, utilized so-called hammer winding, whereby a weight swung in an arc between two banking pins. The breakthrough automatic winding movement via rotor began with the ball bearing Eterna-Matic in the late 1940s, and the technology hasn't changed fundamentally since. Today we speak of unidirectional winding and bi-directionally winding rotors, depending on the type of gear train used.

IWC's automatic Caliber 50611

Balance

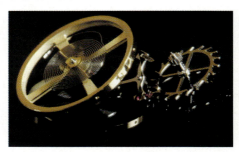

The beating heart of a mechanical watch movement is the balance. Fed by the energy of the mainspring, a tirelessly oscillating little wheel, just a few millimeters in diameter and possessing a spiral-shaped balance spring, sets the rhythm for the escape wheel and pallets with its vibration frequency. Today the balance is usually made of one piece of antimagnetic glucydur, an alloy that expands very little when exposed to heat.

Bar or cock

A metal plate fastened to the base plate at one point, leaving room for a gear wheel or pinion. The balance is usually attached to a bar called the balance cock. Glashütte tradition dictates that the balance cock be decoratively engraved by hand like this one by Glashütte Original.

FRANCK MULLER
GENEVE

Master of complications

8880 AETERNITAS 5
GRAND TOURBILLON WITH ETERNAL CALENDAR
SPLIT-SECONDS CHRONOGRAPH
8 DAY POWER RESERVE
CINTRÉE CURVEX SHAPED AUTOMATIC MOVEMENT
WITH MICRO-ROTOR PLACED AT 6 O'CLOCK
HAND ENGRAVED MOVEMENT

FOR THE NAME AND LOCATION OF AN AUTHORIZED **FRANCK MULLER USA** AGENT, PLEASE CALL 212-463-8898 OR VISIT OUR WEBSITE AT WWW.FRANCKMULLERUSA.COM

Glossary

Beveling

To uniformly file down the sharp edges of a plate, bridge, or bar and give it a high polish. Edges are usually beveled at a 45° angle. As the picture shows, this is painstaking work that needs the skilled hands and eyes of an experienced watchmaker.

Blued screw

Traditional Swiss and Glashütte watchmaking dictates that a movement should contain blued screws for aesthetic reasons. Polished steel screws are heated (or tempered, as it is known in watch parlance) to 290°C. This process relaxes the steel, turning it a deep blue in color. Only a few *manufactures* still put the tempering process into effect with actual heat, others preferring the chemically induced version that assures an even color every time. Jaquet Droz and a few other brands even use blued screws as design elements on their dials.

Bridge

A metal plate fastened to the base plate at two points leaving room for a gear wheel or pinion. This vintage Favre-Leuba movement illustrates the point with three individual bridges.

Caliber

A term, similar to type or model, that refers to different watch movements. Pictured here is Heuer's Caliber 11, the legendary automatic chronograph caliber from 1969. This movement was a coproduction jointly researched and developed for four years by Heuer-Leonidas, Breitling, and Hamilton-Büren. Each company gave the movement a different name after serial production began.

Carbon fiber

A composite material made with carbon filament threads. Carbon fiber is composed of filaments a mere one to two millimeters in diameter. The filament itself comprises several thousand seven-micron carbon fibers held together by resin. The arrangement of the filaments determines the quality of a component, making each unique. The atomic structure of carbon fiber is similar to that of graphite, consisting of sheets of carbon atoms arranged in a regular hexagonal pattern. Carbon fiber is currently being used as a material for dials, cases, and even movement components thanks to its lightness, resilience, and hardness.

Ceramic

An inorganic, nonmetallic material formed by the action of heat and practically unscratchable. Pioneered by Rado, ceramic is a high-tech material generally made from aluminum and zirconium oxide. Today, it is generally used for cases and bezels and now comes in many colors.

Chronograph

From the Greek *chronos* (time) and *graphein* (to write). Originally a chronograph literally wrote, inscribing the time elapsed on a piece of paper with the help of a pencil attached to a type of hand. Today this term is used for watches that show not only the time of day, but also certain time intervals via independent hands that may be started or stopped at will. So-called stopwatches differ from chronographs because they do not show the time of day. This exploded illustration shows the complexity of a Breitling chronograph.

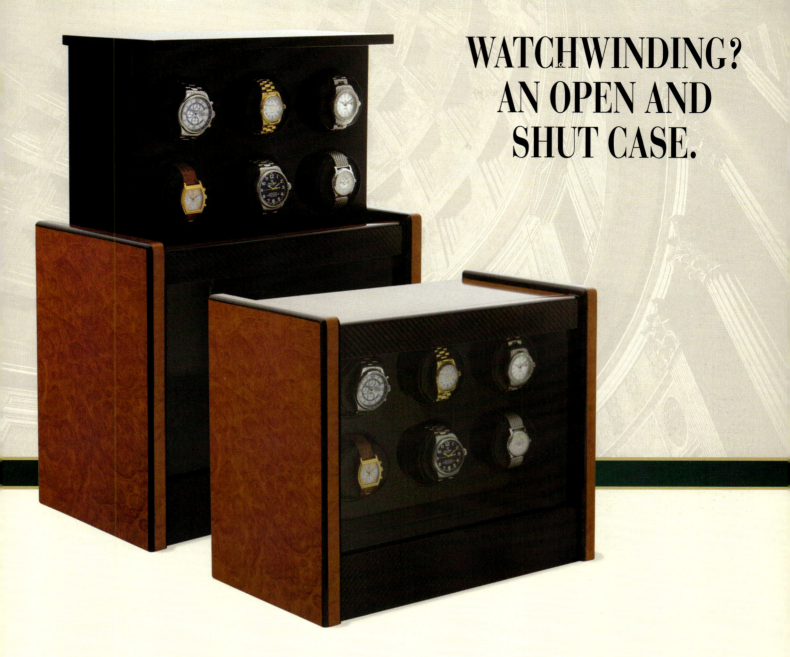

WATCHWINDING? AN OPEN AND SHUT CASE.

the AVANTI 6 WATCHWINDER

Six individually powered winding stations keep your automatic watches fully wound and ready to wear. Each station is microprocessor controlled and easily programmed to meet the winding requirements of your particular watch. There is absolutely no risk of overwinding. The unique case design provides lockable security and easy viewing in the shut position behind a beveled glass window. A simple touch on top of the cabinet releases the complete watchwinder chassis which "floats" upward to the open position allowing for quick and easy mounting of the watches. Choose the elegant Madrona Burl finish (shown) or dramatic Ebony Macassar. Both cases feature durable high gloss finishes with real Carbon Fiber trim panels.

GOING ON A TRIP?
Slip your mounted watch in the Voyager leather case with its own powered mini-winder. You can set it up wherever you are.

ORBITA WATCHWINDERS

Made and Serviced in the USA by Orbita Corporation
1205 Culbreth Drive, Wilmington, NC 28405
Call Toll Free: 800-800-4436 or visit www.orbita.com

© 2007 Orbita Corporation

Glossary

Chronometer

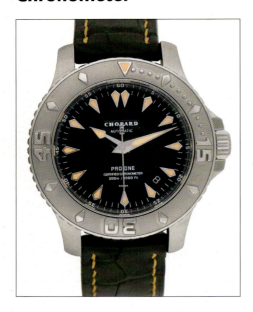

Literally, "measurer of time." As the term is used today, a chronometer denotes an especially accurate watch (one with a deviation of no more than 5 seconds a day for mechanical movements). Chronometers are usually supplied with an official certificate from an independent testing office such as the C.O.S.C. The largest producer of chronometers in 2004 was Rolex with 628,556 officially certified movements. Chopard came in fifth with more than 11,000 certified L.U.C. mechanisms like the 4.96 in the Pro One model shown here.

Column wheel

The component used to control chronograph functions within a true chronograph movement. The presence of a column wheel indicates that the chronograph is fully integrated into the movement. In the modern era, modules are generally used that are attached to a base caliber movement. This particular column wheel is made of blued steel.

Constant force mechanism

Sometimes called a constant force escapement, it isn't really: in most cases this mechanism is "simply" an initial tension spring. It is also known in English by part of its French name, the *remontoir*, which actually means "winding mechanism." In French it would be called the *remontoir d'égalité*, while in German it's the *Nachspannwerk*. This mechanism regulates and portions the energy that is passed on through the escapement, making the rate as even and precise as possible. Shown here is the constant force escapement from Lange & Söhne's Lange 31—a mechanism that gets as close to its name as possible.

C.O.S.C.

The Contrôle Officiel Suisse de Chronométrage, the official Swiss testing office for chronometers. The C.O.S.C. is the world's largest issuer of so-called chronometer certificates, which are only otherwise given out individually by certain observatories (such as the one in Neuchâtel, Switzerland). For a fee, the C.O.S.C. tests the rate of movements that have been adjusted by watchmakers. These are usually mechanical movements, but the office also tests some high precision quartz movements. Those that meet the specifications for being a chronometer are awarded an official certificate as shown here.

Côtes de Genève

Also called *vagues de Genève* and Geneva stripes. This is a traditional Swiss surface decoration comprising an even pattern of parallel stripes, applied to flat movement components with a quickly rotating plastic or wooden peg. Glashütte watchmakers have devised their own version of *côtes de Genève* that is applied at a slightly different angle called Glashütte ribbing.

Crown

The crown is used to wind and set a watch. A few simple turns of the crown will get an automatic movement started, while a manually wound watch is completely wound by the crown. The crown is also used for the setting of

Glossary

various functions, almost always including at least the hours, minutes, seconds, and date. A screwed-down crown like the one on the TAG Heuer Aquagraph pictured here can be tightened to prevent water entering the case or any mishaps while performing extreme sports such as diving.

Equation of time

The mean time that we use to keep track of the passing of the day (24 hours evenly divided into minutes and seconds) is not equal to true solar time. The equation of time is a complication devised to show the difference between the mean time shown on one's wristwatch and the time the sun dictates.
The Équation Marchante by Blancpain very legibly shows this difference via the golden sun-tipped hand that also rotates around the dial in a manner known to watch connoisseurs as *marchant*. Other wristwatch models such as the Eos Boreas by Martin Braun display the difference on an extra scale on the dial.

Escapement

The combination of the balance, balance spring, pallets, and escape wheel, a subgroup which divides the impulses coming from the spring barrel into small, accurately portioned doses. It guarantees that the gear train runs smoothly and efficiently. The pictured escapement is one newly invented by Parmigiani Fleurier containing pallet stones of varying color, though they are generally red synthetic rubies. Here one of them is a colorless sapphire or corundum, the same geological material that ruby is made of.

Flyback chronograph

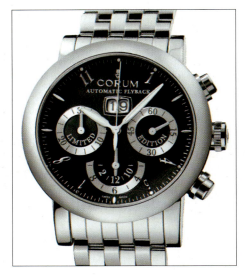

A chronograph with a special dial train switch that makes the immediate reuse of the chronograph movement possible after resetting the hands. It was developed for special timekeeping duties such as those found in aviation, which require the measurement of time intervals in quick succession. A flyback may also be called a *retour en vol*.
An elegant example of this type of chronograph is Corum's Classical Flyback Large Date shown here.

Gear train

A mechanical watch's gear train transmits energy from the mainspring to the escapement. The gear train comprises the minute wheel, the third wheel, the fourth wheel, and the escape wheel.

GMT

GMT, or Greenwich Mean Time, is based on the globe being divided into 24 time zones as established in the Meridian Conference of 1884. The zero meridian runs through the Royal Observatory in the London suburb of Greenwich (pictured). In contemporary watch terminology, GMT is often used to describe a wristwatch that displays a second time zone or a 24-hour indication.

Guilloché

A surface decoration usually applied to the dial and the rotor using a grooving tool with a sharp tip, such as a rose engine, to cut an even pattern onto a level surface. The exact adjustment of the tool for each new path is controlled by a device similar to a pantograph, and the movement of the tool can be controlled either manually or mechanically. Real *guillochis* (the correct term used by a master of guilloché) are very intricate and expensive to produce, which is why most dials decorated in this fashion are produced by stamping machines. Breguet is one of the very few companies to use real guilloché on every one of its dials.

Index

A regulating mechanism found on the balance cock and used by the watchmaker to adjust the movement's rate. The index changes the effective length of the balance spring, thus making it move more quickly or slowly. This is the standard index found on an ETA Valjoux 7750.

Jewel

Glossary

To minimize friction, the hardened steel tips of a movement's rotating gear wheels (called pinions) are lodged in synthetic rubies (fashioned as polished stones with a hole) and lubricated with a very thin layer of special oil. These synthetic rubies are produced in exactly the same way as sapphire crystal using the same material. During the pocket watch era, real rubies with hand-drilled holes were still used, but because of the high costs involved, they were only used in movements with especially quickly rotating gears. The jewel shown here on a bridge from A. Lange & Söhne's Double Split is additionally embedded in a gold chaton secured with three blued screws.

LIGA

The word *LIGA* is actually a German acronym that stands for lithography (*Lithografie*), electroplating (*Galvanisierung*), and plastic molding (*Abformung*). It is a lithographic process exposed by UV or X-ray light that literally "grows" perfect micro components made of nickel, nickel-phosphorus, or 23.5-karat gold atom by atom in a plating bath. The components need no finishing or trimming after manufacture.

Luminous substance

Tritium is a slightly radioactive material used to coat hands, numerals, and hour markers on watch dials in order to make reading the time in the dark possible. Watches bearing tritium must be marked as such, with the letter T on the dial near 6 o'clock. It has now for the most part been replaced by nonradioactive materials such as SuperLumiNova and Traser technology (as seen on this Ball timepiece, a pioneer in the technology) due to medical misgivings and expected governmental regulation of its use.

Mainspring

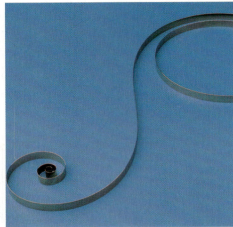

The mainspring, located in the spring barrel, stores energy when tensioned and passes it on to the escapement via the gear train as the tension relaxes. Today, mainsprings are generally made of Nivaflex, an alloy invented by Swiss engineer Max Straumann at the beginning of the 1950s. This alloy basically comprises iron, nickel, chrome, cobalt, and beryllium.

Manufacture

Modern definitions of this word are not clear-cut, but most experts agree that the term should be used for a company that manufactures at least one caliber, or extremely important parts of it such as the base plate, on premises. While ten years ago this constituted only a handful of companies in Switzerland and Germany, today's competitive market has forced a number of other creative souls to invest in developing their own movements. ETA, pictured, is without a doubt the largest *manufacture* in Switzerland. The word itself is derived from Latin (though horologists prefer to use the French variation) and means "made by hand."

Mechanical renaissance

The era following the Swiss quartz crisis of the 1970s. At that point in time, Asian quartz almost put Switzerland out of business. In the mid-1980s, the industry experienced a comeback of the high-end mechanical wristwatch, sparking the mechanical renaissance. This period can be said to have just ended, since mechanical watches are once again "mainstream."

Minute repeater

Glossary

A striking mechanism with hammers and gongs for acoustically signaling the hours, quarter hours, and minutes elapsed since noon or midnight. The wearer pushes a slide, which winds the spring. Normally a repeater uses two different gongs to signal hours (low tone), quarter hours (high and low tones in succession), and minutes (high tone). Some watches have three gongs, called a carillon. The Chronoswiss Répétition à Quarts is a prominent repeating introduction of recent years.

Perlage

Surface decoration comprising an even pattern of partially overlapping dots, applied with a quickly rotating plastic or wooden peg. Also called circular graining, this embellishment had the original use of preventing dust and dirt from gathering on the movement's plates. Today it is mainly a traditional type of decoration. Here it is found on the plates of Frédérique Constant's *manufacture* Caliber FC 910-1.

Perpetual calendar

The calendar module for this type of timepiece automatically makes allowances for the different lengths of each month as well as leap years until the next secular year (in 2100). A perpetual calendar usually shows the date, month, and four-year cycle, and may show the day of the week and moon phase as well, as does this one introduced by George J von Burg at Baselworld 2005.

Plate

A metal platform having several tiers for the gear train. The base plate of a movement usually incorporates the dial and carries the bearings for the primary pinions of the "first floor" of a gear train. The gear wheels are made complete by tightly fitting screwed-in bridges and bars on the back side of the plate. A specialty of the so-called Glashütte school, as opposed to the Swiss school, is the reverse completion of a movement not via different bridges and bars, but rather with a three-quarter plate. Glashütte Original's Caliber 65 (shown) displays a beautifully decorated three-quarter plate.

Power reserve display

A mechanical watch contains only a certain amount of power reserve. A fully wound modern automatic watch usually possesses between 36 and 42 hours of energy before it needs to be wound again. The power reserve display keeps the wearer informed about how much energy his or her watch still has in reserve, a function that is especially practical on manually wound watches with several days of possible reserve. The Nomos Tangente Power Reserve pictured here represents an especially creative way to illustrate the state of the mainspring's tension. On some German watches the power reserve is also displayed with the words "auf" and "ab."

Pulsometer

A scale on the dial, flange, or bezel that, in conjunction with the second hand, may be used to measure a pulse rate. A pulsometer is always marked with a reference number—if it is marked with *gradué pour 15 pulsations*, for example, then the wearer counts fifteen pulse beats. At the last beat, the second hand will show what the pulse rate is in beats per minute on the pulsometer scale. The scale on Sinn's World Time Chronograph (shown) is marked simply with the German world *Puls* (pulse), but the function remains the same.

For the name and location of an authorized **RODOLPHE USA** agent, please call 212-462-4685.

Glossary

Quartz

Timekeeping's technical revolution found its way to the world's wrists in the late 1960s. This was a principally Swiss invention—the first working quartz wristwatches were manufactured by Girard-Perregaux and Piaget as the result of an early joint venture within the Swiss watch industry, but Japanese firms, primarily Seiko, came to dominate the market with new technology. The quartz movement uses the famously stable vibration frequency of a quartz crystal subjected to electronic tension (usually 32,868 Hz) as its norm. The fact that a quartz-controlled second hand jumps to the beat of each second is a concession to the use of outside energy.

Retrograde display

A retrograde display shows the time linearly instead of circularly. The hand continues along an arc until it reaches the end of its scale, at which precise moment it jumps back to the beginning instantaneously. This Nienaber model not only shows the minutes in retrograde form, it is also a regulator display.

Rotor

The rotor is the component that keeps an automatic watch wound. The kinetic motion of this part, which contains a heavy metal weight around its outer edge, winds the mainspring. It can either wind unilaterally or bilaterally (to one or both sides) depending on the caliber. The rotor from this Temption timepiece belongs to an ETA Valjoux 7750.

Sapphire crystal

Synthetic sapphire crystal has become the material of choice to protect the dials of modern wristwatches. This material, known to gemologists as aluminum oxide (Al_2O_3) or corundum, can be colorless (corundum), red (ruby), blue (sapphire), or green (emerald). It is virtually scratchproof with a hardness of 10 on the Mohs scale; only a diamond is harder. Corundum is "grown" using a method invented by Auguste Victore Louis Verneuil in 1902 whereby a process that usually takes a hundred thousand years to complete is accelerated to just a few hours, hence the use of the term synthetic. The innovative Royal Blue Tourbillon by Ulysse Nardin pictured here not only features sapphire crystals on the front and back of the watch, but also actual plates made of both colorless and blue corundum within the movement.

Screw balance

Before the invention of the perfectly weighted balance using a smooth ring, balances were fitted with weighted screws to get the exact impetus desired. Today a screw balance is a subtle sign of quality in a movement due to its costly construction and assembly utilizing minuscule weighted screws.

Seal of Geneva

Glossary

Since 1886 the official seal of this canton has been awarded to Genevan watch *manufactures* who must follow a defined set of high-quality criteria that include the following: polished jewel bed drillings, jewels with olive drillings, polished winding wheels, quality balances and balance springs, steel levers and springs with beveling of 45 degrees and *côtes de Genève* decoration, and polished stems and pinions. This list is not exhaustive, but presents a clear idea of the precise elements needed for a movement to receive the sought-after seal. The pictured seal was awarded to Vacheron Constantin, a traditional Genevan *manufacture*.

Silicium/Silicon

Silicon is an element new to the watchmaking industry. Many companies prefer to call it by its Latin term, *silicium*, but there is absolutely no difference between what is currently being hailed as the next big thing in watchmaking and what Silicon Valley developed for use in electronic micro components in the 1970s. Silicium makes up 28 percent of the earth's crust, and is actually the most common element on earth after oxygen. It is currently being used in the manufacture of precision escapements and other parts, though very much still in the developmental stage.

Skeletonization

The technique of cutting a movement's components down to their weight-bearing basic substance. This is generally done by hand in painstaking hours of microscopic work with a mini handheld saw, though machines can skeletonize parts to a certain degree, such as the version of the Valjoux 7750 that was created for Chronoswiss's Opus and Pathos models. This tourbillon created by Christophe Schaffo is additionally—and masterfully—hand-engraved.

Sonnerie

A variety of minute repeater that—like a tower clock—sounds the time not at the will of the wearer, but rather automatically (*en passant*) every hour (*petite sonnerie*) or quarter hour (*grande sonnerie*). Gérald Genta built the most complicated sonnerie back in the early nineties. Shown is the latest evolution of that model from the front and back.

Split-seconds chronograph

Also known in the watch industry by its French name, the *rattrapante*. A watch with two second hands, one of which can be blocked with a special dial train lever to indicate an intermediate time while the other continues to run. When released, the split-seconds hand jumps ahead to the position of the other second hand. The PTC by Porsche Design illustrates nicely that there are two second hands for the chronograph present on the dial, one red and one white. The exploded illustration shows a rattrapante module.

DB22 POWER

DE BETHUNE

LE FUTUR. MANUFACTURÉ

The newest Automatic calibre featuring: Self-regulating double-barrel mainspring • 3rd generation patented De Bethune ultra light balance wheel • Triple «Parachute» system with titanium balance wheel bridge • A new anti-shock rotor crafted from titanium and platinum • Patented De Bethune isochronic balance spring with terminal plane curve • Power reserve indicator • 120 Hours Power reserve • Entire gear train crafted in gold • 350 feet water-resistant • 28'800 vph •

DE BETHUNE AMERICA – 580 5th Ave, LL 103, New York City, NY 100 19
FOR MORE INFORMATION: Tel. +1 212 729 7152 – Fax +1 201 2391663 – america@debethune.ch

Glossary

Spring barrel

The spring barrel contains the mainspring. It turns freely on an arbor, pulled along by the toothed wheel generally doubling as its lid. This wheel interacts with the first pinion of the movement's gear train. Some movements contain two or more spring barrels for added power reserve.

Swan-neck fine adjustment

A regulating instrument used by the watchmaker to adjust the movement's rate in place of an index and located on top of the balance cock. The swan neck is especially prevalent in fine Swiss and Glashütte watchmaking. Glashütte Original has even invented a duplex version of the swan neck, and Mühle Glashütte has varied the theme with its woodpecker's neck. The swan neck shown here comes from Lang & Heyne's Moritz model.

Tachymeter

A scale on the dial, flange, or bezel of a chronograph that, in conjunction with the second hand, gives the speed of a moving object. A tachymeter takes a value determined in less than a minute and converts it into miles or kilometers per hour. For example, a wearer could measure the time it takes a car to pass between two mile markers on the highway. When the car passes the marker, the second hand will be pointing to the car's speed in miles per hour on the tachymetric scale.

Tourbillon

A technically demanding device invented by Abraham-Louis Breguet in 1801 to compensate for the interference of gravity on the balance of a pocket watch, thus improving its rate. In a tourbillon (from the French word for whirlwind), the entire escapement is mounted on an epicyclic train in a "cage" and rotated completely on its axis over regular periods of time, usually once a minute. Though as good as moot in a wristwatch, this superb horological highlight is seen as a sign of technological know-how in the modern era. Due to the current trend toward this complication in *haute horlogerie*, watchmakers are now introducing creative variations on the theme such as the Gyrotourbillon I by Jaeger-LeCoultre pictured here.

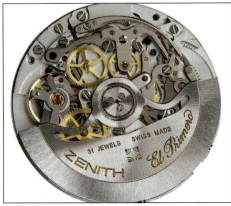

Vibration frequency (vph)

The ring-shaped balance swings around its own axis and acts as the ruling organ of the movement's escapement. Its amplitude (normally about 300 degrees) is restricted by the very thin balance spring, which also provides for the reversing of its direction of rotation. The frequency of the alternating vibrations is measured in Hertz (Hz) or in the more usual vibrations per hour (vph), which is also sometimes written as a/h, the *a* standing for the French *alternance* (change). Most of today's wristwatches tick at frequencies of 28,800 vph (4 Hz) or 21,600 vph (3 Hz). Less usual, but still found in certain models, are vibration frequencies of 18,000 vph (2.5 Hz) and 36,000 vph (5 Hz). Zenith's El Primero, introduced in 1969, was the first serial movement to beat at a frequency of 36,000 vph, and it still does to this day.

Water resistance

Water resistance is an important feature of any timepiece and is usually measured in increments of one atmosphere (atm or bar, equal to 10 meters of water pressure) or meters and is often noted on the dial or case back. Watches resistant to 100 meters are best for swimming and snorkeling. Timepieces resistant to 200 meters are good for scuba diving. To deep-sea dive there are various professional timepieces available for use in depths of 200 meters and more. The Hydromax by Bell & Ross (shown) is water-resistant to a record 11,100 meters.

COMPLICATION

F. Gonet
fabrice Gonet

VULCANIA
Gyrotourbillion
80 Hour Power Reserve
Frequency: 21'600
Rotation 1st axis: 1 min
Rotation 2nd axis: 30 sec
Jewels: 38
Limited edition consisting of
eleven timepieces in titanium and platinum

Westime
BEVERLY HILLS 310.271.0000
LOS ANGELES 310.470.1388
www.westimewatches.com

Barthelay
MONTRE D'EXCEPTION

Lulu
steel, mother of pearl with diamonds

For the name and location of an authorized
Alexis Barthelay USA agent, please call 212-633-4373.

THE NEW SWI LIMITED EDITION COLLECTION

A9240M
Limited Edition of 500
Swiss Automatic ETA 2834-2
Water Resistant to 10ATM / 330 feet
Lage Day Display and Date at 6 o'clock
Mother of Pearl Dial with 10 Top Wesselton Diamonds
Sapphire Crystal Front and Back
MSRP $2,995

A9243M
Limited Edition of 500
Swiss Automatic ETA 2824-2
Water Resistant to 10ATM /330 feet
Date Display at the 6 o'clock position
Mother of Pearl Dial with 10 Top Wesselton Diamonds
Sapphire Crystal Front and Back
MSRP $2,795

THE SWI GROUP

101 South State Road 7, Suite 201 Hollywood, FL 33023
Toll Free 1 866 746 7794 • Tel 1 954 985 3827 • Fax 1 954 985 1828 • sales@swisswatchintl.com

SWI
SWISS WATCH INTERNATIONAL
Limited Edition

A9258
Limited Edition of 500
Swiss Chronograph Automatic ETA 7750
Screw in Crown with Function Pushers
Water Resistant to 20ATM (660 feet)
Luminous Hour and Minute Hands
Sapphire Crystal
MSRP $4,995

A9259
Limited Edition of 250
Swiss Chronograph Automatic ETA 7751
Screw in Crown with Function Pushers
Water Resistant to 20ATM (660 feet)
Luminous Hour and Minute Hands
Sapphire Crystal
MSRP $5,995

THE SWI GROUP

101 South State Road 7, Suite 201 Hollywood, FL 33023
Toll Free 1 866 746 7794 • Tel 1 954 985 3827 • Fax 1 954 985 1828 • sales@swisswatchintl.com

Cellini
A RARE FIND

Cellini's second boutique on Madison Avenue was established in 1987 at the epicenter of the world's most elite shopping district.

The Adams family established a tradition of timeless taste thirty years ago when they began assembling what would become one of the world's most extensive collections of rare European timepieces and bespoke jewelry designs. Over the years, both of Cellini's New York City boutiques have earned raves and respect for their dedication to rarity and sophistication.

With the original location in the Hotel Waldorf-Astoria and a second on Madison Avenue, Cellini's superlative collection of exclusive watches continues to grow, reflecting Cellini president Leon Adams' passion for high horology. Savvy collectors from around the world make the pilgrimage to Cellini to experience the unparalleled selection of rarities and world-class personalized service. More than just a gathering place for the handiwork of today's most acclaimed watchmakers, Cellini has become an arbiter of style and an important proving ground for young watch brands.

Cellini was among the first to offer A. Lange & Söhne, Audemars Piguet, and F.P. Journe, to name but a few, before they were highly successful watch companies. "One of the things I'm most proud of," Adams says, "is that we've never been afraid to take a chance on something new or spend the time nurturing a talented watchmaker."

A rare honor, three highly reputable watch houses will commemorate Cellini's thirty-year anniversary this year. Parmigiani and Panerai will each offer limited edition collections exclusively at Cellini that feature unique executions of their popular models. Audemars Piguet, a featured brand at Cellini right from the start, has created a one-of-a-kind Grande Complication in titanium especially for the occasion. This exceptional timepiece takes every finishing detail to the extreme while combining three of the most difficult complications in watchmaking: the split-seconds chronograph, the perpetual calendar, and the minute repeater.

After spending three decades on the forefront of high horology, it's easy to see why any conversation about the world's best watch shops would be incomplete without a discussion of Cellini.

SCINTILLATING SPARKLE
Watches, however, only tell half of this story. Cellini is also one of New York City's premier jewelers, with a superb selection that ranks among the city's best. "The depth of our collection means our designs

are limited only by our imaginations," Adams says. "We can create pure simplicity with flawless diamond stud earrings, or drama with some of the world's finest colored diamonds or rarest gemstones."

To maintain the jeweler's legendary reputation for excellence, Adams personally selects all of the gemstones featured in Cellini's one-of-a-kind pieces. "I take the responsibility for maintaining our collection very seriously," he says. "Our clients expect an impeccably high standard of excellence, which is why all of Cellini's diamonds are VS1 or better."

Cellini's own willingness to take a chance has served it well for the past three decades. Watch collectors continue to be amazed by this adventurous collection of technically advanced timepieces, while others are spellbound by the bold artistry of the bejeweled objets d'art found here.

The Cellini flagship store was founded in 1977 at the Hotel Waldorf-Astoria.

With two locations in the heart of New York City, Cellini continues to build upon its reputation by offering an unparalleled collection of the world's best timepieces, rare and exotic jewelry, and unsurpassed personalized service.

Awe-inspiring natural fancy colored diamonds in platinum and 18-karat gold from Cellini's exclusive collection.

Cellini is an authorized retailer for

A. Lange & Söhne, Audemars Piguet, Baume & Mercier, Cartier, Chopard, De Bethune, DeWitt, F. P. Journe, Franck Muller, Gérald Genta, Girard-Perregaux, Guy Ellia, H. Moser & Cie., Hublot, IWC, Jaeger-LeCoultre, Jean Dunand, Panerai, Parmigiani Fleurier, Piaget, Pierre Kunz, Richard Mille, Ulysse Nardin, and Vacheron Constantin.

STORE LOCATIONS
509 Madison Avenue at 53rd Street
New York, NY 10022
212-888-0505

Hotel Waldorf-Astoria
301 Park Avenue at 50th Street
New York, NY 10022
212-751-9824

800-CELLINI
www.CelliniJewelers.com

R-50-TN-AJ

BRM North America
Call : 214 231 0144
usa@brm-manufacture.com

SP-44-BN-OR

BRM North America
Call : 214 231 0144
usa@brm-manufacture.com

Spotlight on MB&F

MB&F
Friendly Watches

Maximilian Büsser and Friends sounds more like the name of a pop group than a serious watch firm. But don't be fooled by the odd name—the reasons for it will soon become clear.

After beginning his horological journey at Jaeger-LeCoultre, Büsser became the managing director of Harry Winston Rare Timepieces at the tender age of thirty-one. He was in all reality more than just the company's leader: it was Büsser who lifted Harry Winston from a jewelry watch producer to a real contender in the arena of men's high watchmaking. This he primarily achieved by calling the exclusive Opus line to life in 2000, which featured the Winston company working together with one well-known and creative independent watchmaker per year to produce an extremely limited product the likes of which had never been seen before.

Büsser had a good nose for working with the right independents, and this talent has now helped him to found his own company, MB&F, with the help of all the "friends" he has made in watchmaking over the years. Büsser may not be a watchmaker or a designer, but he knows what is currently moving the *haute horlogerie* market, and this is what he is creating with the help of a team of talented independents and an honest transparency policy behind him.

"We are creating what has never been done," Büsser explains in his quietly self-assured manner. "This is an amazing product that embodies the shared values of exceptional mechanical horology with innovative thinking." Horological Machine Number 1 is the name of the first product to emerge, a series of thirty limited edition watches that has collectors all over the world chomping at the bit. Peter Speake-Marin is just one of the famous names who have helped create this unusually styled tourbillon featuring four spring barrels for seven days of power reserve. Büsser plans on releasing one such masterpiece each year.

As captivating as the phases of the moon. And just as precise.

The incomparable Martin Braun continues his Greek mythology-based line of heavenly complications with Selene. Named for this Greek goddess of the moon, Selene precisely displays the phases of the moon for a previously unimaginable 122 and a half years. But the complication alone was not enough for a designer of Martin Braun's brilliance. Selene is available in three stunning dial variations, including the remarkable Selene Meteorite. Fashioned from the Widmanstatten meteorites found only in Africa, it's extraordinary look comes from the combination of iron, nickel, kamazite and taenite that petrified as the meteorites traveled through space for millions of years. Perhaps it's time one landed on your wrist.

MARTIN BRAUN
1.800.794.4792

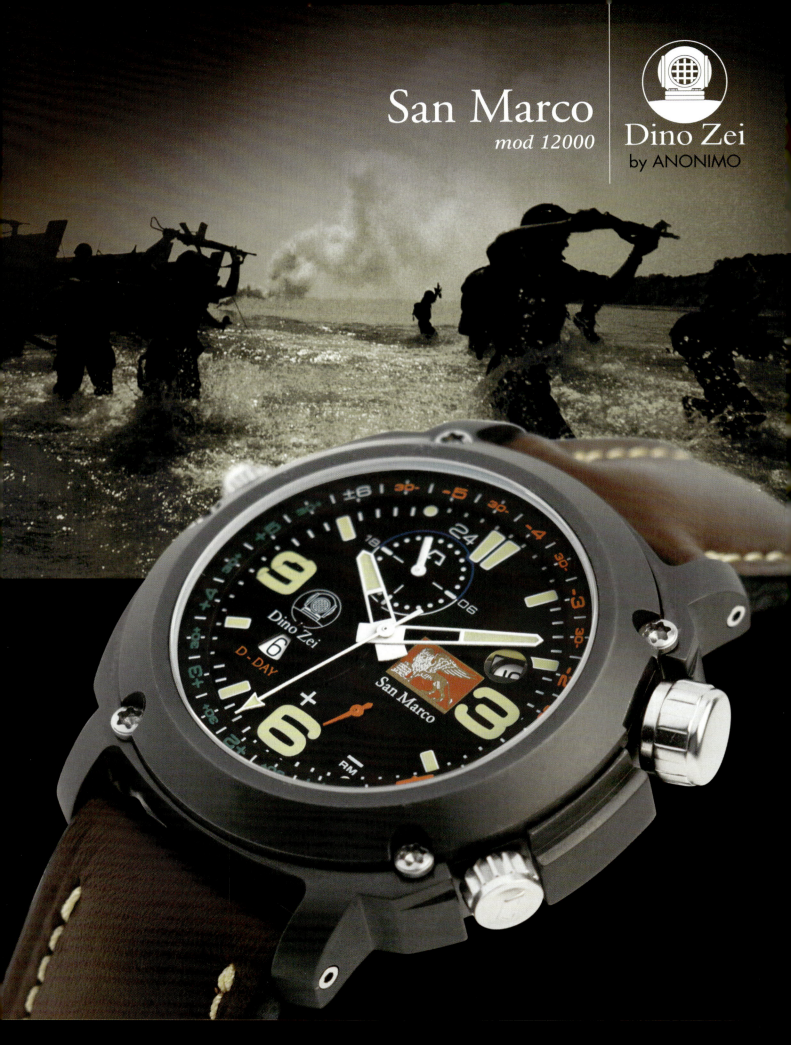

JACQUES LEMANS

Alarm-Chrono F-5007F
Alarm chronograph with tachymeter bezel • Water resistant to 10ATM (330 feet) • 40mm stainless steel case • Luminous hour and minute hands • Date display between 4 and 5 o'clock • 19mm stainless steel bracelet with push button deployant clasp.

Speed-Chrono F-5011A
Speed chronograph with tachymeter bezel • Water resistant to 10ATM (330 feet) • 42mm stainless steel case • Luminous hour and minute hands • Date display at 6 o'clock • 21mm black rubber strap with push button deployant clasp.

GMT F-5012B
Greenwich Mean Time • Water resistant to 10ATM (330 feet) • 43mm Stainless steel case • Carbon fiber dial • Luminous minute and hour hands • Date display at 3 o'clock • 21mm stainless steel bracelet with push button deployant clasp.

OFFICIAL NORTH AMERICAN JACQUES LEMANS DISTRIBUTOR
101 South State Road 7, Suite 201, Hollywood, FL 33023
toll free: 1 866 746 7794 • tel: 1 954 985 3827 • fax: 1 954 985 1828 • sales@swisswatchintl.com • www.jacqueslemans.com

The F1 FORMULA 1 device, FORMULA 1, FORMULA ONE, F1 and devices and the Sweeping Curves device are trademarks of Formula One Licensing BV, a Formula One Group Company. Licensed by Formula One Administration Limited, a Formula One Group Company. All rights reserved. Copyright 2006

Spotlight on Thomas Prescher

Thomas Prescher
Living Art

Thomas Prescher Uhren GmbH came into being in 2000 in the kitchen of the brand's namesake, located in Twann, Switzerland. This cerebral watchmaker has not yet created a "normal" wristwatch in his workshop, a place where complicated functions and original aesthetics are the order of the day. He formally started his company with a creation in the *bras en l'air style*, originally developed in the eighteenth century. This type of watch, which Prescher calls the Tempusvivendi (Latin for "living time") line, involves a centrally located person or animal with moving extremities.

"We don't just make timepieces here," he stresses. "We make art with optimal visibility, design, and taste. It is not necessarily practical, but it makes one's heart beat just a little faster. Here we are really going for the wow-effect."

In the eighteenth century, watchmakers were occupied with developing the first retrograde displays as an alternative to the "regular" round indication. Retrograde displays may be enjoying a revival in the current era, but the *montre en bras* (literally: "watch in arms") often contained another clever specialty that today's retrogrades do not usually deliver. The figures of these—and of Prescher's—timepieces were at rest, in a "nontemporal state," when not indicating the time. When a button found on the crown is pressed, the exquisitely engraved figure's arms automatically jump to show the correct current time on the retrograde arcs. As soon as the button is let go, the arms relax again to return to their original state. Or the wearer can choose to have the figures continuously show the time, as he or she pleases.

Particularly interesting is the fact that Prescher can personalize the Tempusvivendi models to fit the desires of any given customer in terms of dial materials and figure choices, be they animal or human.

In 2003, Prescher exhibited for the first time at Baselworld, showing both his double axis tourbillon pocket watch and the Tempusvivendi timepieces. The positive reactions and "critical applause" he garnered there convinced him it was the correct time to develop something he had been thinking about for a long time: the Tourbillon Trilogy.

"A tourbillon for me is not like a tourbillon for the rest of the industry today. For me it is an expression of art. When I started my career in watchmaking, the tourbillon was still the expression of the highest horological

competence," Prescher says of his predilection for the fascinating whirlwind escapements.

Prescher's Trilogy is a set of three wristwatches comprising a single, a double, and a triple axis tourbillon—all flying tourbillons with a constant force mechanism (*remontoir*), a first in the industry. The double axis example found in the set is the perfected final version of Prescher's original double axis tourbillon pocket watch. The triple axis tourbillon is a sensation, never having existed before.

Men's Collections

The word "Legend" was first used in the English language in the 14th Century and has its origins in the medieval Latin language.

A Legend is a story about mythical events whose heroes and heroines produce extraordinary results that inspire.

For over a quarter of a century the makers of Swiss Legend have created their own legendary reputation by bringing their loyal customers timepieces steeped in tradition, design, and versatility. Swiss Legend is a brand unlike any other.

It is dynamic. It is modern. It is alive.

At the very core of the Swiss Legend design philosophy rests our commitment to stylish, distinctive timepieces for men and women that harmoniously balance cutting edge style with old world precision and accuracy.

Throttle Collection
Swiss Chronograph ETA G10.211, 45mm stainless steel case with a rose or yellow gold ion plated or steel finish, carbon fiber bezel, sapphire crystal, water resistant to 10 ATM (330 feet), screw down crown, date display at 4 o'clock, 28mm stainless steel bracelet with push buttonclasp.

Atlantis 1000 Meter
Swiss Automatic ETA 2824, 48mm solid stainless steel case, unidirectional rotating bezel, sapphire crystal, water resistant to 100 ATM (3,300 feet), screw down crown, date display, 24mm stainless steel bracelet with push button deployant clasp, rubberized strap and Swiss Legend single watch winder included.

Commander Collection
Swiss Quartz Chronograph ETA G10.211, 44.5mm stainless steel case, unidirectional rotating bezel, wtaer resistant to 20 ATM (660 feet), screw down crown, date display at 4 o'clock, 21mm rubber strap with push button dual deployant clasp and also available on a bracelet.

Ladies Collections

Capri Collection
Swiss Quartz ETA 802.101, 34.5mm stainless steel case with yellow gold ion plating or stainless steel finish, bezel set with 208 round diamonds with a total 1.00 carat weight, sapphire crystal, water resistant to 10ATM (330 feet), textured mother of pearl dial in black or white and an 18mm stainless steel bracelet or genuine leather strap with push button butterfly deployant clasp.

All Swiss Legend watches are meticulously crafted to exacting standards and feature the highest quality Swiss Movements.

Beverly Hills Collection
Swiss Quartz ETA 802.101, 39mm stainless steel case with yellow gold ion plating or stainless steel finish, bezel set with 50 round cut diamonds with a total 0.88 carat weight, sapphire crystal, water resistant to 3ATM (99 feet), roman numerals at 12 and 6 o'clock with diamonds at the remaining positions, black or white mother of pearl dial, 33mm genuine leather strap with push button deployant clasp.

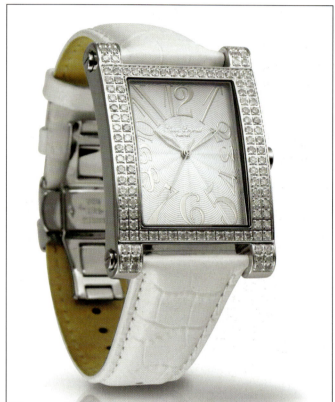

Eleganza Collection
Swiss Quartz ETA 802.111, 31mm stainless steel case with rose or yellow gold ion plating or stainless steel finish, bezel set with 116 full cut round diamonds with a total 2.64 carat weight, sapphire crystal, water resistant to 5ATM (165 feet), textured black or white dial, 22mm genuine leather strap with push button deployant clasp.

Combine this with over 2,000 combinations of styles, materials and functions, and you have a watch collection that offers unparalleled quality, variety, style and functionality.

Watches tick. Legends inspire.

101 South State Road 7, Suite 201 Hollywood, FL 33023
Toll Free 1 866 746 7794 • Tel 1 954 985 3827 • Fax 1 954 985 1828 • sales@swisswatchintl.com

HD3
The Vanguard of Tradition

Three designers with a shared passion for design, a love of liberty, and the inherent need to excel have forged a creative harmony with astounding results. Jörg Hysek, Valérie Ursenbacher, and Fabrice Gonet form the core of HD3—a collective of people inspired by the same passion resulting from fifteen years of working together. The first project to emerge from HD3 comprises one specific timepiece from each of the designers, outfitted with complicated, exclusive La Joux-Perret movements and limited to thirty-three pieces each.

Hysek is no doubt the most well-known of the trio comprising HD3. His work previous to this interesting project is well-documented in both the pen and watch industries. He is a designer whose style is both refined and technically sophisticated.

After working at Rolex for four years, Hysek founded his own design agency called Hysek Styling. He and his team created the looks for Breguet's Marine, the Kirium by TAG Heuer, Ebel's Shanta, the AD 2000 for Dunhill, and—of course—the Jörg Hysek Kilada range for Jörg Hysek's own brand, which received new ownership a couple of years ago.

Prolifically creative, Hysek uninhibitedly builds on the strong identity and immediate recognition of the products he creates. His prestigious works of art are stamped with his own brand of exclusivity and individuality; his timekeepers are designed for those sensitive to these aesthetic qualities—as evidenced by his Idalgo for HD3.

Ursenbacher, passionate about design, was attracted to the watch world from the start. She applied for a position as a designer with Hysek Styling, where it soon became clear that she was exceptionally talented: at just twenty-four years of age, she was promoted to head of the agency's creative department, becoming an associate in 2000. Watchmaking fascinates Ursenbacher because it is an art form full of constraints, where the creator is obliged to constantly search for new forms and ideas. Her Capture timepiece illustrates her way of solving this perfectly.

At the age of only seventeen, Gonet was already a design fanatic, and thus decided to search out Hysek, who became his mentor during his training years with Hysek Styling. Gonet's specific style is aggressive and athletic, inspired by mechanical engineering, particularly the technical and innovative elements of it. This is very obvious in his rectangular Raptor model for HD3.

Three minds, a symbiosis, resulting in exclusive horological creations that are in continual evolution: this is the heart of HD3. As a result of their rarity, HD3 products are coveted by collectors worldwide—each watch in the limited series of just thirty-three comes with a certificate of authenticity. Points of sale are also limited to just three per country, each rigorously selected on the basis of how they harmonize with HD3's philosophy.

The force of the details.

CHRONO 4
Exclusive patent. Revolutionary design.

Manufacture Suisse d'Horlogerie 1887-2007

EBERHARD & CO. S.A. - BIENNE - SUISSE - www.eberhard-co-watches.ch
For additional information call DOMVSHora at 800-967-4050 info@domushora.com

120 years of care and attention to every detail.
Eberhard & Co. celebrates 120 years of a SPECIAL PASSION.

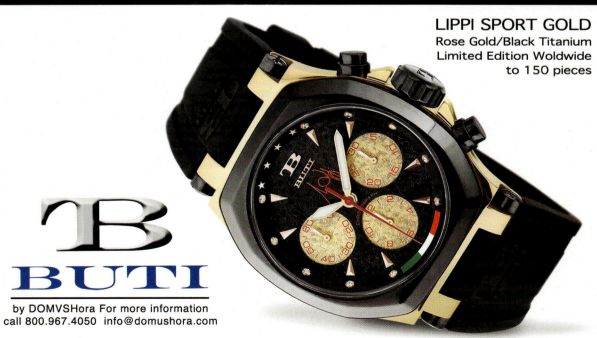

LIPPI SPORT GOLD
Rose Gold/Black Titanium
Limited Edition Woldwide
to 150 pieces

B
BUTI
by DOMVSHora For more information
call 800.967.4050 info@domushora.com

Spotlight on Rodolphe

Rodolphe
Basic Instinct

The fact that the Franck Muller group bought into Rodolphe with a 51 percent majority in 2006 has done nothing to hamper Rodolphe Cattin. In fact, it seems to have allowed him to spread his wings in a much wider and more exciting manner.
Not only has the collaboration with Watchland brought distribution advantages to the Rodolphe brand, but it has also allowed this creative designer from Les Bois, Switzerland access to the group's suppliers, both internal and external, as well as to the business acumen of group CEO Vartan Sirmakes, who works closely with Cattin in repositioning the eponymous brand.
Rodolphe's Instinct line underwent a startling transformation after the merger. While retaining its characteristic Rodolphe look, it was very apparent that these watches also had a breath of fresh air breathed into them, and Rodolphe's typical oblong case shape has become the central instrument in conveying his message. The case is now used to house several designs and functions, from the simple to the complicated, and all in a new way.
The case has also begun to mutate, certainly thanks to Sirmakes's unequaled know-how in this area as well as Watchland's exceptionally outfitted CNC workshops. The new Paninaro line, for example, features a round version of this housing that is simply dazzling. And new cases also abound in the brand's other lines as well.
This is possibly because Cattin takes a different approach to making his watches than others do. He is not a watchmaker, he is a designer. And while watchmakers usually create the technology first, Cattin is principally interested in the visuals of his timepiece. A designer of time, he treats the visible parts of the watch—case, dial, hands, crown, and strap—as elements of a mechanical sculpture. The watchmaker then has to adapt his movement to these aesthetics.
The first line to be revamped was the brand's iconic Instinct, featuring the previously mentioned oblong case. After updating the case by basically "seeing an object (in this case a tonneau watch housing) from a different perspective," as Cattin terms it, he also had the chronograph movement turned 180 degrees to match his concept. Interesting from a technical standpoint as well, the rotated mechanical chronograph movement by Dubois Dépraz is joined by a small quartz movement to show the hours and minutes in the subdial on the right side of the dial.

Sir Ranulph Fiennes
is always in the right place at the right time...

The Phantom.
Stainless steel or titanium case (PVD coated).
Waterproof to 1,000 feet. Antimagnetic.
Automatic-winding chronograph movement.
25 jewels, shock-resistant, tested for 1,000 hours.
Available factory-direct and through select retailers.
Call 1-877-SOARWAY for a free brochure.
www.KoboldWatch.com info@KoboldWatch.com

KOBOLD
Embrace Adventure

AVIATOR
Russian Chronograph

AVIATOR 3133/2704542

23 jewels,
Functions: hours, minutes, seconds,
date calendar, stop watch
with summing up action,
Shock protection,
Stainless steel case;
Mineral glass,
Water resisnant 3 ATM.
Warranty 12 months.

price $989

Détente Distribution Group
48 Main Street, 2nd Floor
Colchester, CT 06415
www.detentewatches.com
1-877-4VOSTOK (486-7865)

Spotlight on Romain Jerome

Romain Jerome
Raising the *Titanic*

New materials, complications, technologies—every high-end watch company is searching for that extra kick to set itself apart from the others.

Romain Jerome's managing director Yvan Arpa has gone to great lengths to establish a legitimate history for his new brand—3,840 meters down to the bottom of the ocean to be precise.

"It is the most luxurious thing, unattainable," Arpa says, explaining the idea behind using a piece of the actual *Titanic* in Romain Jerome's new watches. "It is like a trophy, like wearing a piece of real history on the wrist. It is something unique. In Switzerland there are more than 600 watch brands, and the main message of these 600 Swiss watch brands is tradition: 'We have been making watches for 100, 200, 300 years; that is why we know how to make watches.' We are a new brand: I don't just want to be in this mainstream; I wanted to bring something very different to the mix."

And something different is precisely what he has brought to this industry—one that sees new brands popping up every day—brands that can boast neither the controversy nor the unique quality that Romain Jerome's new Titanic DNA puts on the table. Casting around for a one-of-a-kind idea to set his brand apart from the others, Arpa chose twenty-three unusual concepts, but was fully enamored of the *Titanic* idea right from the get-go. "It must have an emotional value, a story, something behind it. And then I tried to find this piece of *Titanic*. It is really a gentleman's story because now it is forbidden; nobody can go and take pieces anymore. I found someone who had a piece from earlier, and I could buy it from him." The piece of hull that Arpa purchased weighed about one and a half kilograms and was retrieved in 1991. The wreck site of the ocean liner, located in the North Atlantic, has been protected for more than a decade now, but elements were removed on previous diving expeditions.

Once in possession of it, Arpa took his piece of *Titanic* to the Harland & Wolff shipyards in Belfast, Ireland, where the *Titanic* was originally constructed. First he had his piece tested for authenticity, then he had it smelted together with the steel that the shipyard is currently using to make its commemoration *Titanic*, a project that will be ready for public viewing on the luxury liner's hundredth anniversary in 2012. This fusion unites the authentic steel of the luxury liner, which has been resting on the ocean floor for close to a century, and that of the memorial project. The past meets the future: a myth is reborn, just as in mechanical watchmaking. The Titanic DNA timepieces literally wear their oxidized steel on their sleeves, used either as bezel, case band, or dial material. And within the depths of this historic material tick high-quality movements by La Joux-Perret (three-handed watches) or BNB (tourbillon). "The message is very positive," says Arpa. "It's like a rebirth, a tribute, a positive message, fantastic!"

michel Jordi
INNOVATION IN TIME

TWINS TITAN CHRONO
Dual time. Two manufacture movements. Fly-Back Chronograph. Big date. Annual calendar.
Limited Edition: 111 pieces. Fusion of Titanium + 18K red or white gold.

Westime
BEVERLY HILLS 310.271.0000
LOS ANGELES 310.470.1388
www.westimewatches.com

Mechanical Watches Handmade in Germany

In Berlin, life tends to run at a different pace. Fortunately, the highly accurate mechanical masterpieces by ASKANIA—currently making a comeback as part of a manufacturing tradition that stretches back over a century—run at a precise pace you can rely on. The Hauptstadtuhr, dedicated to Germany's exhilarating capital city, ranges in style from elegant to sporty, keeping you up to speed whatever the day—or night—might bring. A timepiece as versatile and fascinating as Berlin itself. www.askania-watches.com

exclusive distribution by

www.detentewatches.com

TEMPELHOF COLLECTION

Spotlight on U-Boat

U-Boat
Aggressive Dimensions in Watchmaking

In the year 1942, the Fontana workshop was poised to produce a professional timepiece for the distinguished officers of the Italian Navy's submarines (also known as U-boats). Though the project was ultimately scrapped, the distinctive drawings, color samples, and original materials were lovingly preserved for more than sixty years. In 2000, Italo Fontana, a cousin of the workshop's late founder, realized a longtime company dream with the launch of the modern U-Boat brand.

U-Boat watches, just like their original namesake, are bold, aggressive, and oversized. These timepieces embody force and style, revealing the unique personality of the man behind the revival, Italo Fontana. "It took me seven years to develop and refine the U-Boat watches. Inspired by eighteenth-century craftsmanship and intricate made-by-hand detailing, we can now produce a timepiece of rare artisanal quality that reaches toward a new dimension in watchmaking."

Character and strength are a hallmark of the U-Boat brand. All of the line's timepieces are designed with the crown on the left side of the case—a unique and unexpected element making this timepiece extremely comfortable to wear despite its extreme size.

Each of the U-Boat timepieces is powered by Swiss ETA movements, automatic and manually wound alike. All of them are housed in full-bodied, over-sized stainless steel cases ranging in size from 45 to 55 millimeters in diameter.

Red, yellow, and orange PVD-treated crystals and precious metals meld beautifully with rubber and steel details, challenging traditional design standards in horology. From the Thousands of Feet collection, with its particular dodecahedral-shaped case, to the latest Nightvision collection that allows the wearer to change out the colored crystal, each watch expresses its own singular personality.

In 2005, Italo Fontana joined forces with Mounir Moufarrige, an acclaimed tastemaker known for his singular work with Montblanc and Chloé. Together, these two are bringing U-Boat into the limelight of today's watch industry, helping to bring about a new feel for Tuscan watchmaking along with other reputable makers from this picturesque region. All of U-Boat's timepieces are designed and assembled in Italy. Found only at the most discriminating of international retailers, U-Boat watches are earning worldwide appreciation from connoisseurs of rare and beloved timepieces and can now be found at 220 select stores around the globe, thirty of which are located in the United States. The U-Boat pieces retail between $1,450 and $6,500, with prices rising along with the number of sparkling gems that may be set into these stately cases.

ROGER DUBUIS

1-800-595-5330 WWW.EXQUISITETIMEPIECES.COM
4380 GULFSHORE BOULEVARD NORTH, SUITE 800, NAPLES, FL 34103

WWW.ROGERDUBUIS.COM

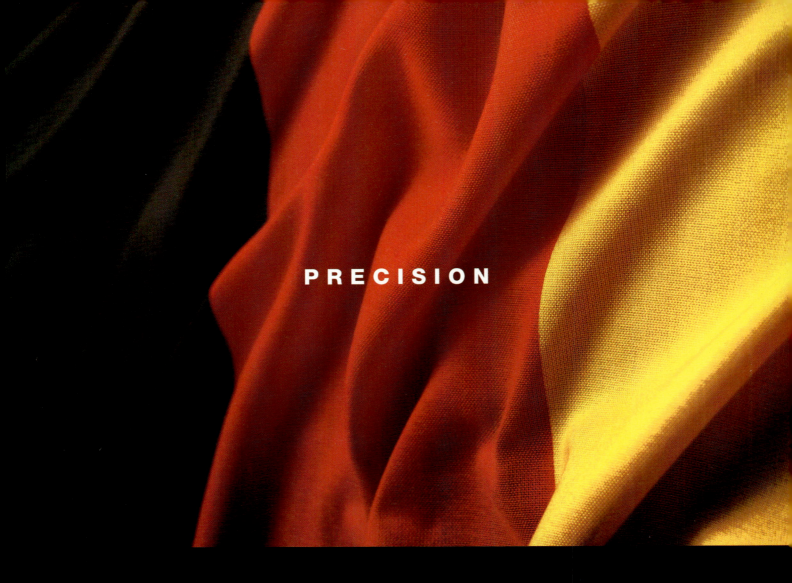

PRECISION

PRESENTING GERMANY'S FINEST WATCHMAKERS:
Sinn ~ Dornblüth & Sohn ~ Jochen Benzinger ~ Jörg Schauer ~ Nomos ~ MeisterSinger
Sothis ~ Limes ~ Mühle Glashütte ~ Schaumburg ~ Brior ~ Jacques Etoile ~ Otium ~ Temption +

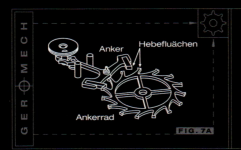

German engineers are obsessed with every detail and world renowned for state-of-the-art design and craftsmanship.

At WatchBuys, we offer the most comprehensive showcase of German mechanical timepieces in North America — all with unparalleled service and product expertise. We're dedicated to helping you find precisely what you want. Right on time.

WATCHBUYS

GERMAN MECHANICAL WATCH SPECIALISTS
watchbuys.com | 888.333.4895

Bozeman Watch Company
Montana Time

A Michigander founding a company in Montana for Swiss watches—this truly seems like a contradiction in terms. But, somehow, it works, making the Bozeman Watch Company one of just a handful in the United States producing high-end timepieces at a time when precision horological design and manufacture is little known as an American enterprise. When founder Christopher Wardle set out to create these Montana-style watches, he decided no other state of mind could be more sought-after than the rugged, yet refined, state of Montana. He also recognized that no expertise other than that found in Switzerland and Germany could be more sought-after in the world of horology. Thus, the Bozeman Watch Company set its sights on bringing the standards of global watchmaking excellence together with the spirit of the American West. With classic Swiss designs, American attitude, and Old World precision manufacturing, the Bozeman Watch Company is a unique whole created of many different parts.

The Bozeman Watch Company was founded a scant four years ago. Right from the beginning, Wardle wanted to make his company holistic in its concept, with distinct distribution and limited editions playing a huge role. Therefore, all of the watches issued until now—seven at last count—have been done so in limited editions of ten, twenty-five, fifty, or one hundred pieces. Obviously, with such low numbers, points of sale will also be automatically limited. So far, watches coming out of Bozeman, Montana, can only be purchased at the downtown Bozeman store, on the brand's website, and at select outlets such as hunting lodges that fit the concept—just going to show that searching out a limited edition watch is half the fun.

The brand's debut timepiece was the Smokejumper Chronograph, a model dedicated to the brave men and women known as smokejumpers who risk their lives fighting forest fires that ravage the region's picturesque landscape with little more than picks and shovels. The relationship between the Bozeman Watch Company and these heroic figures is so close that the Smokejumper Chronograph has even become the official timepiece of the National Smokejumper Association. It is powered by an automatic ETA Valjoux movement that has been certified as a chronometer by Switzerland's official chronometer institute, the C.O.S.C. Housed in a stately 45 mm case water-resistant to 100 meters, the Smokejumper Chronograph comes with both a stainless steel bracelet and the choice of either a brown or a black strap hand-stitched by a saddle maker in Montana. The English bridle leather these straps are made from is actually a stack of three pieces for added durability with waxed edges like tack and saddle gear.

The Bozeman Watch Company already sees some elements characteristic of the Rocky Mountain state flowing into its

rather classic watch designs, making them true American products. Look for even more interesting indigenous elements on new limited editions in the near future.

Prices range between $4,000 and $7,000.

Bell & Ross

NEW BR01 INSTRUMENT TOURBILLON

Ø 46 MM . Regulator . Power reserve: 120 hours . Trust index
Carbon fiber bridges . Titanium case with special carbon finish
Limited edition

Information and Catalog: Bell & Ross Inc. +1.888.307.7887 . e-mail: information@bellrossusa.com . www.bellross.com

A work of art that you can wear...

Pierre DeRoche introduces the world's first triple concentric chronograph indicator, counting the hours, minutes and seconds all on one subdial. The SPLITROCK also features a double glare-proof sapphire crystal, a micro-mini rotor, and a custom-made, one-of-a-kind Dubois Dépraz dual movement accented with hand-engraved Geneva stripes encased in an exquisitely polished satin-brushed surgical stainless steel case. This year only 50 watch connoisseurs worldwide can own one. The SPLITROCK is not only a beautiful timepiece, but a rare work of art.

www.pierrederoche.com   512.457.1563

PIERRE DEROCHE
VALLÉE DE JOUX

Spotlight on Michel Jordi

Michel Jordi
Spirit of Switzerland

This brand, named for its creator, was founded in 1988 in Geneva. In 1989, it literally became an overnight sensation when Jordi launched the ethnically themed and colorful Spirit of Switzerland collection. In the ensuing decade, more than half a million timepieces from this collection were sold worldwide, bringing international fame and recognition to the brand. If you followed the watch scene in the 1990s, you won't find it hard to believe that Michel Jordi enjoys 90 percent brand recognition in Switzerland.

In the late 1990s, it became clear that *haute horlogerie* was the niche that Switzerland would be serving in the wake of the mechanical renaissance after the novelty of Swatch wore off, and Jordi repositioned his brand in 2004, now aiming it at the high-end collector's market. In December of the same year, Jordi presented his first *haute horlogerie* timepiece: a unique and innovative watch named Twins consisting of two "superimposed" watches opening like a fan thanks to its ingenious, patented Twist-Lock system. The first collection, dubbed Heritage, comprised two sets of ninety-nine pieces each in rose and white gold. During this initial launch period, Michel Jordi concentrated on the Swiss market with nine exclusive dealers.

Distribution was gradually expanded internationally in the latter half of 2005. Today, the brand counts thirty exclusive points of sale worldwide in Europe, North America, and Asia. Michel Jordi's goal is to expand the brand's distribution to only fifty very exclusive dealers worldwide. Following the Heritage line, in January 2006 a new piece christened Twins Squelette was introduced to the market that was powered by a collection of rare, historical, mechanical movements no longer produced: Frédéric Piguet Caliber 71 for the upper half of the watch and a Valjoux Caliber 23 for the lower. Production of these movements ceased in 1974.

Created as a genuine artistic homage to the master watchmakers of the Vallée de Joux, these timepieces are genuine collector's items. They also perfectly complement the Twins line as well as Michel Jordi's philosophy of building a brand comprising unique timepieces for collectors and watch aficionados.

This artistic son of a watchmaker continues to add interesting new limited editions to his growing collection of fascinating *haute horlogerie*, a flying tourbillon among them.

"In a globalized world, where everything already exists, I have had the obsession to create an objet d'art, an innovative timepiece with a new function demonstrating Swiss watchmaking skills and know-how," Jordi explains. "This is an exclusive watch equipped with two fine mechanical, hand-wound movements made according to the state of the art that only the most experienced master watchmakers are able to assemble."

Florida's Leading Watch and Jewelry Gallery.

EastCoast Jewelry

Over 20 years of excellence

BOCA RATON 800 329 TIME   PALM BEACH 888 780 TIME   SUNNY ISLES BEACH 888 345 TIME
WWW.EASTCOASTJEWELRY.COM

Florida's Leading Watch and Jewelry Gallery.

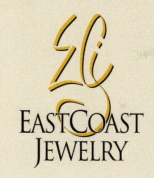

Limited Edition
50 examples

BOCA RATON 800 329 TIME   PALM BEACH 888 780 TIME   SUNNY ISLES BEACH 888 345 TIMETIME
WWW.EASTCOASTJEWELRY.COM

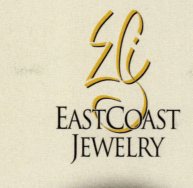

Florida's Leading Watch and Jewelry Gallery.

Limited Edition
21 examples

Glashütte
ORIGINAL
20th anniversary
LIMITED
edition

Boca Raton 800 329 TIME   Palm Beach 888 780 TIME   Sunny Isles Beach 888 345 TIME
www.EastCoastJewelry.com

Florida's Leading Watch and Jewelry Gallery.

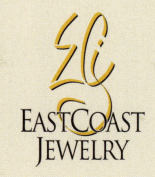

HUBLOT
GENEVE

20th anniversary
LIMITED
edition

Limited Edition
101 examples

BOCA RATON 800 329 TIME   PALM BEACH 888 780 TIME   SUNNY ISLES BEACH 888 345 TIME
www.EastCoastJewelry.com

Alpina

Alpina was purchased several years ago by Aletta and Peter Stas, the active and successful founders of Frédérique Constant. As a second brand, Alpina provides a very sensible addition to the stable with respect to its models and design, but a quick perusal of the two collections makes it easy to see that they complement each other perfectly without infringing on each other's core clientele.

Looking at the very contemporary visuals of modern-day Alpina, it is hard to believe that it is actually a brand rooted in Switzerland's extensive watchmaking history.

Watchmaker Gottlieb Hauser, hailing from Switzerland's Winterthur, discovering that a group was far more effective than an individual, founded the Swiss Watchmaker Corporation (Schweizerische Uhrmacher-Corporation) in 1883.

This group had the joint goal of purchasing watch components to get better prices and distributing finished products together as a group in order to be able to market them more successfully. The concept quickly found recognition, and within just a short time numerous watchmakers had joined the cooperative.

Together with qualified manufacturers, they began to develop their own calibers. Already in 1896 Alpina was registered as a trademark for movements and cases, and in 1901 it was introduced as a trade brand name.

From 1890, the group was headquartered in the watch metropolis of Biel. Right from the beginning, its products were outfitted only with high-quality components such as Breguet balance springs, balances fitted with gold screws, and heavy gold cases.

In order to win over some German watchmakers, the successful cooperative, now called Alpina Union Horlogère, in 1909 founded the Präcisions-Uhrenfabrik Alpina in Glashütte and from then on sustained production workshops in Geneva, Biel, Besançon, and Glashütte. After World War II the name Alpina could no longer be used in Germany by order of the Allies, so Dugena (Deutsche Uhrmacher-Genossenschaft Alpina) was created.

Alpina's current collection rides the wind created by its popular Avalanche line, and rightly so. This reasonably priced timekeeper not only has the right price to attract a broader clientele, it also sports the right look to appeal to men of practically any age thanks to dynamic design and stately case dimensions.

The Avalanche Extreme Régulateur has revealed itself as the true leader of this line, and this is no wonder: the attractive off-center positions of the dial's displays mesh extremely well with the case in its black PVD incarnation. The bezel can be purchased in any number of versions: black, rose gold plate, and even diamond-set, which sells especially well in the United States. Caliber AL-650 is based on a hand-wound ETA Unitas movement, which the factory's head watchmaker Pim Koeslag has modified to accommodate the interesting displays. Like his boss—Peter Stas—Koeslag is also a Dutchman living in Geneva. And hopefully these adaptive modifications are an inkling of what he still has to offer the Swiss watchmaking industry—as well as Alpina and sister brand Frédérique Constant—in the near future.

Alpina

Avalanche Extreme Regulator 48mm
Reference number: AL-650LBBB5BAE6
Movement: manually wound, AL Caliber 650 (base ETA Unitas 6498-1); ø 36.6 mm, height 4.5 mm; 17 jewels; 21,600 vph; finely decorated with côtes de Genève and blued screws
Functions: hours (off-center), minutes, subsidiary seconds
Case: stainless steel, ø 48 mm, height 15 mm; black PVD-coated screwed-down bezel; sapphire crystal; transparent case back; water-resistant to 10 atm
Band: rubber, buckle
Price: $1,790
Variations: black PVD-coated case

Avalanche Extreme Automatic Regulator
Reference number: AL-650LSSS3AEDC4
Movement: automatic, AL Caliber 650-1 (base ETA 2892); ø 25.6 mm, height 3.6 mm; 21 jewels; 28,800 vph; finely decorated with côtes de Genève and blued screws
Functions: hours (off-center), minutes, subsidiary seconds
Case: ceramic, ø 42 mm, height 13 mm; rose gold-plated bezel set with 48 diamonds; sapphire crystal; transparent case back; water-resistant to 20 atm
Band: rubber, buckle
Price: $4,290

Avalanche Extreme Automatic Full Black
Reference number: AL-525LBB5FBAE6
Movement: automatic, AL Caliber 525 (base ETA 2824-2); ø 25.6 mm, height 4.6 mm; 25 jewels; 28,800 vph
Functions: hours, minutes, sweep seconds; date
Case: stainless steel, black PVD-coated, ø 48 mm, height 13 mm; screwed-down bezel; sapphire crystal; screw-in crown; water-resistant to 20 atm
Band: rubber, buckle
Price: $1,690

Avalanche Extreme Automatic
Reference number: AL-525LBS5AE6
Movement: automatic, AL Caliber 525 (base ETA 2824-2); ø 25.6 mm, height 4.6 mm; 25 jewels; 28,800 vph
Functions: hours, minutes, sweep seconds; date
Case: stainless steel, ø 48 mm, height 13 mm; black PVD-coated screwed-down bezel; sapphire crystal; screw-in crown; water-resistant to 20 atm
Band: rubber, buckle
Price: $1,290

Avalanche Regulator
Reference number: AL-650LBBB4A6
Movement: manually wound, AL Caliber 650 (base ETA Unitas 6498-1); ø 36.6 mm, height 4.5 mm; 17 jewels; 21,600 vph; finely decorated with côtes de Genève and blued screws
Functions: hours (off-center), minutes, subsidiary seconds
Case: stainless steel, ø 45 mm, height 12.5 mm; sapphire crystal; transparent case back; water-resistant to 10 atm
Band: rubber, buckle
Price: $1,390
Variations: black PVD-coated case

Avalanche Extreme Regulator 48mm
Reference number: AL-650LBBB5AE4
Movement: manually wound, AL Caliber 650 (base ETA Unitas 6498-1); ø 36.6 mm, height 4.5 mm; 17 jewels; 21,600 vph; finely decorated with côtes de Genève and blued screws
Functions: hours (off-center), minutes, subsidiary seconds
Case: rose gold-plated stainless steel, ø 48 mm, height 15 mm; diamond-set bezel; sapphire crystal; transparent case back; water-resistant to 10 atm
Band: rubber, buckle
Price: $2,190
Variations: black PVD-coated case

Startimer Automatic GMT Chronograph
Reference number: AL-750LWW4R16
Movement: automatic, AL Caliber 750 (base ETA Valjoux 7750); ø 30 mm, height 7.9 mm; 25 jewels; 28,800 vph
Functions: hours, minutes, subsidiary seconds; chronograph; date; 24-hour display (second time zone)
Case: stainless steel, ø 42 mm, height 14.5 mm; bidirectionally rotating bezel under crystal with 24-hour scale; sapphire crystal; transparent case back; water-resistant to 10 atm
Band: leather, buckle
Price: $2,690

Avalanche Ladies Chronograph
Reference number: AL-350LWWW2AD6
Movement: quartz, ETA Caliber 251.471
Functions: hours, minutes, subsidiary seconds; chronograph; date
Case: stainless steel, ø 36 mm, height 12 mm; bezel set with 24 brilliant-cut diamonds; sapphire crystal; water-resistant to 10 atm
Band: rubber, buckle
Price: $2,190
Variations: without diamonds

Angular Momentum

Since its founding in 2001, Angular Momentum has specialized in the creation and manufacture of unique timekeeping works of art. This singular brand's customers are actually more interested in art and craftsmanship than complex mechanics and precision, though these days one does not actually preclude the other. Both classic and new artistic techniques are used in creating Angular Momentum's timepieces. One of this creative little company's newest techniques is *églomisé*, or the art of reverse painting. The reason for using this particular art form is simple: brand founder Martin Pauli is personally interested in it. "During and after my education in industrial art, I spent many years doing scientific painting—insects and the like," the creative entrepreneur recalls. "For many years, I have been doing paintings behind glass as a hobby, the art of which is called *églomisé*." Reverse painting is done backwards on the inside of the sapphire crystal. It is a unique, rare, and difficult art that is brand-new to the horological scene. It was only possible to introduce it here when Pauli finally tracked down the right enamels for painting sapphire crystal that also guarantee longevity and light resistance. What makes this particular technique so difficult is the sequence of paint application necessary to successfully achieve it. The resulting painting is actually seen in reverse from the front, so the paint must be applied opposite to the intended effect, requiring a great deal of imagination, patience, and skill—most especially when using an entire palette of colors, as Angular Momentum certainly does.

Availing itself of ETA movements thus far, Angular Momentum began developing its own caliber in 2006, finally introducing Caliber AM.101 in mid-2007. This 32 mm automatic movement is powered by a microrotor. Pauli's main demand on this movement, as on the watches themselves—aside from reliably keeping the time—is that it can be embellished using Pauli's array of artistic techniques. Only 100 units of Caliber AM.101 are to be released per year, and only as decorated works of art.

Reverse Painted Leopard
Reference number: 16001-D
Movement: automatic, Caliber AM.102-1 (base ETA Unitas 6498); height 4.2 mm; 21 jewels; 21,600 vph; revolving disk with index
Functions: hours, minutes
Case: stainless steel, ø 38 mm; bezel and strap lugs set with diamonds; sapphire crystal with reverse painting on inside; transparent case back; screw-in crown; water-resistant to 5 atm
Band: reptile skin, folding clasp
Price: $18,000
Variations: without diamonds; various unique reverse hand-painted motifs

Reverse Painted Summer Bouquet
Reference number: 19013
Movement: automatic, Caliber AM.102-1 (base ETA Unitas 6498); height 4.2 mm; 21 jewels; 21,600 vph; revolving disk with index
Functions: hours, minutes
Case: stainless steel, ø 38 mm; sapphire crystal with reverse painting on inside; transparent case back; screw-in crown; water-resistant to 5 atm
Band: reptile skin, folding clasp
Price: $9,260
Variations: bezel and strap lugs set with diamonds; various unique reverse hand-painted motifs

Tec & Art Happy Skull
Reference number: 11003-D
Movement: automatic, Caliber AM.102-1 (base ETA Unitas 6498); height 4.2 mm; 21 jewels; 21,600 vph; revolving disk with index
Functions: hours, minutes
Case: stainless steel, ø 38 mm; bezel and strap lugs set with diamonds; sapphire crystal; transparent case back; screw-in crown; water-resistant to 5 atm
Band: reptile skin, folding clasp
Remarks: dial set with diamonds
Price: $18,000
Variations: without diamonds; various motifs

Watch No. 1
Reference number: 17000
Movement: automatic, Caliber AM.101; ø 32 mm height 6.3 mm; 25 jewels; 28,800 vph; micro rotor; Revolving Disk with marker
Functions: hours, minutes
Case: stainless steel; sapphire crystal, partially with metal vapor; transparent case back; screw-in crown; water-resistant to 5 atm
Band: reptile skin, folding clasp
Price: $6,400

Askania

Askania was a much-praised Berlin-based instrument maker during the last German empire and the Weimar Republic, specializing in instruments as diverse as for air travel and machines for the first German cinemas. After World War II ended, things got quiet for the brand. A good 135 years after its founding, the watch brand went back to its origins, starting up production in Berlin in 2006. Now located quite close to the historical Askania courtyards of the nineteenth cen-tury, this company once again produces high-quality mechanical wristwatches.

Now Germany's capital city can also boast a manufacturer of high-quality mechanical wristwatches in Askania, and this young-old brand truly does see itself as the "capital watch," uniting aspects of historical Berlin with the modern day—not unlike the city itself, which was once divided. Old and new places in the city that provide cultural exchange are the force behind the names of Askania's watch models. The Alexanderplatz and Quadriga models created in 2006 stand for the resuscitated bond between the brand's watchmakers with its chairman of the board Leonhard Müller and the capital city.

Additionally, the brand displays its traditional ties with aviation in the models Taifun, Heinkel, and Bremen, which are oriented upon important events and people in aviation history. The air transport corps of the German ministry of defense now also counts on Askania's watchmakers: the Cougar, a reissued pilot's watch from the 1930s, now graces those pilots' wrists.

Taifun Automatic
Reference number: TAI-671
Movement: automatic, ASK 2064 (base ETA 2824); ø 25.6 mm, height 4.6 mm; 25 jewels; 28,800 vph; soft inner core magnetic field protection
Functions: hours, minutes, sweep seconds; date
Case: stainless steel, ø 42 mm, height 12 mm; sapphire crystal; screw-in crown
Band: leather, buckle
Price: $2,999
Variations: black dial; rotating bezel

Taifun Chronograph
Reference number: TAI-683
Movement: automatic, ASK 4062 (base ETA Valjoux 7750); ø 30 mm, height 7.9 mm; 25 jewels; 28,800 vph
Functions: hours, minutes, subsidiary seconds; chronograph; date
Case: stainless steel, ø 45 mm, height 14.5 mm; rotating bezel with 60-minute divisions; sapphire crystal
Band: leather, buckle
Price: $6,259

Bremen Chronograph
Reference number: BRE-722
Movement: automatic, ASK 4063 (base ETA Valjoux 7750); ø 30 mm, height 7.9 mm; 25 jewels, 28,800 vph
Functions: hours, minutes; chronograph; date
Case: stainless steel, ø 43 mm, height 14.5 mm; sapphire crystal
Band: stainless steel, folding clasp
Price: $4,729
Variations: leather strap; black dial

Heinkel Manual Wind
Reference number: HEI-730
Movement: manually wound, ASK 1064 (base ETA Unitas 6497); ø 36.6 mm, height 4.5 mm; 17 jewels; 21,600 vph; finely finished with côtes de Gèneve; blued screws
Functions: hours, minutes, subsidiary seconds
Case: stainless steel, ø 42 mm, height 10.5 mm; sapphire crystal; transparent case back
Band: leather, buckle
Price: $1,759
Variations: cream-colored dial

Anonimo

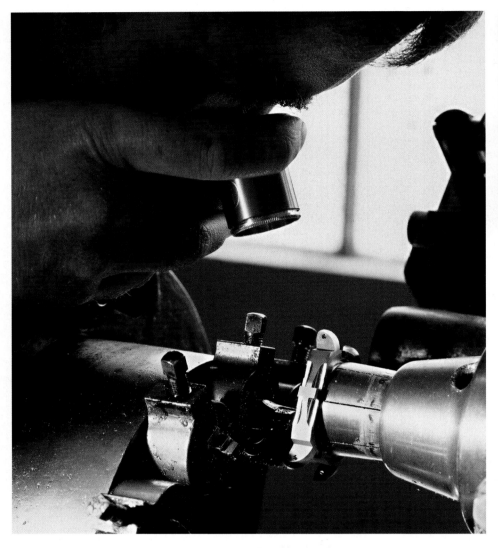

Anonimo was founded in 1997 by Italian luxury goods veteran Federico Massacesi. This was a man with ideas—and also the ambition to become a successful entrepreneur. "A watch is the best accessory a man can have," the well-dressed Massacesi simply states. "I love mechanical watches. "In that year, events conspired to bring Massacesi into this industry. Officine Panerai, which had been waving the flag of Florentine watchmaking most consistently at the time, was bought by the Vendôme Group (later integrated into the Richemont Group), and its production was moved to Switzerland to take advantage of combined resources and synergies.

A great situation for Panerai, but not such a good one for the craftsmen left behind in Florence who had spent years perfecting their handmade crafts for Panerai's distinctive look. It was just then that some friends told Massacesi about the situation. The idea man saw a distinct opportunity and jumped in with both feet. "It's hard to get started in the watch business by yourself," the Italian explains. "It's like a club, and it's all about who you know."

Thanks to his friends, Massacesi knew the right people from the start, craftsmen that Panerai had also depended on for years. "At the time, I didn't realize I was saving such a big tradition," Massacesi admits. "I loved watches and I wanted to be an entrepreneur. I wanted the challenge of making something amazing." His real motivation for striking out on his own was to be able to do business in a different way, with a "targeted objective," as he puts it.

This he has without a doubt achieved. His whole production team now comprises craftsmen and specialists located throughout Tuscany in their original workshops. And the way Massacesi interacts with the personnel found in his Florence head office makes the atmosphere more like that of a family than anything else—something that suits Massacesi just fine. "The real privilege is working with people you like," he explains.

He named his company Anonimo, "anonymous" in Italian, as part of his philosophy to make sure that the watches are not about a brand name, but about the individual who wears them. "They are a testimony to and an expression of the wearer's personality," the Florentine asserts.

This personality starts for Anonimo with its unique cases made by a remarkable father-and-son team that has developed an innovative way of scooping out metal to form a case. Like Massacesi, they believe that it is best to leave the metal's molecules as nature intended. Thus, these case blanks are not stamped or heated as conventional case making processes would dictate. These inventive Tuscans have developed a process over the years utilizing a machine that literally carves out the round case, "scooping" the excess metal away.

"We are always in search of excellence," Massacesi proclaims. "We are curious, and we are skilled. This is our DNA. Swiss movements with Italian case manufacture is a typical combination, and we want to be the best at it."

Anonimo

D-Date II
Reference number: 2026
Movement: automatic, ETA Caliber 2834-2, modified; ø 29.4 mm, height 5.05 mm; 25 jewels; 28,800 vph; power reserve 40 hours; rhodium-plated soigné finish, exclusive rotor
Functions: hours, minutes, sweep seconds; date, day
Case: stainless steel, 42 x 51.4 mm; height 14.8 mm; 18-karat gold bezel; sapphire crystal; screwed-down case back; screw-in crown; water-resistant to 50 atm
Band: Kodiak calfskin leather, gold buckle
Remarks: manual helium expulsion valve
Price: $5,400

Polluce Bronze
Reference number: 2003
Movement: automatic, Anonimo Caliber 01.0 (base Sellita SW200); ø 26 mm, height 4.75 mm; 21 jewels; 28,800 vph; power reserve 40 hours; colimaçon finish, exclusive rotor
Functions: hours, minutes, sweep seconds; date
Case: stainless steel, ø 42 mm; height 14.8 mm; extra-thick sapphire crystal (4 mm); screwed-down case back; screw-in crown; water-resistant to 120 atm
Band: Kodiak calfskin leather, buckle
Remarks: automatic helium expulsion valve
Price: $3,950

Cronoscopio Mark II
Reference number: 2018
Movement: automatic, Anonimo Caliber 01.0 (base Sellita SW200); ø 26 mm, height 4.75 mm; 21 jewels; 28,800 vph; power reserve 40 hours; colimaçon finish
Functions: hours, minutes; chronograph; date, weekday
Case: stainless steel, ø 43.4 mm; height 16.25 mm; sapphire crystal; screwed-down exhibition case back; screw-in crown; water-resistant to 20 atm
Band: Kodiak calfskin leather, buckle
Remarks: telemeter scale to 20 meters
Price: $4,400

Militare Crono Flyback
Reference number: 2016
Movement: automatic, Dubois-Dépraz Caliber 2035 (base ETA 2892-A2); ø 30 mm, height 6.65 mm; 47 jewels; 28,800 vph; power reserve 40 hours; colimaçon finish
Functions: hours, minutes, subsidiary seconds; date; flyback chronograph
Case: stainless steel, ø 43.4 mm; height 15.10 mm; stainless steel, screw-locked bezel; sapphire crystal; transparent case back; water-resistant to 12 atm
Band: Kodiak calfskin leather, buckle
Remarks: patented crown vanishing locking device on left side of case
Price: $5,400

Professionale Crono
Reference number: 6002
Movement: automatic, Dubois Dépraz Caliber 2038 (base ETA 2892-A2); ø 30 mm, height 6.65 mm; 47 jewels; 28,800 vph; power reserve 40 hours; colimaçon finish
Functions: hours, minutes, subsidiary seconds; date; chronograph
Case: stainless steel, ø 46.4 mm; height 15 mm; stainless steel U-Lock bezel; sapphire crystal; screwed-down U-Lock case back; screw-in buttons; screw-in crown with red warning signal; water-resistant to 120 atm
Band: Kodiak calfskin leather, buckle
Remarks: automatic helium expulsion valve; limited edition of 299 pieces
Price: $9,550

Zulu Time
Reference number: 2014
Movement: automatic, Soprod Caliber 9035 (base ETA 2892-A2); ø 25.6 mm, height 5.10 mm; 28 jewels; 28,800 vph; power reserve 42 hours; Soigné finish
Functions: hours, minutes, sweep seconds; date; 24-hour indication (second time zone); power reserve indication
Case: Ox-Pro treated stainless steel, ø 43.4 mm; height 14.75 mm; domed sapphire crystal; screwed-down sapphire crystal case back; crown vanishing locking device; water-resistant to 120 atm
Band: Kodiak calfskin leather, buckle
Price: $4,600

TP Racing
Reference number: 7000
Movement: automatic, ETA Valjoux Caliber 7750; ø 30 mm, height 7.9 mm; 25 jewels; 28,800 vph
Functions: hours, minutes, subsidiary seconds; chronograph; regatta countdown scale
Case: titanium, ø 46 mm; height 19 mm; sapphire crystal; monocoque case construction with no separate case back; water-resistant to 15 atm
Band: Kodiak calfskin leather, buckle
Price: $7,950

Militare Automatico
Reference number: 2010
Movement: automatic, Anonimo Caliber 03.1 (base ETA Valjoux 7750); ø 30 mm, height 7.9 mm; 25 jewels; 28,800 vph; colimaçon finish
Functions: hours, minutes, subsidiary seconds; date; chronograph
Case: Ox-Pro blackened stainless steel, ø 43.4 mm; height 14.4 mm; stainless steel U-Lock bezel; sapphire crystal; screwed-down U-Lock case back; water-resistant to 12 atm
Band: Dinex synthetic, buckle
Price: $3,950
Variations: satin-finished stainless steel; black dial

Arnold & Son

The Swiss watch group The British Masters has resuscitated one of the greatest names in horology with Arnold & Son. The Englishman John Arnold was a contemporary of Abraham-Louis Breguet, the two sharing time that is documented by a lively correspondence. They were also united by a tourbillon that Breguet would present to the late master watchmaker's son: Breguet had mounted his first functioning tourbillon onto a chronometer made by John Arnold and had the following phrase engraved onto its movement: *This combines the first Breguet tourbillon escapement with one of Arnold's earliest movements. It is presented to Arnold's son by Breguet as a tribute to the memory of his beloved father in the year 1808.*

Arnold had a special place among the British watchmakers of his time, for he produced his chronometers on an almost industrial basis, developing standards and hiring numerous other watchmakers During his lifetime, he is said to have manufactured something like 5,000 marine chronometers, selling them at reasonable prices to the British Royal Navy and the West Indies merchant fleet. Arnold chronometers were included in the traveling trunks of great discoverers such as Sir John Franklin, Captain Phipps, Sir Ernest Shackleton, Captain Cook, George Vancouver, Captain W. R. Broughton, Matthew Flinders, George Holbrook, and Dr. Livingstone.

The *manufacture* was known as Arnold & Son from 1787, after John Arnold brought his son John Roger into the company. Until the middle of the nineteenth century, the historical brand remained in the possession of two generations of the great name, after which it was carried on by two further generations of nonrelated master watchmakers.

The ornate logo Arnold & Son was once synonymous with precise timekeeping on the high seas. Thus, the new watch brand Arnold & Son has placed the interplay of time and geography, as well as the basic functions of navigation, at the center of its model policies.

The collection's development is built upon an autonomous manually wound movement (Caliber 294) with seven days of power reserve, exclusively designed and produced for Arnold & Son by the *manufacture* La Joux-Perret in La Chaux-de-Fonds, the brand's joint venture partner. Meanwhile there are other, different reserved watch calibers ready to join it.

Arnold & Son

Grand Tourbillon Perpetual
Reference number: 1GTBP.B01A.C20B
Movement: manually wound, Arnold & Son Caliber 1768; ø 31 mm, height 11.2 mm; 42 jewels; 21,600 vph; one-minute tourbillon; twin spring barrels, power reserve 70 hours
Functions: hours, minutes; perpetual calendar (retrograde date, day, month); equation of time
Case: rose gold, ø 45 mm, height 18.2 mm; bezel under crystal with scale for equation of time bidirectionally rotating via crown; sapphire crystal; transparent case back
Band: reptile skin, folding clasp
Remarks: limited edition of 10 pieces
Price: $252,200
Variations: limited edition of 10 pieces in white gold

True North Perpetual Skeleton
Reference number: 1QPAR.B03A.C40BD
Movement: manually wound, Arnold & Son Caliber 1794; ø 40 mm, height 9.4 mm; 41 jewels; 21,600 vph
Functions: hours, minutes; perpetual calendar (date, month, moon phase, leap year); double equation of time; display of true solar time, display of true direction; power reserve indication
Case: rose gold, ø 45.2 mm, height 13.2 mm; bezel under crystal with longitude scale bidirectionally rotating via crown; sapphire crystal; transparent case back; screw-in crown
Band: reptile skin, folding clasp
Remarks: skeletonized dial
Price: $67,250

True North Perpetual
Reference number: 1QPAW.B01A.C40BD
Movement: manually wound, Arnold & Son Caliber 1794; ø 40 mm, height 9.4 mm; 41 jewels; 21,600 vph
Functions: hours, minutes; perpetual calendar (date, month, moon phase, leap year); double equation of time; displays of true solar time and true direction; power reserve indication
Case: white gold, ø 45.2 mm, height 13.2 mm; bezel under crystal with longitude scale bidirectionally rotating via crown; sapphire crystal; transparent case back; screw-in crown
Band: reptile skin, folding clasp
Price: $70,900
Variations: in rose gold

True Moon
Reference number: 1TMAS.U02A.C40B
Movement: automatic, Arnold & Son Caliber 1788 (base ETA 2893-2); ø 38.6 mm, height 7.4 mm; 21 jewels; 28,800 vph
Functions: hours, minutes, sweep seconds; date; moon phase display
Case: stainless steel, ø 46 mm, height 14.5 mm; sapphire crystal; transparent case back
Band: reptile skin, folding clasp
Remarks: diamond-set dial; realistic depiction of the moon
Price: $15,600
Variations: red gold

Hornet Worldtimer
Reference number: 1H6AP.B04A.C40B
Movement: automatic, Arnold & Son Caliber 1766 (base ETA 2892-A2); ø 38.5 mm, height 7.05 mm; 41 jewels; 28,800 vph
Functions: hours, minutes, sweep seconds; 24-hour display (second time zone); large date; equation of time
Case: rose gold, ø 47 mm, height 13.9 mm; bezel under crystal with world time zones (third time zone), bidirectionally rotating via crown; sapphire crystal; transparent case back
Band: reptile skin, folding clasp
Price: $41,000

Hornet Worldtimer
Reference number: 1H6AS.B03A.C40B
Movement: automatic, Arnold & Son Caliber 1766 (base ETA 2892-A2); ø 38.5 mm, height 7.05 mm; 41 jewels; 28,800 vph
Functions: hours, minutes, sweep seconds; 24-hour display (second time zone); large date; equation of time
Case: stainless steel, ø 47 mm, height 13.9 mm; bezel under crystal with world time zones (third time zone), bidirectionally rotating via crown; sapphire crystal; transparent case back
Band: reptile skin, folding clasp
Price: $20,500

White Ensign Orange & Black
Reference number: 1WEBS.001A.K35B
Movement: manually wound, Arnold & Son Caliber 294E; ø 25.6 mm, height 4.3 mm; 20 jewels; 21,600 vph; power reserve 7 days
Functions: hours, minutes, subsidiary seconds; date; power reserve indication
Case: stainless steel, ø 44.5 mm, height 12 mm; bezel under crystal with 60-minute divisions, bidirectionally rotating via crown; sapphire crystal; transparent case back; screw-in crown; water-resistant to 20 atm
Band: rubber, buckle
Price: $9,000
Variations: various dial variations

Longitude II Black
Reference number: 1L2AS.B02A.A11F
Movement: automatic, Arnold & Son Caliber 714 (base ETA 2892-A2); officially certified chronometer (COSC)
Functions: hours, minutes, sweep seconds; date; 24-hour display/sun compass; current longitude position; hinged case back with indication for setting equation of time
Case: stainless steel, ø 44.5 mm, height 15 mm; bezel under crystal with longitude scale, bidirectionally rotating via crown; sapphire crystal; transparent case back; screw-in crown; water-resistant to 10 atm
Band: stainless steel, double folding clasp
Price: $7,500
Variations: silver or blue dial; rubber strap

Audemars Piguet

Audemars Piguet's current management should have specialized in poker: it was certainly more than just a lucky guess in 2002 when Georges-Henri Meylan, the independent company's far-sighted CEO, signed up as one of the main sponsors for the *Alinghi*, which was at the time the Swiss challenger for the America's Cup.

It was literally unimaginable that the team from the landlocked country could ever hope to take sailing's most important trophy. If Meylan didn't have some sort of inside information, he must have been able to foresee the future. For, lo and behold, Ernesto Bertarelli's team did win the legendary competition on March 2, 2003, against all odds.

Bringing the coveted cup to Europe for the first time in 152 years was good for Switzerland and good for Audemars Piguet, and sailing fans spanning the globe eagerly awaited the thirty-second America's Cup, which took place in Valencia, Spain. The defender was now a safe bet as the next winner, so apparently there were no tarot cards involved a second time when Meylan re-signed with the top-ranked Helvetian team.

Audemars Piguet's partnership with the *Alinghi* has done a lot more than become the focal point of a marketing strategy. It has also inspired the *manufacture* to dedicate a complete set of Royal Oak models in support of the sailing team, the luxury industry's premier sports watch being the perfect choice as a high-profile time-keeping instrument.

While this line has been interesting and attractive thus far, technically it has not been

overly innovative—an element that this *manufacture* is well-known for.

In 2007, Audemars Piguet introduced the limited edition Royal Oak Offshore Alinghi Team Chronograph, a timepiece featuring a bezel and case crafted in forged carbon fiber that could be described as more than interesting. While the term *carbon fiber* might sound like the industry's catchphrase this season, Audemars Piguet is doing a lot more than just putting a supplied carbon fiber dial on an existing model. The word *forged* was chosen carefully to explain the process involving pieces of carbon wire that are pressed and molded together to make the whole. The arrangement of the wire pieces is what determines the quality of the material, and makes each one inherently unique. Not only is this material resistant and strong, a case made of it weighs a mere 100 grams.

The Royal Oak Offshore Alinghi Team Chronograph's 44-millimeter case is available in 18-karat rose gold, platinum, or even entirely in forged carbon fiber, while the typical octagonal bezel of the Royal Oak series on all three models is crafted in the forged carbon fiber material. The case back comprises black PVD-coated titanium engraved with a rendering of the *Alinghi* team at work. The case's crown and chronograph buttons are crafted in durable ceramic, while the eight screws holding the bezel to the case are made of black PVD-coated stainless steel.

This flyback chronograph including a regatta start function using a sweep seconds hand and a regatta countdown function is topped off by a black dial of such interesting proportions and colors—as well as the brand's signature *mega tapisserie* pattern—that the three limited editions are sure to sail out of jeweler's shops as quickly as the *Alinghi* did from Valencia's racing port when it swept its challenger in just four races.

Audemars Piguet

Royal Oak Automatic
Reference number: 15300ST.OO.1220ST.03
Movement: automatic, AP Caliber 3120; ø 26.6 mm, height 4.25 mm; 40 jewels; 21,600 vph
Functions: hours, minutes, sweep seconds; date
Case: stainless steel, ø 39 mm, height 9.35 mm; bezel screwed through to case back with 8 white gold screws; sapphire crystal; screwed-down transparent case back; water-resistant to 5 atm
Band: stainless steel, folding clasp
Price: $11,200
Variations: red gold with crocodile skin strap

Royal Oak Automatic
Reference number: 15300OR.OO.D088CR.01
Movement: automatic, AP Caliber 3120; ø 26.6 mm, height 4.25 mm; 40 jewels; 21,600 vph
Functions: hours, minutes, sweep seconds; date
Case: yellow gold, ø 39 mm, height 9.35 mm; bezel screwed through to case back with 8 white gold screws; sapphire crystal; screwed-down transparent case back; water-resistant to 5 atm
Band: reptile skin, folding clasp
Price: $21,400
Variations: stainless steel with stainless steel bracelet

Royal Oak Automatic
Reference number: 15202ST.OO.0944ST.01
Movement: automatic, AP Caliber 2121; ø 28 mm, height 3.05 mm; 36 jewels; 19,800 vph
Functions: hours, minutes, sweep seconds; date
Case: stainless steel, ø 39 mm, height 7.95 mm; bezel screwed through to case back with 8 white gold screws; sapphire crystal; screwed-down transparent case back; water-resistant to 5 atm
Band: stainless steel, folding clasp
Price: $16,700
Variations: yellow or red gold

Royal Oak Dual Time
Reference number: 26120OR.OO.D002CR.01
Movement: automatic, AP Caliber 2329/2846; ø 26 mm, height 4.9 mm; 37 jewels; 28,800 vph
Functions: hours, minutes; date; second time zone; day/night indication; power reserve display
Case: red gold, ø 39 mm, height 10 mm; bezel screwed through to case back with 8 white gold screws; sapphire crystal; water-resistant to 5 atm
Band: reptile skin, folding clasp
Price: $25,100
Variations: yellow gold; stainless steel with stainless steel bracelet

Royal Oak Chronograph
Reference number: 25860ST.OO.1110ST.03
Movement: automatic, AP Caliber 2385; ø 25.6 mm, height 5.5 mm; 37 jewels; 21,600 vph
Functions: hours, minutes, subsidiary seconds; chronograph; date
Case: stainless steel, ø 40 mm, height 10.95 mm; bezel screwed through to case back with 8 white gold screws; sapphire crystal; screw-in crown and buttons; water-resistant to 5 atm
Band: stainless steel, double folding clasp
Price: $17,200
Variations: yellow or white gold

Royal Oak Chronograph
Reference number: 26022OR.OO.D088CR.01
Movement: automatic, AP Caliber 2385; ø 25.6 mm, height 5.5 mm; 37 jewels; 21,600 vph
Functions: hours, minutes, subsidiary seconds; chronograph; date
Case: yellow gold, ø 40 mm, height 10.95 mm; bezel screwed through to case back with 8 white gold screws; sapphire crystal; screw-in crown and buttons; water-resistant to 5 atm
Band: reptile skin, folding clasp
Price: $29,400
Variations: red or white gold

Royal Oak Chronograph Tourbillon
Reference number: 25977ST.OO.D002CR.01
Movement: manually wound, AP Caliber 2889; ø 29.3 mm, height 7.65 mm; 25 jewels; 21,600 vph; one-minute tourbillon
Functions: hours, minutes, subsidiary seconds; chronograph
Case: stainless steel, ø 44 mm, height 9.8 mm; bezel screwed through to case back with 8 white gold screws; sapphire crystal; screw-in crown
Band: reptile skin, folding clasp
Price: $152,900
Variations: yellow or red gold

Lady Royal Oak
Reference number: 67601ST.ZZ.D012CR.02
Movement: quartz, AP Caliber 2712; finely finished with côtes de Gèneve
Functions: hours, minutes; date
Case: stainless steel, ø 33 mm, height 9.15 mm; bezel screwed through to case back with 8 white gold screws and set with 32 diamonds; sapphire crystal; crown with sapphire cabochon
Band: reptile skin, folding clasp
Price: $17,800
Variations: stainless steel bracelet; in yellow gold with leather strap or stainless steel bracelet

Audemars Piguet

Lady Royal Oak
Reference number: 77321ST.ZZ.1230ST.01
Movement: automatic, AP Caliber 2140; ø 20 mm, height 4 mm; 31 jewels; 28,800 vph; finely finished with côtes de Gèneve
Functions: hours, minutes, sweep seconds; date
Case: stainless steel, ø 33 mm, height 10.37 mm; bezel screwed through to case back with 8 white gold screws and set with 32 diamonds; sapphire crystal; crown with sapphire cabochon
Band: stainless steel, double folding clasp
Price: $13,600
Variations: reptile skin strap; in yellow gold with leather strap or link bracelet

Royal Oak Offshore Chronograph
Reference number: 25721ST.OO.1000ST.08
Movement: automatic, AP Caliber 2326/2840; ø 29.9 mm, height 6.15 mm; 54 jewels; 28,800 vph; soft iron core for protection from magnetic fields
Functions: hours, minutes, subsidiary seconds; chronograph; date
Case: stainless steel, ø 42 mm, height 14.05 mm; bezel screwed through to case back with 8 stainless steel screws; sapphire crystal; screw-in crown with rubber cap; water-resistant to 10 atm
Band: stainless steel, double folding clasp
Price: $20,700
Variations: leather strap; in titanium

Royal Oak Offshore Volcano
Reference number: 26170ST.OO.D101CR.01
Movement: automatic, AP Caliber 3126/3840; ø 29.9 mm, height 7.16 mm; 59 jewels; 21,600 vph; soft iron core for protection from magnetic fields
Functions: hours, minutes, subsidiary seconds; chronograph; date
Case: stainless steel, ø 42 mm, height 14.05 mm; bezel screwed through to case back with 8 stainless steel screws; sapphire crystal; screw-in crown with rubber cap; water-resistant to 10 atm
Band: reptile skin, folding clasp
Price: $18,700

Royal Oak Offshore Chronograph
Reference number: 25940OK.OO.D002CA.01
Movement: automatic, AP Caliber 2326/2840; ø 29.9 mm, height 6.15 mm; 54 jewels; 28,800 vph; soft iron core for protection from magnetic fields
Functions: hours, minutes, subsidiary seconds; chronograph; date
Case: red gold, ø 42 mm, height 14.05 mm; rubber-coated bezel screwed through to case back with 8 stainless steel screws; sapphire crystal; screw-in crown; water-resistant to 10 atm
Band: rubber, folding clasp
Price: $38,700
Variations: stainless steel

Royal Oak Offshore Alinghi Team
Reference number: 26062FS.OO.A002CA.01
Movement: automatic, AP Caliber 2326/2848; ø 26 mm, height 7.3 mm; 50 jewels; 28,800 vph
Functions: hours, minutes; chronograph with flyback and regatta countdown functions
Case: forged carbon fiber, ø 44 mm, height 14.3 mm; bezel screwed through to case back with 8 stainless steel screws; sapphire crystal; screw-in crown, recessed buttons; water-resistant to 10 atm
Band: rubber, buckle
Price: $23,100
Variations: in red gold/carbon fiber; in platinum/carbon fiber

Royal Oak Offshore Lady Chronograph
Reference number: 26048OK.ZZ.D010CA.01
Movement: automatic, AP Caliber 2385; ø 26.2mm, height 5.5 mm; 37 jewels; 21,600 vph
Functions: hours, minutes, subsidiary seconds; chronograph; date
Case: red gold, ø 37 mm, height 14.4 mm; rubber-coated bezel set with 32 diamonds; sapphire crystal; water-resistant to 5 atm
Band: rubber, folding clasp
Price: $40,700
Variations: in stainless steel/rubber

Jules Audemars
Reference number: 15120BC.OO.A002CR.03
Movement: automatic, AP Caliber 3120; ø 26.6 mm, height 4.25 mm; 40 jewels; 21,600 vph; power reserve appx. 60 hours; finely finished with côtes de Gèneve
Functions: hours, minutes, sweep seconds; date
Case: white gold, ø 39 mm, height 9.5 mm; sapphire crystal; transparent case back
Band: reptile skin, buckle
Price: $18,500
Variations: red gold

Jules Audemars Equation du Temps
Reference number: 26003OR.OO.D002CR.01
Movement: automatic, AP Caliber 2120/2808; ø 28 mm, height 5.35 mm; 41 jewels; 19,800 vph
Functions: hours, minutes; perpetual calendar with date, weekday, month, astronomical moon phase, leap year; equation of time, times of sunrise and sunset
Case: red gold, ø 43 mm, height 11.5 mm; sapphire crystal; transparent case back
Band: reptile skin, folding clasp
Price: $78,800
Variations: yellow or white gold

Audemars Piguet

Jules Audemars Tourbillon Minute Repeater
Reference number: 26050PT.OO.D002CR.01
Movement: manually wound, AP Caliber 2874; ø 29.3 mm, height 7.65 mm; 38 jewels; 21,600 vph; one-minute tourbillon
Functions: hours, minutes, subsidiary seconds (on tourbillon cage); chronograph with minute counter; minute repeater
Case: platinum, ø 43 mm, height 11.5 mm; sapphire crystal; transparent case back
Band: reptile skin, folding clasp
Price: $335,700
Variations: red gold

Jules Audemars Jumping Hour Minute Repeater
Reference number: 26151OR.OO.D002CR.01
Movement: manually wound, AP Caliber 2907; ø 37 mm, height 7.6 mm; 35 jewels; 21,600 vph;
Functions: jump hours, minutes, subsidiary seconds; minute repeater
Case: red gold, ø 43 mm, height 12 mm; sapphire crystal; transparent case back
Band: reptile skin, folding clasp
Price: $204,900
Variations: platinum

Millenary
Reference number: 15320OR.OO.D002CR.01
Movement: automatic, AP Caliber 3120; ø 26.6 mm, height 4.25 mm; 40 jewels; 21,600 vph
Functions: hours, minutes, sweep seconds; date
Case: red gold, 45 x 41 mm, height 9 mm; sapphire crystal; transparent case back
Band: reptile skin, folding clasp
Price: $20,300
Variations: white gold

Lady Millenary Ciel Etoilé
Reference number: 77315BC.ZZ.D007SU.01
Movement: automatic, AP Caliber 3123/3908; ø 26 mm, height 5.68 mm; 45 jewels; 21,600 vph
Functions: hours, minutes, sweep seconds; date, moon phase; power reserve indication
Case: white gold, 39.5 x 35.5 mm, height 10.7 mm; bezel and lugs set with 112 brilliant-cut diamonds; sapphire crystal
Band: satin, folding clasp
Price: $36,400
Variations: red gold

Millenary with Deadbeat Seconds
Reference number: 26091OR.OO.D803CR.01
Movement: automatic, AP Caliber 2905; 32.9 x 37.9 mm, height 9.15 mm; 31 jewels; 21,600 vph; Audemars Piguet escapement with deadbeat seconds; double balance spring; twin spring barrels, power reserve 7 days
Functions: hours, minutes, subsidiary seconds
Case: rose gold, 47 x 43 mm, height 15.7 mm; sapphire crystal; transparent case back
Band: reptile skin, folding clasp
Price: $156,100

Edward Piguet Automatic
Reference number: 15121OR.OO.A002CR.02
Movement: automatic, AP Caliber 2140; ø 20 mm, height 4 mm; 31 jewels; 28,800 vph
Functions: hours, minutes, sweep seconds; date
Case: red gold, 29 x 46 mm, height 9.7 mm; sapphire crystal
Band: reptile skin, folding clasp
Remarks: limited availability, must be special ordered
Price: $14,900
Variations: white gold

Edward Piguet Chronograph
Reference number: 25987BC.OO.D002CR.01
Movement: automatic, AP Caliber 2385; ø 25.6 mm, height 5.5 mm; 37 jewels; 21,600 vph
Functions: hours, minutes, subsidiary seconds; chronograph; date
Case: white gold, 29 x 48.7 mm, height 11.9 mm; sapphire crystal
Band: reptile skin, folding clasp
Price: $26,100
Variations: red gold

Edward Piguet Tourbillon Large Date
Reference number: 26009BC.OO.D002CR.01
Movement: manually wound, AP Caliber 2886; 27.65 x 20.9 mm, height 6.1 mm; 20 jewels; 21,600 vph; one-minute tourbillon
Functions: hours, minutes; large date
Case: white gold, 51 x 34 mm, height 12.02 mm; sapphire crystal; transparent case back
Band: reptile skin, folding clasp
Price: $156,500
Variations: red gold

Audemars Piguet

Caliber 3120
Mechanical with automatic winding, bilaterally winding rotor; power reserve 60 hours
Functions: hours, minutes, sweep seconds; date
Diameter: 26.6 mm
Height: 4.25 mm
Jewels: 40
Balance: CuBe (copper-beryllium) with variable inertia
Frequency: 21,600 vph
Balance spring: flat hairspring
Shock protection: Kif Elastor
Remarks: balance bridge; 22-karat gold rotor; beveled and polished steel parts; base plate with perlage, bridges with côtes de Genève

Caliber 2121
Mechanical with automatic winding; bilaterally winding rotor, power reserve 40 hours
Functions: hours, minutes; date
Diameter: 28 mm
Height: 3.05 mm
Jewels: 36
Balance: CuBe (copper-beryllium) with variable inertia
Frequency: 19,800 vph
Balance spring: flat hairspring
Shock protection: Kif Elastor
Remarks: rotor with 22-karat gold oscillating weight; beveled and polished steel parts; base plate with perlage, bridges with côtes de Genève

Caliber 2329/2846
Mechanical with automatic winding; bilaterally winding rotor, power reserve 40 hours
Functions: hours, minutes; date; second time zone; day/night indication
Diameter: 26 mm
Height: 4.9 mm
Jewels: 33
Balance: CuBe (copper-beryllium) with variable inertia
Frequency: 28,800 vph
Balance spring: flat hairspring
Shock protection: Kif Elastor
Remarks: rotor with 22-karat gold oscillating weight; beveled and polished steel parts; base plate with perlage, bridges with côtes de Genève

Caliber 2385
Mechanical with automatic winding; bilaterally winding rotor, power reserve 40 hours
Functions: hours, minutes; date; chronograph
Diameter: 25.6 mm
Height: 5.5 mm
Jewels: 37
Balance: CuBe (copper-beryllium); fine adjustment via index
Frequency: 21,600 vph
Balance spring: flat hairspring
Shock protection: Kif Elastor
Remarks: rotor with 22-karat gold oscillating weight; beveled and polished steel parts; base plate with perlage, bridges with côtes de Genève

Caliber 2326/2840
Mechanical with automatic winding; bilaterally winding rotor, power reserve 40 hours
Functions: hours, minutes; date; chronograph
Diameter: 29.9 mm
Height: 6.15 mm
Jewels: 54
Balance: CuBe (copper-beryllium) with variable inertia
Frequency: 28,800 vph
Balance spring: flat hairspring
Shock protection: Kif Elastor
Remarks: rotor with 22-karat gold oscillating weight; beveled and polished steel parts; base plate with perlage, bridges with côtes de Genève

Caliber 2326/2848
Mechanical with automatic winding; bilaterally winding rotor, power reserve 40 hours
Functions: hours, minutes; chronograph with flyback and regatta countdown functions
Diameter: 26 mm
Height: 7.3 mm
Jewels: 50
Balance: CuBe (copper-beryllium) with variable inertia
Frequency: 28,800 vph
Balance spring: flat hairspring
Shock protection: Kif Elastor
Remarks: rotor with 22-karat gold oscillating weight; beveled and polished steel parts; base plate with perlage, bridges with côtes de Genève

Audemars Piguet

Caliber 2120-2808
Mechanical with automatic winding; extra-flat rotor with side support rollers and 21-karat gold segment, power reserve 48 hours
Functions: hours, minutes; perpetual calendar (date, day, month, moon phase, leap year); sunrise/sunset times, equation of time
Diameter: 28 mm (12 1/2'''); **Height:** 5.35 mm
Jewels: 41; **Frequency:** 19,800 vph
Balance: CuBe (copper-beryllium) with six weights
Balance spring: flat hairspring
Shock protection: Kif Elastor
Number of individual parts: 423
Remarks: beveled and polished steel parts; base plate with perlage, bridges with côtes de Genève

Caliber 2889
Mechanical with manual winding, column-wheel control of chronograph functions; one-minute tourbillon, power reserve 48 hours
Functions: hours, minutes, subsidiary seconds; chronograph
Diameter: 29.3
Height: 7.65 mm
Jewels: 25
Balance: screw balance with variable inertia
Frequency: 21,600 vph
Balance spring: flat hairspring with Phillips terminal curve
Shock protection: Kif Elastor
Remarks: beveled and polished steel parts; base plate with perlage; bridges with côtes de Genève

Caliber 2886
Mechanical with manual winding, power reserve 40 hours; one-minute tourbillon
Functions: hours, minutes, subsidiary seconds; large date
Dimensions: 27.05 x 20.3 mm
Height: 6.1 mm
Jewels: 20
Balance: screw balance with variable inertia
Frequency: 21,600 vph
Balance spring: flat hairspring with Phillips terminal curve
Shock protection: Kif Elastor
Remarks: beveled and polished steel parts; base plate with perlage, bridges with côtes de Genève

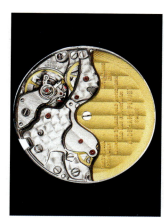

Caliber 2874
Mechanical with manual winding, power reserve 48 hours; one-minute tourbillon
Functions: hours, minutes, subsidiary seconds (on tourbillon cage); chronograph with minute counter; minute repeater
Diameter: 29.3 mm
Height: 7.65 mm
Jewels: 28
Balance: screw balance with variable inertia
Frequency: 21,600 vph
Balance spring: flat hairspring with Phillips terminal curve
Shock protection: Kif Elastor
Remarks: beveled and polished steel parts; base plate with perlage, bridges with côtes de Genève

Caliber 2905
Mechanical with manual winding; Audemars Piguet escapement with deadbeat seconds; twin spring barrels; power reserve 7 days
Functions: hours, minutes, subsidiary seconds
Diameter: 32 x 37 mm
Height: 9.15 mm
Jewels: 31
Balance: with variable inertia
Frequency: 21,600 vph
Balance spring: two flat hairsprings with Phillips terminal curve
Shock protection: Kif Elastor
Remarks: beveled and polished steel parts; base plate with perlage, bridges with côtes de Genève

Caliber 2907
Mechanical with manual winding; power reserve 70 hours
Functions: hours (jump), minutes, subsidiary seconds; minute repeater
Diameter: 37
Height: 7.6 mm
Jewels: 35
Balance: with variable inertia
Frequency: 21,600 vph
Balance spring: flat hairspring with Phillips terminal curve
Shock protection: Kif Elastor
Number of individual parts: 412
Remarks: beveled and polished steel parts; base plate with perlage, bridges with côtes de Genève

Aviator

With a top speed of Mach 2.3 and the dog-fighting maneuverability of an F-16 Fighting Falcon, the Russian MIG 29 Fulcrum is a formidable aircraft in or out of combat. When put to the challenge by the SWIFTS—the Russian equivalent of the U.S. Thunderbirds—in aerial displays testing the limits of both pilot and machine, time itself can seem to stand still.

However, the pilots know it doesn't. In the reality of this split-second world of aerobatic feats and stomach-churning rolls, the watch of choice for the SWIFTS is the Volmax Aviator. Steeped in Russian aviation history, this is the timepiece these world-class pilots trust when flying wingtip to wingtip at speeds pushing 1,500 miles per hour.

At the turn of the new millennium, Aviator—and parent company Volmax—grew out of the slow collapse of Russian watch giant Poljot in the late 1990s. Initially a distributor of Poljot watches abroad, and later heir apparent to the Poljot watch heritage, Volmax now owns and produces watches under the trade names Aviator, Buran, and Sturmanskie. The latter holds the distinction of being the first watch in space on the wrist of Yuri Gagarin.

It's a lineage that goes back seventy-five years to 1932 when the First Moscow Watch Factory began making pocket watches for the Soviet Union Central Air Force Administration. Volmax still manufactures its watches at the same location. This company is the leader in Russian military chronographs along with aviation and space exploration–related timepieces today.

This is not merely an industry for Aviator; it is a passion. Volmax company president Valentin Volodko explains that his company "builds only living watches. Only someone who loves watches can build a mechanical timepiece, and there is a piece of our heart in each and every one."

This is a sentiment that permeates the watchmakers, designers, and distributors of the Aviator line of watches. The majority of the company's models comprises mechanical, manually wound chronographs, a shrinking part of the watch world as automatics become increasingly popular. Commemorating this company's history, Aviator manufactures true military watches and not just military-inspired timepieces. What better proof of this than the fact that they can be found on the wrists of the SWIFTS pilots—accompanying these aviators and their jets in each difficult maneuver.

Guards Colonel Nikolay M. Dyatel, Deputy Head of 237th Aircraft Demonstration Center

Aviator

Hi-Tech
Reference number: 3133/2705965
Movement: manually wound, Poljot Caliber 3133; ø 31 mm, height 7.35 mm; 23 jewels; 21,600 vph; power reserve 42 hours (37 hours with running chronograph)
Functions: hours, minutes, subsidiary seconds; date; chronograph
Case: stainless steel, ø 43 mm, height 12.5 mm; mineral crystal; screwed-down mineral crystal exhibition case back; water-resistant to 30 m
Band: leather, buckle
Price: $929

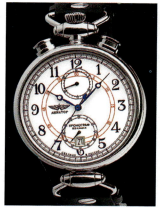

Wright Brothers
Reference number: 3133/2941027
Movement: manually wound, Poljot Caliber 3133; ø 31 mm, height 7.35 mm; 23 jewels; 21,600 vph; power reserve 42 hours (37 hours with running chronograph)
Functions: hours, minutes, subsidiary seconds; date; chronograph
Case: stainless steel, ø 43 mm, height 13.8 mm; mineral crystal; screwed-down mineral crystal exhibition case back; water-resistant to 30 m
Band: leather, buckle
Price: $1,059

Hi-Tech
Reference number: 3133/2704542
Movement: manually wound, Poljot Caliber 3133; ø 31 mm, height 7.35 mm; 23 jewels; 21,600 vph; power reserve 42 hours (37 hours with running chronograph)
Functions: hours, minutes, subsidiary seconds; date; chronograph
Case: stainless steel, ø 43 mm, height 12.5 mm; mineral crystal; screwed-down mineral crystal exhibition case back; water-resistant to 30 m
Band: leather, buckle
Price: $989

Chronograph
Reference number: 31681/6773778B-42
Movement: manually wound, Poljot Caliber 31681; ø 31 mm, height 7.35 mm; 25 jewels; 21,600 vph; power reserve 42 hours (37 hours with running chronograph)
Functions: hours, minutes, subsidiary seconds; date; chronograph; 24-hour display
Case: stainless steel, ø 42 mm, height 13.5 mm; bezel with tachymeter scale; sapphire crystal; screwed-down case back; water-resistant to 50 m
Band: stainless steel, folding clasp
Price: $729

Moon Phase
Reference number: 310579/1166548
Movement: manually wound, Poljot Caliber 310579; ø 31 mm, height 5.05 mm; 17 jewels; 21,600 vph; power reserve 42 hours
Functions: hours, minutes, subsidiary seconds; date; moon phase
Case: gold-plated (10 microns) stainless steel, ø 43 mm, height 13.6 mm; bidirectionally rotating bezel with second time zone; mineral crystal; screwed-down mineral crystal exhibition case back; water-resistant to 30 m
Band: leather, buckle
Price: $599

Three-Hand Propeller Watch
Reference number: 2824-2/2915488
Movement: automatic, ETA Caliber 2824-2; ø 28 mm, height 4.6 mm; 25 jewels; 28,800 vph; power reserve 42 hours (37 hours with running chronograph)
Functions: hours, minutes, sweep seconds; date
Case: stainless steel, ø 42 mm, height 12.4 mm; mineral crystal; water-resistant to 30 m
Band: stainless steel, buckle
Price: $599

Manually Wound
Reference number: 3105/1161544
Movement: manually wound, Poljot Caliber 3105; ø 31 mm, height 5.05 mm; 17 jewels; 21,600 vph; power reserve 42 hours
Functions: hours, minutes, subsidiary seconds; date
Case: stainless steel, ø 43 mm, height 13.6 mm; bidirectionally rotating bezel with second time zone; mineral crystal; screwed-down mineral crystal exhibition case back; water-resistant to 30 m
Band: leather, buckle
Price: $599

Wings
Reference number: 31679/2806432
Movement: manually wound, Poljot Caliber 3133; ø 31 mm, height 7.35 mm; 23 jewels; 21,600 vph; power reserve 42 hours (37 hours with running chronograph)
Functions: hours, minutes, subsidiary seconds; date; chronograph
Case: gold-plated (10 microns) stainless steel, ø 43 mm, height 13.8 mm; sapphire crystal; screwed-down sapphire crystal exhibition case back; water-resistant to 30 m
Band: leather, buckle
Remarks: chronograph buttons decorated with "wing" levers to provide convenient use when wearing gloves
Price: $1,229

Azimuth

Azimuth is a word of Arabic origin meaning "route taken by a traveler" or even "the way." What a fitting name for a company that has chosen a distinct path of its own to follow, forging a course in a country that has a great number of timepiece collectors, but no indigenous watch companies.

Christopher Long and Alvin Lye are two watch enthusiasts of the most passionate sort. Living in Singapore, this bug is not hard to catch. Though small in terms of square mileage, this city-state is a watch lovers' paradise, containing some of the world's most knowledgeable watch junkies and best-stocked shops. It was here that Long and Lye launched Azimuth in 2004.

Azimuth's premise is an easy one: good, traditional design paired with either vintage specialties or the best in modern Swiss technology, which the pair has lovingly had modified to their specifications.

Thus, not only does Azimuth's young collection contain loyal replicas of observation watches, even including the original German wording on the case back for nostalgic purposes, but the Bombardier and Jagdbomber models are also outfitted with vintage Fontainemelon and Schild movements from the 1950s, automatically limiting their numbers.

Azimuth's other strong suit lies in the unusual, in creating concept watches that have truly never been seen before. So far the brand's series of unusual concept watches includes the Gauge Mecha-1 BMF and the SP-1 Mecanique Spaceship. The latter's adventurous mix of displays, powered by a highly modified ETA Unitas caliber 6497, is sure to please fans of horology as much as fans of *Star Trek* with its jump hours against a jet black dial featuring a realistic rendition of the Earth that makes one complete rotation every sixty seconds where the subsidiary seconds display would usually be located.

The classic complications housed in 42 mm cases that the company has also issued until now are not without their own twist: inspired by 1940s style, the mechanical complications found within, such as retrograde and bi-retrograde displays, are decidedly modern.

And because Azimuth places so much emphasis on individuality, the company even offers its own Series Limited program, in which the customer can actually design or have one of Azimuth's designers create components, dials, and other looks for a truly unique timepiece. "When you wear an Azimuth, you not only express your individualism and taste for finer things in life, but you also carry with you a love and passion for horological art. In short, it is a reflection of passion," says Long.

While in North America Azimuth's watches are now going the traditional distribution route via jewelers, in Singapore these models can only be found at the company's own boutique/museum. This tribute to the illustrious past of watchmaking includes a number of historic pilot's watches and artifacts exhibited over more than 1,200 square feet.

Azimuth

Gauge Mecha-1 BMF
Reference number: GM-1
Movement: automatic, very modified ETA Caliber 2836-2; ø 33 mm, height 6 mm; 25 jewels; 28,800 vph; power reserve 36 hours
Functions: hours (revolving disk), minutes (retrograde); 24-hour indication (revolving disk)
Case: stainless steel, 50 x 42 mm, height 13 mm; sapphire crystal; pothole-style exhibition window on case back revealing balance; water-resistant to 50 m
Band: rubber, folding clasp
Price: $3,600
Variations: available with silver-colored dial; alligator skin or leather strap;

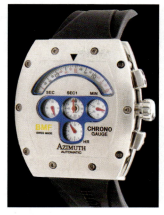

Chrono Gauge Mecha-1 BMF
Reference number: CGM-1
Movement: automatic, very modified ETA Valjoux Caliber 7750; ø 30 mm, height 8 mm; 25 jewels; 28,800 vph
Functions: hours, minutes; chronograph
Case: stainless steel, 50 x 42 mm, height 16 mm; sapphire crystal; pothole-style exhibition window on case back revealing balance; water-resistant to 50 m
Band: rubber, folding clasp
Price: $3,900
Variations: available with black chronograph counters; alligator skin or leather strap

SP-1 Mecanique Spaceship
Reference number: SPACESHIP
Movement: manually wound, ETA Unitas Caliber 6497-1; ø 36.6 mm, height 4.5 mm; 17 jewels; 18,000 vph; 42 hours power reserve
Functions: jump hours, minutes, subsidiary seconds
Case: stainless steel, ø 46 mm; height 13 mm; domed sapphire crystal; sapphire crystal case back; water-resistant to 30 m
Band: calfskin, double folding clasp
Remarks: concept watch with a mystery jump hour carried on a three-dimensional minute hand
Price: $4,300

Heures et Minutes Bi-Retrograde
Reference number: BRHM
Movement: automatic, ETA Caliber 2836-2; ø 33 mm, height 6 mm; 25 jewels; 28,800 vph; power reserve 36 hours; in-house modifications to base movement
Functions: hours (retrograde), minutes (retrograde), sweep seconds
Case: stainless steel, ø 42 mm; mm, height 13.5 mm; sapphire crystal; sapphire crystal case back; water-resistant to 30 m
Band: calfskin, double folding clasp
Price: $4,300
Variations: available in black PVD case with orange markers on the dial

Retrograde Minutes Jour et Nuit
Reference number: RMDN
Movement: automatic, ETA Caliber 2836-2; ø 33 mm, height 6 mm; 25 jewels; 28,800 vph; 36 hours power reserve; in-house modifications to base movement
Functions: hours, minutes (retrograde), sweep seconds; day/night indication
Case: stainless steel, ø 42 mm; height 12.5 mm; sapphire crystal; sapphire crystal case back; water-resistant to 30 m
Band: alligator skin, double folding clasp
Remarks: black mother-of-pearl dial
Price: $3,300
Variations: also available with a silver dial

Calendrier
Reference number: CAL
Movement: automatic, ETA Caliber 2836-2; ø 33 mm, height 5.9 mm; 25 jewels; 28,800 vph; 38 hours power reserve; in-house modifications to base movement
Functions: hours, minutes, sweep seconds; date, day, month; day/night indication
Case: stainless steel, ø 42 mm; height 12.5 mm; sapphire crystal; sapphire crystal case back; water-resistant to 30 m
Band: calfskin, buckle
Price: $2,000

B-Uhr Inner Hour
Reference number: B-UHR
Movement: manually wound, Azimuth Caliber AZ6877 (base movement ETA Unitas 6497-1); ø 36.6 mm, height 5.4 mm; 18 jewels; 18,000 vph; 42 hours power reserve
Functions: hours, minutes, sweep seconds
Case: stainless steel, ø 48 mm; height 15.8 mm; sapphire crystal; hunter lid over exhibition case back; water-resistant to 30 m
Band: buffalo skin with rivets, buckle
Price: $3,800
Variations: other military dial variations; also available in 55 mm case

Bombardier IV
Reference number: BIV-MIL
Movement: manually wound, Marvin Caliber 700; ø 29.4 mm, height 3.3 mm; 17 jewels; 21,600 vph; power reserve 46 hours; vintage movement from the 1960s
Functions: hours, minutes, subsidiary seconds
Case: stainless steel, ø 48 mm; height 10 mm; sapphire crystal; sapphire crystal case back; water-resistant to 30 m
Band: buffalo skin with rivets, buckle
Remarks: limited edition of 99 pieces
Price: $2,200

Backes & Strauss

A new watch brand celebrated its world premier in London's exclusive Two Temple House at the end of 2006: Backes & Strauss was until that point only known as a diamond dealer—the oldest diamond dealer in the world, as a matter of fact, founded in 1789 in Hanau, Germany. Today, Backes & Strauss is headquartered in Antwerp and maintains subsidiaries in London and Dubai among other places.

Vartkess Knadjian, managing director of the Backes & Strauss group, is the son of an Armenian watchmaker and has for years been a close friend of Vartan Sirmakes—better known to watch fans as the head of Franck Muller Watchland. This Genevan concern has purchased some of its diamonds with exclusive cuts—like the Curvex with seventy-three facets—from Backes & Strauss, and now functions as a partner to the company for the diamond profes-sional's first official appearance on the international watch scene.

London was the perfect choice for launching the new watch brand, as the stylish watches crafted with help of Watchland designer Rodolphe Cattin are named for typical London areas such as Berkeley, Piccadilly, and Regent—Knadjian's homage to the life's work of London architect and city planner John Nash.

All Backes & Strauss watches are outfitted with at least one diamond (in the crown), but mainly with many more: a specialty of the new brand is completely paved jewelry watch for both men and women.

Piccadilly
Reference number: PC.40.MA.D.2R
Movement: automatic, Caliber BK200; ø 25.6 mm, height 4.6 mm, 28,800 vph, 26 jewels, 38 hours power reserve, côtes de Genève, blued screws, rotor with platinum segment
Functions: hours, minutes, sweep seconds; date
Case: rose gold, ø 40 mm, height 10.25 mm, sapphire crystal, case set with 106 ideal-cut diamonds (3.6 ct), crown set with ideal-cut diamond
Band: alligator skin strap; 18-karat rose gold folding clasp
Price: $33,300
Variations: white gold ($33,300)

Regent
Reference number: RE.4452.MA.D.1R
Movement: automatic, Caliber BK200; ø 25.6 mm, height 4.6 mm, 28,800 vph, 26 jewels, 38 hours power reserve, côtes de Genève, blued screws, rotor with platinum segment
Functions: hours, minutes, sweep seconds; date
Case: white gold, 44 x 52 mm; height 11.35 mm, sapphire crystal, case set with 54 ideal-cut diamonds (8.5 ct) crown set with ideal-cut diamond
Band: ostrich skin strap; folding clasp
Price: $91,700
Variations: rose gold ($91,700)

Berkeley
Reference number: BY.40.MA.BAG
Movement: automatic, Caliber BK200; ø 25.6 mm, height 4.6 mm, 28,800 vph, 26 jewels, 38 hours power reserve, côtes de Genève, blued screws, rotor with platinum segment
Functions: hours, minutes, sweep seconds; date
Case: white gold, ø 40 mm, height 10.40 mm, sapphire crystal, case set with 56 baguette diamonds (10.5 ct), crown set with ideal-cut diamond
Band: alligator skin strap; 18-karat white gold folding clasp
Price: $166,700
Variations: various dial and diamond varieties

Berkeley
Reference number: BY.37
Movement: automatic, Caliber BK200; ø 25.6 mm, height 4.6 mm, 28,800 vph, 26 jewels, 38 hours power reserve, côtes de Genève, blued screws, rotor with platinum segment
Functions: hours, minutes, sweep seconds; date
Case: white gold, ø 40 mm, height 10 mm, sapphire crystal, case set with 56 baguette diamonds (10.5 ct), crown set with ideal-cut diamond
Band: alligator skin strap; 18-karat white gold folding clasp
Price: $29,200
Variations: various dial and diamond varieties; rose gold

Ball Watch Company

Robust, reliable, and ready for anything—these are the characteristics that grace a modern watch by the Ball Watch Company. The brand's concept of a high-quality, Swiss-made timepiece that puts an emphasis on func-tionality and legibility is one that is finding great favor among American watch fans—especially those looking for the most watch for the money. The brand's American origins may also have something to do with its popularity in North America.

The pocket watch and ensuing wristwatch industry that sprang up in America had a lot to do with the increasing popularity of trains and their need for precise timing. By 1893 many companies had adopted the General Railroad Timepiece Standards. Although these changed from year to year, the Standards included many characteristics found in high-quality Swiss watches: regulation in at least five positions, precision to within 30 seconds in a week, Breguet balance springs, and so on. And an American pocket watch industry emerged that was able to meet these specifications.

One of the chief players in developing these standards, and thus the industry, was Webster Clay Ball, or Webb C. Ball as he preferred to be known. Born in Fredericktown, Ohio, in 1847, Ball grew up on a farm. As a young man, he cast about for a career and became an apprentice to watchmaker George Lewin, the town's jeweler. From there he moved on to a sales position for John Dueber, a manufacturer of watch cases. After purchasing an interest in the firm of Whitcomb and Metten in 1879, he was quick to buy out Metten, then founding the Whitcomb and Ball Jewelry Store with his new partner. Later the same year, he bought out Whitcomb and established the Webb C. Ball Company in Cleveland, Ohio. The enterprising Ball was the first jeweler to use the time signals of the Naval Observatory in Washington after Standard Time was adopted in 1883, thus bringing precise time to Cleveland. Legend has it that he also imported the first chronometer to Ohio, which he put on display in his store window. On July 19, 1891, Ball was appointed chief inspector for Lake Shore Lines. He invented a watch inspection system and a set of timepiece guidelines that most American manufacturers set out to meet. Ball ended up being in charge of governing the precision of at least 175,000 miles of railroad, and he also extended his system into Mexico and Canada.

His inspection system was set up to keep records of a watch's performance using standard forms and uniform regulations, carefully supervising railroad time service with the aid of competent watchmakers. His system called for four standard watches to be present on every train, regardless of whether it was of the passenger or freight variety. These timepieces were in the possession of the conductor, the engineer, the fireman, and the rear brakeman—hence the commemorative names of Ball's modern watch lines.

Ball Watch Company

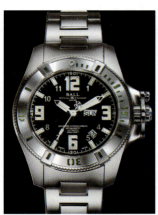

Engineer Hydrocarbon Mad Cow
Reference number: DM1036A-SAJ-BK
Movement: automatic, ETA Caliber 2836-2; ø 25.6 mm, height 5.05 mm; 25 jewels; 28,800 vph; 38 hours power reserve, temperature endurance to -40°C
Functions: hours, minutes, sweep seconds; date, day
Case: titanium, ø 42 mm; height 16.3 mm; unidirectionally rotating stainless steel bezel with 60-minute scale; anti-reflective sapphire crystal; screwed-down case back; screw-in crown with crown protection; water-resistant to 300 m
Band: titanium and stainless steel, folding clasp
Remarks: 32 micro gas tubes on hands and dial, shock-resistant to 7,500 Gs
Price: $1,999

Engineer Hydrocarbon GMT
Reference number: DG1016A-SJ-BK
Movement: automatic, ETA Caliber 2893-2; ø 25.6 mm, height 4.1 mm; 25 jewels; 28,800 vph; 42 hours power reserve; temperature endurance to -40°C
Functions: hours, minutes, sweep seconds; date, second time zone
Case: stainless steel, ø 40 mm; height 14.1 mm; unidirectionally rotating bezel with 24-hour scale; anti-reflective sapphire crystal; screwed-down case back; screw-in crown with patented crown protection; water-resistant to 300 m
Band: stainless steel, folding clasp
Remarks: 17 micro gas tubes on hands and dial; shock-resistant to 7,500 Gs
Price: $2,299

Engineer Hydrocarbon Classic II
Reference number: DM1016A-SIJ-WH
Movement: automatic, ETA Caliber 2892-A2; ø 25.6 mm, height 3.6 mm; 21 jewels; 28,800 vph; 42 hours power reserve, temperature endurance to -40°C
Functions: hours, minutes, sweep seconds; date
Case: titanium, ø 40 mm; height 14.1 mm; unidirectionally rotating stainless steel bezel with 60-minute scale; anti-reflective sapphire crystal; screwed-down case back; screw-in crown with crown protection; water-resistant to 300 m
Band: titanium and stainless steel, folding clasp
Remarks: 16 double-sized micro gas tubes on hands and dial, shock-resistant to 7,500 Gs
Price: $1,899

Engineer Hydrocarbon Chronograph
Reference number: DM1016A-PJ-WH
Movement: automatic, ETA Valjoux Caliber 7750; ø 30 mm, height 7.9 mm; 25 jewels; 28,800 vph; 42 hours power reserve, temperature endurance to -40°C
Functions: hours, minutes, subsidiary seconds; chronograph; date, day
Case: titanium, ø 42 mm; height 18.3 mm; unidirectionally rotating stainless steel bezel with 60-minute scale; anti-reflective sapphire crystal; screwed-down case back; screw-in crown with crown protection; water-resistant to 300 m
Band: rubber, buckle
Remarks: 30 micro gas tubes on hands and dial, shock-resistant to 7,500 Gs
Price: $2,499

Engineer Hydrocarbon TMT Titanium
Reference number: DT1026A-SAJ-BK
Movement: automatic, Ball Caliber 9018 (base ETA 2892-A2); ø 25.6 mm, height 5.1 mm; 25 jewels; 28,800 vph; 38 hours power reserve, temperature endurance to -40°C
Functions: hours, minutes, sweep seconds; date; mechanical thermometer (illuminated)
Case: titanium, ø 42 mm; height 15.8 mm; unidirectionally rotating stainless steel bezel with 60-minute scale; anti-reflective sapphire crystal; screwed-down case back; screw-in crown with crown protection; water-resistant to 300 m
Band: titanium and stainless steel, folding clasp
Remarks: 32 micro gas tubes on hands and dial, shock-resistant to 7,500 Gs
Price: $3,699

Engineer Master II Moonphase
Reference number: NM1082C-SAJ-BK
Movement: automatic, Ball Caliber 963 (base ETA 2836-2); ø 25.6 mm, height 5.05 mm; 25 jewels; 28,800 vph; 38 hours power reserve
Functions: hours, minutes, sweep seconds; date, day; illuminated moon phase
Case: stainless steel, ø 40 mm; height 13.2 mm; anti-reflective sapphire crystal; screwed-down case back; screw-in crown; water-resistant to 100 m
Band: stainless steel, folding clasp
Remarks: 45 micro gas tubes for illuminated moon phase; shock-resistant to 5000 Gs; anti-magnetic to 4,800 A/m
Price: $1,399
Variations: white dial; calfskin strap

Engineer Master II Diver TMT
Reference number: DT1020A-PAJ-BKC
Movement: automatic, Ball Caliber 9018 (base ETA 2892-A2); ø 25.6 mm, height 5.1 mm; 25 jewels; 28,800 vph; 42 hours power reserve
Functions: hours, minutes, sweep seconds; date; illuminated thermometer
Case: titanium coated with DLC (diamond-like carbon), ø 42 mm; height 13.2 mm; anti-reflective sapphire crystal; bidirectionally rotating inner bezel with 60-minute scale; screwed-down case back; screw-in crown; water-resistant to 300 m
Band: rubber, buckle
Remarks: 53 micro gas tubes on hands and dial; shock-resistant to 5000 Gs; anti-magnetic to 4,800 A/m
Price: $3,299

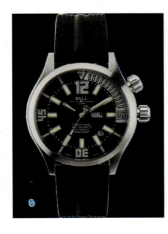

Engineer Master II Diver Chronometer
Reference number: DM1022A-P1CA-BKSL
Movement: automatic, ETA Caliber 2836-2; ø 25.6 mm, height 5.05 mm; 25 jewels; 28,800 vph; 38 hours power reserve; C.O.S.C. certified chronometer
Functions: hours, minutes, sweep seconds; date, day
Case: titanium, ø 44 mm; height 15 mm; sapphire crystal; bidirectionally rotating inner bezel with 60-minute scale; screwed-down case back; screw-in crown; water-resistant to 300 m
Band: rubber, buckle
Remarks: 51 double-sized micro gas tubes on hands and dial; shock-resistant to 5000 Gs; anti-magnetic to 4,800 A/m
Price: $2,299

Ball Watch Company

Trainmaster Cleveland Express
Reference number: NM1058D-LCJ-SL
Movement: automatic, ETA Caliber 2836-2; ø 25.6 mm, height 5.05 mm; 25 jewels; 28,800 vph; 38 hours power reserve; C.O.S.C. certified chronometer
Functions: hours, minutes, sweep seconds; date
Case: stainless steel, ø 41 mm; height 12.5 mm; anti-reflective sapphire crystal; screwed-down exhibition case back; screw-in crown; water-resistant to 50 m
Band: crocodile skin, buckle
Remarks: 15 micro gas tubes on hands and dial; shock-resistant to 5000 Gs; anti-magnetic to 4,800 A/m
Price: $1,899
Variations: blue dial; stainless steel bracelet

Trainmaster Cleveland Express Dual
Reference number: GM1020D-PG-LCJ-SL
Movement: automatic, ETA Caliber 2836-2; ø 25.6 mm, height 5.05 mm; 25 jewels; 28,800 vph; 38 hours power reserve; C.O.S.C. certified chronometer
Functions: hours, minutes, sweep seconds; date; second time zone, military time indication, date warning system
Case: stainless steel, ø 41 mm; height 12.5 mm; sapphire crystal; screwed-down exhibition case back; screw-in crown; water-resistant to 50 m
Band: crocodile skin, buckle
Remarks: 16 micro gas tubes on hands and dial; shock-resistant to 5000 Gs; anti-magnetic to 4,800 A/m
Price: $1,899

Trainmaster Cannonball
Reference number: CM1052D-L1J-BK
Movement: automatic, Ball Caliber 2050 (base Soprod); ø 25.6 mm, height 5.05 mm; 25 jewels; 28,800 vph; 38 hours power reserve
Functions: hours, minutes, subsidiary seconds; date; 45-minute chronograph
Case: stainless steel, ø 43 mm; height 14.8 mm; anti-reflective sapphire crystal; screwed-down case back; screw-in crown; water-resistant to 50 m
Band: crocodile skin, buckle
Remarks: 15 micro gas tubes on hands and dial; shock-resistant to 5000 Gs; enamel dial
Price: $2,599
Variations: white dial; stainless steel bracelet with double folding clasp

Trainmaster Pulsemeter Pro
Reference number: CM1038D-SAJ-BK
Movement: automatic, Ball Caliber 250 (base ETA Valjoux 7750); ø 30 mm, height 7.9 mm; 25 jewels; 28,800 vph; 42 hours power reserve
Functions: hours, minutes, subsidiary seconds; one-button chronograph; date, day; pulsemeter
Case: stainless steel, ø 43 mm; height 15.5 mm; anti-reflective sapphire crystal; screwed-down exhibition case back; screw-in crown with crown protection; water-resistant to 50 m
Band: stainless steel, folding clasp
Remarks: 27 micro gas tubes on hands and dial; shock-resistant to 5,000 Gs
Price: $2,999
Variations: white dial; calfskin strap

Conductor Transcendent Diamond
Reference number: NL1068D-DIA-S2J-PK
Movement: automatic, ETA Caliber 2671; ø 25.6 mm, height 4.8 mm; 25 jewels; 28,800 vph; 38 hours power reserve
Functions: hours, minutes, sweep seconds; date
Case: stainless steel, 28.4 x 38 mm; height 11.6 mm; diamond-set bezel; anti-reflective domed sapphire crystal; screwed-down exhibition case back; screw-in crown; water-resistant to 50 m
Band: stainless steel, double folding clasp
Remarks: 15 micro gas tubes on hands and dial, shock-resistant to 5,000 Gs; mother-of-pearl dial
Price: $3,499
Variations: blue or cream-colored dial; matching crocodile skin strap with buckle

Conductor Chronograph
Reference number: CM1068D-LJ-BK
Movement: automatic, ETA Valjoux Caliber 7750; ø 30 mm, height 7.9 mm; 25 jewels; 28,800 vph; 42 hours power reserve
Functions: hours, minutes, subsidiary seconds; date, day; chronograph
Case: stainless steel, 38.5 x 51 mm, height 16.8 mm; anti-reflective sapphire crystal; exhibition case back; screw-in crown; water-resistant to 50 m
Band: crocodile skin, buckle
Remarks: 18 micro gas tubes on hands and dial; shock-resistant to 5,000 Gs
Price: $2,599
Variations: white dial; stainless steel bracelet with double folding clasp

Fireman Skylab
Reference number: CM1092C-SAJ-BR
Movement: automatic, ETA Valjoux Caliber 7750; ø 30 mm, height 7.9 mm; 25 jewels; 28,800 vph; 42 hours power reserve
Functions: hours, minutes, subsidiary seconds; date, day; chronograph
Case: stainless steel, ø 43 mm, height 14.4 mm; anti-reflective sapphire crystal; screwed-down case back; screw-in crown; water-resistant to 100 m
Band: stainless steel, folding clasp
Remarks: 18 micro gas tubes on hands and dial; shock-resistant to 5,000 Gs; comes in set including calfskin strap
Price: $2,699
Variations: black dial

Fireman Night Train
Reference number: NM1092C-L1B-BK
Movement: automatic, ETA Caliber 2824-2; ø 25.6 mm, height 4.6 mm; 25 jewels; 28,800 vph; 38 hours power reserve
Functions: hours, minutes, sweep seconds; date; military time indication; date warning system
Case: stainless steel covered with DLC (diamond-like carbon), ø 43 mm, height 11.1 mm; anti-reflective sapphire crystal; screwed-down case back; screw-in crown; water-resistant to 100 m
Band: calfskin, buckle
Remarks: 63 micro gas tubes on hands and dial; shock-resistant to 5,000 Gs
Price: $1,399

Reach the World with Timezone.com

International Reach

TimeZone.com is the world's largest and most complete online resource for watch enthusiasts and collectors. Launched in 1994, Time Zone has grown from a small group of enthusiasts to over 45,000 registered users today. More impressive is the number of people who visit TimeZone: in 2006 the site was visited by more than 3 million unique visitors* around the world. TimeZone's reach is truly international, TimeZone's 31 moderators are located in 9 countries and offers discussion in English, French and Japanese. The site is viewed by large numbers of enthusiasts in Italy, France, Germany, Hong Kong, Japan, Singapore, Russia, Switzerland, the UK, Canada, the Netherlands, and many more. There is no other source that covers the world of watches like TimeZone.

TimeZone's viewer traffic has increased dramatically in the past few years. The site receives visits from about 330,000 unique visitors* each month, compared with 32,000 per month in 2002. Today TimeZone generates about 9.5 million page views per month, compared with about 250,000 in 2002. TimeZone averages well over 2,000 new message posts each day, and on some days as many as 3,000 new messages are posted. For watch lovers the world over, TimeZone is the place to be.

Resources Attract a Broad and Affluent Community

TimeZone's extansive resources and many special events attract an affluent group of enthusiast and collectors. TimeZone's brand forums serve as home base for online enthusiasts of the leading watch brands, including Patek Philippe, Rolex, Audemars Piguet, Vacheron Constantin, Breguet, Jaeger LeCoultre, Lange & Söhne, Cartier, Panerai, IWC, and many more. TimeZone's Vintage Watch forum is the meeting place for aficionados of timepieces from the golden age. The Watchmaking Forum provides a place for those with technical interests to seek advice and share information. If you want to open a watch and see what makes it tick, TimeZone offers an online watch school taught by a professional watchmaking instructor. One of TimeZone's most visited pages is Industry News – you can get the all the latest updates here with just a click. The Lifestyle, Automotive and Photography forums offer pleasing and informative diversions.

TimeZone matches its strong online offerings with an industry leading line-up of real world events. TimeZoners around the world host collector get togethers (or "GTGs") where enthusiasts meet others who share their passion, and often leading personalities in the world of watches. Each year TimeZone sends reporters to the Basel and Geneva watch shows to post daily reports. TimeZone's Basel/SIHH Forum is the best place to get real time updates on the newest watches from the top brands. TimeZone also hosts annual Collectors' Tours of Switzerland and Germany. These events take up to 20 collectors on private guided tours of the leading manufacturers and museums, including Patek Philippe, Vacheron Constantin, Audemars Piguet, Jaeger LeCoultre, Lange & Söhne, Glashütte Original, Blancpain, and more. Tours often include a special private dinner with leading independent watchmakers such as Philippe Dufour, Vianney Halter, Felix Baumgartner, Kees Engelbarts, and others.

If you are an advertiser who wants to reach watch enthusiasts, TimeZone.com is the place to be. For more information or to obtain a rate sheet, please e-mail us at advertise@timezone.com

* Unique Visitors: The total number of unique visitors during the report period.
A unique visitor is identified by their IP address or domain name

Baume & Mercier

The traditional brand Baume & Mercier was established in 1830 in western Switzerland by the Baume family, receiving an additional name in 1918 upon merging with Genevan jeweler Mercier. This company earned its reputation during the first heyday of the wristwatch as a manufacturer of sporty chronographs.

The name became official in 1920 when it was registered in Switzerland by William Baume and his friend Paul Mercier. That year was to be a successful one for the company, with the official registry office of the canton of Geneva certifying that this brand had the highest number of movements awarded the Seal of Geneva at the time. This sensational success was the sole work of watchmaker William Baume, grandson of the founder. It is for this reason that the brand has now dedicated a whole collection to him in the modern era: the stylish, elegant William Baume Collection.

Within the larger Richemont Group, Baume & Mercier—along with Cartier and Piaget—forms the nucleus of the watch business. Today, the company is distributed in seventy-five countries, producing about 200,000 watches annually. The European markets—especially Italy, Spain, and France—are particularly important for the brand. In Germany, Baume & Mercier is distributed in 220 exclusive retail shops. And two years ago, Baume & Mercier opened its own production workshops in Les Brenets.

In the last few years, Baume & Mercier has made a name for itself as a watch trendsetter, though in no way only with typical watch fad material. Models like the Riviera and the Hampton—named for the high society beaches of the East Coast—defined a new his and hers watch style in the 1980s and '90s, tempting many brands to follow suit.

Not many watch shapes exist that are accepted right from the get-go. Watches that veer too far from the norm of a circle, or even rectangle, are quickly stamped unserious. The slim, well-proportioned shape of the Hampton goes right up to the line without going over.

For those who may not (yet) dare to embark on the adventure of a rectangular watch, Baume & Mercier introduced a new line of simple, round watches by the name of Executives two years ago.

And at the SIHH 2007, the brand debuted decidedly sporty and technically interesting model variations of the Riviera and Hampton lines, aimed at transporting the successful concept to a new level according to the wishes of designer Alexandre Peraldi.

Baume & Mercier

Riviera XXL Chronograph
Reference number: MOA08755
Movement: automatic, BM Caliber 13750 (base ETA Valjoux 7750); ø 30.4 mm, height 7.9 mm; 25 jewels; 28,800 vph
Functions: hours, minutes, subsidiary seconds; chronograph; date
Case: stainless steel and titanium, ø 43 mm, height 14.65 mm; sapphire crystal; screw-in crown; transparent case back; water-resistant to 20 atm
Band: rubber, security folding clasp
Price: $3,995
Variations: PVD-coated stainless steel; 18-karat rose gold

Classima Executives XL Chronograph
Reference number: MOA08733
Movement: automatic, BM Caliber 13750 (base ETA Valjoux 7750); ø 30.4 mm, height 7.9 mm; 25 jewels; 28,800 vph
Functions: hours, minutes, subsidiary seconds; chronograph; date
Case: stainless steel, ø 42 mm, height 12.95 mm; sapphire crystal
Band: reptile skin, double folding clasp
Price: $2,895
Variations: white dial and stainless steel link bracelet

Classima Executives Power Reserve
Reference number: MOA08736
Movement: automatic, BM Caliber 119094 (base Soprod 9094); ø 25.6 mm, height 5.1 mm; 30 jewels; 28,800 vph
Functions: hours, minutes, sweep seconds; retrograde date, weekday; power reserve display
Case: stainless steel, ø 39 mm, height 11.35 mm; sapphire crystal; transparent case back
Band: reptile skin, buckle
Remarks: limited edition of 1,830 pieces
Price: $4,495
Variations: rose gold

Classima Executives XL GMT
Reference number: MOA08734
Movement: automatic, BM Caliber 11893-2 (base ETA 2893-2); ø 26.2 mm, height 3.6 mm; 25 jewels; 28,800 vph
Functions: hours, minutes, sweep seconds; 24-hour display (second time zone); date
Case: stainless steel, ø 42 mm, height 8.8 mm; sapphire crystal
Band: stainless steel, double folding clasp
Price: $2,295
Variations: leather strap

Hampton Square
Reference number: MOA08749
Movement: automatic, BM Caliber 11651 (base Soprod TT651); ø 25.6 mm, height 5.1 mm, 21 jewels; 28,800 vph
Functions: hours, minutes, sweep seconds; second time zone; large date
Case: stainless steel and titanium, 34.1 x 45 mm, height 12.6 mm; sapphire crystal; screw-in crown with crown protection; transparent case back, water-resistant to 20 atm
Band: rubber, security folding clasp
Price: $3,995

Hampton Classic
Reference number: MOA08747
Movement: quartz, BM Caliber 5001 (base ETA 901.001)
Functions: hours, minutes
Case: stainless steel, 20.4 x 34.2 mm, height 6.8 mm; sapphire crystal
Band: stainless steel, double folding clasp
Price: $1,595
Variations: mother-of-pearl dial and set with diamonds

Hampton Milleis
Reference number: MOA08245
Movement: automatic, BM Caliber 8395 (base ETA 2000); ø 20 mm, height 3.6 mm; 20 jewels; 28,800 vph
Functions: hours, minutes; date
Case: yellow gold, 26 x 40.6 mm, height 8.13 mm; sapphire crystal
Band: reptile skin, folding clasp
Price: $3,495

Diamant
Reference number: MOA08738
Movement: quartz, BM Caliber 7111 (base ETA F03.111/h1)
Functions: hours, minutes; date
Case: stainless steel 22 x 34 mm, height 8.05 mm; oval crown with diamond; sapphire crystal;
Band: stainless steel, folding clasp
Remarks: mother-of-pearl dial with 11 diamond markers
Price: $2,795
Variations: Arabic numerals; case set with brilliant-cut diamonds

Bell & Ross

Instrument BR01 is the name of a three-year-old product line by Bell & Ross, and it really is an impressive instrument—an airplane cockpit board instrument, to be more precise. The square case with its four visible screw heads is reminiscent of the frame of a cockpit instrument, and that is of course absolutely the goal—making the watch seem even more massive on the wrist than it really is, even though 46 mm is not a size to be sneezed at.

Right from the beginning BR01 has been available as a chronograph (ETA Caliber 2894) or as a simple three-hand watch, the latter also available with a large date or power reserve display. The stainless steel case has a satin finish with polished edges or is completely matte black. The choice of dial colors is galvanic black or silver, each in combination with luminous hands and hour markers.

With the advent of Instrument BR01, the French brand is announcing its frontal attack on the wrists of professionals and scene followers alike, for the new watches are in fact as robust as they look after having undergone innumerable tests—something that certainly makes their attractiveness to watch fans outside of pilot's and war buff circles even stronger. The model also comes with its own tools for working on the strap lugs. In this way the watch can be set up on a desk or screwed onto a dashboard in addition to being worn as a wristwatch.

The past two seasons have seen colorfully revamped dials and various new case versions meant to differentiate themselves from the professional military character of the Instruments line using—among other elements—glowing orange and blue tones. An interesting addition to the line is the Phantom, which took its inspiration from Stealth bombers, making the dial more subtle, almost invisible, during the day, while its photoluminescent finish makes it optimal for night reading.

Entering the *haute horlogerie* arena in 2007, Bell & Ross also introduced a limited edition luxury version called the BR01 Instrument Tourbillon. In addition to a tourbillon and power reserve indicator, this regulator-style timepiece also features an interesting addition: a torque indicator the company is calling its trust index. Basically, this display takes the tension of the mainspring into account, giving the wearer a reckoning of the spring's precision based on the amount of torque left in it. The particularly attractive timepiece is housed in a titanium case coated with DLC (diamond-like carbon), which hardens it to 4,000 Vickers. Carbon fiber was also used to craft the dial and the inserts found around the side of the case, lightening the total weight of the case without compromising its robustness—thanks in part to the fact that the movement's base plate is also crafted in carbon fiber. Completing the high-tech look, the visible tourbillon carriage is made of blackened gold.

Changes such as these have gone into effect since perfume and fashion specialist Chanel bought into the company a few years ago, a business deal that also allowed Bell & Ross to call production facilities in La Chaux-de-Fonds its own—something that has opened all pathways for designer Bruno Belamich and his team to develop even more difficult and interesting designs according to Bell & Ross's fundamentals expressed in the professional, instrument-like, yet aesthetic character of the brand's watches.

Bell & Ross

BR 01 Instrument Titanium
Reference number: BR01-94
Movement: automatic, ETA Caliber 2894-2; ø 28.6 mm, height 6.1 mm; 37 jewels; 28,800 vph
Functions: hours, minutes, subsidiary seconds; chronograph; date
Case: titanium, 46 x 46 mm, height 11.5 mm; bezel secured to monocoque case with four screws; sapphire crystal; screw-in crown; water-resistant to 10 atm
Band: rubber, buckle
Remarks: delivered with additional synthetic textile strap
Price: $5,900

BR 01 Instrument Titanium Orange
Reference number: BR01-94
Movement: automatic, ETA Caliber 2894-2; ø 28.6 mm, height 6.1 mm; 37 jewels; 28,800 vph
Functions: hours, minutes, subsidiary seconds; date; chronograph
Case: titanium, 46 x 46 mm, height 11.5 mm; bezel secured to monocoque case with four screws; sapphire crystal; screw-in crown; water-resistant to 10 atm
Band: rubber, buckle
Remarks: delivered with additional synthetic textile strap; limited edition of 500 pieces
Price: $6,500

BR 01 Instrument Phantom
Reference number: BR01-94
Movement: automatic, ETA Caliber 2894-2; ø 28.6 mm, height 6.1 mm; 37 jewels; 28,800 vph
Functions: hours, minutes, subsidiary seconds; date; chronograph
Case: stainless steel with black vacuum carbon coating, 46 x 46 mm, height 11.5 mm; bezel secured to monocoque case with four screws; sapphire crystal; screw-in crown; water-resistant to 10 atm
Band: rubber, buckle
Remarks: delivered with additional synthetic textile strap; dial printed with black luminous substance that fluoresces white; limited edition of 500 pieces
Price: $6,000

BR 03 Instrument Carbon Finish
Reference number: BR03-94
Movement: automatic, ETA Caliber 2894-2; ø 28.6 mm, height 6.1 mm; 37 jewels; 28,800 vph
Functions: hours, minutes, subsidiary seconds; date; chronograph
Case: stainless steel with black vacuum carbon coating, 42 x 42 mm, height 11.5 mm; bezel secured to monocoque case with four screws; sapphire crystal; screw-in crown; water-resistant to 10 atm
Band: rubber, buckle
Price: $5,200
Variations: synthetic textile strap

BR 01 Instrument Diamond
Reference number: BR01-92
Movement: automatic, ETA Caliber 2892-A2; ø 25.6 mm, height 3.6 mm; 21 jewels; 28,800 vph
Functions: hours, minutes, sweep seconds
Case: stainless steel with black vacuum carbon coating, 46 x 46 mm, height 9.5 mm; bezel set with brilliant-cut diamon secured to monocoque case with four screws; sapphire crystal; screw-in crown; water-resistant to 10 atm
Band: rubber, buckle
Price: $10,500
Variations: reptile skin strap

BR 01 Instrument Power Reserve Indicator Full Diamond
Reference number: BR01-97
Movement: automatic, ETA Caliber 2897; ø 25.6 mm, height 4.85 mm; 21 jewels; 28,800 vph
Functions: hours, minutes, sweep seconds; date; power reserve indicator
Case: stainless steel, 46 x 46 mm, height 10.5 mm; bezel and case set with brilliant-cut diamonds; bezel secured to monocoque case with four screws; sapphire crystal; screw-in crown; water-resistant to 10 atm
Band: reptile skin, buckle
Remarks: power reserve indicator set with rubies, diamonds, and sapphires
Price: $28,000

BR 02 Instrument Steel
Reference number: BR02-92
Movement: automatic, ETA Caliber 2892-A2; ø 25.6 mm, height 3.6 mm; 21 jewels; 28,800 vph
Functions: hours, minutes, sweep seconds; date
Case: stainless steel, ø 44 mm; rotating ring under crystal with 60-minute divisions settable via crown; sapphire crystal; screw-in crowns; water-resistant to 100 atm
Band: rubber, buckle
Remarks: automatic helium valve in case
Price: $4,000
Variations: with synthetic textile strap; in black vacuum carbon case finish

BR 02 Instrument Carbon Prodial
Reference number: BR02-92
Movement: automatic, ETA Caliber 2892-A2; ø 25.6 mm, height 3.6 mm; 21 jewels; 28,800 vph
Functions: hours, minutes, sweep seconds; date
Case: stainless steel with black vacuum carbon coating, ø 44 mm; rotating ring under crystal with 60-minute divisions settable via crown; sapphire crystal; screw-in crowns; water-resistant to 100 atm
Band: synthetic textile, buckle
Remarks: automatic helium valve in case
Price: $4,500
Variations: stainless steel

Ernst Benz

It has always been hard to ignore Ernst Benz. This brand was one of the first to create a complete collection housed in 47-millimeter cases, a trend that seems to have found its modern muse in the United States. The large size of this brand's cases had more of a functional reason to them than simple fashion, though: they were created so large to make them legible for pilots. Okay, so we're talking modern hobby aviators here, but still people risking life and limb in small recreational airplanes. Ernst Benz himself was and continues to be one of these pilots. And he loves to invent—so what emerged was an instrument-styled timepiece large enough for hobby aviators to see at a glance.

The response Benz received from fellow aviators for the large-format timepiece was overwhelming, and it went into limited-quantity series—which formed the tentative start to a brand bearing his name. Under new ownership, this concept has now been divided into three families: Traditional, Contemporary, and Diamond—which include new ChronoDiver and ChronoFlite models. The latter can even boast a new GMT variation loyally designed according to one of Benz's own original designs and a World Timer slated for release this winter. Ernst Benz continues to make waves—some that just cannot be ignored as the Ernst Benz brand is now also discovering the world of partnerships. Not only does this young brand enjoy a fruitful relationship with prominent designer John Varvatos, but since mid-2007 also with star chef Mario Batali. The brand partnered with the cook and restaurateur to create a limited edition series of timepieces to benefit the Food Bank For New York City.

The Mario Batali Limited Edition Ernst Benz Great Circle Automatic is an enhanced version of the timepiece's original design, featuring accents in Batali's signature color orange. Batali personally collaborated with Leonid Khankin, Ernst Benz's managing director and chief creative officer, to design and produce the exclusive collection of timepieces. "My partnership with Ernst Benz is born out of my love to celebrate life with simple things of the highest quality, this new watch created by my friend Leonid Khankin is exactly that. To bring art and public service together is a privilege I will never squander; the opportunity to help the Food Bank For New York City provide food for over a quarter million meals a day in New York City is a joyous part of my celebration," Batali explains. This special series of timepieces is available in three Great Circle sizes: 36, 40, and 47 millimeters, each size numbered and limited to 250 pieces. Batali and Khankin personally launched the collection at an exclusive event at the Food & Wine Classic in Aspen on June 15, 2007.

Ernst Benz

ChronoSport 47 mm Roman Contemporary
Reference number: GC 10251/RC
Movement: automatic, ETA Caliber 2836-2; ø 25.6 mm, height 4.6 mm; 25 jewels; 28,800 vph
Functions: hours, minutes, sweep seconds; date, weekday
Case: stainless steel, ø 47mm, height 13.6 mm; sapphire crystal; screw-down sapphire crystal exhibition case back; double O-ring sealed crown; water-resistant to 50 m
Band: alligator skin, buckle
Price: $2,700

ChronoJewel 47 mm
Reference number: GC 10121DD
Movement: automatic, ETA Valjoux Caliber 7750; ø 30 mm, height 7.9 mm; 25 jewels; 28,800 vph
Functions: hours, minutes, subsidiary seconds; date, day; chronograph
Case: stainless steel, ø 47mm, height 16 mm; bezel set with 5 ct brilliant-cut diamonds; sapphire crystal; sapphire crystal exhibition case back; double O-ring sealed crown; water-resistant to 50 m
Band: alligator skin, buckle
Price: $22,500
Variations: optional folding clasp; white dial; stainless steel bracelet; 40 mm case size; 2 ct diamonds

ChronoJewel Roman 47 mm
Reference number: GC 10251TTD
Movement: automatic, ETA Caliber 2836-2; ø 25.6 mm, height 4.6 mm; 25 jewels; 28,800 vph
Functions: hours, minutes, sweep seconds; date, day
Case: yellow gold and stainless steel, ø 47mm, height 14.1 mm; 18-karat yellow gold bezel set with 4 ct brilliant-cut diamonds; sapphire crystal; exhibition sapphire crystal case back; double O-ring sealed crown; water-resistant to 50 m
Band: alligator skin, buckle
Remarks: limited edition of 100 pieces
Price: $18,400

ChronoJewel 36 mm
Reference number: GC 3024ID
Movement: automatic, ETA Caliber 2836-2; ø 25.6 mm, height 4.6 mm; 25 jewels; 28,800 vph
Functions: hours, minutes, sweep seconds; date
Case: stainless steel, ø 36mm, height 12.2 mm; bezel set with 1.15 ct brilliant-cut diamonds; sapphire crystal; exhibition sapphire crystal case back; double O-ring sealed crown; water-resistant to 50 m
Band: alligator skin, buckle
Price: $6,600
Variations: optional folding clasp; white mother-of-pearl dial; stainless steel bracelet

ChronoScope 47 mm Vintage PVD
Reference number: GC 10176N-CF
Movement: automatic, ETA Valjoux Caliber 7750; ø 30 mm, height 7.9 mm; 25 jewels; 28,800 vph; PVD-plated rotor
Functions: hours, minutes, subsidiary seconds; date, day; chronograph
Case: PVD-coated stainless steel, ø 47mm, height 16 mm; sapphire crystal; screw-down sapphire crystal exhibition case back; double O-ring sealed crown; water-resistant to 50 m
Band: carbon fiber, black PVD buckle
Remarks: limited edition of 250 pieces; carbon fiber dial
Price: $5,300
Variations: nylon or black alligator strap with regular dial

ChronoScope 47 mm PVD
Reference number: GC 10171 N
Movement: automatic, ETA Valjoux Caliber 7750; ø 30 mm, height 7.9 mm; 25 jewels; 28,800 vph; PVD-plated rotor
Functions: hours, minutes, subsidiary seconds; date, day; chronograph
Case: PVD-coated stainless steel, ø 47mm, height 16 mm; sapphire crystal; screw-down sapphire crystal exhibition case back; double O-ring sealed crown; water-resistant to 50 m
Band: carbon fiber, black PVD buckle
Remarks: limited edition of 250 pieces; carbon fiber dial
Price: $4,800
Variations: nylon or black alligator strap with regular dial

ChronoScope 47 mm Traditional
Reference number: GC 10114B
Movement: automatic, ETA Valjoux Caliber 7750; ø 30 mm, height 7.9 mm; 25 jewels; 28,800 vph
Functions: hours, minutes, subsidiary seconds; date, day; chronograph
Case: stainless steel, ø 47mm, height 16 mm; sapphire crystal; screw-down exhibition case back; double O-ring sealed crown; water-resistant to 50 m
Band: stainless steel, folding clasp
Price: $4,200
Variations: black or white dial; alligator skin strap; 40 or 44 mm case size

ChronoScope 47 mm Traditional
Reference number: GC 10118A
Movement: automatic, ETA Valjoux Caliber 7750; ø 30 mm, height 7.9 mm; 25 jewels; 28,800 vph
Functions: hours, minutes, subsidiary seconds; date, day; chronograph
Case: stainless steel, ø 47mm, height 16 mm; sapphire crystal; screw-down exhibition case back; double O-ring sealed crown; water-resistant to 50 m
Band: alligator skin, buckle
Price: $4,100
Variations: optional folding clasp; black or white dial; stainless steel bracelet; 40 or 44 mm case size

Ernst Benz

ChronoScope 47 mm Traditional
Reference number: GC 10119A
Movement: automatic, ETA Valjoux Caliber 7750; ø 30 mm, height 7.9 mm; 25 jewels; 28,800 vph
Functions: hours, minutes, subsidiary seconds; date, day; chronograph
Case: stainless steel, ø 47mm, height 16 mm; sapphire crystal; screw-down exhibition case back; double O-ring sealed crown; water-resistant to 50 m
Band: alligator skin, buckle
Price: $4,100
Variations: optional folding clasp; black or white dial; stainless steel bracelet; 40 or 44 mm case size

ChronoScope 40 mm
Reference number: GC 20113D
Movement: automatic, ETA Valjoux Caliber 7750; ø 30 mm, height 7.9 mm; 25 jewels; 28,800 vph
Functions: hours, minutes, subsidiary seconds; date, day; chronograph
Case: stainless steel, ø 40 mm, height 15.8 mm; bezel set with 1.25 ct of brilliant-cut diamonds; sapphire crystal; screw-down sapphire crystal exhibition case back; double O-ring sealed crown; water-resistant to 50 m
Band: alligator skin, buckle
Price: $7,700
Variations: black, white, or mother-of-pearl dial; bracelet; 47 mm case size

ChronoLunar 40 mm
Reference number: GC 20312D
Movement: automatic, ETA Valjoux Caliber 7750; ø 30 mm, height 7.9 mm; 25 jewels; 28,800 vph
Functions: hours, minutes, subsidiary seconds; date, day; chronograph; month; moon phase; 24-hour display
Case: stainless steel, ø 40mm, height 15.8 mm; bezel set with 1.25 ct of brilliant-cut diamonds; sapphire crystal; screw-down sapphire crystal exhibition case back; double O-ring sealed crown; water-resistant to 50 m
Band: alligator skin, buckle
Price: $9,300
Variations: optional folding clasp; black dial; stainless steel bracelet; 47 mm case

ChronoLunar 47 mm
Reference number: GC 10312A
Movement: automatic, ETA Valjoux Caliber 7751; ø 30 mm, height 7.9 mm; 25 jewels; 28,800 vph
Functions: hours, minutes, subsidiary seconds; date, day; chronograph, month, moon phase; 24-hour display
Case: stainless steel, ø 47mm, height 16.3 mm; sapphire crystal; screw-down sapphire crystal exhibition case back; double O-ring sealed crown; water-resistant to 50 m
Band: alligator skin, buckle
Price: $5,800
Variations: optional folding clasp; black dial; stainless steel bracelet

Mario Batali 47 mm
Reference number: GC 10186-MB
Movement: automatic, ETA Valjoux Caliber 7750; ø 30 mm, height 7.9 mm; 25 jewels; 28,800 vph
Functions: hours, minutes, subsidiary seconds; date, day; chronograph
Case: stainless steel, ø 47 mm, height 16 mm; sapphire crystal; screw-down sapphire crystal exhibition case back; double O-ring sealed crown; water-resistant to 50 m
Band: alligator skin, buckle
Remarks: limited edition of 250 pieces
Price: $4,500
Variations: 40 or 36 mm case

ChronoDiver 47 mm
Reference number: GC 10721/CN
Movement: automatic, ETA Valjoux Caliber 7750; ø 30 mm, height 7.9 mm; 25 jewels; 28,800 vph
Functions: hours, minutes, sweep seconds; date, day; chronograph
Case: stainless steel, ø 47 mm, height 15.8 mm; unidirectionally rotating steel bezel; sapphire crystal; screwed-down case back; screw-in crown; double O-ring sealed crown; water-resistant to 200 m
Band: leather, buckle
Price: $4,800
Variations: alligator skin or rubber strap

ChronoFlite World Timer 47 mm
Reference number: GC 10851/CP
Movement: automatic, ETA Caliber 2893-2; ø 25.6 mm, height 4.1 mm; 21 jewels; 28,800 vph
Functions: hours, minutes, sweep seconds; date; world time, second time zone
Case: stainless steel, ø 47 mm, height 12.1 mm; sapphire crystal; screw-down case back; double O-ring sealed crown; water-resistant to 50 m
Band: nylon, buckle
Price: $4,900

ChronoFlite GMT 47 mm
Reference number: GC 10821
Movement: automatic, ETA Caliber 2893-2; ø 25.6 mm, height 4.1 mm; 21 jewels; 28,800 vph
Functions: hours, minutes, sweep seconds; date; second time zone
Case: stainless steel, ø 47 mm, height 11.8 mm; unidirectionally rotating bezel with 24-hour scale; sapphire crystal; screw-down sapphire crystal exhibition case back; double O-ring sealed crown; water-resistant to 200 m
Band: alligator skin, buckle
Price: $3,800

Jochen Benzinger

"Welcome to my industrial museum," Jochen Benzinger sometimes greets visitors to his workshop. What Benzinger says with a laugh actually hits the nail on the head. The forty-four-year-old Pforzheim native maintains an age-old craft with the art of guilloché, using machines that haven't been built for decades. His hand languidly waves toward the 40-foot length of the room, "Back there is the oldest machine that I work with. It's from about 1880, while the youngest is just about sixty years old." All these examples of German and Swiss toolmaking serve one purpose: to decorate watches.

Benzinger learned the art of engraving between 1978 and 1982 from what was Pforzheim's top engraver during that period. Although guilloché is closely related to engraving, at the time it was no longer officially part of the education needed to become an engraver, and Benzinger had to teach himself the art. Fortunately, at the time he was still able to find old, experienced masters of guilloché in some of Pforzheim's jewelry making companies, willing to pass their knowledge on to him. In 1985, Benzinger used this knowledge to found his own company. He created an attractive niche for himself and successfully worked for the local jewelry industry for a long time. For the last five years, the Pforzheim native has worked exclusively in the world of watches, though.

Word of the high quality of his work has gotten around. Even reputable Swiss watch manufacturers contact the introverted engraver to decorate movements and components. Benzinger's company skeletonizes and engraves between 150 and 200 movements for international customers annually, also decorating about 500 rotors for automatic movements. "Industry contracts like that give me the security to keep my company going," Benzinger, who works with his father, two watchmakers, and a freelance master goldsmith, explains. Since this is such a sensitive business, he must naturally remain discreet, refusing to name his contractors. You may well find Benzinger's work in many watches without his name on them.

The engraver also creates one to two unique watches of his own per month. His clients are normal people located all over the world. And it is here that the artist can allow his creativity a great deal of freedom, expressing his personal style. "I skeletonize movements so that you can't necessarily recognize the original movement at first glance. I like that, and it also differentiates me from my Swiss colleagues."

Silver and Blue Subscription
Movement: manually wound, ETA Unitas Caliber 6498; ø 36.6 mm, height 4.5 mm; 17 jewels; 21,600 vph; movement completely skeletonized, engraved, and guilloché by hand; blued screws; skeletonized and blued ratchet wheel; blue coated base plate
Functions: hours, minutes (off-center), subsidiary seconds
Case: stainless steel, ø 42 mm, height 10.5 mm; sapphire crystal; transparent case back
Band: reptile skin, double folding clasp
Price: $8,750
Variations: yellow or red gold

Three-Quarter Skeleton
Movement: manually wound, ETA Unitas Caliber 6498; ø 36.6 mm, height 4.5 mm; 17 jewels; 21,600 vph; movement completely skeletonized, engraved, and guilloché by hand; partially rose gold-plated, blued screws; skeletonized and blued ratchet wheel
Functions: hours, minutes, subsidiary seconds
Case: stainless steel, ø 42 mm, height 10.5 mm; sapphire crystal; transparent case back
Band: reptile skin, double folding clasp
Remarks: silver hand-guilloché dial; partially skeletonized
Price: $8,650
Variations: yellow or red gold

Hand-Engraved Skeleton
Movement: manually wound, ETA Unitas Caliber 6498; ø 36.6 mm, height 4.5 mm; 17 jewels; 21,600 vph; movement completely skeletonized, engraved, and guilloché by hand; blued screws; skeletonized and blued ratchet wheel
Functions: hours, minutes, subsidiary seconds
Case: stainless steel, ø 42 mm, height 10.5 mm; sapphire crystal; transparent case back
Band: reptile skin, double folding clasp
Price: $7,650
Variations: yellow or red gold

Zeitmaschine Chronograph
Movement: automatic, ETA Valjoux Caliber 7750; ø 30 mm, height 7.9 mm; 25 jewels; 28,800 vph; blue coated base plate, partially skeletonized; gold rotor completely skeletonized, engraved, and guilloché by hand
Functions: hours, minutes (off-center), subsidiary seconds; chronograph
Case: stainless steel, ø 42 mm, height 13 mm; sapphire crystal; transparent case back
Band: reptile skin, double folding clasp
Price: $10,600
Variations: yellow or red gold

Rainer Brand

Those who may have had the opportunity to discover the hiking trails of Germany's Spessart region will know Heimbuchenthal. Looking around the idyllic community a little, one could get the impression that time is of special interest here. Heimbuchenthal—the geographic midpoint between Switzerland's Jura region and Germany's Glashütte—is home to a remarkable German watchmaker who loves its peace and quiet to complete his exceptional work: Rainer Brand.

This forty-five-year-old watchmaker is a man of few words; calmness and peace are characteristic of him—and that of his ticking companions. Whether he is talking about his watches or letting them do the talking for him, there is one thing the listener feels without doubt: Brand is modern without feeling obligated to follow fashion. He respects values without being conservative. And he banks on reliability without nostalgia. It soon becomes clear why he has chosen the remoteness of the Spessart forest to develop his watches.

Not only are the parallels between this master watchmaker and his place of business obvious; Brand's watch collection mirrors his spirit and his attitude toward life. Short-lived trends and seasonal preferences aren't what this designer is all about. Instead, his goal is to maintain his own style, and that he has done for fifteen years with flying colors. Brand has remained true to his credo, "style is the product of conscious quality" to this day—much to the joy of his growing clientele. Thus, day in, day out, he creates technically interesting watches of high handcrafted quality. Despite their functionality, these masterpieces always look clean and balanced. Could it be the forest?

Kerala S
Reference number: RB 10 S
Movement: automatic, ETA Valjoux Caliber 7750; ø 30 mm, height 7.9 mm; 25 jewels; 28,800 vph; finely finished with côtes de Genève and blued screws
Functions: hours, minutes, subsidiary seconds; chronograph
Case: stainless steel, ø 40.5 mm, height 15.5 mm; sapphire crystal; transparent case back; water-resistant to 10 atm
Band: Russian leather, buckle
Price: $3,930

Panama DS
Reference number: RB 11 DS
Movement: automatic, ETA Caliber 2892-A2; ø 25.6 mm, height 4.8 mm; 21 jewels; 28,800 vph; finely decorated
Functions: hours, minutes, sweep seconds; second time zone; date
Case: stainless steel, ø 36 mm, height 11 mm; sapphire crystal; transparent case back
Band: Russian leather, buckle
Price: $2,766
Variations: with official C.O.S.C. chronometer certification

Argus Chronometer
Reference number: RB 06 SC
Movement: automatic, ETA Caliber 2892-A2; ø 25.6 mm, height 4.8 mm; 21 jewels; 28,800 vph; officially certified C.O.S.C. chronometer
Functions: hours, minutes, sweep seconds; date
Case: stainless steel, ø 38 mm, height 10.2 mm; sapphire crystal; transparent case back; water-resistant to 10 atm
Band: Russian leather, buckle
Price: $2,766

Ecco Chronometer
Reference number: RB 02 SC
Movement: automatic, ETA Caliber 2892-A2; ø 25.6 mm, height 3.6 mm; 21 jewels; 28,800 vph; officially certified C.O.S.C. chronometer
Functions: hours, minutes, sweep seconds; date
Case: stainless steel, 36 x 31 mm, height 9.2 mm; sapphire crystal; transparent case back
Band: Russian leather, buckle
Price: $2,839

Blancpain

When Blancpain was integrated into the Swatch Group in 1992, the first Fifty Fathoms model, which was perhaps the industry's first modern diver's watch, was already thirty-nine years old. Today, Blancpain is updating this historical line in true horological style, outfitting it with a number of technical delicacies—one of which is without a doubt aimed directly at the collector's market.
Fifty Fathoms was originally created in a cooperative effort by the watch brand and two French personalities: Robert Maloubier and Claude Riffaud, who were assigned the job of creating a military diving unit by the French Ministry of Defense. Since they had no watch that would stand up to the extreme conditions of underwater missions, they gave Blancpain a precise list of details that such a watch should include. The brand's watchmakers and engineers then set to work developing a mechanical watch that was to become the archetype of the diver's watch and that remained water-resistant all the way to 50 fathoms, or 91.45 meters—thus setting the timepiece's name.
This robust watch even accompanied ocean researcher Jacques Cousteau and his team as well as director Louis Malle as they filmed the award-winning movie *The Silent World* in 1956.

In 1997, Blancpain extended the Fifty Fathoms's water resistance to 300 meters. Ten short years later, the Le Brassus–based *manufacture* has decided to relaunch the entire collection, including an automatic model, a chronograph with flyback function, and an extremely water-resistant tourbillon (also 300 meters!).
The automatic model is outfitted with an evolution of Blancpain's *manufacture* movement Caliber 13R0, which was introduced in late 2006. Caliber 1315 was especially developed for use in sports watches with a bimetal rotor for extra weight that ensures highly effective winding and an extra shock-proof balance system. One practical detail is found on this caliber's date: it can be turned both backward and forward without fear of damaging the movement.
The Fifty Fathoms Chronograph Flyback is also outfitted with a unique feature: its chronograph buttons can be used under water thanks to a system of special gaskets.
The Fifty Fathoms Tourbillon is a marriage of *haute horlogerie* and performance: Blancpain's "house specialty"—the flying tourbillon—is housed in a case that is water-resistant to a full 300 meters, just like the other models.
As if that weren't enough water for one season, Blancpain also presents a newly revamped piece for its Léman line: the Léman Répétition Minutes Aqua Lung. Thanks to a fully new case construction, this usually quite sensitive movement containing a full-blown minute repeater can now be treated like any sports watch and taken swimming all the way down to 100 meters. Combining fascinating melodious sounds with inventive and practical technical solutions, this timepiece can be personalized for its wearer with an engraving on the solid case back, which still features a tiny exhibition window for peering at the balance.

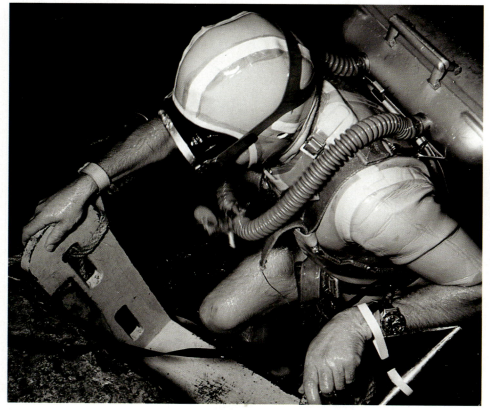

Blancpain

Fifty Fathoms Tourbillon
Reference number: 5025-153052B
Movement: automatic, Blancpain Caliber 25A; ø 25.6 mm, height 4.85 mm; 29 jewels; 21,600 vph; one-minute tourbillon, power reserve 168 hours (eight days)
Functions: hours, minutes, subsidiary seconds (on tourbillon cage); power reserve display
Case: white gold, ø 45 mm, height 15.5 mm; unidirectionally rotating bezel with sapphire crystal inlay; sapphire crystal; screw-in crown; water-resistant to 30 atm
Band: Kevlar, double folding clasp
Price: $102,500
Variations: red gold

Fifty Fathoms
Reference number: 5015-113052B
Movement: automatic, Blancpain Caliber 1315; ø 30.6 mm, height 5.65 mm; 35 jewels; 21,600 vph; protected from magnetic fields by soft iron core
Functions: hours, minutes, sweep seconds; date
Case: stainless steel, ø 45 mm, height 15.5 mm; unidirectionally rotating bezel with sapphire crystal inlay; sapphire crystal; screw-in crown; water-resistant to 30 atm
Band: Kevlar, double folding clasp
Price: $11,100
Variations: red gold

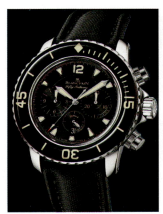

Fifty Fathoms Chronograph
Reference number: 5085F-113052B
Movement: automatic, Blancpain Caliber F185; ø 26.2 mm, height 5.5 mm; 37 jewels; 21,600 vph
Functions: hours, minutes, subsidiary seconds; date; flyback chronograph
Case: stainless steel, ø 45 mm, height 15.5 mm; unidirectionally rotating bezel with sapphire crystal inlay; sapphire crystal; screw-in crown and buttons; water-resistant to 30 atm
Band: Kevlar, double folding clasp
Price: $13,700
Variations: red gold

Léman GMT Alarm
Reference number: 2841-364253B
Movement: automatic, Blancpain Caliber 1241H; ø 31.7 mm, height 6.2 mm; 38 jewels; 28,800 vph; alarm mechanism with automatic winding
Functions: hours, minutes, subsidiary seconds; date; 24-hour display (second time zone); alarm (with power reserve display and indication for alarm function)
Case: rose gold, ø 40 mm, height 13.3 mm; sapphire crystal
Band: reptile skin, folding clasp
Price: $26,500
Variations: white gold

Léman Time Zone
Reference number: 2860-364253B
Movement: automatic, Blancpain Caliber 5L60; ø 26.2 mm, height 3.25 mm; 30 jewels; 21,600 vph
Functions: hours, minutes, subsidiary seconds; date; second time zone; moon phase
Case: rose gold, ø 40 mm, height 11.4 mm; sapphire crystal; transparent case back
Band: reptile skin, double folding clasp
Price: $20,500
Variations: stainless steel

Léman Réveil GMT
Reference number: 2041-12A3064B
Movement: automatic, Blancpain Caliber 1241; ø 31.7 mm, height 6.2 mm; 38 jewels; 28,800 vph
Functions: hours, minutes, subsidiary seconds; date; 24-hour display (second time zone); alarm (with power reserve display and indication for alarm function)
Case: titanium/rose gold, ø 40 mm, height 13.3 mm; sapphire crystal; transparent case back
Band: rubber, folding clasp
Price: $20,100
Variations: in titanium

Le Brassus Perpetual Calendar Tourbillon
Reference number: 4225-364255B
Movement: automatic, Blancpain Caliber 5625A; ø 26.2 mm, height 6.35 mm; 29 jewels; 21,600 vph; one-minute tourbillon; power reserve 7 days
Functions: hours, minutes, subsidiary seconds (on tourbillon cage); perpetual calendar with date, weekday, month, leap year; power reserve display
Case: rose gold, ø 42 mm, height 13 mm; sapphire crystal
Band: reptile skin, double folding clasp
Remarks: corrector buttons on case underneath strap lugs
Price: $128,100

Léman Minute Repeater
Reference number: 2835-123064B
Movement: automatic, Blancpain Caliber 351; ø 23.9 mm, height 4.85 mm; 39 jewels; 21,600 vph
Functions: hours, minutes; minute repeater
Case: titanium, ø 40 mm, height 10.85 mm; sapphire crystal; transparent case back; water-resistant to 10 atm
Band: reptile skin, double folding clasp
Remarks: water-resistant minute repeater
Price: $149,500
Variations: red gold

Blancpain

Fifty Fathoms Air Command Chronograph
Reference number: 5885F-113052B
Movement: automatic, Blancpain Caliber F185; ø 26.2 mm, height 5.5 mm; 37 jewels; 21,600 vph
Functions: hours, minutes, subsidiary seconds; chronograph with flyback function; date
Case: stainless steel, ø 45 mm, height 15.5 mm; unidirectionally rotating bezel with sapphire crystal inlay; sapphire crystal; screw-in crown and buttons; water-resistant to 30 atm
Band: Kevlar, double folding clasp
Price: $14,500

Léman Joaillerie
Reference number: 2850-355455B
Movement: automatic, Blancpain Caliber 6950; ø 32 mm, height 4.75 mm; 35 jewels; 21,600 vph
Functions: hours, minutes, sweep seconds; large date
Case: white gold, ø 40 mm, height 12.6 mm; bezel and strap lugs set with diamonds; sapphire crystal; transparent case back
Band: reptile skin, double folding clasp
Price: $58,10
Variations: red gold

Léman Tourbillon
Reference number: 2925-364253B
Movement: automatic, Blancpain Caliber 3725G; ø 27.6 mm, height 7.05 mm; 35 jewels; 21,600 vph; tourbillon; power reserve 7 days
Functions: hours, minutes; large date, weekday, calendar weeks; power reserve display
Case: rose gold, ø 40 mm, height 14 mm; sapphire crystal; transparent case back
Band: reptile skin, double folding clasp
Price: $108,800
Variations: platinum

Léman Complete Calendar with Moon Phase
Reference number: 2863-112753B
Movement: automatic, Blancpain Caliber 6763; ø 27 mm, height 4.9 mm; 30 jewels; 21,600 vph
Functions: hours, minutes, subsidiary seconds; date, weekday, month, moon phase
Case: stainless steel, ø 40 mm, height 11.5 mm; sapphire crystal
Band: reptile skin, double folding clasp
Price: $10,900
Variations: rose gold

Léman Chrono Flyback
Reference number: 2885F-113053B
Movement: automatic, Blancpain Caliber 69F8; ø 32 mm, height 7 mm; 42 jewels; 21,600 vph
Functions: hours, minutes; chronograph with flyback function; large date
Case: stainless steel, ø 40 mm, height 13.3 mm; sapphire crystal; transparent case back
Band: reptile skin, folding clasp
Price: $11,400

Blancpain Women St. Valentine
Reference number: 3300-454455B
Movement: automatic, Blancpain Caliber 1150; ø 26.2 mm, height 3.25 mm; 28 jewels; 21,600 vph
Functions: hours, minutes, sweep seconds; date
Case: stainless steel, ø 34 mm, height 9.5 mm; bezel set with brilliant-cut diamonds; sapphire crystal; transparent case back
Band: reptile skin, double folding clasp
Price: $13,700

Blancpain Women Lotus
Reference number: 3300-355552B
Movement: automatic, Blancpain Caliber 1150; ø 26.2 mm, height 3.25 mm; 28 jewels; 21,600 vph
Functions: hours, minutes, sweep seconds; date
Case: white gold, ø 34 mm, height 9.5 mm; bezel set with brilliant-cut diamonds; sapphire crystal; transparent case back
Band: satin, double folding clasp
Remarks: dial paved with brilliant-cut diamonds
Price: $33,700
Variations: red gold

Blancpain Women Time Zone
Reference number: 3760-1946A52B
Movement: automatic, Blancpain Caliber 5L60; ø 26.2 mm, height 3.25 mm; 30 jewels; 21,600 vph
Functions: hours, minutes, subsidiary seconds; date; second time zone; day/night indication
Case: white gold, ø 34 mm, height 10.4 mm; bezel set with brilliant-cut diamonds; sapphire crystal; transparent case back
Band: satin, double folding clasp
Remarks: dial paved with brilliant-cut diamonds
Price: $22,200
Variations: stainless steel

Blancpain

Blancpain Women Camélia
Reference number: 3485F-113053B
Movement: automatic, Blancpain Caliber F185; ø 26.2 mm, height 5.5 mm; 37 jewels; 21,600 vph
Functions: hours, minutes, subsidiary seconds; chronograph; date
Case: stainless steel, ø 34 mm, height 11.5 mm; sapphire crystal; transparent case back
Band: reptile skin, double folding clasp
Price: $10,800
Variations: pink or white dial

Le Brassus Perpetual Calendar GMT
Reference number: 4277-344655B
Movement: automatic, Blancpain Caliber 55A5A; ø 27 mm, height 5.95 mm; 28 jewels; 21,600 vph
Functions: hours, minutes; 24-hour display (second time zone); perpetual calendar with date, weekday, month, moon phase, leap year
Case: platinum, ø 42 mm, height 13.5 mm; sapphire crystal; transparent case back
Band: reptile skin, double folding clasp
Price: $68,600

Villeret
Reference number: 6223-1127B5B
Movement: automatic, Blancpain Caliber 1150; ø 26.2 mm, height 3.25 mm; 28 jewels; 21,600 vph; twin spring barrels, power reserve 100 hours
Functions: hours, minutes, sweep seconds; date
Case: stainless steel, ø 38 mm, height 9.2 mm; sapphire crystal
Band: reptile skin, folding clasp
Price: $6,200
Variations: white or red gold

Villeret Moon Phase
Reference number: 6263-3642A55B
Movement: automatic, Blancpain Caliber 6763; ø 27 mm, height 4.9 mm; 30 jewels; 21,600 vph
Functions: hours, minutes, subsidiary seconds; date, weekday, month, moon phase display
Case: rose gold, ø 38 mm, height 10.7 mm; sapphire crystal; transparent case back
Band: reptile skin, folding clasp
Price: $15,700
Variations: stainless steel; white gold

Villeret Retrograde Seconds
Reference number: 4063-154255
Movement: automatic, Blancpain Caliber 7663; ø 26.2 mm, height 4.6 mm; 34 jewels; 28,800 vph
Functions: hours, minutes, subsidiary seconds (30-second retrograde)
Case: white gold, ø 40 mm, height 10.4 mm; sapphire crystal
Band: reptile skin, buckle
Price: $15,900
Variations: red gold

Léman Aqualung Large Date
Reference number: 2850B-113064B
Movement: automatic, Blancpain Caliber 6950; ø 32 mm, height 4.75 mm; 35 jewels; 21,600 vph
Functions: hours, minutes, sweep seconds; large date
Case: stainless steel, ø 40 mm, height 11.4 mm; sapphire crystal; transparent case back
Band: rubber, folding clasp
Price: $15,900

Villeret Time Zone
Reference number: 6260-364A55B
Movement: automatic, Blancpain Caliber 5L60; ø 26.2 mm, height 3.25 mm; 30 jewels; 21,600 vph
Functions: hours, minutes, subsidiary seconds; date; second time zone, day/night indication
Case: rose gold, ø 38 mm, height 10.1 mm; sapphire crystal; transparent case back
Band: reptile skin, buckle
Price: $15,700
Variations: white gold

Léman Perpetual Calendar
Reference number: 2685F-363053B
Movement: automatic, Blancpain Caliber F585; ø 27 mm, height 7.1 mm; 35 jewels; 21,600 vph
Functions: hours, minutes; chronograph; perpetual calendar with date, weekday, month, moon phase, leap year
Case: red gold, ø 40 mm, height 14 mm; sapphire crystal; transparent case back
Band: reptile skin, folding clasp
Price: $36,750
Variations: stainless steel

Blancpain

Caliber 13R0
Mechanical with manual winding, three spring barrels, power reserve 8 days
Functions: hours, minutes, sweep seconds; date
Diameter: 30.6 mm (13 1/2''')
Height: 4.8 mm
Jewels: 30
Balance: titanium with four gold regulating screws
Frequency: 28,800 vph
Balance spring: Breguet hairspring
Remarks: regulated in 5 positions; base plate with côtes de Genève; gold-plated chamfering with chaton effect

Caliber 1315
Mechanical with automatic winding, three spring barrels, power reserve 120 hours (appx. 5 days); bi-metallic rotor
Functions: hours, minutes, sweep seconds; date
Diameter: 30.6 mm (13 1/2''')
Height: 5.65 mm
Jewels: 35
Balance: glucydur, with four regulating screws
Frequency: 28,800 vph
Balance spring: Breguet hairspring
Remarks: regulated in five positions; base plate and rotor decorated with perlage; 222 individual components

Caliber 1151
Mechanical with automatic winding, twin spring barrels, power reserve to 100 hours
Functions: hours, minutes, sweep seconds; date
Diameter: 26.8 mm (12''')
Height: extra-flat, 3.25 mm
Jewels: 29
Balance: beryllium copper
Frequency: 21,600 vph
Balance spring: flat hairspring with fine adjustment via micrometer screw
Remarks: regulated in five positions; base plate and rotor decorated with côtes de Genève; 185 individual components
Related calibers: 1161 (with subsidiary seconds); 1106 (manually wound, subsidiary seconds, date, power reserve)

Caliber 21
Mechanical with manual winding, power reserve 40 hours
Functions: hours, minutes
Diameter: 20.4 mm (9''')
Height: extra-flat, 1.73 mm
Jewels: 18
Balance: beryllium copper
Frequency: 21,600 vph
Balance spring: flat hairspring
Shock protection: Kif (balance), Duofix (escape wheel)
Remarks: regulated in five positions; base plate decorated with perlage, bridges with côtes de Genève; 132 individual components
Related caliber: 21 S (skeletonized)

Caliber 1185
Mechanical with automatic winding, power reserve 40 hours; rotor in 18-karat gold
Functions: hours, minutes; date, chronograph
Diameter: 25.6 mm (12'''), **Height:** 5.5 mm
Jewels: 37
Balance: beryllium copper
Frequency: 21,600 vph
Remarks: regulated in five positions; 304 individual components
Related calibers: 1186 (with rattrapante), F185 (flyback function), F585 (flyback, perpetual calendar), 1180 (manual winding), 1181 (manual winding, rattrapante), 5580 (manual winding, perpetual calendar), 5581 (perpetual calendar, rattrapante), 5585 (perpetual calendar), 23F9A (flyback, rattrapante, tourbillon)

Caliber 23
Mechanical with manual winding, tourbillon, power reserve eight days
Functions: hours, minutes, subsidiary seconds (above tourbillon cage); date, power reserve display
Diameter: 25.6 mm
Height: 3.5 mm
Jewels: 19
Balance: monometallic with regulating screws
Frequency: 21,600 vph
Shock protection: Kif
Remarks: regulated in five positions; 195 individual components
Related caliber: 25 (mechanical with automatic winding)

Caliber 33
Mechanical with manual winding, power reserve 44 hours
Functions: hours, minutes, subsidiary seconds; minute repeater
Diameter: 23.6 mm (10 1/2'''), **Height:** 3.3 mm
Jewels: 31
Frequency: 21,600 vph
Balance: monometallic with masselotte and regulating screws
Balance spring: Breguet hairspring
Remarks: regulated in five positions; base plate decorated with perlage, beveled bridges with côtes de Genève; 320 individual components; fourth wheel, escape wheel, and balance under separate bridges
Related caliber: 35 (automatic winding)

Caliber 6.15
Mechanical with automatic winding, power reserve 42 hours
Functions: hours, minutes
Diameter: 15.3 mm
Height: 3.9 mm
Jewels: 29
Frequency: 21,600 vph
Balance: beryllium copper
Balance spring: flat hairspring
Shock protection: Kif
Remarks: regulated in five positions; base plate and rotor decorated with côtes de Genève; 152 individual components; platinum rotor

World One
International Watch & Jewellery Journal

www.worldone-journal.com

The business magazine of the watch, clock and jewellery sector for specialist retailers sourcing globally and also for the industry, along with importers and exporters, wholesalers and distributors.

4 issues a year

You are looking for a magazine that does not simply focus on the products, but also on the associated services and marketing campaigns?

Subscribe now!

Yearly subscription rate incl. postage:
- Europe: 36.00 €
- Overseas (airmail postage): 54.60 €

To place your order please call, fax or e-mail!

Rühle-Diebener-Verlag | P.O. Box 70 04 50 | 70574 Stuttgart / Germany | Phone: +49 (0) 711 976670
Fax: +49 (0) 711 9766749 | email: info@worldone-journal.com | www.rdv-online.com

blu–source du temps

Bernhard Lederer was born in 1958 in Kornwestheim, Germany—not far from Stuttgart—and by the age of fifteen he was already taking mechanical things apart and putting them back together—repairing clocks by feel and with the aid of books borrowed from the local public library. One year after completing an apprenticeship at the Museum of Historical Watches and Clocks in Wuppertal, Lederer opened his first little company. He made everything himself by hand, specializing in the restoration and reconstruction of vintage watches and clocks. It was also here that Lederer began to work on some of his own designs.

Having earned the title of master watchmaker, Lederer joined the celebrated A.H.C.I. at its founding in 1985. The Académie Horlogère des Créateurs Indépendents (Horological Academy of Independent Creators) was a group of some of the watch industry's most interesting and creative watchmakers—all of whom were not affiliated in any solid way with an existing brand.

By 1990, Lederer was manufacturing small series of about ten pieces for his newly created models, but it was in 1993 that Lederer created what was to become his most well-known timepiece: the Time Dimension. This timepiece came about thanks to a cooperative venture he had started with Hans Donner in 1993, and the common creative juices later led him to other interesting projects such as a set of monumental clocks in Brazil to celebrate the 500th anniversary of that country's discovery. In 1996, the Time Dimension earned tenth place in watch magazine *ArmbandUhren's* prestigious Watch of the Year award.

By the year 1999, Lederer was ready to exchange his handmade, personal way of manufacturing timepieces for true serial production and decided to take a decisive step. Relocating to Switzerland, he established blu-source du temps with a silent part-ner and became the company's technical director.

Since its official founding at the dawn of the new millennium, blu—which could stand for "Bernhard Lederer's Universe" or even "Bernhard Lederer's Uhren" (*Uhren* being German for "watches")—has introduced one interesting model after another based on the master watchmaker's unique concept of revolving time.

The basic idea behind the blu-Planet line, which is the company's most popular series, is that time is never-ending; perpetually revolving rather than finitely enclosed like on a conventional watch dial with hands.

Stepping up the concept a gear last year, Lederer introduced a tourbillon version of the Planet called blu-Majesty, which revolves on three different axes and beats with a frequency that is half that of a conventional modern watch. Lederer set the frequency at 14,400 vph (2 Hertz) so that the beating of the balance could be seen by the naked eye. "A king strides," he explains, "while servants scurry."

Baselworld 2007 saw the evolution of this model: the majestic T3, a true masterpiece in transparency and spatial depth. Twelve visible pillars "support" the gold bezel and simultaneously function as hour markers. Encircling time like the famous Parthenon, the T3 is a beautifully sculpted piece of architectural horology.

blu–source du temps

Blu Majesty Tourbillon MT3
Reference number: MT3 / 990.60.7/D
Movement: automatic, Caliber Blu MT3; ø 30 mm, height 11.8 mm; 26 jewels; 14,400 vph; three tourbillons with parallel axes and different speeds of rotation; twin spring serially operating barrels, power reserve 72 hours
Functions: hours (on the 12-hour carriage's plate), minutes (on the cage of the small hour tourbillon)
Case: rose gold with sapphire crystal case sides, ø 44 mm, height 15 mm; sapphire crystal; monocoque case without separate case back
Band: reptile skin; buckle
Price: $240,000
Variations: white gold; limited edition of 10 in platinum

Blu Majesty Tourbillon MT2
Reference number: MT2 / 285.60.7/D
Movement: automatic, Caliber Blu MT2; ø 36 mm, height 11.8 mm; 26 jewels; 14,400 vph; three tourbillons with parallel axes and different speeds of rotation; twin spring serially operating barrels, power reserve 72 hours
Functions: hours (on the rotating plate), minutes (on the cage of the small hour tourbillon)
Case: white gold, ø 44 mm, height 15 mm; sapphire crystal
Band: reptile skin; buckle
Remarks: rotating dial made of aventurine
Price: $190,000
Variations: limited edition of 50 in rose gold; limited edition of 10 in platinum

Blu Majesty MT1
Reference number: MT1 / 1.60.7/D
Movement: automatic, Caliber Blu MT1; ø 36 mm, height 11.8 mm; 26 jewels; 14,400 vph; three tourbillons with parallel axes and different speeds of rotation; twin spring serially operating barrels, power reserve 72 hours
Functions: hours (diamond marker on the rotating dial), minutes (on the cage of the small hour tourbillon)
Case: white gold, ø 44 mm, height 15 mm; sapphire crystal
Band: reptile skin; buckle
Remarks: silver dial with spectrolite
Price: $190,000
Variations: limited edition of 50 in rose gold; limited edition of 10 in platinum

Blu Galaxy
Reference number: H62/281.50.9/L
Movement: automatic, Caliber Blu-Orbit (base ETA 2892-A2); ø 25.6 mm, height 3.6 mm; 25 jewels; 28,800 vph; exclusive in-house automatic module with fine côtes de Genève
Functions: hours, minutes, seconds—all shown by three concentric aventurine disks with diamond markers
Case: red gold, ø 39 mm, height 13 mm; movable strap lugs; sapphire crystal; transparent case back; recessed crown
Band: reptile skin; buckle
Price: $21,900
Variations: stainless steel with aventurine and mother-of-pearl dial; white gold

Blu Duett
Reference number: H12/710.10.9/D
Movement: automatic, Caliber Blu-Orbit (base ETA 2892-A2); ø 25.6 mm, height 3.6 mm; 25 jewels; 28,800 vph
Functions: hours, minutes (off-center), date
Case: stainless steel, ø 44 mm, height 10.5 mm; movable strap lugs; sapphire crystal; transparent case back; recessed crown
Band: reptile skin; buckle
Price: $6,800

Blu Quartett
Reference number: H14/740.10.9/D
Movement: automatic, Caliber Blu-Orbit (base ETA 2892-A2); ø 25.6 mm, height 3.6 mm; 25 jewels; 28,800 vph; exclusive in-house automatic module with fine côtes de Genève
Functions: hours (off-center), minutes (off-center, retrograde), sweep seconds; date
Case: stainless steel, ø 42 mm, height 10.5 mm; movable strap lugs; sapphire crystal; transparent case back; recessed crown
Band: reptile skin; buckle
Price: $9,300
Variations: rose gold

Blu Open Planet
Reference number: H26/260.10.9/D
Movement: automatic, Caliber Blu-Orbit (base ETA 2892-A2); ø 25.6 mm, height 3.6 mm; 25 jewels; 28,800 vph; in-house dial train module
Functions: hours (on rotating dial), minutes (off-center, in small rotating dial)
Case: stainless steel, ø 44 mm, height 10.5 mm; movable strap lugs; sapphire crystal; transparent case back; recessed crown
Band: reptile skin; buckle
Remarks: carbon fiber dial
Price: $10,750
Variations: dial galvanically treated with palladium

Blu Winter Dream
Reference number: G41/171.12.9/L
Movement: automatic, Caliber Blu-Orbit (base ETA 2892-A2); ø 25.6 mm, height 3.6 mm; 25 jewels; 28,800 vph; in-house dial train module
Functions: hours (ruby marker on rotating dial), minutes (off-center, in small rotating dial with diamond pavé and ruby markers)
Case: stainless steel, ø 39 mm, height 10.5 mm; case, bezel, and strap lugs completely paved with diamonds; sapphire crystal; transparent case back; recessed crown
Band: reptile skin; buckle
Remarks: mother-of-pearl dial
Price: $31,800
Variations: rose gold with black mother-of-pearl dial

Martin Braun

The past twelve months have been important ones for Martin Braun—perhaps the most important ones of his entire career. Three events came together in an advantageous way, with the result that Braun now belongs to one of the watch industry's biggest luxury groups. Anticipating the coming movement crunch, Braun had decided that it was time to create his own base movement to power his astronomical complications: an $11\frac{1}{2}$-line automatic mechanism, very classic in both appearance and technology, that maintains a distinct focus on reliability. Caliber MAB 88 possesses a single spring barrel offering 42 hours of power reserve. At 3.6 mm in height, it can be fitted into even the most elegant of cases—especially those featuring a sapphire crystal case back revealing the movement's elements of fine finishing, which include blued screws, blued winding wheels, and a decorated plate featuring Martin Braun's stylized sunburst logo over the rotor's ball bearings. Braun will now use this movement in place of the ETA 2892-A2 as his base, as evidenced by the new Selene and Classic models introduced at the 2007 Baselworld and WPHH.

Discovering that working with Swiss suppliers is much easier when the company in question is actually located in Switzerland, Braun changed his destiny by deciding to move his company to the motherland of watchmaking. Firmly ensconced in his new factory in Porrentruy, and emblazoning his dials with the predicate "Swiss made," Braun was approached by one of the industry's most active CEOs: Vartan Sirmakes. Sirmakes, head of the Franck Muller Group, had been keeping an eye on Braun's astronomical complications for a while. His goal was to make the German master watchmaker hailing from the Black Forest area part of his Franck Muller Watchland family.

Signing the papers in February 2007, Braun sees this move positively: the merger—Watchland now owns 51 percent of Martin Braun Uhren—presents Braun with untold opportunities in research, development, and distribution. "With this new situation, we can now invest in our ideas and our future. I have hired a developmental engineer that previously worked at some of the industry's top addresses. When I introduced my ideas to him, he was speechless. He said he had never experienced anything like this. He said that to get this far in other companies, there would first have to be meetings, meetings, and more meetings. Here, we take an idea and run with it," Braun enthuses.

These resources include Watchland's in-house case and sapphire crystal making abilities—the former is a Sirmakes specialty; the latter, definitively a unique element for a manufacturer—and outside suppliers purchased in recent years by the Franck Muller Group for crowns, buttons, bracelets, movement components, and dials. Naturally, should Braun want it, he will also have access to Franck Muller's own formidable R&D department located within Watchland's picturesque Genthod walls.

"We will certainly be using Watchland's resources as best we can to complete our plans," Braun reveals. "We are already preparing a brand-new, innovative design, one that will remain secret until the time is ripe.

"It is not our goal to try to top Franck Muller's Revolution tourbillon. We have other goals that are completely different and wholly within the established Martin Braun concept. The Franck Muller watchmakers won't be contributing any ideas. That will continue to come from me. Martin Braun will remain Martin Braun."

Martin Braun

EOS
Reference number: GP
Movement: automatic, MAB Caliber 88; ø 25.6 mm, height 3.8 mm; 25 jewels; 28,800 vph; autonomous module MAB 1; finely finished movement; gold rotor
Functions: hours, minutes; date; times of sunrise and sunset
Case: stainless steel, ø 42 mm, height 13 mm; sapphire crystal; transparent case back
Band: reptile skin, buckle
Price: $11,950
Variations: various dial versions; rose gold 39 mm case size ($19,750) or 42 mm ($20,950); platinum ($35,450); with diamonds

EOS Boreas
Reference number: PB
Movement: automatic, MAB Caliber 88; ø 25.6 mm, height 3.8 mm; 25 jewels; 28,800 vph; autonomous module MAB 2; finely finished movement; gold rotor
Functions: hours, minutes; date; times of sunrise and sunset; equation of time
Case: stainless steel, ø 42 mm, height 13 mm; bezel and case lugs set with diamonds; sapphire crystal; transparent case back
Band: reptile skin, buckle
Price: $25,400
Variations: 39 mm ($24,200); various dial versions; rose gold 39 mm case size ($24,759) or 42 mm ($25,950); platinum ($39,850)

Heliozentric
Reference number: PB
Movement: automatic, MAB Caliber 88; ø 25.6 mm, height 3.8 mm; 25 jewels; 28,800 vph; autonomous module MAB 3; gold rotor
Functions: hours, minutes; annual calendar with date, month, zodiac display; illustration of the Earth on its elliptic orbit around the sun as a month display
Case: stainless steel, ø 42 mm, height 13 mm; sapphire crystal; transparent case back
Band: reptile skin, buckle
Remarks: diamonds on blued steel dial make constellations Orion and Ursa Major
Price: $19,750
Variations: rose gold ($28,750); platinum ($43,050); various dial versions; with diamonds

Astraios
Reference number: S RGC Royal
Movement: automatic, MAB Caliber 88; ø 25.6 mm, height 3.8 mm; 25 jewels; 28,800 vph; autonomous module MAB 4; gold rotor
Functions: hours, minutes; times of sunrise and sunset; annual calendar with date, month; illustration of the Earth on its elliptic orbit around the sun as a month display
Case: stainless steel, ø 42 mm, height 13 mm; bezel and lugs set with diamonds; sapphire crystal; transparent case back
Band: reptile skin, buckle
Price: $27,950
Variations: rose gold ($36,950); platinum ($43,050); various dial versions; without diamonds

Notos
Reference number: W RGC RG
Movement: automatic, MAB Caliber 88; ø 25.6 mm, height 3.8 mm; 25 jewels; 28,800 vph; autonomous module MAB 5; finely finished movement
Functions: hours, minutes; date; equation of time display, visualization of the equation of time as month display; display of declination
Case: rose gold, ø 42 mm, height 13 mm; sapphire crystal; transparent case back
Band: reptile skin, buckle
Remarks: bipartite dial with real onyx or Cocoolong stone
Price: $28,850
Variations: stainless steel ($19,850); platinum ($43,350); with diamonds; various dial variations

Selene
Reference number: FC B Royal
Movement: automatic, MAB Caliber 88; ø 25.6 mm, height 3.8 mm; 25 jewels; 28,800 vph; autonomous module MAB 6t; gold rotor
Functions: hours, minutes; date; moon phase
Case: stainless steel, ø 44 mm, height 14 mm; sapphire crystal; transparent case back
Band: reptile skin, buckle
Remarks: photorealistic depiction of the surface of the moon, settable to the minute
Price: $11,250
Variations: stainless steel with black or silver dial ($11,250) or meteorite dial ($12,750); rose gold with black or silver dial ($20,250) or meteorite dial ($21,750); platinum with black or silver dial ($34,550) or meteorite dial ($36,250)

Benzol
Reference number: Y
Movement: automatic, ETA Valjoux Caliber 7750; ø 30 mm, height 7.9 mm; 25 jewels; 28,800 vph; special rotor design
Functions: hours, minutes, subsidiary seconds; chronograph; date
Case: stainless steel, ø 44 mm, height 16 mm; sapphire crystal; transparent case back; water-resistant to 5 atm
Band: leather/nylon, buckle
Remarks: carbon fiber dial
Price: $5,750
Variations: various dial colors

Falcon Claw
Reference number: Royal
Movement: automatic, ETA Valjoux Caliber 7750; ø 30 mm, height 7.9 mm; 25 jewels; 28,800 vph; special rotor design
Functions: hours, minutes, subsidiary seconds; chronograph; date
Case: stainless steel, ø 44 mm, height 16 mm; bezel and strap lugs set with diamonds; sapphire crystal; transparent case back
Band: reptile skin, buckle
Remarks: hour markers in the shape of a falcon claw grasping a diamond
Price: $24,950
Variations: without diamonds on case ($8,350)

Breguet

With the whole industry currently searching out silicon solutions, Breguet's CEO and Swatch Group chairman Nicolas G. Hayek just leans back and smiles. Breguet was part of one of the original groups formed to research silicon components, and the investment made at that time is now beginning to bear real fruit.

While other companies seem to be just flirting with the newfangled high-tech material at this time, this historically based brand with an established reputation for innovation is doing a lot more than dabbling: Breguet has introduced two watches with more than one silicon component in the past year. The Classique 5177 contains a new base movement—automatic Caliber 777Q—which leaves plenty of room and opportunity for later complications. But right now it has an escape wheel and pallet fork made of high-tech silicon—in addition to a ceramic ball bearing, a new balance shock protection system by the name of Nivachoc, and DLC coating on the inside of the spring barrel.

Sibling timepiece Classique 5157 is even outfitted with a slim, twin spring barrel movement (Caliber 591A) that houses a veritable array of silicon components including an escape wheel, a pallet fork, and even a balance spring.

All this technical progress should really come as no surprise to watch lovers. Abraham-Louis Breguet, who originally founded his own company in 1775, was one of the watch industry's greatest innovators. To this day, he probably remains the world's most talented and creative watchmaker. His inventions and patents cannot be counted with two hands, and many are still regularly used in watchmaking today—one example being the tourbillon. Others include such important elements as the constant-force escapement, the *pare-chute*, the upward pointing terminal curve of the balance spring, jump seconds and hours, the perpetual calendar, the idea of twin spring barrels, and a lubrication-free escapement.

It was Breguet who patented the tourbillon in 1801 as a way of improving the rate of pocket watches hampered by the effects of gravity. Contrary to wristwatches, pocket watches stand straight up and stationary in a pocket. Since pocket watches are unable to move around as wristwatches do, gravity takes its toll on their accuracy, a status quo that the tourbillon was created to cheat: It was Breguet who came up with the idea of rotating the escapement around its own axis once every minute to this end.

Nowhere is this heritage clearer than in 2007's La Tradition tourbillon, the most complicated evolution of the La Tradition model originally introduced in 2005. This unusual and very vintage-looking wristwatch contains not only a *pare-chute* mechanism, but also a very obvious tourbillon at the top of the practically nonexistent dial.

It is joined by sister tourbillon Messidor, which is a very transparent regulator model—so transparent, in fact, that the tourbillon seems to literally float between two sheets of sapphire crystal.

Abraham-Louis Breguet would have been proud.

Breguet

Tradition Tourbillon Fusée
Reference number: 7047 BA 11 9ZU
Movement: manually wound, Breguet Caliber 569; ø 36 mm; height 10.82 mm; 43 jewels; 21,600 vph; movement design according to historical model; tourbillon, balance with Breguet titanium balance spring, chain and fusée
Functions: hours, minutes; power reserve display
Case: yellow gold, ø 41 mm, height 16 mm; sapphire crystal; exhibition case back
Band: reptile skin, buckle
Price: $146,800

Tourbillon Messidor
Reference number: 5335 BR 42 9W6
Movement: manually wound, Breguet Caliber 558; ø 34.5 mm, height 6.83 mm; 25 jewels; 18,000 vph; tourbillon cage encased within two sapphire crystal bridges; movement completely skeletonized
Functions: hours, off-center minutes, subsidiary seconds (on tourbillon cage)
Case: red gold, ø 40 mm, height 9.65 mm; sapphire crystal; transparent case back
Band: reptile skin, folding clasp
Price: $129,500
Variations: platinum

Marine Chronograph
Reference number: 5827 BR Z2 5ZU
Movement: automatic, Breguet Caliber 583 Q/1; ø 34.5 mm, height 6.83 mm; 25 jewels; 28,800 vph; sweep minute counter
Functions: hours, minutes, subsidiary seconds; flyback chronograph; date
Case: red gold, ø 42 mm, height 14.1 mm; sapphire crystal; transparent case back; screw-in crown; water-resistant to 10 atm
Band: rubber, folding clasp
Remarks: black rhodium-plated, hand-guilloché gold dial
Price: $26,400
Variations: leather strap; red gold link bracelet

Marine Tourbillon Chronograph
Reference number: 5837 BR 92 5ZU
Movement: manually wound, Breguet Caliber 554.3; one-minute tourbillon; silicon balance spring, pallet fork, and escape wheel
Functions: hours, minutes, subsidiary seconds (on tourbillon cage); chronograph
Case: red gold, ø 42 mm, height 14 mm; sapphire crystal; transparent case back; screw-in crown; water-resistant to 10 atm
Band: rubber, folding clasp
Price: $134,500
Variations: red gold link bracelet

Reine de Naples
Reference number: 8928 BB 51 844 DD0D
Movement: automatic, Breguet Caliber 586; ø 20 mm, height 3.6 mm; 29 jewels; 21,600 vph
Functions: hours, minutes
Case: white gold, 33 x 25 mm, height 8.6 mm; bezel, lugs, and flange set with diamonds; sapphire crystal; transparent case back; crown with briolette-cut diamond
Band: satin, folding clasp
Remarks: mother-of-pearl dial
Price: $30,300
Variations: yellow gold

Reine de Naples
Reference number: 8928 BB 8D 844 DD0D
Movement: automatic, Breguet Caliber 586; ø 20 mm, height 3.6 mm; 29 jewels; 21,600 vph
Functions: hours, minutes
Case: white gold, 33 x 25 mm, height 8.6 mm; bezel, lugs, flange and dial set with diamonds; sapphire crystal; transparent case back; crown with briolette-cut diamond
Band: satin, folding clasp
Remarks: mother-of-pearl scale ring
Price: $33,900
Variations: yellow gold

Classique
Reference number: 5177 BA 29 9V6
Movement: automatic, Breguet Caliber 777 Q; ø 28, height 3.8; 35 jewels; 28,800 vph; silicon pallet fork and escape wheel
Functions: hours, minutes, sweep seconds; date
Case: yellow gold, ø 38 mm, height 7.35 mm; sapphire crystal; transparent case back
Band: reptile skin, folding clasp
Remarks: enamel dial
Price: $19,100
Variations: white gold

Classique
Reference number: 5157 BA 12 9V6
Movement: automatic, Breguet Caliber 777 Q; ø 27.9, height 2.62; 35 jewels; 28,800 vph; silicon pallet fork and escape wheel
Functions: hours, minutes, sweep seconds; date
Case: yellow gold, ø 38 mm, height 7.35 mm; sapphire crystal; transparent case back
Band: reptile skin, folding clasp
Remarks: hand-guilloché gold dial
Price: $19,100
Variations: white gold

Breguet

Classique
Reference number: 5157 BA 11 9V6
Movement: automatic, Breguet Caliber 502.3; ø 27.9, height 2.62; 35 jewels; 28,800 vph; extra-flat movement design
Functions: hours, minutes
Case: yellow gold, ø 38 mm, height 5.4 mm; sapphire crystal; transparent case back
Band: reptile skin, buckle
Remarks: hand-guilloché gold dial
Price: $15,000
Variations: white gold

Classique
Reference number: 5207 BB 12 9V6
Movement: automatic, Breguet Caliber 516 DRSR; ø 32, height 4.62; 34 jewels; 28,800 vph; finely finished
Functions: hours, minutes, retrograde seconds; power reserve display
Case: white gold, ø 39 mm, height 9.85 mm; sapphire crystal; transparent case back
Band: reptile skin, folding clasp
Remarks: hand-guilloché gold dial
Price: $18,900
Variations: yellow gold

Tourbillon Automatique
Reference number: 5317 PT 12 9V6
Movement: automatic, Breguet Caliber 587 DR; ø 27.6, height 6.3; 32 jewels; 21,600 vph; one-minute tourbillon with Breguet balance spring; power reserve of 5 days; hand-engraved movement
Functions: hours, minutes, subsidiary seconds (on tourbillon cage); power reserve display
Case: platinum, ø 39 mm, height 11.15 mm; sapphire crystal; transparent case back
Band: reptile skin, folding clasp
Remarks: hand-guilloché gold dial
Price: $116,500
Variations: yellow gold

Ladies' Tourbillon
Reference number: 3358 52 986 DD00
Movement: manually wound, Breguet Caliber 557; ø 30.5, height 6.35; 21 jewels; 21,600 vph; one-minute tourbillon with Breguet balance spring; hand-engraved movement
Functions: hours, off-center minutes, subsidiary seconds (on tourbillon cage)
Case: white gold, ø 35 mm, height 9.15 mm; bezel and lugs set with 74 diamonds; sapphire crystal; transparent case back
Band: reptile skin, folding clasp
Remarks: hand-guilloché mother-of-pearl dial
Price: $94,700

Double Tourbillon
Reference number: 5347 PT 11 9ZU
Movement: manually wound, Breguet Caliber 588; ø 37.8 mm, height 12.35; 69 jewels; two independent tourbillons coupled via a differential gear, but revolving on a common base plate
Functions: hours (rotating dial), minutes
Case: platinum, ø 44 mm, height 18.65; sapphire crystal; transparent case back
Band: reptile skin, folding clasp
Price: $347,100
Variations: set with baguette-cut diamonds

La Tradition Breguet
Reference number: 7027 BB 11 9V6
Movement: manually wound, Breguet Caliber 507 DR; ø 32.6 mm, height 6.8 mm; 34 jewels; 21,600 vph; movement design according to historical model; balance with weighted screws, Breguet balance spring, parechute shock protection; central spring barrel
Functions: hours, minutes; double power reserve display (front and back)
Case: white gold, ø 37 mm, height 12 mm; sapphire crystal; transparent case back
Band: reptile skin, buckle
Price: $23,000
Variations: yellow gold

Perpetual Calendar
Reference number: 5327 1E 9V6
Movement: automatic, Breguet Caliber 502.3 DRP1; ø 32.4 mm, height 4.72; 38 jewels; 21,600 vph; hand-engraved movement
Functions: hours, minutes; perpetual calendar with date, weekday, month, moon phase display, and leap year; power reserve display
Case: yellow gold, ø 39 mm, height 9.05 mm; sapphire crystal; transparent case back
Band: reptile skin, folding clasp
Price: $58,200
Variations: red or white gold

Minute Repeater Perpetual Calendar
Reference number: 5447 PT 1E 9V6
Movement: manually wound, Breguet Caliber 567 RMP; ø 27.6 mm, height 8.5 mm; 31 jewels; 21,600 vph; Breguet balance spring; hand-engraved movement
Functions: hours, minutes; perpetual calendar with date, day, month, moon phase display, leap year; minute repeater
Case: platinum, ø 40 mm, height 14.9 mm; sapphire crystal; transparent case back
Band: reptile skin, folding clasp
Price: $265,400

Breguet

Type XXI
Reference number: 3810 BR 92 9ZU
Movement: automatic, Breguet Caliber 584 Q; ø 31, height 6.4 mm; 25 jewels; 28,800 vph; sweep minute counter
Functions: hours, minutes, subsidiary seconds; chronograph with flyback function; date
Case: red gold, ø 42 mm, height 15.2 mm; unidirectionally rotating bezel with 60-minute divisions; sapphire crystal; screw-in crown; water-resistant to 10 atm
Band: reptile skin, folding clasp
Price: $17,600

Type XXI
Reference number: 3810 ST 92 SZ9
Movement: automatic, Breguet Caliber 584 Q; ø 31, height 6.4 mm; 25 jewels; 28,800 vph; sweep minute counter
Functions: hours, minutes, subsidiary seconds; chronograph with flyback function; 24-hour display; date
Case: stainless steel, ø 42 mm, height 15.2 mm; unidirectionally rotating bezel with 60-minute divisions; sapphire crystal; screw-in crown; water-resistant to 10 atm
Band: reptile skin, folding clasp
Price: $9,800
Variations: stainless steel bracelet

Marine Large Date
Reference number: 5817 ST 12 5V8
Movement: automatic, Breguet Caliber 517 GG; ø 26.2 mm, height 3.37 mm; 35 jewels; 28,800 vph;
Functions: hours, minutes, sweep seconds; large date
Case: stainless steel, ø 39 mm, height 11.85 mm; sapphire crystal; transparent case back; screw-in crown; water-resistant to 10 atm
Band: rubber, folding clasp
Price: $12,150
Variations: stainless steel bracelet; in red gold; in white gold with red gold bezel

Marine Chronograph
Reference number: 5827 BB 12 5Z0
Movement: automatic, Breguet Caliber 583 Q; ø 31, height 6.4 mm; 25 jewels; 28,800 vph; sweep minute counter
Functions: hours, minutes, subsidiary seconds; flyback chronograph; date
Case: white gold, ø 42 mm, height 14.1 mm; sapphire crystal; transparent case back; screw-in crown; water-resistant to 10 atm
Band: white gold, double folding clasp
Remarks: hand-guilloché gold dial
Price: $37,700
Variations: rubber or leather strap; in yellow gold (with rubber or leather strap, or gold bracelet)

Ladies' Marine
Reference number: 8818 BB 59 864 DD0D
Movement: automatic, Breguet Caliber 537/1; ø 20 mm, height 3.6 mm; 20 jewels; 21,600 vph
Functions: hours, minutes, sweep seconds
Case: white gold, ø 30 mm, height 9.4 mm; bezel and lugs set with 58 diamonds; sapphire crystal; transparent case back; crown with sapphire cabochon
Band: satin, buckle
Remarks: wave pattern mother-of-pearl dial set with diamonds
Price: $31,900
Variations: in yellow or white gold with rubber strap

Reine de Naples
Reference number: 8909 BB VD J29 DDD0
Movement: automatic, Breguet Caliber 537 DRL1; ø 20 mm, height 5 mm; 20 jewels; 21,600 vph
Functions: hours, minutes; moon phase; power reserve display
Case: white gold, 38.5 x 30.45 mm, height 10 mm; bezel and case, lug and flange set with diamonds; sapphire crystal; transparent case back; crown with briolette-cut diamond
Band: white gold with diamonds, folding clasp
Remarks: mother-of-pearl dial paved with diamonds
Price: $196,800
Variations: satin strap; bracelet set with 11 diamond cabochons

Heritage Large Date
Reference number: 5480 BB 12 996
Movement: automatic, Breguet Caliber 516 GG; ø 26.2 mm, height 4.47 mm; 30 jewels; 21,600 vph
Functions: hours, minutes, subsidiary seconds; large date
Case: white gold, 40.4 x 34 mm, height 9.25 mm; sapphire crystal
Band: reptile skin, folding clasp
Price: $21,300
Variations: in yellow or red gold

Ladies' Heritage
Reference number: 3661 BR 12 984 DD00
Movement: automatic, Breguet Caliber 537/2; ø 20 mm, height 3.6 mm; 22 jewels; 21,600 vph
Functions: hours, minutes, subsidiary seconds
Case: red gold, 29.6 x 35 mm, height 11.2 mm; bezel and lugs set with 56 diamonds; sapphire crystal
Band: reptile skin, buckle
Price: $27,300
Variations: in white gold with or without diamonds; in red gold without diamonds
Chopard

Breitling

Though Breitling's primary focus has always been on aviation, and will probably always remain so, a new partnership begun five years ago has pulled this skywriter back down to earth for the time being.

Now Breitling also speeds along on land, having paired with noble automaker Bentley to create an outstanding collection aptly named Breitling for Bentley. Thus far, this automotive-inspired line of watches has spawned chronographs featuring characteristics taken from the refined cars, such as the typical colors and woods found on the dial and case, and interesting embossing on case backs looking astoundingly like engine turbines. A main characteristic of the line has also been the tremendous size of the timepieces, measuring 45 mm and more in diameter.

Last year saw a continuation on the theme that was as surprising as it was striking. For the first time, Breitling presented a watch that is not round: the rectangular Breitling for Bentley Flying B with its machined look and refined jump hour movement by Dubois Dépraz is also an officially certified C.O.S.C. chronometer. And although it can't fly, it does take off at 38.5 x 57.3 mm. In the past year, Breitling upped its ante by presenting a chronograph version sure to make men's hearts speed along with fascination.

Simultaneously, Breitling also decided to conquer the oceans with a reissue of the brand's Superocean model. Originally deciding the watery element was worth triumphing over in 1957, Breitling introduced a diver's watch in a monocoque case and armored crystal that guaranteed water resistance to a depth of 200 meters, a technical feat back in the day. Over the years, Breitling has even developed chronographs and simple versions for the line that were water-resistant to depths of 500, 1000, and even 2000 meters.

Superocean Héritage is the name of the 2007 version, which appears both modern and nostalgic at the same time—due in great part to the bracelet and strap that the new model comes on: it is available on a beautifully contrasting contemporary rubber strap or a supple, smooth Milanaise bracelet crafted in woven steel. It is the mesh bracelet in combination with the simple, colorful look of the dial and bezel that creates a slight nostalgic tinge. The bracelet is outfitted with a modern folding clasp, and a new screw system enables the wearer to shorten and lengthen it in the way a good diver's watch should. Fittingly, the Superocean Héritage comes in two case diameters: 38 and 46 mm—one a classic size, and one a trendy larger size that complements this aviation specialist's collection as a whole. And, of course, the automatic movement powering this seafaring timepiece is an officially certified C.O.S.C. chronometer, as are all of Breitling's movements.

Breitling

Navitimer Montbrillant Légende
Reference number: A2334012
Movement: automatic, Breitling Caliber 23 (base ETA Valjoux 7750); ø 30 mm, height 7.9 mm; 25 jewels; 28,800 vph; officially certified chronometer (COSC)
Functions: minutes, subsidiary seconds; chronograph; date
Case: stainless steel, ø 47 mm, height 15 mm; bidirectionally rotating rose gold bezel with integrated slide rule and tachymeter scale; sapphire crystal
Band: stainless steel/rose gold, folding clasp
Price: $5,600
Variations: stainless steel

Navitimer Montbrillant Datora
Reference number: A21330-12
Movement: automatic, Breitling Caliber 21 (base ETA Valjoux 7751); ø 30 mm, height 7.9 mm; 25 jewels; 28,800 vph; officially certified chronometer (COSC)
Functions: hours, minutes, subsidiary seconds; chronograph; date, weekday, month, 24-hour display
Case: stainless steel, ø 43 mm, height 14.1 mm; bidirectionally rotating bezel with integrated slide rule and tachymeter scale; sapphire crystal
Band: stainless steel, folding clasp
Price: $5,930
Variations: leather strap

Navitimer World
Reference number: A24322-12
Movement: automatic, Breitling Caliber 24 (base ETA Valjoux 7754); ø 30 mm, height 7.9 mm; officially certified chronometer (COSC)
Functions: hours, minutes, subsidiary seconds; chronograph; date; 24-hour display (second time zone)
Case: stainless steel, ø 46 mm, height 15.6 mm; bidirectionally rotating bezel with integrated slide rule and 60-minute divisions; sapphire crystal
Band: leather, buckle
Price: $4,770
Variations: red gold; white gold

Navitimer
Reference number: A23322-12
Movement: automatic, Breitling Caliber 23 (base ETA Valjoux 7750); officially certified chronomete (COSC)
Functions: hours, minutes, subsidiary seconds; chronograph; date
Case: stainless steel, ø 41.8 mm, height 14.6 mm; bidirectionally rotating bezel with integrated slide rule and tachymeter scale; sapphire crystal
Band: leather, buckle
Price: $4,450
Variations: steel bracelet; red gold with reptile skin strap

Navitimer Montbrillant
Reference number: A41330-12
Movement: automatic, Breitling Caliber 41 (base ETA 2892-A2); officially certified C.O.S.C. chronometer
Functions: hours, minutes, subsidiary seconds; chronograph; date
Case: stainless steel, ø 38 mm, height 13 mm; bidirectionally rotating bezel with tachymeter scale; sapphire crystal
Band: leather, buckle
Price: $3,800
Variations: stainless steel bracelet; red gold with leather strap

Montbrillant Olympus
Reference number: A1935012
Movement: automatic, Breitling Caliber 19 (base ETA 2892-A2); officially certified C.O.S.C. chronometer
Functions: hours, minutes, subsidiary seconds; chronograph; four-year calendar with date, day, month, moon phase display
Case: stainless steel, ø 43 mm, height 15.3 mm; bidirectionally rotating bezel with integrated slide rule and tachymeter scale; sapphire crystal
Band: reptile skin, buckle
Price: $6,690
Variations: stainless steel bracelet; red gold with leather strap

Emergency Mission
Reference number: A73321
Movement: quartz, Breitling Caliber 73 (base ETA 251.262); officially certified C.O.S.C. chronometer
Functions: hours, minutes, subsidiary seconds; chronograph; date; retractable micro antenna with aviation emergency frequency 121.5 MHz
Case: stainless steel, ø 45 mm, height 19.2 mm; bidirectionally rotating bezel with 60-minute divisions; sapphire crystal; screw-in crown; water-resistant to 10 atm
Band: stainless steel, folding clasp
Remarks: extendable emergency antenna
Price: $5,420
Variations: leather strap

Cockpit
Reference number: A49350-11
Movement: automatic, Breitling Caliber 49 (base ETA 2892-A2); ø 25.6 mm, height 3.9 mm; 22 jewels; 28,800 vph; officially certified C.O.S.C. chronometer
Functions: hours, minutes, sweep seconds; large date
Case: stainless steel, ø 41 mm, height 14 mm; unidirectionally rotating bezel with 60-minute divisions; sapphire crystal; screw-in crown; water-resistant to 30 atm
Band: stainless steel, folding clasp
Price: $4,600
Variations: leather strap; stainless steel/yellow gold; yellow gold

Breitling

Chrono Cockpit
Reference number: A13358-12
Movement: automatic, Breitling Caliber 13 (base ETA Valjoux 7750); officially certified C.O.S.C. chronometer
Functions: hours, minutes, subsidiary seconds; chronograph; date
Case: stainless steel, ø 39 mm, height 14.8 mm; unidirectionally rotating bezel with 60-minute divisions; sapphire crystal; screw-in crown; water-resistant to 10 atm
Band: stainless steel, folding clasp
Price: $4,640
Variations: stainless steel/yellow gold; yellow gold

Super Avenger
Reference number: A13370-11
Movement: automatic, Breitling Caliber 13 (base ETA Valjoux 7750); officially certified C.O.S.C. chronometer
Functions: hours, minutes, subsidiary seconds; chronograph; date
Case: stainless steel, ø 48.4 mm, height 18.6 mm; unidirectionally rotating bezel with 60-minute divisions; sapphire crystal; screw-in crown; water-resistant to 30 atm
Band: leather, buckle
Price: $3,725
Variations: with steel bracelet

Chronomat Evolution
Reference number: B13356-11
Movement: automatic, Breitling Caliber 13 (base ETA Valjoux 7750); officially certified C.O.S.C. chronometer
Functions: hours, minutes, subsidiary seconds; chronograph; date
Case: stainless steel, ø 43.7 mm, height 14.7 mm; unidirectionally rotating bezel with gold elements; sapphire crystal; screw-in gold crown and buttons; water-resistant to 30 atm
Band: stainless steel/yellow gold, folding clasp
Price: $7,145
Variations: leather strap; white gold; rose gold

Colt GMT
Reference number: A32350-11
Movement: automatic, Breitling Caliber 32 (base ETA 2893-2); ø 25.6 mm, height 4.1 mm; 21 jewels; 28,800 vph; officially certified C.O.S.C. chronometer
Functions: hours, minutes, sweep seconds; date; 24-hour display (second time zone)
Case: stainless steel, ø 40.5 mm, height 13.2 mm; unidirectionally rotating bezel with 60-minute divisions; sapphire crystal; screw-in crown; water-resistant to 50 atm
Band: leather, buckle
Price: $2,225
Variations: stainless steel bracelet

Avenger Seawolf
Reference number: E17370-18
Movement: automatic, Breitling Caliber 44 (base ETA 2892-A2); ø 25.6 mm, height 3.6 mm; 21 jewels; 28,800 vph; officially certified chronometer (COSC)
Functions: hours, minutes, sweep seconds; date
Case: titanium, ø 44 mm, height 18.4 mm; unidirectionally rotating bezel with 60-minute divisions; sapphire crystal; screw-in crown; water-resistant to 30 atm
Band: rubber, buckle
Price: $2,695
Variations: titanium bracelet

Chrono Avenger M1
Reference number: E73360-09
Movement: quartz, Breitling Caliber 73 (base ETA 251.262); officially certified C.O.S.C. chronometer
Functions: hours, minutes, subsidiary seconds; chronograph; date; ten-minute countdown for regattas
Case: titanium, ø 44 mm, height 17.2 mm; unidirectionally rotating bezel with 60-minute divisions; sapphire crystal; screw-in crown; water-resistant to 100 atm
Band: rubber, buckle
Price: $3,075
Variations: titanium bracelet

Avenger Skyland
Reference number: A13380-12
Movement: automatic, Breitling Caliber 13 (base ETA Valjoux 7750); ø 30 mm, height 7.9 mm; 25 jewels; 28,800 vph; officially certified chronometer (COSC)
Functions: hours, minutes, subsidiary seconds; chronograph; date
Case: titanium, ø 45 mm, height 17.9 mm; unidirectionally rotating bezel with 60-minute divisions; sapphire crystal; screw-in crown; water-resistant to 30 atm
Band: leather, buckle
Price: $3,650
Variations: various dial variations; black case

Chrono Superocean
Reference number: A13340-11
Movement: automatic, Breitling Caliber 13 (base ETA Valjoux 7750); officially certified C.O.S.C. chronometer
Functions: hours, minutes, subsidiary seconds; chronograph; date, weekday
Case: stainless steel, ø 42 mm, height 15.1 mm; unidirectionally rotating bezel with 60-minute divisions; sapphire crystal; screw-in crown and buttons; water-resistant to 50 atm
Band: stainless steel, folding clasp
Price: $3,540
Variations: leather strap

Breitling

Blackbird
Reference number: A44359-10
Movement: automatic, Breitling Caliber 44 (base ETA 2892-A2); officially certified C.O.S.C. chronometer
Functions: hours, minutes, subsidiary seconds; chronograph; large date
Case: stainless steel, ø 43.7 mm; height 14.5 mm unidirectionally rotating bezel with tachymeter scale; sapphire crystal; screw-in crown and buttons; water-resistant to 30 atm
Band: stainless steel, folding clasp
Price: $6,050
Variations: white gold

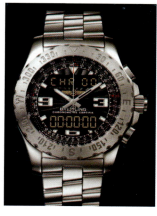

Airwolf
Reference number: A78363-38
Movement: quartz, Breitling Caliber 78; officially certified chronometer (COSC)
Functions: hours, minutes, sweep seconds (analogue); digital display for chronograph with backlighting, perpetual calendar (date, day, month, year); second time zone (world time); timer with alarm signal
Case: stainless steel, ø 43.5 mm, height 17.1 mm; bidirectionally rotating bezel with 360-degree divisions/directions; sapphire crystal; screw-in crown; water-resistant to 5 atm
Band: stainless steel, folding clasp
Price: $3,820

Superocean Heritage 38
Reference number: A37320-16
Movement: automatic, Breitling Caliber 37 (base ETA 2824); ø 25.6, height 4.6 mm; 25 jewels; 28,800 vph; officially certified C.O.S.C. chronometer
Functions: hours, minutes, subsidiary seconds; date
Case: stainless steel, ø 38 mm, height 12.1 mm; unidirectionally rotating bezel with reference marker; sapphire crystal; screw-in crown and buttons; water-resistant to 20 atm
Band: Milanaise stainless steel bracelet, folding clasp
Price: $3,040
Variations: rubber strap

Superocean Heritage 46
Reference number: A17320-16
Movement: automatic, Breitling Caliber 37 (base ETA 2824); ø 25.6, height 4.6 mm; 25 jewels; 28,800 vph; officially certified C.O.S.C. chronometer
Functions: hours, minutes, sweep seconds; date
Case: stainless steel, ø 38 mm, height 13.8 mm; unidirectionally rotating bezel with reference marker; sapphire crystal; screw-in crown and buttons; water-resistant to 20 atm
Band: rubber, buckle
Price: $3,120
Variations: stainless steel bracelet

Bentley Mark VI
Reference number: P26362-12
Movement: automatic, Breitling Caliber 26B (base ETA 2892-A2); officially certified chronometer (COSC)
Functions: hours, minutes, subsidiary seconds; chronograph; date
Case: stainless steel, ø 42 mm, height 16.3 mm; bezel in platinum; sapphire crystal; screw-in crown; water-resistant to 5 atm
Band: reptile skin, buckle
Price: $10,450
Variations: stainless steel bracelet; rose gold

Bentley Mulliner Tourbillon
Reference number: K18841-0412
Movement: automatic, Breitling Caliber 18B; one-minute tourbillon; officially certified chronometer (COSC)
Functions: hours, minutes, subsidiary seconds; chronograph (30-minute counter); date
Case: yellow gold, ø 48.7 mm, mm; bidirectionally rotating bezel with integrated slide rule; sapphire crystal; transparent case back with wood decoration; screw-in crown; water-resistant to 5 atm
Band: reptile skin, buckle
Remarks: hand-cut mother-of-pearl markers
Price: upon request
Variations: platinum

Bentley GT
Reference number: A13362-12
Movement: automatic, Breitling Caliber 13B (base ETA Valjoux 7750); officially certified chronometer (COSC)
Functions: hours, minutes, subsidiary seconds; chronograph; date, weekday
Case: stainless steel, ø 44.8 mm, height 15.6 mm; bidirectionally rotating bezel with integrated slide rule; sapphire crystal; screw-in crown; water-resistant to 5 atm
Band: stainless steel, folding clasp
Price: $7,000
Variations: in yellow gold

The Flying B
Reference number: A28362-12
Movement: automatic, Breitling Caliber 28B; officially certified chronometer (COSC)
Functions: hours (jump), minutes, subsidiary seconds
Case: stainless steel 38.5 x 57.3 mm, height 14.7 mm; sapphire crystal; transparent case back; screw-in crown; water-resistant to 5 atm
Band: reptile skin, buckle
Price: $12,670
Variations: red gold

Brior

The design typical of Holger Wecker's watches remains just as fresh today as it was in 1987 when he crafted his first watch case in wood.

Exotic woods had always cast a spell on Wecker, a master watchmaker and goldsmith. Thanks to their light weight, a good feel on the skin even in the face of allergies, and an almost metallically hard surface, exotic woods such as mahogany and briarwood are very suitable for making watch cases. Working them is just like working gold or other precious metals. A water-resistant case made of exotic wood comprises up to fifteen different components. Every piece of wood is checked along its grain for suitability, as only a small percentage of the natural material is fit for being made into a case.

Evolution and innovation meet in the Mammut model: its case is made of mammoth bone that is more than 10,000 years old and combined with finely skeletonized movements. Openly and transparently, the gold-plated, skeletonized automatic movement of Fin Calendrier allows the observant eye to follow the filigreed calendar disk with its underlaid plate of onyx at 3 o'clock. The rotating diamond used for the date hand on the Diamond Date model—an in-house development with a special module for the calendar—is also quite interesting.

Brior's collection meanwhile comprises more than thirty-two models for which individual customer desires can be realized at any time. At heart, though, every Brior is a unique piece—thanks to Wecker's artistic creativity and the material's natural grain.

Brior

Tarlo Skeleton
Reference number: T 21 111
Movement: manually wound, ETA Caliber 2801-2; ø 26 mm, height 3.35 mm; 17 jewels; 28,800 vph; skeletonized, hand-engraved, gold-plated
Functions: hours, minutes
Case: stainless steel/wood, ø 38.2 mm, height 9.2 mm; sapphire crystal; transparent case back; crown with gemstone cabochon
Band: saddle leather, snap buckle
Price: $1,950
Variations: dial with choice of Arabic or Roman numerals

Engraved Fin Calendrier
Reference number: T 23 121
Movement: automatic, ETA Caliber 2892; ø 26.2 mm, height 3.8 mm; 21 jewels; 28,800 vph; skeletonized, gold-plated calendar disk inlaid with onyx
Functions: hours, minutes, sweep seconds; date
Case: stainless steel/wood, ø 38.2 mm, height 9.2 mm; sapphire crystal; transparent case back; crown with gemstone cabochon
Band: saddle leather, snap buckle
Price: $3,950
Variations: dial with choice of Arabic or Roman numerals

Diamond Date
Reference number: TE 11 042
Movement: automatic, ETA Caliber 2824-2, modified; ø 25.6 mm, height 4.6 mm; 25 jewels; 28,800 vph; revolving date mother-of-pearl disk with a diamond marker
Functions: hours, minutes, sweep seconds; date
Case: stainless steel, ø 34.7 mm, height 9 mm; sapphire crystal; transparent case back; crown with gemstone cabochon
Band: reptile skin, buckle
Price: $1,500
Variations: various mother-of-pearl dial colors

Mammut
Reference number: M 23 122
Movement: automatic, ETA Caliber 2892; ø 26.2 mm, height 3.8 mm; 21 jewels; 28,800 vph; skeletonized, gold-plated calendar disk inlaid with onyx
Functions: hours, minutes, sweep seconds; date
Case: stainless steel/mammoth ivory, ø 38 mm, height 9.2 mm; sapphire crystal; transparent case back; crown with gemstone cabochon
Band: shark skin, snap buckle
Remarks: the mammoth ivory is 10,000 years old, originating from a find in the Ukraine
Price: $3,950
Variations: with manually wound movement; with Roman numerals

Perla
Reference number: P 31 410
Movement: manually wound, ETA Caliber 2801-2; ø 26 mm, height 3.35 mm; 17 jewels; 28,800 vph; skeletonized, rhodium-plated
Functions: hours, minutes, sweep seconds
Case: stainless steel/mother-of-pearl, ø 38 mm, height 9.1 mm; sapphire crystal; transparent case back; crown with gemstone cabochon
Band: leather, buckle
Price: $1,950
Variations: with automatic movement; with Arabic numerals

Cavaletto Automatic
Reference number: C 32 412
Movement: automatic, ETA Caliber 2892; ø 26.2 mm, height 3.8 mm; 21 jewels; 28,800 vph; skeletonized, rhodium-plated
Functions: hours, minutes, sweep seconds
Case: stainless steel/mahogany wood, ø 38 mm, height 9.1 mm; sapphire crystal; transparent case back; crown with gemstone cabochon
Band: shark skin, snap buckle
Price: $2,950
Variations: dial with choice of Arabic or Roman numerals; with manually wound movement

Cavaletto Chronograph
Reference number: C 12 432
Movement: automatic, ETA Valjoux Caliber 7751; ø 30 mm, height 7.9 mm; 25 jewels; 28,800 vph; finely finished
Functions: hours, minutes, subsidiary seconds; chronograph; date, weekday, month, moon phase, 24-hour display
Case: stainless steel/mahogany wood, ø 42.5 mm, height 14.2 mm; sapphire crystal; transparent case back; crown with gemstone cabochon
Band: shark skin, snap buckle
Price: $4,150
Variations: with briarwood

Tempio
Reference number: TE 33 412
Movement: automatic, ETA Caliber 2892; ø 26.2 mm, height 3.8 mm; 21 jewels; 28,800 vph; partially skeletonized, côtes de Genève
Functions: hours, minutes, sweep seconds
Case: stainless steel, ø 34.7 mm, height 9 mm; sapphire crystal; transparent case back; crown with gemstone cabochon
Band: shark skin, snap buckle
Price: $1,750
Variations: dial with choice of Arabic or Roman numerals

B.R.M

"The success of BRM watches will not hinge on mass production. Quality, not quantity, is our goal," Bernard Richards proudly proclaims. For him, the true sign of luxury lies in "technical skills and perfection in all stages of manufacture." All major operations needed for making a wristwatch—such as encasing, assembling, setting, and polishing—are performed by hand in his little factory, one that looks much like an automotive garage located outside Paris in Magny-sur-Vexin. None of the components found in a B.R.M watch are off-the-rack. These are all custom-designed and -made, fitting perfectly into his automotive ideal of the wristwatch.

"Instead of just soldering lugs to the case, we manufacture each element separately, and then screw them onto the case," Richards explains. "Thus it is possible to utilize different materials and colors." One example of this is black or grey titanium cases with polished stainless steel lugs—a striking combination most manufacturers simply cannot achieve.

Richards is a self-taught designer who does not follow any certain school of thought or philosophy, setting out in 2002 to completely dedicate his energies to the wristwatch. The charming Frenchman sees things and is immediately inspired by them. "I never learned designing formally—in fact, I was a very bad boy in school. I just do what comes into my head. And it often comes quickly," he reveals. This, in fact, also extends to working with his hands, as Richards makes all his own prototypes as well.

The unusual timepieces he introduced during the last five years were mainly based on the tried and trusted Valjoux 7750—the mechanical chronograph movement most often utilized in watch production. Richards has set lofty goals for himself and his young venture, for it is fully his intention to set up a true *manufacture* in his French factory. His Birotor model is thus outfitted with an autonomous caliber fully manufactured and conceived on French soil.

This movement is as unique as the materials that have gone into attaining its visuals. B.R.M calls its four new shock absorbers mounted on conical springs its Isolastic system. This not only provides a soft bed for the movement, but looks ultra-machine-like. The movement's plates and bridges are crafted in Arcap, while the rotors are made of Fortale and tantalum.

The twin set of rotors, found at 12 and 6 o'clock, are mounted on double rows of ceramic bearings that require no lubrication. Their lighter Arcap structure allows them to wind more efficiently, and to top it all off, they function using a differential that was developed from automobile technology.

Baselworld 2007 saw the introduction of the R50 T, a power-reserve movement that also utilizes the company's Isolastic system technology. Shaped like an engine with a cylinder on the left side, it is held in place by three triangles of carbon fiber and fiberglass. A spring placed upon each of these triangles absorbs any vibration inside the case.

In keeping with his extreme love of motor sports, Richards is also embarking on a partnership with the racing team of Henri Pescarolo, four-time winner of the Le Mans 24 Hours. The B.R.M Pescarolo timepiece is limited to a total of forty-eight pieces—twenty-four each for the two cars built by Pescarolo Sports that took part in the 2007 edition.

B.R.M

BR 01
Movement: automatic, Precitime Caliber Birotor; 24 x 32 mm; 35 jewels; 28,800 vph; 45 hours power reserve; double rotors in Fortale HR and tantalum on ceramic ball bearings, patented Isolastic system with four shock absorbers, arcap plates and bridges
Functions: hours, minutes, subsidiary seconds
Case: titanium with stainless steel crown, lugs, and screws, 40 x 48 mm, height 9.9 mm, domed sapphire crystal, anti-reflective on both sides; domed sapphire crystal exhibition case back; water-resistant to 30 m
Band: reptile skin, buckle
Price: $52,450
Variations: with rose gold elements; in a rose gold case; with checkered leather strap

R50 T
Movement: automatic, heavily modified ETA Caliber 2161; ø 38 mm; 35 jewels; 28,800 vph; 48 hours power reserve; patented Isolastic system with three shock absorbers, rotor made of Fortale HR, tantalum and aluminum
Functions: hours, minutes, sweep seconds; power reserve indication
Case: titanium, ø 50 mm, height 13.2 mm, sapphire crystal, anti-reflective on both sides; exhibition case back; water-resistant to 30 m
Band: leather, buckle
Remarks: three-year guarantee
Price: $21,150
Variations: with yellow, orange, or red hands

SP44 OR
Movement: automatic, ETA Valjoux Caliber 7753; ø 30 mm, height 7.9 mm; 25 jewels; 28,800 vph; 42 hours power reserve
Functions: hours, minutes, subsidiary seconds; chronograph
Case: stainless steel with rose gold buttons, crown, and lugs, ø 44 mm, sapphire crystal, anti-reflective on both sides; exhibition case back; water-resistant to 100 m
Band: reptile skin, buckle
Remarks: three-year guarantee
Price: $9,950
Variations: in a black high-gloss PVD case with orange or white elements

MTD
Movement: two automatic movements, ETA Caliber 2671; ø 17.20 mm, height 4.80 mm; 25 jewels; 28,800 vph; 38 hours power reserve
Functions: hours, minutes, sweep seconds; second time zone
Case: titanium, 53 x 35 mm, height 14 mm; sapphire crystal; water-resistant to 100 m
Band: rubber, buckle
Remarks: three-year guarantee
Price: $7,850
Variations: extra-hard PVD black titanium case

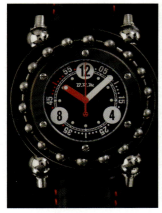

RL45
Movement: automatic, ETA Caliber 2671; ø 17.20 mm, height 4.80 mm; 25 jewels; 28,800 vph; 38 hours power reserve
Functions: hours, minutes, subsidiary seconds
Case: stainless steel / titanium, coated with black PVD, ø 45 mm, sapphire crystal; exhibition case back; water-resistant to 100 m
Band: rubber, buckle
Remarks: three-year guarantee; stainless steel balls around the perimeter of the dial
Price: $5,650
Variations: also available with ceramic balls around the dial

3MVT
Movement: three automatic movements, ETA Caliber 2671; ø 17.20 mm, height 4.80 mm; 25 jewels; 28,800 vph; 38 hours power reserve
Functions: hours, minutes, subsidiary seconds
Case: titanium, ø 52 mm, sapphire crystal; exhibition case back; water-resistant to 100 m
Band: leather, buckle
Remarks: three-year guarantee
Price: $9,500

CR44
Movement: automatic, ETA Valjoux Caliber 7753; ø 30 mm, height 7.9 mm; 27 jewels; 28,800 vph; 46 hours power reserve
Functions: hours, minutes, subsidiary seconds; chronograph
Case: stainless steel, 44 x 44 mm, sapphire crystal; exhibition case back; water-resistant to 100 m
Band: leather, buckle
Remarks: three-year guarantee
Price: $6,050
Variations: in a black case covered with extra-hard PVD coating

V8 Competition
Movement: automatic, ETA Valjoux Caliber 7753; ø 30 mm, height 7.90 mm; 27 jewels; 28,800 vph; 42 hours power reserve
Functions: hours, minutes, subsidiary seconds; date; chronograph
Case: stainless steel, ø 44 mm, sapphire crystal; exhibition case back; water-resistant to 100 m
Band: leather, buckle
Remarks: carbon fiber dial; three-year guarantee
Price: $6,100
Variations: also available as Campione model with black dial

Carl F. Bucherer

Relying on the technical competence and strong identity garnered in more than eighty years of existence, the individualistic Carl F. Bucherer watch brand proudly bears the full name of its company founder with good reason.

In 1919, visionary entrepreneur Carl Friedrich Bucherer introduced his first watch collection, a line into which he poured not only his knowledge of watchmaking, but also his special feel for the needs of his demanding clientele. Bucherer was an exceptional man, and he possessed the courage to veer off the beaten path. With creativity and wild enthusiasm, both he and the ensuing two generations of his family created a very successful company, displaying a unique talent for uniting traditional values with new ideas and a Swiss passion for watchmaking.

A good modern example of this is the new Patravi Chronograde, introduced at Baselworld 2007. This mechanical masterpiece unites six functions including a chronograph, a flyback function, a large date, an annual calendar, a power reserve indicator, and the retrograde display of the chronograph's hour counter, a combination that has never been seen before. CEO Thomas Morf's ambitious team worked for over two years on its development. "This timepiece embodies far more than the sum of its components," he confirms.

The company also launched a new watch in the Manero product line called Tribute to MaBu. Behind this somewhat unusual name lies a completely restored original vintage Valjoux 92 movement from the early 1950s. This exclusive chronograph outfitted with the original manually wound caliber dedicated to Carl's brother Max Bucherer (1883–1974) is restricted to 100 pieces thanks to the limited availability of the movement.

Though Carl F. Bucherer has been a great friend to women throughout its history, including the modern era—aptly proven by the successful Alacria line—2007 marks the year that the brand finally makes a splash in the world of women's complications. A sensational timepiece belonging to the Manero line, which is a mere 36 mm in diameter, is not only outfitted with a mechanical chronograph, but a rare one-button variety of stopwatch. And, naturally, it can be purchased in any decorative variation from purist stainless steel to the lavish jeweled timepieces the Bucherer dynasty has always been famous for.

Outshining the other fabulous spring introductions, however, is an evolution of a watch first presented two years ago: the Travel Tec. This practical time zone traveler with the ultra-complicated case has been upgraded and improved to such a degree that its current 46 mm palladium and

ceramic incarnation can be described as nothing short of eye-catching. "I believe overall that it is this watch's design that people are attracted to," Morf says to explain the avid interest in the company's flagship timepiece. "The Travel Tec is now the epitome of the whole collection. Timeless, bold design: it is this combination that people really like."

Carl F. Bucherer

Patravi TravelTec GMT
Reference number: 00.10620.08.33.01
Movement: automatic, CFB Caliber 1901 (base ETA 2894-2); ø 28.6 mm, height 7.3 mm; 39 jewels; 28,800 vph; officially certified C.O.S.C. chronometer
Functions: hours, minutes, subsidiary seconds; chronograph; 24-hour display; date
Case: stainless steel, ø 46.6 mm, height 15.5 mm; ring under crystal with 24-hour scale (third time zone), bidirectionally rotating via button; sapphire crystal; screw-in crown; water-resistant to 5 atm
Band: leather, folding clasp
Price: $10,900
Variations: stainless steel bracelet; diamond-set bezel

Patravi TravelTec GMT
Reference number: 00.10620.03.33.01
Movement: automatic, CFB Caliber 1901 (base ETA 2894-2); ø 28.6 mm, height 7.3 mm; 39 jewels; 28,800 vph; officially certified C.O.S.C. chronometer
Functions: hours, minutes, subsidiary seconds; chronograph; 24-hour display (second time zone); date
Case: red gold, ø 46.5 mm, height 15.5 mm; ring under crystal with 24-hour scale (third time zone), bidirectionally rotating via button; sapphire crystal; screw-in crown; water-resistant to 5 atm
Band: leather, folding clasp
Price: $39,500

Patravi Chronograph Big Date Annual Calendar
Reference number: 00.10619.03.13.01
Movement: automatic, CFB Caliber 1957.1 (base ETA 2892-A2); ø 30 mm, height 7.3 mm; 49 jewels; 28,800 vph; officially certified C.O.S.C. chronometer
Functions: hours, minutes, subsidiary seconds; chronograph; annual calendar with large date and month display
Case: red gold, ø 42 mm, height 13.5 mm; sapphire crystal; screw-in crown; water-resistant to 5 atm
Band: leather, folding clasp
Price: $21,900
Variations: black dial; red gold link bracelet

Patravi T-Graph
Reference number: 00.10615.08.53.21
Movement: automatic, CFB Caliber 1960 (base ETA 2892-A2); ø 30 mm, height 7.3 mm; 47 jewels; 28,800 vph
Functions: hours, minutes, subsidiary seconds; chronograph; large date; power reserve display
Case: stainless steel, 39 x 52 mm, height 13.8 mm; sapphire crystal; screw-in crown; water-resistant to 5 atm
Band: stainless steel, folding clasp
Price: $7,300
Variations: calfskin strap

Patravi T-Graph
Reference number: 00.10615.08.53.01
Movement: automatic, CFB Caliber 1960 (base ETA 2892-A2); ø 30 mm, height 7.3 mm; 47 jewels; 28,800 vph
Functions: hours, minutes, subsidiary seconds; chronograph; large date; power reserve display
Case: stainless steel, 39 x 52 mm, height 13.8 mm; sapphire crystal; screw-in crown; water-resistant to 5 atm
Band: calfksin, folding clasp
Price: $6,900
Variations: with diamond-set bezel; red gold

Patravi T24 Power Reserve
Reference number: 00.10612.08.33.01
Movement: automatic, CFB Caliber 1953 (base ETA 2892-A2); ø 25.6 mm, height 5.1 mm; 28 jewels; 28,800 vph
Functions: hours, minutes, sweep seconds; date; 24-hour display (second time zone); power reserve display
Case: stainless steel, 36 x 48 mm, height 10.8 mm; sapphire crystal; screw-in crown; water-resistant to 5 atm
Band: alligator skin, folding clasp
Price: $4,500
Variations: with diamond-set bezel; stainless steel bracelet

Patravi Chronograde
Reference number: 00.10623.08.33.01
Movement: automatic, CFB Caliber 1902 (base ETA 2892-A2); ø 30 mm, height 7.3 mm; 51 jewels; 28,800 vph
Functions: hours, minutes, subsidiary seconds; chronograph with flyback function and retrograde hour counter; annual calendar with large date and month display; power reserve indicator
Case: stainless steel, ø 44 mm, height 13.5 mm; sapphire crystal; screw-in crown; water-resistant to 5 atm
Band: leather, folding clasp
Price: $12,200
Variations: stainless steel bracelet

Manero Perpetual Calendar
Reference number: 00.10902.03.16.01
Movement: automatic, CFB Caliber 1955.1 (base ETA 2892-A2); ø 25.6 mm, height 5.2 mm; 21 jewels; 28,800 vph; officially certified chronometer (COSC)
Functions: hours, minutes, sweep seconds; perpetual calendar with date, weekday, month, moon phase scale and leap year
Case: red gold, ø 40 mm, height 11.5 mm; sapphire crystal; screw-in crown
Band: alligator skin, buckle
Price: $27,000
Variations: red gold bracelet; diamond-set bezel

Carl F. Bucherer

Manero Retrograde
Reference number: 00.10901.08.26.01
Movement: automatic, CFB Caliber 1903 (base ETA 2892-A2); ø 25.6 mm, height 5.1 mm; 34 jewels; 28,800 vph
Functions: hours, minutes, sweep seconds; date (retrograde), day; 24-hour display (second time zone); power reserve display
Case: stainless steel, ø 40 mm, height 11.5 mm; sapphire crystal; water-resistant to 3 atm
Band: alligator skin, buckle
Price: $6,300
Variations: with diamond-set bezel

Manero Retrograde
Reference number: 00.10901.08.26.21
Movement: automatic, CFB Caliber 1903 (base ETA 2892-A2); ø 25.6 mm, height 5.1 mm; 34 jewels; 28,800 vph
Functions: hours, minutes, sweep seconds; date (retrograde), day; 24-hour display (second time zone); power reserve display
Case: stainless steel, ø 40 mm, height 11.5 mm; sapphire crystal; water-resistant to 3 atm
Band: stainless steel, folding clasp
Price: $6,700
Variations: with diamond-set bezel

Manero Tribute to MaBu
Reference number: 00.10903.03.01
Movement: automatic, Valjoux Caliber 92; ø 29.5 mm, height 6 mm; 17 jewels; 18,000 vph; column-wheel control of chronograph functions; vintage, re-worked manufacture movement
Functions: hours, minutes, subsidiary seconds; chronograph
Case: red gold, ø 40 mm, height 13 mm; domed sapphire crystal; water-resistant to 3 atm
Band: alligator skin, buckle
Remarks: limited edition of 100 pieces
Price: $24,000

Manero Monograph
Reference number: 00.10904.03.97.11
Movement: automatic, CFB Caliber 1962; ø 24.6 mm, height 4.2 mm; 21 jewels; 21,600 vph; one-button control of the chronograph functions (start-stop-reset)
Functions: hours, minutes, subsidiary seconds; chronograph
Case: red gold, ø 35 mm, height 10.5 mm; bezel set with 50 diamonds; sapphire crystal; crown with chronograph button; water-resistant to 3 atm
Band: snake skin and leather, buckle
Remarks: dial set with diamonds
Price: $46,500

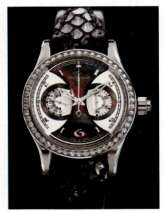

Manero Monograph
Reference number: 00.10904.08.16.01
Movement: automatic, CFB Caliber 1962; ø 24.6 mm, height 4.2 mm; 21 jewels; 21,600 vph; one-button control of the chronograph functions (start-stop-reset)
Functions: hours, minutes, subsidiary seconds; chronograph
Case: stainless steel, ø 35 mm, height 10.5 mm; bezel set with 50 diamonds; sapphire crystal; crown with chronograph button; water-resistant to 3 atm
Band: snake skin and leather, buckle
Remarks: mother-of-pearl dial
Price: $20,500

Alacria Diva
Reference number: 00.10705.01.21.12
Movement: quartz
Functions: hours, minutes
Case: yellow gold, 31.3 x 45 mm, height 8 mm; case sides set with 128 brilliant-cut diamonds; sapphire crystal; water-resistant to 3 atm
Band: python skin, buckle
Price: $24,900
Variations: with snake or lizard skin strap; case set with 46 brilliant-cut diamonds

Alacria Fancy Diva
Reference number: 00.10705.02.11.13
Movement: quartz
Functions: hours, minutes
Case: white gold, 31.3 x 45 mm, height 8 mm; bezel and case sides set with 154 brilliant-cut diamonds; sapphire crystal; water-resistant to 3 atm
Band: alligator skin, buckle
Price: $165,000

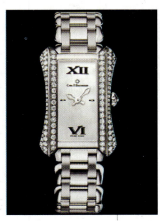

Alacria Midi
Reference number: 00.10701.02.71.32
Movement: quartz
Functions: hours, minutes
Case: white gold, 26.5 x 38 mm, height 7 mm; case sides set with 102 brilliant-cut diamonds; sapphire crystal; water-resistant to 3 atm
Band: white gold, folding clasp
Price: $27,300
Variations: yellow gold

Camilla Lindh, model.
Not afraid of getting older.

The Alacria in 18 K yellow gold, set with 102 diamonds FC Top Wesselton vvs 1.6 ct is a perfect example of Carl F. Bucherer's unique philosophy. As an independent family business in Lucerne since 1919, our passion for perfection and love of detail have never changed.

CARL F. BUCHERER

FOR PEOPLE WHO DO NOT GO WITH THE TIMES.

www.carl-f-bucherer.com   info@cfbnorthamerica.com   800 395 4306

Bulgari

Breathtaking jewelry pieces, scents to beguile the senses, elegant sunglasses, luxurious leather bags, and, as the crowning jewel, hotels: Anyone with a penchant for exclusivity is well served by the Italian luxury brand Bulgari's fine tradition. The brand's concept follows a distinct system within the family-owned company where president Paolo Bulgari and his brother Nicola firmly hold the reins. No idea goes into production that the two brothers have not personally consented to.

The Greek silversmith Sotirio Bulgari settled in Rome at the beginning of the last century and founded a shop called Old Curiosity Shop, named after the novel by Charles Dickens, in order to attract British and American tourists in the Eternal City. His selection of jewelry and accessories was impressive even then, and he soon opened another branch in St. Moritz. In order to continue developing and perfecting his jewelry art and the production of silver wares, he made his shop on Via Condotti in Rome the flagship store, which it has remained until today.

In the 1990s Bulgari extended its product portfolio to include perfumes and accessories, supporting its international expansion by going public and putting the holding company Bulgari S.p A. on the stock index.

Watches were already part of the program in the 1940s, but only in the '70s did a systematic collection become apparent. The most famous example is the Bulgari-Bulgari model: Created by designer Gérald Genta in 1977, it was not only a groundbreaking success for the company, but also the first watch produced in a large series under the company's own insignia. The double logo engraved into the bezel still continues to influence the company's watch design today. Shortly thereafter the family founded Bulgari Time S.A. in Switzerland's Neuchâtel. In 1993 Bulgari embarked upon a new strategy and since then has distributed its watches worldwide through a network of exclusive dealers.

The next step in the evolution followed in mid-2000, when Bulgari purchased Daniel Roth S.A. and Gérald Genta S.A., both established names in the production and manufacture of complicated and unusual watches.

In 2004 Bulgari introduced the first *grande complication* completely developed and manufactured within the group. The following year Bulgari took a 50 percent interest in the company Cadrans Design S.A., a Swiss manufacturer of high-quality dials, as well as a 51 percent interest in Prestige d'Or S.A., a market leader in the manufacture of stainless steel bracelets for complicated watches, thus once again underscoring the company's position within the high watchmaking sector.

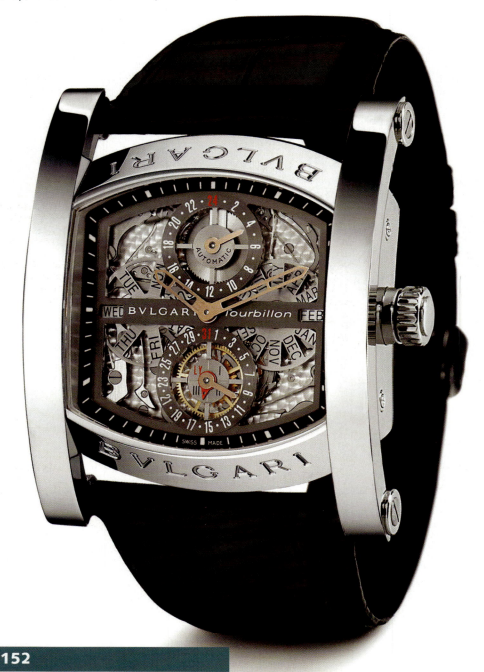

Bulgari

Bulgari-Bulgari Tourbillon
Reference number: BB 40 C6PLTB
Movement: manually wound, Caliber BVL 200 (base Daniel Roth Caliber R&G 052); ø 28 mm, height 4.4 mm; 20 jewels; 21,600 vph; power reserve 64 hours; one-minute tourbillon
Functions: hours, minutes; subsidiary seconds (on tourbillon cage); power reserve display (on back)
Case: platinum, ø 40 mm, height 9.6 mm; engraved bezel; sapphire crystal; transparent case back
Band: reptile skin, double folding clasp
Remarks: limited edition of 20 numbered pieces
Price: $102,000

Bulgari-Bulgari Répétition Minutes
Reference number: BBW 40 C6GLRM
Movement: manually wound, Caliber BVL 300 (base Parmigiani Caliber 9950); ø 28 mm, height 5.7 mm; 31 jewels; 18,000 vph; power reserve 47 hours
Functions: hours, minutes, subsidiary seconds; hour, quarter hour, and minute repeater
Case: white gold, ø 40 mm, height 11 mm; engraved bezel; sapphire crystal; transparent case back
Band: reptile skin, double folding clasp
Remarks: limited edition of 15 numbered pieces
Price: $145,000

Bulgari-Bulgari Moon Phases
Reference number: BBW 38 GLMP/C3
Movement: automatic, La Joux-Perret Caliber 3103 (base ETA 2892-A2); ø 27 mm, height 5.35 mm; 26 jewels; 28,800 vph
Functions: hours, minutes, subsidiary seconds; date; moon phase
Case: white gold, ø 38 mm, height 9.2 mm; engraved bezel; sapphire crystal
Band: reptile skin, buckle
Remarks: limited edition of 99 pieces
Price: $18,400
Variations: unlimited white gold version; limited or unlimited yellow gold versions

Bulgari-Bulgari Annual Calendar
Reference number: BB 38 GLAC 4/C1
Movement: automatic, Dubois Dépraz Caliber 5733 (base ETA 2892-A2); ø 25.6 mm, height 5.2 mm; 21 jewels; 28,800 vph
Functions: hours, minutes, sweep seconds; annual calendar with date, month
Case: yellow gold, ø 38 mm, height 9.8 mm; engraved bezel; sapphire crystal
Band: reptile skin, buckle
Remarks: limited edition of 99 pieces
Price: $18,400
Variations: unlimited yellow gold version; limited or unlimited white gold versions

Bulgari-Bulgari Réserve de Marche
Reference number: BBP 41 BGL
Movement: manually wound, Caliber BVL 131 (base Frédéric Piguet Caliber 1103.4); ø 26.2 mm, height 2.8 mm; 21 jewels; 28,800 vph; power reserve 72 hours
Functions: hours, minutes, sweep seconds; power reserve display
Case: rose gold, ø 41 mm, height 7.3 mm; engraved bezel; sapphire crystal
Band: reptile skin, double folding clasp
Price: $15,850
Variations: white gold

Rettangolo Réserve de Marche
Reference number: RT 49 PLD
Movement: manually wound, Parmigiani Caliber 115; 29.3 x 23.6 mm, height 6.55 mm; 28 jewels; 28,800 vph; power reserve eight days
Functions: hours, minutes, subsidiary seconds; date; power reserve display
Case: platinum, 47.65 x 29 mm, height 10.35 mm; sapphire crystal; transparent case back
Band: reptile skin, double folding clasp
Remarks: limited edition of 99 pieces
Price: $44,700

Anfiteatro Tourbillon
Reference number: AT 40 GLTB
Movement: manually wound, Caliber MVT 9902 TB (base Girard-Perregaux 9902); ø 28.8 mm, height 6.75 mm; 20 jewels; 21,600 vph, power reserve 75 hours; one-minute tourbillon; completely hand-worked and engraved
Functions: hours, minutes
Case: yellow gold, ø 40 mm, height 10.6 mm; engraved flange; sapphire crystal
Band: reptile skin, buckle
Price: $82,000
Variations: platinum

Diagono Professional Tachymeter Rattrapante
Reference number: CHW 40 C6GLTARA
Movement: automatic, La Joux-Perret Caliber 8601 (base ETA Valjoux 7750); ø 30.4 mm, height 8.4 mm; 31 jewels; 28,800 vph; officially certified chronometer (COSC)
Functions: hours, minutes, subsidiary seconds; split-seconds chronograph
Case: white gold, ø 40 mm, height 14.65 mm; bezel engraved with tachymeter scale; sapphire crystal; transparent case back; screw-in crown; water-resistant to 10 atm
Band: reptile skin, double folding clasp
Price: $34,600
Variations: yellow gold

Bulgari

Diagono Professional GMT Flyback
Reference number: GMT 40 C6SVD/FB
Movement: automatic, Dubois Dépraz Caliber 21340 (base ETA 2892-A2); ø 30 mm, height 7.6 mm; 21 jewels; 28,800 vph; officially certified chronometer (COSC)
Functions: hours, minutes, subsidiary seconds; chronograph with flyback function; date; 24-hour display (second time zone)
Case: stainless steel, ø 40 mm, height 15.6 mm; bidirectionally rotating bezel with 24-hour scale; sapphire crystal; screw-in crown and buttons; water-resistant to 10 atm
Band: rubber/stainless steel, double folding clasp
Price: $7,200
Variations: with black dial and flange in blue/red

Diagono Professional Regatta
Reference number: SD 40 BSV/RE
Movement: automatic, Dubois Dépraz Caliber 42028 (base ETA 2892-A2); ø 30 mm, height 7.6 mm; 39 jewels; 28,800 vph
Functions: hours, minutes, subsidiary seconds; chronograph with flyback function and count-down display
Case: stainless steel, ø 40 mm, height 15.6 mm; bidirectionally rotating bezel with 360-degree divisions and display of directions; sapphire crystal; screw-in crown and buttons; water-resistant to 30 atm
Band: rubber/stainless steel, double folding clasp
Price: $6,700
Variations: white dial

Diagono Professional Scuba Chrono
Reference number: GMT 40 C5 SSD
Movement: automatic, Caliber B 224 (base ETA 2892-A2); ø 30 mm, height 7.4 mm; 49 jewels, 28,800 vph; officially certified chronometer (COSC); sweep chronograph minute counter
Functions: hours, minutes, subsidiary seconds; chronograph with flyback function; 24-hour display
Case: yellow gold, ø 40 mm, height 16.3 mm; unidirectionally rotating bezel with 60-minute divisions; sapphire crystal; screw-in crown and buttons; water-resistant to 30 atm
Band: rubber/yellow gold, double folding clasp
Price: $18,100
Variations: stainless steel; yellow gold/stainless steel

Ergon Chrono
Reference number: EGW 40 C5 GLD CH
Movement: automatic, Caliber B 130 (base ETA 2894-2); ø 28.6 mm, height 6.1 mm; 37 jewels; 28,800 vph
Functions: hours, minutes, subsidiary seconds; chronograph; date
Case: white gold, 40.4 x 51 mm, height 12.3 mm; sapphire crystal
Band: reptile skin, double folding clasp
Price: $15,100
Variations: with diamond pavé; yellow gold; stainless steel

Assioma Chrono
Reference number: AA 48 C13 GLDCH
Movement: automatic, Caliber B 130 (base ETA 2094); ø 28.6 mm, height 6.1 mm; 33 jewels, 28,800 vph; individualized for Bulgari
Functions: hours, minutes, subsidiary seconds; chronograph; date
Case: yellow gold, ø 48 mm, height 13.35 mm; sapphire crystal
Band: reptile skin, double folding clasp
Price: $12,600
Variations: in 44 mm case size; stainless steel with reptile skin strap or stainless steel bracelet; stainless steel/yellow gold with reptile skin strap or gold bracelet

Assioma Petite Complication
Reference number: AAP 48 GLHR
Movement: automatic, Caliber BVL 261 (base Girard-Perregaux 3100); ø 26.2 mm, height 4.8 mm; 44 jewels; 28,800 vph; retrograde hour display (240°), anthracite-colored movement
Functions: hours (retrograde), minutes, subsidiary seconds; day/night indication
Case: rose gold, 47.7 x 38.8 mm, height 13.25 mm; engraved bezel; sapphire crystal; transparent case back
Band: reptile skin, double folding clasp
Remarks: limited edition of 99 numbered pieces
Price: $19,000
Variations: yellow gold, limited edition of 99 pieces in white gold

Assioma Multi Complication
Reference number: AA 48 PLTB
Movement: automatic, Caliber BVL 416 (base GG12011); ø 30 mm, height 7.6 mm; 39 jewels; 21,600 vph; power reserve 64 hours; one-minute tourbillon
Functions: hours, minutes; perpetual calendar with date, day, month, leap year; 24-hour display (second time zone)
Case: platinum, 47.7 x 38.8 mm, height 14.8 mm; engraved bezel; sapphire crystal; transparent case back
Band: reptile skin, double folding clasp
Remarks: limited and numbered edition of 25 pieces
Price: $137,000

Assioma Multi Complication (back)
Movement: Caliber BVL 416 is the first autonomous multi-complication movement developed, produced, and assembled by the Bulgari Group. It comprises 416 individual components. Both the transparent case back and the skeletonized rotor allow for an unimpeded view of the tourbillon cage and the lavishly decorated, anthracite-colored movement.

The insider's guide to luxury

www.goldarths.com

Buti

Viva Italia! These calls were heard especially loud and clear spanning the entire globe from the time between June 9 and July 9, 2006: Italy had won the soccer World Cup, an event of untold importance throughout the world, and nowhere more significant than in Italy. During the month-long event held in Germany's largest soccer stadiums, Italy's head coach was without a doubt one of the figures most often on camera. And Marcello Lippi was wearing a colorful Buti on his wrist, his own personal example of great Italian design coupled with Swiss engineering.

This six-year-old company was founded by Italian Tommaso Buti, a well-known name in the Italian fashion industry. Buti's hot concept includes designing these striking watches in Florence and having them manufactured in Switzerland using Swiss parts. This combination of Italian flair for design and Swiss love of detail and precision has produced a line of watches like no other. "Time is an endless succession of moments in which events and the changing of things take place," says Buti, emphasizing that this visible concept of time is one that is all his own. Buti, a watch aficionado and collector, lives and works in Florence, a city that has been highly prized for its association with art, style, and design for centuries. Buti's own showroom is located in a historic palazzo in the city center. The movements utilized are of the finest quality: ETA bases with modifications made by the masters, La Joux-Perret, under the direction of an Italian watchmaker who cooperates with Buti and who has been practicing the craft of watchmaking since 1939. This watchmaker was also one of those whose skilled hands breathed life into the first Panerai collection, also created in Florence.

The highlight of Buti's collection is without a doubt the Black Gold flyback chronograph, limited to fifty pieces worldwide. Buti has devised a process involving vacuum ionization that turns an ordinary 18-karat yellow gold case a dramatic black color. The exact process naturally remains secret, but suffice it to say that the results are quite stunning. When such cases are paired with Buti's strikingly colored, galvanized and marbled-relief dials, the outcome remains truly unique. This timekeeper features a Jaquet 8112 movement, which is based on the Valjoux 7750 and modified by the addition of a GMT display requiring an additional plate. Its elegant black dial prominently displays the limitation number underneath the company's logo, and eight of the dial markers are represented by eight natural diamonds. The Black range also contains one other model featuring a split-seconds complication.

Only available in Europe and Asia until three years ago, Buti is currently being distributed in the United States by DOMUSHora, specialists for Italian timepieces. DOMUSHora's vice president of marketing Umberto Cipolla describes Buti's collection as the ultimate in Italian sophistication and high-tech watchmaking, "We believe there is a niche market for these very special watches. Our plan is to limit distribution to selective (and selected) luxury retailers whose clientele includes collectors and those who appreciate very special timepieces."

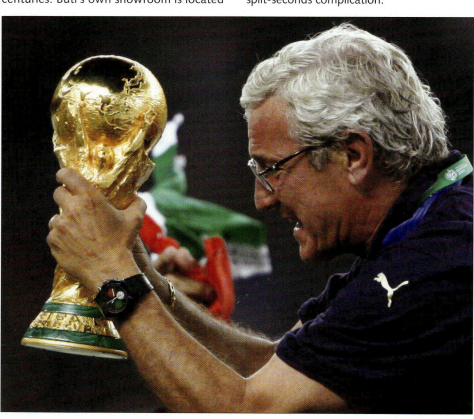

Magnum
Movement: automatic, ETA Valjoux Caliber 7750; ø 30 mm, height 7.9 mm; 25 jewels; 28,800 vph; power reserve 40 hours; soigné finishing
Functions: hours, minutes, subsidiary seconds; chronograph
Case: black PVD-coated titanium, ø 48 mm, height 16 mm; sapphire crystal; case back secured with eight 18-karat gold screws; 18-karat gold crown and buttons
Band: sharkskin, buckle
Remarks: flange set with brilliant-cut diamonds
Price: $16,900

Black Rain GMT
Movement: automatic, modified ETA Valjoux Caliber 7750; ø 30 mm, height 7.9 mm; 25 jewels; 28,800 vph; power reserve 40 hours; soigné-finished black PVD rotor
Functions: hours, minutes, subsidiary seconds; chronograph with flyback function; second time zone
Case: black PVD-coated titanium, ø 42 mm, height 16 mm; sapphire crystal; sapphire case back secured with eight gold screws; black PVD crown and buttons
Band: rubber, buckle
Remarks: flange set with brilliant-cut diamonds; marbled dial
Price: $9,500
Variations: black or white marbled dial

Black Rain Rattrapante
Movement: automatic, modified ETA Valjoux Caliber 7750; ø 30 mm, height 7.9 mm; 25 jewels; 28,800 vph; power reserve 40 hours; soigné finished black PVD rotor
Functions: hours, minutes, subsidiary seconds; split-seconds chronograph with flyback function; second time zone
Case: black PVD-coated titanium, ø 42 mm, height 16 mm; sapphire crystal; sapphire case back secured with eight gold screws; black PVD crown and buttons
Band: rubber, buckle
Remarks: flange set with brilliant-cut diamonds; marbled dial
Price: $11,900

Lippi Sport Gold
Reference number: YKOSPORT-LIPPI
Movement: automatic, Jaquet Caliber 8147 (base ETA Valjoux 7750); ø 30 mm, height 7.9 mm; 25 jewels; 28,800 vph
Functions: hours, minutes, subsidiary seconds; chronograph
Case: rose gold, ø 42 mm, height 15 mm; black titanium bezel; sapphire crystal; screw-down case back with commemorative world cup engraving; screw-in crown; water-resistant to 200 m
Band: rubber, buckle
Remarks: special marbled dial with Italian national soccer coach Marcello Lippi's signature; limited edition of 75 pieces
Price: appx. $14,900

Shark
Movement: automatic, modified ETA Valjoux Caliber 7750; ø 30 mm, height 7.9 mm; 25 jewels; 28,800 vph; power reserve 40 hours; soigné-finished and engraved rotor
Functions: hours, minutes, subsidiary seconds; chronograph
Case: stainless steel, ø 42 mm, height 16 mm; black PVD bezel; sapphire crystal; case back secured with eight screws
Band: rubber, buckle
Remarks: dial set with eight brilliant-cut diamonds
Price: $7,400
Variations: stainless steel bracelet with folding clasp; rubber-coated crown

Competition
Reference number: YKcompetition
Movement: automatic, Jaquet Caliber 8147 (base ETA Valjoux 7750); ø 30 mm, height 7.9 mm; 25 jewels; 28,800 vph; power reserve 40 hours
Functions: hours, minutes, subsidiary seconds; chronograph
Case: black titanium, ø 42 mm, height 15 mm; 18-karat gold bezel; sapphire crystal; screw-down exhibition case back; screw-in gold buttons and crown; water-resistant to 200 m
Band: rubber, buckle
Price: $10,500

Mister One
Reference number: MOTXTT grey
Movement: automatic, Jaquet Caliber 8147 (base ETA Valjoux 7750); ø 30 mm, height 7.9 mm; 25 jewels; 28,800 vph; power reserve 40 hours
Functions: hours, minutes, subsidiary seconds; chronograph
Case: titanium, ø 40 mm, height 14.5 mm; sapphire crystal; screw-down exhibition case back; screw-in crown; water-resistant to 200 m
Band: rubber, buckle
Price: $6,500

Black Fausto
Reference number: FTOATXB
Movement: automatic, Jaquet Caliber 8147 (base ETA Valjoux 7750); ø 30 mm, height 7.9 mm; 25 jewels; 28,800 vph; power reserve 40 hours
Functions: hours, minutes; chronograph
Case: stainless steel, ø 42 mm, height 15 mm; sapphire crystal; screw-down exhibition case back; screw-in crown; water-resistant to 200 m
Band: crocodile skin, buckle
Price: $8,100

Cartier

The blue cabochon in the crown has been a signature element for Cartier since the beginning of the 1930s when the Pasha of Marrakesh ordered a watch from Louis Cartier that he wished to take swimming with him. The cabochon in the crown sealed it, making it more water-resistant, and not only was the Pasha line born, but also an element that makes a timepiece by Cartier recognizable even at a distance.

Cartier is now introducing a new classic for men and women in the same vein as the Tank, the most outstanding feature of which is the placement of the crown and its blue cabochon within a crown protection that looks distinctly like a bubble—or a small balloon. This is perfect, for it exactly coincides with the absolute roundness of the Ballon Bleu's case, while simultaneously breaking up the—well—roundness of the whole. Available in three sizes, this new Cartier classic can be easily and beautifully worn by men or women. The perfection of shapes this famed company has conceived combined with movements crafted in the art of *haute horlogerie* have always been the secret to Cartier's success, beginning with the first models created in the Paris workshops in 1853. The watches now found in the brand's Collection Privée Cartier Paris are crafted in the most precious materials and outfitted with mechanical *manufacture* movements made according to traditional watchmaker practices. Within Cartier's large product palette, they make up their own little colorful collection, one that most especially aims for aficionados of literally beautiful examples of watchmaking. Cartier produces and assembles its own watches in its factory in Switzerland's La Chaux-de-Fonds. However, as in the past, the company continues to enjoy taking the opportunity to combine its own know-how with the expertise of other great *manufactures* in order to develop and realize unusual technical ideas. These partners count among the most reputable Swiss *manufactures* and specialist workshops: Piaget, Renaud et Papi, Dubois Dépraz, Girard-Perregaux, Frédéric Piguet, and of course Jaeger-LeCoultre.

Jaeger-LeCoultre is today—once again—Cartier's main partner with regard to the Collection Privée Cartier Paris. Already in 1903 Cartier represented Jaeger-LeCoultre's most important customer, and in 1907 the Cartier brothers signed a contract with Edmond Jaeger that guaranteed them exclusive production of chronometers, watches with flat movements, and future inventions as long as they continued to order a certain number of pieces. The relationship between Jaeger-LeCoultre and Cartier was to last more than three-quarters of a century. From 1927 until 1979, Jaeger-LeCoultre supplied more than thirty-two different calibers to the European Watch Company, which was founded in 1919 by Cartier in New York. With the advent of quartz technology, the relationship between the two companies weakened toward the end of the 1970s. However, for many years now a new chapter in the story of this long and fruitful cooperation between Cartier and Jaeger-LeCoultre has been taking place—much to the joy of demanding connoisseurs who expect very special pieces from the label Collection Privée Cartier Paris.

Cartier

Rotonde de Cartier Grand Date
Reference number: W1550751
Movement: manually wound, Cartier Caliber 9602 MC (base Jaeger-LeCoultre); ø 25.6 mm, height 4 mm; 22 jewels; 28,800 vph
Functions: hours, minutes, subsidiary seconds; large date
Case: red gold, ø 42 mm, height 11.3 mm; sapphire crystal; crown with sapphire cabochon; transparent case back
Band: reptile skin, double folding clasp
Price: $21,300
Variations: white gold

Rotonde de Cartier Grande Complication
Reference number: W1553251
Movement: manually wound, Cartier Caliber 9433 MC (Renaud et Papi); ø 33.8 mm, height 9.85 mm; 35 jewels; one-minute tourbillon; chronograph button in crown; power reserve eight days
Functions: hours, minutes, sweep seconds; chronograph; perpetual calendar with date, weekday, month, and leap year display
Case: platinum, ø 43.5 mm, height 16.25 mm; sapphire crystal; crown with sapphire cabochon; transparent case back
Band: reptile skin, double folding clasp
Remarks: limited edition of 10 numbered pieces
Price: $400,000

Tank Louis Cartier XL 2 Fuseaux
Reference number: W1553051
Movement: manually wound, Cartier Caliber 9901 MC; 26 x 20.3 mm, height 3.1 mm; 18 jewels, 21,600 vph
Functions: hours, minutes (two sets of each)
Case: rose gold, 30 x 39.2 mm, height 7 mm; mineral crystal; crown with sapphire cabochon; transparent case back
Band: reptile skin, double folding clasp
Price: $20,300
Variations: white gold

Cloche 1922
Reference number: W1551151
Movement: manually wound, Cartier Caliber 9970 MC (base Jaeger-LeCoultre); 12.8 x 15.2 mm, height 2.9 mm; 18 jewels, 21,600 vph
Functions: hours, minutes
Case: yellow gold, 28.8 x 37.2 mm, height 6.1 mm; mineral crystal; crown with sapphire cabochon; transparent case back
Band: reptile skin, folding clasp
Price: $24,200

Tortue XL 8 Days Power Reserve
Reference number: W1545851
Movement: manually wound, Cartier Caliber 9910 MC (base Jaeger-LeCoultre); ø 30 mm, height 5.3 mm; 25 jewels; 28,800 vph; twin spring barrels, power reserve eight days
Functions: hours, minutes, subsidiary seconds; large date; power reserve display
Case: red gold, 38 x 48 mm, height 11.6 mm; mineral crystal; crown with sapphire cabochon; transparent case back
Band: reptile skin, folding clasp
Price: $34,100
Variations: white gold

Rotonde Jour et Nuit
Reference number: W1550151
Movement: manually wound, Cartier Caliber 9903 MC (base Jaeger-LeCoultre); ø 26.2 mm, height 4.72 mm; 25 jewels, 28,800 vph; day/night hour display via hand-engraved disk with marker
Functions: hours (day/night), minutes (retrograde)
Case: white gold, ø 42 mm, height 11.3 mm; sapphire crystal; transparent case back
Band: reptile skin, folding clasp
Price: $16,100
Variations: red gold

Tortue XL
Reference number: W1546051
Movement: manually wound, Cartier Caliber 9601 MC (base Jaeger-LeCoultre); ø 25.6 mm, height 3.3 mm; 20 jewels; 21,600 vph
Functions: hours, minutes
Case: red gold, 38 x 48 mm, height 10.8 mm; mineral crystal; crown with sapphire cabochon; transparent case back
Band: reptile skin, folding clasp
Price: $16,100
Variations: platinum

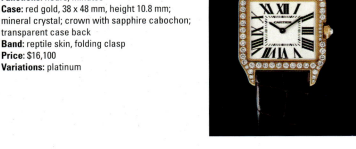

Santos Dumont SM
Reference number: WH100351
Movement: quartz, Cartier Caliber 690
Functions: hours, minutes
Case: red gold, 38 x 48 mm, height 10.3 mm; bezel set with 62 diamonds; sapphire crystal; screw-in crown with diamond cabochon
Band: reptile skin, buckle
Price: $21,950
Variations: yellow or white gold

Cartier

Tonneau LM
Reference number: WE400831
Movement: manually wound, Cartier Caliber 8970 MC; ø 23.3 mm, height 2.5 mm; 18 jewels; 21,600 vph
Functions: hours, minutes
Case: white gold, 26.2 x 46.7 mm, height 8 mm; bezel set with 63 diamonds; mineral crystal; crown with diamond cabochon
Band: reptile skin, folding clasp
Price: $26,300

Santos 100 MM
Reference number: WM503251
Movement: automatic, Cartier Caliber 076 MC (base ETA 2671); ø 17.2 mm, height 4.8 mm; 25 jewels; 28,800 vph
Functions: hours, minutes, sweep seconds
Case: white gold, 33 x 44.2 mm; bezel and lugs set with 285 diamonds; sapphire crystal; screw-in crown
Band: reptile skin, folding clasp
Remarks: mother-of-pearl dial
Price: $37,300

La Doña SM
Reference number: WE600351
Movement: quartz, Cartier Caliber 059
Functions: hours, minutes
Case: white gold, 20 x 22 mm, height 7.2 mm; bezel set with 52 diamonds; sapphire crystal; crown with diamond cabochon
Band: reptile skin, folding clasp
Price: $16,200
Variations: red or yellow gold

La Doña LM
Reference number: W6400456
Movement: quartz, Cartier Caliber 690
Functions: hours, minutes
Case: red gold, 26 x 28 mm, height 8.2 mm; sapphire crystal
Band: reptile skin, folding clasp
Price: $9,100
Variations: yellow gold

La Doña LM
Reference number: W6600221
Movement: quartz, Cartier Caliber 690
Functions: hours, minutes
Case: stainless steel, 26 x 28 mm, height 8.2 mm; sapphire crystal
Band: stainless steel, double folding clasp
Price: $4,600
Variations: as small model (SM)

Santos Dumont SM
Reference number: W2012851
Movement: manually wound, Cartier Caliber 430 MC (base Piaget); ø 20.5 mm, height 2.1 mm, 18 jewels, 21,600 vph
Functions: hours, minutes
Case: red gold, 44.5 x 38.5 mm, height 10 mm; bezel; sapphire crystal; crown with faceted sapphire
Band: reptile skin, folding clasp
Price: $12,300

Roadster Chronograph
Reference number: W62042Y5
Movement: automatic, Cartier Caliber 8510 (base ETA 2894); ø 12.5 mm, height 6.1 mm; 37 jewels; 28,800 vph
Functions: hours, minutes, subsidiary seconds; chronograph; date
Case: red gold, 42 x 37.4 mm, height 12.2 mm; sapphire crystal with magnifying lens; screw-in crown; water-resistant to 10 atm
Band: reptile skin, double folding clasp
Remarks: patented exchangeable band system
Price: $20,000

Pasha Seatimer Chronograph
Reference number: W301970M
Movement: automatic, Cartier Caliber 8630 MC (base ETA Valjoux 7753); ø 30 mm, height 7.9 mm; 27 jewels; 28,800 vph
Functions: hours, minutes, subsidiary seconds; chronograph; date
Case: yellow gold, ø 42.5 mm, height 14.5 mm; unidirectionally rotating bezel with ceramic ring; sapphire crystal; crown with protective cap and cabochon, screw-in buttons; water-resistant to 10 atm
Band: yellow gold with intermediate rubber links, double folding clasp
Price: $38,400

Ballon Bleu MM
Reference number: W69004Z2
Movement: automatic, Cartier Caliber 076 MC (base ETA 2671); ø 17.2 mm, height 4.8 mm; 25 jewels; 28,800 vph
Functions: hours, minutes, sweep seconds
Case: red gold, ø 36.5 mm, height 9.8 mm; sapphire crystal; crown with sapphire cabochon
Band: red gold, double folding clasp
Price: $22,000
Variations: yellow gold

Ballon Bleu LM
Reference number: W69013Z2
Movement: automatic, Cartier Caliber 049 MC (base ETA 2892-A2); ø 25.6 mm, height 3.6 mm; 21 jewels; 28,800 vph
Functions: hours, minutes, sweep seconds; date
Case: white gold, ø 42 mm, height 10.5 mm; sapphire crystal; crown with sapphire cabochon
Band: white gold, double folding clasp
Price: $28,200
Variations: yellow or red gold

Ballon Bleu Jewellry SM
Reference number: WE9002Z3
Movement: quartz, Cartier Caliber 057 MC
Functions: hours, minutes
Case: red gold, ø 28.5 mm, height 9.2 mm; bezel set with 30 diamonds; sapphire crystal; crown with sapphire cabochon
Band: red gold, double folding clasp
Price: $23,700
Variations: white or yellow gold

Pasha 42
Reference number: W3019551
Movement: automatic, Cartier Caliber 8000 MC (base Jaeger-LeCoultre); ø 25.6 mm, height 3.85 mm; 27 jewels; 28,800 vph; twin spring barrels
Functions: hours, minutes, sweep seconds
Case: yellow gold, ø 42 mm, height 8.6 mm; sapphire crystal; crown with protective cap and cabochon
Band: reptile skin, folding clasp
Price: $16,300
Variations: red gold

Santos 100 Chrono
Reference number: W20090X8
Movement: automatic, Cartier Caliber 8630 MC (base ETA Valjoux 7753); ø 30 mm, height 7.9 mm; 27 jewels; 28,800 vph
Functions: hours, minutes, subsidiary seconds; chronograph; date
Case: stainless steel, 41.2 x 54.3 mm, height 14.3 mm; sapphire crystal; water-resistant to 10 atm
Band: reptile skin, double folding clasp
Price: $7,700

Santos 100 LM
Reference number: W20121U2
Movement: automatic, Cartier Caliber 8630 MC (base ETA Valjoux 7753); ø 25.6 mm, height 3.6 mm; 21 jewels; 28,800 vph
Functions: hours, minutes, sweep seconds
Case: stainless steel, 38.3 x 51.1 mm, height 13 mm; bezel covered with rubber; sapphire crystal; water-resistant to 10 atm
Band: rubber, buckle
Price: $5,450

Chronoscaph PM
Reference number: W1ß197U2
Movement: quartz, Cartier Caliber 471 CC
Functions: hours, minutes, subsidiary seconds; chronograph; date
Case: stainless steel, ø 32 mm, height 12 mm; sapphire crystal; crown with rubber cabochon; water-resistant to 10 atm
Band: stainless steel/rubber, folding clasp
Price: $3,450
Variations: black dial, applied rubber elements

Roadster PM
Reference number: W62053V3
Movement: quartz, Cartier Caliber 688 CC
Functions: hours, minutes; date
Case: stainless steel, 30 x 36.7 mm, height 9.8 mm; sapphire crystal with magnifying lens; screw-in crown; water-resistant to 10 atm
Band: nylon, buckle
Remarks: patented exchangeable band system
Price: $4,500

Chase-Durer

Chase-Durer was founded in 1992 by Brandon and Marianne Chase, who took the other half of the company name from their mentor and associate, watchmaker Stefan Durer. The company has spent the last fifteen years establishing itself on the cutting edge of design paired with function—at a reasonable price for the consumer.

Since these previous movie-industry specialists began a decade and a half ago, Chase-Durer has become known as a company specializing in Swiss-made watches housed in solid stainless steel cases featuring scratchproof sapphire crystals and SuperLumiNova illumination for greater legibility. The design and production elements involved in each timepiece made by Chase-Durer are engineered to deliver the ultimate in dependability, performance, and legibility. Chase-Durer offers a variety of Swiss mechanical movements in automatic and manually wound watches as well as many high-grade Swiss quartz movements for greater variety. There are many models for the discriminating enthusiast to choose from—such as the Apogee powered by a modified ETA 2892-A2 movement with quick adjustment for the GMT function and the automatic Combat Command GMT featuring a chronograph and three time zones. Those who love vintage-style timepieces are enthusiastic about the new Warhawk, housed in a 50-millimeter titanium case and powered by the classic ETA Unitas 6497 manually wound movement. A left-handed version of the Warhawk is also available in a limited edition.

Chase-Durer's Conquest Automatic is a C.O.S.C. officially certified chronometer, which proves the superlative precision of its Sellita SW200 mechanism, a 26-jewel movement that can be viewed through the timepiece's sapphire crystal case back. The timepiece's handsome design includes a distinctive titanium bezel, SuperLumiNova-coated hands, and a rubber bracelet containing solid engraved steel inserts and a folding clasp.

Chase-Durer is so confident of the quality of its wristwatches that the company offers a full two-year guarantee on its timepieces—a rare occurrence in an industry that advertises timepieces meant to be passed down through generations. "Chase-Durer's commitment to fine watchmaking will never end," explains the brand's designer Marianne Chase. "Rest assured, many new designs with new and unique movements are in store for the future—designs that will continue to underscore our commitment to provide the best value in the marketplace." Chase's philosophy guarantees that the fine timepieces this Los Angeles–based company produces will be around for years to come, ensuring that all watch enthusiasts can enjoy the style, value, and durability of Chase-Durer.

Apogee Gold
Reference number: CD.499.8
Movement: automatic, CD Caliber 9055 (base ETA 2892-A2); ø 25.6 mm, height 5.10 mm; 30 jewels; 28,800 vph; 42 hours power reserve; 18-karat rose gold rotor with côtes de Genève, blued screws
Functions: hours, minutes, sweep seconds; date, day, second time zone, power reserve display
Case: rose gold, ø 44 mm, height 11.05 mm; sapphire crystal; screwed-down exhibition case back; screw-in crown; water-resistant to 50 m
Band: reptile skin, 18-karat rose gold folding clasp
Price: $13,900

Apogee Steel
Reference number: CD.499.1
Movement: automatic, CD Caliber 9055 (base ETA 2892-A2); ø 25.6 mm, height 5.10 mm; 30 jewels; 28,800 vph; 42 hours power reserve; côtes de Genève on rotor, blued screws
Functions: hours, minutes, sweep seconds; date, day, second time zone, power reserve display
Case: stainless steel, ø 44 mm, height 11.05 mm; sapphire crystal; screwed-down exhibition case back; screw-in crown; water-resistant to 50 m
Band: reptile skin, folding clasp
Price: $6,900

Conquest
Reference number: CD777
Movement: automatic, Sellita Caliber SW 200; ø 25.6 mm, height 4.6 mm; 26 jewels; 28,800 vph; 42 hours power reserve
Functions: hours, minutes, sweep seconds; date
Case: stainless steel, ø 48 mm, height 11 mm; titanium bezel; sapphire crystal, anti-reflective on both sides; sapphire crystal exhibition case back; screw-in crown; water-resistant to 100 m
Band: rubber, double folding clasp
Price: $1,295
Variations: available in 5 dial colors: silver, yellow, orange, green, black; also available in rose or yellow gold-plated case

Warhawk
Reference number: CD.607.1
Movement: manually wound, ETA Unitas Caliber 6497, ø 36 mm, height 4.5 mm; 17 jewels; 18,000 vph, 42 hours power reserve
Functions: hours, minutes, subsidiary seconds
Case: titanium, ø 50 mm, height 18 mm; domed mineral crystal, anti-reflective on both sides; screwed-down case back; water-resistant to 100 m
Band: leather, buckle
Price: $895
Variations: four dial colors: black, brown, antique silver, burgundy; mother-of-pearl dial; carbon fiber dial; limited edition of 199 pieces with left-hand crown

Combat Command GMT
Reference number: CD251
Movement: automatic, ETA Valjoux Caliber 7754; ø 30 mm, height 7.9 mm; 25 jewels; 28,800 vph
Functions: hours, minutes, subsidiary seconds; date; chronograph; second and third time zones
Case: stainless steel, ø 40 mm, height 13 mm; unidirectionally rotating bezel with 24-hour divisions; sapphire crystal, anti-reflective on both sides; screw-down exhibition case back; screw-in crown and buttons; water-resistant to 100 m
Band: stainless steel, folding clasp
Price: $1,995

Combat Command Chronograph
Reference number: CD250
Movement: automatic, ETA Valjoux Caliber 7750; ø 30 mm, height 7.9 mm; 25 jewels; 28,800 vph; 42 hours power reserve
Functions: hours, minutes, subsidiary seconds; date, day; chronograph
Case: stainless steel, ø 40 mm, height 13 mm; unidirectionally rotating bezel with 60-minute divisions; sapphire crystal; screwed-down sapphire crystal case back; screw-in crown and buttons; water-resistant to 30 m
Band: stainless steel, folding clasp
Price: $1,350

Starburst
Reference number: CD990
Movement: automatic, Sellita Caliber SW 200; ø 25.6 mm, height 4.6 mm; 26 jewels; 28,800 vph; 42 hours power reserve
Functions: hours, minutes, sweep seconds; date
Case: stainless steel, ø 46 mm, height 13 mm; sapphire crystal, anti-reflective on both sides; sapphire crystal exhibition case back; water-resistant to 100 m
Band: reptile skin, buckle
Remarks: carbon fiber dial with magnifying lens above date display
Price: $895
Variations: available in 7 dial variations; rubber strap also available

Cloud Chaser
Reference number: CD330
Movement: automatic, Sellita Caliber SW 200; ø 25.6 mm, height 4.6 mm; 26 jewels; 28,800 vph; 42 hours power reserve
Functions: hours, minutes, sweep seconds; date
Case: stainless steel, ø 50 mm, height 12 mm; sapphire crystal, anti-reflective on both sides; sapphire crystal exhibition case back; rose gold-plated bezel; water-resistant to 100 m
Band: stainless steel, double folding clasp
Price: $995
Variations: available with black or silver-colored dial; all-black PVD case version; 18-karat rose gold plated case; limited-edition diamond-set version; leather strap

Chopard

In honor of the tenth year of his L.U.C. *manufacture*, Chopard co-president Karl-Friedrich Scheufele threw a party last fall. It was a big party that included eighty or so of his closest friends, one of these being Belgian racing legend Jacky Ickx: all were on hand to celebrate one entrepreneur taking a courageous step at a time when it may not have been so easy to come to such a decision.

In the early 1990s, Chopard was an established Swiss brand—regardless of the fact that it was owned by a German family from Pforzheim—specializing in elegant men's watches, jewelry watches, and jewelry. But Scheufele, a connoisseur of mechanical watchmaking, longed to bring the brand his father acquired in 1963 back to the place it once was, regardless of the fact that mechanical watches weren't overly popular at the time.

Enlisting the aid of renowned master watchmaker Michel Parmigiani, Scheufele began to spend a great deal of time in a small town in Switzerland's Val de Travers, Fleurier. The early '90s saw Scheufele's small team create a new automatic base movement featuring an elegant micro rotor. In 1996, after several years of trial and error, Scheufele was ready to present his "baby" to the waiting watch world.

"Creating the L.U.C. movement was an additional opportunity for Chopard to become a recognized brand in the world of *haute horlogerie*, and I think in order to be really recognized and accepted, one had to go this direction. Naturally this means conceiving, making, and producing our own movement. We believe in substance. I saw an opportunity for Chopard as a brand to go back to its roots. Louis-Ulysse Chopard made movements, his own movements, in the old days. Because of the development after the takeover of my family, Chopard was more known as a ladies' watch, more known even as a jewelry brand, and not so much known as a men's watch any longer. And in order to be really credible in that field, I thought the best thing would be to make our own movements," Scheufele explains of his decision to go down the *manufacture* path. The success of this move has only proved Scheufele right over the course of time: the latest in this decade-old family of movements is the Chrono One, a fully new flyback chronograph development, which by the day of its introduction at the above-mentioned event had already needed 16,000 hours of manpower from a team of twenty-five watchmakers in the company's Fleurier and Geneva technical departments as well as a grand total of seventy different drawings until one ex-

actly fit the bill. This movement was christened Caliber L.U.C. 10 CF in honor of the anniversary it was created to celebrate.

As if that weren't enough, the Mille Miglia car race that Chopard has sponsored since 1988 celebrated its eightieth anniversary. Chopard's gift to vintage automobile fans everywhere in its honor was the Mille Miglia GT XL 2007, a resolutely contemporary timepiece with a powerful charm and a certified chronometer movement.

Chopard

L.U.C. XP
Reference number: 161902-1001 WG
Movement: automatic, L.U.C. Caliber 96 HM; ø 27.4 mm, height 3.3 mm; 29 jewels; 28,800 vph; twin spring barrels, micro rotor; power reserve 65 hours
Functions: hours, minutes
Case: white gold, ø 39.5 mm, height 6.8 mm; sapphire crystal; transparent case back; water-resistant to 3 atm
Band: reptile skin, buckle
Price: $8,660
Variations: yellow or rose gold

L.U.C. Fleurier
Reference number: 161896-5001 RG
Movement: automatic, L.U.C. Caliber 9.96; ø 27.4 mm, height 3.3 mm; 29 jewels; 28,800 vph; twin spring barrels; micro rotor; officially certified chronometer (COSC); qualité Fleurier; power reserve 65 hours
Functions: hours, minutes, subsidiary seconds
Case: red gold, ø 39.5 mm, height 8.66 mm; sapphire crystal; water-resistant to 3 atm
Band: reptile skin, buckle
Remarks: limited edition of 250 pieces
Price: $12,520
Variations: white gold

L.U.C. Twin
Reference number: 161880-1001 WG
Movement: automatic, L.U.C. Caliber 4.96; ø 27.4 mm, height 3.3 mm; 32 jewels; 28,800 vph; twin spring barrels; micro rotor; officially certified chronometer (COSC)
Functions: hours, minutes, sweep seconds; date
Case: white gold, ø 39 mm, height 9.2 mm; sapphire crystal; transparent case back; water-resistant to 3 atm
Band: reptile skin, buckle
Price: $9,210
Variations: yellow gold ($8,765)

L.U.C. Twist
Reference number: 161888-5001 RG
Movement: automatic, L.U.C. Caliber 1.96; ø 27.4 mm, height 3.3 mm; 32 jewels; 28,800 vph; twin spring barrels; micro rotor; officially certified chronometer (COSC); Seal of Geneva
Functions: hours, minutes, subsidiary seconds; date
Case: red gold, ø 41 mm, height 10 mm; sapphire crystal; transparent case back
Band: reptile skin, buckle
Price: $12,000
Variations: white gold

Strike One
Reference number: 161912-5002 RG
Movement: automatic, L.U.C. Caliber 96 SH; ø 33 mm, height 5.7 mm; 33 jewels; 28,800 vph; hour repeater; twin spring barrels; micro rotor; officially certified chronometer (COSC); Seal of Geneva
Functions: hours, minutes; date; hour repeater; power reserve display
Case: rose gold, ø 40.5 mm, height 10.6 mm; sapphire crystal
Band: reptile skin, buckle
Remarks: limited edition of 100 pieces
Price: $37,050
Variations: white gold, also limited to 100 pieces

L.U.C. Quattro Mark
Reference number: 161903-001 GG
Movement: manually wound, L.U.C. Caliber 1.96; ø 28.6 mm, height 3.7 mm; 44 jewels; 28,800 vph; 4 spring barrels, power reserve more than 200 hours; officially certified chronometer (COSC); Seal of Geneva
Functions: hours, minutes, subsidiary seconds; date; power reserve display
Case: yellow gold, ø 38 mm, height 10 mm; sapphire crystal; transparent case back
Band: reptile skin, buckle
Price: $24,440
Variations: white gold

L.U.C. Chrono One
Reference number: 161916-1001 WG
Movement: automatic, L.U.C. Caliber 10 CF; ø 28.8 mm, height 7.6 mm; 45 jewels; 28,800 vph; column-wheel control of chronograph functions; officially certified chronometer (COSC); Seal of Geneva
Functions: hours, minutes, subsidiary seconds; date; chronograph with flyback function
Case: white gold, ø 42 mm, height 14.25 mm; sapphire crystal; transparent case back
Band: reptile skin, buckle
Remarks: launched in 2006 on the occasion of the L.U.C. Manufacture's ten-year anniversary
Price: $44,050

L.U.C. Lunar One
Reference number: 161894-9001 Platinum
Movement: automatic, L.U.C. Caliber 96 QP; ø 33 mm, height 6 mm; 35 jewels; 28,800 vph; twin spring barrels; micro rotor; officially certified chronometer; Seal of Geneva
Functions: hours, minutes, subsidiary seconds; perpetual calendar with large date, weekday, month, orbital moon phase display, leap year; 24-hour display
Case: rose gold, ø 40.5 mm, height 11.4 mm; sapphire crystal; transparent case back
Band: reptile skin, buckle
Remarks: limited edition of 250 pieces
Price: $54,930

Chopard

L.U.C. Regulator
Reference number: 168449-3001
Movement: manually wound, L.U.C. Caliber 4RT; ø 30.4 mm, height 4.9 mm; 39 jewels; 28,800 vph; 4 spring barrels, power reserve more than 200 hours; officially certified chronometer (COSC)
Functions: hours (off-center), minutes, subsidiary seconds; date; 24-hour display (second time zone); power reserve display
Case: stainless steel, ø 38.5 mm, height 9.75 mm; sapphire crystal; transparent case back
Band: reptile skin, buckle
Remarks: limited edition of 250 pieces
Price: $30,590

L.U.C. Tech Twist
Reference number: 168490-3002
Movement: automatic, L.U.C. Caliber 1.96 TB; ø 27.4 mm, height 3.3 mm; 32 jewels; 28,800 vph; twin spring barrels, micro rotor; bridges with côtes de Genève; officially certified chronometer (COSC); Seal of Geneva
Functions: hours, minutes, subsidiary seconds; date
Case: stainless steel, ø 41 mm, height 10 mm; sapphire crystal; transparent case back
Band: reptile skin, buckle
Remarks: limited edition of 250 pieces
Price: $10,570

L.U.C. Tourbillon Steel Wings
Reference number: 161906-1001 WG
Movement: manually wound, L.U.C. Caliber 4T; ø 29.1 mm, height 6.5 mm; 33 jewels; 28,800 vph; one-minute tourbillon; Variner balance with weights, 4 spring barrels, power reserve more than 216 hours; officially certified chronometer (C.O.S.C.)
Functions: hours, minutes, subsidiary seconds (on tourbillon cage); power reserve display
Case: white gold, ø 40.5 mm, height 11 mm; sapphire crystal; transparent case back
Band: reptile skin, folding clasp
Remarks: limited edition of 100 pieces
Price: $104,930

L.U.C. Tourbillon Titanium SL
Reference number: 168502-3001
Movement: manually wound, L.U.C. Caliber 4T; ø 29.1 mm, height 6.5 mm; 33 jewels; 28,800 vph; one-minute tourbillon; Variner balance with weights, 4 spring barrels, power reserve more than 216 hours; officially certified C.O.S.C. chronometer
Functions: hours, minutes, subsidiary seconds (on tourbillon cage); power reserve display
Case: titanium, ø 40.5 mm, height 11 mm; sapphire crystal; transparent case back
Band: reptile skin, folding clasp
Remarks: limited edition of 100 pieces
Price: $112,900

Chronograph Mille Miglia
Reference number: 158992-3002
Movement: automatic, ETA Caliber 2894-2; ø 28.6 mm, height 6.1 mm; 37 jewels; 28,800 vph; officially certified chronometer (COSC)
Functions: hours, minutes, subsidiary seconds; chronograph; date
Case: stainless steel, ø 42.5 mm, height 13.9 mm; bezel engraved with tachymeter scale; sapphire crystal; water-resistant to 5 atm
Band: rubber, buckle
Price: $5,995
Variations: stainless steel bracelet

Mille Miglia GT XL Chrono 2007
Reference number: 168459-3001
Movement: automatic, ETA Caliber A07.111; ø 36.6 mm, height 7.9 mm; 24 jewels; 28,800 vph; officially certified chronometer (COSC)
Functions: hours, minutes, subsidiary seconds; date; chronograph
Case: stainless steel, ø 44 mm; bezel engraved with tachymeter scale; sapphire crystal; water-resistant to 10 atm
Band: leather, buckle
Price: $5,980
Variations: rubber strap

Mille Miglia Gran Turismo XL
Reference number: 161902-5002 RG
Movement: automatic, ETA Caliber A07.111; ø 36.6 mm, height 7.9 mm; 24 jewels; 28,800 vph; officially certified chronometer (COSC)
Functions: hours, minutes, sweep seconds; date
Case: stainless steel, ø 44 mm; bezel screw-in crown; sapphire crystal; water-resistant to 10 atm
Band: rubber with Dunlop tire tread, folding clasp
Price: $6,240
Variations: leather strap

L.U.C. Pro One GMT
Reference number: 168912-3002
Movement: automatic, L.U.C. Caliber 4.96 H24 Pro One; ø 27.4 mm, height 3.3 mm; 31 jewels; 28,800 vph; twin spring barrels; black micro rotor; officially certified chronometer (COSC)
Functions: hours, minutes, sweep seconds; date; 24-hour display (second time zone)
Case: stainless steel, ø 42 mm, height 13.1 mm; rotating bezel with 24-hour divisions; screw-in crown; sapphire crystal; transparent case back; water-resistant to 30 atm
Band: reptile skin, folding clasp
Price: $7,365

Chopard

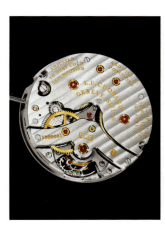

L.U.C. 1.02
Mechanical with manual winding, one-minute tourbillon; power reserve appx. 200 hours
Functions: hours, minutes, subsidiary seconds; power reserve display
Diameter: 29.1 mm
Height: 6.1 mm
Jewels: 33
Balance: Variner with adjustable eccentric weights
Frequency: 28,800 vph
Individual components: 224
Remarks: two stacked, serially operating spring barrels; base plate with perlage; beveled bridges with côtes de Genève, polished steel parts and screw heads; Seal of Geneva; official chronometer with C.O.S.C. certificate

L.U.C. 1.98
Mechanical with manual winding, power reserve appx. 200 hours
Functions: hours, minutes, subsidiary seconds; date; power reserve display
Diameter: 28.6 mm, **Height:** 3.7 mm
Jewels: 39
Balance: glucydur
Frequency: 28,800 vph
Balance spring: Breguet hairspring
Index system: swan-neck fine adjustment
Remarks: two stacked, serially operating spring barrels, micro rotor in 22-karat gold; base plate with perlage; beveled bridges with côtes de Genève, polished steel parts and screw heads; Seal of Geneva; official chronometer with C.O.S.C. certificate

L.U.C. 1.96
Mechanical with automatic winding, power reserve 65 hours
Functions: hours, minutes, subsidiary seconds; date
Diameter: 27.4 mm, **Height:** 3.3 mm
Jewels: 32
Balance: glucydur
Frequency: 28,800 vph
Balance spring: Breguet hairspring
Index system: swan-neck fine adjustment
Remarks: two stacked, serially operating spring barrels, micro rotor in 22-karat gold; base plate with perlage; beveled bridges with côtes de Genève, polished steel parts and screw heads; Seal of Geneva; official chronometer with C.O.S.C. certificate

L.U.C. 4.96
Mechanical with automatic winding, power reserve 65 hours
Functions: hours, minutes, sweep seconds; date
Diameter: 27.4 mm
Height: 3.3 mm
Jewels: 34
Balance: glucydur
Frequency: 28,800 vph
Balance spring: flat hairspring, Nivarox I
Index system: micrometer screw
Remarks: two stacked, serially operating spring barrels, micro rotor in 18-karat gold; base plate with perlage; beveled bridges with côtes de Genève, polished steel parts and screw heads; official chronometer with C.O.S.C. certificate

L.U.C. 10 CF
Mechanical with automatic winding, power reserve 65 hours; column-wheel control of chronograph functions; vertical clutch; stop-seconds with automatic reset
Functions: hours, minutes, subsidiary seconds; date; chronograph with flyback function
Diameter: 28.8 mm
Height: 7.6 mm
Jewels: 45
Balance: Variner with four weighted screws
Frequency: 28,800 vph
Balance spring: flat hairspring
Remarks: base plate with perlage; beveled bridges with côtes de Genève, polished steel parts and screw heads; official chronometer with C.O.S.C. certificate

L.U.C. 3.97
Mechanical with automatic winding, power reserve 65 hours
Functions: hours, minutes, subsidiary seconds; date
Dimensions: 28.15 x 27.6 mm
Height: 3.3 mm
Jewels: 29
Balance: glucydur
Frequency: 28,800 vph
Balance spring: flat hairspring, Nivarox I
Index system: micrometer screw
Remarks: two stacked, serially operating spring barrels, micro rotor in 18-karat gold; base plate with perlage; beveled bridges with côtes de Genève, polished steel parts and screw heads; official chronometer with C.O.S.C. certificate

L.U.C. 1.97
Mechanical with automatic winding, power reserve 65 hours
Functions: hours, minutes, subsidiary seconds; date
Dimensions: 28.15 x 27.6 mm
Height: 3.3 mm
Jewels: 29
Balance: glucydur
Frequency: 28,800 vph
Balance spring: flat hairspring, Nivarox I
Index system: micrometer screw
Remarks: two stacked, serially operating spring barrels, micro rotor in platinum; base plate with perlage; beveled bridges with côtes de Genève, polished steel parts and screw heads; official chronometer with C.O.S.C. certificate

L.U.C. QP96
Mechanical with automatic winding, power reserve 65 hours
Functions: hours, minutes, subsidiary seconds; perpetual calendar with large date, weekday, month, orbital moon phase display, leap year, 24-hour display
Diameter: 33 mm, **Height:** 6 mm, **Jewels:** 32
Balance: glucydur, **Frequency:** 28,800 vph
Balance spring: flat hairspring, Nivarox I
Index system: micrometer screw
Remarks: two stacked, serially operating spring barrels, 22-karat gold micro rotor; base plate with perlage; beveled bridges with côtes de Genève, polished steel parts and screw heads; official chronometer with C.O.S.C. certificate; Seal of Geneva

Chronoswiss

Gerd-Rüdiger Lang fulfilled a lifelong dream for himself when he finally built a generous factory for his brand on the outskirts of Munich. After this company's modest beginnings in the basement of Lang's family home there, he moved to rented premises on Elly-Staegmeyr-Strasse. Thanks to a stupendous pe- riod of growth that has lasted twenty years, the "man with the tick" finally reached his most important finish line.

Building this watch factory is something like signing the "generational contract" for his family: Lang and his daughter Natalie, the two managing directors, have their corner offices on the second floor across from each other. Both—father and daughter—have direct contact to the company's "gear train," the watchmaker workshops. Here, ideas and plans conceived by the lead duo are translated into watches. The production department has twelve workspaces where watchmakers assemble components delivered from Switzerland—completely in the tradition of the company—to make a ticking whole. The watchmaker workshops—both production and service—are not only outfitted with large windows on the outside walls to let light in, the walls separating the workshops are also outfitted with large windows to let visitors observe the watchmakers at work without disturbing them.

Obligated to their name, Chronoswiss's watches must fulfill the prerequisites of the predicate "Swiss made"—and more. Despite this, the fully outfitted and functional watch factory on German soil is an important prerequisite for underscoring the term "made in Germany"—which has always subconsciously accompanied all the products of this company. What might sound contrary at first is actually the end of a large circle that began in 1958 in Braunschweig and led through Switzerland to Frankfurt and then Munich. Not only does the person of Gerd-Rüdiger Lang join respect for German precision standards with the joy of the Swiss art of watchmaking, but so do his watches. Despite all his love of Swiss watchmaking, Lang never really seriously debated moving his company to Switzerland. And despite all he feels for Munich—his chosen home since 1974—the Swiss quality standard "Swiss made" has always been the only goal worth striving for in his watches.

Lang's dream of building his own factory has now finally come true. And with it, Swiss watches made in Germany.

Chronoswiss

Imperia
Reference number: CH 2071 W rg
Movement: automatic, ETA Caliber 2000-1; ø 19.4 mm, height 3.6 mm; 20 jewels; 28,800 vph
Functions: hours, minutes, sweep seconds; date
Case: white gold, 30 x 48 mm, height 9 mm; anti-reflective sapphire crystal; transparent case back
Band: reptile skin, buckle
Price: upon request
Variations: rose-colored dial; stainless steel; red gold; various strap variations; folding clasp

Imperator
Reference number: CH 2871 R si
Movement: automatic, ETA Caliber 2892-A2; ø 25.6 mm, height 3.6 mm; 21 jewels; 28,800 vph
Functions: hours, minutes, sweep seconds; date
Case: red gold, 36.7 x 56 mm, height 10 mm; anti-reflective sapphire crystal; transparent case back
Band: reptile skin, buckle
Price: upon request
Variations: silver dial; stainless steel; white gold; various strap variations; folding clasp

Répétition à Quarts Diamonds
Reference number: CH 1643 D bk
Movement: automatic, Chronoswiss Caliber C.126 (base Enicar 165 with repeater module E 94 by Dubois Dépraz); ø 28 mm, height 8.35 mm; 38 jewels; 21,600 vph
Functions: hours, minutes, subsidiary seconds; quarter hour repeater
Case: stainless steel, ø 40 mm, height 14 mm; diamond-set bezel; anti-reflective sapphire crystal; transparent case back
Band: reptile skin, buckle
Price: upon request
Variations: platinum; yellow, red or white gold; various dial and strap variations; folding clasp

Répétition à Quarts
Reference number: CH 1641 R
Movement: automatic, Chronoswiss Caliber C.126 (base Enicar 165 with repeater module E 94 by Dubois Dépraz); ø 28 mm, height 8.35 mm; 38 jewels; 21,600 vph
Functions: hours, minutes, subsidiary seconds; quarter hour repeater
Case: red gold, ø 40 mm, height 14 mm; anti-reflective sapphire crystal; transparent case back
Band: reptile skin, buckle
Price: $29,500
Variations: yellow or white gold; stainless steel; platinum (limited edition); various dial and strap variations; folding clasp

Chronograph Rattrapante
Reference number: CH 7323
Movement: automatic, Chronoswiss Caliber C.732 (base ETA Valjoux 7750); ø 30 mm, height 8.3 mm; 28 jewels; 28,800 vph; patented rattrapante mechanism; movement finished with côtes de Genève; individually numbered
Functions: hours, minutes, off-center subsidiary seconds; split-seconds chronograph
Case: stainless steel, ø 38 mm, height 15.25 mm; anti-reflective sapphire crystal; transparent case back
Band: reptile skin, buckle
Price: $10,500
Variations: gold/stainless steel (red or yellow); yellow or red gold; platinum (limited edition); various dial and strap variations

Chronoscope
Reference number: CH 1523 bw
Movement: automatic, Chronoswiss Caliber C.125 (base Enicar 165); ø 26.8 mm, height 6.8 mm; 30 jewels; 21,600 vph; chronograph with column-wheel control of the functions integrated into base movement; one button on crown
Functions: off-center hours, minutes, subsidiary seconds; chronograph
Case: stainless steel, ø 38 mm, height 12 mm; sapphire crystal; transparent case back; crown with integrated chronograph button
Band: reptile skin, buckle
Price: $8,150
Variations: gold/stainless steel (red or yellow); yellow, white, or red gold; platinum (limited edition); various dial and strap variations

Delphis
Reference number: CH 1421 R
Movement: automatic, Chronoswiss Caliber C.124 (base Enicar 165); ø 28.6 mm, height 6.9 mm; 32 jewels; 21,600 vph
Functions: hours (digital, jump), minutes (retrograde), subsidiary seconds (analogue)
Case: red gold, ø 38 mm, height 11 mm; anti-reflective sapphire crystal; transparent case back
Band: reptile skin, buckle
Price: $8,150
Variations: stainless steel; gold/stainless steel (red or yellow); yellow, white, or red gold; platinum (limited edition), diverse dial variations, folding clasp

Kairos Lady
Reference number: CH 2023 K
Movement: automatic, ETA Caliber 2000-1; ø 19.4 mm, height 3.6 mm; 20 jewels; 28,800 vph
Functions: hours, minutes, sweep seconds; date
Case: stainless steel, ø 30 mm, height 8 mm; anti-reflective sapphire crystal; transparent case back
Band: reptile skin, buckle
Price: $13,500
Variations: with diamonds; stainless steel/red gold with diamonds; red gold; black dial; various strap variations; folding clasp

Chronoswiss

Klassik Chronograph
Reference number: CH 7403
Movement: automatic, Chronoswiss Caliber C.741 (base ETA Valjoux 7750); ø 30 mm, height 5.4 mm; 25 jewels; 28,800 vph
Functions: hours, minutes, subsidiary seconds; chronograph; date
Case: stainless steel, ø 37 mm, height 14.2 mm; anti-reflective sapphire crystal; transparent case back
Band: reptile skin, buckle
Price: $3,400
Variations: with tachymeter or pulsometer scale; stainless steel/red gold, red gold; various dial variations; folding clasp

Lunar Complete Calendar
Reference number: CH 9323
Movement: automatic, Chronoswiss Caliber C.931 (base ETA 2892-A2 with calendar module by Dubois Dépraz); ø 25.6 mm, height 5.75 mm; 21 jewels; 28,800 vph
Functions: hours, minutes, sweep seconds; date, weekday, month, moon phase display
Case: red gold, ø 38 mm, height 10.65 mm; anti-reflective sapphire crystal; transparent case back
Band: reptile skin, buckle
Price: $12,700
Variations: stainless steel; gold/stainless steel (yellow or red); yellow or white gold; platinum (limited edition); with matte black dial, various strap variations; folding clasp

Lunar Chronograph
Reference number: CH 7521 R
Movement: automatic, Chronoswiss Caliber C.755 (base ETA Valjoux 7750); ø 30 mm, height 7.9 mm; 25 jewels; 28,800 vph
Functions: hours, minutes, subsidiary seconds; chronograph; date; moon phase display
Case: red gold, ø 38 mm, height 15 mm; anti-reflective sapphire crystal; transparent case back
Band: reptile skin, buckle
Price: $12,950
Variations: stainless steel; gold/stainless steel (yellow or red); yellow or white gold; platinum (limited edition)

Perpetual Calendar
Reference number: CH 1723
Movement: automatic, Chronoswiss Caliber C.127 (base ETA 2892-A2 with calendar module 5800 C by Dubois Dépraz); ø 26.8 mm, height 8.79 mm; 30 jewels; 21,600 vph
Functions: hours, minutes, sweep seconds; perpetual calendar with date, weekday, month, moon phase display, leap year display
Case: stainless steel, ø 40 mm, height 13 mm; anti-reflective sapphire crystal; transparent case back
Band: reptile skin, buckle
Price: $24,500
Variations: yellow, white, or red gold; platinum (limited edition), various strap variations; folding clasp

Opus
Reference number: CH 7521 SR
Movement: automatic, Chronoswiss Caliber C.741 S (base ETA Valjoux 7750); ø 30 mm, height 7.9 mm; 25 jewels; 28,800 vph; movement completely skeletonized and decorated
Functions: hours, minutes, subsidiary seconds; chronograph
Case: red gold, ø 38 mm, height 15 mm; anti-reflective sapphire crystal; transparent case back
Band: reptile skin, buckle
Price: $16,950
Variations: stainless steel; gold/stainless steel (yellow or red); yellow or white gold; platinum (limited edition); various dial and strap variations; folding clasp

Orea Automatique
Reference number: CH 1263
Movement: automatic, Chronoswiss Caliber C.121 (base Enicar 165); ø 26.8 mm, height 5.3 mm; 30 jewels; 21,600 vph
Functions: hours, minutes, subsidiary seconds
Case: stainless steel, ø 37 mm, height 10 mm; anti-reflective sapphire crystal; transparent case back
Band: reptile skin, buckle
Remarks: genuine enameled dial
Price: $4,200
Variations: stainless steel; gold/stainless steel (yellow or red); yellow, white, or red gold; diverse strap variations, folding clasp; also as Orea Lady and Orea Manual Wind

Grand Régulateur Chronomètre
Reference number: CH 6721 R
Movement: automatic, Chronoswiss Caliber C.673 (base ETA Unitas 6497); ø 36.6 mm, height 4.7 mm; 17 jewels; 21,600 vph; officially certified chronometer (COSC)
Functions: off-center hours, minutes, subsidiary seconds
Case: red gold, ø 44 mm, height 13.45 mm; anti-reflective sapphire crystal; transparent case back
Band: reptile skin, buckle
Price: $11,950
Variations: stainless steel

Régulateur
Reference number: CH 1221 R
Movement: automatic, Chronoswiss Caliber C.122 (base Enicar 165); ø 26.8 mm, height 5.3 mm; 30 jewels; 21,600 vph
Functions: off-center hours, minutes, subsidiary seconds
Case: yellow gold, ø 38 mm, height 10.5 mm; anti-reflective sapphire crystal; transparent case back
Band: reptile skin, buckle
Price: $10,200
Variations: stainless steel; red gold/stainless steel; white gold; various strap and dial variations

Chronoswiss

Timemaster Chronograph Date
Reference number: CH 7533 lu
Movement: automatic, Chronoswiss Caliber C.751 (base ETA Valjoux 7750); ø 30 mm, height 7.9 mm; 25 jewels; 28,000 vph
Functions: hours, minutes, subsidiary seconds; chronograph; date
Case: stainless steel, ø 44 mm, height 16 mm; bidirectionally rotating bezel with reference marker; anti-reflective sapphire crystal; transparent case back; screw-in crown; water-resistant to 10 atm
Band: stainless steel, folding clasp
Price: $7,950
Variations: with black dial; with water-resistant strap

Timemaster Automatic
Reference number: CH 2833 mp
Movement: automatic, Chronoswiss Caliber ETA 2892-A2; ø 25.6 mm, height 3.6 mm; 21 jewels; 28,800 vph
Functions: hours, minutes, sweep seconds; date
Case: stainless steel, ø 40 mm, height 12 mm; bidirectionally rotating bezel with reference marker; sapphire crystal; transparent case back; screw-in crown; water-resistant to 10 atm
Band: leather, buckle
Price: upon request
Variations: with colorful dials and matching straps

Timemaster Flyback
Reference number: CH 7633 OR
Movement: automatic, Chronoswiss Caliber C.763 (base ETA Valjoux 7750); ø 30 mm, height 7.9 mm; 29 jewels; 28,800 vph
Functions: hours, minutes, subsidiary seconds; chronograph with flyback function
Case: stainless steel, ø 40 mm, height 16 mm; bidirectionally rotating bezel with reference marker; sapphire crystal; transparent case back; screw-in crown (left); water-resistant to 10 atm
Band: stainless steel, folding clasp
Remarks: available in versions for left- and right-handers; dial available in black or completely luminescent
Price: $8,150

Tora Chronograph
Reference number: CH 7423
Movement: automatic, Chronoswiss Caliber C.743 (base ETA Valjoux 7750); ø 30 mm, height 8.1 mm; 25 jewels; 28,800 vph
Functions: hours, minutes, subsidiary seconds, chronograph; date; 24-hour display (second time zone)
Case: stainless steel, ø 38 mm, height 15.1 mm; anti-reflective sapphire crystal; transparent case back
Band: reptile skin, buckle
Price: $7,600
Variations: red gold/stainless steel; yellow, white, or red gold; platinum (limited edition)

Tora
Reference number: CH 1321
Movement: automatic, Chronoswiss Caliber C.123 (base Enicar 165); ø 26.8 mm, height 5.65 mm; 30 jewels; 21,600 vph
Functions: hours (two sets of hour displays for two time zones, off-center, independently settable), minutes, sweep seconds
Case: yellow gold, ø 38 mm, height 10.8 mm; anti-reflective sapphire crystal; transparent case back
Band: reptile skin, buckle
Price: $11,700
Variations: yellow gold/stainless steel; stainless steel; black dial; various strap variations; folding clasp

Régulateur à Tourbillon Squelette
Reference number: CH 3121 S R
Movement: manually wound, Chronoswiss Caliber C.361 (base STT); ø 30 mm, height 5.4 mm; 23 jewels; 28,800 vph, power reserve appx. 72 hours; one-minute flying tourbillon in ball bearing; twin spring barrels; movement completely skeletonized and engraved
Functions: off-center hours, minutes
Case: red gold, ø 38 mm, height 10.6 mm; anti-reflective sapphire crystal; transparent case back
Band: reptile skin, buckle
Price: $67,500
Variations: yellow or white gold; platinum (limited edition of 50 pieces); various strap variations; folding clasp

Régulateur à Tourbillon
Reference number: CH 3123
Movement: manually wound, Chronoswiss Caliber C.361 (base STT); ø 30 mm, height 5.4 mm; 23 jewels; 28,800 vph, power reserve appx. 72 hours; one-minute flying tourbillon in ball bearing; twin spring barrels
Functions: off-center hours, minutes
Case: stainless steel, ø 38 mm, height 10.6 mm; anti-reflective sapphire crystal; transparent case back
Band: reptile skin, buckle
Price: upon request
Variations: yellow, white or red gold; platinum (limited edition); various strap variations; folding clasp

Pathos
Reference number: CH 7323 SD
Movement: automatic, Chronoswiss Caliber C.732 (base ETA Valjoux 7750); ø 30 mm, height 8.3 mm; 28 jewels; 28,800 vph; movement completely skeletonized and decorated
Functions: hours, minutes, subsidiary seconds; split-seconds chronograph
Case: stainless steel, ø 38 mm, height 15.25 mm; diamond-set bezel; anti-reflective sapphire crystal; transparent case back
Band: reptile skin, buckle
Price: upon request
Variations: stainless steel without diamonds ($14,500); gold/stainless steel (yellow or red); yellow gold; platinum (limited edition); various dial and strap variations, folding clasp

Chronoswiss

Caliber C.126 (dial side)
Base caliber: C.122 (Enicar 165) with strike train module E 94 by Dubois Dépraz
Mechanical with automatic winding, power reserve 35 hours; ball-bearing rotor in platinum, skeletonized and gold-plated
Functions: hours, minutes, subsidiary seconds; quarter-hour repeater
Diameter: 28 mm, **Height:** 8.35 mm, **Jewels:** 38
Balance: glucydur, three-legged
Frequency: 21,600 vph
Shock protection: Incabloc
Balance spring: Nivarox I flat hairspring, with fine adjustment via eccentric screw
Remarks: all-or-nothing strike train; two gongs; base plate and beveled bridges with perlage; côtes de Genève; rotor with côtes de Genève

Caliber C.125 (dial side)
Base caliber: C.122 (Enicar 165)
Mechanical with automatic winding, power reserve 35 hours; ball-bearing rotor in platinum, skeletonized and gold-plated
Functions: hours (off-center), minutes, subsidiary seconds; chronograph
Diameter: 26.8 mm, **Height:** 7.85 mm, **Jewels:** 30
Balance: glucydur, three-legged
Frequency: 21,600 vph
Shock protection: Incabloc
Balance spring: Nivarox I flat hairspring, with fine adjustment via eccentric screw
Remarks: integrated column-wheel chronograph; crown button for start-stop-reset; ball-bearing chronograph center wheel; base plate and beveled bridges with perlage; côtes de Genève

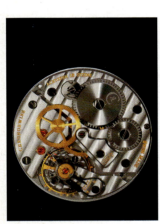

Caliber C.111
Base caliber: Marvin 700
Mechanical with manual winding, power reserve 46 hours
Functions: hours, minutes, subsidiary seconds
Diameter: 29.4 mm (13′′′)
Height: 3.3 mm
Jewels: 17
Balance: glucydur, three-legged
Frequency: 21,600 vph
Shock protection: Incabloc
Balance spring: Nivarox I flat hairspring
Remarks: bridges with perlage; polished pallet fork, escape wheel, and screws

Caliber C.122
Base caliber: Enicar 165
Mechanical with automatic winding, power reserve 40 hours; ball-bearing rotor, skeletonized and gold-plated
Functions: hours, minutes, subsidiary seconds
Diameter: 26.8 mm (11 3/4′′′)
Height: 5.3 mm
Jewels: 30
Balance: glucydur, three-legged
Frequency: 21,600 vph
Shock protection: Incabloc
Balance spring: Nivarox I flat hairspring
Remarks: base plate with perlage; beveled bridges with perlage and côtes de Genève; rotor with côtes de Genève; polished pallet fork, escape wheel, and screws

Caliber C.672
Base caliber: ETA Unitas 6497-1
Mechanical with manual winding, power reserve appx. 50 hours; stop-seconds (hacking balance stop)
Functions: hours, minutes, sweep seconds
Diameter: 36.6 mm (16 1/2′′′)
Height: 5.4 mm; **Jewels:** 18
Balance: glucydur, three-legged
Frequency: 18,000 vph
Shock protection: Incabloc
Balance spring: Nivarox I flat hairspring, swan-neck fine adjustment
Remarks: beveled bridges with côtes de Genève; polished pallet fork, escape wheel, and screws; escape bridge with perlage

Caliber C.361
Base caliber: STT 6361
Mechanical with manual winding, power reserve 72 hours; twin spring barrels; one-minute tourbillon, ruby ball bearing
Functions: hours (off-center), minutes
Diameter: 30 mm (13 3/4′′′)
Height: 5.4 mm
Jewels: 23, three of which are embedded in gold chatons
Balance: glucydur, with weighted screws
Frequency: 28,800 vph
Shock protection: Incabloc
Balance spring: Nivarox I flat hairspring
Remarks: bridges with côtes de Genève

Frédérique Constant

Peter and Aletta Stas have been doing just what their tagline says they should since the end of the 1980s: "live your passion."

This Dutch couple started out as a small watch manufacturer with big ideas. Seeing those ideas grow first into an iconic timepiece in the Heart Beat model and then into a factory housing enough technology to call the brand a *manufacture*, this company is now entering a really interesting stage of its development.

Frédérique Constant currently manufactures something like 55,000 timepieces per year. Not all of these come from the company's leading line, Heart Beat, nor do a high percentage contain the brand's *manufacture* movement developed in 2004 in conjunction with specialists from some of Europe's leading watchmaker schools.

Little by little, however, this brand is finding its footing, developing interesting new timepieces positioned at the top of the pyramid. The success of the Heart Beat *manufacture* caliber spurred the Stases on to further research. In 2007, after two years of R&D, the company introduced a model containing new materials—a trend that is currently rampaging through the industry's high-end manufacturers. "This will help us create even better, more precise, and more reliable mechanical watches," Peter Stas explains.

The first Frédérique Constant timepiece featuring high-tech materials is a limited edition of wristwatches containing a silicon escape wheel: the HBM Silicium Moon Phase Date. *Silicium* is the Latin word for the element silicon, which is the second most prevalent element found on earth, making up 28 percent of our planet's crust (oxygen is first). Used for many years in the production of integrated circuits, it has only been in recent years that suppliers have thought to apply the process to make perfect friction-free watch components. The watch industry currently prefers to call this "high-tech" material by its Latin name, though it remains silicon. The crafting of a silicium escape wheel requires the use of a new technology called deep reactive ion etching (DRIE). Using a computer-generated mask, multiple images of the component are produced and projected onto a silicium wafer 100 millimeters in diameter and 0.5 millimeters high. The wafer can hold about 250 of the miniscule components, which are released from it after development by a process called isotropic etching. The components that emerge are perfect and need no finishing other than a little cleaning on the surface. In theory, they are all identical and need no polishing.

Why silicium? The main benefit is that components made of this element do not need lubrication, which has always been the bane of watchmakers in every age. In addition, silicium components are very light and produce next to no friction.

This timepiece is not the only member of the Heart Beat family presently making waves. The Ladies Double Heart Beat introduced in 2006 has been so successful for the Genevan brand that a number of new colors were added in 2007 for the line featuring a double heart-shaped cutaway over the balance and fifty-two diamonds on the bezel.

Frédérique Constant

Healey Chronograph
Reference number: FC-392HBS6B6
Movement: automatic, ETA Valjoux Caliber 7750; ø 30 mm, height 7.9 mm; 25 jewels; 28,800 vph
Functions: hours, minutes, subsidiary seconds; date; chronograph
Case: stainless steel, ø 43 mm, height 14.5 mm; sapphire crystal; transparent case back
Band: leather, buckle
Price: $2,595

Healey Automatic
Reference number: FC-303HBS6B6
Movement: automatic, ETA Caliber 2824-2; ø 25.6 mm, height 4.6 mm; 25 jewels; 28,800 vph
Functions: hours, minutes, sweep seconds; date
Case: stainless steel, ø 43 mm, height 10.5 mm; sapphire crystal
Band: leather, buckle
Price: $1,395

Classic Chronograph
Reference number: FC-393M6B6
Movement: automatic, ETA Valjoux Caliber 7750; ø 30 mm, height 7.9 mm; 25 jewels; 28,800 vph
Functions: hours, minutes; date; chronograph
Case: stainless steel, ø 43 mm, height 14.2 mm; sapphire crystal; transparent case back
Band: leather, buckle
Price: $2,195

Heart Beat Manufacture Moon Phase with Silicium
Reference number: FC-935SABS4H9
Movement: automatic, Frédérique Constant Caliber FC 935; ø 30.5 mm, height 5.25 mm; 27 jewels; 28,800 vph; manufacture caliber with "upside down" positioning of the balance and escapement on the dial side
Functions: hours, minutes; date; moon phase
Case: red gold, ø 42 mm, height 12 mm; sapphire crystal; transparent case back
Band: reptile skin, buckle
Remarks: limited edition of 188 pieces
Price: $14,850

Heart Beat Manufacture Moon Phase Date Côtes de Genève
Reference number: FC-915CDG4H9
Movement: manually wound, Frédérique Constant Caliber FC 915; ø 30.5 mm, height 3.5 mm; 17 jewels; 28,800 vph; manufacture caliber with "upside down" positioning of the balance and escapement on the dial side
Functions: hours, minutes; date; moon phase
Case: red gold, ø 41 mm, height 10 mm; sapphire crystal; transparent case back
Band: reptile skin, buckle
Price: $11,595

Heart Beat Manufacture Moon Phase Date
Reference number: FC-935MC4H6
Movement: manually wound, Frédérique Constant Caliber FC 935; ø 30.5 mm, height 5.25 mm; 27 jewels; 28,800 vph; manufacture caliber with "upside down" positioning of the balance and escapement on the dial side
Functions: hours, minutes; date; moon phase
Case: stainless steel, ø 42 mm, height 12.1 mm; sapphire crystal; transparent case back
Band: reptile skin, buckle
Price: $5,995

Ladies Double Heart Beat
Reference number: FC-310DHB2PD4
Movement: automatic, Frédérique Constant Caliber FC 310H2G-2 (base ETA 2892); ø 25.6 mm, height 3.6 mm; 21 jewels; 28,800 vph; modified with partial skeletonization
Functions: hours, minutes, sweep seconds
Case: rose gold-plated stainless steel ø 34 mm, height 10 mm; bezel set with 56 diamonds; sapphire crystal; transparent case back
Band: reptile skin, buckle
Remarks: mother-of-pearl dial with diamond markers
Price: $3,750
Variations: stainless steel; without diamonds

Persuasion Big Date Dual Time Large Carrée
Reference number: FC-325BS4C24
Movement: automatic, Frédérique Constant Caliber FC 325 (base ETA 2892); ø 25.6 mm, height 3.6 mm; 21 jewels; 28,800 vph
Functions: hours, minutes, sweep seconds; large date; second time zone
Case: stainless steel with PVD gold plating, 30.6 x 39.1 mm, height 10.5 mm; sapphire crystal; transparent case back
Band: leather, buckle
Price: $2,550
Variations: stainless steel

Corum

Corum seems like a bird of paradise among established Swiss watch brands. Right from the beginning, this brand distinguished itself from other marques with original watch design. This has not changed since the company's first appearance more than fifty years ago. In 1955, as the company was established in La Chaux-de-Fonds, located in the Swiss Jura region, the gifted watchmaker Gaston Ries and his nephew René Bannwart transformed this small, private-label company into a watch *manufacture* featuring its own brand: Corum.

A scant one year later in 1956, the young watch *manufacture* presented its first Corum watches to the public. All of the models were excitingly original, garnering immediate and intense attention, and the foundation was laid for the company's reputation as a trendsetter among watch brands. Delicate watch movements enclosed in artfully sliced and hollowed gold coins or literally encased between completely transparent sapphire crystal plates were the specialty of creative minds. Rising watchmakers and designers with a will to excel could not avoid at least one stint with Corum. Creations of iconic importance such as the watches of the Admiral's Cup line were achieved, a series that has long represented the public image of Corum with nautical flags in place of numerals.

The new Admiral's Cup Tides 48 is the successor model to the tide watch Marées, first introduced in 1992. The three individual mechanisms that make up the tide movement are the result of a development period that took place from about 1988 to 1991 in cooperation with the Geneva Observatory and the French navy's hydrographic and oceanographic service (SHOM) in Brest where a difference in water level of more than eight meters between ebb and tide can be observed—and where a tide watch is a particularly practical accessory.

The new Admiral's Cup Tides 48 runs on an ETA automatic movement outfitted with tide module CO 277, which was developed fifteen years ago exclusively for Corum by Dubois Dépraz, Switzerland's largest supplier of specialty modules for movements.

Even though the case became clearly bigger, the weight of the watch has remained almost the same since the company chose a light, though very robust and corrosion-proof material in titanium for the case and clasp. Combined with vulcanized rubber for the strap and as a coating for the bezel and crown protection, this timepiece is as comfortable as t is attractive.
In January 2000, forty-five years after the brand's founding, Severin Wunderman took over Corum, and since that day the brand has experienced a fresh period of growth. The experienced and renowned watch business professional (Wunderman developed and produced Gucci's phenomenally successful watches) reflected on the roots of the family business and brought his son Michael on board, who now assumes more and more of the responsibility at Corum.
Since 2004, Michael Wunderman has been the company's managing director. While introducing his own individual style, he continues, in the best Corum tradition, to emphasize the special features and unusual slant for which the company has long stood.

Admiral's Cup Competition 48
Reference number: 947.931.04 V700 AN 12
Movement: automatic, Corum Caliber CO 947 (base modified ETA Valjoux 7750); ø 30 mm, height 7.9 mm; 25 jewels; 28,800 vph; officially certified chronometer (COSC)
Functions: hours, minutes, subsidiary seconds; date and day
Case: titanium, ø 48 mm, height 18 mm; sapphire crystal; screw-in crown; water-resistant to 30 atm
Band: titanium, double folding clasp
Price: $6,200
Variations: blue dial; red gold with leather strap

Admiral's Cup Challenge 44
Reference number: 753.691.20 V701 AA 92
Movement: automatic, Corum Caliber CO 753 COSC (base modified ETA Valjoux 7750); ø 30 mm, height 7.9 mm; 27 jewels; 28,800 vph; officially certified chronometer (COSC)
Functions: hours, minutes, subsidiary seconds; chronograph; date
Case: stainless steel, ø 44 mm, height 13 mm; sapphire crystal; screw-in crown; water-resistant to 10 atm
Band: stainless steel, double folding clasp
Price: $6,000
Variations: black or blue dial; red gold with leather strap, rubber strap, or link bracelet

Admiral's Cup Tides 48
Reference number: 277.931.91 0371 AG 32
Movement: automatic, Corum Caliber CO 277 (base ETA 2892-A2 with exclusive tide module by Dubois Dépraz); ø 26.2 mm, height 5.2 mm; 21 jewels; 28,800 vph; officially certified C.O.S.C. chronometer
Functions: hours, minutes, sweep seconds; date; moon phase; tides and strength of tides
Case: red gold, ø 48 mm, height 12 mm; rubber-coated bezel; sapphire crystal; transparent case back; screw-in crown; water-resistant to 5 atm
Band: rubber, folding clasp
Price: $20,000
Variations: titanium with rubber strap or link bracelet

Admiral's Cup Competition 40
Reference number: 082.961.20 F379 AA 12
Movement: automatic, Corum Caliber CO 082 (base ETA 2892-A2); ø 25.6 mm, height 3.6 mm; 21 jewels; 28,800 vph
Functions: hours, minutes, sweep seconds; date
Case: stainless steel, ø 40 mm, height 10 mm; sapphire crystal; screw-in crown; water-resistant to 10 atm
Band: rubber, folding clasp
Price: $3,800
Variations: with diamond-set bezel

Romulus
Reference number: 373.515.20 F101 BN 57
Movement: automatic, Corum Caliber CO 373 (base ETA 2897); ø 26.2 mm, height 4.85 mm; 21 jewels; 28,800 vph
Functions: hours, minutes, sweep seconds; date; power reserve display
Case: stainless steel, ø 42 mm, height 11 mm; bezel engraved with Roman numerals; sapphire crystal; screw-in crown; water-resistant to 5 atm
Band: leather, double folding clasp
Price: $3,400
Variations: silver-colored dial; stainless steel link bracelet

Romulus Dual Time
Reference number: 283.510.55 0001 BN 56
Movement: automatic, Corum Caliber CO 283 (base Frédéric Piguet 5K60); ø 26.2 mm, height 5.7 mm; 30 jewels; 28,800 vph
Functions: hours, minutes, subsidiary seconds; date; second time zone
Case: red gold, ø 41 mm, height 10 mm; bezel engraved with Roman numerals; sapphire crystal; transparent case back
Band: reptile skin, buckle
Price: $17,000
Variations: white gold; without second time zone in red or white gold

Golden Bridge
Reference number: 113.550.55 0001 000R
Movement: manually wound, Corum Caliber CO GB 001; 34 x 4.9 mm, height 3 mm; 15 jewels; 18,000 vph; baton movement with crown at 6 o'clock; hand-engraved bridges and plates
Functions: hours, minutes
Case: red gold, 37 x 32 mm, height 10 mm; case with sapphire crystal on the sides; sapphire crystal; transparent case back
Band: reptile skin, buckle
Price: $22,000
Variations: red gold link bracelet; yellow or white gold; platinum

Golden Tourbillon Panoramique
Reference number: 382.850.59 0F01 0000
Movement: manually wound, Corum Caliber CO 382 (base La Joux-Perret 7951); 16 jewels; 18,000 vph; one-minute tourbillon; all bridges and cocks made of sapphire crystal; power reserve 90 hours
Functions: hours, minutes
Case: white gold, 38 x 53 mm, height 14 mm; case with sapphire crystal on the sides; sapphire crystal; transparent case back
Band: reptile skin, buckle
Price: $158,000
Variations: red gold

Cuervo y Sobrinos

Havana—the name has the magic sound of Caribbean joie de vivre to it, of tropical temperatures and music, that doesn't really jibe in every way with today's reality. Despite this, the romantic picture of La Habana, as the Cuban capital city is known by its residents, seems to effortlessly survive all times, even the hardest of them. Against a background of fading affluence and the peeling facades of a societal model, the epoch of rich tobacco plantations and sugar barons seems more like a fairy tale than anything else. Ramón Rio y Cuervo and his sister's sons kept a watchmaking workshop and an elegant shop on Quinto Avenida where they sold fine Swiss pocket watches (and, of course, less fine American models as well). Along with the advent of tourism from the nearby coast of Florida at the beginning of the twentieth century, the business developed with wristwatches, whose dials Don Ramón soon had printed with his own name, as did other jewelers in New York, Paris, and even Lucerne. And Cuervo y Sobrinos—Cuervo and Nephews—was born.

Numerous international personalities of literature, science, film, theater, and politics visited "Casa Cuervo" on their trips to the Caribbean paradise. From the guest book and photographs that were found only a few years ago in the basement of the former store, Ernest Hemingway, Enrico Caruso, Clark Gable, Winston Churchill, and even Albert Einstein seemed to have been customers of Cuervo y Sobrinos.

Upon the initiative of an Italian watch enthusiast and a Spanish businessman, the traditional brand was resuscitated a few years ago. In cooperation with various Swiss workshops, Don Ramón's heirs have developed a new wristwatch collection, striking in its unusual case shapes and dial details and definitely awakening nostalgic memories of the 1940s.

Tobacco and cigars, the two typical products of the island, play an important role in the new watches' identity. For one, all the watches are delivered in a prestigious and, of course, fully functional humidor made of precious woods. For another, the individual model families are all named after famous cigar formats. For example, there is the Espléndido, whose case, with its strongly tailored shape, reminds one of the immense popularity of the "hourglass" models of the '40s, which almost all big Genevan brands carried in their programs. With a length of 47 mm including lugs and a width of 32.5 mm at the narrowest spot of the "hourglass," this watch is anything but delicate even though its long lugs make the leather strap comfortably hug even the smallest of wrists.

Prominente's case shape is reminiscent of 1930s style. It's slightly domed, making it comfortable to wear despite its respectable length of 52 mm.

Cuervo y Sobrinos's watch model Torpedo doesn't display the pointed ends of the cigar of the same name, rather it illustrates a cultivated, round case with very striking lugs in which the original shape of the previously mentioned Espléndido is recognizable. The Robusto line is new to the collection and features classic three-hand models, sporty diving pieces, and a clever complete calendar. While the world continues to wait for the end of the Cuban revolution, this new yet old watch brand looks back over the past, at the same time foreshadowing innovations to come.

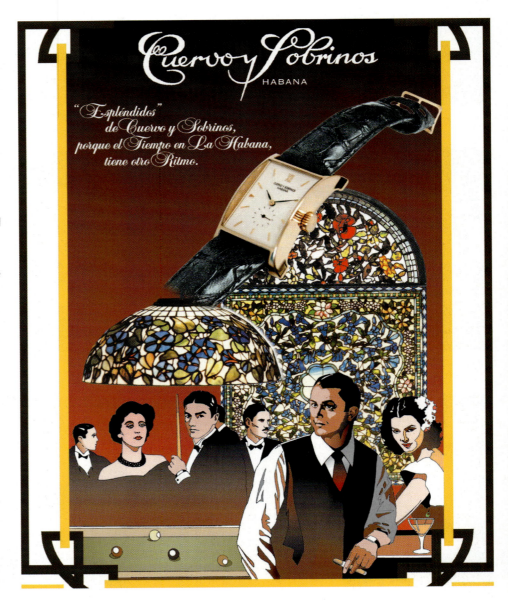

Espléndidos Small Seconds
Reference number: 2451.1RG
Movement: automatic, ETA Caliber 2895-2; ø 26.2 mm, height 4.5 mm; 27 jewels; 28,800 vph; exclusive rotor
Functions: hours, minutes, subsidiary seconds; date
Case: stainless steel, 47 x 37 mm, height 10.3 mm; sapphire crystal; transparent case back
Band: reptile skin, double folding clasp
Price: $3,400
Variations: various dial versions; yellow or rose gold

Espléndidos Power Reserve Retrograde Date
Reference number: 2452.1A
Movement: automatic, Soprod Caliber 9094 (base ETA Caliber 2892-A2); ø 25.6 mm, height 5.10 mm; 30 jewels; 28,800 vph; exclusive rotor
Functions: hours, minutes, sweep seconds; date, weekday; power reserve indicator
Case: stainless steel, 47 x 37 mm, height 13.86 mm; sapphire crystal; transparent case back
Band: reptile skin, double folding clasp
Price: $4,400
Variations: various dial versions; yellow or rose gold

Espléndidos Monopulsante
Reference number: 2450.9GO
Movement: automatic, CYS Caliber 2450 (base La Joux-Perret 5000); ø 29 mm, height 5.60 mm; 21 jewels; 21,600 vph; one-button control of chronograph functions; finely finished movement
Functions: hours, minutes, subsidiary seconds; chronograph
Case: rose gold, 47 x 37 mm, height 13.86 mm; sapphire crystal; transparent case back; crown with chronograph button
Band: reptile skin, double folding clasp
Price: $19,500
Variations: limited edition of 10 pieces in white gold

Prominente Chronograph
Reference number: 1014.1NLE
Movement: automatic, ETA Caliber 2094; ø 23.3 mm, height 5.5 mm; 33 jewels; 28,800 vph; exclusive rotor
Functions: hours, minutes, subsidiary seconds; date; chronograph
Case: stainless steel, 31 x 52 mm, height 12.4 mm; sapphire crystal; transparent case back
Band: reptile skin, double folding clasp
Remarks: limited edition of 125 pieces for brand's 125th anniversary; dial with carbon fiber segment
Price: $5,800

Prominente Data
Reference number: 1012.1CG
Movement: automatic, ETA Caliber 2892-A2; ø 25.6 mm, height 3.6 mm; 21 jewels; 28,800 vph; exclusive rotor
Functions: hours, minutes, sweep seconds; date
Case: stainless steel, 31 x 52 mm, height 10.5 mm; sapphire crystal; transparent case back
Band: reptile skin, double folding clasp
Price: $3,300
Variations: various dial versions; yellow or rose gold

Robusto Chronograph
Reference number: 2859.1NLE
Movement: automatic, ETA Caliber 2892-A2 with Dubois Dépraz module 2359; ø 31.15 mm, height 7.2 mm; 48 jewels; 28,800 vph; exclusive rotor
Functions: hours, minutes, subsidiary seconds; date; chronograph; weekday, month, moon phase
Case: stainless steel, ø 43 mm, height 15.6 mm; sapphire crystal; transparent case back
Band: reptile skin, double folding clasp
Remarks: carbon fiber dial
Price: $6,500

Espléndidos 1882
Reference number: 2412.1N82
Movement: automatic, ETA Caliber 2824-2; ø 25.6 mm, height 4.6 mm; 25 jewels; 28,800 vph
Functions: hours, minutes (disk display in window); date
Case: stainless steel, 47 x 37 mm, height 13.86 mm; sapphire crystal; transparent case back
Band: reptile skin, double folding clasp
Price: $3,600
Variations: various dial versions

Espléndidos 1882
Reference number: 2412.1RH82
Movement: automatic, modified ETA Caliber 2824-2; ø 25.6 mm, height 4.6 mm; 25 jewels; 28,800 vph
Functions: hours, minutes (disk display in window); date
Case: stainless steel, 47 x 37 mm, height 13.86 mm; sapphire crystal; transparent case back
Band: reptile skin, double folding clasp
Price: $3,600
Variations: various dial versions

Cvstos

The timepieces of this young brand cultivate an exceptionally "technical" look that veers sharply from the appearance of traditional *haute horlogerie*, approaching a clientele that doesn't necessarily include elements such as *côtes de Genève*, gold, and guilloché in their idea of watchmaking. The tonneau-shaped cases made of stainless steel, gold, and even palladium have a strong character and demonstrate with visible screw heads, rubber gaskets, and brushed surfaces the origins of their modern metal workings. Thanks to a transparent case back and a conscious decision not to use dials in the regular sense, these watches' mechanical insides are attractively put on show. And it soon becomes clear to the observer that movement components don't necessarily need to be shiny in order to be interesting. The matte gray surfaces bear witness to great attention to detail, even if the presented technology is not nearly as innovative as its futuristic appearance may suggest.

A great deal of tradition goes into the making of a Cvstos, and that is no wonder for a brand that is the spiritual child of Sassoun Sirmakes, son of Vartan Sirmakes, the man who led Genevan watchmaker Franck Muller to world fame and who today rules over Watchland with its more than 600 employees. Young Mr. Sirmakes learned the craft of watchmaking at his father's side, and when kindred spirit Antonio Terranova, designer and movement engineer, found him, Sirmakes's dream of making his own watches turned into reality. That was in 2004, and Sassoun Sirmakes was only twenty-one years old.

Cvstos is headquartered in Meyrin, a suburb of Geneva where this brand is free to unfold its unusual mixture of high-tech and luxurious elements, created in an electric field between idyll and machine, tradition and modernity.

Challenge QP-S
Movement: automatic, Cvstos Caliber 6510; 28,800 vph; special movement finish, rotor in palladium and titanium
Functions: hours, minutes, sweep seconds; perpetual calendar with date, day, month, moon phase, leap year
Case: palladium, 53.7 x 41 mm, height 15.5 mm; sapphire crystal; transparent case back; screw-in crown; water-resistant to 10 atm
Band: rubber, folding clasp
Price: $28,300
Variations: stainless steel ($23,300); rose gold ($32,500); blackened stainless steel

Challenge Chrono
Movement: automatic, Cvstos Caliber 577; 28,800 vph; special movement finish, rotor in palladium and titanium
Functions: hours, minutes, subsidiary seconds; chronograph; date; power reserve indication
Case: rose gold, 53.7 x 41 mm, height 15.5 mm; sapphire crystal; transparent case back; screw-in crown; water-resistant to 10 atm
Band: rubber, folding clasp
Price: $23,300
Variations: blackened stainless steel ($13,300); stainless steel ($12,500); 18-karat white gold with diamonds ($40,000)

Challenge Twin-Time
Reference number: CH TWIN-TIME 5N B
Movement: automatic, Cvstos Caliber 551; 28,800 vph; special movement finish, rotor in palladium and titanium
Functions: hours, minutes, sweep seconds; large date; second time zone
Case: rose gold, 53.7 x 41 mm, height 14.3 mm; sapphire crystal; transparent case back; screw-in crown; water-resistant to 10 atm
Band: rubber, folding clasp
Price: $20,800
Variations: stainless steel ($10,000); blackened steel ($10,800)

Challenge-R Chrono
Movement: automatic, Cvstos Caliber 577; 28,800 vph; special movement finish, rotor in palladium and titanium
Functions: hours, minutes, subsidiary seconds; chronograph; date; power reserve indication
Case: stainless steel, ø 50 mm, height 15.5 mm; sapphire crystal; transparent case back; screw-in crown; water-resistant to 10 atm
Band: rubber, folding clasp
Price: $17,500
Variations: rose gold

Cyclos

Engineer, architect, and designer John C. Ermel was searching for a way of showing the time on a conventional and intuitively legible 12-hour dial where the hours of the day and night would be unmistakably distinguishable from each other. During his search he happened upon a long-forgotten technology that was never developed far enough to become functional.

The DualPhase display by Cyclos (realized together with master watchmakers Robert Greubel and Stephen Forsey of Compli-Time) is made possible by two spiral-shaped, overlapping 12-hour numeral circles of varying diameters and an hour hand that can grow and shrink as necessary. Its double-looped curve creates this effect by combining a clockwise rotation with a movement in radial direction. In mathematics, this is called a Pascal Spiral, and since it follows a strict law, it was possible to construct a mechanism that moves hands in the same way.

The effect of this interesting technology is surprising: when the date changes, the outer tip of the hour hand begins its path around the inner numeral circle, changing at six o'clock in the morning to the outer scale. By the time noon has come along, the hand has "grown" almost 3.5 millimeters and runs along the outer scale. At 6 o'clock in the evening it has once again "shrunk" to half its length and from then until midnight displays the time on the inner ring.

Sometimes you just have to look at things twice to get them.

a.m./p.m. dark
Reference number: APD-SS
Movement: automatic, Cyclos Caliber CW 1 (base ETA 2892-A2); ø 33 mm, height 6.6 mm; 21 jewels; 28,800 vph; patented Dual Phase 24-hour display with hour hand that changes in length; officially certified chronometer (COSC)
Functions: hours (24-hour display), minutes, sweep seconds; date
Case: stainless steel, ø 39 mm, height 12.8 mm; sapphire crystal; transparent case back; water-resistant to 5 atm
Band: leather, folding clasp
Price: $7,900
Variations: silver-colored dial

day&night Parity
Reference number: PAR-WG
Movement: automatic, Cyclos Caliber CW 1 (base ETA 2892-A2); ø 33 mm, height 6.6 mm; 21 jewels; 28,800 vph; patented Dual Phase 24-hour display with hour hand that changes in length; officially certified chronometer (COSC)
Functions: hours (24-hour display), minutes, sweep seconds; date
Case: white gold, ø 39 mm, height 12.8 mm; sapphire crystal; transparent case back; water-resistant to 5 atm
Band: reptile skin, folding clasp
Price: $19,350
Variations: stainless steel

day&night Classic dark
Reference number: CLD-RG
Movement: automatic, Cyclos Caliber CW 1 (base ETA 2892-A2); ø 33 mm, height 6.6 mm; 21 jewels; 28,800 vph; patented Dual Phase 24-hour display with hour hand that changes in length; officially certified chronometer (COSC)
Functions: hours (24-hour display), minutes, sweep seconds; date
Case: red gold, ø 39 mm, height 12.8 mm; sapphire crystal; transparent case back; water-resistant to 5 atm
Band: reptile skin, folding clasp
Price: $18,850
Variations: yellow gold ($17,750); light dial

day&night Transparent light
Reference number: TRL-YG
Movement: automatic, Cyclos Caliber CW 1 (base ETA 2892-A2); ø 33 mm, height 6.6 mm; 21 jewels; 28,800 vph; patented Dual Phase 24-hour display with hour hand that changes in length; officially certified chronometer (COSC)
Functions: hours (24-hour display), minutes, sweep seconds; date
Case: yellow gold, ø 39 mm, height 12.8 mm; sapphire crystal; transparent case back; water-resistant to 5 atm
Band: reptile skin, folding clasp
Remarks: skeletonized dial reveals hand mechanics
Price: $19,350
Variations: light dial

De Bethune

This little company speaks softly and carries a huge stick—in the form of its powerful movements, which are the subject of so many patents and hold so many elements of new technology that you really have to wonder exactly how many people work in the little factory located in the middle of the Jura village of La Chaux l'Auberson.

And in most cases, those asking that question would be extremely surprised to hear the answer: in general just one person is working on De Bethune's movements. The company's technical director, Denis Flageollet, has more than twenty years of experience under his belt with regard to the research, conception, and successful implementation of more than 120 different, extremely prestigious timepieces—for other companies, of course.

Flageollet, who had been working for complication think tank THA, and David Zanetta, a well-known consultant for a number of prestigious watch brands, founded their own company in 2002, and De Bethune was born. Together, they bought what used to be the village pub and turned it into one of the most amazing factories to be found that far in the hills. The modern CNC machinery combined with the expertise of an experienced watchmaking team allows Flageollet to produce prototypes in the blink of an eye and make small movement series without delays. In order to become more independent of suppliers, the little factory now also makes its own cases, dials, and hands, which guarantees a high level of excellence with regard to production and quality control.

In the five years since its founding, De Bethune has developed a manually wound caliber with five or eight days of power reserve, a self-regulating double barrel, a balance wheel in titanium and platinum that allows for an ideal inertia mass ratio, a balance spring including a patented De Bethune terminal curve, and a triple parachute system. In the same time frame, the little company has also developed an automatic movement that it has brought to serial production. This includes five or ten days of power reserve, a platinum and titanium oscillating weight mounted on a ceramic ball bearing, a self-adjusting twin spring barrel, a titanium and platinum balance spring with De Bethune's patented terminal curve, and solid 18-karat gold gear wheels—which are a unique addition to a serially manufactured movement. Additionally, the company has also patented its revolving moon mechanism, which represents the moon phases in a three-dimensional manner; its titanium and platinum balance wheel; the special terminal curve on its balance spring; and its silicon balance wheel including a balance spring and pallet fork made of the high-tech material.

"Our studies of the silicon balance spring were done here in-house at De Bethune for the last one and a half years," Flageollet explains. "It is the logical result of the studies of the titanium-platinum balance with De Bethune's terminal curve. We chose to use silicon because it is the best material for the great precision and perfect control needed for working with numerous laboratories all over the world. This technology has been used for more than thirty years by high-tech industries, adapted for electronics, for example. De Bethune's silicon elements are manufactured by a process developed by De Bethune in a foreign laboratory completely independent of any other research currently taking place in the industry."

De Bethune

Perpetual Calendar with Revolving Moon Phase
Reference number: DB 15 WS1
Movement: manually wound, De Bethune Caliber DB 2004; ø 30 mm, height 5.9 mm; 26 jewels; 28,800 vph; twin spring barrels, 5 day power reserve; triple shock protection; titanium balance with platinum weights; completely finished by hand
Functions: hours, minutes; perpetual calendar with date, day, month, moon phase (3D), leap year display
Case: red gold, ø 43 mm, height 13 mm; sapphire crystal; transparent case back
Band: reptile skin, buckle
Price: $95,000
Variations: white gold; platinum

DBL Jewellery
Reference number: DBL J1WS2
Movement: manually wound, De Bethune Caliber DB 2014; ø 34 mm, height 6 mm; 29 jewels; 21,600 vph; twin spring barrels, power reserve approx. 192 hours; balance made of titanium and platinum weights; completely finished by hand
Functions: hours, minutes; moon phase (3D)
Case: white gold, 45 x 42.5 mm, height 11 mm; case, bezel, and lugs set with baguette-cut diamonds; screw-in crown set with diamonds; sapphire crystal
Band: reptile skin, buckle
Remarks: dial with diamonds and blue sapphire cabochon markers; diamond and sapphire moon
Price: upon request

8 Days Power Reserve with Revolving Moon
Reference number: DBS PS5
Movement: manually wound, De Bethune Caliber DB 2014; ø 34 mm, height 6 mm; 31 jewels; 21,600 vph; twin spring barrels, power reserve 192 hours; balance made of titanium with platinum weights; completely finished by hand
Functions: hours, minutes; moon phase (3D); power reserve display (on the back)
Case: rose gold, 45 x 42.5 mm, height 11 mm; sapphire crystal
Band: reptile skin, buckle
Price: $50,000
Variations: platinum; white gold

Beat Quantième
Reference number: DB20Q1
Movement: automatic, De Bethune Caliber DB 2024; ø 30 mm; 53 jewels; 28,800 vph; twin spring barrels, power reserve over 140 hours; balance made of titanium with platinum weights; titanium rotor with platinum oscillating weight on ceramic ball bearings
Functions: hours, minutes; date; power reserve display (linear)
Case: white gold, ø 45.5 mm, height 11.6 mm; sapphire crystal; transparent case back
Band: reptile skin, buckle
Price: $39,000
Variations: titanium

Power
Reference number: DB22
Movement: automatic, De Bethune Caliber DB 2024; ø 30 mm; 53 jewels; 28,800 vph; twin spring barrels, power reserve 6 days; balance made of titanium with platinum weights; titanium rotor with platinum oscillating weight on ceramic ball bearings
Functions: hours, minutes; power reserve display
Case: white gold, ø 45.5 mm, height 11.3 mm; sapphire crystal; transparent case back; water-resistant to 10 atm
Band: reptile skin, buckle
Price: $35,000
Variations: rose gold and titanium

8 Days Power Reserve with Revolving Moon
Reference number: DBS RS1
Movement: manually wound, De Bethune Caliber DB 2014; ø 34 mm, height 6 mm; 31 jewels; 21,600 vph; twin spring barrels, power reserve 192 hours; balance made of titanium with platinum weights; completely finished by hand
Functions: hours, minutes; moon phase (3D); power reserve display (on the back)
Case: platinum, 45 x 42.5 mm, height 11 mm; sapphire crystal
Band: reptile skin, buckle
Price: $65,000
Variations: platinum; rose gold

Digital
Reference number: DB DIGITAL R
Movement: manually wound, De Bethune Caliber DB 2044; ø 30 mm, height 6 mm; 35 jewels; 28,800 vph; twin spring barrels, power reserve 6 days, balance made of titanium with platinum weights; completely finished by hand
Functions: hours (jump), minutes (disk display); day, date and month in windows; moon phase (on case back)
Case: white gold, ø 42.5 mm, height 11 mm; sapphire crystal
Band: reptile skin, buckle
Price: $ 70,000
Variations: rose gold

Classic 2
Reference number: DB25C2WS3
Movement: automatic, De Bethune Caliber DB 2024-J10; ø 30 mm; 53 jewels; 28,800 vph; twin spring barrels, power reserve appx. 240 hours; balance made of titanium with platinum weights; titanium rotor with platinum oscillating weight
Functions: hours, minutes; power reserve display
Case: white gold, ø 44 mm, height 11.5 mm; sapphire crystal; transparent case back
Band: reptile skin, buckle
Price: upon request
Variations: rose gold

De Grisogono

Certain men dazzle because of their discretion. Others because of their exuberance, Fawaz Gruosi, owner and founder of de Grisogono explains. "Today's man, whether athletic or dreamy, mischievous or serious, ardent or thoughtful, is no longer afraid to assert his difference. With the de Grisogono watch collections, I wanted to give him a watch according to his image, a timepiece that resembles him and distinguishes him from others. Nonconformist at times, yet always audacious, the collections—conceived in our own workshops—reveal the unique character of each man. The watches, perfectly anchored between traditional craftsmanship and technical innovation, marvelously reflect the values of our brand: to reinvent elegance and to jostle new ideas in order to transform the timekeeper into a true art of savoir vivre."

Gruosi ought to know what he is talking about. Previously an employee of Chopard, Gruosi discovered he had his very own style slumbering within him, and decided to strike out on his own to realize these unique designs. But not before meeting his future wife through his work, today's co-president of Chopard, Caroline Gruosi-Scheufele.

This marriage made in jewelry ensures cooperation between the two companies, especially in terms of manufacturing and marketing. The cooperation is not too close, however, for the concepts of the two companies diverge sharply from each other.

Gruosi first made a name for himself with the black diamond, a precious stone that was not regularly being used by any other brand at the time. Though critics were divided, Gruosi knew how to make his organically inspired creations come to life with the black carbon-based gem. This success was quickly followed by the use of "icy" diamonds—gems that have so many inclusions that they are not clear and brilliant, but rather matte and icy in appearance. Usually thought of as stones of inferior quality, Gruosi masterfully utilized the gems to advantage in his unique jewelry creations and was able to chalk up another success toward building his own distinct look.

Naturally it was not long before Gruosi decided to enter the market for men's luxury wristwatches. The first of these were decidedly marked by Gruosi's style—and an extremely large case that immediately made waves.

Though de Grisogono continues to use these signature elements in the brand's wristwatches—characteristically including black diamonds, red and other flamboyantly colored golds, and stately dimensions—this is not all the brand has to offer, and in the last decade a fairly wide collection has come to life.

From the premiere timepiece Instrumento Numero Uno through the *haute horlogerie* minute repeater Occhio (created with the aid of Christophe Claret) all the way to the most recent of Gruosi's unique timepieces FG One and Power Breaker, the de Grisogono collection features timepieces for every man—provided his pockets are deep enough. And naturally there is also a collection of matching jewelry including cufflinks, tie pins, and rings for these men to choose from.

De Grisogono

Instrumento Novantatre
Reference number: N02
Movement: automatic, ETA Caliber 2892-A2 with module for large date and month; ø 25.6 mm, height 3.6 mm (base caliber); 21 jewels; 28,800 vph
Functions: hours, minutes, subsidiary seconds; large date, month
Case: stainless steel, 40 x 48 mm, height 12 mm; sapphire crystal; transparent case back
Band: leather, double folding clasp
Price: $10,900

Instrumento Novantatre
Reference number: N07
Movement: automatic, ETA Caliber 2892-A2 with module for large date and month; ø 25.6 mm, height 3.6 mm (base caliber); 21 jewels; 28,800 vph
Functions: hours, minutes, subsidiary seconds; large date, month
Case: rose gold, 40 x 48 mm, height 12 mm; sapphire crystal; transparent case back
Band: leather, double folding clasp
Price: $21,700

Instrumento Grande
Reference number: N06
Movement: automatic, ETA Caliber 2892-A2 with module for large date; ø 25.6 mm, height 3.6 mm (base caliber); 21 jewels; 28,800 vph; black movement finish with blued screws
Functions: hours, minutes; large date
Case: rose gold, 41.1 x 48.3 mm, height 12.5 mm; case with sapphire crystal on the sides; sapphire crystal; transparent case back
Band: reptile skin, double folding clasp
Price: $21,900
Variations: stainless steel

Instrumento Grande Open Date
Reference number: N05
Movement: automatic, ETA Caliber 2892-A2 with module for large date; ø 25.6 mm, height 3.6 mm (base caliber); 21 jewels; 28,800 vph; cutaway in dial displays shape and arrangement of both date disks
Functions: hours, minutes; large date
Case: rose gold, 41.1 x 48.3 mm, height 12.5 mm; case with sapphire crystal on the sides; sapphire crystal; transparent case back
Band: reptile skin, double folding clasp
Price: $24,300

Instrumento No. Uno
Reference number: UNO DF/N1
Movement: automatic, ETA Caliber 2892-A2 with module for large date and second time zone; ø 25.6 mm, height 3.6 mm; 21 jewels; 28,800 vph; black movement finish with blued screws
Functions: hours, minutes; large date; second time zone
Case: stainless steel, 57 x 33 mm, height 10.9 mm; sapphire crystal; transparent case back
Band: reptile skin, double folding clasp
Price: $10,900
Variations: various dial versions, case materials, and straps

Uno Grande Seconde
Reference number: N03
Movement: automatic, ETA Caliber 2892-A2; ø 25.6 mm, height 3.6 mm; 21 jewels; 28,800 vph
Functions: hours, minutes (off-center), sweep seconds
Case: stainless steel, 57 x 33 mm, height 10.9 mm; sapphire crystal; transparent case back; crown with black diamond cabochon
Band: reptile skin, double folding clasp
Price: $10,000
Variations: rose gold

FG One
Reference number: N01
Movement: automatic, ETA Caliber 2892-A2 with module for extra time zone and dial train; ø 25.6 mm, height 3.6 mm; 21 jewels; 28,800 vph
Functions: hours (jump), minutes (retrograde), seconds (retrograde); second time zone (24-hour disk); day/night indication
Case: stainless steel, 33 x 58 mm, height 11.75 mm; fluted case; sapphire crystal
Band: reptile skin, double folding clasp
Price: $13,300
Variations: rose gold

Power Breaker
Reference number: N02
Movement: automatic, ETA Caliber 2892-A2 with chronograph module by Dubois Dépraz; ø 30 mm, height 6.5 mm; 47 jewels; 28,800 vph
Functions: hours, minutes; chronograph
Case: stainless steel, polished and PVD coated, 54.2 x 43.3 mm, height 15.2 mm; sapphire crystal
Band: rubber, double folding clasp
Remarks: the first 500 pieces bear the signature of Formula 1 Renault team manager Flavio Briatore engraved on the case back
Price: $14,400
Variations: in Browny Brown gold with brown rubber strap

DeWitt

Since its founding, this exclusive little watch *manufacture* has been at home in the servants' house of the family that gives it its name located in the noble Genevan suburb of Vandoeuvres. This past year, that structure definitively became too small, and the company moved to a generous new building created for it on a green field in Vernier's industrial quarter near the Geneva airport. It is especially the production department for individual components and the ever-expanding research and development department—which determines the future of the brand's model development and technical innovation—that will profit from the extra room.
In not quite five years, this brand has achieved incredible feats as well as being able to launch several remarkably complicated watches—a minute repeater, a tourbillon, a split-seconds chronograph with an isolator, and a perpetual calendar with two retrograde displays—all based upon the finest *ébauches* by the most reputable makers. In 2005, DeWitt laid the cornerstone for a collection that would permanently coin the image of the brand: the Tourbillon Différentiel Académia. By introducing the striking Académia case, the brand set a unique, individual image. The complex component—comprising screwed elements—is a mirror image of the complicated technology that it houses. Thus, the Tourbillon Différentiel is not only outfitted with an exclusively complicated tourbillon escapement, but also an in-house, three-dimensional differential to communicate between the two spring barrels and the power reserve display. Jerôme De Witt is, however, an incorrigible perfectionist: therefore, his master watchmakers built him the new Tourbillon à Force Constante in the winter of 2006. This masterpiece contains an additional regulating organ that first saves up the energy coming from the spring barrel and then portions it out precisely before passing it on to the tourbillon carriage. The very masculine Académia collection is an excellent platform for technical gadgets and very fine display complications. These creations have earned a great deal of praise in the expert press, both for their technical and aesthetic elements.
This incredible success story is also the reason why these engineers, watchmakers, case makers, and gem setters have voluntarily given up their ideal working conditions in the renovated manor house in Vandoeuvres for a modern factory. In Vernier, they have 1,500 square meters on two floors at their disposal—five times as much space as before. In addition to the usual production departments—component manufacture, polishing, assembly, finishing, decoration, rate adjustment, water resistance testing, and quality control—this company will now also entertain a genuine research and development center to design, test, and produce its own base movements.

DeWitt

Academia Seconde Rétrograde
Reference number: AC.1102.53/102.M680/102
Movement: automatic, DeWitt Caliber DW 1102 (base ETA 2892-A2 with module for retrograde seconds); ø 29.2 mm, height 5.45 mm; 21 jewels; 28,800 vph
Functions: hours, minutes, subsidiary seconds (retrograde)
Case: rose gold, ø 43 mm, height 12 mm; case, bezel, and strap lugs set with diamonds; sapphire crystal
Band: reptile skin, buckle
Price: $45,900
Variations: white gold with grey carbon fiber dial; without diamonds

Academia Double Fuseau GMT 2
Reference number: AC.2002.48.M687
Movement: automatic, DeWitt Caliber DW 2002 (base ETA 2892-A2 with module for second time zone and 24-hour display); ø 26.2 mm, height 4.95 mm; 21 jewels; 28,800 vph
Functions: hours, minutes, sweep seconds; date; two 24-hour displays (second time zone)
Case: white gold, ø 43 mm, height 14 mm; sapphire crystal
Band: reptile skin, folding clasp
Remarks: mother-of-pearl dial
Price: $24,500
Variations: rose gold; with diamonds

Academia Tourbillon Différentiel
Reference number: AC.8002.28A.M954
Movement: manually wound, DeWitt Caliber DW 8002; ø 30 mm, height 8.9 mm; 24 jewels; 21,600 vph; flying one-minute tourbillon; patented differential winding gear; power reserve 120 hours; finely finished, côtes de Genève
Functions: hours, minutes; power reserve display
Case: titanium/red gold, ø 43 mm, height 12 mm; bezel in titanium with rubber inlay; sapphire crystal
Band: rubber, double folding clasp
Price: $177,900
Variations: titanium; white gold

Academia Tourbillon à Force Constante
Reference number: AC.800.3.48.M120
Movement: manually wound, DeWitt Caliber DW 8003; ø 30 mm, height 7.8 mm; 24 jewels; 21,600 vph; flying one-minute tourbillon with constant force mechanism; power reserve 72 hours; finely finished, côtes de Genève
Functions: hours, minutes (off-center)
Case: white gold, ø 43 mm, height 12.85 mm; sapphire crystal
Band: reptile skin, folding clasp
Price: $199,000
Variations: rose gold; with diamonds

Academia Triple Complication GMT 3
Reference number: AC.2041.21.M006
Movement: automatic, DeWitt Caliber DW 2041 (base ETA 2893 with module for second time zone and day/night indication); ø 26.2 mm, height 9.2 mm; 25 jewels; 28,800 vph
Functions: hours, minutes (off-center); second time zone (12-hour display); large date; day/night disk display
Case: palladium, ø 43 mm, height 14 mm; sapphire crystal; screw-in crown; water-resistant to 10 atm
Band: rubber, triple folding clasp
Price: $49,900
Variations: red gold

Academia Silicium Grande Date
Reference number: AC.1501.53/01.M622
Movement: automatic, DeWitt Caliber DW 1501 (base ETA 2892); ø 30.2 mm, height 5.3 mm; 22 jewels; 28,800 vph; gold rotor
Functions: hours, minutes, sweep seconds; large date, weekday
Case: rose gold, ø 39 mm, height 11.15 mm; case, bezel, and strap lugs set with diamonds; sapphire crystal
Band: reptile skin, triple folding clasp
Remarks: unique dial made of pure gold-plated silicon
Price: $54,900
Variations: white gold; without diamonds

Academia Silicium Hora Mundi
Reference number: AC.2021.48.M623
Movement: automatic, DeWitt Caliber DW 2021 (base ETA 2892-A2 with world time module); ø 26.2 mm, height 5 mm; 21 jewels; 28,800 vph
Functions: hours, minutes, sweep seconds; date; world time (24-hour display)
Case: white gold, ø 39 mm, height 11.15 mm; sapphire crystal
Band: reptile skin, triple folding clasp
Remarks: unique dial made of pure silicon
Price: $36,900
Variations: rose gold; with diamonds

Tourbillon Mystérieux Haute Joaillerie
Reference number: AC.8400.48/03.M950
Movement: manually wound, DeWitt Caliber DW 8001; ø 28 mm, height 5.18 mm; 19 jewels; 21,600 vph; one-minute tourbillon; patented differential winding gear; power reserve 110 hours; blued base plate and bridges
Functions: hours, minutes
Case: white gold, ø 43 mm, height 14 mm; case, bezel, and strap lugs set with baguette-cut sapphires; crown set with sapphires; sapphire crystal
Band: reptile skin, triple folding clasp set with sapphires
Price: upon request

Pierre DeRoche

Oftentimes, high-quality watchmaking nestles in a secret valley—usually somewhere in the Jura—waiting to be discovered. The Pierre DeRoche brand is just such an example, born of a watchmaking dynasty that has been located in Le Lieu since 1901 when Marcel Frédérich Dépraz officially founded his workshop specializing in chronographs in this tiny Vallée de Joux town.

The Pierre DeRoche story is inextricably entwined with a determination to continue and expand a legacy. Its founder, Pierre Dubois, is one of three brothers who are today living proof that Switzerland's best watchmakers can remain under the roof of a family-owned and -managed business. Pierre's two brothers, Pascal and Jean-Philippe, are the fourth-generation directors of the Helvetian country's most venerable supplier of mechanical complications: Dubois Dépraz.

Pierre Dubois did not join the family business like his brothers at the beginning of the 1990s, but chose a different route instead. However, he did not abandon watchmaking, which truly seemed to be in his blood as well. He went to work for Audemars Piguet—located just kilometers away in Le Brassus—eventually becoming that company's CFO.

Coming from such a well-established family tradition with international legitimacy and recognition, Dubois need not look too far to recognize the love he feels for complicated watches, precision, and the development of models with significant added value. And so it is that his Pierre DeRoche brand—magnificently run in the truest sense of family traditions—and its small collection of timepieces have far more than just excellent design and quality components behind them: they are also outfitted with complicated Dubois Dépraz calibers that have been created solely for the use of Pierre DeRoche, evident in the brand's first timepiece: the SplitRock.

GrandCliff Flyback
Reference number: GRC10001AC10-003CRO
Movement: automatic, Dubois Dépraz Caliber 44525 (base ETA 2892-A2); ø 25.6 mm, height 3.6 mm; 49 jewels, 28,800 vph; power reserve 42 hours; skeletonized and engraved rotor
Functions: hours, minutes, subsidiary seconds; large date; flyback chronograph
Case: stainless steel, ø 42.5 mm, height 14.5 mm; screw-in crown and buttons; anti-reflective sapphire crystal; screw-down sapphire crystal case back; water-resistant to 100 m
Band: crocodile skin, folding clasp
Price: $9,015
Variations: 18-karat rose gold with 22-karat gold rhodium-plated rotor; black dial; Barenia leather strap

GrandCliff GMT Power Reserve
Reference number: GRC10002AC10-001CRO
Movement: automatic, Dubois Dépraz Caliber 333 (base ETA 2897); ø 26.2 mm, height 6.45 mm; 21 jewels, 28,800 vph; power reserve 42 hours; skeletonized and engraved rotor
Functions: hours, minutes, subsidiary seconds; date; 24-hour indication (second time zone); power reserve indicator
Case: stainless steel, ø 42.5 mm, height 14.5 mm; screw-in crown and buttons; anti-reflective sapphire crystal; screw-down sapphire crystal case back; water-resistant to 100 m
Band: crocodile skin, folding clasp
Price: $8,360
Variations: Barenia leather strap

SplitRock
Reference number: SPR30001ORO0-001 CRO
Movement: automatic, Dubois Dépraz Caliber 475 (base ETA 2671); ø 31.5 mm, height 6.95 mm; 39 jewels, 28,800 vph; power reserve 42 hours; skeletonized and engraved rotor
Functions: hours, minutes, subsidiary seconds; date; chronograph
Case: rose gold, 32 x 46 mm, height 14 mm; anti-reflective sapphire crystal; sapphire crystal case back; water-resistant to 30 m
Band: crocodile skin, folding clasp
Remarks: limited edition of 21 pieces
Price: $31,105
Variations: Barenia leather strap

GrandCliff GMT Heures Retro
Reference number: GRC10001AC10-002CRO1
Movement: automatic, Dubois Dépraz Caliber 4525 (base ETA 2892); ø 30 mm, height 7.3 mm; 49 jewels, 28,800 vph; power reserve 42 hours; skeletonized and engraved rotor
Functions: hours, minutes, subsidiary seconds; large date; chronograph (retrograde 12-hour counter)
Case: stainless steel, ø 42.5 mm, height 14.5 mm; bezel set with 64 diamonds (1.28 ct); screw-in crown and buttons; anti-reflective sapphire crystal; sapphire crystal case back; water-resistant to 100 m
Band: Barenia leather, folding clasp
Price: $10,555

D. Dornblüth & Sohn

Remarkable wristwatches are lavishly created by hand in Kalbe (near Magdeburg) that feature large manually wound movements with three-quarter plates, screw balances, swan-neck fine adjustments, and a clever power reserve display called the UP and DOWN function according to vintage German watchmaking tradition.

The history of the Dornblüth caliber reaches back to the 1960s in the Erzgebirge mountains. Back then, father Dieter Dornblüth had just laid down the first sketches of his own movement on paper. However, this movement was only completed with the help of his son Dirk in a reunited Germany. Kalbe, located today in the German state Saxony-Anhalt, is not exactly a traditional hotbed of watchmaking, but Dieter and Dirk Dornblüth are not exactly planning on going into competition with Glashütte. The strengths of their small workshop are completely different.

The two new bridges of the good little Unitas base caliber they use have mutated into a three-quarter plate, the words engraved on it done so by hand and flushed out with gold. Its flat surfaces have been decorated with a clean wave pattern, and the lower "stories" of the movement are embellished with perlage. The jewel bearings of the gear train reside in gold chatons, secured by screws featuring blued heads. The hand-engraved balance cock holds an authentic screw balance in place, oscillating with a frequency of 18,000 vph, that is finely adjusted by a screw that pushes the index against a swan neck.

The watchmaking pair has recently come up with an interesting feature for their handmade movements: the Quattro Arret. During the final control phase before delivery, the Dornblüths uncovered a problem: precisely adjusting the seconds so they could regulate the watch. The Quattro Arret is a device they devised to stop the seconds without just having them hack, which is far less technically demanding. Now it is possible to precisely stop and start a Dornblüth timepiece in increments of 90 degrees, or every fifteen seconds.

99.3
Reference number: 99.3 (1) 750 RG
Movement: manually wound, Dornblüth Caliber 99.3 (base ETA Unitas 6497); ø 37 mm, height 4.4 mm; 20 jewels; 18,000 vph; indirect subsidiary seconds; combo lever, recessed corrector; screw balance; swan-neck fine adjustment; finely finished movement with screw-mounted gold chatons
Functions: hours, minutes, subsidiary seconds; date; power reserve display
Case: rose gold, ø 42 mm, height 11.5 mm; sapphire crystal; transparent case back
Band: reptile skin, buckle
Price: $14,800
Variations: stainless steel; various dial variations

99.2
Reference number: 99.2 (6) ST
Movement: manually wound, Dornblüth Caliber 99.2 (base ETA Unitas 6497); ø 37 mm, height 4.4 mm; 20 jewels; 18,000 vph; indirect subsidiary seconds; combo lever, recessed corrector; screw balance; swan-neck fine adjustment; finely finished movement with screw-mounted gold chatons
Functions: hours, minutes, subsidiary seconds; power reserve display
Case: stainless steel, ø 42 mm, height 11.5 mm; sapphire crystal; transparent case back
Band: reptile skin, buckle
Price: $7,950
Variations: stainless steel bracelet; rose gold; various dial variations

99.1
Reference number: 99.1 (2) DR ST
Movement: manually wound, Dornblüth Caliber 99.1 (base ETA Unitas 6498); ø 37 mm, height 4.4 mm; 20 jewels; 18,000 vph; indirect subsidiary seconds; combo lever, recessed corrector; screw balance; swan-neck fine adjustment; finely finished movement with screw-mounted gold chatons
Functions: hours, minutes, subsidiary seconds
Case: stainless steel, ø 42 mm, height 11.5 mm; sapphire crystal; transparent case back
Band: reptile skin, buckle
Price: $5,100
Variations: stainless steel bracelet; rose gold; various dial variations

99.4
Reference number: 99.4 (2) ST
Movement: manually wound, Dornblüth Caliber 99.4 (base ETA Unitas 6497); ø 37 mm, height 4.4 mm; 20 jewels; 18,000 vph; indirect subsidiary seconds; combo lever, recessed corrector; screw balance; swan-neck fine adjustment; finely finished movement with screw-mounted gold chatons
Functions: hours, minutes, subsidiary seconds; date
Case: stainless steel, ø 42 mm, height 11.5 mm; sapphire crystal; transparent case back
Band: reptile skin, buckle
Price: $6,850
Variations: stainless steel bracelet; rose gold; various dial variations

Doxa

In 1889, Georges Ducommun, at barely the age of twenty, founded his own re-assembly atelier in Le Locle. It was the stepping-stone to a career which might be termed typically American by a European in this day and age. Within just a few years, Ducommun's backyard workshop had been turned into a veritable factory, over whose door the proud brand name Doxa was emblazoned.

The industrious craftsman obviously knew how to enjoy the good things in life as well, for he made his home in the idyllic Château des Monts castle high above Le Locle, where today the world-famous watch museum is housed. He managed the steep path to the factory in the mornings and evenings by horse-drawn buggy—so it's no wonder that the talented designer showed a very early interest in automobiles. Ducommun was one of the first in the entire canton of Neuchâtel to possess an "iron carriage." It was his car that led him to one of his most successful business ideas: Doxa was soon manufacturing large numbers of clocks for automobile dashboards, outfitted with eight-day movements that Ducommun patented in 1908. Very clever.

These historical anecdotes were very important for the new launch of the traditional Doxa brand; thus there exists once again a pocket watch with an eight-day movement at Doxa. And there is also a sporty chronograph named for the legendary automobile race: The Coppa Milano-San Remo, which was attended by Europe's racing elite in the years between the two world wars.

A further highlight of the company's history, also commemorated by the contemporary owners, was the success of the diver's watch Sub 300T. When this watch was issued in 1967, it was clearly very different from most of the other so-called professional diver's watches. The U.S. Diving Association turned out to be a valuable consultant, and the American frogmen obviously knew exactly what they needed: a light-colored dial for mid-range diving depths, where it is not yet dark enough for luminous numerals, and a wide case base that lays securely on the arm. The special feature of this watch, however, is the two rows of numerals found on the unidirectionally rotating bezel: The inner ring of numbers is a conventional *minuterie*, but the outer set constitutes a display of depth in meters. When used with the minute display found on the inner half of the bezel, it is a functional decompression table: When, at the beginning of the dive, both markers are set to the top of the minute display, it is possible to read from the bezel that at a diving depth of 30 meters it is about time to think about slowly getting back to the surface after about 25 minutes; at 40 meters, after 15 minutes; and, correspondingly, at 20 meters, only after 50 minutes. Very, very clever.

The contemporary Doxa product developers who pulled the striking '60s design of the Sub 300T out of the drawer and are now offering it to watch collectors and traditionally minded divers in various limited editions were also very clever. The limited edition Sub 300T is delivered with a certificate signed by Clive Cussler, author of the Dirk Pitt series, whose hero of the same name wears a Doxa diving watch during his fictitious paperback adventures.

DOXA SUB 300 Tested on the rocks

Doxa

SUB 1000T Professional
Reference number: 10000330001
Movement: automatic, Doxa Caliber 24-2 (base ETA 2824-2); ø 25.6 mm, height 4.6 mm; 25 jewels; 28,800 vph
Functions: hours, minutes, sweep seconds; date
Case: stainless steel, ø 42.7 mm, height 14.6 mm; unidirectionally rotating bezel with engraved decompression table (patented); sapphire crystal; screw-in crown; water-resistant to 1000 m
Band: stainless steel, folding clasp
Remarks: limited edition of 5,000 pieces; rubber dive strap included
Price: $2,290

SUB 1000T Sharkhunter
Reference number: 10000330002
Movement: automatic, Doxa Caliber 24-2 (base ETA 2824-2); ø 25.6 mm, height 4.6 mm; 25 jewels; 28,800 vph
Functions: hours, minutes, sweep seconds; date
Case: stainless steel, ø 42.7 mm, height 14.6 mm; unidirectionally rotating bezel with engraved decompression table (patented); sapphire crystal; screw-in crown; water-resistant to 1000 m
Band: stainless steel, folding clasp
Remarks: limited edition of 5,000 pieces; rubber dive strap included
Price: $2,290

SUB 1000T Divingstar
Reference number: 10000330004
Movement: automatic, Doxa Caliber 24-2 (base ETA 2824-2); ø 25.6 mm, height 4.6 mm; 25 jewels; 28,800 vph
Functions: hours, minutes, sweep seconds; date
Case: stainless steel, ø 42.7 mm, height 14.6 mm; unidirectionally rotating bezel with engraved decompression table (patented); sapphire crystal; screw-in crown; water-resistant to 1000 m
Band: stainless steel, folding clasp
Remarks: limited edition of 5,000 pieces; rubber dive strap included
Price: $2,290

SUB 1000T Caribbean
Reference number: 10000330003
Movement: automatic, Doxa Caliber 24-2 (base ETA 2824-2); ø 25.6 mm, height 4.6 mm; 25 jewels; 28,800 vph
Functions: hours, minutes, sweep seconds; date
Case: stainless steel, ø 42.7 mm, height 14.6 mm; unidirectionally rotating bezel with engraved decompression table (patented); sapphire crystal; screw-in crown; water-resistant to 1000 m
Band: stainless steel, folding clasp
Remarks: limited edition of 5,000 pieces; rubber dive strap included
Price: $2,290

SUB 600T Professional
Reference number: 6000330005
Movement: automatic, Doxa Caliber 94-2 (base ETA 2894-2); ø 28.6 mm, height 6.1 mm; 37 jewels; 28,800 vph
Functions: hours, minutes, subsidiary seconds; chronograph; date
Case: stainless steel, ø 45 mm, height 18 mm; unidirectionally rotating bezel with engraved decompression table (patented); sapphire crystal; screw-in crown and buttons; water-resistant to 600 m
Band: stainless steel, folding clasp
Remarks: limited edition of 250 pieces; diver's rubber strap included in set
Price: $3,490
Variations: 40-year anniversary edition

SUB 600T Sharkhunter
Reference number: 6000330005
Movement: automatic, Doxa Caliber 94-2 (base ETA 2894-2); ø 28.6 mm, height 6.1 mm; 37 jewels; 28,800 vph
Functions: hours, minutes, subsidiary seconds; chronograph; date
Case: stainless steel, ø 45 mm, height 18 mm; unidirectionally rotating bezel with engraved decompression table (patented); sapphire crystal; screw-in crown and buttons; water-resistant to 600 m
Band: stainless steel, folding clasp
Remarks: limited edition of 250 pieces; diver's rubber strap included in set
Price: $3,490
Variations: 40-year anniversary edition

SUB 750T Professional
Reference number: 750GMT330002
Movement: automatic, Doxa Caliber 93-2 (base ETA 2993-2); ø 25.6 mm, height 4.6 mm; 25 jewels; 28,800 vph
Functions: hours, minutes, sweep seconds; date; three time zones
Case: stainless steel, ø 45 mm, height 13 mm; unidirectionally rotating bezel with engraved decompression table (patented); sapphire crystal; screw-in crown; water-resistant to 750 m
Band: stainless steel, folding clasp
Remarks: limited edition of 1,000 pieces
Price: $2,490
Variations: yellow dial (Divingstar model)

SUB 750T Sharkhunter
Reference number: 750GMT330003
Movement: automatic, ETA Caliber 2824-A2; ø 25.6 mm, height 4.6 mm; 25 jewels; 28,800 vph
Functions: hours, minutes, sweep seconds; date; three time zones
Case: stainless steel, ø 45 mm, height 13 mm; unidirectionally rotating bezel with engraved decompression table (patented); sapphire crystal; screw-in crown; water-resistant to 750 m
Band: stainless steel, folding clasp
Remarks: limited edition of 1,000 pieces
Price: $2,490
Variations: blue dial (Caribbean model)

Du Bois & Fils

Philippe Du Bois founded the watch company Du Bois & Fils with his sons in the family's house in Le Locle in 1785. As a merchant he had already established extensive business ties all over Europe and in the United States, providing his new watch business with an excellent start. In the nineteenth century, he pursued building up his own subsidiaries in countries such as Germany, Holland, Spain, and the United States, and Du Bois & Fils bloomed. The Frankfurt subsidiary was particularly important thanks to its proximity to the fair. The watches still in existence from this era clearly illustrate Du Bois & Fils's design tendencies: the company very obviously preferred to distribute elegant, decorative pocket watches with additional mechanisms in simple, genteel, classic cases like those that were found on Genevan luxury watches of the same time period. A very rare pocket watch by Du Bois & Fils featuring a mock pendulum can be dated from around 1800. This resting escapement outfitted with a double escape wheel caused quite an uproar at the time. However, the company's most valuable timepiece from this period was a gold one-minute tourbillon that featured a thermometer display.

For eight generations the watch brand remained remarkably true to its principles and today continues to illustrate these venerable values: the brand's watches are chiefly made in limited editions. Du Bois & Fils continues to innovate with the times—as long as it serves to extend the company's excellent tradition. Thus, current movements enrich the contemporary collection's models with interesting complications. Looking at the brand's best-sellers, one continues to find fine, elegant wristwatches of classic design. Several models have already been awarded prizes in international competitions. All the brand's watches are naturally Swiss made, created by masters of their craft.

With two centuries of history at its beck and call, Du Bois & Fils continues to count on high quality, careful details, and solid continuity. In today's world, it is important to be able to orient oneself on lasting values.

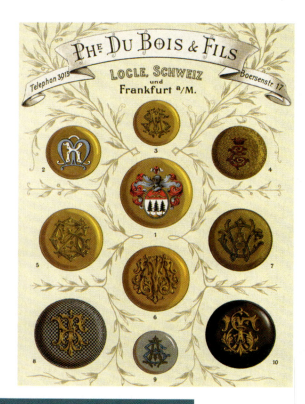

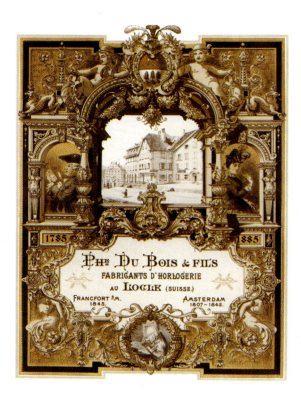

Du Bois & Fils

Le Chronographe 1910
Reference number: 38570
Movement: automatic, ETA Valjoux Caliber 7751; ø 30 mm, height 7.9 mm; 25 jewels; 28,800 vph
Functions: hours, minutes, subsidiary seconds; chronograph; date, weekday, month, moon phase display; 24-hour display
Case: red gold, ø 38 mm, height 14 mm; sapphire crystal; hinged case back
Band: reptile skin, buckle
Price: $11,745
Variations: yellow or white gold

Grande Date
Reference number: 90390
Movement: automatic, ETA Caliber 2892-A2 with module 4900 by Dubois Dépraz; ø 25.6 mm, height 7.3 mm; 49 jewels; 28,800 vph
Functions: hours, minutes, subsidiary seconds; chronograph; annual calendar with large date and month display
Case: yellow gold, ø 40 mm, height 14 mm; sapphire crystal; transparent case back
Band: reptile skin, buckle
Price: $12,145
Remarks: limited edition of 300 pieces
Variations: white gold

Montre Calendrier
Reference number: 63017
Movement: automatic, ETA Caliber 2892-A2 with module 9000 by Dubois Dépraz; ø 25.6 mm, height 6 mm; 21 jewels; 28,800 vph
Functions: hours, minutes, sweep seconds; date, weekday, month, moon phase display
Case: stainless steel, ø 40 mm, height 12 mm; sapphire crystal
Band: reptile skin, buckle
Price: $2,745
Variations: with date and moon phase only

Virage
Reference number: 45036
Movement: manually wound, La Joux-Perret Caliber 736.6; 17.5 x 25 mm, height 2.9 mm; 18 jewels; 28,800 vph; finely decorated and engraved
Functions: hours, minutes; moon phase display; power reserve indication
Case: stainless steel, 37 x 30 mm, height 9 mm; sapphire crystal; transparent case back
Band: reptile skin, buckle
Price: $5,850
Variations: yellow gold

Tonneau Grande Date
Reference number: 74002
Movement: automatic, ETA Caliber 2892-A2 with module TT 651 by Soprod; ø 25.6 mm, height 4 mm; 21 jewels; 28,800 vph; finely finished with perlage and côtes de Gèneve
Functions: hours, minutes, sweep seconds; large date; second time zone
Case: stainless steel, 42 x 35 mm, height 9 mm; sapphire crystal; transparent case back
Band: reptile skin, buckle
Price: $2,750
Variations: with complete calendar

Racing IV
Reference number: 90118
Movement: automatic, ETA Valjoux Caliber 7750; ø 30 mm, height 7.9 mm; 25 jewels; 28,800 vph; côtes de Gèneve
Functions: hours, minutes; chronograph; date
Case: stainless steel, ø 40 mm, height 14 mm; mineral crystal; transparent case back
Band: leather, buckle
Price: $2,250
Variations: white dial, black dial

Chronograph Henry Du Bois
Reference number: 72251
Movement: automatic, ETA Valjoux Caliber 7750; ø 30 mm, height 7.9 mm; 25 jewels; 28,800 vph; côtes de Gèneve
Functions: hours, minutes, subsidiary seconds; chronograph; date
Case: gold-plated stainless steel, ø 39 mm, height 14 mm; sapphire crystal; transparent case back
Band: leather, buckle
Price: $2,785
Variations: stainless steel

La Réctangulaire
Reference number: 45324
Movement: automatic, ETA Caliber 2000; ø 19.4 mm, height 3.6 mm; 20 jewels; 28,800 vph; gold-plated
Functions: hours, minutes, sweep seconds; date
Case: yellow gold, 38 x 27 mm, height 10 mm; sapphire crystal; transparent case back
Band: reptile skin, buckle
Price: $7,245
Variations: stainless steel

Dubey & Schaldenbrand

When watchmakers Georges Dubey and René Schaldenbrand invented a little spring that they found worthy of patenting on March 12, 1946, they surely never thought that the company they would form around it would still be in existence sixty years later. But a good idea never dies, and the simple mechanism they developed to enhance a stopwatch's split-seconds function became a cult object, bringing the pair a reputation as innovative watchmakers offering classic, affordable timepieces. But it was perhaps the visible spring on the front of the watch's dial that fascinated people most.

Dubey, an instructor at the reputable school of watchmaking in La Chaux-de-Fonds, and watchmaker Schaldenbrand had wound the spirally shaped spring around the stem of the sweep second hand of a Landeron chronograph caliber. This little spring was the ingenious main ingredient of the reset system for the large second hand of the rattrapante. This "people's rattrapante," a mechanism less expensive to manufacture than the traditional variation, took the hearts of watch fans by storm, and its official name, Index Mobile, became synonymous with that of the Dubey & Schaldenbrand brand.

Today the Dubey & Schaldenbrand philosophy is not only cemented in the ingenious invention of its founding fathers, but also rests in the anachronistic, affectionate care for production founded on the principles of the classic art of making beautiful watches. The owner of the company, Cinette Robert, a daughter of the watchmaker dynasty Meylan-LeCoultre and an absolute expert on early watch masterpieces, has an impressive talent for combining the technology of modern mechanical movements with timeless and classic lines.

Inspired by a new feel for hues and textures available in this modern age of watchmaking, Robert has now created a colorful model that appeals not only to a new generation of watch fans, but also to dyed-in-the-wool mechanical traditionalists looking for something a little different.

The new Coupe's stately case perfectly hugs the wrist thanks to its aerodynamic shape. But the stunning dial is actually what immediately draws the eye to this timepiece. This component is as meticulously finished as the timepiece's movement, featuring twenty-four shining guilloché rays emanating from the center, intertwined with a wavy guilloché pattern, known in Switzerland as *vagues*, giving the white dial its very special gleam. The eye-catcher is, however, the twelve rare, painstakingly hand-painted rainbow numerals that range from "warm" hues of red and yellow at the top of the dial to "cold" colors green, blue, and violet opposite them. These numerals of the Rainbow Coupe interplay with the oval-shaped minute scale encircling the center portion of the dial and containing the subdial for subsidiary seconds at the bottom and the double window for the large date at the top, a style that makes the date extremely legible without being overly obtrusive. The numerals are also available in a silver or gold powdered style.

This model's hands are also of special note, for they are based on a design found in a vintage Dubey & Schaldenbrand advertisement. "La montre DS marche bien," it read: "the DS watch works well." And it still does, outfitted as this model is with a finely finished ETA-based automatic movement with a chronometer-quality escapement.

Dubey & Schaldenbrand

Coupé 06
Reference number: ACO/ST/SIC
Movement: automatic, ETA Caliber 2892-A2, modified; ø 25.6 mm, height 4.8 mm; 26 jewels; 28,800 vph
Functions: hours, minutes, subsidiary seconds; large date
Case: stainless steel, domed, 38 x 50 mm, height 12.4 mm; sapphire crystal; transparent case back
Band: reptile skin, buckle
Price: $5,950
Variations: rose gold

Coupé Caprice
Reference number: ACOC/ST/BKG
Movement: automatic, ETA Caliber 2892-A2, modified; ø 25.6 mm, height 4.9 mm; 22 jewels; 28,800 vph
Functions: hours, minutes, sweep seconds; large date; power reserve display
Case: stainless steel, domed, 38 x 50 mm, height 12.4 mm; sapphire crystal; transparent case back; crown on the left side of the case
Band: reptile skin, buckle
Price: $6,950

Aerodyn Date
Reference number: ACL/RG/WHG
Movement: automatic, ETA Caliber 2895; ø 25.6 mm, height 4.35 mm; 30 jewels; 28,800 vph
Functions: hours, minutes, subsidiary seconds; large date
Case: rose gold, domed, 33 x 44 mm, height 11.5 mm; sapphire crystal
Band: reptile skin, buckle
Price: $10,950
Variations: stainless steel ($4,750)

Aerodyn Duo
Reference number: ADUO/ST/BKG
Movement: automatic, ETA Caliber 2892-A2, modified; ø 25.6 mm, height 4.9 mm; 26 jewels; 28,800 vph
Functions: hours, minutes, sweep seconds; date; second time zone (24-hour display)
Case: stainless steel, domed, 33 x 44 mm, height 11.7 mm; sapphire crystal
Band: reptile skin, buckle
Price: $4,750
Variations: rose gold

Aerochrono
Reference number: AERO/RG/SIG
Movement: automatic, ETA Caliber 2094; ø 23.9 mm, height 5.5 mm; 33 jewels; 28,800 vph
Functions: hours, minutes, subsidiary seconds; chronograph; date
Case: rose gold, domed, 33 x 44 mm, height 12.2 mm; sapphire crystal; transparent case back
Band: reptile skin, buckle
Price: $13,950
Variations: stainless steel ($6,350)

Gran' Chrono Astro
Reference number: AGCA/RG/SIB
Movement: automatic, ETA Valjoux Caliber 7751; ø 30 mm, height 7.9 mm; 25 jewels; 28,800 vph; hand-engraved bridges, rotor skeletonized with company logo
Functions: hours, minutes; chronograph; date, day, month, moon phase
Case: rose gold, domed, 38 x 50 mm, height 15.5 mm; sapphire crystal; transparent case back
Band: reptile skin, buckle
Price: $17,500
Variations: stainless steel

Spiral Cap
Reference number: SCAP/ST/WHB
Movement: automatic, ETA Caliber 2892-A2, modified; ø 25.6 mm, height 4.9 mm; 22 jewels; 28,800 vph; second hand with a visible, though functionless, return spring
Functions: hours, minutes, sweep seconds; large date; power reserve indicator
Case: stainless steel, with movable lugs, ø 35.5 mm, height 10.7 mm; sapphire crystal; transparent case back; crown on left side of case with sapphire cabochon
Band: ostrich skin, buckle
Price: $5,450

Diplomatic
Reference number: CCDI/RG/WHB
Movement: automatic, ETA Caliber 2892-A2, modified; ø 25.6 mm, height 4.9 mm; 23 jewels; 28,800 vph
Functions: hours, minutes, sweep seconds; date; second time zone (24-hour display)
Case: stainless steel, 34 x 34 mm, height 9.9 mm; sapphire crystal
Band: reptile skin, buckle
Price: upon request
Variations: rose gold ($8,500)

Roger Dubuis

The meteoric developmental speed of this *manufacture* located just outside Geneva and the incredible frequency of its new introductions—even technical ones—seem absolutely sensational to the traditional, rather conservative watch industry.

This company was founded in 1995 as SOGEM SA (Société Genevoise des Montres) by name giver Roger Dubuis and its current president Carlos Dias, though it has only been a *manufacture* since 1999. "We place very strict demands upon ourselves," Dias explains, "which is why I only wanted to use this term—for which I have the utmost respect—when it was truly justified."

Today, Roger Dubuis not only develops all of its own movements (now twenty-eight different mechanical calibers), but also produces just about all of their individual components in-house, from the base plate to the escapement and including balance springs. All of this *manufacture's* movements bear the Seal of Geneva as a statement of quality and mark of origin.

The company boasts 450 employees, a good thirty of whom work in quality control, while another 180 professional tool makers and machinery specialists operate more than 100 highly complex and modern production machines. Up to 1.4 million movement components are permanently in production at the factory.

Dias, the restless lord of this manor, has a lot of plans for Roger Dubuis Manufacture, currently including two more large extensions to the factory—despite all the recent additions that have been made. Some have had trouble keeping up with Dias's terrific pace, including Roger Dubuis himself, who has gone into well-deserved retirement. At the beginning, these two created a complete collection of unusual watches in no time flat—watches with unheard-of dimensions and incomparable display complications.

Brave design and clever technical solutions have remained the hallmarks of this brand, even if the model families seem to be exploding under Dias's creative exuberance: The collection now comprises more than 7,000 references, a number that can be chalked up to some of the extreme limitations of individual variations, of course. Select models of high technical complexity are produced in editions of only twenty-eight pieces. Luxurious avant-garde timepieces are restricted to amounts of 280, and trend-setting highlights are usually limited to 888 units.

Meanwhile, Dias has even begun using the brand name Roger Dubuis for establishing a jewelry line and various objets d'art. The path to success has led through powerful shapes, stately dimensions, and a pinch of humor that reveals the desire to create without taking oneself too seriously. Perhaps it is the delicate balance between frivolity and know-how that has allotted Roger Dubuis's watches their exceptional place in the industry: without the Meyrin-based *manufacture's* technical and design competence, these extreme horological complications may not have been dared. Others who may theoretically have the technical know-how for such constructions often don't have the unbridled joy in creation that is necessary to make horological masterpieces housed in cases as big as a bar of Swiss chocolate or packed within a cross from a Swiss flag.

Roger Dubuis

Excalibur Double Tourbillon
Reference number: EX45 01 0 N9.671
Movement: manually wound, RD Caliber 01; ø 37 mm; 52 jewels; 21,600 vph; two flying one-minute tourbillons coupled via a differential gear; Seal of Geneva
Functions: hours (jump, retrograde), minutes (retrograde); power reserve display (on back)
Case: white gold, ø 45 mm, height 16 mm; sapphire crystal; transparent case back
Band: reptile skin, folding clasp
Remarks: limited edition of 28 pieces
Price: $226,300

Excalibur Tourbillon Minute Repeater
Reference number: EX45 08 5 G33.2A
Movement: automatic, RD Caliber 08; ø 33 mm; 42 jewels; 21,600 vph; flying one-minute tourbillon; two micro rotors; Seal of Geneva
Functions: hours, minutes; hour, quarter hour and minute repeater
Case: rose gold, ø 45 mm, height 16.3 mm; sapphire crystal; transparent case back
Band: reptile skin, folding clasp
Remarks: limited edition of 28 pieces
Price: $454,900

Excalibur Split-Seconds Chronograph
Reference number: EX45 79 9 9.71R
Movement: automatic, RD Caliber 79; ø 30 mm; 38 jewels; 21,600 vph; platinum micro rotor; column-wheel control of the chronograph functions; Seal of Geneva
Functions: hours, minutes, subsidiary seconds; split-seconds chronograph
Case: stainless steel, ø 45 mm, height 15.3 mm; sapphire crystal; transparent case back
Band: rubber, folding clasp
Remarks: limited edition of 280 pieces
Price: $69,400

Excalibur Chronograph
Reference number: EX45 78 7.9.3.7AR
Movement: automatic, RD Caliber 78; ø 30 mm; 36 jewels; 21,600 vph; micro rotor; column-wheel control of the chronograph functions; Seal of Geneva
Functions: hours, minutes, subsidiary seconds; chronograph
Case: titanium/stainless steel, ø 45 mm, height 15.3 mm; stainless steel bezel; sapphire crystal; transparent case back
Band: rubber, folding clasp
Remarks: limited edition of 280 pieces
Price: $27,800

Excalibur World Time
Reference number: EX45 1448 5 3.7ATT.28
Movement: automatic, RD Caliber 1448; ø 25.6 mm; 33 jewels; 28,800 vph; Seal of Geneva
Functions: hours, minutes (central); two additional time zones with reference city display
Case: rose gold, ø 45 mm, height 13.8 mm; sapphire crystal; transparent case back
Band: reptile skin, folding clasp
Remarks: limited edition of 28 pieces
Price: $51,800

Excalibur Just for Kings
Reference number: EX45 06 5 3 7A
Movement: manually wound, RD Caliber 06; ø 33.8 mm; 53 jewels; 21,600 vph; flying one-minute tourbillon; one-button chronograph; Seal of Geneva
Functions: hours, minutes, subsidiary seconds (on tourbillon cage); chronograph with two retrograde counters; large date
Case: rose gold, ø 45 mm, height 16 mm; sapphire crystal; transparent case back; crown with chronograph button
Band: reptile skin, folding clasp
Remarks: limited edition of 28 pieces
Price: $259,900

Excalibur Minute Repeater Perpetual Calendar
Reference number: EX45 0829 0 N9C.71R
Movement: automatic, RD Caliber 0829; ø 33.8 mm, height 8.8 mm; 52 jewels; 21,600 vph; flying one-minute tourbillon; two micro rotors; Seal of Geneva
Functions: hours, minutes; perpetual calendar with large date, weekday, month, moon phase, leap year, 24-hour display (second time zone), day/night indication; minute repeater
Case: white gold, ø 45 mm, height 17 mm; sapphire crystal; transparent case back
Band: reptile skin, folding clasp
Remarks: limited edition of 28 pieces
Price: $543,400

Excalibur Ladies' Tourbillon
Reference number: EX39 09 5 3.7A
Movement: manually wound, RD Caliber 09; ø 23.6 mm; 19 jewels; 21,600 vph; flying one-minute tourbillon; Seal of Geneva
Functions: hours, minutes, subsidiary seconds (on tourbillon cage)
Case: rose gold, ø 39 mm, height 13 mm; sapphire crystal; transparent case back
Band: reptile skin, folding clasp
Remarks: limited edition of 28 pieces
Price: $90,700

Roger Dubuis

Excalibur
Reference number: EX39 21 0 FFD N91D 7AH-HE
Movement: automatic, RD Caliber 21; ø 23.6 mm, height 3.8 mm; 29 jewels; 28,800 vph; Seal of Geneva
Functions: hours, minutes, subsidiary seconds
Case: white gold, ø 39 mm, height 13 mm; bezel, case lugs, and case sides set with diamonds; sapphire crystal; transparent case back; crown set with ruby cabochon
Band: reptile skin, folding clasp
Remarks: limited edition of 28 pieces; dial set with a diamond heart and mother-of-pearl inlay
Price: $66,800

Excalibur
Reference number: EX39 21 9 15.7AR
Movement: automatic, RD Caliber 21; ø 23.6 mm, height 3.8 mm; 29 jewels; 28,800 vph; Seal of Geneva
Functions: hours, minutes, subsidiary seconds
Case: stainless steel, ø 39 mm, height 13 mm; sapphire crystal; transparent case back; screw-in crown
Band: reptile skin, folding clasp
Remarks: limited edition of 28 pieces
Price: $14,500

Excalibur
Reference number: EX39 21 0-FFD N1D.7A
Movement: automatic, RD Caliber 21; ø 23.6 mm, height 3.8 mm; 29 jewels; 28,800 vph; Seal of Geneva
Functions: hours, minutes
Case: white gold, ø 39 mm, height 13 mm; bezel, case lugs, and case sides set with diamonds; sapphire crystal; transparent case back; crown set with ruby cabochon
Band: Raso calfskin, folding clasp
Remarks: limited edition of 28 pieces; mother-of-pearl dial paved with diamonds
Price: $56,600

Sympathie Chronograph
Reference number: SYM43 78 9 9R.53
Movement: automatic, RD Caliber 78; ø 30 mm; 36 jewels; 28,800 vph; platinum micro rotor; column-wheel control of chronograph functions; Seal of Geneva
Functions: hours, minutes, subsidiary seconds; chronograph
Case: white gold, ø 43 mm, height 15.4 mm; sapphire crystal; transparent case back
Band: reptile skin, buckle
Remarks: limited edition of 280 pieces
Price: $25,100

Hommage Perpetual Calendar
Reference number: HO43 1429 0 5R.7A
Movement: automatic, RD Caliber 1429; ø 26.2 mm; 31 jewels; 21,600 vph; Seal of Geneva
Functions: hours, minutes; perpetual calendar with date, weekday, month, moon phase, leap year; 24-hour display (second time zone), day/night indication
Case: white gold, ø 43 mm, height 13 mm; sapphire crystal; transparent case back
Band: reptile skin, buckle
Remarks: limited edition of 28 pieces
Price: $108,700

MuchMore Flying Tourbillon
Reference number: M34 09 5 OB.RD.71
Movement: manually wound, RD Caliber 09; ø 23.3 mm; 19 jewels; 21,600 vph; flying one-minute tourbillon; Seal of Geneva
Functions: hours, minutes
Case: rose gold, domed, 56 x 34 mm, height 14 mm; sapphire crystal; transparent case back
Band: reptile skin, buckle
Remarks: limited edition of 28 pieces
Price: $86,800

Golden Square
Reference number: G40 03 7 GN9G.61
Movement: manually wound, RD Caliber 03; ø 33.8 mm; 27 jewels; 21,600 vph; flying one-minute tourbillon; Seal of Geneva
Functions: hours, minutes, subsidiary seconds (on tourbillon cage); large date; power reserve indication
Case: polished titanium, domed, 40 x 40 mm, height 14 mm; sapphire crystal; transparent case back
Band: leather, folding clasp
Remarks: limited edition of 280 pieces
Price: $80,400

Golden Square Jewellery
Reference number: G37 09 0-SDC DGCN9
Movement: manually wound, RD Caliber 09; ø 25.6 mm; 19 jewels; 21,600 vph; flying one-minute tourbillon; Seal of Geneva
Functions: hours, minutes, subsidiary seconds (on tourbillon cage)
Case: white gold, domed, 37 x 37 mm, height 14 mm; bezel and strap lugs set with brilliant-cut diamonds; sapphire crystal; transparent case back
Band: reptile skin, folding clasp
Remarks: limited edition of 28 pieces; dial in chess board pattern of diamond pavé
Price: $115,300

Roger Dubuis

Golden Square Jewellery
Reference number: G34 21 5 FFD DGCN9.61
Movement: automatic, RD Caliber 21; ø 23.6 mm, height 3.8 mm; 29 jewels; 28,800 vph; Seal of Geneva
Functions: hours, minutes
Case: rose gold, domed, 37 x 37 mm, height 14 mm; bezel, strap lugs, and case sides set with brilliant-cut diamonds; sapphire crystal; transparent case back
Band: reptile skin with Swarovsky stones, folding clasp
Remarks: limited edition of 28 pieces; dial in chess board pattern of diamond pavé
Price: $42,400

EasyDiver
Reference number: SE48 05 7.N/9 K9/K10
Movement: manually wound, RD Caliber 05; ø 33.8 mm; 20 jewels; 21,600 vph; flying one-minute tourbillon; Seal of Geneva
Functions: hours, minutes, sweep seconds
Case: titanium, ø 48 mm, height 16 mm; unidirectionally rotating bezel in stainless steel with 60-minute divisions; sapphire crystal; transparent case back
Band: rubber, folding clasp
Remarks: limited edition of 280 pieces
Price: $69,000

AcquaMare
Reference number: GA35 21 9 1.13C
Movement: automatic, RD Caliber 21; ø 25.6 mm; 29 jewels; 28,800 vph; Seal of Geneva
Functions: hours, minutes
Case: stainless steel, domed, 35 x 35 mm, height 15 mm; bezel with 60-minute divisions; sapphire crystal; screw-in crown; water-resistant to 30 atm
Band: rubber, folding clasp
Remarks: limited edition of 888 pieces
Price: $12,800

SeaMore
Reference number: MS34 21 9 9.53C
Movement: automatic, RD Caliber 14; ø 25.6 mm, height 3.43 mm; 31 jewels; 28,800 vph; Seal of Geneva
Functions: hours, minutes
Case: stainless steel, domed, 43 x 43 mm, height 15 mm; bezel in white gold with 60-minute divisions; sapphire crystal; screw-in crown; water-resistant to 30 atm
Band: reptile skin, buckle
Remarks: limited edition of 280 pieces
Price: $14,000

TooMuch
Reference number: T22 54 5 FFD NR1LOD25
Movement: manually wound, RD Caliber 54; ø 18 mm; 19 jewels; 21,600 vph; Seal of Geneva
Functions: hours, minutes
Case: rose gold, domed, 22 x 34 mm, height 7 mm; bezel, strap lugs, and case sides set with brilliant-cut diamonds; sapphire crystal
Band: reptile skin, folding clasp
Remarks: mother-of-pearl dial with ruby and diamond pavé; limited edition of 28 pieces
Price: $39,800

TooMuch
Reference number: T26 86 0-FD NR1LO.D/25
Movement: quartz, RD Caliber 86
Functions: hours, minutes
Case: white gold, domed, 26 x 38 mm, height 7 mm; bezel set with brilliant-cut diamonds; sapphire crystal
Band: white gold, completely paved with diamonds, folding clasp
Remarks: dial set with rubies; limited edition of 28 pieces
Price: $37,400

Follow Me
Reference number: F17 54 0-SDC N1.63
Movement: manually wound, RD Caliber 54; ø 18 mm; 19 jewels; 21,600 vph; Seal of Geneva
Functions: hours, minutes
Case: white gold, cross-shaped, domed, 40 x 40 mm, height 10 mm; bezel and strap lugs set with diamonds; sapphire crystal; transparent case back
Band: double reptile skin, double buckle
Remarks: limited edition of 28 pieces
Price: $32,900
Variations: various dial versions

Golden Square
Reference number: G34 98 5-SDC GCN114.7A
Movement: manually wound, RD Caliber 98; ø 23.3 mm; 19 jewels; 21,600 vph; Seal of Geneva
Functions: hours, minutes
Case: rose gold, domed, 34 x 34 mm, height 9 mm; bezel set with brilliant-cut diamonds; sapphire crystal
Band: reptile skin, buckle
Remarks: limited edition of 28 pieces; mother-of-pearl inlay on dial
Price: $32,100
Variations: white gold; various dial variations

Ebel

In 1911, Eugène and Alice Blum, née Levy, founded Ebel. The four letters of their new brand name were taken from their own: Eugène Blum et Levy. After its founding in La Chaux-de-Fonds, Ebel made a name for itself among the established brands above all as a supplier for quality movements. The originality and technical perfection of the brand's models were awarded prizes at many international watch fairs.

Charles Blum, son of the founders, took over Ebel in 1932. Striving for care and precision in his manufacturing, he worked with a team of talented watchmakers. He extended Ebel's collection with great attention and sensibility to the demands of the market, putting creativity and quality in the foreground and even launching the brand internationally.

In the 1970s, the Swiss watch industry was experiencing a serious crisis. When Pierre-Alain Blum, grandson of the founding couple, took over the reins, he banked on innovation. Reducing the number of models in the collection, he launched the legendary Sport Classique in 1977—today known as the Ebel Classic. Absolutely unmistakable, marked as it is by its inimitable wave-design bracelet in combination with a monocoque case, the model became a design icon of the modern era. These "architects of time" have found the way back to their own style with the Ebel Classic line after it looked for a while as if the brand wanted to burn every bridge to the past. Since being integrated into the Movado Group Inc. (MGI) in 2004, the brand has returned to its roots, its traditional philosophy, and its characteristic elements: soft, sensual shapes, flowing lines, and balanced proportions paired with high quality standards and exacting technology. Coming out with its own demanding, complicated watches outfitted with *manufacture* movements, Ebel today is well on the way to winning back a place around the top of the luxury watch segment.

1911 BTR Chronograph
Reference number: 5137L73/15335145
Movement: automatic, Ebel Caliber 137; ø 31 mm, height 6.4 mm; 27 jewels; 28,800 vph; officially certified chronometer (COSC)
Functions: hours, minutes, subsidiary seconds; chronograph; date
Case: rose gold, ø 44.5 mm, height 13 mm; rubber-coated bezel; sapphire crystal; transparent case back; screw-in crown; buttons with rubber elements; water-resistant to 10 atm
Band: reptile skin, folding clasp
Price: $23,900
Variations: stainless steel with rubber strap

1911 BTR Chronograph
Reference number: B137L73/15335N92
Movement: automatic, Ebel Caliber 137; ø 31 mm, height 6.4 mm; 27 jewels; 28,800 vph; officially certified chronometer (COSC)
Functions: hours, minutes, subsidiary seconds; chronograph; date
Case: titanium, ø 44.5 mm, height 13 mm; rubber-coated bezel; sapphire crystal; transparent case back; screw-in crown; buttons with rubber elements; water-resistant to 10 atm
Band: synthetic, folding clasp
Price: $7,700
Variations: various dial and band variations

1911 BTR Chronograph
Reference number: 5139L72/15135145
Movement: automatic, Ebel Caliber 139 (base Ebel 137); ø 31 mm, height 7.4 mm; 27 jewels; 28,800 vph; officially certified chronometer (COSC)
Functions: hours, minutes, subsidiary seconds; chronograph; date
Case: rose gold, ø 44.5 mm, height 13.6 mm; bezel engraved with tachymeter scale; sapphire crystal; transparent case back; screw-in crown; buttons with rubber elements; water-resistant to 10 atm
Band: reptile skin, folding clasp
Remarks: limited edition of 100 pieces
Price: $26,800
Variations: stainless steel

1911 BTR Perpetual Calendar
Reference number: 5288L70/0335186
Movement: automatic, Ebel Caliber 288 (base Ebel 137); ø 31 mm, height 8 mm; 27 jewels; 28,800 vph; officially certified COSC chronometer
Functions: hours, minutes, subsidiary seconds; chronograph; perpetual calendar with date, weekday, month, astronomical moon phase display, leap year
Case: rose gold, ø 44.5 mm, height 14.3 mm; sapphire crystal; transparent case back; screw-in crown; water-resistant to 10 atm
Band: reptile skin, folding clasp
Remarks: limited edition of 20 pieces
Price: $47,750
Variations: limited edition of 20 pieces in white gold; stainless steel

1911 Discovery
Reference number: 9750L62/53B60
Movement: automatic, Ebel Caliber 750 (base ETA Valjoux 7750); ø 30 mm, height 7.9 mm; 29 jewels; 28,800 vph; officially certified chronometer (COSC)
Functions: hours, minutes, subsidiary seconds; chronograph; date, weekday
Case: stainless steel, ø 43 mm, height 14.2 mm; bezel with tachymeter scale; sapphire crystal; screw-in crown; water-resistant to 10 atm
Band: leather, folding clasp
Price: $4,200
Variations: rubber strap; stainless steel/yellow gold on leather strap or link bracelet

Ebel Classic Hexagon GMT
Reference number: 9301F60/5335P06GS
Movement: automatic, Ebel Caliber 301; ø 26.2 mm, height 5.25 mm; 21 jewels; 28,800 vph
Functions: hours, minutes, sweep seconds; large date; 24-hour display (second time zone)
Case: stainless steel, ø 45.4 mm, height 11.2 mm; sapphire crystal; water-resistant to 5 atm
Band: leather, folding clasp
Price: $3,850

Ebel Classic Hexagon Régulateur
Reference number: 9300F61/6335P86US
Movement: automatic, Ebel Caliber 300; ø 26.2 mm, height 5.25 mm; 21 jewels; 28,800 vph
Functions: off-center hours, minutes, subsidiary seconds
Case: stainless steel, ø 45.4 mm, height 11.2 mm; sapphire crystal; water-resistant to 5 atm
Band: leather, folding clasp
Price: $3,850

Brasilia Gent Chrono
Reference number: 9126M52/54BR35606
Movement: automatic, Ebel Caliber 126 (base ETA 2894-A2); ø 28 mm, height 6.1 mm; 37 jewels; 28,800 vph
Functions: hours, minutes, subsidiary seconds; chronograph; date
Case: stainless steel, 44 x 32.5 mm, height 13.4 mm; sapphire crystal; rubber cap on buttons; water-resistant to 5 atm
Band: rubber, folding clasp
Price: $4,750
Variations: various dial and band variations; as three-handed automatic timepiece

Eberhard & Co.

Watches made by Eberhard & Co. combine Swiss precision with Italian flair for elegance, and this brand's name has been inseparably linked with sports timekeeping from its early days. Just a few years after the company was founded in the Swiss mountain town of La Chaux-de-Fonds in 1887, Eberhard was commissioned to time one of the first competitive motor races, with the result that the chronograph specialists soon earned an excellent reputation among car enthusiasts as well as watch aficionados.

Special models have recently strengthened this reputation for connoisseurs. Two examples are the Tazio Nuvolari and Tazio Nuvolari Vanderbilt Cup, chronographs that the founder's successor, a motor sports enthusiast, named after the wiry race driver from Mantua. The watches of this collection commemorate this popular Italian hero, known as the Flying Mantuan, who piloted his car to numerous successes in the 1930s. Developments such as the Traversetolo, an extra-large manually wound watch containing a vintage *manufacture* caliber, prove not only Eberhard's sense of tradition but also its soft spot for collectors with smaller pockets.

The year 2007 was a historical one for La Maison Suisse d'Horlogerie Eberhard & Co.: it was this brand's 120th anniversary. These 120 years have been marked by a special passion for precise and fascinating art: 120 years of a glorious past that aids the brand in mastering the challenges of the future, and 120 years that have been marked by a timeless personality.

Since its founding in 1887, Eberhard & Co. has used these values as its sounding board for the creation of classic, but also innovative, watch models that mirror the complete richness of a legendary history. To celebrate this important milestone, Eberhard & Co. has created a series of surprising initiatives in various areas, from advertising in cinemas to special events climaxing in the launch of a select horological specialty: a unique chronograph with a special movement that was created just for this anniversary.

Eberhard & Co.

Chrono 4
Reference number: 31041
Movement: automatic, Eberhard Caliber EB 200 (base ETA 2894-2); ø 33 mm, height 7.5 mm; 53 jewels; 28,800 vph; four totalizers arranged in a row
Functions: hours, minutes, subsidiary seconds; chronograph; date; 24-hour display
Case: stainless steel, ø 40 mm, height 13.8 mm; sapphire crystal; screw-in crown; water-resistant to 5 atm
Band: reptile skin, buckle
Price: $4,850
Variations: stainless steel bracelet

Chrono 4
Reference number: 31041
Movement: automatic, Eberhard Caliber EB 200 (base ETA 2894-2); ø 33 mm, height 7.5 mm; 53 jewels; 28,800 vph; four totalizers arranged in a row
Functions: hours, minutes, subsidiary seconds; chronograph; date; 24-hour display
Case: stainless steel, ø 40 mm, height 13.8 mm; sapphire crystal; screw-in crown; water-resistant to 5 atm
Band: stainless steel, folding clasp
Price: $5,520
Variations: reptile skin strap

Chrono 4 Temerario
Reference number: 31047
Movement: automatic, Eberhard Caliber EB 250 (base ETA 2894-2); 33 x 28 mm, height 7.5 mm; 53 jewels; 28,800 vph; four totalizers arranged in a row; crown located between upper lugs
Functions: hours, minutes, subsidiary seconds; chronograph; date; 24-hour display
Case: stainless steel, 41.5 x 37 mm, height 12.9 mm; sapphire crystal
Band: reptile skin, folding clasp
Price: $6,500
Variations: stainless steel bracelet ($6,800)

Chrono 4 Bellissimo Coeur Vitré
Reference number: 31043
Movement: automatic, Eberhard Caliber EB 200 (base ETA 2894-2); ø 33 mm, height 7.5 mm; 53 jewels; 28,800 vph; four totalizers arranged in a row; finely finished movement, rotor with côtes de Genève
Functions: hours, minutes, subsidiary seconds; chronograph; date; 24-hour display
Case: stainless steel, ø 40 mm, height 14 mm; sapphire crystal; transparent case back; screw-in crown; water-resistant to 5 atm
Band: reptile skin, buckle
Price: $5,130
Variations: stainless steel bracelet ($5,780)

Chrono 4 Bellissimo
Reference number: 39060
Movement: automatic, Eberhard Caliber EB 200 (base ETA 2894-2); ø 33 mm, height 7.5 mm; 53 jewels; 28,800 vph; four totalizers arranged in a row; finely finished movement, rotor with côtes de Genève
Functions: hours, minutes, subsidiary seconds; chronograph; date; 24-hour display
Case: white gold, ø 40 mm, height 14 mm; sapphire crystal; transparent case back; screw-in crown
Band: reptile skin, buckle
Price: $ 11,650

Tazio Nuvolari Gold Car Collection
Reference number: 31037
Movement: automatic, ETA Valjoux Caliber 7750; ø 30 mm, height 7.9 mm; 25 jewels; 28,800 vph
Functions: hours, minutes; chronograph
Case: stainless steel, ø 43 mm, height 16.3 mm; bezel engraved with tachymeter scale; sapphire crystal; transparent case back
Band: stainless steel, folding clasp
Price: $4,700
Variations: reptile skin strap ($3,880)

Tazio Nuvolari Vanderbilt Cup
Reference number: 31045
Movement: automatic, Eberhard Caliber 8102 (base ETA Valjoux 7750); ø 30 mm, height 7.9 mm; 25 jewels; 28,800 vph; chronograph reset via crown button
Functions: hours, minutes, subsidiary seconds; chronograph
Case: stainless steel, ø 42 mm, height 16.3 mm; sapphire crystal; transparent case back
Band: leather, buckle
Price: $5,780
Variations: stainless steel bracelet ($6,320); rose gold with leather strap

Extra-Fort Roue à Colonnes Grand Date
Reference number: 30062
Movement: automatic, Eberhard Caliber 8150 (base ETA Valjoux 7750); ø 30 mm, height 7.9 mm; 25 jewels; 28,800 vph; column-wheel control of chronograph functions
Functions: hours, minutes, subsidiary seconds; chronograph; large date
Case: rose gold, ø 41 mm, height 15 mm; sapphire crystal; transparent case back
Band: reptile skin, buckle
Price: $ 11,600

Eberhard & Co.

Extra-Fort Rattrapante Edition Limitée
Reference number: 31049
Movement: automatic, Eberhard Caliber 8601 (base ETA Valjoux 7750); ø 30 mm, height 8.4 mm; 31 jewels; 28,800 vph; rhodium-plated rotor; côtes de Genève
Functions: hours, minutes, subsidiary seconds; split-seconds chronograph
Case: stainless steel, ø 41.2 mm, height 15.3 mm; sapphire crystal; screw-in crown; water-resistant to 5 atm
Band: reptile skin, buckle
Price: $12,420
Variations: stainless steel bracelet ($12,980)

Extra Fort Grande Date
Reference number: 41024
Movement: automatic, Eberhard Caliber 3532 (base ETA 2892-A2); ø 25.6 mm, height 5.1 mm; 26 jewels; 28,800 vph
Functions: hours, minutes, subsidiary seconds; large date
Case: stainless steel, ø 37.5 mm, height 10.25 mm; sapphire crystal; transparent case back; screw-in crown; water-resistant to 5 atm
Band: reptile skin, buckle
Price: $3,260
Variations: stainless steel bracelet; rose gold; various dial versions

Extra Fort Grande Date RDM
Reference number: 41036
Movement: automatic, Eberhard Caliber 3531 (base ETA 2892-A2); ø 25.6 mm, height 5.1 mm; 22 jewels; 28,800 vph
Functions: hours, minutes, sweep seconds; large date; power reserve display
Case: stainless steel, ø 39 mm, height 10.7 mm; sapphire crystal; transparent case back; screw-in crown; water-resistant to 5 atm
Band: reptile skin, buckle
Price: $3,620
Variations: stainless steel bracelet; white or rose gold

Extra Fort Grande Date Édition Bleuet
Reference number: 41037
Movement: automatic, ETA Caliber 3531 (base ETA 2892-A2); ø 25.6 mm, height 4.95 mm; 22 jewels; 28,800 vph; rotor with blue outline; côtes de Genève
Functions: hours, minutes, sweep seconds; date; power reserve display
Case: stainless steel, domed, ø 39 mm, height 10.6 mm; sapphire crystal; transparent case back; water-resistant to 5 atm
Band: reptile skin, buckle
Price: $3,850
Variations: stainless steel bracelet

Scafodat
Reference number: 41025
Movement: automatic, ETA Caliber 2824-2; ø 26 mm, height 4.6 mm; 25 jewels; 28,800 vph
Functions: hours, minutes, sweep seconds; date
Case: stainless steel, ø 44 mm, height 15 mm; bidirectionally rotating ring under crystal, settable via screw-in crown; sapphire crystal; screw-in crown
Band: stainless steel, folding clasp with wetsuit extension
Remarks: comes with rubber strap in set
Price: $4,650
Variations: rubber strap

Chrono Traversetolo
Reference number: 31051
Movement: automatic, ETA Caliber A07.211; ø 37 mm, height 7.9 mm; 25 jewels; 28,800 vph; côtes de Genève
Functions: hours, minutes, subsidiary seconds; date; chronograph
Case: stainless steel, ø 43 mm, height 14.5 mm; sapphire crystal; transparent case back
Band: stainless steel, folding clasp
Price: upon request
Variations: reptile skin or rubber strap

Traversetolo Vitré
Reference number: 21020 VZ
Movement: manually wound, ETA Unitas Caliber 6498; ø 36.6 mm, height 4.5 mm; 17 jewels; 21,600 vph; finely finished, côtes de Genève
Functions: hours, minutes, subsidiary seconds
Case: stainless steel, ø 43 mm, height 10.7 mm; sapphire crystal; transparent case back
Band: leather, buckle
Price: $1,900
Variations: stainless steel bracelet

8 Days
Reference number: 21017
Movement: manually wound, Eberhard Caliber EB 896 (base ETA Peseux 7001, modified); ø 34 mm, height 5 mm; 25 jewels; 21,600 vph; two mainsprings; power reserve 192 hours (8 days)
Functions: hours, minutes, subsidiary seconds; power reserve display
Case: stainless steel, ø 39.4 mm, height 11.55 mm; sapphire crystal
Band: stainless steel, folding clasp
Price: $3,100
Variations: leather strap; yellow gold

Stylus 2008 Annual
Writing Instruments Directory

The editorial team of *Stylus* magazine has created the only comprehensive and current global reference to the leading fine writing instrument manufacturers.

The *2008 Stylus Pen Annual Volume III* includes brand histories and full-color photos and descriptions of products from over 70 companies worldwide. It also includes:

- Glossary of pen terminology
- Care and maintenance guide
- Accessories
- Ink reference guide

Order before November 1st, 2007 for free shipping (North America Only)

To order, please use tear-out order form in this issue or send check or money order, along with name, shipping address and telephone number, to:

Fine Life Media, 363 Reef Road, Suite 2E, Fairfield, CT 06824, or call **203-259-8100 x200** to reserve your copy. $24.95 plus $10 s+h. (Shipping outside North America $25)

Visa, MasterCard, American Express and Discover are accepted.

To place your online order visit: www.stylusmag.com or www.iwmagazine.com

Edox

In 1884, Christian Rüefli-Flury from the Swiss watchmaking city Grenchen decided to found his own company. He moved to Biel where he opened a small workshop for refining and decorating *ébauches*, or base movements. A short time later, Rüefli had the brand name Edox officially registered. This was a concise name, easy to pronounce in every language, and short enough to elegantly grace a dial. Edox comes from ancient Greek and means "the hour" in the furthest sense of its meaning. As one of the first Swiss wristwatch manufacturers, Edox specialized in making elegant, thin wristwatches, even in the early 1920s. Entering the era of the wristwatch accelerated the brand's success, and in 1927 Edox was turned into a joint-stock company. After World War II, the demand for Edox watches grew by leaps and bounds. Production bottlenecks ensued, and in the spring of 1955 the company moved into a new, larger building.

In 1961, Edox's engineers developed a crown system with a double O-ring gasket that made screwing in superfluous. This technical innovation coupled with a double case back led to the birth of the sporty Dolphin model which possessed a water resistance of at least 200 meters—at that time this was a technical feat of the highest sort! With sporty watches such as the Bluebird (1969) and world time watches such as the Geoscope, featuring a rotating view of the globe integrated into the dial, Edox secured a solid reputation. In 1973, Edox's stock was sold to ASUAG, the largest association of Swiss watch manufacturers at the time and the predecessor of today's Swatch Group. The success hoped for by this maneuver remained out of reach, however, and Edox's current president Victor Strambini put the brand back on independent terms in 1983. He then moved the headquarters to Les Genevez, located in the heart of the Swiss Jura, the cradle of the watch industry.

In Les Genevez today there are two different buildings containing modern workshops with more than 140 employees, of which about 110 are qualified watchmakers. The employees make sure that a great deal of attention to detail is paid in everything Edox does.

Edox has been the official watch partner of *Spirit of Norway*, the current U.I.M. Class 1 Offshore World Powerboat world champion, since 2006, and a new line called Class 1 has been created out of this partnership. The crowning glory of this elegant, sporty family is the Edox Spirit of Norway, a series that is water-resistant to 500 meters and features a power reserve display, a large date, a helium valve, and an almost scratchproof ceramic bezel.

Speed on both land and sea is currently a big topic for Edox: the Swiss manufacturer has also entered into cooperation with Koenigsegg automobiles, the visible result of which is a very limited, newly developed chronograph featuring rev-

olutionary side doors that open like on the car.

The brand's most wonderful new addition this year has been Edox's Classe-Royale in a striking, very complicated case measuring 42 x 42 mm. The top model here is a stunning new five-minute repeater, parts of which are visible through a strategically placed cut-away in the dial.

Edox

Class 1 Spirit of Norway
Reference number: 01104 3 TIN TIN
Movement: automatic, Edox Caliber 011 (base ETA Valjoux 7750); ø 30 mm, height 7.9 mm; 25 jewels; 28,800 vph
Functions: hours, minutes, subsidiary seconds; chronograph; date, weekday
Case: titanium, ø 45 mm, height 17 mm; unidirectionally rotating ceramic bezel with 60-minute divisions; sapphire crystal; screw-in crown; water-resistant to 50 atm
Band: rubber, folding clasp
Remarks: limited edition; screw-in helium valve; carbon fiber dial
Price: $3,995
Variations: blue carbon fiber dial

Class 1 Day Date
Reference number: 83002 TIN TIN
Movement: automatic, Edox Caliber 83 (base ETA 2834); ø 29.4 mm, height 5.05 mm; 25 jewels; 28,800 vph
Functions: hours, minutes, sweep seconds; date, weekday
Case: titanium, ø 45 mm, height 14.5 mm; unidirectionally rotating ceramic bezel with 60-minute divisions; sapphire crystal; screw-in crown; water-resistant to 50 atm
Band: rubber, folding clasp
Remarks: screw-in helium valve
Price: $1,795
Variations: white dial; titanium bracelet

Class 1 GMT Titanium
Reference number: 93002 3 TIN TIN
Movement: automatic, Edox Caliber 93 (base ETA 2893); ø 25.6 mm, height 4.1mm; 49 jewels; 28,800 vph
Functions: hours, minutes, sweep seconds; date; 24-hour display (second time zone)
Case: titanium, ø 45 mm, height 14 mm; ceramic bezel with 24-hour divisions; sapphire crystal; screw-in crown; water-resistant to 50 atm
Band: rubber, folding clasp
Remarks: screw-in helium valve
Price: upon request
Variations: white dial; titanium bracelet

Edox Koenigsegg Limited Edition
Reference number: 45002 / 3 NIN
Movement: automatic, Edox Caliber 45 (base ETA 2892-A2 with chronograph module by Dubois Dépraz); ø 28 mm, height 7.3 mm; 49 jewels; 28,800 vph; officially certified COSC chronometer
Functions: hours, minutes, subsidiary seconds; large date; chronograph
Case: stainless steel/titanium, ø 46 mm; sapphire crystal; screw-in crown; buttons protected underneath bipartite bezel that can be opened; water-resistant to 5 atm
Band: rubber, folding clasp
Remarks: limited edition of 30 pieces; carbon fiber dial
Price: $16,000
Variations: case set with brilliant-cut diamonds

Classe Royale Five-Minute Repeater
Reference number: 87002 / 357 NIN
Movement: automatic, Edox Caliber 87 (base ETA 2892-A2 with repeater module by Dubois Dépraz); ø 36 mm, height 7.35 mm; 49 jewels; 28,800 vph
Functions: hours, minutes; five-minute repeater
Case: partially PVD-coated stainless steel, 45 x 45 mm, height 14 mm; sapphire crystal; screw-in crown; transparent case back
Band: reptile skin, folding clasp
Price: $16,500

Classe Royale Chronograph
Reference number: 01105 357 NIN
Movement: automatic, Edox Caliber 011 (base ETA Valjoux 7750); ø 30 mm, height 7.9 mm; 25 jewels; 28,800 vph
Functions: hours, minutes, subsidiary seconds; date, weekday; chronograph
Case: partially PVD-coated stainless steel, 40 x 40 mm, height 14 mm; sapphire crystal; screw-in crown; transparent case back
Band: rubber, folding clasp
Price: $3,295

Classe Royale Ultra Slim
Reference number: 270293 NIN
Movement: quartz, Edox Caliber 27; height 1.4 mm; world's flattest movement with date display
Functions: hours, minutes; date
Case: stainless steel, 37 x 39 mm, height 4.6 mm; sapphire crystal
Band: leather, buckle
Price: $1,495
Variations: folding clasp; also available in ladies' size

Classe Royale Ladies' Chronograph
Reference number: 01924 3D AIN
Movement: quartz, Ronda caliber
Functions: hours, minutes, subsidiary seconds; date; chronograph
Case: stainless steel, 37 x 39 mm, bezel set with 24 brilliant-cut diamonds; sapphire crystal
Band: leather, buckle
Price: $2,495
Variations: without diamonds; with PVD coating

Epos

With interesting new complications and attractive, modern, and simple designs, Epos has proven itself the cream of the crop in its price segment, a development that has been enthusiastically received—especially among Europe's watch fans, but also elsewhere. Thus, the brand continues to realize true technical and aesthetic specialties with comparatively simple means such as a graphically convincing jump hour model based on a vintage manually wound AS movement (Caliber 1727) and a large date with double digits that are not placed next to each other, but rather one on top of the other, based on a finely finished ETA Unitas pocket watch movement. The best thing about it is that even watch fans with shallower pockets can afford these specialties.

Epos's roots extend back to the year 1925 when James Aubert founded a watchmaking workshop in Switzerland's Jura region. He worked as a movement designer for the movement *manufactures* Landeron and Lémania, passing his extensive knowledge on to his nephew Jean Aubert and his son-in-law Jean Fillon, who continues to design movements for the independent company as its chief engineer to this day. In Fillon's workshop many modules are created for Epos, ingenious mechanisms such as the jump hour, large date, and power reserve, as well as dial train modifications for the regulator and a regulator with moon phase. When, at the beginning of the 1980s, quartz watches flooded the market and traditional Swiss watchmaking was thrown into a crisis, Peter Hofer was one of the few to swim against the current, founding the brand Epos together with his wife Erna in 1983 in the bilingual city of Biel. Thanks to his good relationships with suppliers and independent movement designers such as Jean Fillon as well as his profound knowledge of global markets, Hofer achieved successfully positioning the young brand with its exclusively mechanical collection. When, after twenty years, Hofer looked for someone to take over his family business, he came across Ursula Forster, a woman hailing from a watchmaking family who shares Hofer's love of the mechanical watch. Together with her husband, Tamdi Chonge, a man who has also been involved in the Swiss watchmaking industry for many years, she took over the Epos brand in August 2002 and laid down new distribution structures in the most important European and world markets—like the United States, where GNT Incorporated handles these especially attractive watches, which are also sold at especially attractive prices.

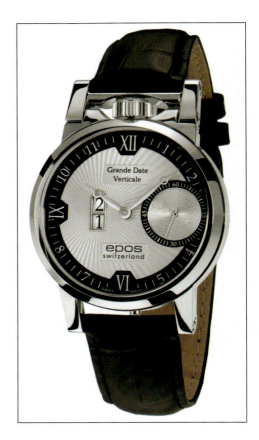

Epos

Sophistiquée Large Date
Reference number: 3383
Movement: manually wound, Epos Caliber GDV (base ETA Unitas 6498); ø 36.6 mm, height 3.9 mm; 17 jewels; 21,600 vph; finely finished with côtes de Genève and blued screws
Functions: hours, minutes, subsidiary seconds; large date
Case: stainless steel, ø 41 mm, height 11.2 mm; sapphire crystal; transparent case back
Band: leather, buckle
Price: $2,750
Variations: with silver-colored dial

Sophistiquée Jump Hour
Reference number: 3385
Movement: automatic, Epos Caliber HS (base ETA 2892-A2); ø 25.6 mm, height 3.6 mm; 21 jewels; 28,800 vph; finely finished
Functions: hours (digital, jump), minutes, sweep seconds; date
Case: stainless steel, ø 41 mm, height 11 mm; sapphire crystal; transparent case back
Band: leather, buckle
Remarks: individually numbered
Price: $2,750
Variations: with black dial

Sophistiquée Retrograde Minute
Reference number: 3379
Movement: manually wound, ETA Unitas Caliber 6498, modified; ø 36.6 mm, height 3.9 mm; 17 jewels; 21,600 vph; finely finished with côtes de Genève and blued screws
Functions: hours, minutes (retrograde), subsidiary seconds
Case: stainless steel, ø 41 mm, height 11.6 mm; sapphire crystal; transparent case back
Band: leather, buckle
Remarks: individually numbered
Price: $2,950
Variations: with black dial

Sophistiquée Automatic
Reference number: 3386
Movement: automatic, ETA Caliber 2824-2; ø 25.6 mm, height 4.6 mm; 25 jewels; 28,800 vph; finely finished
Functions: hours, minutes, small sweep seconds; date
Case: stainless steel, ø 41 mm, height 10.7 mm; sapphire crystal; transparent case back
Band: leather, buckle
Remarks: individually numbered
Price: $1,050
Variations: with black dial

Passion Heure Sautante
Reference number: 3370
Movement: manually wound, AS Caliber 1727; ø 19.4 mm, height 3 mm; 17 jewels; 21,600 vph; finely finished historical movement with côtes de Genève and blued screws
Functions: hours (digital, jump), minutes (off-center), subsidiary seconds
Case: stainless steel, ø 42.6 mm, height 8.8 mm; sapphire crystal; transparent case back
Band: leather, buckle
Remarks: individually numbered
Price: $2,500
Variations: white dial

Passion
Reference number: 3369
Movement: manually wound, ETA Unitas Caliber 6498; ø 36.6 mm, height 3.9 mm; 17 jewels; 21,600 vph; partially skeletonized above the balance; finely finished historical movement with blued screws
Functions: hours, minutes, subsidiary seconds
Case: stainless steel, ø 42.7 mm, height 9.5 mm; sapphire crystal; transparent case back
Band: leather, buckle
Remarks: individually numbered editions
Price: $1,350
Variations: white dial; also available with Roman numerals

Elégance Power Reserve
Reference number: 3362
Movement: manually wound, Peseux Caliber 7046 with in-house power reserve indicator; 17 jewels; 21,600 vph; finely finished with blued screws
Functions: hours, minutes, subsidiary seconds; date; power reserve display
Case: stainless steel, 33 x 40 mm, height 9.1 mm; sapphire crystal; transparent case back
Band: leather, buckle
Price: $3,050
Variations: with black or copper-colored dial

Elégance Régulateur
Reference number: 3363
Movement: manually wound, Peseux Caliber 7046 with in-house regulator modification; 17 jewels; 21,600 vph; finely finished with blued screws
Functions: hours (off-center), minutes, subsidiary seconds; date; moon phase display
Case: stainless steel, 33 x 40 mm, height 8.9 mm; sapphire crystal; transparent case back
Band: leather, buckle
Price: $3,150
Variations: with black or copper-colored dial

Louis Erard

The heart of watch company Louis Erard has beaten for nearly three years with the heightened rhythm of its resuscitation: new owners, new managers, new developmental directions, a new philosophy, a new collection, new positioning, and new products. The work done under the watchful eye of Alain Spinedi is based on Louis Erard's interesting and successful history. Since the renaissance of mechanical watches began somewhat more than fifteen years ago, numerous watch brands have concentrated on watches in the upper price class. Obviously, however, there is a growing number of well-informed watch fans searching for watches manufactured according to traditional Swiss watchmaking at affordable prices. They are Louis Erard's clientele.

A Swiss watchmaking firm with a long tradition, Louis Erard is named after the founder of the company, a man who started up a small movement reassembly business of his own in 1931, just after the world economic crisis of that era. Erard, the son of a well-known watchmaking family, remained behind the scenes for his entire working life as a supplier to a number of distinguished watch manufacturers. However, he encouraged his sons René and Jean-Louis to distance themselves from movement reassembly and concentrate on the design and manufacture of watch movements. Thus, modern technology was continually being introduced into the small factory, the name of which only few insiders had ever heard. It was Louis Erard's grandson Paul who thought of employing lucrative marketing for the company's high-quality products in the late 1970s, putting together a complete line of his own watches as an independent brand.

Good things come to those who wait in the Swiss world of watches, and it was indeed a number of years before Paul was able to present his own completed collection under the slogan "l'espirit du temps." In 1978 the company changed its name from Louis Erard et Fils to plain Louis Erard, and almost fifty years after the original founding, an independent brand with a complete watch line was presented to the general public. The firm located in Le Noirmont once again owns its own workshops where nine experienced watchmakers are always hard at work. Louis Erard is available in several key markets in Europe, Asia, and, of course, the United States. Thanks to a strengthened presence in these markets and the opening of new ones, in 2005 the brand was available at more than 600 points of sale in about thirty-five countries. By the end of 2006, 800 points of sale had been achieved, and by 2010 the company expects to have another 2,000 retailers selling Louis Erard.

Louis Erard

1931 Anniversary Regulator
Reference number: 52 206 AA 20
Movement: manually wound, ER Caliber 1001 (base ETA Peseux Caliber 7001); ø 23.3 mm, height 2.5 mm; 17 jewels; 21,600 vph; finely finished, blued screws, dial side with côtes de Genève
Functions: hours (off-center), minutes, subsidiary seconds
Case: stainless steel, ø 40 mm, height 9 mm; sapphire crystal; transparent case back; water-resistant to 5 atm
Band: leather, folding clasp
Price: $1,300
Variations: yellow gold

La Carrée Chronograph
Reference number: 77 502 AA 12
Movement: automatic, ETA Valjoux Caliber 7750; ø 30 mm, height 7.9 mm; 25 jewels; 28,800 vph
Functions: hours, minutes; chronograph; date
Case: stainless steel, 39 x 39 mm, height 15 mm; sapphire crystal; water-resistant to 5 atm
Band: leather, folding clasp
Price: $1,600
Variations: silver-colored dial

La Sportive Day Date
Reference number: 72 411 AA 02
Movement: automatic, ETA Caliber 2836-2; ø 25.6 mm, height 5.05 mm; 25 jewels; 28,800 vph
Functions: hours, minutes, sweep seconds; date, weekday
Case: stainless steel, ø 42 mm, height 11 mm; ring under crystal with 60-minute divisions, unidirectionally rotating via crown; sapphire crystal; water-resistant to 10 atm
Band: leather, folding clasp
Price: $730
Variations: stainless steel bracelet ($800); white dial; also available as GMT or chronograph models

1931 Small Seconds
Reference number: 47 207 AA 12
Movement: manually wound, ETA Peseux Caliber 7001; ø 23.3 mm, height 2.5 mm; 17 jewels; 21,600 vph; finely finished, blued screws
Functions: hours, minutes, subsidiary seconds
Case: stainless steel, ø 40 mm, height 8 mm; sapphire crystal; transparent case back; water-resistant to 5 atm
Band: leather, folding clasp
Price: $850
Variations: silver dial; yellow gold

1931 Complete Calendar Moon Phase
Reference number: 44 203 AA 11
Movement: automatic, ETA Caliber 2824-2 with module 9000 by Dubois Dépraz; ø 25.6 mm, height 4.6 mm; 25 jewels; 28,800 vph
Functions: hours, minutes, sweep seconds; date, weekday, month, moon phase
Case: stainless steel, ø 40 mm, height 12 mm; sapphire crystal; transparent case back; water-resistant to 5 atm
Band: leather, folding clasp
Price: $1,700
Variations: black dial

1931 GMT Large Date
Reference number: 82 205 AA 12
Movement: automatic, ETA Caliber 2824-2 with module TT 651 by Technotime; ø 25.6 mm, height 4.6 mm; 25 jewels; 28,800 vph
Functions: hours, minutes, sweep seconds; large date; second time zone
Case: stainless steel, ø 40 mm, height 12 mm; sapphire crystal; transparent case back; water-resistant to 5 atm
Band: leather, folding clasp
Price: $1,670
Variations: silver-colored dial

Heritage Day-Date Chronograph
Reference number: 78 259 AA01
Movement: automatic, ETA Valjoux Caliber 7750; ø 30 mm, height 7.9 mm; 25 jewels; 28,800 vph
Functions: hours, minutes, subsidiary seconds; chronograph; date, weekday
Case: stainless steel, ø 40 mm, height 13.5 mm; sapphire crystal; water-resistant to 5 atm
Band: leather, folding clasp
Price: $1,350
Variations: stainless steel bracelet ($1,440); black or bronze-colored dial

Les Asymétriques Chronograph
Reference number: 73 320 AA 02
Movement: automatic, ETA Valjoux Caliber 7750; ø 30 mm, height 7.9 mm; 25 jewels; 28,800 vph
Functions: hours, minutes; chronograph; date
Case: stainless steel, ø 40.3 mm, height 14 mm; sapphire crystal; water-resistant to 50 m
Band: leather, folding clasp
Price: $1,390
Variations: white dial

Jacques Etoile

Master watchmaker Klaus Jakob's heart beats above all for old traditions—and vintage movements that are no longer in production. This tireless collector somehow always manages to unearth old hand-assembled calibers, or perhaps only parts of them, on remote dusty shelves or in some forgotten box on his extensive travels through the Swiss watchmaking countryside. Then he lovingly reworks them and places the end result in attractive, classic cases. Thanks to a respectable pricing policy, these limited editions of exceptional watches are snapped up immediately by interested buyers.

On the occasion of the small Lörrach-based watch company's ten-year anniversary, founder Jakob introduced a special series of reworked sixty-four-year-old automatic movements. The innovative watch movement factory Felsa, which was at home in Lengnau, Switzerland, had already developed a bidirectionally winding movement wound by rotor and brought it to a serial stage at the beginning of the 1940s when other reputable companies were still fooling around with ungainly "hammer" automats featuring pendulum oscillating weights in order to get around Rolex's patent (unidirectional winding). Felsa's winding mechanism, grandiosely christened the Bidynator, wrote its own chapter of watch history during its time. The new Lunamatic models, and the Lune & Etoile that was derived from them, see the master watchmaker leaving his beaten path of classic motifs to combine cutting-edge design elements with traditional production technology. Jacques Etoile's modernly designed model family utilizes the case of the previous Indianapolis model, though it includes graphically unusual and cleanly designed dials. Three different large circles touch or even cut into the central minute scale in several places. The dials are classically manufactured by Schätzle in Weil am Rhein, a neighboring town to Lörrach, and can also be personalized with the potential owner's sign of the zodiac, for example.

Meanwhile, Jakob has (re)discovered the regulator dial. This dial has its origins in the precision pendulum clocks that were located in the regulating departments of large watch factories about 100 years ago to keep "normed" time. The watchmakers regulated their freshly assembled movements according to the fastidiously set and wound clocks, making sure that their rates matched up. In order to do this, the watchmakers basically only needed to check out the position of the minute hand in comparison with the time shown on the dials of the new watches. Thus, workshop clocks whose hour hands were banned to a small subdial in order to keep the view of the much more important minute hand free of obstruction became popular. The "regulator" that resulted became a synonym for precision.

Precision has also always been a domain of large watch movements with large, stable, swinging balances. And this is why it fits so perfectly that Jacques Etoile uses a reworked pocket watch movement (ETA Unitas 6498) in his Régulateur. On top, the caliber is decorated with *côtes de Genève* on both bridges and the balance cock and garnished with blued screws—*comme il faut*, fitting for a fine Swiss movement.

There is hardly anything left of the good little worker movement except the somewhat coarse, straight cut of the bridges. The Super Soigné finish that Jakob also offers features fine elements such as a swan-neck fine adjustment, a screw balance, screw-mounted gold chatons, and a sunburst pattern on the ratchet and winding wheels.

Jacques Etoile

Grand Régulateur
Movement: manually wound, ETA Unitas Caliber 6498; ø 36.6 mm, height 4.5 mm; 17 jewels; 21,600 vph; finished with côtes de Genève and blued screws
Functions: off-center hours, minutes, subsidiary seconds
Case: stainless steel, ø 47 mm, height 14 mm; Hardlex crystal; transparent case back
Band: leather, buckle
Price: $1,550
Variations: Super Soigné movement finish with screw balance, swan-neck fine adjustment and screw-mounted gold chatons; black dial

Réserve de Marche
Movement: manually wound, ETA Unitas Caliber 6498; ø 36.6 mm, height 4.5 mm; 17 jewels; 21,600 vph
Functions: hours, minutes, subsidiary seconds; moon phase display; power reserve display
Case: stainless steel, ø 47 mm, height 14 mm; Hardlex crystal; transparent case back
Band: leather, buckle
Price: $2,400
Variations: cream-colored dial

Bidynator 72
Movement: automatic, ETA Caliber 2824-2; ø 25.6 mm, height 4.6 mm; 25 jewels; 28,800 vph
Functions: hours, minutes, sweep seconds
Case: stainless steel, ø 38 mm, height 9.7 mm; sapphire crystal; transparent case back
Band: leather, buckle
Price: $990
Variations: various band and dial variations

Metropolis Applique
Movement: manually wound, Unitas Caliber 6300; ø 29.4 mm, height 4.62 mm; 19 jewels; 18,000 vph; lavishly re-worked rare vintage manufacture movement
Functions: hours, minutes, sweep seconds
Case: stainless steel, ø 38 mm, height 10 mm; sapphire crystal; transparent case back
Band: leather, buckle
Price: $2,300
Variations: various band and dial variations

Plongeur VII
Movement: automatic, ETA Caliber 2824-2; ø 25.6 mm, height 4.6 mm; 25 jewels; 28,800 vph
Functions: hours, minutes, sweep seconds; date
Case: stainless steel, ø 40 mm, height 10 mm; unidirectionally rotating bezel with 60-minute divisions; sapphire crystal; screw-in crown; water-resistant to 20 atm
Band: stainless steel, double folding clasp
Price: $850
Variations: black dial

Atlantis
Movement: automatic, ETA Caliber 2824-2; ø 25.6 mm, height 4.6 mm; 25 jewels; 28,800 vph; magnetic field protection
Functions: hours, minutes, sweep seconds; date
Case: stainless steel, ø 43 mm, height 13.3 mm; unidirectionally rotating bezel with 60-minute divisions; sapphire crystal; screw-in crown; water-resistant to 50 atm
Band: rubber, buckle
Price: $2,150
Variations: orange dial; stainless steel bracelet

Lune & Etoile
Movement: automatic, ETA Caliber 2824-2 with Dubois Dépraz module 9231; ø 25.6 mm, height 4.6 mm; 25 jewels; 28,800 vph; Super Soigné finish
Functions: hours, minutes, sweep seconds; date; moon phase display
Case: stainless steel, ø 38 mm, height 9.7 mm; sapphire crystal; transparent case back
Band: leather, buckle
Remarks: can be personalized with one's own sign of the zodiac
Price: $2,350
Variations: black dial

Imola Chronograph
Movement: automatic, ETA Valjoux Caliber 7750; ø 30 mm, height 7.9 mm; 25 jewels; 28,800 vph; Super Soigné finish
Functions: hours, minutes, subsidiary seconds; chronograph
Case: stainless steel, ø 42 mm, height 13 mm; sapphire crystal; transparent case back
Band: leather, buckle
Price: $3,700
Variations: silver-colored dial

Fabergé

After an absence from the watch market of almost ninety years, Fabergé made its comeback in 2005. In the ensuing three years, the brand has been able to establish itself with a medium-sized production of exceptional timepieces that are not only made by watchmakers, but also very importantly by goldsmiths, engravers, enamelers, and guillocheurs. These watches' solid gold or platinum cases are the perfect partner for their exquisite dials, which are guilloché by hand in the company's workshops. A great many of them are then given a translucent coating of enamel—a legendary technique that Fabergé continues to practice on its eggs, jewelry, and watches.

Fabergé became famous for its jeweled eggs, which were originally manufactured solely for the family of the Russian czars. After the October Revolution of 1917, production was halted and only in the recent past has it been taken up again. Now the revival of the brand as a manufacturer of wristwatches is also a reality thanks to craftsman Victor Mayer. The current licensee of this name is located in Pforzheim, Germany, and enjoys an excellent reputation in the industry for enamel work. Today, Victor Mayer is managed by Dr. Marcus O. Mohr, a fourth-generation Mayer.

The name of the men's collection, Agathon, is an homage to Peter Carl Fabergé's younger brother, who, with his brilliant creative ideas, contributed conclusively to the first great successes of the brand at the end of the nineteenth century. Another line from the men's collection is the Carrée—timepieces that fascinate with their fine, square cases. These are crafted in gold, inspired stylistically from art deco, and also available, if so desired, with a square enameled dial. The women's collection Anastasia, a word that is actually Greek for "the risen," is, for one thing, dedicated to the youngest daughter of the last czar and, for another, symbolic of the revival of the traditional watchmaking art practiced by Fabergé.

The design of the watch collection was inspired by early sketches for Fabergé watches. While creating details such as the crown, buckle, and rotor, design elements typical of the brand such as the Romanov eagle, the sign of the last czar's court jeweler, and above all the characteristic egg shape were utilized. The outline of the buckle is derived from the oval shape, as is the signet featuring the blue-enameled Cyrillic letter *F*.

Each individual piece achieves uniqueness through the microscopic irregularities of the enamel, which bear witness to the authenticity of the handwork done on it. This mature collection of timepieces has been distinctly created in the style that Peter Carl Fabergé would have given to them had he lived to create more than just a handful of the first wristwatches for women. Beautiful enamels, rich golds, aesthetic designs, and collaborations with reputable movement makers and modifiers give this collection a look like no other—thanks in great part to the experience and depth of Victor Mayer's own workshops.

Fabergé

Anastasia
Reference number: M 1009 GG/58
Movement: quartz, Fabergé Caliber F1600 (base ETA 976.001)
Functions: hours, minutes
Case: yellow gold, 29 x 24.5 mm, height 7.8 mm; bezel set with 48 brilliant-cut diamonds; sapphire crystal; crown set with sapphire cabochon
Band: stingray, buckle with enameled emblem
Remarks: mother-of-pearl dial, guilloché by hand
Price: $10,700
Variations: white gold

Agathon Medium Chronograph
Reference number: M 1020 WG/AU
Movement: automatic, Fabergé Caliber F1702 (base ETA 2094); ø 23.9 mm, height 5.5 mm; 33 jewels; 28,800 vph; finely finished; rotor engraved in the shape of a Romanoff eagle
Functions: hours, minutes, subsidiary seconds; chronograph
Case: white gold, ø 34.7 mm, height 13 mm; bezel and strap lugs set with 137 diamonds; sapphire crystal; transparent case back; crown and buttons with sapphire cabochons
Band: reptile skin, buckle with enameled emblem
Remarks: gold dial, guilloché by hand, paved with brilliant-cut diamonds
Price: $24,000

Agathon Medium
Reference number: M 1021 RG/BR
Movement: automatic, Fabergé Caliber F1703 (base ETA 2895-2); ø 25.6 mm, height 4.35 mm; 27 jewels; 28,800 vph; finely finished; rotor engraved in the shape of a Romanoff eagle
Functions: hours, minutes, subsidiary seconds
Case: rose gold, ø 34.7 mm, height 11 mm; bezel and strap lugs set with 84 brilliant-cut diamonds; sapphire crystal; transparent case back; crown set with sapphire cabochon
Band: stingray, buckle with enameled emblem
Remarks: gold dial, guilloché by hand, high fire enamel
Price: $18,200
Variations: yellow or white gold; various dial variations

Agathon
Reference number: M 1102 RG/00
Movement: automatic, Fabergé Caliber F1700 (base ETA 2892-A2); ø 25.6 mm, height 3.6 mm; 21 jewels; 28,800 vph; finely finished; rotor engraved in the shape of a Romanoff eagle
Functions: hours, minutes, sweep seconds; date
Case: rose gold, ø 40 mm, height 10.5 mm; sapphire crystal; transparent case back; crown set with sapphire cabochon
Band: reptile skin, buckle with enameled emblem
Remarks: silver dial, guilloché by hand
Price: $10,800
Variations: yellow or white gold

Agathon
Reference number: M 1109 WG/BL
Movement: automatic, Fabergé Caliber F1842 (base Frédéric Piguet 1163); ø 25.6 mm, height 3.25 mm; 30 jewels; 21,600 vph; finely finished with côtes de Genève; rotor engraved in the shape of a Romanoff eagle
Functions: hours, minutes, subsidiary seconds
Case: white gold, ø 40 mm, height 10 mm; sapphire crystal; transparent case back; crown set with sapphire cabochon
Band: reptile skin, buckle with enameled emblem
Remarks: gold dial, guilloché by hand, high fire enamel
Price: $16,400
Variations: yellow gold

Agathon Chronograph
Reference number: M 1115 RG/BR
Movement: automatic, Fabergé Caliber F1701 (base ETA 2894-A2); ø 28.6 mm, height 6.1 mm; 37 jewels; 28,800 vph; rotor engraved in the shape of a Romanoff eagle
Functions: hours, minutes, subsidiary seconds; chronograph
Case: rose gold, ø 40 mm, height 13 mm; sapphire crystal; transparent case back; crown set with sapphire cabochon
Band: stingray, buckle with enameled emblem
Remarks: gold dial, guilloché by hand, high fire enamel
Price: $19,400

Carrée
Reference number: M 1117 RG/OP
Movement: manually wound, Fabergé Caliber F1933 (base Frédéric Piguet 810); ø 18.8 mm, height 2 mm; 20 jewels; 28,800 vph; finely finished; gold guilloché movement holder ring
Functions: hours, minutes
Case: rose gold, 36 x 28.5 mm, height 8 mm; bezel set with 80 brilliant-cut diamonds; sapphire crystal; transparent case back; crown set with sapphire cabochon
Band: stingray, buckle with enameled emblem
Remarks: gold dial, guilloché by hand, high fire enamel
Price: $19,600

Agathon Excentris
Reference number: M 1120 WG/00
Movement: manually wound, Fabergé Caliber F1933 (base Frédéric Piguet 810); ø 18.8 mm, height 2 mm; 20 jewels; 28,800 vph; finely finished; gold guilloché movement holder ring
Functions: hours, minutes (off-center)
Case: white gold, ø 40 mm, height 9 mm; sapphire crystal; transparent case back; crown set with sapphire cabochon
Band: stingray, buckle with enameled emblem
Remarks: silver dial, guilloché by hand
Price: $17,500
Variations: rose gold

Ferrari

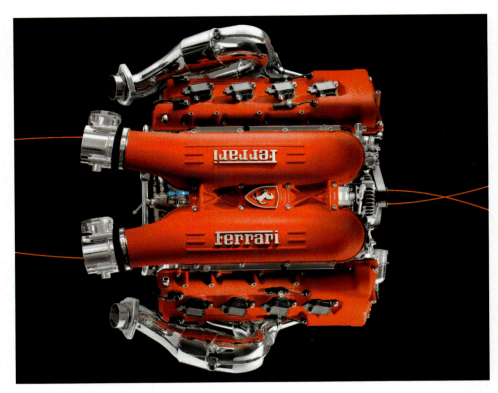

In May 1947 a fascinating chapter in automobile history was written when the first Ferrari rolled from the automotive factory in Maranello. Since then, what are probably the world's most famous sports cars have been created here all wearing their world-renowned emblem: the Cavallino Rampante.

Ferrari—engineered by Officine Panerai: what Panerai's managing director Angelo Bonati and Jean Todt, director of Ferrari SpA, presented in March 2006 in Maranello is more than a new model series; it is a new watch brand and a modern piece of traditional Italian culture.

"A brand like Ferrari deserves more than a simple logo on the dial," began Bonati in his speech at the press conference in the Ferrari racing department hall located in the historical building complex in the middle of their own test track. "Our Ferrari watches have the same DNA as Ferrari's cars," Bonati said, explaining the approach to the big job of designing watches able to bear Ferrari's signature confidently on their dials.

The starting point for the development of the Ferrari watch collection was a deep reflection on the tradition and culture of the Scuderia Ferrari. The new watches needed to justify in every way the high demands that Ferrari made upon their concept, development, and manufacture. Only by occupying itself with the Ferrari brand and its products could Panerai capture and convey the inimitable style and character of Ferrari's automobiles in the much smaller dimensions of a wristwatch.

Thus, the visuals of the Ferrari watches by Panerai are oriented upon the shapes and aesthetics of the automobiles, and you don't have to be a passionate Ferrarista to discover the subtle lines of the chassis and motor details in the watch's design. The convex shape of the bezel and the slim case band featuring geometric strap lugs underscore the aerodynamics of the case; alternating satin-finished and polished surfaces round off the image. Even the clever fluting of the crown and chronograph buttons mirrors the details of a Ferrari dashboard—these watches are unmistakably the product of their automotive inspiration.

Especially noteworthy is the fluted crown, screwed-down for better water resistance with a very short bayonet thread: a quarter turn is enough to loosen or to tighten the seal, and a colored mark helps the wearer to find the correct positions of the crown. Just as the Ferrari automobile's model range is divided into two main sections, so is the Ferrari watch collection. As on the cars, the Scuderia line is uncompromisingly sporty, corresponding to the products of the automobile company's racing department, which generally cause global furor on the track—especially in Formula 1—under the shining yellow coat of arms containing the famed prancing horse. The Gran Turismo range comprises sports cars that personify the legendary brand, forever representing the be-all and end-all for sport-oriented automobile enthusiasts. Celebrating the sixtieth anniversary of the sports car brand in Maranello, Officine Panerai has created a perpetual calendar, limited to sixty pieces, to underscore the robustness and continuity of these precious objects of Italian origin.

Ferrari

Granturismo GMT/Alarm
Reference number: FER00017
Movement: automatic, Panerai Caliber OP XXIV (base La Joux-Perret 590/ETA Valjoux 7750); ø 30.4 mm, height 7.5 mm; 31 jewels; 28,800 vph; automatic winding of both movement and alarm
Functions: hours, minutes, sweep seconds; 24-hour display (second time zone); date; alarm
Case: stainless steel, ø 45 mm; sapphire crystal; transparent case back; crown with screw-in bayonet technology
Band: reptile skin, double folding clasp
Price: $10,400

Perpetual Calendar
Reference number: FER00015
Movement: automatic, Panerai Caliber OP XXII
Functions: hours, minutes, subsidiary seconds; perpetual calendar with date, month, leap year
Case: stainless steel, ø 45 mm; sapphire crystal; transparent case back; crown with screw-in bayonet technology
Band: reptile skin, double folding clasp
Price: $26,000

Scuderia Chronograph 40 mm
Reference number: FER00019
Movement: automatic, Panerai Caliber OP XIII (base ETA Valjoux 7750); ø 30 mm, height 7.9 mm; 27 jewels; 28,800 vph; officially certified chronometer (COSC)
Functions: hours, minutes, subsidiary seconds; chronograph
Case: stainless steel, ø 45 mm; sapphire crystal; crown with screw-in bayonet technology, screw-in buttons; water-resistant to 10 m
Band: leather, double folding clasp
Price: $7,850

Scuderia Chronograph 40 mm
Reference number: FER00018
Movement: automatic, Panerai Caliber OP XIII (base ETA Valjoux 7750); ø 30 mm, height 7.9 mm; 27 jewels; 28,800 vph; officially certified chronometer (COSC)
Functions: hours, minutes, subsidiary seconds; chronograph
Case: stainless steel, ø 45 mm; sapphire crystal; crown with screw-in bayonet technology, screw-in buttons; water-resistant to 10 atm
Band: leather, double folding clasp
Price: $7,850

Granturismo 8 Days GMT
Reference number: FER00012
Movement: manually wound, Panerai Caliber P2002/2; ø 30 mm, height 6.5 mm; 21 jewels; 28,800 vph; three serially operating spring barrels; power reserve 8 days
Functions: hours, minutes, subsidiary seconds; second time zone (12-hour hand), day/night indication; date; power reserve display
Case: stainless steel, ø 45 mm; sapphire crystal; transparent case back; crown with screw-in bayonet technology; water-resistant to 100 atm
Band: reptile skin, double folding clasp
Price: $12,900

Scuderia Chronograph Flyback
Reference number: FER00014
Movement: automatic, Panerai Caliber OP XIX (base ETA Valjoux 7750); ø 30 mm, height 7.9 mm; 31 jewels; 28,800 vph; officially certified chronometer (COSC)
Functions: hours, minutes, subsidiary seconds; chronograph with flyback function
Case: stainless steel, ø 45 mm; sapphire crystal; transparent case back; crown with screw-in bayonet technology, screw-in buttons; water-resistant to 10 atm
Band: leather, double folding clasp
Remarks: carbon fiber dial
Price: $10,300

Granturismo Chronograph
Reference number: FER00011
Movement: automatic, Panerai Caliber OP XII (base ETA Valjoux 7750); ø 30 mm, height 7.9 mm; 27 jewels; 28,800 vph; officially certified chronometer (COSC)
Functions: hours, minutes, subsidiary seconds; chronograph
Case: stainless steel, ø 45 mm; sapphire crystal; crown with screw-in bayonet technology, screw-in buttons; water-resistant to 10 atm
Band: leather, double folding clasp
Price: $8,000

Granturismo Chronograph
Reference number: FER00013
Movement: automatic, Panerai Caliber OP XII (base ETA Valjoux 7750); ø 30 mm, height 7.9 mm; 27 jewels; 28,800 vph; officially certified chronometer (COSC)
Functions: hours, minutes, subsidiary seconds; chronograph
Case: stainless steel, ø 45 mm; sapphire crystal; crown with screw-in bayonet technology, screw-in buttons; water-resistant to 10 atm
Band: leather, double folding clasp
Price: $8,000

Fortis

Fifteen years ago Fortis began working with space specialists. In their search for a partner for the development of a watch made particularly for use in space, Fortis's managers were invited to come to Russia's Star City, a secret place north of Moscow not to be found on any map, to formulate a profile. After extensive tests at the borders of that which is physically possible, the first generation of official space chronographs by Fortis were certified with an official seal for use in orbit on board the space station *Mir*.

The fascination of space borders on that which humans can imagine with their limited experience, and it therefore holds great attraction. Perfection determines the daily routine in space, and reliability is the most important fundamental principle. This is demanded of Fortis's watches both in space and on Earth. Aesthetics, functionality, and authenticity characterize the new generation of space travel watches. They belong to the official equipment on board the first outpost of humanity in orbit: the *International Space Station* (ISS), which makes its rounds in the clear night sky like a great shining star.

The third generation of the Cosmonaut line is crafted in titanium and—according to the demands of space travelers—carries as little weight as possible. The specific material characteristics—above all high stability and a hypoallergenic quality—are not only appreciated by people whose jobs happen to be in orbit.

"Developed for space, used by people on Earth." This credo is the base of Fortis's space partnership—one that has lent the brand its pioneering position on the way toward the future.

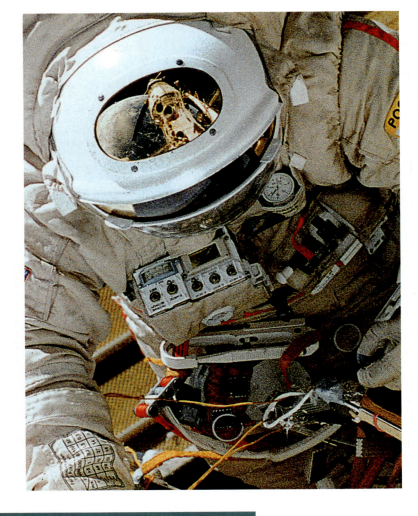

B-42 Flieger Automatic Day/Date
Reference number: 655.10.11 L 01
Movement: automatic, ETA Caliber 2836-2; ø 25.6 mm, height 5.05 mm; 25 jewels; 28,800 vph
Functions: hours, minutes, sweep seconds; date, weekday
Case: stainless steel, ø 42 mm, height 15 mm; sapphire crystal; transparent case back; water-resistant to 20 atm
Band: leather, buckle
Price: $1,200
Variations: various strap and bracelet options

B-42 Flieger Chronograph
Reference number: 656.10.11 L 08
Movement: automatic, ETA Valjoux Caliber 7750; ø 30 mm, height 7.9 mm; 25 jewels; 28,800 vph
Functions: hours, minutes, subsidiary seconds; chronograph; date
Case: stainless steel, ø 42 mm, height 15 mm; sapphire crystal; transparent case back; water-resistant to 20 atm
Band: leather, buckle
Price: $2,300
Variations: various strap and bracelet options

B-42 Flieger Chronograph Alarm
Reference number: 657.10.11 LC 01
Movement: automatic, Fortis Caliber 2001-5 (base ETA Valjoux 7750); ø 30 mm, height 7.9 mm; 32 jewels; 28,800 vph; integrated alarm mechanism with automatic winding; officially certified chronometer (COSC)
Functions: hours, minutes, subsidiary seconds; chronograph; date; alarm
Case: stainless steel, ø 42 mm, height 15 mm; sapphire crystal; transparent case back; water-resistant to 20 atm
Band: reptile skin, buckle
Price: $8,150
Remarks: limited edition of 300 pieces
Variations: various strap and bracelet options

B-42 Flieger Chronograph Alarm
Reference number: 636.10.12 LC 05
Movement: automatic, Fortis Caliber 2001-5 (base ETA Valjoux 7750); ø 30 mm, height 7.9 mm; 32 jewels; 28,800 vph; integrated alarm mechanism with automatic winding
Functions: hours, minutes, subsidiary seconds; chronograph; date; alarm
Case: stainless steel, ø 42 mm, height 17 mm; button protection; sapphire crystal; individually numbered; transparent case back; water-resistant to 20 atm
Band: reptile skin, buckle
Price: $6,250
Variations: various strap and bracelet options

B-42 Official Cosmonauts Day/Date Titanium
Reference number: 658.27.11 K
Movement: automatic, ETA Caliber 2836-2; ø 25.6 mm, height 5.05 mm; 25 jewels; 28,800 vph
Functions: hours, minutes, sweep seconds; date, weekday
Case: titanium, ø 42 mm, height 13 mm; rubber-coated crown and buttons; sapphire crystal; water-resistant to 20 atm
Band: rubber, double folding clasp
Price: $2,025
Variations: various strap and bracelet options; in original Cosmonaut set with tools and exchangeable bands

B-42 Official Cosmonauts Chronograph Titanium
Reference number: 659.27.11 M
Movement: automatic, ETA Valjoux Caliber 7750; ø 30 mm, height 7.9 mm; 25 jewels; 28,800 vph
Functions: hours, minutes, subsidiary seconds; chronograph; date, weekday
Case: titanium, ø 42 mm, height 15 mm; rubber-coated crown and buttons; sapphire crystal; water-resistant to 20 atm
Band: titanium, folding clasp with extension
Price: $3,350
Variations: various strap and bracelet options; in original Cosmonaut set with tools and exchangeable bands

Official Cosmonauts Chronograph Alarm Platinum
Reference number: 607.70.12 LC 05
Movement: automatic, Fortis Caliber 2001-5 (base ETA Valjoux 7750); ø 30 mm, height 7.9 mm; 32 jewels; 28,800 vph; integrated alarm mechanism with automatic winding
Functions: hours, minutes, subsidiary seconds; chronograph; date; alarm
Case: platinum, ø 38 mm, height 15 mm; sapphire crystal; water-resistant to 10 atm
Band: reptile skin, buckle
Remarks: limited edition of 100 pieces
Price: $19,100
Variations: in set with tools and exchangeable bands

Official Cosmonauts Chronograph
Reference number: 630.10.11 L 01
Movement: automatic, ETA Valjoux Caliber 7750; ø 30 mm, height 7.9 mm; 25 jewels; 28,800 vph
Functions: hours, minutes, subsidiary seconds; chronograph; date, weekday
Case: stainless steel, ø 38 mm, height 13 mm; rubber-coated crown and buttons; sapphire crystal; water-resistant to 20 atm
Band: leather, buckle
Price: $2,195
Variations: various strap and bracelet options; in original Cosmonaut set with tools and exchangeable bands

Fortis

B-42 Marinemaster Day/Date
Reference number: 647.11.42 Si 02
Movement: automatic, ETA Caliber 2836-2; ø 25.6 mm, height 5.05 mm; 25 jewels; 28,800 vph
Functions: hours, minutes, sweep seconds; date, weekday
Case: stainless steel, ø 42 mm, height 13 mm; unidirectionally rotating bezel with 60-minute divisions; sapphire crystal; water-resistant to 20 atm
Band: silicon, double folding clasp
Remarks: white SuperLumiNova dial with blue luminescent effect in darkness
Price: $1,425
Variations: rubber strap

B-42 Marinemaster Chronograph Alarm
Reference number: 639.10.41 Si 20
Movement: automatic, Fortis Caliber 2001-5 (base ETA Valjoux 7750); ø 30 mm, height 7.9 mm; 32 jewels; 28,800 vph; integrated alarm mechanism with automatic winding; officially certified C.O.S.C. chronometer
Functions: hours, minutes, subsidiary seconds; chronograph; date; alarm
Case: stainless steel, ø 42 mm, height 15 mm; unidirectionally rotating bezel with 60-minute divisions; sapphire crystal; water-resistant to 20 atm
Band: silicon, double folding clasp
Price: $8,275
Variations: various strap and bracelet options

Flieger Cockpit
Reference number: 654.10.13 L 01
Movement: manually wound, ETA Caliber 2801-2, ø 25.6 mm, height 3.35 mm; 17 jewels; 28,800 vph
Functions: hours, minutes, sweep seconds
Case: stainless steel, ø 40 mm, height 13 mm; sapphire crystal; water-resistant to 20 atm
Band: leather, buckle
Price: $900
Remarks: limited edition of 950 pieces
Variations: stainless steel bracelet

Flieger Chronograph
Reference number: 597.11.11 L 08
Movement: automatic, ETA Valjoux Caliber 7750; ø 30 mm, height 7.9 mm; 25 jewels; 28,800 vph
Functions: hours, minutes, subsidiary seconds; chronograph; date, weekday
Case: stainless steel, ø 40 mm, height 15 mm; sapphire crystal; water-resistant to 10 atm
Band: leather, buckle
Price: $1,800
Variations: stainless steel bracelet; in a numbered gold edition

B-42 Diver GMT 3 Time Zones
Reference number: 650.10.12 M
Movement: automatic, ETA 2893-2; ø 25.6 mm, height 4.1 mm; 21 jewels; 28,800 vph
Functions: hours, minutes, sweep seconds; 24-hour display (second time zone); date, weekday
Case: stainless steel, ø 42 mm, height 15 mm; rotating bezel with 24-hour divisions (third time zone); sapphire crystal; water-resistant to 20 atm
Band: stainless steel, folding clasp with wetsuit extension
Price: $1,900
Variations: various strap and bracelet options

B-42 Diver Chronograph Alarm
Reference number: 641.10.92 Si 05
Movement: automatic, Fortis Caliber 2001-5 (base ETA Valjoux 7750); ø 30 mm, height 7.9 mm; 32 jewels; 28,800 vph; integrated alarm mechanism with automatic winding; officially certified chronometer (COSC)
Functions: hours, minutes, subsidiary seconds; chronograph; date; alarm
Case: stainless steel, ø 42 mm, height 15 mm; unidirectionally rotating bezel with 60-minute divisions; sapphire crystal; water-resistant to 20 atm
Band: silicon, double folding clasp
Price: $7,600
Remarks: limited edition of 300 pieces
Variations: various strap and bracelet options

B-42 Pilot Professional Chronograph
Reference number: 635.10.11 L 01
Movement: automatic, ETA Valjoux Caliber 7750; ø 30 mm, height 7.9 mm; 25 jewels; 28,800 vph
Functions: hours, minutes, subsidiary seconds; chronograph; date, weekday
Case: stainless steel, ø 42 mm, height 15 mm; button protection; sapphire crystal; transparent case back; water-resistant to 20 atm
Band: leather, buckle
Price: $2,200
Variations: various strap and bracelet options

Square
Reference number: 653.10.41 L 16
Movement: automatic, ETA Caliber 2836-2, ø 25.6 mm, height 5.05 mm; 25 jewels; 28,800 vph
Functions: hours, minutes, sweep seconds; date, weekday
Case: stainless steel, 38 x 38 mm, height 13 mm; sapphire crystal; transparent case back, water-resistant to 10 atm
Band: leather, buckle
Price: $1,400

Rob's Report
A Wealth of Information—Watches Online

Congratulations . . . you are holding the best single learning resource about watches in your hands right now. In fact, in addition to *Wristwatch Annual*, hundreds of excellent books have been published about watches, including two of my favorites: James Dowling and Jeffrey Hess's *The Best of Time—Rolex Wristwatches: An Unauthorized History* and Gerd-Rüdiger Lang's *Chronograph Wristwatches: To Stop Time*. Watch books make great learning tools and wonderful gifts for all watch lovers.

While books about watches are an excellent resource, the online watch world offers unlimited learning opportunities with two key advantages over its printed counterparts: once the Is are dotted and the Ts are crossed, a book is final (at least until the next edition is published). The Internet offers up-to-the-minute information 24/7. And, unless you take Abbie Hoffman's advice and "steal this book," books cost money, while reading online watch sites is free.

So, what exactly does the Internet offer, in terms of learning about watches? There are almost countless watch websites available online, and educational opportunities can seem almost infinite. Remember, though, that knowledge is power; if you are a serious watch collector, or just looking for information before you buy your first fine wristwatch, it always pays to be informed. With that bit of advice, we present for you here the best of the online watch world's educational websites.

The biggest online watch news in 2007 was the merger of two category leaders: Antiquorum (Antiquorum.com) and Timezone.com. Antiquorum, the world's leading watch auction firm, bought Timezone.com, the world's most popular watch forum. Both sites offer vast and well-structured information.

Antiquorum.com has an archive of watch auction results going back to the 1990s, complete with a picture and details of each watch. Antiquorum is the best venue for buying serious collector's pieces, and the company's auctions in New York, Geneva, Hong Kong, and Singapore regularly set price records. The good news is that everyone with an Internet connection can both follow the auctions in real time and bid online.

Timezone.com is a forum-based site where visitors can read what other people have written in "posts" and reply if they wish. In addition to each day's posts, Timezone.com features archived posts too, including watch reviews, technical analyses of different calibers, articles from notable watch journalists, a forum dedicated to watch photography, brand-specific forums, an industry news forum, and—my favorite—an online watchmaking class that is overseen by a skilled watchmaker.

An obvious source of information is watch manufacturers' websites, although some are much better than others. Among the best from a learning perspective are: Blancpain.com, with its own forum; IWC.ch, also with its own forum and members area; Glashuette-Original.com, a particularly informative site containing everything you'd ever want to know about watchmaking in Glashütte; Panerai.com; Vacheron-Constantin.com; Richard Mille.com; and PatekPhilippe.com, which does an excellent job of keeping up to date with Patek Philippe's ever-changing collection. All of these websites offer comprehensive data on their current collection of timepieces along with slick pictures, and most also offer historical and collector's information as well.

A recent development is watch-related blogs, where collectors express themselves regarding their passion for watches and give their thoughts, feelings, and opinions along with news from their particular niche of the collector's world. Watch blogs are as unique as the collectors behind them. Some of the most interesting blogs can be found here: Wristwatchreview.com; Fratellowatches.com; the excellent Tapestry of Time (http://timetapestry.blogspot.com); and—my favorite—the colorful, brutally honest: Kronos Blog (http://kronosclub.blogspot.com).

The online watch world encompasses many areas, not least among them commercial. While commercial websites are primarily motivated by profit, most educational watch websites are owned and operated by passionate collectors. For the price of an Internet connection, anyone can learn enough about watches to become a genuine expert. This kingdom of information is current and ever-expanding. Here is a partial list of other highly recommended, interesting, and educational websites in no particular order . . . let your passion lead where it may and enjoy the learning:

Jayhawk's Watch Photograph Database: (www.ittc.ku.edu/~jgauch/watch/index.html)

Seiko & Citizen Watch Forum: (www.network54.com/Forum/78440)

Poor Man's Watch Forum (www.pmwf.com)

Paneristi.com's Public Forum (www.network54.com/Forum/353391)

VintageRolexForum.com

EquationOfTime.com, which features the popular Dive Watch Forum and collector's photo galleries

SteveG's Watch Launchpad with incredible pictures (http://ninanet.net/watches/launchpad.html)

Watchfinder.net, a comprehensive portal to all things watches

---

ROB SPAYNE HAS BEEN WORKING ON THE INTERNET FOR EIGHT YEARS, FOUNDING WWW.WATCHFINDER.NET IN 2000. HE IS ALSO AN EXPERIENCED WATCH ENTHUSIAST WHO HAS SUCCESSFULLY CREATED A PROFESSION FROM HIS TWO PASSIONS. HIS WEBSITE IS AN AUTHORITATIVE AND WELL-VISITED PORTAL FOR THE HOROLOGICALLY MINDED.

Gérald Genta

Gérald Genta has been one of the most influential designers working in the field of *haute horlogerie* since 1969—the year that he began creating unique designs for famous brands such as Patek Philippe and Audemars Piguet. He officially founded a company bearing his name at the beginning of the 1990s and went on to make fast friends with master watchmaker Daniel Roth. The two ended up sharing workshop space in Le Sentier and then sold both companies to Singaporean distributor Hour Glass at the end of the decade. In 2000, both brands were purchased by the Bulgari Group.

Gérald Genta's premises are still located in Le Sentier, a village in Switzerland's famed Vallée de Joux. This small factory is still shared with Daniel Roth so that the two brands can profit equally from the synergies created by each of their concepts and master watchmakers. These synergies also often spill over to the Bulgari brand, which can now proudly boast a small collection of *haute horlogerie* timepieces.

Gérald Roden, CEO of the Gérald Genta and Daniel Roth brands, has made absolutely sure that the brand's watches continue to contain the same type of elements and feel that Genta's original designs did. Therefore, the company has retained the unusual case shapes and dial designs that are part of Genta's legacy, while allowing them to evolve in a way that makes them continue to stand out in today's world market.

"I believe our success at this has to do with good team management within the scope of a company vision and challenging projects," Roden reveals. "The role of the leader, in other words, the management, is important as he or she is the one to make sure the DNA of the project is respected and that the teams work together."

Genta was a pioneer in the watch industry, and Roden guarantees that this basic fact is respected by continuing the brand's free-spirited choice of materials for dials and cases. This company was the first in the high-end segment to use rubber, glass fibers, wood, liquid ceramics, tantalum, and bronze in its products—long foreshadowing contemporary trends in the industry.

The latter material—bronze—is one that Gérald Genta is daring to resuscitate in 2007. Nineteen years ago, Genta presented a model called Gefica. This was a timepiece created from a discussion he had had with some friends during an African hunt; the first two letters of each of these friends' surnames led to the unusual moniker for the timepiece. Since it was intended as a hunter's watch, bronze was chosen as the non-shiny material for the case to avoid any glinting. PVDs and ceramics were not available in 1988, so it was up to Genta to find the appropriate matte-colored metal. It also has a beautiful patina and an unusual look to make it a true standout.

Inspired by the original, the new Gefica contains a resolutely twenty-first-century spirit: profoundly urban with earthy shapes, materials, and colors.

Gérald Genta

Octo 48-Month Perpetual Calendar
Reference number: OQM.Y.60.515.CN.BD
Movement: automatic, Gérald Genta Caliber GG 7080; ø 35.6 mm, height 4.6 mm; 26 jewels; 28,800 vph; hand-engraved and colorfully anodized movement
Functions: hours, minutes; calendar programmed for four years with date, day, month, moon phase
Case: white gold, ø 42.5 mm, height 11.55 mm; sapphire crystal; transparent case back; crown with hawk's eye cabochon
Band: reptile skin, folding clasp
Price: $61,700
Variations: red gold

Arena Spice
Reference number: RSP.X.156.CA.BD.SR1
Movement: automatic, Gérald Genta Caliber GG 7510; ø 26.2 mm, height 5.9 mm; 21 jewels; 28,800 vph; perlage
Functions: hours (digital, jump); minutes (retrograde), sweep seconds
Case: stainless steel, ø 41 mm, height 11 mm; rubber-coated bezel set with diamonds; sapphire crystal; screw-in crown
Band: rubber, folding clasp
Remarks: mother-of-pearl dial with brass and sapphire inlay
Price: $13,250

Arena Biretro Gold
Reference number: BSP.Y.66.269.CN.BD
Movement: automatic, Gérald Genta Caliber GG 7724; ø 26.2 mm, height 5.28 mm; 27 jewels; 28,800 vph; perlage
Functions: hours (digital, jump); minutes (retrograde), sweep seconds; date (retrograde)
Case: white gold, ø 45 mm, height 12.8 mm; tantalum bezel; sapphire crystal; transparent case back; screw-in crown
Band: reptile skin, folding clasp
Price: $24,500

Octo Chrono Quattro Retro
Reference number: OQC.Z.50.581.CN.BD
Movement: automatic, Gérald Genta Caliber GG 7800; ø 36 mm, height 8.5 mm; 37 jewels; 21,600 vph; four retrograde functions (two chronograph counters, minute hand, date hand), date coupled to jump hour
Functions: hours (digital, jump); minutes (retrograde); date (retrograde); chronograph (two retrograde counters)
Case: red gold, ø 44.5 mm, height 14.85 mm; sapphire crystal; transparent case back; crown with hawk's eye cabochon
Band: reptile skin, folding clasp
Price: $44,400
Variations: white gold

Retro Sport Fantasy Navigator
Reference number: RSF.X.10.173.CA.BD
Movement: automatic, Gérald Genta Caliber GG 7510; ø 26.2 mm, height 5.9 mm; 21 jewels; 28,800 vph; perlage
Functions: hours (digital, jump); minutes (retrograde)
Case: stainless steel, ø 41 mm, height 11 mm; sapphire crystal; transparent case back; screw-in crown
Band: leather, buckle
Price: $8,300
Variations: with rubber bezel and strap

Octo Biretro
Reference number: OBR.Y.60.520.CN.BD
Movement: automatic, Gérald Genta Caliber GG 7722; ø 26.2 mm, height 5.28 mm; 27 jewels; 28,800 vph; hand-engraved and colorfully anodized movement
Functions: hours (digital, jump); minutes (retrograde); date (retrograde)
Case: white gold, ø 42.5 mm, height 11.9 mm; sapphire crystal; transparent case back; crown with hawk's eye cabochon
Band: reptile skin, folding clasp
Price: $28,850
Variations: red gold; 39 mm case size

Arena Chrono Quattro Retro
Reference number: ABC.Y.80.290.CN.BD
Movement: automatic, Gérald Genta Caliber GG 7800; ø 36 mm, height 8.5 mm; 37 jewels; 21,600 vph
Functions: hours (digital, jump); minutes (retrograde); date (retrograde); chronograph (two retrograde counters)
Case: titanium, ø 45 mm, height 15.4 mm; sapphire crystal; transparent case back; screw-in crown, flat buttons integrated into case sides; water-resistant to 100 m
Band: reptile skin, folding clasp
Price: $25,350
Variations: titanium/white gold with diamonds

Arena Retro Sport
Reference number: RSP.L.10.262.CJ.BD
Movement: automatic, Gérald Genta Caliber GG 7510; ø 26.2 mm, height 5.9 mm; 21 jewels; 28,800 vph; hand-engraved and colorfully anodized movement
Functions: hours (digital, jump); minutes (retrograde), sweep seconds
Case: stainless steel, ø 38 mm, height 11 mm; sapphire crystal; screw-in crown
Band: rubber, folding clasp
Price: $7,950

Girard-Perregaux

Swiss watch metropolis La Chaux-de-Fonds is where Girard-Perregaux is located. An Art Nouveau building on Rue Numa Droz erected in 1904 today houses the lion's share of the production department. The building, the length of which stretches almost all the way down the block, once served as the offices for the Tavannes watch factory outside the city, which employed around 2,000 people during its heyday. "We could have built a new factory on the outskirts like many of our competitors do," owner Luigi Macaluso remarks, before adding, "that would probably have been much cheaper too."

The building was completely renovated in order to recreate its original look. Old style elements were restored with great care. The majority of the 360 employees moved to various other locations on Rue Numa Droz at the beginning of 2003.

In manufacturing movements, Girard-Perregaux is for the most part autonomous, and even movement design is done in-house. Naturally mainsprings, gear wheel sets, balances, and escapement parts are purchased. Base plates, however, are cre-ated on modern CNC machines. All flat components are hand-finished with dec-orations like *perlage* and *côtes circulaires*, and all edges are beveled at a 45-degree angle before they are polished and treated with a galvanic precious metal coating. The edges of steel components are pol-ished and given fine tin polishing. All this work is chiefly done in-house at Girard-Perregaux. Alongside movements, cases and metal bracelet elements are also cre-ated in the building on Rue Numa Droz. Additionally, the departments for research and development and "*méthode*" are also housed here—the latter occupying itself with purchasing tools and machines as well as developing them when they are not regularly available. The eight employees in the research and development and *mé-thode* sections dispose of a budget that on average comprises about 10 percent of the company's annual turnover. *Haute horlogerie* watches are manufactured in another building located on a hill above the *manufacture*. Especially talented watchmakers occupy themselves with assembling complicated watches such as models belonging to the repeater family Opera and the Tourbillon with Three Golden Bridges.

The delicacy of a tourbillon and the clever sound and motion technology of a repeater are united in the new Vintage 1945 Jackpot model, lustily crossing the border between tool and toy. This watch is namely an authentic slot machine for the wrist, inspired by a vintage American slot machine. The lever on the right side of the case sets three little cylinders in motion that are each printed with five different symbols. The system disposes of a stop mechanism that halts the cylinders randomly. At the same time, a chime is activated whose little hammer hits a gong, making a little "ding" sound when one of the cylinders stops.

A fully new movement was developed to realize this charming complication: *manufacture* caliber GPFAY08 Jackpot Tourbillon measures 38.6 x 32.6 mm, beats at a frequency of 21,600 vph, and has a power reserve of four days (96 hours).

Girard-Perregaux

Laureato EVO3 Tourbillon
Reference number: 99071-27-000-21A
Movement: automatic, GP Caliber 9600; ø 28.6 mm, height 6.22 mm; 30 jewels; 21,600 vph; one-minute tourbillon with three bridges made of sapphire crystal; micro rotor
Functions: hours, minutes, subsidiary seconds (on tourbillon cage)
Case: titanium, ø 42 mm, height 12.6 mm; platinum bezel; sapphire crystal; transparent case back
Band: titanium, folding clasp
Price: $160,000
Variations: leather strap

Vintage 1945 Tourbillon with Three Gold Bridges
Reference number: 99890-53-000-BA6A
Movement: automatic, GP Caliber 9600CS; 28.6 x 28.6 mm, height 6.25 mm; 30 jewels; 21,600 vph; one-minute tourbillon; micro rotor
Functions: hours, minutes
Case: white gold, 32 x 32 mm, height 11.95 mm; sapphire crystal; transparent case back
Band: reptile skin, folding clasp
Price: $160,000
Variations: yellow or rose gold

Opera II
Reference number: 99741-52-831-BAEA
Movement: manually wound, GP Caliber 9897; ø 28 mm, height 8.8 mm; 37 jewels; 21,600 vph; one-minute tourbillon; repeater movement with Westminster carillon
Functions: hours, minutes; perpetual calendar with date, day, month, leap year; minute repeater
Case: rose gold, ø 42 mm, height 14.15 mm; sapphire crystal; transparent case back
Band: reptile skin, folding clasp
Price: $510,000
Variations: white gold; platinum

Vintage 1945 Jackpot Tourbillon
Reference number: 99720-52-651-BA6A
Movement: manually wound, GP Caliber FAY08; 38.6 x 32.6 mm; 21,600 vph; one-minute tourbillon; "slot machine" with three cylinders that are tensioned and activated by a lever on the right side of the case, gong when display stops; power reserve 96 hours
Functions: hours, minutes, subsidiary seconds (on tourbillon); slot machine
Case: rose gold, 43.95 x 43 mm, height 17.3 mm; sapphire crystal
Band: reptile skin, folding clasp
Price: $565,000

Cat's Eye Tourbillon with Three Gold Bridges
Reference number: 99495D53B000-JK6A
Movement: manually wound, GP Caliber 9700.0A; 32 x 27 mm, height 6.1 mm; 20 jewels; 21,600 vph; one-minute tourbillon; power reserve 72 hours
Functions: hours, minutes, subsidiary seconds (on tourbillon cage)
Case: white gold, 31.3 x 36.3 mm, height 10.8 mm; bezel, lugs and case sides set with 84 baguette-cut diamonds; sapphire crystal; crown set with diamond
Band: satin, folding clasp set with 14 diamonds
Remarks: front of case paved with diamonds
Price: $195,000

Tourbillon with Three Gold Bridges
Reference number: 99250-53-000-BA6A
Movement: automatic, GP Caliber 9600; ø 28.6 mm, height 6.25 mm; 30 jewels; 21,600 vph; one-minute tourbillon; micro rotor
Functions: hours, minutes
Case: white gold, ø 38 mm, height 9.9 mm; sapphire crystal; transparent case back
Band: reptile skin, folding clasp
Price: $120,000
Variations: yellow or rose gold; platinum

Vintage 1945 XXL Perpetual Calendar
Reference number: 90270-52-821-BA6A
Movement: automatic, GP Caliber 3170; ø 29.3 mm, height 6.28 mm; 44 jewels; 28,800 vph
Functions: hours, minutes; chronograph; 24-hour display; perpetual calendar with date, weekday, month, moon phase, leap year
Case: rose gold, 36 x 37 mm, height 14.9 mm; sapphire crystal; transparent case back
Band: reptile skin, folding clasp
Price: $48,750

Vintage 1945 XXL Chronograph
Reference number: 25840-52-111-BAED
Movement: automatic, GP Caliber 33CO (base GP 3300); ø 29.3 mm, height 8.48 mm; 63 jewels; 28,800 vph
Functions: hours, minutes, subsidiary seconds; chronograph; date
Case: rose gold, 36 x 37 mm, height 12.9 mm; sapphire crystal; transparent case back
Band: reptile skin, folding clasp
Price: $22,500
Variations: white gold; stainless steel

Girard-Perregaux

Vintage 1945 Large Date Moon Phase
Reference number: 25800-52-651-BCGD
Movement: automatic, GP Caliber 3330; 28.8 x 26.5 mm, height 4.9 mm; 32 jewels; 28,800 vph
Functions: hours, minutes, subsidiary seconds; large date; moon phase
Case: white gold, 32 x 32 mm, height 11.2 mm; sapphire crystal; transparent case back
Band: reptile skin, folding clasp
Price: $18,000
Variations: yellow gold; rose gold

Vintage 1945 Power Reserve
Reference number: 25850-52-611-BA6A
Movement: automatic, GP Caliber 33RO (base GP 3300); ø 25.6 mm, height 4.55 mm; 27 jewels; 28,800 vph
Functions: hours, minutes, subsidiary seconds; date; power reserve display
Case: white gold, 32 x 32 mm, height 11.2 mm; sapphire crystal; transparent case back
Band: reptile skin, folding clasp
Price: $15,500
Variations: yellow gold; white gold

Vintage 1945 Carree Triple Date
Reference number: 25810-52-651-BA6A
Movement: automatic, GP Caliber 33MO; ø 25.6 mm, height 4.55 mm; 27 jewels; 28,800 vph
Functions: hours, minutes, sweep seconds; date, weekday, month
Case: rose gold, 32 x 34.5 mm, height 12 mm; sapphire crystal; transparent case back
Band: reptile skin, folding clasp
Price: $16,000
Variations: stainless steel

Vintage 1945 Carree Chronograph
Reference number: 25820-53-651-BA6A
Movement: automatic, GP Caliber 30CO; ø 23.3 mm, height 6.28 mm; 38 jewels; 28,800 vph; column-wheel control of chronograph functions
Functions: hours, minutes, subsidiary seconds; chronograph
Case: white gold, 32 x 34.5 mm, height 13.5 mm; sapphire crystal; transparent case back
Band: reptile skin, folding clasp
Price: $21,500
Variations: rose gold

Vintage 1945 Carree Small Seconds
Reference number: 25815-52-111-BACA
Movement: automatic, GP Caliber 4500; ø 30 mm, height 3.95 mm; 27 jewels; 28,800 vph
Functions: hours, minutes, sweep seconds; date
Case: rose gold, 32 x 34.5 mm, height 11.5 mm; sapphire crystal; transparent case back
Band: reptile skin, folding clasp
Price: $14,600
Variations: stainless steel

Vintage 1945
Reference number: 25932D11AB61-11A
Movement: automatic, GP Caliber 3290; ø 23.3 mm, height 3.2 mm; 28 jewels; 28,800 vph
Functions: hours, minutes, subsidiary seconds; date
Case: stainless steel, 28.2 x 28.6 mm, height 10.45 mm; bezel set with diamonds; sapphire crystal; transparent case back
Band: stainless steel, folding clasp
Price: $10,500
Variations: reptile skin strap; rose gold

Cat's Eye Bi-Retro
Reference number: 80485D53A761-KK7A
Movement: automatic, GP Caliber 3390; ø 26.2 mm, height 3.2 mm; 36 jewels; 28,800 vph
Functions: hours, minutes, subsidiary seconds (retrograde); date, weekday (retrograde); moon phase
Case: white gold, 35.25 x 30.25 mm, height 10.45 mm; bezel set with 68 diamonds; sapphire crystal; transparent case back; crown with cabochon
Band: satin, folding clasp
Remarks: mother-of-pearl dial with diamond markers
Price: $25,000
Variations: rose gold; with completely paved case

Cat's Eye
Reference number: 80480D53A761-KK9A
Movement: automatic, GP Caliber 33RO; ø 25.6 mm, height 4.55 mm; 27 jewels; 28,800 vph
Functions: hours, minutes, subsidiary seconds; date; power reserve display
Case: white gold, 35.25 x 30.25 mm, height 10.45 mm; bezel set with 68 baguette-cut diamonds; sapphire crystal; transparent case back; crown with cabochon
Band: satin, folding clasp
Remarks: mother-of-pearl dial with diamond markers
Price: $22,500

Girard-Perregaux

ww.tc Chronograph
Reference number: 49805-52-151-BA6A
Movement: automatic, GP Caliber 33CO; ø 29.3 mm, height 8.48 mm; 63 jewels; 28,800 vph
Functions: hours, minutes, subsidiary seconds; chronograph; date; 24-hour display (world time)
Case: white gold, ø 43 mm, height 13.4 mm; bidirectionally rotating bezel under crystal with world reference city names; sapphire crystal; transparent case back; screw-in crown
Band: reptile skin, folding clasp
Price: $25,500
Variations: rose gold

ww.tc Financial
Reference number: 49805-52-253-BACA
Movement: automatic, GP Caliber 33CO; ø 29.3 mm, height 8.48 mm; 63 jewels; 28,800 vph
Functions: hours, minutes, subsidiary seconds; chronograph; date; 24-hour display (world time)
Case: rose gold, ø 43 mm, height 13.4 mm; bidirectionally rotating bezel under crystal with visualization of market opening times; sapphire crystal; transparent case back; screw-in crown
Band: reptile skin, folding clasp
Remarks: limited edition of 500 pieces
Price: $23,500
Variations: stainless steel

ww.tc Titanium
Reference number: 49805-21-652-BA6A
Movement: automatic, GP Caliber 33CO; ø 29.3 mm, height 8.48 mm; 63 jewels; 28,800 vph
Functions: hours, minutes, subsidiary seconds; chronograph; date; 24-hour display (world time)
Case: titanium, ø 43 mm, height 13.4 mm; bidirectionally rotating bezel under crystal with world reference city names; sapphire crystal; transparent case back; screw-in crown
Band: reptile skin, folding clasp
Price: $13,000

Girard-Perregaux 1966
Reference number: 49525-53-631-BK6A
Movement: automatic, GP Caliber 3300; ø 26 mm, height 3.28 mm; 27 jewels; 28,800 vph
Functions: hours, minutes, sweep seconds; date
Case: white gold, ø 38 mm, height 8.5 mm; sapphire crystal; transparent case back
Band: reptile skin, folding clasp
Price: $10,250

Girard-Perregaux 1966
Reference number: 49525-53-131-BK6A
Movement: automatic, GP Caliber 3300; ø 26 mm, height 3.28 mm; 27 jewels; 28,800 vph
Functions: hours, minutes, sweep seconds; date
Case: rose gold, ø 38 mm, height 8.5 mm; sapphire crystal; transparent case back
Band: reptile skin, folding clasp
Price: $9,250

Girard-Perregaux 1966 Complete Calendar
Reference number: 49535-52-151-BK6A
Movement: automatic, GP Caliber 33M0; ø 25.6 mm; 27 jewels; 28,800 vph
Functions: hours, minutes, sweep seconds; date, weekday, month, moon phase
Case: rose gold, ø 40 mm, height 10.7 mm; sapphire crystal; transparent case back
Band: reptile skin, folding clasp
Price: $14,250

Laureato USA 98 DLC
Reference number: 80175-24-251-FK6A
Movement: automatic, GP Caliber 33CO; ø 29.3 mm, height 8.48 mm; 63 jewels; 28,800 vph; sweep minute counter
Functions: hours, minutes, subsidiary seconds; flyback chronograph
Case: black DLC-coated titanium, ø 46 mm, height 15.6 mm; rubber-coated bezel; sapphire crystal; screw-in crown; water-resistant to 10 atm
Band: rubber, double folding clasp
Remarks: limited edition of 150 pieces
Price: $13,300

Laureato USA 98
Reference number: 80175-11-151-FK7A
Movement: automatic, GP Caliber 33CO; ø 29.3 mm, height 8.48 mm; 63 jewels; 28,800 vph; sweep minute counter
Functions: hours, minutes, subsidiary seconds; flyback chronograph
Case: stainless steel, ø 46 mm, height 15.1 mm; sapphire crystal; transparent case back; screw-in crown; water-resistant to 10 atm
Band: rubber, folding clasp
Remarks: limited edition of 250 pieces
Price: $11,500

Girard-Perregaux

Caliber 2700
Mechanical with automatic winding, rotor with ceramic ball bearing, unilaterally winding; double third wheel; stop-seconds, power reserve 40 hours
Functions: hours, minutes, sweep seconds or subsidiary seconds at 9 or 11 o'clock; jumping date
Diameter: 8 3/4''' (19.4 mm)
Height: 4 mm
Jewels: 32
Balance: glucydur
Frequency: 28,800 vph
Balance spring: flat hairspring, fine adjustment
Shock protection: Kif
Remarks: 214 components

Caliber 3200
Mechanical with automatic winding, rotor with ceramic ball bearing, unilaterally winding; stop-seconds, power reserve 42 hours
Functions: hours, minutes, sweep seconds or subsidiary seconds at 9 or 11 o'clock; date
Diameter: 10 1/2''' (23.3 mm)
Height: 3.2 mm
Jewels: 27
Balance: glucydur
Frequency: 28,800 vph
Balance spring: flat hairspring, fine adjustment
Shock protection: Kif
Remarks: 185 components

Caliber 3300
Mechanical with automatic winding, rotor with ceramic ball bearing, unilaterally winding; stop-seconds, power reserve 46 hours
Functions: hours, minutes, sweep seconds or subsidiary seconds at 9 or 11 o'clock; date
Diameter: 11 1/2''' (25.6 mm)
Height: 3.2 mm
Jewels: 27
Balance: glucydur
Frequency: 28,800 vph
Balance spring: flat hairspring, fine adjustment
Shock protection: Kif
Remarks: 191 components

Caliber 4500
Mechanical with automatic winding, rotor with ceramic ball bearing, unilaterally winding; double third wheel; stop-seconds, power reserve 56 hours
Functions: hours, minutes, sweep seconds or subsidiary seconds at 9 or 11 o'clock; date
Diameter: 13 1/4''' (30 mm)
Height: 3.95 mm
Jewels: 27
Balance: glucydur
Frequency: 28,800 vph
Balance spring: flat hairspring, fine adjustment
Shock protection: Kif
Remarks: 190 components

Caliber 9600
Mechanical with automatic winding; one-minute tourbillon; power reserve 48 hours
Functions: hours, minutes, subsidiary seconds (on tourbillon cage)
Diameter: 28.6 mm
Height: 6.22 mm
Jewels: 30
Frequency: 21,600 vph
Remarks: patented design of the tourbillon under three gold bridges; automatic winding with platinum micro rotor

Caliber GPFAY08
Mechanical with manual winding; one-minute tourbillon; "slot machine" with three cylinders that are wound and activated by a hand lever, gong when display stops spinning; power reserve 96 hours
Functions: hours, minutes, subsidiary seconds (on tourbillon cage); slot machine function
Dimensions: 38.6 x 32.6 mm
Height: 8.02 mm
Jewels: 38
Balance: glucydur
Frequency: 21,600 vph

From the same watch experts that bring you **Wristwatch Annual**—the definitive book of modern watch models—now comes an equally invaluable resource for the vintage watch collector: **Classic Wristwatches**

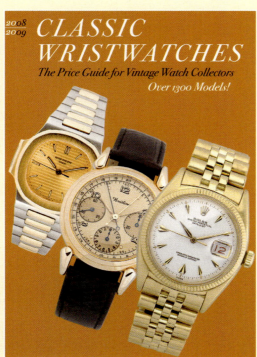

Praise for the Wristwatch Annual series

"The must-have annual.... A huge 432-page feast for the eyes."
—London Times

"An invaluable source of information for anyone who wants a thorough survey of the new additions to the market. Each year a plethora of luxury mechanical watches are launched and each year new manufacturers take up the flight with the veterans."
—Plaza Watch

Classic Wristwatches 2008/2009

Classic Wristwatches contains extensive chapters on approximately 50 of the most historically interesting brands sought after on today's secondary and auction markets. Updated and revised every two years, it contains the most current information on 1,100 vintage watches and their approximate value, including details on the movement, case, special characteristics, and estimated price of each piece.

By Stefan Muser and Michael Ph. Horlbeck
1,100 full-color illustrations
232 pages, 8¼ × 11¾ in.
ISBN: 978-0-7892-0935-1
$35.00 · Paperback

Published by ABBEVILLE PRESS
137 Varick Street, New York, NY 10013
1-800-Artbook (in U.S. only)
Also available wherever fine books are sold
www.abbeville.com/wristwatches

Glashütte Original

The Glashütte Original *manufacture* is a specialist in elegant, modern, and luxurious mechanical wristwatches featuring exclusive and innovative watch movements. Its timepieces embody typical German virtues such as precision, functionality, and reliability. They also symbolize traditional values like quality, exclusivity, and authenticity and 160 years of continuous, fascinating, and eventful watchmaking in Saxony's Müglitz Valley. Glashütte Original's focus for 2007 was chronograph Caliber 99. The *manufacture* had previously presented the unusual PanoRetroGraph in 2000 outfitted with manually wound Caliber 60, an exceptional, highly complicated chronograph with a countdown function and gong to signify when time is up. Now the *manufacture* has concentrated on conceiving a new manually wound movement with more down-to-earth features—though movement designer Christian Schmied-chen obviously didn't want to limit himself that much after all, in the end pro-ducing a demanding split-seconds chronograph with flyback function and pan-orama date.

The mechanics of a split-seconds chronograph are a special challenge for movement designers, for they literally contain two stopwatches in one that need to be coupled to each other. When creating the dial, the designers oriented themselves on historical pocket watches. When the split-seconds button is pressed, the red rattrapante hand follows its silver-colored counterpart along the red minute scale, which can also find its origins in historical precision watches.

The now more tonneau-shaped Karree models of the Senator line have been added on to with the ad-dition of a fully newly devel-oped manually wound movement: *manufacture* Caliber 22 premieres Glashütte Original's typical panorama date at 6 o'clock. Alongside the characteristic Glashütte three-quarter plate, a screw balance outfitted with eigh-teen gold weighted screws, a swan-neck fine adjustment, and some screw-mounted gold chatons can also be recognized through the sapphire crystal case back of this watch. Instead of applied baton markers, like on the pre-vious automatic variations, here one finds applied Roman numerals. Thus, just one glance is enough to recognize that this Senator Karree is outfitted with a manually wound movement instead of the usual automatic variation.

The most surprising new introduction of the year is called Senator Sixties and literally awakens memories of the joie de vivre of the 1960s—even if the historical model of this watch still ticked behind the Iron Curtain. Typically sixties is the domed dial above which a strongly domed sapphire crystal juts. The shaped crystal case back is also new: it not only allows a direct view into automatic *manufacture* Caliber 39-52, but also for the first time makes it possible to have a side view of the rotating oscillating weight.

Glashütte Original

Julius Assmann 4
Reference number: 46-12-01-01-04
Movement: manually wound, Glashütte Original Caliber 46-12; ø 32.2 mm, height 5.8 mm; 19 jewels; 21,600 vph; one-minute tourbillon; hand-engraved and skeletonized movement
Functions: hours (jump, retrograde), minutes, subsidiary seconds (on tourbillon cage)
Case: rose gold, ø 45 mm, height 12.7 mm; sapphire crystal; transparent case back under hinged lid
Band: reptile skin, buckle
Remarks: can be removed from frame and worn as pocket watch; limited edition of 25 pieces
Price: $135,000

Tourbillon Regulator
Reference number: 46-02-03-03-04
Movement: manually wound, Glashütte Original Caliber 46-02; ø 32.2 mm, height 5.8 mm; 19 jewels; 21,600 vph; one-minute tourbillon
Functions: hours (jump, retrograde), minutes, subsidiary seconds
Case: platinum, ø 39.4 mm, height 11.4 mm; sapphire crystal; transparent case back
Band: reptile skin, buckle
Remarks: limited edition of 100 pieces
Price: $98,000

PanoMaticTourbillon XL
Reference number: 41-03-04-04-04
Movement: manually wound, Glashütte Original Caliber 41-03; ø 30.95 mm, height 5.53 mm (without tourbillon carriage); 37 jewels; 21,600 vph; flying one-minute tourbillon
Functions: hours, off-center minutes, subsidiary seconds (on tourbillon cage); date (retrograde); power reserve display
Case: white gold, ø 42 mm, height 11.5 mm; sapphire crystal; transparent case back
Band: reptile skin, double folding clasp
Price: $110,000

Senator Karree Tourbillon
Reference number: 43-01-12-12-04
Movement: manually wound, Glashütte Original Caliber 43-01; 26.2 x 20.5 mm, height 4.3 mm (without tourbillon carriage); 18 jewels; 21,600 vph; flying one-minute tourbillon
Functions: hours, off-center minutes, subsidiary seconds (on tourbillon cage)
Case: platinum, 40 x 36.3 mm, height 10.8 mm; sapphire crystal; transparent case back
Band: reptile skin, buckle
Remarks: limited edition of 50 pieces
Price: $108,000

Senator Rattrapante
Reference number: 99-01-03-03-04
Movement: manually wound, Glashütte Original Caliber 99-01; ø 32.3 mm, height 8.4 mm; 47 jewels; 28,800 vph
Functions: hours, minutes, subsidiary seconds; split-seconds chronograph; panorama date
Case: platinum, ø 42 mm, height 15 mm; sapphire crystal; crown with onyx cabochon; transparent case back
Band: reptile skin, buckle
Remarks: limited edition of 100 pieces
Price: $55,000

Senator Perpetual Calendar
Reference number: 100-02-11-01-04
Movement: automatic, Glashütte Original Caliber 100-02; ø 31.15 mm, height 7.1 mm; 59 jewels; 28,800 vph; reset mechanism
Functions: hours, minutes, sweep seconds; perpetual calendar with panorama date, weekday, month, moon phase display, leap year
Case: rose gold, ø 40 mm, height 13 mm; sapphire crystal; transparent case back
Band: reptile skin, double folding clasp
Price: $24,500
Variations: platinum; stainless steel

Senator Calendar Week
Reference number: 100-05-13-02-04
Movement: automatic, Glashütte Original Caliber 100-05; ø 31.15 mm, height 7.1 mm; 71 jewels; 28,800 vph; reset mechanism
Functions: hours, minutes, sweep seconds; panorama date, calendar weeks
Case: stainless steel, ø 40 mm, height 13 mm; sapphire crystal; transparent case back
Band: reptile skin, double folding clasp
Price: $13,100
Variations: rose gold

Senator Meissen
Reference number: 100-10-01-01-04
Movement: automatic, Glashütte Original Caliber 100-10; ø 31.15 mm, height 4.3 mm; 32 jewels; 28,800 vph
Functions: hours, minutes
Case: rose gold, ø 40 mm, height 9.8 mm; sapphire crystal; transparent case back
Band: reptile skin, buckle
Remarks: handcrafted and hand-painted Meissen porcelain dial; numbered
Price: $17,000

Glashütte Original

Senator Karree Perpetual Calendar
Reference number: 39-50-52-51-04
Movement: automatic, Glashütte Original Caliber 39-54; ø 31.15 mm, height 7.3 mm; 48 jewels; 28,800 vph
Functions: hours, minutes, sweep seconds; perpetual calendar with panorama date, weekday, month, moon phase display, leap year
Case: rose gold, 40 x 36.6 mm, height 13 mm; sapphire crystal; transparent case back
Band: reptile skin, double folding clasp
Price: $23,500
Variations: stainless steel

Senator Karree Panorama Date Manual Wind
Reference number: 22-02-52-51-04
Movement: manually wound, Glashütte Original Caliber 22-02; 28.5 x 23 mm, height 5.76 mm; 35 jewels; 28,800 vph
Functions: hours, minutes, sweep seconds; panorama date
Case: rose gold, 40 x 36.3 mm, height 12.2 mm; sapphire crystal; transparent case back
Band: reptile skin, double folding clasp
Price: $17,000
Variations: stainless steel

Senator Sixties
Reference number: 39-52-02-01-04
Movement: automatic, Glashütte Original Caliber 39-52; ø 26 mm, height 4.3 mm; 25 jewels; 28,800 vph
Functions: hours, minutes, sweep seconds
Case: rose gold, ø 39 mm, height 9.4 mm; domed sapphire crystal; domed transparent case back
Band: reptile skin, buckle
Price: $11,800
Variations: stainless steel

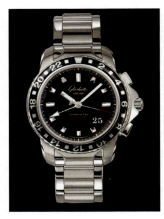

Sport Evolution GMT
Reference number: 39-55-43-03-14
Movement: automatic, Glashütte Original Caliber 39-55; ø 32.1 mm, height 5.9 mm; 40 jewels; 28,800 vph
Functions: hours, minutes, sweep seconds; panorama date; 24-hour display (second time zone)
Case: stainless steel, ø 42 mm, height 14.4 mm; bidirectionally rotating bezel with 24-hour divisions (third time zone); sapphire crystal; transparent case back; screw-in crown; water-resistant to 10 atm
Band: stainless steel, folding clasp with fine adjustment mechanism
Price: $9,900
Variations: Trieste or rubber strap

Senator Karree Chronograph
Reference number: 39-31-53-52-04
Movement: automatic, Glashütte Original Caliber 39-31; ø 31.15 mm, height 7.2 mm; 51 jewels; 28,800 vph
Functions: hours, minutes, subsidiary seconds; chronograph
Case: stainless steel, 40 x 36.6 mm, height 13.3 mm; sapphire crystal; transparent case back
Band: reptile skin, double folding clasp
Price: $7,100
Variations: rose gold

Senator Navigator Panorama Date
Reference number: 100-03-07-04-04
Movement: automatic, Glashütte Original Caliber 100-03; ø 31.15 mm, height 5.8 mm; 51 jewels; 28,800 vph; reset mechanism
Functions: hours, minutes, sweep seconds; panorama date
Case: stainless steel, ø 44 mm, height 13.9 mm; sapphire crystal
Band: reptile skin, buckle
Price: $8,500

Senator Sixties
Reference number: 39-52-01-02-04
Movement: automatic, Glashütte Original Caliber 39-52; ø 26 mm, height 4.3 mm; 25 jewels; 28,800 vph
Functions: hours, minutes, sweep seconds
Case: stainless steel, ø 39 mm, height 9.4 mm; domed sapphire crystal; domed transparent case back
Band: reptile skin, buckle
Price: $5,800
Variations: rose gold

Sport Evolution M
Reference number: 39-21-01-02-14
Movement: automatic, Glashütte Original Caliber 39-21; ø 26 mm, height 4.3 mm; 25 jewels; 28,800 vph
Functions: hours, minutes, sweep seconds; date
Case: stainless steel, ø 37 mm, height 12 mm; aluminum salmon-colored bezel; sapphire crystal; transparent case back; screw-in crown; water-resistant to 10 atm
Band: stainless steel, folding clasp with fine adjustment mechanism
Price: $6,900
Variations: silver-colored dial and diamond-set bezel; Trieste strap

Glashütte Original

PanoMaticChrono XL
Reference number: 95-01-31-24-05
Movement: automatic, Glashütte Original Caliber 95-01; ø 32.2 mm, height 7.2 mm; 57 jewels; 28,800 vph; central bilaterally winding rotor rotor via stepped gear
Functions: hours, minutes, subsidiary seconds; chronograph with flyback function; panorama date
Case: white gold, ø 42 mm, height 13.5 mm; sapphire crystal; transparent case back
Band: reptile skin, buckle
Price: $50,000
Variations: rose gold

PanoMaticReserve XL
Reference number: 90-03-31-11-05
Movement: automatic, Glashütte Original Caliber 90-03; ø 32.6 mm, height 7 mm; 61 jewels; 28,800 vph; off-center rotor; duplex swan-neck fine adjustment; screw balance
Functions: hours, off-center minutes, subsidiary seconds; panorama date; power reserve display
Case: rose gold, ø 42 mm, height 12.5 mm; sapphire crystal; transparent case back
Band: reptile skin, double folding clasp
Price: $20,000
Variations: white gold

PanoMaticVenue
Reference number: 90-04-01-01-04
Movement: automatic, Glashütte Original Caliber 90-04; ø 32.6 mm, height 7 mm; 47 jewels; 28,800 vph; off-center rotor; duplex swan-neck fine adjustment
Functions: hours, off-center minutes, subsidiary seconds; 24-hour display (second time zone)
Case: rose gold, ø 39.4 mm, height 12 mm; sapphire crystal; transparent case back
Band: reptile skin, double folding clasp
Price: $15,200
Variations: limited edition of 200 pieces in platinum; stainless steel

Lady Serenade
Reference number: 39-22-03-22-04
Movement: automatic, Glashütte Original Caliber 39-22; ø 26 mm, height 4.3 mm; 25 jewels; 28,800 vph
Functions: hours, minutes, sweep seconds; date
Case: stainless steel, ø 36 mm, height 10.2 mm; diamond-set bezel; sapphire crystal; transparent case back; diamond in crown
Band: reptile skin, double folding clasp
Price: $10,300
Variations: without diamond-set bezel; in rose gold (with or without diamonds)

PanoMaticLunar XL
Reference number: 90-02-31-14-05
Movement: automatic, Glashütte Original Caliber 90-02; ø 32.6 mm, height 7 mm; 47 jewels; 28,800 vph; off-center rotor; duplex swan-neck fine adjustment
Functions: hours, off-center minutes, subsidiary seconds; panorama date; moon phase display
Case: white gold, ø 42 mm, height 12.5 mm; sapphire crystal; transparent case back
Band: reptile skin, double folding clasp
Price: $21,300
Variations: rose gold

PanoMaticCentral XL
Reference number: 100-03-21-11-04
Movement: automatic, Glashütte Original Caliber 100-03; ø 31.15 mm, height 5.8 mm; 51 jewels; 28,800 vph; reset mechanism
Functions: hours, minutes, sweep seconds; panorama date
Case: rose gold, ø 42 mm, height 11.6 mm; sapphire crystal; transparent case back
Band: reptile skin, buckle
Price: $17,500
Variations: white gold

PanoMaticLunar
Reference number: 90-02-01-01-04
Movement: automatic, Glashütte Original Caliber 90-02; ø 32.6 mm, height 7 mm; 47 jewels; 28,800 vph; off-center rotor; duplex swan-neck fine adjustment
Functions: hours, off-center minutes, subsidiary seconds; panorama date; moon phase display
Case: rose gold, ø 39.4 mm, height 12 mm; sapphire crystal; transparent case back
Band: reptile skin, double folding clasp
Price: $17,000
Variations: stainless steel; limited edition of 200 pieces in platinum

Pretty Butterfly
Reference number: 65-01-70-70-04
Movement: manually wound, Glashütte Original Caliber 65-01; ø 32.2 mm, height 6.1 mm; 48 jewels; 28,800 vph
Functions: hours, off-center minutes, subsidiary seconds; panorama date; power reserve display
Case: white gold, ø 39.4 mm, height 12 mm; diamond-set bezel; sapphire crystal; transparent case back; diamond-set crown
Band: reptile skin, buckle set with brilliant-cut diamonds
Remarks: mother-of-pearl dial set with diamonds
Price: $38,200

Glashütte Original

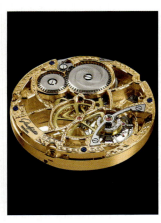

Caliber 46-12
Mechanical with manual winding, one-minute tourbillon; power reserve 60 hours, hand-skeletonized and engraved
Functions: jump retrograde hours, minutes, subsidiary seconds
Diameter: 32.2 mm; **Height:** 5.8 mm
Jewels: 19 plus two diamond endstones
Balance: screw balance with gold screws in tourbillon cage, one revolution per minute
Frequency: 21,600 vph
Balance spring: Breguet hairspring
Remarks: very finely finished components, beveled edges, polished steel parts, screw-mounted gold chatons, blued screws, winding wheels with double sunburst pattern; hand-skeletonized and engraved

Caliber 99
Mechanical with manual winding; power reserve 45 hours
Functions: hours, minutes, subsidiary seconds; split-seconds chronograph; panorama date
Diameter: 32.3 mm; **Height:** 8.4 mm
Jewels: 47
Balance: screw balance with 18 gold screws
Frequency: 28,800 vph
Balance spring: flat hairspring, swan-neck fine adjustment
Remarks: very finely finished movement, beveled edges, polished steel parts, screw-mounted gold chatons, blued screws, winding wheels with double sunburst pattern; bridges and cocks decorated with Glashütte ribbing; balance cock engraved by hand

Caliber 93
Mechanical with automatic winding, flying one-minute tourbillon; off-center rotor; power reserve 48 hours
Functions: hours, minutes (off-center), subsidiary seconds (on tourbillon cage); panorama date
Diameter: 32.2 mm; **Height:** 7.65 mm
Jewels: 46 plus two diamond endstones
Balance: screw balance with 18 gold screws in tourbillon carriage, one revolution per minute
Frequency: 21,600 vph
Balance spring: Breguet hairspring
Remarks: beveled edges, polished steel parts, screw-mounted gold chatons, blued screws, winding wheels with double sunburst decoration, bridges and cocks with Glashütte ribbing

Caliber 41-03
Mechanical with manual winding, flying one-minute tourbillon; power reserve 48 hours
Functions: hours, minutes (off-center), subsidiary seconds (on tourbillon cage); date (retrograde); power reserve indication
Diameter: 26.2 mm
Height: 5.53 mm (without tourbillon cage)
Jewels: 35 plus two diamond endstones
Balance: screw balance with 18 gold screws in tourbillon cage, one revolution per minute
Frequency: 21,600 vph
Balance spring: Breguet hairspring
Remarks: components finely finished, beveled edges, polished steel parts, screw-mounted gold chatons, blued screws, winding wheels with double sunburst pattern

Caliber 46-02
Mechanical with manual winding, one-minute tourbillon; power reserve 60 hours
Functions: hours (jump, retrograde), minutes, subsidiary seconds
Diameter: 32.2 mm
Height: 5.8 mm (without tourbillon cage)
Jewels: 17 plus two diamond endstones
Balance: screw balance with 18 gold balance screws in tourbillon cage, one revolution per minute
Frequency: 21,600 vph
Balance spring: Breguet hairspring
Remarks: components finely finished, beveled edges, polished steel parts, blued screws, winding wheels with double sunburst pattern; hand-engraved base plate

Caliber 95
Mechanical with automatic winding, twin spring barrels with bilaterally winding step gear in two speeds
Functions: hours, minutes (off-center), subsidiary seconds; chronograph with flyback function; panorama date
Diameter: 32.2 mm; **Height:** 7.2 mm; **Jewels:** 57
Balance: screw balance with 18 gold screws
Frequency: 28,800 vph
Balance spring: flat hairspring, swan-neck fine adjustment
Remarks: separate wheel bridges for winding and chronograph; screw-mounted gold chatons, blued screws, winding wheels with double sunburst decoration, bridges and cocks with Glashütte ribbing, hand-engraved balance cock

Caliber 90 (base caliber)
Mechanical with automatic winding; power reserve 42 hours
Functions: hours, minutes (off-center), sweep seconds; panorama date, moon phase
Diameter: 32.6 mm; **Height:** 5.4 mm; **Jewels:** 28
Balance: screw balance with 18 gold weighted screws
Balance spring: flat hairspring, Duplex swan-neck fine adjustment (for beat and rate)
Frequency: 28,800 vph
Balance spring: flat hairspring, duplex swan-neck fine adjustment (for rate and beat)
Shock protection: Incabloc
Remarks: hand-engraved balance cock; three-quarter plate with Glashütte ribbing; off-center skeletonized rotor with 21-karat gold weight

Caliber 60
Mechanical with manual winding, power reserve 42 hours
Functions: hours, minutes, subsidiary seconds; panorama date; chronograph with flyback and countdown functions (30 minutes, acoustic signal via gong)
Diameter: 32.2 mm; **Height:** 7.2 mm; **Jewels:** 54
Balance: screw balance with 18 gold weighted screws
Frequency: 28,800 vph
Balance spring: flat hairspring, swan-neck fine adjustment
Remarks: screw-mounted gold chatons, blued screws, winding wheels with double sunburst pattern, bridges and cocks decorated with Glashütte ribbing, balance cock engraved by hand

Glashütte Original

Caliber 65
Mechanical with manual winding, power reserve 42 hours
Functions: hours, minutes, subsidiary seconds; power reserve indication
Diameter: 32.2 mm; **Height:** 6.1 mm; **Jewels:** 48
Balance: screw balance with 18 gold weighted screws
Frequency: 28,800 vph
Balance spring: flat hairspring, Duplex swan-neck fine adjustment (for beat and rate)
Remarks: immaculately finished movement, beveled edges, polished steel parts, blued screws, screw-mounted gold chatons, winding wheels with double sunburst pattern, bridges and cocks with Glashütte ribbing; balance cock engraved by hand

Caliber 43
Mechanical with manual winding, flying one-minute tourbillon; power reserve 48 hours
Functions: hours, minutes (off-center), subsidiary seconds (on tourbillon cage)
Dimensions: 26.2 x 20.5 mm
Height: 4.3 mm (without tourbillon cage)
Jewels: 16 plus two diamond endstones
Balance: screw balance with 18 gold balance screws in tourbillon cage, one revolution per minute
Frequency: 21,600 vph
Balance spring: Breguet hairspring
Remarks: movement skeletonized and engraved by hand, beveled edges, polished steel parts, screw-mounted gold chatons, blued screws, winding wheels with double sunburst pattern

Caliber 100
Mechanical with automatic winding; skeletonized rotor; reset mechanism for second hand via button on case; power reserve 55 hours
Functions: hours, minutes, sweep seconds; panorama date
Diameter: 31.15 mm; **Height:** 7.1 mm; **Jewels:** 59
Balance: screw balance with 18 gold weighted screws; **Frequency:** 28,800 vph
Balance spring: flat hairspring
Remarks: screw-mounted gold chatons, blued screws, winding wheels with double sunburst decoration, bridges, cocks with Glashütte ribbing
Related calibers: 100-01 (power reserve display); 100-02 (perpetual calendar); 100-03 (panorama date); 100-04 (moon phase); 100-05 (calendar weeks); 100-06 (complete calendar)

Caliber 69
Mechanical with manual winding, power reserve 42 hours
Functions: hours, minutes, subsidiary seconds; flyback chronograph; panorama date
Diameter: 32.2 mm; **Height:** 7.2 mm; **Jewels:** 41
Balance: screw balance with 18 gold weighted screws
Frequency: 28,800 vph
Balance spring: flat hairspring, swan-neck fine adjustment
Remarks: immaculately finished movement, beveled edges, polished steel parts, blued screws, screw-mounted gold chatons, three-quarter plate decorated with Glashütte ribbing; winding wheels with double sunburst pattern; balance cock engraved by hand

Caliber 22-02
Mechanical with manual winding, power reserve 40 hours
Functions: hours, minutes, sweep seconds; flyback panorama date
Dimensions: 28.5 x 23 mm; **Height:** 5.76 mm
Jewels: 35
Balance: screw balance with 18 gold weighted screws
Frequency: 28,800 vph
Balance spring: flat hairspring, swan-neck fine adjustment
Remarks: immaculately finished movement, beveled edges, polished steel parts, blued screws, screw-mounted gold chatons, bridges and cocks decorated with Glashütte ribbing; winding wheels with double sunburst pattern

Caliber 39-50 (dial side)
Mechanical with automatic winding, power reserve 40 hours, stop-seconds
Functions: hours, minutes, sweep seconds; flyback perpetual calendar with panorama date, weekday, month, moon phase, and leap year
Diameter: 31.15 mm; **Height:** 7.2 mm
Jewels: 48
Balance spring: flat hairspring, swan-neck fine adjustment
Frequency: 28,800 vph
Shock protection: Incabloc
Remarks: beveled edges, polished steel parts, three-quarter plate decorated with Glashütte ribbing; winding wheels with sunburst pattern; skeletonized rotor with 21-karat gold oscillating weight

Glycine

Large watches have always been one of Glycine's specialties. Founded in the year 1914 by Eugène Meylan, the brand at first produced voluminous timepieces with gold and platinum cases for solvent men. The production of watches containing mechanical movements was continued into the 1970s, even though the consumer was by then demanding quartz watches almost exclusively.

Glycine Watch SA is known more today as a specialist for making pilot's watches, as once again illustrated by the plenitude of pilot-style timepieces introduced in 2007. The Airman 7 Plaza Mayor is a new take on Glycine's signature theme, exhibiting a beguiling overall simplicity and a stately size—in a square case measuring 53 x 53 mm. It utilizes three independent mechanical movements to achieve the display of four time zones: an automatic ETA 2893 and two smaller, decorated ETA 2671s. It is available in black stainless steel with a black carbon fiber dial and in a satin-finished stainless steel case with dark red or dark blue carbon fiber dials. An 18-karat gold version of this timepiece is slated for release at the end of 2007.

The classically round Airman 17 features a stately case diameter of 46 mm and a new, technically interesting crown at 4 o'clock to set the timepiece's second and third time zones and ensure that they remain unchanged.

Katherina Brechbühler, co-owner and man-ager with her father Hans, describes the Combat family "as one of the company's most popular lines." Within the past year, the pair has added a diver's watch, a chro-nograph, and an automatic timepiece to the line that retain the typical look of the reli-able, quality-conscious, and reasonably priced ETA-driven timepieces.

Glycine has always been one of the front-runners in new trends in mechanical watches. For example, in 1938 Glycine was one of the twenty-nine exhibitors at the first Basel Fair after the Great Depression and ensuing world economic crisis in the early 1930s. Since then, Glycine hasn't missed a single Basel Fair. After the war, Glycine was one of the first Swiss brands to put its money on the automatic movement. In 1948 the company was already able to show an entire range of automatic watches. In the year 1996 the company once again took up designing large-format watches, something that represented one of the traditional firm's most important production arms in the '50s and '60s. On the American and, especially, the Italian markets, Glycine has been strongly represented since the middle of the 1990s with oversized chronographs and sports watches.

Glycine

Airman 17
Reference number: 3852.19-LB9
Movement: automatic, ETA A07.171; ø 36.6 mm, height 7.6 mm; 24 jewels; 28,800 vph
Functions: hours, minutes, sweep seconds; date; 24-hour display (second time zone)
Case: stainless steel, ø 46 mm, height 15 mm; unidirectionally rotating bezel with 24-hour scale (third time zone); sapphire crystal; transparent case back; screw-in crown; water-resistant to 20 atm
Band: leather, buckle
Price: $3,375
Variations: stainless steel bracelet; various dial variations

Airman 7 Plaza Mayor
Reference number: 3861.19-LB9
Movement: automatic, ETA Caliber 1 x 2893-2, 2 x 2671-2; three independent ETA automatic movements, one with an additional 24-hour display
Functions: hours, minutes, sweep seconds; date; three time zones; additional 24-hour display (fourth time zone)
Case: stainless steel, 53 x 53 mm, height 12.5 mm; sapphire crystal; transparent case back; screw-in crowns at 2 o'clock; water-resistant to 5 atm
Band: leather, buckle
Price: $5,690
Variations: in various dial versions; steel-colored movement holder

Combat SUB Automatic
Reference number: 3863.19ATN-D9
Movement: automatic, ETA Caliber 2824-2; ø 25.6 mm, height 4.6 mm; 25 jewels; 28,800 vph
Functions: hours, minutes, sweep seconds; date
Case: stainless steel, ø 42 mm, height 10.6 mm; unidirectionally rotating bezel with 60-minute divisions; sapphire crystal; screw-in crown; water-resistant to 20 atm
Band: rubber, buckle
Price: $925
Variations: stainless steel bracelet; various dial variations

Combat 07 Chronograph
Reference number: 3869.196AT-LB9
Movement: automatic, ETA Valjoux Caliber 7750; ø 30 mm, height 7.9 mm; 25 jewels; 28,800 vph
Functions: hours, minutes, subsidiary seconds; chronograph; date
Case: stainless steel, ø 43 mm, height 14.5 mm; sapphire crystal; transparent case back; screw-in crown; water-resistant to 10 atm
Band: leather, buckle
Price: $1,575
Variations: various dial versions; stainless steel bracelet

Incursore Chrono Day Date
Reference number: 3867.19SL-LB9
Movement: automatic, ETA Valjoux Caliber 7750; ø 30 mm, height 7.9 mm; 25 jewels; 28,800 vph
Functions: hours, minutes, subsidiary seconds; date, weekday; chronograph
Case: stainless steel, ø 46 mm, height 15 mm; sapphire crystal; transparent case back; screw-in crown; water-resistant to 10 atm
Band: leather, buckle
Price: $2,600
Variations: various dial versions

Incursore 46 mm manual
Reference number: 3873.19SL-LB9
Movement: automatic, ETA Unitas Caliber 6497-1; ø 36.6 mm, height 4.5 mm; 17 jewels; 18,000 vph
Functions: hours, minutes, subsidiary seconds
Case: stainless steel, ø 46 mm, height 12 mm; sapphire crystal; transparent case back; water-resistant to 20 atm
Band: leather, buckle
Price: $1,525

Lagunare Automatic
Reference number: 3819.19-LB7
Movement: automatic, ETA Caliber 2824-2; ø 25.6 mm, height 4.6 mm; 25 jewels; 28,800 vph
Functions: hours, minutes, sweep seconds; date
Case: stainless steel, ø 46 mm, height 12.5 mm; unidirectionally rotating ring under crystal with 60-minute divisions, settable via crown; sapphire crystal; screw-in crown; water-resistant to 30 atm
Band: leather, buckle
Price: $1,250
Variations: rubber strap; stainless steel bracelet

Lagunare 1000
Reference number: 3850.19-D9
Movement: automatic, ETA Caliber 2824-2; ø 25.6 mm, height 4.6 mm; 25 jewels; 28,800 vph
Functions: hours, minutes, sweep seconds; date
Case: stainless steel, ø 46 mm, height 13 mm; unidirectionally rotating ring under crystal with 60-minute divisions, settable via crown; sapphire crystal; screw-in crown; water-resistant to 30 atm
Band: rubber, buckle
Price: $1,850
Variations: various dial variations

Graham

The Swiss group The British Masters has breathed new life into the old name Graham with unusual watch creations. The moniker is derived from one of the most important figures in the history of watchmaking: the great George Graham was not only the namesake of the cylinder escapement from the eighteenth century, but was also said to be the inventor of the chronograph and may justifiably be called one of the most important men in the history of watchmaking.

Graham began working for the famous Thomas Tompion in 1695, but soon started his own business—with the ambition of outdoing his master. Most of the watches that were made at this time deviated in rate precision by up to ten minutes per day. Graham was one of the first whose watches didn't deviate more than one second per day. Graham even received the contract from the Greenwich Royal Observatory to build its master clock. He was also inducted into the Royal Society, an organization that was originally reserved for scientists and astronomers only.

His inventions made Graham famous throughout Europe, even if he had none of them patented—his moral ideals did not allow him to! He preferred to share his knowledge with his colleagues. Because of his great deeds performed in the name of his homeland, the English Parliament agreed to inter his earthly remains in Westminster Abbey's nave, where they still reside today.

Despite his merits earned in the development of precision timekeeping, it was one of the short-term measuring devices Graham invented that would coin the image of the new wristwatch brand. To this day, nothing has changed in the base concept of the chronograph, which includes a second set of hands that can be coupled or decoupled to join or leave the flow of energy in the movement as desired. Therefore, various chronographs play the main role in the modern Graham model palette.

There is, for example, the Chronofighter model, whose unusual thumb lever mechanism is an enduring fascination in this most popular of boy toy watches. Similar buttons were built sixty years ago for British bomber pilots, who couldn't reliably press the comparatively small crown button of their pilot's chronographs with their big gloves on.

The chronograph family keeps on growing—now completed with the Swordfish chronograph, also available for lefties and outfitted with a very special visual: In this case it's the applied magnifying lenses over the two chronograph counters, whereby it is worth mentioning that the little crystals are each surrounded by a lavishly constructed bezel. The new chronograph for 2007 is named for one of the famous curves of England's legendary race course, Silverstone: Woodcote. Whole races, championships, and careers have been decided in this curve, and among motor sports fans the name alone commands a great deal of respect. The Grand Silverstone Woodcote's sporty dial made of carbon fiber, displaying large date and sweep GMT indications, is striking. Its energy is supplied by the reliable bi-compax chronograph movement Graham Caliber 1721. This timepiece also includes an incredibly practical flyback function that means the chronograph no longer needs to be stopped, reset, and started again—all of these steps are united in one simple, flowing gesture. The sporty watch is secured to the wrist by a black rubber strap with a tire tread motif.

Last year's King George saw Graham daring to create a true *grande complication* for the first time: a split-second chronograph with a minute repeater.

Swordfish Big 12/6 Left
Reference number: 2SWAS.B14A.K06B
Movement: automatic, Graham Caliber G 1710 (base ETA Valjoux 7750); ø 30 mm, height 8.75 mm; 34 jewels; 28,800 vph
Functions: hours, minutes, subsidiary seconds; chronograph
Case: stainless steel, ø 46 mm, height 18 mm; sapphire crystal with two magnifying lenses over the chronograph totalizers; screw-in crown; water-resistant to 10 atm
Band: rubber, buckle
Price: $7,750
Variations: crown and buttons on the right; diverse dial and band variations

Swordfish Big 12/6 Right
Reference number: 2SWAS.B21A.K06B
Movement: automatic, Graham Caliber G 1710 (base ETA Valjoux 7750); ø 30 mm, height 8.75 mm; 34 jewels; 28,800 vph
Functions: hours, minutes, subsidiary seconds; chronograph
Case: PVD-coated stainless steel, ø 46 mm, height 18 mm; red gold bezel, crown, and case; sapphire crystal with two magnifying lenses over the chronograph totalizers; screw-in crown; water-resistant to 10 atm
Band: rubber, buckle
Price: $16,450
Variations: red gold; diverse dial variations

Chronofighter Oversize Commander
Reference number: 20VATCO.B01A.K10B
Movement: automatic, Graham Caliber G 1732 (base ETA Valjoux 7750); ø 30 mm, height 8.75 mm; 30 jewels; 28,800 vph
Functions: hours, minutes, subsidiary seconds; chronograph
Case: titanium, ø 46 mm, height 18 mm; bezel coated with carbon fiber; sapphire crystal; crown with chronograph button and security device; water-resistant to 10 atm
Band: rubber, buckle
Price: $10,400

Chronofighter Oversize Diver Orange Seal
Reference number: 20VDIVAS.B02A.K10B
Movement: automatic, Graham Caliber G 1732 (base ETA Valjoux 7750); ø 30 mm, height 8.75 mm; 30 jewels; 28,800 vph
Functions: hours, minutes, subsidiary seconds; chronograph
Case: stainless steel, ø 46 mm, height 18 mm; unidirectionally rotating bezel with 60-minute divisions; sapphire crystal; crown with chronograph button and security device; helium valve on case; water-resistant to 30 atm
Band: rubber, buckle
Price: $7,500
Variations: blackened stainless steel; partially blackened stainless steel

Chronofighter Oversize Overload Mark III
Reference number: 20VAS.G01A.K10B
Movement: automatic, Graham Caliber G 1732 (base ETA Valjoux 7750); ø 30 mm, height 8.75 mm; 30 jewels; 28,800 vph
Functions: hours, minutes, subsidiary seconds; chronograph
Case: stainless steel, ø 46 mm, height 18 mm; sapphire crystal; crown with chronograph button and security device; water-resistant to 30 atm
Band: rubber, buckle
Remarks: limited edition of 500 pieces
Price: $9,500

Chronofighter R.A.C. Skeleton
Reference number: 2CRBS.BK1A.K25B
Movement: automatic, Graham Caliber G 1742SQ (base ETA Valjoux 7750); ø 30 mm, height 8.75 mm; 30 jewels; 28,800 vph; column-wheel control of chronograph functions
Functions: hours, minutes, subsidiary seconds; chronograph
Case: stainless steel, ø 43 mm, height 16 mm; sapphire crystal; transparent case back; crown with chronograph button and security device
Band: rubber, buckle
Remarks: dial partially skeletonized
Price: $11,050
Variations: with silver-colored dial

Grand Silverstone Woodcote II
Reference number: 2GSIUBR.B07A.K07B
Movement: automatic, Graham Caliber G 1721 (base ETA Valjoux 7750); ø 30.05 mm, height 8.75 mm; 28 jewels; 28,800 vph
Functions: hours, minutes, subsidiary seconds; chronograph with flyback function; large date; 24-hour display (second time zone)
Case: PVD-coated stainless steel, ø 44 mm, height 15 mm; red gold bezel coated with carbon fiber coating and tachymeter scale; sapphire crystal; screw-in crown; water-resistant to 10 atm
Band: rubber, buckle
Remarks: limited edition of 500 pieces
Price: $15,000
Variations: stainless steel (limited edition of 500)

Chronofighter RAC Black Speed
Reference number: 2CRBS.B01A.L30B
Movement: automatic, Graham Caliber G 1732 (base ETA Valjoux 7750); ø 30 mm, height 8.75 mm; 30 jewels; 28,800 vph; column-wheel control of chronograph functions
Functions: hours, minutes, subsidiary seconds; chronograph; date
Case: stainless steel, ø 43 mm, height 16.4 mm; sapphire crystal; transparent case back; crown with chronograph button and security device; water-resistant to 5 atm
Band: leather, buckle
Price: $8,400
Variations: diverse dial variations; red gold

Greubel Forsey

Not another tourbillon, some watch experts may have groaned when they heard of Alsatian Robert Greubel and Englishman Stephen Forsey's invention during Baselworld 2004—an invention that comprised two tourbillon carriages working at an incline of 30 degrees. Forsey and Greubel have not only taken up Abraham-Louis Breguet's basic concept in their designs—one that sees deviation of the balance cancelled out by the rotation of the tourbillon carriage. These two master watchmakers go not only one step further with their inventions, but two at once.

Forsey and Greubel work on several levels of varying structures all at once, though they are also involved in a network of external contacts.

Thanks to their second venture, CompliTime SA, they are closely associated with the leading brands of the Swiss watchmaking industry, which the two creative watchmakers also supply with complicated movements and mechanisms. The Richemont Group recently bought into this company—which should come as no surprise since the world's largest luxury watch group has been a good customer for years, profiting from the know-how these inventive young watchmakers readily offer. The watch brand Greubel Forsey, however, remains exclusively all their own.

Double Tourbillon 30°
Movement: manually wound, Caliber GF 02, ø 36.4 mm, height 9.65 mm; 39 jewels; 21,600 vph; balance with variable inertia; four-minute tourbillon inside of which a one-minute tourbillon inclined by 30° can be found; twin spring barrels; power reserve 72 hours
Functions: hours, minutes, subsidiary seconds; four-minute indication on large tourbillon; power reserve display
Case: platinum, ø 43.5 mm, height 15.76 mm; sapphire crystal; transparent case back
Band: reptile skin, folding clasp
Price: $425,000
Variations: red or white gold with various dial variations ($360,000)

Double Tourbillon 30° Secret
Movement: manually wound, Caliber GF 02, ø 36.4 mm, height 9.65 mm; 39 jewels; 21,600 vph; balance with variable inertia; four-minute tourbillon inside of which a one-minute tourbillon inclined by 30° can be found; twin spring barrels; power reserve 72 hours
Functions: hours, minutes, subsidiary seconds; four-minute indication on large tourbillon; power reserve display
Case: white gold, ø 43.5 mm, height 15.84 mm; sapphire crystal; transparent case back
Band: reptile skin, folding clasp
Remarks: limited edition of 11 pieces
Price: $380,000

Invention Piece 1
Movement: manually wound, Caliber GF 02n, ø 36.4 mm, height 12.72 mm; 38 jewels; 21,600 vph; balance with variable inertia; four-minute tourbillon inside of which a one-minute tourbillon inclined by 30° can be found; twin spring barrels; power reserve 72 hours
Functions: hours, minutes (sectoral), subsidiary seconds; power reserve display
Case: white gold, ø 43.5 mm, height 16.64 mm; sapphire crystal; transparent case back
Band: reptile skin, folding clasp
Remarks: limited edition of 11 pieces
Price: $450,000
Variations: limited edition of 11 pieces in red gold

Tourbillon 24 Secondes Incliné
Movement: manually wound, Caliber GF 01, ø 36.4 mm, height 9.65 mm; 36 jewels; 21,600 vph; 24-second tourbillon inside of which a balance with variable inertia inclined by 25° can be found; twin spring barrels; power reserve 72 hours
Functions: hours, minutes, subsidiary seconds; power reserve display
Case: white gold, ø 43.5 mm, height 15.76 mm; sapphire crystal; transparent case back
Band: reptile skin, folding clasp
Price: $250,000
Variations: black or silver dial

Hautlence

Renaud de Retz and Guillaume Tetu were simply two young men employed in the Swiss watch industry until about three years ago when they discovered they had a common passion. Experienced enough to understand where to find the know-how they had jointly envisioned to create their own unique brand of *haute horlogerie*, they began work on their premier watch, resulting in something truly new in an industry where the wheel rarely gets reinvented.

De Retz, who is in charge of marketing and communications, maintains that the company has "a far-sighted and avant-garde approach" to its timepiece, which is simply called HL and currently available in twelve different versions. Elucidating this view, de Retz explains, "The fact that we are not watchmakers allows us to have a completely new approach. With Hautlence, we started from scratch and said to ourselves, 'let's do what we want to see in a watch and what kind of watch we would like to egotistically have.' This product, from our point of view, is 'avant-garde' because this is a new way of telling time and of showing beautiful mechanics." The movement is a brand-new construction featuring an element that has not yet been used in watchmaking and which Tetu, who is in charge of product development, calls the connecting rod. Literally speaking, the hand-wound movement is regulator-style, but the hour disk, located on the left, is propelled by the connecting rod (visible horizontally along the bottom of the dial) between the hour disk and the retrograde minutes. When the minute hand reaches the end of its arc, its movement sets the connecting rod into motion and propels the disk forward one space. The mechanism is framed by an attractive 16/9 TV screen case.

HL 05
Movement: manually wound, Hautlence Caliber HL (base ETA Peseux 7001); 37.3 x 30.4 mm, height 3.8 mm; 24 jewels; 21,600 vph; power reserve 40 hours; sandblasted, rhodium-plated, decorated with perlage and côtes de Genève
Functions: hours (jump), minutes (retrograde), subsidiary seconds
Case: white gold, 43.5 x 37 mm, height 10.5 mm; sapphire crystal, anti-reflective on the inside; water-resistant to 3 atm
Band: alligator skin, white gold triple folding clasp with extension
Remarks: limited and numbered edition of 88 pieces
Price: $42,900

HL 06
Movement: manually wound, Hautlence Caliber HL (base ETA Peseux 7001); 37.3 x 30.4 mm, height 3.8 mm; 24 jewels; 21,600 vph; power reserve 40 hours; sandblasted, rhodium-plated, decorated with perlage and côtes de Genève
Functions: hours (jump), minutes (retrograde), subsidiary seconds
Case: white gold, 43.5 x 37 mm, height 10.5 mm; sapphire crystal, anti-reflective on the inside; water-resistant to 3 atm
Band: alligator skin, white gold triple folding clasp with extension
Remarks: limited and numbered edition of 88 pieces
Price: $42,900

HLs 04
Movement: manually wound, Hautlence Caliber HL (base ETA Peseux 7001); 37.3 x 30.4 mm, height 3.8 mm; 24 jewels; 21,600 vph; power reserve 40 hours; sandblasted, rhodium-plated, decorated with perlage and côtes de Genève
Functions: hours (jump), minutes (retrograde), subsidiary seconds
Case: white gold, 43.5 x 37 mm, height 10.5 mm; bezel in stainless steel with black DLC coating; sapphire crystal, anti-reflective on the inside; water-resistant to 5 atm
Band: rubber, white gold triple folding clasp with extension
Remarks: limited and numbered edition of 88 pieces
Price: $48,900

HLs 06
Movement: manually wound, Hautlence Caliber HL (base ETA Peseux 7001); 37.3 x 30.4 mm, height 3.8 mm; 24 jewels; 21,600 vph; power reserve 40 hours; sandblasted, rhodium-plated, decorated with perlage and côtes de Genève
Functions: hours (jump), minutes (retrograde), subsidiary seconds
Case: rose gold, 43 x 45 mm, height 12.5 mm; sapphire crystal, anti-reflective on the inside; water-resistant to 5 atm
Band: rubber, rose gold triple folding clasp with extension
Remarks: limited and numbered edition of 88 pieces
Price: $44,900
Variations: alligator skin strap

Hamilton

Hamilton Watch Co., established in 1892 in Lancaster, Pennsylvania, had developed into one of the biggest watch manufacturers in the world shortly after its founding. Around the turn of the century, every second railway employee in the United States wore a watch by Hamilton in his vest pocket so that he could not only register the trains' punctuality, but also oversee and coordinate them.

Hamilton secured its good reputation with a continuous stream of new customers, including expedition travelers, ocean-crossers, mail carrier pilots, and other daring adventurers. And, of course, the military. There were even times when Hamilton had to halt production of civilian timepieces, as the demand from the military was so great. Hamilton's Lancaster factory produced an estimated one million watches during World War II.

The triangular Ventura remains unforgettable; in 1957 it was one of the first wristwatches outfitted with an electronic movement that not only banked on progressive technology, but also progressive design. For the fiftieth anniversary of this spectacular watch, Hamilton this year launched two limited special edition models, one outfitted with quartz and one with an automatic movement, each limited to 1,957 pieces.

Khaki Action 44 mm
Reference number: H63516135
Movement: automatic, ETA Valjoux Caliber 7753; ø 30 mm, height 7.9 mm; 27 jewels; 28,800 vph
Functions: hours, minutes, subsidiary seconds; chronograph; date
Case: stainless steel, ø 44 mm, height 12.2 mm; black PVD-coated unidirectionally rotating bezel with 60-minute divisions; sapphire crystal; transparent case back; screw-in crown and buttons
Band: stainless steel; double folding clasp
Price: $1,445
Variations: various strap and bracelet variations

Khaki Twilight
Reference number: H62515793
Movement: automatic, ETA Caliber 2893; ø 25.6 mm, height 4.1 mm; 21 jewels; 28,800 vph
Functions: hours, minutes, sweep seconds; date; 24-hour display (second time zone)
Case: stainless steel, ø 44 mm, height 14.5 mm; sapphire crystal; transparent case back; screw-in crown with security bow
Band: stainless steel; double folding clasp
Price: $795
Variations: rubber strap

Jazzmaster Square Auto Chrono
Reference number: H32666535
Movement: automatic, ETA Caliber 2894; ø 28.6 mm, height 6.1 mm; 37 jewels; 28,800 vph
Functions: hours, minutes, subsidiary seconds; date; chronograph
Case: stainless steel, 40 x 40 mm, height 14.95 mm; sapphire crystal; screw-in crown
Band: stainless steel; double folding clasp
Price: $1,795
Variations: silver-colored dial; leather strap

Maestro Day-Date
Reference number: H32716839
Movement: automatic, ETA Valjoux Caliber 7750; ø 30 mm, height 7.9 mm; 25 jewels; 28,800 vph
Functions: hours, minutes, subsidiary seconds; chronograph; date, day
Case: stainless steel, ø 45 mm, height 15 mm; sapphire crystal; transparent case back; screw-in crown
Band: leather, folding clasp
Price: $1,345
Variations: silver-colored dial

Hermès

Parisian company Hermès does things quite differently than its fashionable competition with subsidiaries in the French capital. One of the most fundamental differences is the fact that Hermès has never been bought by a large concern. This company has a holding structure managed by Jean-Louis Dumas, a fifth-generation member of the founding family.

Hermès was established in 1837 by Thierry Hermès in Paris. This company specialized in robust leather utensils that gentlemen needed for travel at the time.

The production of watches, begun with the founding of Biel-based subsidiary La Montre Hermès in 1978, is easily explained: the company's workshops in Paris were already producing straps for watches in the 1920s, thereby even influencing watch fashions.

Different from other manufacturers of lifestyle products, Hermès does not have its watches simply assembled by so-called private labelers, but strives to have 100 percent control over its products. The factory located in a Biel suburb can soon celebrate twenty years of continuously growing autonomy.

Last year, Hermès invested 25 million Swiss francs in its movement production, thus securing 25 percent of Manufacture Vaucher's stock. This didn't particularly surprise insiders, especially since Hermès began working with this arm of the Sandoz empire two years previously, when investment was the order of the day.

Dressage
Reference number: DR 1.770.218 M
Movement: automatic, Vaucher Caliber P 1928; ø 25.6 mm, height 3.5 mm; 32 jewels; 28,800 vph; red gold rotor
Functions: hours, minutes, sweep seconds; date
Case: red gold, ø 40 mm, height 9.72 mm; sapphire crystal; transparent case back; screw-in crown; water-resistant to 5 atm
Band: reptile skin, folding clasp
Price: $18,100
Variations: yellow gold; white gold with mother-of-pearl dial

Dressage Moon Phase
Reference number: DR 2.765.712M
Movement: automatic, Vaucher Caliber P 1929; ø 25.6 mm, height 5.5 mm; 28,800 vph; red gold rotor
Functions: hours, minutes, sweep seconds; date (retrograde); moon phase
Case: platinum, 40 x 46 mm, height 9.72 mm; sapphire crystal; transparent case back; screw-in crown; water-resistant to 5 atm
Band: reptile skin, folding clasp
Price: $39,950
Variations: red gold

Cape Cod 1928
Reference number: CD 1.890.670/MNO
Movement: automatic, Vaucher Caliber P 1928; ø 25.6 mm, height 3.5 mm; 32 jewels; 28,800 vph; finished with Hermès decoration
Functions: hours, minutes, sweep seconds; date
Case: white gold, 37 x 36 mm, height 9.7 mm; sapphire crystal
Band: reptile skin, folding clasp
Price: $22,500
Variations: rose gold

Cape Cod 8 Days
Reference number: CD 2.965.722/M
Movement: automatic, Vaucher Caliber H 8928; 29.3 x 23.6 mm, height 4.9 mm; 28 jewels; 21,600 vph; twin spring barrels; 8 days power reserve; finished with Hermès decoration
Functions: hours (jump, in window), minutes, subsidiary seconds; power reserve display
Case: platinum, 37 x 32 mm, height 13.4 mm; sapphire crystal; transparent case back
Band: reptile skin, folding clasp
Price: $53,500
Variations: rose or white gold

Hanhart

In 1882 Robert Koch discovered the tuberculosis bacillus, Franklin D. Roosevelt was born, and the Bayreuth Festival House saw Richard Wagner premiere *Parsifal*. The same year in the little Black Forest town Gütenbach, a company entered the horological scene that was to develop into a reputable specialist for timekeeping technology.

Hanhart celebrates 125 years of existence and a corresponding anniversary watch edition along the topic of *in memoriam fontis et origins* (Latin for "thinking about the source and origin"). The origin referred to is in the 1920s when stopwatches were introduced to the Gütenbach-based company, laying the cornerstone for a continuing leading world reputation in short-term time measurement.

In the late 1930s, Hanhart began manufacturing pilot's chronographs, the aesthetic style of which is mirrored in diverse replicas and new models of the present day. Thus, it is no wonder that Hanhart is presenting a series of limited edition watches in honor of its 125th anniversary, a series that stylistically and qualitatively represents all the values for which Hanhart stands.

The flagship of the Hanhart collection, the platinum Opus 41, was developed especially for the anniversary to underscore the brand's competence in the art of high-quality watchmaking. The manually wound chronograph unites the historical origins of the brand with stylistic developments reaching to the modern era with high aesthetic and mechanical value. It's not only the attractive design with a solid, two-tone silver dial with sunray guilloché and valuable platinum case that makes this chronograph interesting. Inside a case featuring characteristic asymmetric distances between the buttons there ticks an original Hanhart column-wheel movement, Caliber 41 from the 1950s. The limited quantity of the rare chronograph movement alone will make the watch—restricted to a mere thirty-nine pieces—advance as a favorite among connoisseurs.

The spirit of 125 years of timekeeping for sports events is currently being honored in the form of a twin set edition of 125 pieces. A black painted collector's box contains the Minos, a Hanhart wristwatch classic, in a special edition kept to the style of classic sports car instruments. It is outfitted with an automatic movement, subsidiary seconds, and a date display. The Minos's partner is a special edition split-seconds chronograph with flyback function. Both stainless steel watches reveal their movements under a transparent case back, and it is especially the stopwatch with its lavishly decorated Hanhart *manufacture* movement featuring blued screws and *côtes de Genève* that attracts the eye. The case backs of both edition watches bear the anniversary inscription "125 Jahre Spirit of Racing" and are numbered in pairs.

In the Black Forest's Gütenbach they have been doing the impossible for 125 years—stopping time.

Hanhart

Hanhart Pioneer Caliber II
Reference number: 716.0100-00
Movement: automatic, Hanhart Caliber 716 (base ETA Valjoux 7750); ø 30 mm, height 7.9 mm; 28 jewels; 28,800 vph; modified button positions
Functions: hours, minutes, subsidiary seconds; chronograph
Case: stainless steel, ø 40 mm, height 15 mm; bidirectionally rotating bezel with reference marker; sapphire crystal; transparent case back
Band: leather, buckle
Price: $5,000
Variations: various leather straps; stainless steel bracelet

Red X Red
Reference number: 718.060N-00
Movement: automatic, Hanhart Caliber 718 (base ETA Valjoux 7750); ø 30 mm, height 7.9 mm; 28 jewels; 28,800 vph
Functions: hours, minutes, subsidiary seconds; chronograph
Case: stainless steel, ø 40 mm, height 15 mm; bidirectionally rotating bezel with reference marker; sapphire crystal; transparent case back
Band: leather, buckle
Remarks: limited edition of 747 pieces
Price: $5,000
Variations: stainless steel bracelet

Sirius Automatic
Reference number: 710.020A-00
Movement: automatic, Hanhart Caliber 710 (base ETA Valjoux 7750); ø 30 mm, height 7.9 mm; 28 jewels; 28,800 vph; modified button positions
Functions: hours, minutes, subsidiary seconds; chronograph; date
Case: stainless steel, ø 40 mm, height 15.4 mm; bidirectionally rotating bezel with reference marker; sapphire crystal; transparent case back
Band: stainless steel, folding clasp
Price: $5,400
Variations: various strap and bracelet variations

M 39 Mother-of-Pearl
Reference number: 760.05PF-00
Movement: automatic, Hanhart Caliber 760 (base ETA 2895-A2); ø 25.6 mm, height 4.5 mm; 27 jewels; 28,800 vph
Functions: hours, minutes, subsidiary seconds
Case: stainless steel, 47.5 x 34.5 mm, height 9.7 mm; sapphire crystal; transparent case back
Band: leather, buckle
Remarks: replica of a Hanhart watch from the 1930s; mother-of-pearl dial
Price: $2,600
Variations: black or silver-colored mother-of-pearl; dial set with diamonds

M 39 Diamonds
Reference number: 760.110I-00
Movement: automatic, Hanhart Caliber 760 (base ETA 2895-A2); ø 25.6 mm, height 4.5 mm; 27 jewels; 28,800 vph
Functions: hours, minutes, subsidiary seconds
Case: stainless steel, 47.5 x 34.5 mm, height 9.7 mm; case sides set with 28 diamonds; sapphire crystal; transparent case back
Band: leather, buckle
Remarks: replica of a Hanhart watch from the 1930s
Price: $7,500

Attaché
Reference number: 756-040V-00
Movement: automatic, Hanhart Caliber 756 (base ETA 2892-A2 with Soprod module); ø 25.6 mm, height 3.9 mm; 28 jewels; 28,800 vph
Functions: hours, minutes, sweep seconds; large date; power reserve display
Case: stainless steel, ø 40 mm, height 12.7 mm; sapphire crystal; transparent case back; screw-in crown
Band: leather, buckle
Price: $3,500
Variations: stainless steel bracelet

Gold Chronograph
Reference number: 719.0303.00
Movement: automatic, Hanhart Caliber 717 (base ETA Valjoux 7750); ø 30 mm, height 7.9 mm; 28 jewels; 28,800 vph
Functions: hours, minutes, subsidiary seconds; chronograph
Case: rose gold, ø 40 mm, height 15 mm; bidirectionally rotating bezel with reference marker; sapphire crystal; transparent case back
Band: reptile skin, buckle
Remarks: limited anniversary edition of 125 pieces
Price: $21,000
Variations: black dial

Opus 41
Reference number: 704.0408-00
Movement: manually wound, Hanhart Caliber 41; ø 34 mm, height 6.4 mm, 17 jewels; 18,000 vph; authentic Hanhart chronograph movement from the 1950s; column-wheel control of chronograph; swan-neck fine adjustment and Breguet balance spring
Functions: hours, minutes, subsidiary seconds; chronograph with flyback function
Case: platinum, ø 42 mm, height 15.7 mm; sapphire crystal; transparent case back
Band: reptile skin, platinum buckle
Remarks: limited anniversary edition of 39 pieces
Price: on request

Hublot

Jean-Claude Biver was already speaking of a "Big Bang" when he was initially asked about his recipe for freshening up Hublot's collection, the prestigious brand that had turned down a bit of a dead-end street. Hublot's owner, Carlo Crocco, had given the charismatic watch executive who had so successfully repositioned Blancpain extensive authority and then entrusted him with his life's work.

When Crocco realized his vision of a watch as a "porthole" (French: *hublot*) in matte brushed metal on a rubber strap that smelled lightly of vanilla twenty-five years ago, he called it "la montre des montres"—the "watch of all watches." This is also what the company was named until just recently. Simplicity was trump among the avant-garde, and thanks to the demonstrative nonconformism of the Hublot watch, the company was able to utilize the luxury theme in a carefree manner. But times have changed, and for this reason Biver has set off his "Big Bang," as promised.

Meanwhile the two-year-old "Hublot of all Hublots" has retained the technical attitude of its predecessors, but pulls way ahead of them in the choice of design materials. The case of the Big Bang is built in several layers of different high-tech materials and precious metals, expressed both in the fissured case shape as well as in the daring color composition, including black PVD coatings, Kevlar, carbon fiber, and aluminum contrasted against red gold, platinum, and white ceramic. Even the rubber strap, which until now was only available in black, has finally taken on all the colors of the rainbow—and then some. The *manufacture* La Joux-Perret is in charge of the technology found in the chronograph module and an oscillating weight made from the heavy metal tungsten.

Biver's first act was received with a great deal of critical and popular applause. The industry's opinion makers are pleased with the fact that Hublot has been able to continue in an innovative fashion without completely giving up on its original concept, while the general public has been buying up Big Bangs like they're going out of style—which they most definitely are not. In fact, the Big Bang has just about tripled Hublot's annual turnover, with demand far exceeding the available supply in 2007. Part of the success of the fusion-oriented timepiece is the brand's magic touch in making a whole collection out of just one watch—something that Hublot has been good at since first launching its understated gold-and-rubber porthole in 1980. Biver has meanwhile introduced the Bigger Bang featuring a BNB-manufactured tourbillon chronograph that contains scads of new technology and materials. Then he went on to use even more new materials and technology to change the color, feel, and shape of these two models—using elements such as magnesium, tantalum, and new ways to finish gold. A 48 mm Big Bang, a million-dollar Big Bang, a Bigger Bang All Black, and even a Big Bang Cappuccino have meanwhile hit retail shops, with no end in sight to the demand. How could they possibly top this for next year? By reissuing the classic Hublot, of course, which will give consumers still waiting for their Bangs a chance to own a modern Hublot while spending about $5,000 less.

Hublot

Big Bang
Reference number: 301.PX.130.RX
Movement: automatic, Caliber HUB 44 (base ETA Valjoux 7750); ø 30 mm, height 7.9 mm; 25 jewels; 28,800 vph; column-wheel control of chronograph functions; rhodium-plated base plate; rotor coated black
Functions: hours, minutes, subsidiary seconds; chronograph; date
Case: red gold and Kevlar, 44.5 mm, height 16 mm; red gold bezel; sapphire crystal; transparent case back; water-resistant to 10 atm
Band: rubber, folding clasp
Price: $20,000

Big Bang Black Magic
Reference number: 301.CX.130.RX
Movement: automatic, Caliber HUB 44 (base ETA Valjoux 7750); ø 30 mm, height 7.9 mm; 25 jewels; 28,800 vph; column-wheel control of chronograph functions; rhodium-plated base plate; rotor coated black
Functions: hours, minutes, subsidiary seconds; chronograph; date
Case: ceramic and Kevlar, ø 44.5 mm, height 16 mm; black ceramic bezel; sapphire crystal; transparent case back; water-resistant to 10 atm
Band: rubber, folding clasp
Price: $11,900

Big Bang Cappuccino
Reference number: 341.PC.1007.RX
Movement: automatic, ETA Caliber 2894; ø 28.6 mm, height 6.1 mm; 37 jewels; 28,800 vph
Functions: hours, minutes, subsidiary seconds; chronograph; date
Case: red gold and Kevlar, ø 41 mm, height 14.3 mm; bezel set with brilliant-cut diamonds; sapphire crystal; transparent case back; water-resistant to 10 atm
Band: rubber, folding clasp
Price: $17,900

Big Bang Ice Bang
Reference number: 301.CT.130.RX
Movement: automatic, Caliber HUB 44 (base ETA Valjoux 7750); ø 30 mm, height 7.9 mm; 25 jewels; 28,800 vph; column-wheel control of chronograph functions; rhodium-plated base plate; rotor coated black
Functions: hours, minutes, subsidiary seconds; chronograph; date
Case: ceramic and Kevlar, ø 44.5 mm, height 16 mm; tantalum bezel; sapphire crystal; transparent case back; water-resistant to 10 atm
Band: rubber, folding clasp
Price: $13,500

Bigger Bang Tourbillon
Reference number: 308.CX.130.RX
Movement: manually wound, Caliber HUB 1400CT (base La Joux-Perret); ø 30 mm, height 7.8 mm; 33 jewels; 21,600 vph; flying one-minute tourbillon; twin spring barrels, power reserve 120 hours
Functions: hours, minutes, subsidiary seconds; chronograph
Case: platinum and Kevlar, ø 44.5 mm, height 16 mm; black ceramic bezel; sapphire crystal; transparent case back; water-resistant to 10 atm
Band: rubber, folding clasp
Remarks: limited edition of 18 pieces
Price: $150,000
Variations: red gold/ceramic; ceramic

Big Bang Monaco Yacht Club
Reference number: 301.AM.130.RX.YCM07
Movement: automatic, Caliber HUB 44 (base ETA Valjoux 7750); ø 30 mm, height 7.9 mm; 25 jewels; 28,800 vph; base plate, bridges, and screws coated with black PVD
Functions: hours, minutes, subsidiary seconds; chronograph; date
Case: tantalum and Kevlar, ø 44.5 mm, height 16 mm; black ceramic bezel; sapphire crystal; transparent case back; water-resistant to 10 atm
Band: rubber, folding clasp
Price: $15,600

Bat Bang Tourbillon All Black
Reference number: 308.CI.134.RXO
Movement: manually wound, Caliber HUB 1000SB; ø 30 mm, height 7.4 mm; 24 jewels; 21,600 vph; flying one-minute tourbillon hovering 2.8 mm over the base plate; power reserve 120 hours
Functions: hours, minutes
Case: ceramic and Kevlar, ø 44.5 mm, height 14.5 mm; sapphire crystal; water-resistant to 10 atm
Band: rubber, folding clasp
Remarks: limited edition of 50 pieces
Price: $190,000

Big Bang Platinum Matte Big Date
Reference number: 308.TX.130.RX-I
Movement: manually wound, Caliber HUB 1050GD (base HUB1050); ø 30 mm, height 7.4 mm; 27 jewels; 21,600 vph; flying one-minute tourbillon hovering 2.8 mm over the base plate; power reserve 120 hours
Functions: hours, minutes; large date; power reserve display
Case: platinum and Kevlar, ø 44.5 mm, height 16.3 mm; sapphire crystal; transparent case back; water-resistant to 10 atm
Band: rubber, folding clasp
Remarks: limited edition of 18 pieces
Price: $190,000

Hublot

Big Bang 41 mm Aspen
Reference number: 341.CH.230.RW
Movement: automatic, ETA Caliber 2894; ø 28.6 mm, height 6.1 mm; 37 jewels; 28,800 vph
Functions: hours, minutes, subsidiary seconds; chronograph; date
Case: ceramic and Kevlar, ø 41 mm, height 14.3 mm; white ceramic bezel; sapphire crystal; transparent case back; water-resistant to 10 atm
Band: rubber, folding clasp
Price: $10,500

Big Bang Aspen Diamonds Baguette
Reference number: 341.CW.230.RW.190
Movement: automatic, ETA Caliber 2894; ø 28.6 mm, height 6.1 mm; 37 jewels; 28,800 vph
Functions: hours, minutes, subsidiary seconds; chronograph; date
Case: ceramic and Kevlar, ø 41 mm, height 14.3 mm; bezel set with baguette-cut diamonds; sapphire crystal; transparent case back; water-resistant to 10 atm
Band: rubber, folding clasp
Price: $41,500

Big Bang 41 mm Porto Cervo
Reference number: 341.PE.230.R.194
Movement: automatic, ETA Caliber 2894; ø 28.6 mm, height 6.1 mm; 37 jewels; 28,800 vph
Functions: hours, minutes, subsidiary seconds; date; chronograph
Case: red gold and Kevlar, ø 41 mm, height 14 mm; bezel set with baguette-cut diamonds; sapphire crystal; transparent case back; water-resistant to 10 atm
Band: rubber, folding clasp
Price: $21,200

Chrono SuperB
Reference number: 1926.BF30.1
Movement: automatic, Dubois Dépraz Caliber 2021 (base ETA 2892-A2); ø 31.15 mm, height 7.2 mm; 48 jewels; 28,800 vph
Functions: hours, minutes, subsidiary seconds; date; chronograph
Case: stainless steel, ø 42.5 mm, height 13.1 mm; sapphire crystal; transparent case back; crown and buttons covered with natural rubber; water-resistant to 10 atm
Band: reptile skin, folding clasp
Price: $7,200
Variations: also available in black, Bordeaux, and green

Classic
Reference number: 1915.NE.10.1
Movement: automatic, ETA Caliber 2892-A2; ø 25.6 mm, height 3.6 mm; 21 jewels; 28,800 vph
Functions: hours, minutes, sweep seconds; date
Case: stainless steel, ø 39 mm, height 11 mm; sapphire crystal; water-resistant to 5 atm
Band: rubber, double folding clasp
Price: $4,800

Classic
Reference number: 1915.NE.10.1
Movement: automatic, ETA Caliber 2892-A2; ø 25.6 mm, height 3.6 mm; 21 jewels; 28,800 vph
Functions: hours, minutes, sweep seconds; date
Case: red gold, ø 39 mm, height 11 mm; sapphire crystal; water-resistant to 5 atm
Band: rubber, double folding clasp
Price: $11,900

Big Bang King Palladium
Reference number: PT 322.LX.100.RX
Movement: automatic, HUB Caliber 21 (base Caliber 2892); ø 25.6 mm, height 3.6 mm; 23 jewels; 28,800 vph
Functions: hours, minutes, sweep seconds; date
Case: palladium and Kevlar, ø 48 mm, height 11 mm; unidirectionally rotating bezel with 60-minute divisions; sapphire crystal; water-resistant to 30 atm
Band: rubber, folding clasp
Price: $22,900

Big Bang King Porto Cervo
Reference number: 322.PH.230.RW
Movement: automatic, Caliber HUB 21 (base ETA 2892); ø 25.6 mm, height 3.6 mm; 23 jewels; 28,800 vph
Functions: hours, minutes, sweep seconds; date
Case: red gold and Kevlar, ø 48 mm, height 11 mm; unidirectionally rotating ceramic bezel with 60-minute divisions; sapphire crystal; water-resistant to 30 atm
Band: rubber, folding clasp
Price: $26,400

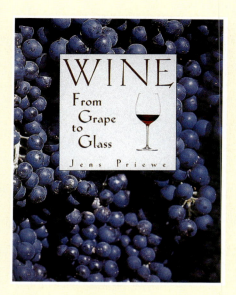

Wine: From Grape to Glass

"The ultimate gift for any wine lover." —*Touring & Tasting Magazine*

Tailor-made for the contemporary wine consumer who drinks what he or she likes, this vividly illustrated text discusses not only awe-inspiring vintages, but also unknown wines from countries only recently included on the wine maps of the world. Half the book is devoted to the wine-making process itself; the other half examines the best wines of the world, country by country, and guides the reader to an understanding of the intricacies of wine tasting and appreciation.

By Jens Priewe
1,000 full-color illustrations
256 pages · 9 x 11⅞ in. · Hardcover
ISBN: 978-0-7892-0917-7
$45.00

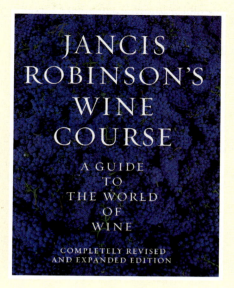

Jancis Robinson's Wine Course: A Guide to the World of Wine

"She has an encyclopedic grasp of her subject and doesn't put a foot wrong… a splendid introduction to the world of wine." —Stephen Brook, *Decanter Magazine*

"Witty, brilliant, authoritative." —Robert M. Parker, Jr., *The Wine Advocate*

Dedicated to ensuring that you get the most out of every glass, Jancis Robinson's Wine Course explains how to taste and store wine, what to serve on special occasions at home, and how to order the best value from a restaurant wine list. Robinson also describes the distinctive characteristics of hundreds of different grape varieties and studies the traditional and innovative methods employed in the creation of great wines.

By Jancis Robinson
170 full-color illustrations
352 pages · 8 x 11 in. · Paperback
ISBN: 978-0-7892-0883-5
$29.95

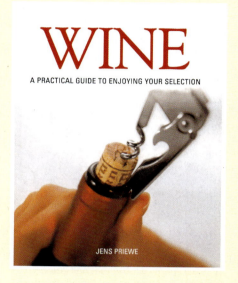

Wine: A Practical Guide to Enjoying Your Selection

Following the success of the author's *Wine: From Grape to Glass*, this new book offers a treasury of invaluable information for the contemporary wine consumer who would like to know more about caring for wine and serving it properly. In this essential guide, internationally acclaimed expert Jens Priewe fully describes, with lively text and striking photographs, the correct way to handle wine, from uncorking and tasting to serving and storing.

By Jens Priewe
200 full-color illustrations
128 pages · 7¾ x 10 in. · Hardcover
ISBN: 978-0-7892-0745-6
$32.50

Published by ABBEVILLE PRESS
137 Varick Street, New York, NY 10013
1-800-Artbook (in U.S. only)
Also available wherever fine books are sold
Visit us at www.abbeville.com

IWC

The name Da Vinci has been inseparable from IWC since 1985 when the Schaffhausen-based brand chose to use the last name of the genius artist, inventor, and researcher Leonardo from Vinci (near Florence). They justifiably assumed that everyone would automatically associate the name of this watch line with the Renaissance's universal genius.

When the "old" Da Vinci was presented on the first day of the Basel fair in 1985, those in charge of the Swiss German company were fairly sure that they would attract a good deal of attention. The Da Vinci was the horological sensation of the year. The special attraction of the watch—a chronograph with a perpetual calendar—was its four-digit display of the year. Displaying the first two digits on the dial demanded a great deal of additional technical effort, which Kurt Klaus—longtime head watchmaker at IWC—overcame with a few brilliant tricks. The highlight of the new Da Vinci collection is the chronograph outfitted with a newly constructed movement. Its automatic mechanism, *manufacture* Caliber 89360, has a power reserve of 68 hours. The tension necessary to wind the mainspring is provided by a progression of the Pellaton winding system that has been in use again at IWC for a few years now. The double ratchet winding system functions with four clicks, two of which are always engaging the winding wheel to convey the energy of the rotor to the ratchet wheel with a back-and-forth motion. Its effectiveness was thus improved by about 30 percent, and the automatic mechanism's freewheeling is just about zero.

The chronograph, controlled by a classic column wheel, is of a flyback nature and is outfitted with a long sweep chronograph second hand that moves above a combination totalizer featuring a short hand (12 hours) and a longer one (60 minutes) on a common axis in the center of a small sub-sidiary dial underneath the 12 o'clock position. For the first time, this makes it possible to read the stopped time interval like an analogue display, which the schooled human eye can recognize at a glance.

The new line's case interprets the classic tonneau shape in a unique way, thus representing a revolutionary step for IWC. "I think that we have waited too long with the Da Vinci—the product has not been seriously changed since 1985. That was a mistake. Today the intervals are much shorter—five, six years," explains IWC head Georges Kern, who loves to speak of "evolution" when talking about his

watches, and must now admit that the new Da Vinci is not a small evolutionary step, but rather a giant leap that needed a giant portion of courage to complete.

IWC

Da Vinci Perpetual Calendar Kurt Klaus Edition
Reference number: 376203
Movement: automatic, IWC Caliber 79261 (base ETA Valjoux 7750 with module), ø 30 mm, height 7.9 mm; 25 jewels; 28,800 vph
Functions: hours, minutes, subsidiary seconds; chronograph; perpetual calendar with date, weekday, month, four-digit year, moon phase
Case: red gold, 43 x 50 mm, height 15.2 mm; sapphire crystal; screw-in crown
Band: reptile skin, folding clasp
Remarks: homage to the designer of the perpetual calendar with four-digit date display; limited edition of 500 pieces
Price: $32,000
Variations: platinum (limited edition of 50)

Da Vinci Chronograph
Reference number: 376401
Movement: automatic, IWC Caliber 89360; ø 30 mm; 40 jewels; 28,800 vph; Pellaton winding, shock proofed rotor
Functions: hours, minutes, subsidiary seconds; chronograph with flyback function; date
Case: white gold, 43 x 50 mm, height 14.35 mm; sapphire crystal; transparent case back; screw-in crown
Band: reptile skin, folding clasp
Price: $25,000
Variations: stainless steel; red gold; limited edition of 500 pieces in platinum

Da Vinci Automatic
Reference number: 42303
Movement: automatic, IWC Caliber 30130; ø 25.6 mm, height 4.85; 22 jewels; 28,800 vph
Functions: hours, minutes, sweep seconds; large date
Case: stainless steel, 35.6 x 44 mm, height 10.9 mm; sapphire crystal; screw-in crown
Band: reptile skin, folding clasp
Price: $5,500
Variations: white gold or red gold

Portofino Automatic
Reference number: 356302
Movement: automatic, IWC Caliber 30110 (base ETA 2892-A2); ø 25.6 mm, height 3.6; 21 jewels; 28,800 vph
Functions: hours, minutes, sweep seconds; date
Case: red gold, ø 39 mm, height 8.6 mm; sapphire crystal
Band: reptile skin, buckle
Price: $7,000
Variations: stainless steel

Portofino Midsize
Reference number: 356404
Movement: automatic, IWC Caliber 30110 (base ETA 2892-A2); ø 25.6 mm, height 3.6; 21 jewels; 28,800 vph
Functions: hours, minutes, sweep seconds; date
Case: stainless steel, ø 34 mm, height 8.2 mm; sapphire crystal
Band: reptile skin, buckle
Price: $2,700
Variations: red gold

Portofino Chronograph
Reference number: 378303
Movement: automatic, IWC Caliber 79320 (base ETA Valjoux 7750); ø 30 mm, height 7.9 mm; 25 jewels; 28,800 vph
Functions: hours, minutes, sweep seconds; chronograph; date, weekday
Case: stainless steel, ø 41 mm, height 13.5 mm; sapphire crystal
Band: reptile skin, buckle
Price: $3,900

Big Ingenieur
Reference number: 500501
Movement: automatic, IWC Caliber 51112; ø 38.2 mm, height 7.44; 44 jewels; 21,600 vph; Pellaton winding; power reserve mechanically limited to seven days
Functions: hours, minutes, sweep seconds; date; power reserve display
Case: stainless steel, ø 45.5 mm, height 15 mm; sapphire crystal; transparent case back; screw-in crown
Band: reptile skin, buckle
Price: $11,800

Ingenieur Automatic
Reference number: 323401
Movement: automatic, IWC Caliber 80111; ø 30 mm, height 7.25; 28 jewels; 28,800 vph; Pellaton winding, shock-proofed rotor; soft iron core for protection from magnetic fields
Functions: hours, minutes, sweep seconds; date
Case: stainless steel, ø 44 mm, height 14 mm; ceramic bezel; sapphire crystal; screw-in crown; water-resistant to 12 atm
Band: textile, buckle
Price: $7,500

IWC

Ingenieur Automatic
Reference number: 322801
Movement: automatic, IWC Caliber 80111; ø 30 mm, height 7.25; 28 jewels; 28,800 vph; Pellaton winding, shock-proofed rotor; soft iron core for protection from magnetic fields
Functions: hours, minutes, sweep seconds; date
Case: stainless steel, ø 40 mm, height 13.5 mm; sapphire crystal; transparent case back; screw-in crown; water-resistant to 12 atm
Band: stainless steel, folding clasp
Price: $5,600

Pilot's Watch Automatic Edition Antoine de Saint-Exupéry
Reference number: 320104
Movement: automatic, IWC Caliber 30140 (base ETA 2892-A2 with module); ø 25.6 mm, height 3.6 mm (base movement); 21 jewels; 28,800 vph
Functions: hours, minutes, sweep seconds; date; power reserve display
Case: stainless steel, ø 44 mm, height 12.6 mm; sapphire crystal
Band: leather, buckle
Remarks: homage to author and pilot Antoine de Saint-Exupéry; limited edition of a total of 1,929 pieces
Price: $4,500
Variations: limited edition of 250 pieces in white gold; limited edition of 500 pieces in red gold

Pilot's Watch Double Chronograph Top Gun
Reference number: 379901
Movement: automatic, IWC Caliber 79230 (base ETA Valjoux 7750); ø 30 mm, height 7.9 mm; 25 jewels; 28,800 vph; soft iron core for protection from magnetic fields
Functions: hours, minutes, subsidiary seconds; split-seconds chronograph; date, weekday
Case: ceramic, ø 46 mm, height 17.6 mm; sapphire crystal; screw-in crown; water-resistant to 6 atm
Band: nylon, buckle
Remarks: cooperation with the pilots' school of the U.S. Marines
Price: $10,400

Pilot's Watch Laureus Sport for Good Foundation Edition
Reference number: 371712
Movement: automatic, IWC Caliber 79230 (base ETA 7750); ø 30 mm, height 7.9 mm; 25 jewels; 28,800 vph
Functions: hours, minutes, subsidiary seconds; chronograph; date, weekday
Case: stainless steel, ø 42 mm, height 14.7 mm; sapphire crystal; screw-in crown; water-resistant to 6 atm
Band: reptile skin, buckle
Remarks: special edition for the Laureus Foundation; limited edition of 2,500 pieces
Price: $4,700

Pilot's Watch Chrono Automatic
Reference number: 371713
Movement: automatic, IWC Caliber 79230 (base ETA Valjoux 7750); ø 30 mm, height 7.9 mm; 25 jewels; 28,800 vph
Functions: hours, minutes, subsidiary seconds; chronograph; date, weekday
Case: red gold, ø 42 mm, height 14.7 mm; sapphire crystal; screw-in crown; water-resistant to 6 atm
Band: reptile skin, buckle
Price: $4,700
Variations: stainless steel with leather strap; stainless steel with stainless steel bracelet

Big Pilot's Watch
Reference number: 500402
Movement: automatic, IWC Caliber 51110; ø 38.2 mm, height 7.44 mm; 44 jewels; 21,600 vph; Pellaton winding; power reserve mechanically limited to seven days
Functions: hours, minutes, sweep seconds; date; power reserve display
Case: white gold, ø 46.2 mm, height 15.8 mm; sapphire crystal
Band: reptile skin, folding clasp
Price: $25,000
Variations: stainless steel

Spitfire Double Chronograph
Reference number: 371802
Movement: automatic, IWC Caliber 79230 (base ETA Valjoux 7750); ø 30 mm, height 7.9 mm; 25 jewels; 28,800 vph; soft iron core for protection from magnetic fields
Functions: hours, minutes, subsidiary seconds; split-seconds chronograph; date, weekday
Case: stainless steel, ø 44 mm, height 17 mm; sapphire crystal; screw-in crown; water-resistant to 6 atm
Band: leather, buckle
Price: $9,500

Aquatimer Chrono Cousteau Divers
Reference number: 371802
Movement: automatic, IWC Caliber 79320 (base ETA Valjoux 7750); ø 30 mm, height 7.9 mm; 25 jewels; 28,800 vph
Functions: hours, minutes, subsidiary seconds; split-seconds chronograph; date, weekday
Case: stainless steel, ø 44 mm, height 17 mm; bezel under crystal with 60-minute divisions, unidirectionally rotating via crown; sapphire crystal; screw-in crown; water-resistant to 12 atm
Band: rubber, buckle
Remarks: limited edition of 2,500 pieces
Price: $5,800

IWC

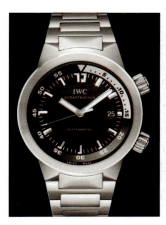

Aquatimer Automatic
Reference number: 354805
Movement: automatic, IWC Caliber 30110 (base ETA 2892-A2); ø 25.6 mm, height 3.6 mm; 23 jewels; 28,800 vph
Functions: hours, minutes, sweep seconds; date
Case: stainless steel, ø 42 mm, height 12.8 mm; bezel under crystal with 60-minute divisions, unidirectionally rotating via crown; sapphire crystal; screw-in crown; water-resistant to 100 atm
Band: stainless steel, folding clasp with security button
Price: $5,000
Variations: rubber strap

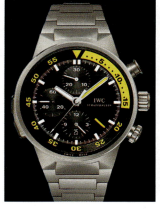

Aquatimer Split Minute Chronograph
Reference number: 372301
Movement: automatic, IWC Caliber 79470 (base ETA Valjoux 7750); ø 30 mm, height 8.2 mm; 30 jewels; 28,800 vph
Functions: hours, minutes, subsidiary seconds; chronograph with additional separately stoppable minute hand (flyback)
Case: titanium, ø 44 mm, height 16.3 mm; bezel under crystal with 60-minute divisions, unidirectionally rotating via crown; sapphire crystal; screw-in crown; water-resistant to 12 atm
Band: titanium, folding clasp with security button
Price: $9,800
Variations: rubber strap

Portuguese Chronograph Automatic
Reference number: 371401
Movement: automatic, IWC Caliber 79350 (base ETA Valjoux 7750); ø 30 mm, height 7.9 mm; 25 jewels; 28,800 vph
Functions: hours, minutes, subsidiary seconds; chronograph
Case: stainless steel, ø 40.9 mm, height 12.3 mm; sapphire crystal
Band: reptile skin, buckle
Price: $6,600
Variations: yellow, red, or white gold

Portuguese Automatic
Reference number: 500101
Movement: automatic, IWC Caliber 51010; ø 38.2 mm, height 7.44 mm; 44 jewels; 21,600 vph; Pellaton winding; theoretical power reserve of 8 days; power reserve mechanically limited to 7 days
Functions: hours, minutes, subsidiary seconds; date; power reserve display
Case: red gold, ø 42.3 mm, height 13.9 mm; sapphire crystal
Band: reptile skin, folding clasp
Price: $17,600
Variations: white gold; stainless steel

Portuguese Régulateur
Reference number: 544404
Movement: manually wound, IWC Caliber 98245; ø 38.2 mm; 22 jewels; 18,000 vph; modeled after an historical IWC pocket watch movement
Functions: hours, off-center minutes, subsidiary seconds
Case: white gold, ø 43.1 mm, height 11.7 mm; sapphire crystal; transparent case back
Band: reptile skin, buckle
Price: $17,900
Variations: stainless steel; red gold; limited edition of 500 pieces in platinum

Portuguese Perpetual Calendar
Reference number: 502119
Movement: automatic, IWC Caliber 51612; ø 38.2 mm; 64 jewels; 18,000 vph; Pellaton winding; power reserve mechanically limited to seven days
Functions: hours, minutes, subsidiary seconds; perpetual calendar with date, day, month, four-digit year display, double moon phase (for the earth's northern and southern hemispheres)
Case: red gold, ø 44.2 mm, height 15.5 mm; sapphire crystal; transparent case back
Band: reptile skin, folding clasp
Price: $29,800
Variations: white gold

Portuguese Tourbillon Mystère
Reference number: 504207
Movement: automatic, IWC Caliber 50900; ø 38.2 mm, height 7.44 mm; 44 jewels; 19,800 vph; flying one-minute tourbillon, Breguet balance spring; Pellaton winding; power reserve mechanically limited to seven days
Functions: hours, minutes, subsidiary seconds; power reserve display
Case: white gold, ø 44.2 mm, height 14.2 mm; sapphire crystal; transparent case back
Band: reptile skin, folding clasp
Remarks: limited edition of 250 pieces
Price: $98,000

Portuguese Minute Repeater
Reference number: 524204
Movement: manually wound, IWC Caliber 95290; 54 jewels; 18,000 vph
Functions: hours, minutes; minute repeater
Case: platinum, ø 43 mm, height 12.35 mm; sapphire crystal; transparent case back
Band: reptile skin, folding clasp
Remarks: limited edition of 100 pieces
Price: $103,000
Variations: 250 pieces in white gold; 250 pieces in red gold

Jaeger-LeCoultre

A sensational prototype introduced in April 2007 underscores this Le Sentier–based *manufacture's* justifiable position as one of the leaders within a select circle of the industry's highly innovative brands. In the company's new research and development lab, forty-five engineers, technicians, and watchmakers systematically work with the discovery and development of futuristic materials and methods for use in watchmaking. The first product to spring from this research took two years and is called the Master Compressor Extreme LAB.

The movement of this incredible timepiece needs absolutely no lubrication. In order to guarantee perfect functioning without oil and grease, the correct materials for individual components with compatible friction coefficients had to be chosen; traditional materials are not in the mix. Searching for alternative, suitable materials resulted in a colorful combination of substances. Modern ceramics and a carbon nitride bearing the name Easium play a central role. Easium is temperature-stable, doesn't corrode, and is almost as hard as diamond or tungsten carbide, making it extremely friction-free and resistant to wear. All these characteristics predestined it to be the ideal material for use as bearings.

In order to further reduce friction in the movement's quickly rotating wheels' bearings, all steel pivots and pinions—already finely polished—received additional special surface coatings.

The escape wheel is made of silicon; the pallets—transforming the rotation of the gear train into the pendulum motion necessary to drive the balance—are made of synthetic black diamond. And the technicians used Easium for the shockproof balance bearing of Caliber 983C.

The movement itself, which includes a tourbillon escapement and a special date whose hand makes a big jump across the tourbillon cage between the fifteenth and sixteenth of the month, also includes more new materials: Ticalium (an aluminum-titanium carbide alloy) was used for the flat parts, while the tourbillon carriage is crafted of a magnesium alloy.

The new balance has no balance wheel, but rather bears streamlined satellites made of heavy platinum and iridium at the end of its two arms. The balance spring of Caliber 988C was not only outfitted with a carefully calculated Phillips terminal curve but also burnished at a specially calculated position near the roller. The "bend" that resulted has a changed microstructure and thus a different elasticity coefficient, ensuring that the balance spring "breathes" in an absolutely concentric manner.

The oscillating weight of the automatic rotor is also crafted in heavy platinum and iridium, while the carbon rotor body coated with nickel polytetrafluorethylene is not only extremely flat, but also light and attractive thanks to its shape.

Jaeger-LeCoultre registered no fewer than eleven patents for the Master Compressor Extreme LAB, among others for the special case made of carbon fiber and a titanium ring that is outfitted with a bezel made of a silicon-carbon nitride.

Jaeger-LeCoultre

Duomètre à Chronographe
Reference number: 601 24 20
Movement: automatic, JLC Caliber 380; ø 33.7 mm, height 6.95 mm; 48 jewels; 21,600 vph; twin spring barrels and two separate gear trains for watch and chronograph; chronograph functions controlled by switch on foudroyante mechanism
Functions: hours, minutes (off-center), sweep seconds; chronograph with foudroyante sixth-second counter; double power reserve display
Case: red gold, ø 42 mm, height 13.4 mm; sapphire crystal; transparent case back
Band: reptile skin, folding clasp
Price: $35,800
Variations: limited edition of 300 pieces in yellow gold; platinum

Master Compressor Extreme LAB
Reference number: 179 T4 70
Movement: automatic, JLC Caliber 988C; ø 30 mm, height 7.05 mm; 26 jewels; 28,800 vph; lubrication-free experimental movement with one-minute tourbillon; flat and functional parts made of ceramic, silicon and new alloys; wheel-less balance with weights; carbon fiber rotor with platinum/iridium oscillating weight; several patents pending
Functions: hours, minutes; date; 24-hour display (day/night indication)
Case: carbon fiber in titanium frame, ø 45 mm, height 14.8 mm; silicon/carbon nitride bezel; sapphire crystal; transparent case back
Band: Alcantara leather, buckle
Price: $300,000

Master Compressor Diving Pro Geographic
Reference number: 185 T7 70
Movement: automatic, JLC Caliber 979; height 7.3 mm; 29 jewels; 28,800 vph; power reserve 48 hours
Functions: hours, minutes, subsidiary seconds; date; second time zone; depth gauge (80 meters)
Case: titanium, ø 46.3 mm, height 19.8 mm; unidirectionally rotating diver's bezel; sapphire crystal; crowns with patented compression key system; water-resistant to 30 atm
Band: titanium links with steel core, double folding clasp
Remarks: additional Cordura diver's strap
Price: $22,000
Variations: leather strap; rubber link bracelet

Master Compressor Diving Chronograph
Reference number: 186 T1 70
Movement: automatic, JLC Caliber 751D; ø 26.2 mm, height 5.65 mm; 41 jewels; 28,800 vph; twin spring barrels, power reserve 65 hours
Functions: hours, minutes; function display; date; chronograph
Case: titanium, ø 44 mm, height 16.25 mm; unidirectionally rotating diver's bezel; sapphire crystal; crown and buttons with patented compression key system; water-resistant to 100 atm
Band: titanium, double folding clasp, extendable
Remarks: additional Cordura diver's strap
Price: $11,000
Variations: rubber link bracelet; rubber strap; red gold with rubber strap

Master Compressor Diving GMT
Reference number: 187 T6 70
Movement: automatic, JLC Caliber 975D; height 5.7 mm; 29 jewels; 28,800 vph; power reserve 48 hours
Functions: hours, minutes; function display; date; 24-hour display (second time zone)
Case: titanium, ø 44 mm, height 16.25 mm; unidirectionally rotating diver's bezel; sapphire crystal; crowns with patented compression key system; water-resistant to 100 atm
Band: rubber, buckle
Price: $8,200
Variations: titanium link bracelet

Master Compressor Diving GMT Lady
Reference number: 189 84 20
Movement: automatic, JLC Caliber 971D; height 5.7 mm; 29 jewels; 28,800 vph; power reserve 48 hours
Functions: hours, minutes; function display; date; 24-hour display (second time zone)
Case: stainless steel, ø 38 mm, height 14.1 mm; unidirectionally rotating diver's bezel set with 16 diamonds; sapphire crystal; crowns with patented compression key system; water-resistant to 30 atm
Band: reptile skin; folding clasp
Price: $6,950
Variations: rubber or stainless steel link bracelet; red gold with leather strap

Master Compressor Extreme W-Alarm
Reference number: 177 84 70
Movement: automatic, JLC Caliber 912; ø 28 mm, height 7.78 mm; 28 jewels; 28,800 vph; two separate spring barrels for movement and alarm
Functions: hours, minutes, sweep seconds; date; alarm (hours and minutes); 24 time zones
Case: titanium/stainless steel, ø 46.3 mm, height 16.5 mm; ring with world time zones under bezel that is bidirectionally rotating via crown; sapphire crystal; patented Compressor key system on crown; water-resistant to 10 atm
Band: rubber, double folding clasp
Price: $12,400
Variations: reptile skin strap; stainless steel bracelet; limited editions in titanium and red gold/titanium

Master Compressor Chronograph
Reference number: 175 84 70
Movement: automatic, JLC Caliber 751; ø 25.6 mm, height 5.6 mm; 41 jewels; 28,800 vph; ceramic ball bearing rotor
Functions: hours, minutes, subsidiary seconds; chronograph; date
Case: stainless steel, ø 41.5 mm, height 13.65 mm; sapphire crystal; patented Compressor key system on crown and buttons; water-resistant to 10 atm
Band: reptile skin, folding clasp
Price: $8,750
Variations: in red gold on leather strap or red gold bracelet; stainless steel bracelet

Jaeger-LeCoultre

Reverso Squadra Chronograph GMT
Reference number: 701 86 8P
Movement: automatic, JLC Caliber 754; height 6.27 mm; 39 jewels; 28,800 vph
Functions: hours, minutes; chronograph; large date
Case: stainless steel, 50.5 x 35 mm, height 14 mm; case can be turned and rotated 180°; sapphire crystal; black PVD-coated crown and buttons; water-resistant to 5 atm
Band: rubber, buckle
Price: $9,150
Variations: rubber link bracelet; in red gold with rubber strap or rubber link bracelet

Reverso Squadra Hometime Black
Reference number: 700 26 72
Movement: automatic, JLC Caliber 977; height 5.7 mm; 29 jewels; 28,800 vph
Functions: hours, minutes, subsidiary seconds; date; separately settable hour hand (second time zone); day/night display (coupled to second time zone)
Case: red gold, 50.5 x 35 mm, height 14 mm; case can be turned and rotated 180°; sapphire crystal
Band: rubber, buckle
Price: $15,650
Variations: rubber link bracelet; in stainless steel with rubber strap or rubber link bracelet

Reverso Duetto Classique
Reference number: 256 84 02
Movement: manually wound, JLC Caliber 865; 18.4 x 17.2 mm, height 3.45 mm; 19 jewels; 21,600 vph
Functions: hours, minutes, subsidiary seconds (front); hours, minutes (back)
Case: red gold, 38.7 x 23 mm, height 9.4 mm; case can be turned and rotated 180°; two sapphire crystals
Band: reptile skin, folding clasp
Remarks: top and bottom of case set with diamonds
Price: $14,150
Variations: red gold link bracelet; with metal bracelet; yellow gold; stainless steel

Master Tourbillon
Reference number: 165 24 20
Movement: automatic, JLC Caliber 978; height 7.05 mm; 33 jewels; 28,800 vph; one-minute tourbillon; date hand jumps from the 15th to the 16th
Functions: hours, minutes, subsidiary seconds (on tourbillon cage); date; 24-hour display (second time zone)
Case: stainless steel, ø 41.5 mm, height 12.5 mm; sapphire crystal; transparent case back
Band: reptile skin, folding clasp
Price: $49,000
Variations: red gold; platinum

Master World Geographic
Reference number: 152 24 20
Movement: automatic, JLC Caliber 936; height 4.9 mm; 38 jewels; 28,800 vph
Functions: hours, minutes, sweep seconds; date; second time zone (world time); power reserve display
Case: red gold, ø 41.5 mm, height 12.3 mm; ring under crystal with world time zone scale, unidirectionally rotating via crown; sapphire crystal; transparent case back
Band: reptile skin, folding clasp
Price: $19,900
Variations: stainless steel

Reverso Squadra World Chrono
Reference number: 702 T4 70
Movement: automatic, JLC Caliber 753; 33.5 x 31.15 mm, height 7.57 mm; 44 jewels; 28,800 vph
Functions: hours, minutes, subsidiary seconds; chronograph; large date; day/night indication; world time display (back)
Case: titanium, 53 x 36.5 mm, height 16.5 mm; case can be turned and rotated 180°; sapphire crystal; transparent case back; water-resistant to 5 atm
Band: reptile skin, double folding calsp
Price: $14,500
Variations: rubber link bracelet

Master Calendar
Reference number: 151 24 2D
Movement: automatic, JLC Caliber 924; ø 26 mm, height 6.5 mm; 41 jewels; 28,800 vph
Functions: hours, minutes, subsidiary seconds; date, weekday, month, moon phase; power reserve display
Case: red gold, ø 40 mm, height 13.1 mm; sapphire crystal; transparent case back; water-resistant to 5 atm
Band: reptile skin, folding clasp
Price: $15,500
Variations: stainless steel on leather strap or link bracelet

Master Eight Days Perpetual Squelette
Reference number: 161 64 SQ
Movement: manually wound, JLC Caliber 876 SQ; ø 32 mm, height 6.6 mm; 37 jewels; 28,800 vph; twin spring barrels, power reserve eight days; completely skeletonized
Functions: hours, minutes; perpetual calendar with date, weekday, month, moon phase, four-digit year; day/night indication; power reserve display
Case: platinum, ø 41.5 mm, height 11.8 mm; sapphire crystal; transparent case back
Band: reptile skin, double folding clasp
Remarks: limited edition
Price: $96,100

Jaeger-LeCoultre

Reverso Grande Automatique
Reference number: 303 84 20
Movement: manually wound, JLC Caliber 970; 22.6 x 25.6 mm, height 5.3 mm; 29 jewels; 28,800 vph
Functions: hours, minutes, subsidiary seconds; large date; separately settable hour hand (second time zone); day/night indication (coupled to second time zone)
Case: stainless steel, 46.5 x 29.3 mm, height 12 mm; case can be turned and rotated 180°; sapphire crystal
Band: reptile skin, folding clasp
Price: $8,250
Variations: stainless steel bracelet; in red gold on leather strap or red gold bracelet

Reverso Grande Sun Moon
Reference number: 304 24 20
Movement: manually wound, JLC Caliber 873; height 5.3 mm; 25 jewels; 28,800 vph; twin spring barrels, power reserve eight days
Functions: hours, minutes, subsidiary seconds; day/night indication; moon phase; power reserve display
Case: red gold, 46.5 x 29.3 mm, height 12 mm; case can be turned and rotated 180° back decorated with starry sky; sapphire crystal
Band: reptile skin, folding clasp
Price: $17,600
Variations: metal bracelet; stainless steel on strap or bracelet

Reverso Grande Complication à Triptyque
Reference number: 232 64 20
For the 75th anniversary of the Reverso, Jaeger-LeCoultre presented a *grande complication* that uses the company's complicated revolving case as its base. The main movement features a tourbillon with a special escapement, displaying the time on both dials as well as solar time along with a depiction of the heavens that includes the signs of the zodiac, the times of sunrise and sunset, and the equation of time. The perpetual calendar displays (date, day, month, moon phases) are stored in the case's base since they only move forward once a day. This very limited masterpiece (dimensions 37.7 x 55 mm, height 17.9 mm) retails for $375,000 in platinum.

AMVOX 2 Chronograph
Reference number: 192 T4 70
Movement: automatic, JLC Caliber 751B; ø 25.6 mm, height 5.6 mm; 39 jewels; 28,800 vph; chronograph controlled by pressure on crystal (transmission to the inside of the case via a lever connecting the button axles)
Functions: hours, minutes, subsidiary seconds; chronograph; date
Case: blackened titanium, ø 44 mm, height 15.1 mm; sapphire crystal; water-resistant to 5 atm
Band: calfskin, folding clasp
Price: $14,950
Variations: titanium; titanium/platinum

Idéale
Reference number: 460 21 84
Movement: manually wound, JLC Caliber 846; 15.2 x 13 mm, height 2.9 mm, 18 jewels; 21,600 vph
Functions: hours, minutes
Case: red gold, 39.7 x 17 mm, height 9 mm; lugs set with 24 diamonds; sapphire crystal; crown with sapphire cabochon
Band: red gold, folding clasp
Price: $15,000
Variations: leather strap; yellow gold on leather strap or metal bracelet; stainless steel on leather strap or metal bracelet

Reverso Duetto Duo
Reference number: 269 24 20
Movement: manually wound, JLC Caliber 854; 22 x 17.2 mm, height 3.8 mm; 21 jewels; 21,600 vph
Functions: hours, minutes; second time zone; day/night indication
Case: red gold, 40.2 x 25 mm, height 9.85 mm; case can be turned and rotated 180°; case sides set with diamonds; sapphire crystal
Band: reptile skin, folding clasp
Price: $14,450
Variations: red gold link bracelet; yellow gold, also with metal bracelet; white gold on leather strap or metal bracelet

Master Minute Repeater
Reference number: 164 T4 50
Movement: manually wound, JLC Caliber 947; ø 34.7 mm, height 8.95 mm; 43 jewels; 21,600 vph; twin spring barrels, fifteen days power reserve
Functions: hours, minutes; minute repeater; power reserve display, display of torque
Case: platinum, ø 44 mm, height 15.8 mm; sapphire crystal; transparent case back
Band: reptile skin, folding clasp
Remarks: limited edition
Price: $135,000

Reverso Duoface
Reference number: 303 84 20
Movement: manually wound, JLC Caliber 854; 22 x 17.2 mm, height 3.8 mm; 21 jewels; 21,600 vph
Functions: hours, minutes, subsidiary seconds (front); second time zone; day/night indication (back)
Case: yellow gold, 42.2 x 26 mm, height 9.4 mm; sapphire crystal; case can be turned and rotated 180°
Band: reptile skin, folding clasp
Price: $12,400
Variations: stainless steel or red gold on leather strap or metal bracelet; yellow gold bracelet

Jaeger-LeCoultre

Caliber 380
Mechanical with manual winding, twin spring barrels and two separate gear trains for watch and chronograph; one-button chronograph functions controlled by switch on foudroyante mechanism
Functions: hours, minutes (off-center), sweep seconds; chronograph with foudroyante sixth-second counter; double power reserve display
Diameter: 33.7 mm
Height: 6.95 mm
Jewels: 48
Balance: screw balance with weights
Frequency: 21,600 vph
Remarks: plates with perlage, bridges with côtes de Genève

Caliber 978
Mechanical with automatic winding; one-minute tourbillon
Functions: hours, minutes, subsidiary seconds (on tourbillon cage); date hand (jumps from 15th to 16th of the month); 24-hour display (second time zone)
Diameter: 31 mm
Height: 7.05 mm
Jewels: 33
Balance: screw balance with four weights
Frequency: 28,800 vph
Remarks: plates with perlage, bridges with côtes de Genève

Caliber 752
Mechanical with automatic winding, twin spring barrels; power reserve 65 hours
Functions: hours, minutes, subsidiary seconds; chronograph; date, world time
Diameter: 25.6 mm
Height: 5.6 mm
Jewels: 41
Balance: screw balance with four weights
Frequency: 28,800 vph
Mainspring: flat hairspring
Shock protection: Kif
Remarks: plates with perlage, bridges with côtes circulaires

Caliber 936 (dial side)
Mechanical with automatic winding; twin spring barrels; power reserve 43 hours
Functions: hours, minutes, sweep seconds; date, second time zone
Diameter: 31.35 mm
Height: 4.9 mm
Jewels: 38
Balance: glucydur
Frequency: 28,800 vph
Mainspring: flat hairspring
Shock protection: Kif
Remarks: plates with perlage, bridges with côtes de Genève

Caliber 873
Mechanical with automatic winding; twin spring barrels, power reserve 43 hours
Functions: hours, minutes, sweep seconds; date; second time zone
Diameter: 31.35 mm
Height: 4.9 mm
Jewels: 38
Balance: glucydur
Frequency: 28,800 vph
Balance spring: flat hairspring
Shock protection: Kif
Remarks: plates with perlage, bridges with côtes de Genève

Caliber 970
Mechanical with automatic winding; power reserve 45 hours
Functions: hours, minutes, subsidiary seconds; separately settable hour hand (second time zone); day/night indication (coupled to second time zone), large date
Dimensions: 22.6 x 25.6 mm
Height: 5.3 mm
Jewels: 29
Balance: glucydur
Frequency: 28,800 vph
Balance spring: flat hairspring
Shock protection: Kif
Remarks: plate with perlage, rotor with côtes de Genève

Caliber 177
Mechanical with manual winding, patented spherical tourbillon; twin spring barrels; power reserve eight days
Functions: hours, minutes, subsidiary seconds (on tourbillon cage); perpetual calendar with date (two retrograde hands) and month; display of true solar time (equation); retrograde leap year display on back
Diameter: 36.3 mm
Height: 10.85 mm
Jewels: 77
Frequency: 21,600 vph
Remarks: 659 individual parts; plates with perlage, bridges with côtes de Genève

Caliber 876
Mechanical with manual winding; twin spring barrels, power reserve eight days
Functions: hours, minutes; perpetual calendar with date, day, month, year (four-digit), day/night indication; power reserve display
Diameter: 32 mm
Height: 6.6 mm
Jewels: 37
Balance: glucydur with compensation screws
Frequency: 28,800 vph
Balance spring: flat hairspring
Shock protection: Kif

Jaeger-LeCoultre

Caliber 751B
Mechanical with automatic winding; chronograph functions controlled by pushing on watch crystal; power reserve 65 hours
Functions: hours, minutes, subsidiary seconds; separately chronograph; date
Diameter: 26.2 mm
Height: 5.6 mm
Jewels: 39
Balance: screw balance with four weights
Frequency: 28,800 vph
Balance spring: flat hairspring
Shock protection: Kif

Caliber 849
Mechanical with manual winding, power reserve 35 hours
Functions: hours, minutes
Diameter: 21.1 mm
Height: 1.85 mm
Jewels: 19
Balance: glucydur
Frequency: 21,600 vph
Balance spring: flat hairspring
Shock protection: Kif
Remarks: ultra-flat movement; base plate with perlage, bridges with côtes de Genève

Caliber 899
Mechanical with automatic winding, power reserve 43 hours
Functions: hours, minutes, sweep seconds; date
Diameter: 26.6 mm
Height: 3.3 mm
Balance spring: screw balance with four weights
Frequency: 28,800 vph
Shock protection: Kif
Remarks: base plate with perlage, bridges with côtes circulaires

Caliber 753
Mechanical with automatic winding, twin spring barrels, power reserve 65 hours
Functions: hours, minutes, subsidiary seconds; large date; chronograph; day/night indication; world time (back)
Dimensions: 33.5 x 31.15 mm
Height: 7.57 mm
Jewels: 44
Balance: glucydur
Frequency: 28,800 vph
Balance spring: flat hairspring
Shock protection: Kif
Remarks: base plate with perlage

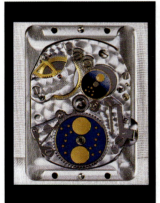

Caliber 923
Mechanical with automatic winding, power reserve 43 hours
Functions: hours, minutes, sweep seconds; date hand; second time zone with names of world reference cities; day/night indication
Diameter: 26 mm
Height: 4.9 mm
Jewels: 31
Balance: glucydur
Frequency: 28,800 vph
Balance spring: flat hairspring with fine adjustment via micrometer screw
Shock protection: Kif
Remarks: 281 individual components; base plate with perlage, bridges with côtes de Genève, blued screws

Caliber 848
Mechanical with manual winding, one-minute tourbillon (on back); power reserve 45 hours
Functions: hours, minutes, subsidiary seconds; power reserve display
Dimensions: 23.4 x 28.9 mm
Height: 4.9 mm
Jewels: 25
Balance: glucydur with weighted screws
Frequency: 21,600 vph
Balance spring: flat hairspring
Shock protection: Kif
Remarks: 200 individual components; plates and bridges in white gold with ray-shaped côtes de Genève

Caliber 909/1
Mechanical with automatic winding, power reserve 45 hours
Functions: hours, minutes, sweep seconds; date, alarm (vibration or sound); 24-hour display; perpetual calendar with date, day, month, double moon phase, four-digit year
Diameter: 31 mm
Balance: glucydur
Frequency: 28,800 vph
Balance spring: flat hairspring with fine adjustment
Shock protection: Kif
Remarks: 363 individual parts; plate with perlage, bridges with côtes de Genève, blued screws

Caliber 844
Mechanical with manual winding; power reserve 45 hours
Functions: hours, minutes with dial train on both sides
Dimensions: 22.6 x 17.2 mm
Height: 3.45 mm
Jewels: 18
Balance: glucydur
Frequency: 21,600 vph
Balance spring: flat hair spring
Shock protection: Kif

Jacob & Co.

American pop culture would currently be unthinkable without Jacob & Co. From hip-hop to mainstream, and from sports hero to movie diva, anyone who's anyone wears a watch by "Jacob the Jeweler" these days.

This type of attention positively smacks of the short-lived and cheap. And even though Jacob's masterfully designed, overly large timepieces kicked off a trend all their own—even calling to life a great deal of "icy" copycats, certainly the purest form of flattery—they are anything but cheap and faddish.

Jacob Arabo grew up in Russia, where his passion for creating jewelry developed during his formative years. After immigrating to the United States as a teenager, Arabo enrolled in a jewelry design course with the intent of developing his natural talents. Showing exceptional aptitude, he was urged to begin his career in earnest and thus immediately began designing for a number of jewelry labels and private clients. In 1986, a short five years after that, Arabo opened his current company, Diamond Quasar, and from then on designed exclusively for his own label, Jacob & Co.

The year 2006 marked Jacob's full frontal attack on the established watch industry. Creating a number of wild tourbillons and jeweled and non-jeweled five time zone automatics and manually wound models in 2005—practically heralding what was to come—Jacob took the entire industry by storm at Baselworld 2006. The question, "Have you seen what Jacob is showing?" was heard throughout the entire show—and justifiably asked. Jacob & Co.'s innovative introduction, the Quenttin, incorporated so many firsts in such a newfangled look that the observer needed to rub his or her eyes before going for a second glance.

Gone was any trace of diamond, Jacob's shining hallmark, replaced by a mechanical monster resembling something more along the lines of a small adding machine. This machine, actually not so small at 56 x 47 x 21 mm, *only* shows the hours and minutes on the main digital disk displays, and the power reserve display at far left, which could conceivably also be used as the date, since it comprises a full thirty-one days. This tremendous autonomy is achieved by seven—count 'em, you can see 'em—spring barrels above the time display.

The following Baselworld proved that Jacob's beloved sparklers weren't actually gone, but just set aside for a time. His new Crystal Tourbillon wowed audiences at the world's largest watch fair with its almost transparent movement thanks to the fact that the mechanism's bridges are crafted in pure sapphire crystal. The bezel and crown are completely and invisibly set with Jacob's hallmark top-grade diamonds, lending the timepiece a fully ethereal feel. Insiders were also allowed a sneak peak at what complicated timepiece Jacob has cooked up to amaze his adoring audiences next: the Quadra, a timepiece featuring four separate tourbillons emulating the brand's signature Five Time Zone look.

Jacob & Co.

Quenttin
Movement: manually wound, Jacob & Co. Caliber 5; height 15.35 mm, 40 jewels; 21,000 vph; 31 days power reserve; seven spring barrels; vertical tourbillon
Functions: hours, minutes; power reserve display
Case: rose gold, 56 x 47 mm; height 21.35 mm; sapphire crystal; water-resistant to 30 m
Band: rubber, double folding clasp
Remarks: manual winding by key, comes with special custom box
Price: $360,000
Variations: white gold ($360,000); red, blue, or black magnesium ($350,000)

Crystal Tourbillon
Movement: manually wound, Jacob & Co. Caliber 8; ø 32.6 mm, height 5.4 mm; 17 jewels; 21,600 vph; power reserve 120 hours; transparent tourbillon movement with sapphire crystal bridges and plates
Functions: hours, minutes
Case: white gold, ø 47 mm, height 14.5 mm; bezel, case, and crown set with 17.48 ct of baguette-cut diamonds; sapphire crystal; sapphire crystal exhibition case back
Band: alligator skin, buckle set with 2.22 ct of baguette-cut diamonds
Remarks: limited edition
Price: $1,200,000

Revealed Hour
Movement: automatic, Jacob & Co. Caliber 6 (base caliber ETA 2892-A2); ø 34.8 mm, height 6.6 mm; 21 jewels; 28,800 vph; power reserve 42 hours
Functions: jump hours, minutes
Case: rose gold, ø 43 mm, height 11 mm; case and lugs set with 2.19 ct of diamonds; sapphire crystal; sapphire crystal exhibition case back; water-resistant to 30 m
Band: alligator skin, folding clasp
Remarks: limited edition
Price: $84,000
Variations: case available in 18-karat white gold

H24 Five Time Zone Automatic
Movement: automatic, Jacob & Co. Caliber 2 (base caliber ETA A07.111); ø 37.2 mm, height 9.9 mm; 24 jewels; 28,800 vph; power reserve 46 hours
Functions: hours, minutes, sweep seconds; date; four additional time zones
Case: stainless steel, ø 47.5 mm, height 15.95 mm; sapphire crystal; sapphire crystal exhibition case back; water-resistant to 30 m
Band: alligator skin; folding clasp
Remarks: limited edition
Price: $14,800
Variations: available in 18-karat rose, yellow or white gold; available in platinum

The Standard Automatic
Movement: automatic, ETA Caliber 2892-A2; ø 25.6 mm, height 3.6 mm; 21 jewels; 28,800 vph; 40 hours power reserve
Functions: hours, minutes, sweep seconds; date
Case: rose gold, ø 40 mm; bezel set with double row of diamonds (2.6 ct); sapphire crystal; screw-down case back; water-resistant to 100 m
Band: reptile skin, folding clasp
Remarks: mother-of-pearl dial with .12 ct diamonds
Price: $36,000
Variations: in 57.5 mm case size; available in 18-karat white gold; with full pavé case or diamond-set bezel

Five Time Zone Collection
Movement: quartz, ETA Caliber 956.112 for main display; ø 17.5 mm, height 3.5 mm; four additional quartz movements (ETA 280.002) for small time zone displays
Functions: hours, minutes, sweep seconds; date; four additional time zones
Case: stainless steel, ø 47 mm, height 13.25 mm; mineral crystal; water-resistant to 100 m
Band: stainless steel fully paved with diamonds, folding clasp
Remarks: full pavé dial, case, bezel, and bracelet
Price: $85,500
Variations: available in 40 and 47 mm case sizes

Five Time Zone Collection
Movement: quartz, ETA Caliber 956.112 for main display; ø 17.5 mm, height 3.5 mm; four additional quartz movements (ETA 280.002) for additional time zone displays
Functions: hours, minutes, sweep seconds; date; four additional time zones
Case: stainless steel with diamond-set rose gold bezel (5 ct), ø 47 mm, height 13.25 mm; sapphire crystal; diamond-set case lugs; water-resistant to 100 m
Band: snake skin, folding clasp
Remarks: interchangeable diamond and non-diamond bezel; dial is diamond-set map of the world
Price: $77,000
Variations: white or rose gold; without diamonds

Manhattan
Movement: quartz, ETA Caliber E01.701; ø 17.5 mm, height 3.5 mm
Functions: hours, minutes
Case: white gold, 37 x 37 mm, height 11.5 mm; sapphire crystal; diamond-set bezel and case lugs; no visible crown: setting done from the back
Band: reptile skin, buckle
Remarks: unusual dial with three-dimensional skyline in diamonds; limited edition
Price: $90,000
Variations: available in 18-karat rose gold

Jaquet Droz

A dial is what gives any watch its character, its face, so to speak. A connoisseur often unconsciously opts to buy or pass on a watch based on the emotions he or she feels upon looking at the dial. The creative designers at Jaquet Droz have taken the "faces" of their timepieces a step further and incorporated this all-important component into the company's comprehensive concept of luxury.

The La Chaux-de-Fonds–based brand sells luxury, but what is it exactly that makes these products so luxurious? Their rarity, of course. Not only are Jaquet Droz timepieces themselves uncommon, but they are made of components that are also unique in nature—literally—starting with the dial. Jaquet Droz limits some of its small series, editions called "Numerus Clausus," to eight or eighty-eight. A series containing eight pieces is often made all the more luxurious by the use of rare and precious materials on the dials. Jaquet Droz goes even further: The Swatch Group–owned company also offers made-to-order dials in materials as rare as meteorite, nuumite, and spectrolite.

At the company's refounding, Jaquet Droz often presented unique dials with uncommon types of enameling according to historical examples. Now the company's focus has turned to semiprecious geological materials.

Jaquet Droz and its experienced dial maker search everywhere for rare and exotic materials to offer the company's discerning customers, traveling not only to famed jewel cities like Idar-Oberstein in Germany, but also to faraway places like Hong Kong. Manuel Emch, Jaquet Droz's CEO, not infrequently visits the little dial workshop to choose the exact cuts of stone he would like the next Numerus Clausus or unique dials to be made of.

Not all of Jaquet Droz's current dials are made of exotic materials, some of them are created using the traditional *grande feu* (high fire) art of enameling. This look, which can only be achieved using a difficult process of painting and firing many times in a high-temperature kiln, characterizes the face of the brand—as does the use of tempered blue elements on the dial such as screws and hands. Jaquet Droz's latest creation, the Date Astrale model, adds a new element to the brand's signature features. A discrete diamond acts as a retrograde hand, traveling across a display that is one of only two elements on this secretive black opaline dial with a circular satin finish. The brand's emphasis on the dial's distinct appearance does not preclude the use of discriminating movements and even a few very complicated timepieces in the collection such as an equation of time and even a tourbillon minute repeater—with the regulating whirlwind naturally hidden on the back of the watch to preserve the brand's low-key identity. Turning this seemingly simple watch around, the wearer can experience the fascination of watchmaking's highest complication, but only when he or she is not wearing the piece.

Jaquet Droz

Grande Seconde Céramique Noir Absolu
Reference number: J003035201
Movement: automatic, Jaquet Droz Caliber 2663; ø 26.2 mm; 30 jewels; 28,800 vph; twin spring barrels, power reserve 68 hours; black PVD-coated white gold rotor
Functions: hours, minutes (off-center), large subsidiary seconds
Case: ceramic, ø 43 mm, height 12.3 mm; sapphire crystal; transparent case back
Band: rubber, folding clasp
Remarks: black Grand Feu enamel dial; limited edition of 88 pieces
Price: $15,000

Grande Seconde Medium Météorite Sertie
Reference number: J014014224
Movement: automatic, Jaquet Droz Caliber 2663; ø 26.2 mm; 30 jewels; 28,800 vph; twin spring barrels, power reserve 68 hours
Functions: hours, minutes (off-center), large subsidiary seconds
Case: white gold, ø 39 mm, height 11.5 mm; bezel and strap lugs set with diamonds; sapphire crystal
Band: reptile skin, buckle
Remarks: meteorite dial; subdial rings set with 88 diamonds; limited edition of 8 pieces
Price: $43,300

L'Origine
Reference number: J022030201
Movement: automatic, Jaquet Droz Caliber 1153; ø 26.2 mm; 28 jewels; 28,800 vph; twin spring barrels, power reserve 68 hours
Functions: hours, minutes, sweep seconds
Case: stainless steel, ø 43 mm, height 11 mm; sapphire crystal
Band: reptile skin, buckle
Price: $7,000

Grande Heure Minute Medium Noire
Reference number: J017010201
Movement: automatic, Jaquet Droz Caliber 1169; ø 26.2 mm; 32 jewels; 28,800 vph; twin spring barrels, power reserve 68 hours
Functions: hours, minutes, subsidiary seconds
Case: stainless steel, ø 41 mm, height 11.35 mm; sapphire crystal
Band: reptile skin, buckle
Remarks: limited edition of 88 pieces
Price: $9,100

La Date Astrale
Reference number: J021010201
Movement: automatic, Jaquet Droz Caliber 2650R; ø 26.2 mm; 28 jewels; 28,800 vph; twin spring barrels, power reserve 68 hours
Functions: hours, minutes (off-center); date (retrograde)
Case: stainless steel, ø 39 mm, height 11.5 mm; sapphire crystal
Band: reptile skin, buckle
Remarks: retrograde date display with diamond marker
Price: $14,000

La Fleur de Lotus
Reference number: J014014202
Movement: automatic, Jaquet Droz Caliber 2663; ø 26.2 mm; 30 jewels; 28,800 vph; twin spring barrels, power reserve 68 hours
Functions: hours, minutes (off-center)
Case: white gold, ø 39 mm, height 11.5 mm; sapphire crystal
Band: reptile skin, buckle
Remarks: dial set with tsavorites, sapphires, and diamonds
Price: $33,000

Quantième Perpétuel Email Noir
Reference number: J008334210
Movement: automatic, Jaquet Droz Caliber 5863; ø 26.2 mm; 33 jewels; 28,800 vph; twin spring barrels, power reserve 68 hours
Functions: hours, minutes, subsidiary seconds; date, weekday (retrograde), month, leap year display
Case: white gold, ø 43 mm, height 12 mm; sapphire crystal
Band: reptile skin, buckle
Remarks: black Grand Feu enamel dial; limited edition of 88 pieces
Price: $49,300

Tourbillon
Reference number: J023033201
Movement: automatic, Jaquet Droz Caliber JD2; ø 34.4 mm; 16 jewels; 21,600 vph; twin spring barrels, power reserve 88 hours; one-minute tourbillon
Functions: hours, minutes (off-center)
Case: red gold, ø 44 mm, height 13.8 mm; sapphire crystal; transparent case back
Band: reptile skin, buckle
Remarks: limited edition of 28 pieces
Price: $119,000

JeanRichard

According to legend, Daniel Jean-Richard was fourteen years old when he held his first watch in his hand in 1679. And it didn't even work. A horse dealer on his way through town had noticed the filigreed iron wares and silver jewelry that young Daniel had put together. The man had an English pocket watch in his baggage that had stopped working somewhere between London and Basel. The young JeanRichard with his obvious talent appeared trustworthy to him, and he gave Daniel the valuable timepiece to repair. He wanted to pick it up again a few weeks later on his way home from Geneva.

And Daniel JeanRichard actually did repair the watch with his primitive tools. During the process he also memorized all of the details, allowing him to build an exact replica of the watch during the following winter.

In the middle of nowhere, somewhere between Geneva and the French border in the Jura region of Switzerland, where the snow piled so high in the winter that the farms were covered and their residents sometimes didn't see their neighbors for weeks at a time, in the village of La Sagne, nestled in a valley between La Chaux-de-Fonds and Le Locle, is exactly where a boy achieved that which no one in the entire canton of Neuchâtel had accomplished until then: he made an entire pocket watch from scratch, using just his memory.

Today Massimo Macaluso, who was just a few years older than the brand's namesake when his father first introduced him to the world of watches, directs JeanRichard's business. Massimo's father, Luigi Macaluso bought his own Swiss watch brand after working for many years in an import business for Swiss watches. Using the Girard-Perregaux *manufacture* as a springboard, he created JeanRichard as a second brand and systematically extended the collection, heading it ever more upscale—so that it now even includes a tourbillon.

The next big step was taken under the aegis of Massimo: the introduction of an autonomous movement by the name of Caliber JR 1000, produced exclusively for JeanRichard by the Sowind Group's movement *manufacture*. We are not talking about a modified caliber for another group brand, either, which would have been far too expensive for what was intended. No, Caliber JR 1000 displays a number of unique characteristics, such as subsidiary seconds driven outside the flow of energy by a micromodule gear wheel with a special tooth shape that can also double as the driving source for additional complications if necessary.

This source is now being heavily tapped as the next generation of JeanRichard timepieces is introduced. These begin with the incredibly creative Paramount Time Square, a watch that innovatively uses hypocycloids and planetary gears to display the hours on

a square track following the shape of the Paramount case. It could be considered a regulator display were it round, as it separates all three main displays—hours, minutes, and seconds.

Another good example of the versatility of Caliber JR 1000 is the Bressel line's Flying Hands model. In 2007 wonderfully interpreted for women, the Flying Hands represents a true regulator display with the addition of date and power reserve indications.

JeanRichard

Paramount JR 1000
Reference number: 61108-11-60A-AA6
Movement: automatic, JR Caliber 1000; ø 25.6 mm; height 5.1 mm; 32 jewels; 28,800 vph
Functions: hours, minutes, subsidiary seconds; date
Case: stainless steel, 34.3 x 36.5 mm, height 11.15 mm; sapphire crystal
Band: reptile skin, buckle
Price: $4,200
Variations: limited edition of 25 pieces in rose gold

Paramount Sebring
Reference number: 62118-11-61B-EE6D
Movement: automatic, JR Caliber 1000; ø 25.6 mm; height 5.1 mm; 33 jewels; 28,800 vph; linear display of power reserve
Functions: hours, minutes, subsidiary seconds; date; power reserve display
Case: stainless steel, 36.3 x 36.3 mm, height 12.05 mm; sapphire crystal; transparent case back
Band: leather and rubber, folding clasp
Remarks: carbon fiber dial
Price: $6,250

Paramount Square
Reference number: 62118-11-61A-AAE
Movement: automatic, JR Caliber 10RJ (base 1000); ø 25.6 mm; height 4.9 mm; 25 jewels; 28,800 vph; linear display of power reserve
Functions: hours, minutes, sweep seconds; date; power reserve display (linear)
Case: stainless steel, 36.3 x 36.9 mm, height 12.05 mm; sapphire crystal; transparent case back
Band: reptile skin, buckle
Price: $6,250
Variations: white dial

Bressel 1665
Reference number: 63112-49-60A-AAED
Movement: automatic, JR Caliber 1020; ø 25.6 mm; height 5.1 mm; 34 jewels; 28,800 vph
Functions: off-center hours, minutes, subsidiary seconds; date; power reserve display
Case: stainless steel, ø 42 mm, height 10.5 mm; sapphire crystal; transparent case back
Band: reptile skin, folding clasp
Price: $6,950
Variations: limited edition of 100 pieces in rose gold

Bressel Alternative
Reference number: 64112-11-EOA-AACD
Movement: automatic, JR Caliber 1000; ø 25.6 mm; height 5.1 mm; 29 jewels; 28,800 vph
Functions: hours, off-center minutes, subsidiary seconds; date; power reserve display
Case: stainless steel, ø 42 mm, height 10.5 mm; sapphire crystal; transparent case back
Band: reptile skin, folding clasp
Price: $7,250
Variations: rose gold

Paramount Time Square
Reference number: 67118-79-61A-AA6D
Movement: automatic, JR Caliber 1100; ø 25.6 mm; 33 jewels; 28,800 vph; hours marked with revolving triangular reference marker thanks to special gear train
Functions: hours, minutes, sweep seconds; date
Case: stainless steel/titanium, 36.3 x 36.3 mm, height 12.05 mm; sapphire crystal; transparent case back
Band: reptile skin, folding clasp
Price: $7,500

2 Time Zones
Reference number: 68130-11-61A-AAED
Movement: automatic, JR Caliber 1060 (base JR 1000); 31 jewels; 28,800 vph; world time display settable via separate crown
Functions: hours, minutes, sweep seconds; date; 24-hour display (second time zone) with world reference cities
Case: stainless steel, ø 43 mm mm, height 13.2 mm; sapphire crystal; transparent case back
Band: reptile skin, folding clasp
Price: $7,650
Variations: various band and dial variations

Bressel Flying Hand
Reference number: 63112D11A70DAF8D
Movement: automatic, JR Caliber 1020; ø 25.6 mm, height 5.1 mm; 34 jewels; 28,800 vph
Functions: off-center hours, minutes, subsidiary seconds; date; power reserve display
Case: stainless steel, ø 42 mm, height 10.5 mm; bezel set with 52 diamonds; sapphire crystal; transparent case back
Band: stingray skin, folding clasp
Remarks: mother-of-pearl dial with diamond markers
Price: $12,500
Variations: without diamonds; various band and dial variations

F.-P. Journe

Born in 1957 in Marseille, France, François-Paul Journe would not have prophesied a career as a watchmaker and movement designer for himself at a young age. If he had been a better student, he might have done something completely different with his life: he only embarked upon an apprenticeship as a watchmaker because he had been expelled from school—and because his uncle had already gone down the same path. So perhaps it was something like genetic talent that got passed to him after all? He ended his education in Paris at the above-mentioned uncle's workshop, but soon there-after discovered that re-pairing watches as a simple technician was no longer enough for him. He began to build his own movements, all the while dreaming of a tourbillon and then actually achieving it. He was barely twenty years old at the time. In order to realize his ambition of making his own watches—an entire collection of them, as a matter of fact—Journe opened his first workshop in the Paris suburb of Saint-Germain-des-Près, where he completed highly specialized instruments with numerous technical and aesthetic refinements for a very special type of collector clientele, with all work on the pieces done lavishly by hand. Additionally, he continued to work as a restorer of watches and clocks and for quite a while was in charge of caring for the timekeepers found in the Musée des Arts et Métiers.

In 1986 he joined the Academy of Independent Horologists, the world-renowned A.H.C.I., which provided a springboard to greater international fame. He moved from Paris to Geneva, where he founded his own brand, establishing it with a consistently developed collection and a logical, aesthetic language of the highest degree. Characteristic of Journe's design is the off-center arrangement of the dials, held by screwed-on, polished frames. While it is possible that these elements are also being reproduced by other reputable brands, this should be viewed as a form of flattery and not a reason for retreating from the unmistakable design. The most remarkable thing—and for a watchmaker the most unusual—is that Journe designs his watches from the outside in. This means that he first creates the "face" of the watch and arranges the displays purely from an aesthetic standpoint. Only at the end does he slip on the shoes of movement designer in order to arrange the functions correspondingly found inside the watch. Journe's latest work of genius is a complicated chronograph with a lightning fast display of seconds: the Centigraphe Souverain is outfitted with three totalizers that display the passage of time to the hundredth of a second—thanks to the *seconde foudroyante* located in the counter at 2 o'clock that makes one revolution per second along a scale with 100 divisions. Like the other two counters, it is also outfitted with a tachymeter scale allowing the wearer to visualize speeds to 360,000 km/h. The chronograph is activated using an innovative rocking bar on the case near 2 o'clock, which is outfitted with a clever isolator mechanism that decouples the stopwatch mechanism from the running movement. With such horological specialties, Journe has secured the undivided attention of collectors, who literally allow themselves to be added to waiting lists in the hopes of being able to purchase one of his reputable timepieces—his entire annual production is generally sold out at least one year in advance, with no more than 700 to 1,000 watches being produced at this little *manufacture* located in the heart of Geneva each year.

F. P. Journe

Octa Réserve de Marche
Movement: automatic, FP Journe Caliber 1300-2; ø 30 mm, height 5.7 mm; 30 jewels; 21,600 vph; twin spring barrels, power reserve 120 hours; plate and bridges crafted in 18-karat gold
Functions: hours, minutes (off-center), subsidiary seconds; large date; power reserve display
Case: platinum, ø 38 mm, height 10 mm; sapphire crystal; transparent case back
Band: reptile skin, platinum buckle
Price: $31,700
Variations: red gold ($28,200); 40 mm case size in platinum ($33,000) or red gold ($28,700)

Octa Calendrier
Movement: automatic, FP Journe Caliber 1300-2; ø 30 mm, height 5.7 mm; 32 jewels; 21,600 vph; twin spring barrels, power reserve 120 hours; plate and bridges crafted in 18-karat gold
Functions: hours, minutes (off-center), subsidiary seconds; annual calendar with date (retrograde), weekday and month; power reserve display
Case: platinum, ø 38 mm, height 10 mm; sapphire crystal; transparent case back
Band: reptile skin, platinum buckle
Price: $44,300
Variations: red gold ($40,700); 40 mm case size in platinum ($45,500) or red gold ($41,300)

Octa Divine
Movement: automatic, FP Journe Caliber 1300-3; ø 30 mm, height 5.7 mm; 30 jewels; 21,600 vph; twin spring barrels, power reserve 120 hours; plate and bridges crafted in 18-karat gold
Functions: hours, minutes, subsidiary seconds; large date; power reserve display
Case: platinum, ø 36 mm, height 10 mm; sapphire crystal; transparent case back
Band: reptile skin, platinum buckle
Price: $37,000
Variations: red gold ($33,500); 40 mm case size in platinum ($38,300) or red gold ($34,000)

Octa Automatic Reserve
Movement: automatic, FP Journe Caliber 1300-3; ø 30.4 mm, height 5.86 mm; 37 jewels; 21,600 vph; twin spring barrels, power reserve 120 hours; plate and bridges crafted in 18-karat gold
Functions: hours, minutes, subsidiary seconds; large date; power reserve display
Case: platinum, ø 38 mm, height 10 mm; sapphire crystal; transparent case back
Band: reptile skin, platinum buckle
Price: $30,100
Variations: red gold ($26,600); 40 mm case size in platinum ($31,400) or red gold ($27,100)

New Chronomètre à Resonance
Movement: manually wound, FP Journe Caliber 1499-2; ø 32 mm, height 4.8 mm; 36 jewels; 21,600 vph; unique movement concept featuring two escapements that influence and stabilize each other; plate and bridges crafted in 18-karat gold
Functions: hours, minutes, subsidiary seconds (double for two time zones); power reserve display
Case: platinum, ø 40 mm, height 9 mm; sapphire crystal; transparent case back
Band: reptile skin, platinum buckle
Price: $65,400
Variations: red gold ($60,900)

New Tourbillon Souverain
Movement: manually wound, FP Journe Caliber 1403; ø 32 mm, height 6.35 mm; 26 jewels; 21,600 vph; one-minute tourbillon; escapement with deadbeat seconds and jump second display; patented constant force mechanism; plate and bridges crafted in 18-karat gold
Functions: hours, minutes (off-center), subsidiary seconds; power reserve display
Case: platinum, ø 40 mm, height 10 mm; sapphire crystal; transparent case back
Band: reptile skin, platinum buckle
Price: $119,100
Variations: red gold

Chronomètre Souverain
Movement: automatic, FP Journe Caliber 1304; ø 30 mm, height 3.7 mm; 21 jewels; 21,600 vph; plate and bridges crafted in 18-karat gold; chronometer balance with "invisible" connection to gear train; twin spring barrels
Functions: hours, minutes, subsidiary seconds; power reserve display
Case: platinum, ø 40 mm, height 6.5 mm; sapphire crystal; transparent case back
Band: reptile skin, platinum buckle
Price: $26,700
Variations: red gold ($22,800)

Sonnerie Souveraine
Movement: automatic, FP Journe Caliber 1505; ø 35.8 mm, height 7.8 mm; 21,600 vph; plate and bridges crafted in 18-karat gold; repeater chimes hours and quarter hours en passant, on/off function; 408 individual components, 10 patents pending
Functions: hours, minutes (off-center), subsidiary seconds; grande sonnerie; power reserve display; display of sonnerie function
Case: stainless steel, ø 40 mm, height 14 mm; sapphire crystal
Band: reptile skin, platinum buckle
Price: 650,000 Swiss francs plus taxes

Kobold

The popularity of Kobold watches among both hard-core professionals in exploration like Sir Ranulph Fiennes and Will Cross and watch connoisseurs is somewhat unusual, given the company's background.

Founded by a teenager attending his first year of college and based in the United States, Kobold is an anomaly among luxury watch com-panies, most of which are headquartered in classic watchmaking countries like Switzerland and Germany. Yet perhaps it is this circumstance that draws such es-teemed clients as former U.S. president Bill Clinton and rock star Bruce Springsteen to the quirky brand—not to mention actor James Gandolfini, best known for his tele-vision role in The Sopranos, now one of Kobold's brand ambassadors and a self-declared fan of the company. Yet Michael Kobold continues to be unimpressed by all this celebrity. "To me, it's far more im-portant that a person wears one of my watches who is actually in need of that particular timepiece for his or her specific job," he explains, "than when someone famous wears it to the Oscars."

Nonetheless, it is without a doubt his friend Gandolfini who has done the most for the name recognition of Kobold's timepieces since 2003. Hanging around at a photo shoot with him one day, Kobold began snapping some of his own shots. Gandolfini laughingly flipped him the bird, which Kobold got on film. Using it as an ad motif with the appropriate tagline, "James Gandolfini thinks Kobold is no. 1," Kobold sparked controversy and drew a great deal of attention to his brand.

Gandolfini also unwittingly helped Kobold create one of his most popular models: the Soarway Diver SEAL, a wristwatch manufactured especially for deep-sea divers. The SEAL is a timepiece of generous proportions, measuring 44 mm in diameter and 17.75 mm in height. Its size was determined by Gandolfini, a man of generous proportions himself. "Jim told me that my watches were too small for him, so we set out to design a watch for big people like him," explains the company's founder. The watch was later named after this particular sea creature because it most resembled "what Jim would look like in a diver's suit," Kobold adds with mirthful enthusiasm.

The SEAL, boasting a water resistance of 1,000 meters, was well received among professional and amateur divers, collectors, and a host of celebrities. Bill Clinton was seen wearing his SEAL shortly after the watch made its debut, and actor Kiefer Sutherland wore one in the popular prime-time TV series 24. Kobold has meanwhile introduced titanium and PVD-coated versions of the SEAL as well as a limited edition of five rose gold models.

Right from his first day in business, Kobold vowed to hold on to the strict production limit he originally set. "In the beginning, even this low number seemed hard to achieve," the young watch manufacturer laughingly recalls. Now, almost a decade after he began selling watches out of his student apartment at Carnegie Mellon University, Kobold's line includes some eighteen different models, and production is nearing capacity.

Kobold

Mid-Size Chronograph
Reference number: KD 037167
Movement: automatic, ETA Caliber 2094, modified; ø 23.3 mm, height 5.5 mm; 28 jewels; 28,800 vph; power reserve 42 hours; tested for 1,000 hours
Functions: hours, minutes, subsidiary seconds; chronograph
Case: 18-karat white gold, ø 36 mm, height 11 mm; screw-in crown with protection, buttons with protection; sapphire crystal; sapphire crystal case back; water-resistant to 100 m
Band: alligator skin, gold buckle
Price: $12,500
Variations: 18-karat red gold; matching metal bracelet; diamonds available upon request

Phantom Tactical Chronograph
Reference number: KD 924453
Movement: automatic, ETA Valjoux Caliber 7750; ø 30 mm, height 8.1 mm; 25 jewels; 28,800 vph, power reserve 46 hours; côtes de Genève, perlage, tested for 1,000 hours
Functions: hours, minutes, subsidiary seconds; date, day; chronograph
Case: PVD-coated stainless steel, ø 41 mm, height 15.5 mm; unidirectionally rotating bezel with 60-minute scale; screw-in crown and buttons; extra-thick sapphire crystal, anti-reflective on the back; screw-down case back; water-resistant to 300 m
Band: PVD-coated stainless steel, folding clasp
Price: $4,850
Variations: titanium case

Spirit of America
Reference number: KD 637122
Movement: manually wound, Kobold Caliber K.644 (base ETA Unitas 6497, modified); ø 36 mm, height 8.1 mm; 17 jewels; 18,000 vph; power reserve 50 hours; côtes de Genève, gold-plated engraving on bridge; tested for 1,000 hours
Functions: hours, minutes
Case: titanium, ø 44.35 mm, height 14 mm; sapphire crystal, anti-reflective on the back; screw-down case back; water-resistant to 100 m
Band: leather, buckle
Price: $2,950
Variations: dial available in blue, red, and ivory; mother-of-pearl dial ($3,200)

Soarway Diver Red Gold
Reference number: KD 242126
Movement: automatic, ETA Caliber 2892-A2; ø 25.6 mm, height 4.35 mm; 21 jewels; 28,800 vph; power reserve 46 hours; côtes de Genève, perlage; tested for 1,000 hours
Functions: hours, minutes, sweep seconds, date
Case: 18-karat red gold, ø 42 mm, height 12.5 mm; unidirectionally rotating bezel with 60-minute scale; screw-in crown; sapphire crystal, anti-reflective on the back; screw-down case back; water-resistant to 300 m
Band: alligator skin, gold buckle
Price: $11,500
Variations: in stainless steel; with or without second hand; ivory or black dial

Pulsometer Chronograph
Reference number: KD 942161
Movement: automatic, Kobold Caliber K.752 (base modified ETA Valjoux 7750); ø 30 mm, height 8.1 mm; 28 jewels; 28,800 vph, power reserve 46 hours; côtes de Genève, perlage, tested for 1,000 hours
Functions: hours, minutes, subsidiary seconds; date; chronograph, pulsometer
Case: stainless steel, ø 41 mm, height 16 mm; unidirectionally rotating bezel with 60-minute scale; screw-in crown and buttons; sapphire crystal, anti-reflective on the back; screw-down case back; water-resistant to 100 m
Band: alligator skin, buckle
Price: $4,250

Soarway Diver Seal
Reference number: KD 832121
Movement: automatic, ETA Caliber 2824; ø 25.6 mm, height 4.35 mm; 22 jewels; 28,800 vph; power reserve, 46 hours; côtes de Genève, perlage, tested for 1,000 hours
Functions: hours, minutes, sweep seconds
Case: stainless steel, ø 44.5 mm, height 17.5 mm; unidirectionally rotating bezel with 60-minute scale; screw-in crown; sapphire crystal, anti-reflective on the back; screw-down case back; water-resistant to 1,000 m
Band: leather, buckle
Price: $2,850
Variations: stainless steel bracelet ($3,450)

Rattrapante Stirling Moss
Reference number: KD 971172
Movement: automatic, modified ETA Valjoux Caliber 7750; ø 30 mm, height 8.1 mm; 25 jewels; 28,800 vph, power reserve 46 hours; côtes de Genève, perlage; tested for 1,000 hours
Functions: hours, minutes, subsidiary seconds; date; split-seconds chronograph
Case: titanium, ø 41 mm, height 16 mm; screw-in crown; button protection; extra-thick sapphire crystal; screw-down case back; water-resistant to 100 m
Band: alligator skin, buckle
Remarks: limited edition of 250 pieces; first 50 come in a wood collector's box signed by Stirling Moss and Michael Kobold
Price: $7,450

Spirit of America
Reference number: KD 637122
Movement: manually wound, Kobold Caliber K.421 (base ETA Unitas 6497, modified); ø 36 mm, height 8.1 mm; 17 jewels; 18,000 vph; power reserve 50 hours; côtes de Genève, gold-plated engraving on bridge; tested for 1,000 hours
Functions: hours, minutes
Case: titanium, ø 44 mm, height 14 mm; sapphire crystal, anti-reflective on the back; screw-down case back; water-resistant to 100 m
Band: Louisiana alligator skin, signed buckle
Remarks: genuine mother-of-pearl dial
Price: $3,200

Pierre Kunz

Pierre Kunz is a master watchmaker who would seem to have gone the usual route in the watchmaking world. Initiated into the mechanical mysteries of horology at a young age, Kunz first studied watchmaking officially at the Vallée de Joux school. Upon completing his studies, he worked for a prestigious supplier of mechanical complications, Victorin Piguet. The name of this workshop founded in Le Sentier in the 1920s may not be familiar to too many watch fans, since watches have never been produced under the company's own name, but this workshop has always specialized in complicated *ébauches* such as minute repeaters, perpetual calendars, and single-button chronographs. Historically, the company has made this type of complicated horology for the very top tier of the watch industry—which is exactly the job Kunz was entrusted with for a number of years. He designed and completed perpetual calendars by hand for one of the industry's top-level companies.

After that, Kunz went into business for himself, restoring old clocks, but it wasn't long before his penchant for great complications got the better of him. After working for a few different companies famous in the world of watches, he finally ended up at Franck Muller's Watchland, and the quality of his work led him quickly up the ladder.

He was soon entrusted with working on some of Franck Muller's own unique pieces. And this is the spot where luck and legend take over. It was precisely in this department where Watchland's CEOs, Franck Muller and Vartan Sirmakes, "discovered" him. They saw the talent slumbering within him and presented him with the opportunity of having a brand bearing his own name, under the aegis and with the support of the Franck Muller Group. Considering the resources at hand within this group, Kunz would have been crazy to refuse.

Muller and Sirmakes gave him carte blanche to create according to his instincts. And thus Kunz chose the retrograde complication as his signature. This dynamic example of mechanics not only adds a great deal of enthusiastic movement to the dial, it also combines tradition with modernity to give Kunz's timepieces a look and feel that is both contemporary and classic—not only for now, but certainly in the future as well.

But that is not all this veritable artist is capable of. Housed in one of Watchland's smaller manor buildings, Kunz and his just about twenty employees have created some of the most interesting horology to leave Switzerland in the last few years. These designs have included the Square Tourbillon, featuring a square balance wheel and tourbillon carriage and—what else?—a retrograde function, in this case as a second time zone display.

Pierre Kunz

Second Time Zone
Reference number: A017 FHR GD
Movement: automatic, Caliber PK 2001-1521-3 (base ETA 2892); ø 25.6 mm, height 3.6 mm (base movement); 38 jewels; 28,800 vph
Functions: hours, minutes; large date; second time zone (jump, retrograde) with day/night indication
Case: white gold, ø 41 mm, height 11.7 mm; sapphire crystal
Band: reptile skin, buckle
Price: $22,300
Variations: platinum ($30,700); various dial variations

Second Time Zone
Reference number: G017 FHR GD
Movement: automatic, Caliber PK 2001-1523 (base ETA 2892); ø 25.6 mm, height 3.6 mm (base movement); 38 jewels; 28,800 vph
Functions: hours, minutes; large date; second time zone (jump, retrograde) with day/night indication
Case: red gold, ø 44 mm, height 11.85 mm; sapphire crystal
Band: reptile skin, buckle
Price: $24,800
Variations: platinum ($34,800); various dial variations

Tahiti Moon
Reference number: A014 HMRL
Movement: automatic, Caliber PK 2001-1521-3 (base ETA 2892); ø 25.6 mm, height 3.6 mm (base movement); 38 jewels; 28,800 vph
Functions: hours (retrograde), minutes (retrograde); moon phase
Case: red gold, ø 41 mm, height 10.7 mm; sapphire crystal
Band: reptile skin, buckle
Price: $22,300
Variations: white gold ($22,300); stainless steel ($14,000), platinum ($30,700)

Metropolitan Tourbillon
Reference number: O800T
Movement: manually wound, Caliber PK 2102; ø 31 mm, height 5.3 mm; 20 jewels; 18,000 vph; flying one-minute tourbillon with square cage
Functions: hours, minutes
Case: white gold, 41 x 41 mm, height 11.45 mm; sapphire crystal
Band: reptile skin, buckle
Price: $90,000
Variations: red gold ($90,000); platinum ($101,700)

Chrono Sport
Reference number: G403
Movement: automatic, Caliber PK 2010-2328 (base ETA Valjoux 7750); ø 30.4 mm, height 9.18 mm; 37 jewels; 28,800 vph
Functions: hours, minutes; chronograph with retrograde counters
Case: stainless steel, ø 44 mm, height 15 mm; bezel engraved with hour markers; sapphire crystal; water-resistant to 10 atm
Band: rubber, double folding clasp
Remarks: dial crafted in anthracite-colored texalium
Price: $15,800
Variations: dial in red, copper-colored, or silver-colored texalium or in colored Plexiglas; in gold

Grande Date Sport
Reference number: G016 GD
Movement: automatic, Caliber PK 2001-1520 (base ETA 2892); ø 25.6 mm, height 6.05 mm; 30 jewels; 28,800 vph; officially certified chronometer (C.O.S.C.)
Functions: hours, minutes, seconds (retrograde); large date
Case: stainless steel, ø 44 mm, height 12.35 mm; sapphire crystal; screw-in crown; water-resistant to 10 atm
Band: rubber, double folding clasp
Price: $12,300
Variations: dial in blue, black, or silver-colored texalium

Grande Date
Reference number: G009 GD
Movement: automatic, Caliber PK 2001-1522 (base ETA 2892); ø 25.6 mm, height 6.05 mm; 40 jewels; 28,800 vph
Functions: hours, minutes, seconds (double retrograde); large date, weekday (retrograde)
Case: white gold, ø 44 mm, height 11.55 mm; sapphire crystal
Band: reptile skin, buckle
Price: $30,600
Variations: red gold ($30,600); platinum ($40,000)

Cupidon
Reference number: M102 STR
Movement: manually wound, Caliber PK 2005-2392; 32.4 x 23.3 mm, height 4 mm; 31 jewels; 21,600 vph
Functions: hours, minutes; three retrograde second hands with sectoral displays of 120° each, designed as a love barometer
Case: white gold, 31 x 40 mm, height 9.55 mm; sapphire crystal; bezel, strap lugs, and case sides set with brilliant-cut diamonds; dial set with rubies
Band: reptile skin, buckle
Price: $12,500
Variations: with mother-of-pearl dial; in red gold; in stainless steel ($7,500)

Maurice Lacroix

The watchmaking industry is currently confronted with numerous influences from every other possible type of industry in its current search for new and better means of construction and utilization of different materials. During the years of the mechanical renaissance—and basically lasting until about yesterday—it was enough to refine traditional methods and principles of watchmaking, optimize them, and rationalize them. Now the time has come to think about true progress.

A good example of this imperative is Maurice Lacroix, a brand that can thank its comet-like ascension in the 1990s to its clever interpretations of "classic" pocket watch characteristics. Meanwhile, this recent addition to the ranks of *manufacture* brands has completely redesigned its full collection, banning every lick of Breguet-style bliss from the designs of its watches. And more: president Philippe Merck backs down neither from costs nor effort in modernizing the technology involved in the company's own movements, naturally banking on up-to-date production methods like LIGA—a German acronym standing for lithography (*Lithographie*), electroplating (*Galvanisierung*), and plastic molding (*Abformung*)—and similar processes for manufacturing hard synthetic materials. In Montfaucon, located not far from the company's factory in Saignelégier, Maurice Lacroix has set up a workshop for the production of highly precise individual movement components. This new company is called La Manufacture des Franches-Montagnes SA and is outfitted with the newest in CNC technology.

While the rest of the industry continues to bank on the fascination of transparent mechanics, Maurice Lacroix has gone a step further: at Baselworld 2007, the company allowed a small circle of specialists a sneak peek at the concept watch Mémoire 1. Its mechanical movement allows it to go between displaying the regular time and that of a chronograph just by pressing a button. Thus, two hands (for minutes and seconds) and a disk (for hours) are enough to display the functions of both. A complicated mechanism comprising more than five hundred individual components—among them nine heart cams—guarantees the simultaneous motion of both programs, adjusting the display corresponding to the wishes of the wearer.

Technology is no longer visible on the Mémoire 1's dial, retreating completely to the depths of the movement and creating room for an array of new, unused design ideas that creative director and product developer Sandro Reginelli can now realize—like in models such as the new Pontos Décentrique GMT.

Maurice Lacroix once made an important contribution to the cultivation of the traditional timepiece with its Masterpiece Collection, and now this young *manufacture* is doing the same thing with just as much élan for the future of mechanical watchmaking.

Maurice Lacroix

Masterpiece Le Chronograph
Reference number: MP7008-PG101-120
Movement: manually wound, Maurice Lacroix Caliber ML 106; ø 36.6 mm, height 6.9 mm; 20 jewels; 18,000 vph; column-wheel control of chronograph functions; swan-neck fine adjustment; hand-decorated
Functions: hours, minutes, subsidiary seconds; chronograph
Case: rose gold, ø 45 mm, height 16 mm; sapphire crystal; transparent case back; water-resistant to 3 atm
Band: reptile skin, rose gold folding clasp
Remarks: limited edition of 250 pieces
Price: $24,800

Masterpiece Le Chronograph
Reference number: MP7128-SS001-320
Movement: manually wound, Maurice Lacroix Caliber ML 106; ø 36.6 mm, height 6.9 mm; 20 jewels; 18,000 vph; column-wheel control of chronograph functions; swan-neck fine adjustment; hand-decorated
Functions: hours, minutes, subsidiary seconds; chronograph
Case: stainless steel, ø 45 mm, height 16 mm; sapphire crystal; transparent case back; water-resistant to 3 atm
Band: reptile skin, folding clasp
Price: $15,000

Masterpiece Masterchrono
Reference number: MP6348-SS002-12E
Movement: automatic, Maurice Lacroix Caliber ML 67 (base ETA Valjoux 7750); ø 30 mm, height 7.9 mm; 26 jewels; 28,800 vph
Functions: hours, minutes, subsidiary seconds; chronograph; date, weekday
Case: stainless steel, ø 43 mm, height 15 mm; sapphire crystal; transparent case back; screw-in crown; water-resistant to 10 atm
Band: stainless steel, folding clasp
Price: $7,500
Variations: leather strap; various dial variations

Masterpiece Jours Rétrogrades
Reference number: MP6358-SS001-31E
Movement: automatic, Maurice Lacroix Caliber ML 102 (base ETA 2892-A2); ø 25.6 mm, height 7.9 mm; 22 jewels; 28,800 vph; decorated by hand
Functions: hours, minutes, sweep seconds; large date, weekday (retrograde)
Case: stainless steel, ø 40 mm, height 12.5 mm; sapphire crystal; transparent case back; water-resistant to 5 atm
Band: reptile skin, folding clasp
Price: $6,900
Variations: various dial variations

Masterpiece Lune Rétrograde
Reference number: MP7078-SS001-120
Movement: manually wound, Maurice Lacroix Caliber ML 104 (base ETA Unitas 6498-2); ø 36.6 mm, height 6.1 mm; 36 jewels; 21,600 vph; decorated by hand
Functions: hours, minutes; date (retrograde), weekday, moon phase; power reserve display (retrograde)
Case: stainless steel, ø 43.5 mm, height 13 mm; sapphire crystal; transparent case back
Band: reptile skin, buckle
Price: $7,500
Variations: stainless steel/rose gold; various dial variations

Masterpiece Double Rétrograde
Reference number: MP7018-SS001-110
Movement: manually wound, Maurice Lacroix Caliber ML 100 (base ETA Unitas 6497-1); ø 36.6 mm, height 6.3 mm; 50 jewels; 21,600 vph; decorated by hand
Functions: hours, minutes, subsidiary seconds; date (retrograde); 24-hour display (second time zone, retrograde); power reserve display
Case: stainless steel, ø 43.5 mm, height 12 mm; sapphire crystal; transparent case back; water-resistant to 5 atm
Band: reptile skin, folding clasp
Price: $8,000
Variations: rose gold; stainless steel/rose gold

Masterpiece Calendrier Rétrograde
Reference number: MP7068-SS001-191
Movement: manually wound, Maurice Lacroix Caliber ML 76 (base ETA Unitas 6498-1); ø 37 mm; height 6.3 mm; 33 jewels; 18,000 vph; decorated by hand
Functions: hours, minutes, subsidiary seconds; date (retrograde)
Case: stainless steel, ø 43 mm, height 11.5 mm; sapphire crystal; transparent case back; water-resistant to 3 atm
Band: reptile skin, folding clasp
Price: $5,900
Variations: stainless steel/rose gold; rose gold; black dial

Masterpiece Rectangulaire Petite Seconde
Reference number: MP7009-PG101-110
Movement: manually wound, Maurice Lacroix Caliber ML 126 (base La Joux-Perret); 25.6 x 17.6 mm, height 3.85 mm; 20 jewels; 21,600 vph; decorated by hand
Functions: hours, minutes, subsidiary seconds
Case: rose gold, 36.7 x 28 mm, height 10 mm; sapphire crystal; transparent case back
Band: reptile skin, folding clasp
Price: $12,500
Variations: stainless steel; various dial variations

Maurice Lacroix

Masterpiece Phase de Lune
Reference number: MP6428-SS001-11E
Movement: automatic, Maurice Lacroix Caliber ML 37 (base ETA 2824-2); ø 26 mm, height 6.3 mm; 25 jewels; 28,800 vph; decorated by hand
Functions: hours, minutes, sweep seconds; date, weekday, month, moon phase
Case: stainless steel, ø 40 mm, height 13.5 mm; sapphire crystal; transparent case back; water-resistant to 5 atm
Band: reptile skin, folding clasp
Price: $6,600
Variations: various dial variations

Masterpiece Flyback Aviator
Reference number: MP6178-SS001-32E
Movement: automatic, Maurice Lacroix Caliber ML 15 (base ETA 2892-A2); ø 30 mm, height 7.45 mm; 49 jewels; 28,800 vph; finely finished with blued screws and côtes de Genève
Functions: hours, minutes, subsidiary seconds; chronograph with flyback function; large date, month
Case: stainless steel, ø 42 mm, height 14 mm; bezel engraved with tachymeter scale; sapphire crystal; transparent case back; water-resistant to 10 atm
Band: reptile skin, folding clasp
Price: $8,300
Variations: rubber strap; various dial variations

Pontos Décentrique GMT
Reference number: PT6118-SS001-330
Movement: automatic, Maurice Lacroix Caliber ML 121 (base Sellita SW 200); ø 33.5 mm, height 7.34 mm; 30 jewels; 28,800 vph; decorated by hand; plates and bridges plated in black gold
Functions: hours, minutes (off-center), sweep seconds; date; second time zone (off-center) with day/night indication
Case: stainless steel, ø 43 mm, height 14 mm; sapphire crystal
Band: reptile skin, folding clasp
Price: $5,700

Pontos Valgranges
Reference number: PT6128-SS001-130
Movement: automatic, ETA Valgranges Caliber A07; ø 36.6 mm, height 7.9 mm; 25 jewels; 28,800 vph; decorated by hand
Functions: hours, minutes, subsidiary seconds; chronograph; date
Case: stainless steel, ø 47 mm, height 15.6 mm; sapphire crystal; transparent case back; water-resistant to 5 atm
Band: reptile skin, folding clasp
Price: $4,400
Variations: various dial variations

Pontos Rectangulaire Chronographe
Reference number: PT6197-TT003-331
Movement: automatic, Maurice Lacroix Caliber ML 112/3 (base ETA Valjoux 7750); ø 30 mm, height 7.9 mm; 25 jewels; 28,800 vph; decorated by hand
Functions: hours, minutes, subsidiary seconds; date; chronograph
Case: titanium, 38.21 x 42.85 mm, height 15.25 mm; sapphire crystal; transparent case back; water-resistant to 5 atm
Band: reptile skin, folding clasp
Price: $3,700
Variations: stainless steel; various dial variations

Pontos Grande Guichet GMT
Reference number: PT6098-SS001-330
Movement: automatic, Maurice Lacroix Caliber ML 129 (base ETA 2892-2); ø 26.2 mm, height 5.25 mm; 21 jewels; 28,800 vph; decorated by hand
Functions: hours, minutes, sweep seconds; large date; second time zone
Case: stainless steel, ø 40 mm, height 13 mm; sapphire crystal; transparent case back; water-resistant to 5 atm
Band: reptile skin, folding clasp
Price: $3,000
Variations: stainless steel bracelet; various dial variations

Pontos Limited Edition 2007
Reference number: PT6198-SS001-83G
Movement: automatic, ETA Caliber 2836-2; ø 25.6 mm, height 5.2 mm; 25 jewels; 28,800 vph; decorated by hand
Functions: hours, minutes; date, weekday
Case: stainless steel, ø 40 mm, height 12 mm; sapphire crystal; transparent case back; water-resistant to 5 atm
Band: leather, buckle
Remarks: limited edition of 2,007 pieces
Price: upon request

Miros Diver
Reference number: MI6028-SS062-331
Movement: automatic, Sellita Caliber SW 200; ø 25.6 mm, height 4.6 mm; 26 jewels; 28,800 vph; officially certified C.O.S.C. chronometer
Functions: hours, minutes, sweep seconds; date
Case: stainless steel, ø 40 mm, height 12 mm; unidirectionally rotating bezel with 60-minute divisions; screw-in crown; water-resistant to 20 atm
Band: stainless steel, folding clasp with wetsuit extension
Remarks: limited edition of 999 pieces
Price: $1,750
Variations: various dial and bezel variations

"Visually ravishing." —*Sea History*

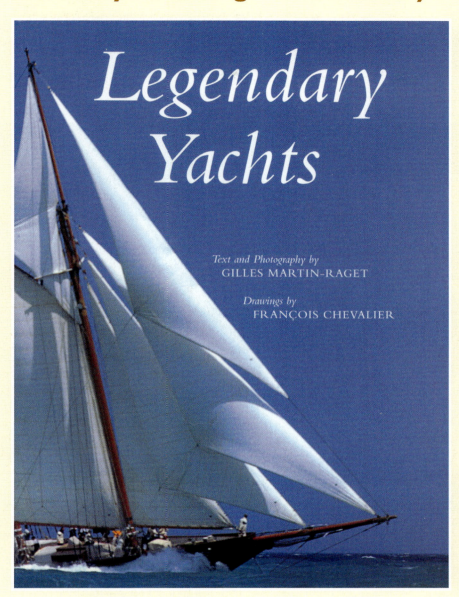

Text and photography by
Gilles Martin-Raget
Drawings by François Chevalier
300 full-color illustrations,
90 black-and-white drawings
200 pages · 9 x 12¼ in. · Cloth
ISBN: 978-0-7892-0637-4
$65.00

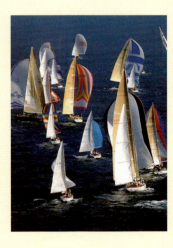

Legendary Yachts

Legendary Yachts is a tribute to the great racing yachts of the past, their current renaissance, and today's new enthusiasm for the classic regatta.

This vibrantly illustrated volume provides an insider's perspective on five top regattas and delves into the histories of over a dozen classic boats like *Pen Duick* and *Shenandoah*. The book also details the restoration of these wooden boats, using ninety precise drawings from a variety of perspectives to reveal the structure of each vessel.

Published by **ABBEVILLE PRESS**
137 Varick Street, New York, NY 10013
1-800-Artbook (in U.S. only)
Also available wherever fine books are sold
Visit us at www.abbeville.com

A. Lange & Söhne

"One neither flies nor drives a zeppelin. One simply travels in the most comfortable way that one can attach to the word 'travel,'" Hugo Eckener, legendary aviation pioneer and successor to Ferdinand Graf von Zeppelin, summarized his impressions of traveling in a dirigible. It was with a zeppelin over Dresden that A. Lange & Söhne celebrated the introduction of the company's Richard Lange model—at the same time reminiscing about the historical tie between the Saxon watch *manufacture* and the airship yard located on Lake Constance.

In 1935, the Zeppelin shipyard received the first two of fifteen large observation watches that Lange had manufactured for navigating the queen of the skies. This tradition of highly precise timekeepers is continued in A. Lange & Söhne's newest model—a timepiece named for the scientifically ambitious Richard Lange for good reason.

On the occasion of the reacquaintance of these two brands—both of which escaped the public eye for a short time thanks to historical circumstances and both of which experienced a comeback in the 1990s—a zeppelin outfitted for the modern technological era arrived in Dresden for the first time. Walter Lange, great-grandson of the founder of A. Lange & Söhne, personally greeted Wolfgang von Zeppelin, previous managing director of the Zeppelin shipyard, presenting him with a Richard Lange, which—like its larger predecessor—will once again accompany the captains on board the these vessels.

The brand's grand introduction of 2007 was the new Lange 31, a watch very precisely named for its function: when it is wound just once, it will run for a full month—a complete thirty-one days—and thus longer than any other mechanical wristwatch.

In order to save up enough energy for this feat, the Lange 31 has two stacked spring barrels that take up three-quarters of the entire surface of the movement. The two mainsprings found in them are each 1,850 millimeters long (about six feet), and thus seven and a half times as long as the mainsprings used in conventional mechanical watch movements. Winding such strong springs with the fine mechanics of a crown winding mechanism would be a tedious venture; therefore the brand's innovative movement designers came up with the idea of using key technology from early pocket watches. The lever energy of the key allows the transmission to be smaller than that of a conventional crown winding mechanism. The key is inserted into the proper opening on the sapphire crystal case back, allowing the energy to move directly to the spring barrel. This system features the same fluid winding motion as a crown.

In order to evenly dose the great energy of these powerful springs to the rest of the movement, a constant force mechanism is located between the twin spring barrels and the escapement, functioning just like an escapement with a *remontoir*. This is a lavish design that ensures that the same amount of energy is passed on to the escapement and balance regardless of the current state of the mainspring's tension. The result: even energy, even amplitude, and an even rate all the way to the thirty-first day.

A. Lange & Söhne

Lange 1
Reference number: 101.021
Movement: manually wound, Lange Caliber L901.0; ø 30.4 mm, height 5.9 mm; 53 jewels; 21,600 vph; hand-engraved balance cock; hand-finished components; 72 hours power reserve; twin spring barrels
Functions: hours, minutes, subsidiary seconds; patented large date; power reserve display
Case: yellow gold, ø 38.5 mm, height 10 mm; sapphire crystal; transparent case back
Band: reptile skin, yellow gold buckle
Price: $25,200
Variations: white or rose gold; platinum

Lange 1
Reference number: 101.025
Movement: manually wound, Lange Caliber L901.0; ø 30.4 mm, height 5.9 mm; 53 jewels; 21,600 vph; hand-engraved balance cock; hand-finished components; 72 hours power reserve; twin spring barrels
Functions: hours, minutes, subsidiary seconds; patented large date; power reserve display
Case: platinum, ø 38.5 mm, height 10 mm; sapphire crystal; transparent case back
Band: reptile skin, platinum buckle
Price: $37,200
Variations: yellow, white, or rose gold

Grand Lange 1 Luminous
Reference number: 115.029
Movement: manually wound, Lange Caliber L901.2; ø 30.4 mm, height 5.9 mm; 53 jewels; 21,600 vph; 72 hours power reserve; twin spring barrels
Functions: hours, minutes, subsidiary seconds; patented large date; power reserve display; luminous hands and applied elements
Case: white gold, ø 41.9 mm, height 11 mm; sapphire crystal; transparent case back
Band: calfskin, white gold buckle
Price: $26,800
Variations: as Lange 1 Luminous in yellow gold, red gold, or platinum

Lange 1 Moonphase
Reference number: 109.021
Movement: manually wound, Lange Caliber L901.5; ø 30.4 mm, height 5.9 mm; 54 jewels; 21,600 vph; hand-engraved balance cock; hand-finished components; 72 hours power reserve; twin spring barrels; moon phase display with continuous drive via hour wheel; button for quick-setting date
Functions: hours, minutes, subsidiary seconds; patented large date; moon phase display; power reserve display
Case: yellow gold, ø 38.5 mm, height 10.4 mm; sapphire crystal; transparent case back
Band: reptile skin, yellow gold buckle
Price: $29,500
Variations: red gold; platinum

Lange 1 Time Zone
Reference number: 116.025
Movement: manually wound, Lange Caliber L031.1; ø 34.1 mm, height 6.65 mm; 54 jewels; 21,600 vph; hand-engraved balance cock; home time with day/night indication, local time (hours, minutes) with day/night indication and reference city ring settable via button; twin spring barrels; power reserve 72 hours
Functions: hours, minutes, subsidiary seconds; second time zone; patented large date; power reserve display; day/night indication for both time zones
Case: platinum, ø 41.9 mm, height 11 mm; sapphire crystal; transparent case back
Band: reptile skin, platinum buckle
Price: $46,900

Lange 1 Time Zone
Reference number: 116.032
Movement: manually wound, Lange Caliber L031.1; ø 34.1 mm, height 6.65 mm; 54 jewels; 21,600 vph; hand-engraved balance cock; hand-finished components; home time with day/night indication, local time (hours, minutes) with day/night indication display and reference city ring settable via button; twin spring barrels
Functions: hours, minutes, subsidiary seconds; second time zone; patented large date; power reserve display; day/night indication for both time zones
Case: red gold, ø 41.9 mm, height 11 mm; sapphire crystal; transparent case back
Band: reptile skin, red gold buckle
Price: $34,300

Little Lange 1 Soirée
Reference number: 813.043
Movement: manually wound, Lange Caliber L901.4; ø 30.4 mm, height 5.9 mm; 53 jewels; 21,600 vph; hand-engraved balance cock; hand-finished components; 72 h power reserve; twin spring barrels
Functions: hours, minutes, subsidiary seconds; patented large date; power reserve display
Case: red gold, ø 36.1 mm, height 10 mm; bezel set with 52 brilliant-cut diamonds; sapphire crystal; transparent case back
Band: stingray skin; red gold buckle
Remarks: genuine mother-of-pearl dial
Price: $39,400

Lange 31
Reference number: 130.025
Movement: manually wound by key, Lange Caliber L034.1; ø 37.3 mm, height 9.6 mm; 61 jewels; 21,600 vph; 31 day power reserve; twin spring barrels; constant force escapement (patent pending); hand-engraved balance cock; hand-finished components
Functions: hours, minutes, subsidiary seconds; patented large date; power reserve display
Case: platinum, ø 45.9 mm, height 15.9 mm; sapphire crystal; transparent case back
Band: reptile skin, platinum buckle
Price: $140,000

A. Lange & Söhne

Saxonia
Reference number: 215.021
Movement: manually wound, Lange Caliber L941.3; ø 25.6 mm, height 3.2 mm; 21 jewels; 21,600 vph; hand-engraved balance cock; hand-finished components; 45 hours power reserve
Functions: hours, minutes, subsidiary seconds
Case: yellow gold, ø 37 mm, height 7.34 mm; sapphire crystal; transparent case back
Band: reptile skin, yellow gold buckle
Price: $15,100
Variations: white or red gold

Saxonia Automatic
Reference number: 315.032
Movement: automatic, Lange Caliber L921.4 SAX-O-MAT; ø 30.4 mm, height 5.55 mm; 45 jewels; 21,600 vph; hand-engraved balance cock; hand-finished components; Zero Reset hand-setting mechanism; 46 hours power reserve
Functions: hours, minutes, subsidiary seconds; patented large date
Case: red gold, ø 37 mm, height 9.7 mm; sapphire crystal; transparent case back
Band: reptile skin, red gold buckle
Price: $24,100
Variations: white or yellow gold

Grand Saxonia Automatic
Reference number: 307.029
Movement: automatic, Lange Caliber L921.4 SAX-O-MAT; ø 30.4 mm, height 3.8 mm; 36 jewels; 21,600 vph; hand-engraved balance cock; hand-finished components; Zero Reset hand-setting mechanism; 46 hours power reserve
Functions: hours, minutes, subsidiary seconds
Case: white gold, ø 40.6 mm, height 8.2 mm; sapphire crystal; transparent case back
Band: reptile skin, white gold buckle
Price: $21,400
Variations: red gold

Richard Lange
Reference number: 232.021
Movement: manually wound, Lange Caliber L041.2; ø 30.6 mm, height 6 mm; 26 jewels; 21,600 vph; hand-engraved balance cock; hand-finished components; in-house balance spring with balance spring stud (patent pending); 38 hours power reserve
Functions: hours, minutes, sweep seconds
Case: yellow gold, ø 40.5 mm, height 10.6 mm; sapphire crystal; transparent case back
Band: reptile skin, yellow gold buckle
Price: $22,500
Variations: red gold; platinum

Richard Lange
Reference number: 232.025
Movement: manually wound, Lange Caliber L041.2; ø 30.6 mm, height 6 mm; 26 jewels; 21,600 vph; hand-engraved balance cock; hand-finished components; in-house balance spring with balance spring stud (patent pending); 38 hours power reserve
Functions: hours, minutes, sweep seconds
Case: platinum, ø 40.5 mm, height 10.6 mm; sapphire crystal; transparent case back
Band: reptile skin, platinum buckle
Price: $34,400
Variations: yellow or red gold

Langematik Perpetual
Reference number: 310.032
Movement: automatic, Lange Caliber L922.1 SAX-O-MAT; ø 30.4 mm, height 5.7 mm; 43 jewels; 21,600 vph; hand-engraved balance cock; Zero Reset hand-setting mechanism; main button for synchronizing the correction of all calendar functions, three individual buttons; 46 hours power reserve
Functions: hours, minutes, subsidiary seconds; perpetual calendar with patented large date, day, month, moon phase, leap year; 24-hour display
Case: red gold, ø 38.5 mm, height 10.2 mm; sapphire crystal; transparent case back
Band: reptile skin, red gold buckle
Price: $62,900
Variations: metal bracelet

Langematik Perpetual
Reference number: 310.225
Movement: automatic, Lange Caliber L922.1 SAX-O-MAT; ø 30.4 mm, height 5.7 mm; 43 jewels; 21,600 vph; hand-engraved balance cock; Zero Reset hand-setting mechanism; main button for synchronizing the correction of all calendar functions, three individual buttons; 46 hours power reserve
Functions: hours, minutes, subsidiary seconds; perpetual calendar with patented large date, day, month, moon phase, leap year; 24-hour display
Case: platinum, ø 38.5 mm, height 10.2 mm; sapphire crystal; transparent case back
Band: platinum, folding clasp
Price: $113,100
Variations: reptile skin strap

Datograph
Reference number: 403.035
Movement: manually wound, Lange Caliber L951.1; ø 30.6 mm, height 7.5 mm; 40 jewels; 18,000 vph; hand-engraved balance cock; hand-finished components; 36 hours power reserve; column-wheel control of chronograph functions
Functions: hours, minutes, subsidiary seconds; chronograph with flyback function and precisely jumping minute counter; patented large date
Case: platinum, ø 39 mm, height 12.8 mm; sapphire crystal; transparent case back
Band: reptile skin, platinum buckle
Price: $60,100
Variations: metal bracelet

A. Lange & Söhne

Datograph
Reference number: 403.032
Movement: manually wound, Lange Caliber L951.1; ø 30.6 mm, height 7.5 mm; 40 jewels; 18,000 vph; hand-engraved balance cock; hand-finished components; 36 hours power reserve; column-wheel control of chronograph functions
Functions: hours, minutes, subsidiary seconds; chronograph with flyback function and precisely jumping minute counter; patented large date
Case: red gold, ø 39 mm, height 12.8 mm; sapphire crystal; transparent case back
Band: red gold, folding clasp
Price: $61,600
Variations: reptile skin strap

Datograph Perpetual
Reference number: 410.425
Movement: manually wound, Lange Caliber L952.1; ø 32 mm, height 8 mm; 45 jewels; 18,000 vph; hand-engraved balance cock; hand-finished components; column-wheel control of chronograph functions
Functions: hours, minutes, subsidiary seconds; chronograph with flyback function; perpetual calendar with patented large date, weekday, month, moon phase display, leap year; 24 hour display with day/night indication
Case: platinum, ø 41 mm, height 13.5 mm; sapphire crystal; transparent case back
Band: platinum, folding clasp
Price: $176,400
Variations: reptile skin strap

Lange Double Split
Reference number: 404.035
Movement: manually wound, Lange Caliber L001.1; ø 30.6 mm, height 9.45 mm; 40 jewels; 21,600 vph; two column wheels to control chronograph double rattrapante functions; precisely jumping minute counter; hand-engraved balance cock; hand-finished components
Functions: hours, minutes, subsidiary seconds; chronograph with flyback function, split-seconds and -minute counters; power reserve display
Case: platinum, ø 43.2 mm, height 15.3 mm; sapphire crystal; transparent case back
Band: reptile skin, platinum buckle
Price: $116,700

Tourbograph Pour le Mérite
Reference number: 702.025
Movement: manually wound, Lange Caliber L903.0; ø 30 mm, height 8.9 mm; 43 jewels; 21,600 vph; hand-engraved balance cock; hand-finished components; one-minute tourbillon; motive power regulated by chain and fusee as well as stepped planetary gear; 36 hours power reserve
Functions: hours, minutes; split-seconds chronograph; power reserve display
Case: platinum, ø 41.2 mm, height 14.3 mm; sapphire crystal; transparent case back
Band: reptile skin, platinum folding clasp
Remarks: limited edition of 51 pieces in platinum; later edition of another 50 in gold
Price: $460,000

Cabaret Soirée
Reference number: 827.043
Movement: manually wound, Lange Caliber L931.3; 25.6 x 17.6 mm, height 4.95 mm; 30 jewels; 21,600 vph; hand-engraved balance cock; hand-finished components; 42 hours power reserve
Functions: hours, minutes, subsidiary seconds; patented large date
Case: red gold, 36.3 x 26.5 mm, height 9.3 mm; bezel set with 70 brilliant-cut diamonds; sapphire crystal; transparent case back
Band: stingray skin, red gold buckle
Remarks: mother-of-pearl dial
Price: $35,700

Cabaret
Reference number: 107.031
Movement: manually wound, Lange Caliber L931.3; 25.6 x 17.6 mm, height 4.95 mm; 30 jewels; 21,600 vph; hand-engraved balance cock; hand-finished components; 42 hours power reserve
Functions: hours, minutes, subsidiary seconds; patented large date
Case: red gold, 36.3 x 25.5 mm, height 9.1 mm; sapphire crystal; transparent case back
Band: reptile skin, red gold buckle
Price: $20,100
Variations: yellow gold

Cabaret Moon Phase
Reference number: 118.021
Movement: manually wound, Lange Caliber L931.5; 25.6 x 17.6 mm, height 5.05 mm; 31 jewels; 21,600 vph; hand-engraved balance cock; hand-finished components; 42 hours power reserve
Functions: hours, minutes; subsidiary seconds; patented large date; moon phase display
Case: yellow gold, 36.3 x 25.5 mm, height 9.1 mm; sapphire crystal; transparent case back
Band: reptile skin, yellow gold buckle
Price: $24,000
Variations: red gold

Arkade
Reference number: 103.021
Movement: manually wound, Lange Caliber L911.4; 25.6 x 17.6 mm, height 4.95 mm; 30 jewels; 21,600 vph; hand-engraved balance cock; hand-finished components; 42 hours power reserve
Functions: hours, minutes, subsidiary seconds; patented large date
Case: yellow gold, 29 x 22 mm, height 8.4 mm; sapphire crystal; transparent case back
Band: reptile skin, buckle
Price: $14,000
Variations: white gold; diamond-set bezel

A. Lange & Söhne

Caliber L901.0 (Lange 1)
Mechanical with manual winding; twin serially operating spring barrels, power reserve 72 hours, stop-seconds
Functions: hours, minutes, subsidiary seconds; large date; power reserve indicator
Diameter: 30.4 mm; **Height:** 5.9 mm
Jewels: 53, including nine screw-mounted gold chatons
Balance: glucydur with weighted screws
Frequency: 21,600 vph
Balance spring: Nivarox 1 with special terminal curve and swan-neck fine adjustment; beat adjustment via regulating screw
Shock protection: Incabloc
Remarks: chiefly manufactured, assembled, and decorated by hand

Caliber L901.5 (Lange 1 Moon Phase)
Mechanical with manual winding; twin serially operating spring barrels, power reserve 72 hours, stop-seconds
Functions: hours, minutes, subsidiary seconds; large date; moon phase
Diameter: 30.4 mm; **Height:** 5.9 mm
Jewels: 54, including nine screw-mounted gold chatons
Balance: glucydur with weighted screws
Frequency: 21,600 vph
Balance spring: Nivarox 1 with special terminal curve, swan-neck fine adjustment; beat adjustment via regulating screw
Remarks: moon phase driven by hour wheel, thus continuously in motion; precise dial train with deviation of only one day in 122.6 years

Caliber L031.1 (Lange Time Zone)
Mechanical with manual winding; twin serially operating spring barrels, power reserve 72 hours, stop-seconds
Functions: hours, minutes, subsidiary seconds; large date; second time zone with reference city ring; day/night indication for both time zones
Diameter: 34.1 mm; **Height:** 6.65 mm
Jewels: 54, including nine screw-mounted gold chatons
Balance: glucydur with weighted screws
Frequency: 21,600 vph
Balance spring: Nivarox 1 with special terminal curve, swan-neck fine adjustment; beat adjustment via regulating screw
Shock protection: Incabloc

Caliber L034.1 (Lange 31)
Mechanical with manual winding; key winding; twin serially operating spring barrels, power reserve 31 days, constant force escapement with patent pending; stop-seconds
Functions: hours, minutes, subsidiary seconds; date; power reserve indication
Diameter: 30.4 mm; **Height:** 5.9 mm
Jewels: 61, one of which is a transparent corundum bearing
Balance: glucydur with weighted screws
Frequency: 21,600 vph
Balance spring: Nivarox 1 with special terminal curve, swan-neck fine adjustment; beat adjustment via regulating screw
Shock protection: Incabloc
Remarks: key for winding with torque limiter

Caliber L921.4 (SAX-O-MAT)
Mechanical with automatic winding, bidirectionally winding three-quarter rotor in 21-karat gold and platinum, winding mechanism with four micro-ball bearings; power reserve 46 hours, hand-setting mechanism with automatic return to zero (Zero Reset)
Functions: hours, minutes, subsidiary seconds; patented large date
Diameter: 30.4 mm; **Height:** 5.55 mm; **Jewels:** 45
Balance: glucydur with weighted screws
Frequency: 21,600 vph
Balance spring: Nivarox 1 with swan-neck fine adjustment; beat adjustment via regulating screw
Shock protection: Kif
Remarks: three-quarter plate with Glashütte ribbing, hand assembled and decorated

Caliber 041.2 (Richard Lange)
Mechanical with manual winding, power reserve 38 hours, stop-seconds
Functions: hours, minutes, sweep seconds
Diameter: 30.4 mm
Height: 6 mm
Jewels: 27, including two in screw-mounted gold chatons
Balance: shock-proofed glucydur with eccentric regulating cams
Frequency: 21,600 vph
Balance spring: in-house manufacture with collet (patent pending), beat adjustment via fine adjustment screw
Remarks: Glashütte three-quarter plate, bridges with Glashütte ribbing

A. Lange & Söhne

Caliber L951.1 (Datograph)
Mechanical with manual winding; power reserve 36 hours, stop-seconds
Functions: hours, minutes, subsidiary seconds; patented large date; chronograph with flyback mechanism and precise minute counter
Diameter: 30.6 mm; **Height:** 7.5 mm
Jewels: 40, including four in screw-mounted gold chatons
Balance: glucydur with weighted screws
Frequency: 18,000 vph
Balance spring: Nivarox 1 with special terminal curve, swan-neck fine adjustment; beat adjustment via regulating screw
Remarks: chiefly manufactured, assembled, and decorated by hand; column-wheel control of chronograph functions

Caliber L922.1 Sax-O-Mat (Perpetual)
Mechanical with automatic winding, bidirectionally winding three-quarter rotor in 21-karat gold and platinum, winding mechanism with four micro-ball bearings; power reserve 46 hours, hand-setting mechanism with automatic return to zero (Zero Reset)
Functions: hours, minutes, subsidiary seconds; perpetual calendar with patented large date, day, month, moon phase, leap year, 24-hour display with day/night indication
Diameter: 30.4 mm; **Height:** 5.7 mm; **Jewels:** 43
Balance: glucydur with weighted screws
Frequency: 21,600 vph
Balance spring: Nivarox 1 with swan-neck fine adjustment; beat adjustment via regulating screw
Shock protection: Incabloc

Caliber L952.1 (Datograph Perpetual)
Mechanical with manual winding; stop-seconds; power reserve 36 hours
Functions: hours, minutes, subsidiary seconds; perpetualcalendar (large date, day, month, moon phase, leap year, day/night indication); chronograph with flyback mechanism and precisely jumping minute counter
Diameter: 32 mm; **Height:** 8 mm
Jewels: 45, including four in screw-mounted gold chatons
Balance: glucydur with eccentric regulating cam
Frequency: 18,000 vph
Balance spring: in-house manufacture with collet (patent pending), patented beat regulation via regulating screw
Remarks: column-wheel control of chronograph

Caliber L001.1 (Lange Double Split)
Mechanical with manual winding; power reserve 36 hours, stop-seconds; isolator mechanism, jumping minute counter
Functions: hours, minutes, subsidiary seconds; large date; chronograph with flyback function and double rattrapante for seconds and minutes
Diameter: 30.6 mm; **Height:** 9.54 mm
Jewels: 40 including four in screw-mounted gold chatons
Balance: glucydur with eccentric regulating screws; **Shock protection:** Incabloc
Frequency: 21,600 vph
Balance spring: in-house manufacture with collet (patent pending), swan-neck fine adjustment, patented beat regulation via regulating screw

Caliber L903.0 (Pour le Mérite)
Mechanical with manual winding; one-minute tourbillon; chain and fusée as well as stepped planetary gear; power reserve 36 hours
Functions: hours, minutes, split-seconds chronograph; power reserve display
Diameter: 30 mm; **Height:** 8.9 mm
Jewels: 43, including six in screw-mounted gold chatons, tourbillon cage bearing with two diamond endstones
Balance: glucydur with weighted screws
Frequency: 21,600 vph
Balance spring: Nivarox 1
Remarks: chiefly manufactured, assembled, and decorated by hand; chronograph bridge engraved by hand; three-quarter plate with Glashütte ribbing; 14 different types of perlage

Caliber L931.5 (Cabaret Moon Phase)
Mechanical with manual winding, power reserve 42 hours, stop-seconds
Functions: hours, minutes, subsidiary seconds; large date; moon phase
Dimensions: 25.6 x 17.6 mm; **Height:** 5.05 mm
Jewels: 31, including three in screw-mounted gold chatons
Balance: glucydur with weighted screws
Frequency: 21,600 vph
Balance spring: Nivarox 1 with swan-neck fine adjustment; beat adjustment via regulating screw
Shock protection: Kif
Remarks: chiefly manufactured, assembled, and decorated by hand according to highest quality criteria; three-quarter plate with Glashütte ribbing

Jacques Lemans

Good Swiss quality and moderate prices may not always be two things that go together, but in Jacques Lemans's case, they are in no way contradictory. This represents the philosophy of the company founded by Alfred Riedl three decades ago. Though the watches are manufactured in Wallbach, Switzerland, to ensure proper Swiss quality, this brand is headquartered in St. Veit, Austria. Well-known in Europe, the Middle East, and Asia, where it has done its main business until now, the company is currently giving Americans the opportunity to get to know its watches and its version of good value. Jacques Lemans is now being distributed in the United States by Swiss Watch International, a company that can proudly look back on two generations and more than thirty years of experience in the distribution of European timepieces. SWI's involvement with the brand since introducing it stateside in 2003 has been extremely prosperous, certainly in part due to the great success of the company's show on ShopNBC and the other occasions SWI is so adept at organizing for its brands.

All of Jacques Lemans's mechanical watches are outfitted with either ETA calibers in the three-hand models or ETA Valjoux movements in the chronographs, such as those of the traditionally styled Jacques Lemans Classic series. These round 40 mm cases are classically designed with fluted bezels and case backs. The chronograph pushers and crown are vintage-styled for an extra touch of class. Their dials are embellished with an attractive guilloché pattern. The subdials located at 9 o'clock on some of the models contain GMT displays, which can either be used as 24-hour displays or second time zones. The scale shown on the flange (outside of the date ring) of the chronograph is a tachymeter scale used for measuring distances and speeds.

In 2006 Jacques Lemans CEO Alfred Riedl was able to secure the rights to manufacture the world's only Formula 1–licensed wristwatches, with Formula 1 boss Bernie Ecclestone personally flying to St. Veit to sign the licensing agreement. The following year saw a white gold limited edition chronograph model emerge from the partnership.

The models introduced so far reflect the legendary feel of Formula 1 through their use of materials also found in Formula 1 vehicles, such as carbon fiber, rubber, titanium, and ceramic. Fitting into a general price range between $200 and $500, the Jacques Lemans F1 watches are mainly all quartz driven.

Jacques Lemans wristwatches have a full five-year guarantee in North America. In addition to being sold on ShopNBC, these timepieces can also be found in North American retail jewelry stores for the same prices, which start at $350 and average up to about $1,400, though certain deluxe models set with gemstones can range up to $6,000.

Jacques Lemans

F5000 Limited Edition
Movement: automatic, ETA Caliber 2894-2; ø 28 mm, height 6.1 mm; 37 jewels; 28,800 vph; 36 hours power reserve
Functions: hours, minutes, subsidiary seconds; date; chronograph
Case: white gold, ø 43 mm; sapphire crystal; screwed-down case back, screw-in crown and buttons; water-resistant to 10 atm
Band: reptile skin, buckle
Price: $18,000

G163C
Movement: automatic, Claro 888 (base ETA); ø 25.6 mm, height 5.73 mm; 18 jewels; 21,600 vph; 36 hours power reserve
Functions: hours, minutes, subsidiary seconds; date
Case: rose gold-plated stainless steel, ø 42 mm; sapphire crystal; screw-down case back
Band: reptile skin, buckle
Price: $1,895

G163E
Movement: automatic, Claro 888 (base ETA); ø 25.6 mm, height 5.73 mm; 18 jewels; 21,600 vph; 36 hours power reserve
Functions: hours, minutes, subsidiary seconds; date
Case: rose gold-plated stainless steel, ø 42 mm; sapphire crystal; screwed-down mother-of-pearl case back
Band: reptile skin, buckle
Remarks: mother-of-pearl dial
Price: $1,895

G179A
Movement: automatic, Sellita Caliber SW 200; ø 25.6 mm, height 4.6 mm; 25 jewels; 28,800 vph; 36 hours power reserve
Functions: hours, minutes, subsidiary seconds; date
Case: stainless steel, ø 42 mm; sapphire crystal; screwed-down case back; water-resistant to 5 atm
Band: leather, buckle
Price: $1,295

G180D
Movement: automatic, Sellita Caliber SW 200; ø 25.6 mm, height 4.6 mm; 25 jewels; 28,800 vph; 36 hours power reserve
Functions: hours, minutes, subsidiary seconds
Case: stainless steel, ø 42 mm; sapphire crystal; screwed-down case back; water-resistant to 5 atm
Band: stainless steel, double folding clasp
Remarks: "open heart" aperture in dial
Price: $1,895

G186C
Movement: automatic, Sellita Caliber SW 200; ø 25.6 mm, height 4.6 mm; 25 jewels; 28,800 vph; 36 hours power reserve
Functions: hours, minutes, subsidiary seconds
Case: stainless steel, 43 x 32 mm; sapphire crystal; screwed-down case back; water-resistant to 5 atm
Band: stainless steel, double folding clasp
Remarks: "open heart" aperture in dial
Price: $1,795

G189B
Movement: automatic, ETA Valjoux Caliber 7750; ø 30 mm, height 7.9 mm; 25 jewels; 28,800 vph; 36 hours power reserve
Functions: hours, minutes, subsidiary seconds; date; chronograph
Case: stainless steel, ø 42 mm; sapphire crystal; screwed-down case back; water-resistant to 10 atm
Band: leather, buckle
Price: $3,195

G211B
Movement: automatic, Claro 888 (base ETA); ø 25.6 mm, height 5.73 mm; 18 jewels; 21,600 vph; 36 hours power reserve
Functions: hours, minutes, subsidiary seconds; date
Case: stainless steel, ø 40 mm; ceramic bezel; sapphire crystal; screwed-down case back
Band: stainless steel with ceramic, double folding clasp
Price: $1,795

Limes

Ickler GmbH was founded in 1924 by Karl Ickler, a trained chain maker who worked as a production foreman in foreign companies at the beginning of his career. He set up the watch case manufacturing company upon returning to Pforzheim. After World War II, the company was rebuilt by the founder's sons, Heinz and Kurt. Today, the concern is managed by a third-generation Ickler, Thomas, an industrial engineer who at the end of the 1990s decided to not only manufacture high-quality cases, but also complete watches.

The advent of private label watches came in 1990 for this company. Decades-long ex-perience in the watch industry, a high level of quality, an already established production capability, and the compelling desire to create something of his own led Thomas Ickler to the development of the watch brand Limes a few years later. The concept was clear: high-quality Swiss movements in lavish *manufacture* cases by Ickler.

The lion's share of the Limes collection, in stainless steel and titanium, can be purchased for between $500 and $2,500. Watches in 18-karat rose or white gold can cost up to the $6,000 mark. For this amount of money, the customer gets high-quality, well-outfitted, and stylistically attractive watches, which cultivate their own aesthetic apart from short-lived fashion trends and need not fear any comparison to products from the established competition.

The Pharo Full Calendar Moonphase Chronograph is certainly a highlight of the Limes collection and combines technology and sophistication at an elevated level. The Pharo line has recently been completely reworked, now housed in a new stainless steel "manufacture" case in either round or *carré cambré* shapes, impressive with their elegant fluting.

Limes's designers have created a very elegant timekeeper in the Pharo Balancier Visible, in which a beating heart can be seen through an aperture at 12 o'clock. Another important model family contains the sporty, robust timepieces called Endurance 1000. Both the pure diver's watches and the GMT models featuring second and third time zones are water-resistant to 1,000 meters. The latter are thus not only suitable for frequent travelers, but also those active in water sports.

Limes now also offers an elegant ladies' line: the Artemisia collection features cases with artfully curved fluting ornaments and bezels set with brilliant-cut diamonds—for elegance and a hint of luxury on the wrist.

Pharo DayDate
Reference number: U6282C-LA2.1
Movement: automatic, ETA Caliber 2834-2; ø 29.4 mm, height 5.5 mm; 25 jewels; 28,800 vph; finely finished with côtes de Genève and blued screws
Functions: hours, minutes, sweep seconds; date, weekday
Case: stainless steel, ø 40.5 mm, height 11 mm; sapphire crystal; transparent case back; water-resistant to 5 atm
Band: leather, buckle
Price: $1,475
Variations: various band and dial variations; bezel set with brilliant-cut diamonds

Pharo Balancier Visible
Reference number: U6282C-LA3.2
Movement: automatic, ETA Caliber 2824-2; ø 25.6 mm, height 4.6 mm; 25 jewels; 28,800 vph; modified with partial skeletonization; finely finished with côtes de Genève and blued screws
Functions: hours, minutes, sweep seconds
Case: stainless steel, ø 40.5 mm, height 10.7 mm; sapphire crystal; transparent case back; water-resistant to 5 atm
Band: leather, buckle
Price: $1,475
Variations: various dial variations, bezel set with brilliant-cut diamonds

Pharo Automatic
Reference number: U6282C-D-LA1.1
Movement: automatic, ETA Caliber 2824-2; ø 25.6 mm, height 4.6 mm; 25 jewels; 28,800 vph; finely finished with côtes de Genève and blued screws
Functions: hours, minutes, sweep seconds; date
Case: stainless steel, ø 40.5 mm, height 10.7 mm; bezel set with 65 brilliant-cut diamonds; sapphire crystal; transparent case back; water-resistant to 5 atm
Band: leather, buckle
Price: $4,100
Variations: various dial variations; without diamonds on bezel

Pharo Carré
Reference number: U4040-LA1.1
Movement: automatic, ETA Caliber 2824-2; ø 25.6 mm, height 4.6 mm; 25 jewels; 28,800 vph; finely finished with côtes de Genève
Functions: hours, minutes, sweep seconds; date
Case: stainless steel, 36.7 x 36.7 mm, height 9.5 mm; sapphire crystal; transparent case back; water-resistant to 5 atm
Band: leather, buckle
Price: $1,475
Variations: various strap and dial variations

Endurance 1000
Reference number: U8787-LA2.4M
Movement: automatic, ETA Caliber 2824-2; ø 25.6 mm, height 4.6 mm; 25 jewels; 28,800 vph
Functions: hours, minutes, sweep seconds; date
Case: stainless steel, ø 41.2 mm, height 12.2 mm; sapphire crystal; unidirectionally rotating bezel with 60-minute divisions; screw-in crown; water-resistant to 1,000 meters (100 atm)
Band: rubber, folding clasp with security pin
Price: $1,175
Variations: black, navy blue, Imola yellow dial colors; stainless steel bracelet

Endurance 1000 Chrono
Reference number: U8787-LA2.4M
Movement: automatic, ETA Valjoux Caliber 7750; ø 30 mm, height 7.9 mm; 25 jewels; 28,800 vph
Functions: hours, minutes, subsidiary seconds; chronograph; date
Case: stainless steel, ø 41.2 mm, height 15.5 mm; sapphire crystal; unidirectionally rotating bezel with 60-minute divisions; screw-in crown and buttons; water-resistant to 1,000 meters (100 atm)
Band: stainless steel, double folding clasp
Price: $2,475
Variations: orange dial; rubber strap

Endurance 1000 GMT 4
Reference number: U8787-LG3.2M
Movement: automatic, ETA Caliber 2893-2; ø 25.6 mm, height 4.1 mm; 21 jewels; 28,800 vph
Functions: hours, minutes, sweep seconds; date; 24-hour display (second time zone)
Case: stainless steel, ø 41.8 mm, height 12.6 mm; sapphire crystal; unidirectionally rotating bezel with 60-minute divisions; screw-in crown; water-resistant to 1,000 meters (100 atm)
Band: rubber, folding clasp with security pin
Price: $1,475
Variations: stainless steel bracelet; 24-hour divisions on the bezel

Endurance Rallye Limited Edition
Reference number: U4515_IC1.1
Movement: automatic, ETA Valjoux Caliber 7750; ø 30 mm, height 7.9 mm; 25 jewels; 28,800 vph; finely finished with côtes de Genève
Functions: hours, minutes, subsidiary seconds; chronograph; date
Case: stainless steel, ø 41 mm, height 13.3 mm; bezel engraved with tachymeter scale; sapphire crystal; transparent case back; water-resistant to 10 atm
Band: buffalo leather, buckle
Remarks: carbon fiber dial; limited edition of 99 pieces
Price: $1,995
Variations: brown leather strap; stainless steel bracelet

Longines

Longines actually gets its name from the natural setting surrounding its factory: the building is located in Saint-Imier on fields that abut a little river called Les Longines. In 1866, Ernest Francillon purchased the above-mentioned piece of property on the banks of the Schüss in Saint-Imier and promptly made the term *Les Longines* the brand name for his watches. And there is hardly a family in this little town that has not at some time or another been financially dependent upon this company's watch production.

In the spring of 2007, this brand celebrated its 175th anniversary with the extension of the museum located in that factory building. This company museum, in existence since the 1990s, was extended by another four departments, giving it exhibition space on several floors. Alongside the original collection located there, which delivers a general overview of the incredible depth of Longines timepieces throughout the years, as well as watch technology and its development in the previous 175 years, the books relating to the business end of the watches on display are kept in another department. The shelves stretching from the floor of an expansive room are filled to the ceiling with the large-format, heavy books that contain handwritten entries regarding hundreds of thousands of watches, production and sales dates, the names of the customers supplied, and a series of other notes.

Another museum section is dedicated solely to the development of the watch in the last fifty years. Much of this may appear a little strange to the visitor, and this might be because a great deal of the Swiss watch industry gets its inspiration for the design of new watches from models dating from the 1950s, '60s, and '70s.

Another department allows interested parties to immerse themselves in Longines advertising through the years with the display of old posters, catalogues, packaging, and pictures of famous people wearing Longines watches—as well as those whose job it was to make the consumer enthusiastic enough to buy one themselves.

The fifth museum department provides a look into the impressive history of the Longines brand in sports timekeeping. Here stopwatches are on display alongside watches combined with modern photo finish cameras. The exhibition provides an informative look into a time around one hundred years ago when modern sports timekeeping was still in its infancy. For decades, it was unimaginable to think of sports without calling to mind these stopwatches from Saint-Imier, and in the second half of the past century the *manufacture's* specially developed products were in regular use at the Olympic Games.

A visit to this company museum quickly makes it clear that Longines has had a grand history—thanks in great part to the towering imagination and inventive spirit of its people in the factory buildings located on the edge of the little Jura city Saint-Imier. It also becomes clear that Longines was active in practically every area of watch technology, often as a pioneer and setting numerous trends.

Longines

Weems
Reference number: L2.713.4.13.0
Movement: automatic, Caliber L699 (base ETA A07.111); ø 36.6 mm, height 7.9 mm; 24 jewels; 28,800 vph
Functions: hours, minutes, sweep seconds
Case: stainless steel, ø 47.5 mm, height 15.6 mm; sapphire crystal; hinged transparent case back
Band: reptile skin, buckle
Price: $3,700

Lindbergh Hour Angle Watch
Reference number: L2.678.4.11.0
Movement: automatic, Caliber L699 (base ETA A07.111); ø 36.6 mm, height 7.9 mm; 24 jewels; 28,800 vph
Functions: hours, minutes, sweep seconds
Case: stainless steel, ø 47.5 mm, height 16.2 mm; bezel with longitude divisions; sapphire crystal; hinged transparent case back
Band: reptile skin, buckle
Remarks: rotating dial center for synchronizing the second hand
Price: upon request

Longines Legend Diver
Reference number: L3.674.4.56.0
Movement: automatic, Caliber L633 (base ETA 2824-2); ø 25.6 mm, height 4.6 mm; 25 jewels; 28,800 vph
Functions: hours, minutes, sweep seconds
Case: stainless steel, ø 42 mm, height 13.5 mm; inner bezel with 60-minute divisions rotating via crown; sapphire crystal; water-resistant to 30 atm
Band: synthetic, buckle
Price: $1,900

HydroConquest
Reference number: L3.642.4.96.6
Movement: automatic, Caliber L633 (base ETA 2824-2); ø 25.6 mm, height 4.6 mm; 25 jewels; 28,800 vph
Functions: hours, minutes, sweep seconds; date
Case: stainless steel, ø 41 mm, height 11.85 mm; unidirectionally rotating bezel with 60-minute divisions; sapphire crystal; screw-in crown; water-resistant to 30 atm
Band: stainless steel, double folding clasp
Price: $1,050
Variations: black dial

HydroConquest Chronograph
Reference number: L3.644.4.56.6
Movement: automatic, Caliber L667 (base ETA Valjoux 7750); ø 30 mm, height 7.9 mm; 25 jewels; 28,800 vph
Functions: hours, minutes, subsidiary seconds; chronograph; date
Case: stainless steel, ø 41 mm, height 15.55 mm; unidirectionally rotating bezel with 60-minute divisions; sapphire crystal; screw-in crown; water-resistant to 30 atm
Band: stainless steel, double folding clasp
Price: $1,725
Variations: blue dial

HydroConquest Chronograph
Reference number: L3.673.4.76.6
Movement: automatic, Caliber L667 (base ETA Valjoux 7750); ø 30 mm, height 7.9 mm; 25 jewels; 28,800 vph
Functions: hours, minutes, subsidiary seconds; chronograph; date
Case: stainless steel, ø 41 mm, height 15.55 mm; unidirectionally rotating bezel with 60-minute divisions; sapphire crystal; screw-in crown; water-resistant to 30 atm
Band: stainless steel, double folding clasp
Price: $2,000

HydroConquest Maxi
Reference number: L3.665.4.76.2
Movement: automatic, Caliber L696 (base ETA A07.231); ø 36.6 mm, height 7.9 mm; 25 jewels; 28,800 vph
Functions: hours, minutes, subsidiary seconds; chronograph; date
Case: stainless steel, ø 47.5 mm, height 15.55 mm; unidirectionally rotating bezel with 60-minute divisions; sapphire crystal; screw-in crown; water-resistant to 30 atm
Band: rubber, double folding clasp
Price: $2,350

Conquest Chronograph
Reference number: L3.661.4.56.6
Movement: automatic, Caliber L667 (base ETA Valjoux 7750); ø 30 mm, height 7.9 mm; 25 jewels; 28,800 vph
Functions: hours, minutes, subsidiary seconds; chronograph; date
Case: stainless steel, ø 41 mm, height 15.25 mm; ceramic bezel; sapphire crystal; screw-in crown; water-resistant to 30 atm
Band: stainless steel, double folding clasp
Price: $2,150
Variations: rubber or leather strap

Longines

Conquest
Reference number: L3.657.4.56.2
Movement: automatic, Caliber L633 (base ETA 2824-2); ø 25.6 mm, height 4.6 mm; 25 jewels; 28,800 vph
Functions: hours, minutes, sweep seconds; date
Case: stainless steel, ø 41 mm, height 11.55 mm; ceramic bezel; sapphire crystal; screw-in crown; water-resistant to 30 atm
Band: rubber, double folding clasp
Price: upon request
Variations: leather band or stainless steel bracelet

Master Collection Chronograph
Reference number: L2.629.4.78.3
Movement: automatic, Caliber L651 (base ETA 2894-2); ø 28.6 mm, height 6.1 mm; 37 jewels; 28,800 vph
Functions: hours, minutes, subsidiary seconds; chronograph; date
Case: stainless steel, ø 40 mm, height 11.6 mm; sapphire crystal; transparent case back
Band: reptile skin, double folding clasp
Price: $2,200
Variations: stainless steel bracelet

Master Collection
Reference number: L2.128.4.78.6
Movement: automatic, Caliber L595 (base ETA 2000-1); ø 19.4 mm, height 3.6 mm; 20 jewels; 28,800 vph
Functions: hours, minutes, sweep seconds; date
Case: stainless steel, ø 25.5 mm, height 8.4 mm; sapphire crystal
Band: stainless steel, double folding clasp
Price: upon request
Variations: reptile skin strap

Master Collection GMT
Reference number: L2.631.4.70.3
Movement: automatic, Caliber L704 (base ETA A07.171); ø 36.6 mm, height 7.9 mm; 24 jewels; 28,800 vph
Functions: hours, minutes, sweep seconds; 24-hour display (second time zone); date
Case: stainless steel, ø 42 mm, height 14.2 mm; sapphire crystal; transparent case back
Band: stainless steel, double folding clasp
Price: $2,300
Variations: reptile skin strap

Master Collection Moonphase
Reference number: L2.673.4.78.3
Movement: automatic, Longines Caliber L678 (base ETA Valjoux 7750); ø 30 mm, height 7.9 mm; 25 jewels; 28,800 vph
Functions: hours, minutes, subsidiary seconds; chronograph; date, day, month, moon phase; 24-hour display
Case: stainless steel, ø 40 mm, height 14.25 mm; sapphire crystal; transparent case back
Band: reptile skin, double folding clasp
Price: $2,700
Variations: stainless steel bracelet

Master Collection Maxi
Reference number: L2.640.4.51.3
Movement: manually wound, Longines Caliber L512 (base ETA Unitas 6498-2); ø 36.6 mm, height 4.5 mm; 17 jewels; 21,600 vph
Functions: hours, minutes, subsidiary seconds
Case: stainless steel, ø 47.5 mm, height 14 mm; sapphire crystal; transparent case back
Band: reptile skin, double folding clasp
Price: upon request
Variations: stainless steel bracelet

Master Collection Chronograph
Reference number: L2.693.4.51.6
Movement: automatic, Longines Caliber L696 (base ETA A07.231); ø 36.6 mm, height 7.9 mm; 25 jewels; 28,800 vph
Functions: hours, minutes, subsidiary seconds; chronograph; date
Case: stainless steel, ø 44mm, height 14.2 mm; sapphire crystal; transparent case back
Band: stainless steel, double folding clasp
Price: $2,500
Variations: reptile skin strap

Evidenza
Reference number: L2.142.4.73.4
Movement: automatic, Longines Caliber L595 (base ETA 2000-1); ø 19.4 mm, height 3.6 mm; 20 jewels; 28,800 vph
Functions: hours, minutes, sweep seconds; date
Case: stainless steel, 26 x 30.6 mm, height 8.1 mm; sapphire crystal
Band: reptile skin, double folding clasp
Price: $1,625
Variations: stainless steel bracelet

Evidenza
Reference number: L2.670.4.73.4
Movement: automatic, Longines Caliber L599 (base ETA 2892-A2); ø 25.6 mm, height 5.35 mm; 30 jewels; 28,800 vph
Functions: hours, minutes, subsidiary seconds; large date
Case: stainless steel, 33.1 x 38.75 mm, height 10.45 mm; sapphire crystal
Band: reptile skin, double folding clasp
Price: $2,000
Variations: stainless steel bracelet

Evidenza Power Reserve
Reference number: L2.672.4.73.4
Movement: automatic, Longines Caliber L602 (base ETA 2897-5); ø 25.6 mm, height 4.95 mm; 21 jewels; 28,800 vph
Functions: hours, minutes, sweep seconds; date; power reserve display
Case: stainless steel, 33.1 x 38.75 mm, height 10.49 mm; sapphire crystal
Band: reptile skin, double folding clasp
Price: $2,250
Variations: stainless steel bracelet

Evidenza Chronograph
Reference number: L2.643.4.73.4
Movement: automatic, Longines Caliber L650 (base ETA 2894-2); ø 28.6 mm, height 6.25 mm; 37 jewels; 28,800 vph
Functions: hours, minutes, subsidiary seconds; chronograph; date
Case: stainless steel, 34.9 x 40 mm, height 12.45 mm; sapphire crystal
Band: reptile skin, double folding clasp
Price: $2,425
Variations: stainless steel bracelet

Evidenza Maxi
Reference number: L2.701.4.78.4
Movement: automatic, Longines Caliber L674 (base ETA Valjoux 7750); ø 30 mm, height 7.9 mm; 25 jewels; 28,800 vph
Functions: hours, minutes, subsidiary seconds; chronograph; date; weekday
Case: stainless steel, 40.6 x 47.4 mm, height 14.9 mm; sapphire crystal
Band: reptile skin, double folding clasp
Price: upon request
Variations: stainless steel bracelet

La Grande Classique
Reference number: L4.708.2.11.2
Movement: automatic, Longines Caliber L593 (base ETA 2000-1); ø 19.4 mm, height 3.6 mm; 20 jewels; 28,800 vph
Functions: hours, minutes
Case: stainless steel, PVD gold-plated; ø 34 mm, height 7.05 mm; sapphire crystal
Band: reptile skin, buckle
Price: $895
Variations: PVD gold-plated or two-tone stainless steel bracelet

La Grande Classique
Reference number: L4.708.4.72.6
Movement: automatic, Longines Caliber L593 (base ETA 2000-1); ø 19.4 mm, height 3.6 mm; 20 jewels; 28,800 vph
Functions: hours, minutes
Case: stainless steel, ø 34 mm, height 7.05 mm; sapphire crystal
Band: stainless steel, folding clasp
Price: $1,050
Variations: reptile skin strap

DolceVita
Reference number: L5.657.4.71.2
Movement: automatic, Longines Caliber L595 (base ETA 2000-1); ø 19.4 mm, height 3.6 mm; 20 jewels; 28,800 vph
Functions: hours, minutes, sweep seconds; date
Case: stainless steel, 26.6 x 32.1 mm, height 8.25 mm; sapphire crystal
Band: reptile skin, buckle
Price: upon request
Variations: stainless steel bracelet

DolceVita
Reference number: L5.657.6.16.0
Movement: automatic, Longines Caliber L595 (base ETA 2000-1); ø 19.4 mm, height 3.6 mm; 20 jewels; 28,800 vph
Functions: hours, minutes, sweep seconds; date
Case: yellow gold, 26.6 x 32.1 mm, height 8.25 mm; sapphire crystal
Band: reptile skin, buckle
Price: upon request
Variations: yellow gold link bracelet

Lang & Heyne

This small Dresden-based watch brand was founded in 2001 by two watchmaking "soul mates." Mirko Heyne had just finished his apprenticeship at a grand Glashütte manufacture where he had met instructor Rolf Lang and his son, Marco. Marco Lang had been infected by the watch bug in his early childhood and as a journeyman made fine precision pendulum clocks with Ihno Fleßner, a northern German watch expert. In Dresden, he maintained a small business as a watch creator and restorer.

Lang and Heyne saw an entrepreneurial possibility with their combined horological talent and predilections; this would be something completely different from that which was already available in Glashütte: their creations would be even more personal, contain even more work done by hand, and be even more traditional than the others.

A year later, Lang & Heyne introduced their first automatic watches at Baselworld. In the blink of an eye, they had written more orders than they had the capacity for. As nice as the success was, it seemed to stultify the creativity of the two watchmakers, and they became discordant with regard to the future of their little *manufacture*. In the summer of 2002, Heyne left the company. However, Lang & Heyne continues to display the spirit along with the name of both talented watchmakers

Lang & Heyne's products are as classic as classic can be in the Saxon style prevalent at the end of the nineteenth century, the heyday of the pocket watch.

Marco Lang, whose favorite spot is the watchmaker bench, has meanwhile closed down his retail shop in order to fully concentrate on the creation of his watches. The small Lang & Heyne team is at home now in a villa in Dresden. The exclusive collection of only thirty to forty watches annually only leaves the workshop after Lang personally assembles and adjusts them.

Friedrich August I
Movement: manually wound, Caliber I; ø 36.6 mm, height 5.4 mm; 19 jewels; 18,000 vph; three-quarter plate with traditional Saxon silver frosted finish; balance with diamond endstone
Functions: hours, minutes; subsidiary seconds
Case: rose gold, ø 43.6 mm, height 10.5 mm; sapphire crystal; transparent case back
Band: crocodile skin, buckle
Remarks: hand-engraved Louis XV hands; genuine enamel dial
Price: $23,500
Variations: white or yellow gold

Johann
Movement: manually wound, Caliber I; ø 36.6 mm, height 5.4 mm; 19 jewels; 18,000 vph; three-quarter plate with traditional Saxon silver frosted finish; swan-neck fine adjustment
Functions: hours, minutes; subsidiary seconds
Case: white gold, ø 43.6 mm, height 10.5 mm; sapphire crystal; transparent case back
Band: crocodile skin, buckle
Remarks: hand-filed pear-shaped hands; genuine enamel dial
Price: $24,800
Variations: yellow or rose gold

Moritz
Movement: manually wound, Caliber III; ø 36.6 mm, height 6.9 mm; 19 jewels; 18,000 vph; three-quarter plate; swan-neck fine adjustment; module plate (1.5 mm)
Functions: hours, minutes; subsidiary seconds; date, weekday, month, moon phase; declination (inclination of pole axis over the course of the year)
Case: rose gold, ø 43.8 mm, height 12.5 mm; sapphire crystal; transparent case back
Band: crocodile skin, buckle
Remarks: silver dial
Price: $40,800
Variations: declination motifs: Europe/Africa, Asia, North America

Albert
Movement: manually wound, Caliber IV; ø 36.6 mm, height 6.9 mm; 22 jewels; 18,000 vph; column-wheel control of chronograph functions; sweep second and minute counters
Functions: hours, minutes; subsidiary seconds; chronograph
Case: platinum, ø 43.6 mm, height 13 mm; sapphire crystal; transparent case back; crown with chronograph button
Band: crocodile skin, buckle
Remarks: hand-engraved Louis XV hands; genuine enamel dial
Price: $59,500

Giuliano Mazzuoli

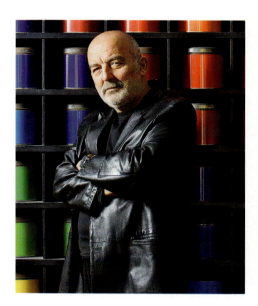

Florentine designer and cult creator Giuliano Mazzuoli developed his own concrete idea of what a wristwatch should look like at the beginning of the new millennium. In 2004, he debuted his watch brand to an exclusive circle of retailers with the Manometro model. The rich and beautiful of Northern Italy literally tore these watches out of their retailers' hands: Fiat heir Lapo Elkann, soccer star Roberto Baggio, TV anchorwoman Cesara Buonamici, and even Prince Victor Emmanuel of Savoy proudly displayed their new acquisitions on their wrists—for getting them was less a question of money than of good connections.

Even today Mazzuoli instructs his retailers not to put the Manometro in the display window but rather just to offer it discreetly to select clientele.

Mazzuoli gets the ideas for his products from objects for everyday use. His writing instruments are famous, especially those that look a lot like a lengthened espresso pot and are therefore called Moka and Mokina. "I don't study or conceive the things that I make," the fifty-eight-year-old autodidact explains. "I just find them." He found one, for example, at the sick bed of one of his relatives: the blood pressure measuring mechanism with its cleanly designed manometer appealed to him, and the idea for the basic design of his new watch was born.

The Manometro watch models are characteristic in their simple, monocoque, pot-shaped case. The crystal is secured to the flange on the inside and has no separate bezel. The case back is secured with eight screws. At a diameter of 42.5 mm and a height of 14.8 mm the watch has a lot of confidence.

On the occasion of the presentation of the new 8C sports car by Alfa Romeo, Mazzuoli produced a watch called Contagiri (Italian for "rpm speed counter") that is wound and set by the bezel and has a switch for going between these functions recessed into the case.

Manometro S
Movement: automatic, ETA Caliber 2824-2; ø 25.6 mm, height 4.6 mm; 25 jewels; 28,800 vph
Functions: hours, minutes, sweep seconds; date
Case: carbon fiber, ø 45.2 mm, height 14.8 mm; sapphire crystal; titanium case back; screw-in crown; water-resistant to 5 atm
Band: rubber, double folding clasp
Remarks: carbon fiber dial
Price: $5,950

Manometro
Movement: automatic, ETA Caliber 2824-2; ø 25.6 mm, height 4.6 mm; 25 jewels; 28,800 vph
Functions: hours, minutes, sweep seconds
Case: stainless steel, ø 45.2 mm, height 14.8 mm; sapphire crystal
Band: leather, buckle
Price: $3,500
Variations: satin-finished case; crown at 10 o'clock; various dial and band colors

Manometro Chronograph
Movement: automatic, ETA Caliber 2892 with chronograph module 2030 by Dubois Dépraz; ø 31.15 mm; 48 jewels; 28,800 vph; buttons at 8 and 10 o'clock
Functions: hours, minutes, subsidiary seconds; chronograph
Case: stainless steel, ø 45.2 mm, height 14.8 mm; sapphire crystal
Band: reptile skin; double folding clasp
Price: $6,950

Manometro Limited Edition
Movement: automatic, ETA Caliber 2824-2; ø 25.6 mm, height 4.6 mm; 25 jewels; 28,800 vph
Functions: hours, minutes, sweep seconds; date
Case: bronze-coated titanium, ø 45.2 mm, height 14.8 mm; sapphire crystal; titanium case back; screw-in crown; water-resistant to 5 atm
Band: reptile skin; double folding clasp
Price: $4,950

MeisterSinger

"Perfection should not be noticed, but rather missed when not there." The great violinist Jascha Heifetz could be discussing MeisterSinger's one-handed watches with this statement.
It is, in fact, renunciation of decorative embellishments that creates the generosity of these watches from Münster. Manfred Brassler, owner and founder of this company, returns to the source of watchmaking with his one-handed watches—the point in time when everything started with one hand, before man and machine were subjected to the dictatorship of an ever faster society with ever more precise watches—all the way to atomic time.
For the past six years, Brassler has reduced the day to the rhythmic succession of five-minute intervals. His watches serve as a symbol of slowing time down in a period of swiftly accelerating society.
The exaggerated simplicity of these dials tempts one to put the one-handed watches in a drawer as an archetype: the sole needle-shaped hand cannot be reduced anymore no matter how hard one tries, and the 144 lines symbolizing the five-minute intervals of a twelve-hour period have something normative about them.

"A customer once wrote me that his MeisterSinger was a symbol of leisure time for him," Brassler grins. "It measures the time in intervals of five minutes; you don't need to know what time it is any more precisely than that." Thanks to the precise hand and the exact intervals shown on the dial, no one will ever need to think they will miss a train because of this watch. It's better for your stress level to be at the train station five minutes early anyway.
Until now, these minimalist timekeepers have been outfitted with manually wound movements. No. 01 is powered by the rarely used ETA Caliber 2801, which is somewhat larger in diameter than its well-known sister, ETA Peseux 7001, while the No. 02 is served well by the robust ETA Unitas 6498, originally created for pocket watches. The new MeisterSinger No. 03 housing an auto-matic movement completes the small collection of one-handed watches—with which this German brand has attained worldwide recognition in just a couple of years.
The youngest member of the family is the Monograph, which derives it legitimacy from the fundamental difference between measured time and experienced time: you should not plan your day to the minute or

have to justify every second, but when ascertaining a time interval, the stopped time must be correct—to the second. For this reason, the Monograph includes hands for the stopped minutes and seconds, while the time is read—like on the other models in the collection—from one single, long hour hand.

MeisterSinger

No. 01 Single Hand
Reference number: AM304
Movement: manually wound, ETA Caliber 2801-2; ø 25.6 mm, height 3.35 mm; 17 jewels; 28,800 vph
Functions: hours (each index line stands for five minutes)
Case: stainless steel, ø 43 mm, height 11.7 mm; sapphire crystal; transparent case back
Band: leather, buckle
Price: $1,200
Variations: silvery white, black, or ivory-colored dial; in 38 mm case

Single Hand Unitas 02
Reference number: AM602
Movement: manually wound, ETA Unitas Caliber 6497-1; ø 36.6 mm, height 4.5 mm; 17 jewels; 18,000 vph; finely finished with perlage and blued screws
Functions: hours (each index line stands for five minutes)
Case: stainless steel, ø 43 mm, height 12.5 mm; sapphire crystal; transparent case back
Band: leather, buckle
Price: $1,750
Variations: silvery white, copper, or ivory-colored dial

Single Hand Automatic
Reference number: AM903
Movement: automatic, ETA Caliber 2824-2; ø 25.6 mm, height 4.6 mm; 25 jewels; 28,800 vph; rotor with côtes de Genève
Functions: hours (each index line stands for five minutes)
Case: stainless steel, ø 43 mm, height 11.2 mm; sapphire crystal; transparent case back
Band: leather, buckle
Price: $1,450
Variations: silvery white or black-coppery brown dial; in 38 mm case

Karelia
Reference number: CM101
Movement: manually wound, ETA Peseux Caliber 7001; ø 23.3 mm, height 2.5 mm; 17 jewels; 21,600 vph
Functions: hours, minutes, subsidiary seconds
Case: stainless steel, ø 34 mm, height 7.5 mm; sapphire crystal; transparent case back
Band: leather, buckle
Price: $1,600
Variations: black, copper, or ivory-colored dial; 38 mm case diameter

Monograph Single Hand Chronograph
Reference number: MM102
Movement: automatic, ETA Valjoux Caliber 7750; ø 30 mm, height 7.9 mm; 25 jewels; 28,800 vph
Functions: hours (each index line stands for five minutes); chronograph
Case: stainless steel, ø 43 mm, height 14.8 mm; sapphire crystal; transparent case back
Band: reptile skin, buckle
Price: $3,500
Variations: silver or ivory-colored dial

Unomatik
Reference number: UM103
Movement: automatic, ETA Caliber A07.161; ø 36.6 mm, height 4.5 mm; 24 jewels; 28,800 vph
Functions: hours (each index line stands for five minutes); power reserve display
Case: stainless steel, ø 45 mm, height 11.7 mm; sapphire crystal; transparent case back
Band: calfskin, buckle
Price: $3,100
Variations: white dial

Archao Gold
Reference number: AMAG1
Movement: automatic, ETA Unitas Caliber 6497-1; ø 36.6 mm, height 4.5 mm; 17 jewels; 18,000 vph; hand-guilloché fermata design
Functions: hours (each index line stands for five minutes)
Case: red gold, ø 43 mm, height 12.5 mm; sapphire crystal; transparent case back
Band: reptile skin, buckle
Price: $9,500
Variations: black numerals; stainless steel

Edition 2007
Reference number: ED07B
Movement: automatic, Sellita SW 200; ø 25.6 mm, height 4.6 mm; 25 jewels; 28,800 vph; rotor with côtes de Genève
Functions: hours (each index line stands for five minutes)
Case: stainless steel, ø 43 mm, height 11.5 mm; sapphire crystal; transparent case back
Band: leather, buckle
Remarks: limited edition of 333 pieces per dial variation
Price: $1,600
Variations: white dial with silver or copper-colored elements

Richard Mille

Richard Mille is not an engineer by profession, but rather a marketing expert who earned his first paychecks in the watch segment of the French arms, automobile, and space travel concern Matra in the early 1980s. This was a time of fundamental changes in technology, and the European watch industry was being confronted with gigantic challenges. Mille was responsible for traditional French watch brands such as Yema and Jaz, for which he created completely new product palettes in the lowest price segment. When Matra dissolved its watch division and sold it to Seiko, Mille went to Paris to work for the reputable jeweler Mauboussin, for whom he developed an original watch collection. The highlight of that series was a tourbillon with plates and bridges made of rock crystal, which Mille had designed and made at the specialty workshop of Renaud & Papi, already a subsidiary of Audemars Piguet at the time.

His experiences and collaborations with APRP, as Renaud & Papi is now known, and Audemars Piguet were to help form the way Mille would work from that point on. Though he has also forged strong bonds with movement makers Vaucher and Soprod—"I use the movement company that best suits my needs for a given project," he openly explains—it is to APRP that he continues to turn for the projects that are furthest removed from the established watch industry.

Now these relationships have come full circle, for in early 2007 Audemars Piguet has finally invested in Mille's future in a monetary sense. One of the most traditional companies in the Swiss watchmaking industry, Audemars Piguet purchased 20 percent of the forward-thinking brand, which has become something of a favorite among acquisitive collectors.

Seen in this light, it seems strange when Mille says things like, "I have absolutely no historical relationship to watchmaking—and therefore no obligations either. The mechanics of my watches orient themselves on that which is technically possible, and at best on that which Formula 1 automobiles and space travel technology have to offer."

He does not make such statements out of any desire to provoke; that is never the impetus for the fifty-six-year-old Frenchman to say something inflammatory about his watches. Mille does indeed have a relationship with traditional watchmaking, even if the appearance of his products and his company's philosophy may not feature anything recognizable from it.

Mille is to watchmaking what Enzo Ferrari was to automobile design. Like the famous sports car manufacturer and racing team owner, he has a clear idea of what he wants, and his goals are certainly comparable to those of the technological excellence of Formula 1. Mille, the passionate automobile fan, has transposed the technical aesthetics of racing cars and airplanes to the world of watches and has created in his short career as a watch manufacturer numerous "conversation pieces" that are not only exciting because of their breathtaking technical specialties, but also because of their exclusive price tags.

Movement plates made of highly resilient carbon nanofibers; ultra-light aluminum silicon carbide (called Alusic); springs, bars, levers, and chronograph column wheels made of titanium; and new tooth shapes with reduced pressure angles are just some of the things that Mille has thought up to test watchmakers and take them to their limits.

Richard Mille

Automatic Rectangular
Reference number: RM 016
Movement: automatic, Richard Mille Caliber RM 005-S (base Vaucher 331); ø 25.6 mm, height 3.5 mm; 32 jewels; 28,800 vph; skeletonized; surfaces PVD coated; rotor with adjustable inertia
Functions: hours, minutes; large date
Case: red gold, 49.8 x 38 mm, height 8.25 mm; sapphire crystal; transparent case back
Band: rubber, folding clasp
Price: $46,000
Variations: titanium ($44,000); white gold ($50,000)

Perini Navi Cup
Reference number: RM 015
Movement: manually wound, Richard Mille Caliber RM 015; 30.2 x 28.6 mm, height 7.8 mm; 23 jewels; 21,600 vph; one-minute tourbillon; carbon nanofiber base plate; function button for winding (C), neutral (N), and hand-setting (L)
Functions: hours, minutes; power reserve and torque displays; 24-hour display (second time zone); function selection (C-N-L)
Case: white gold, 48 x 39 mm, height 13.85 mm; sapphire crystal; transparent case back
Band: rubber, folding clasp
Price: $268,000
Variations: red gold ($260,000); platinum ($303,000)

Flyback Chronograph Felipe Massa
Reference number: RM 011 FM
Movement: automatic, Richard Mille Caliber RM 011S; 30.3 x 32.75 mm, height 9 mm; 62 jewels; 28,800 vph; twin spring barrels; rotor with adjustable inertia; base plate and bridges in titanium; skeletonized, PVD coated
Functions: hours, minutes, subsidiary seconds; chronograph with flyback function; annual calendar with large date and month
Case: titanium, 40 x 50 mm, height 16.15 mm; sapphire crystal; transparent case back
Band: rubber, folding clasp
Price: $68,000
Variations: red gold ($72,000); white gold ($76,000)

Architectural Tourbillon
Reference number: RM 012
Movement: manually wound, Richard Mille Caliber RM 012; 30.2 x 28.6 mm, height 6.35 mm; 19 jewels; 21,600 vph; one-minute tourbillon; spring barrel, gear train, and tourbillon cage crafted in aluminum Anticorodal 100; pipe-shaped bridge structure in steel and titanium
Functions: hours, minutes
Case: platinum, 48 x 39.3 mm, height 13.85 mm; sapphire crystal; transparent case back
Band: rubber, folding clasp
Remarks: limited edition of 30 pieces
Price: $450,000

Tourbillon RM 002-V2
Reference number: RM 002-V2
Movement: manually wound, Richard Mille Caliber RM 002-V2; 30.2 x 28.6 mm, height 6.35 mm; 23 jewels; 21,600 vph; one-minute tourbillon with ceramic endstone; base plate in carbon nanofiber; gear train bridge in Arcap; white gold chatons; function button for winding (W), neutral (N), and hand-setting (H)
Functions: hours, minutes; power reserve and torque indicator; function selection
Case: white gold, 45 x 38.3 mm, height 11.85 mm; sapphire crystal; transparent case back
Band: rubber, folding clasp
Price: $220,000
Variations: titanium ($208,000); red gold ($212,000); platinum ($255,000)

Tourbillon RM 003-V2
Reference number: RM 003-V2
Movement: manually wound, Richard Mille Caliber RM 003-V2; 30.2 x 28.6 mm, height 6.35 mm; 23 jewels; 21,600 vph; one-minute tourbillon with ceramic endstone; base plate in carbon nanofiber; gear train bridge in Arcap; white gold chatons; function button for winding (W), neutral (N), and hand-setting (H)
Functions: hours, minutes; 12-hour display (second time zone); power reserve and torque indicator; function selection
Case: white gold, 48 x 39.3 mm, height 13.85 mm; sapphire crystal; transparent case back
Band: rubber, folding clasp
Price: $250,000
Variations: titanium; red gold; platinum ($285,000)

Split-Seconds Chronograph
Reference number: RM 004-V2
Movement: manually wound, Richard Mille Caliber RM 004-V2; 30.2 x 28.6 mm, height 8.9 mm; 37 jewels; 21,600 vph; carbon nanofiber base plate, titanium gear train bridge and column wheels; function button for winding (W), neutral (N), and hand setting (H)
Functions: hours, minutes, subsidiary seconds; split-seconds chronograph, power reserve and torque displays; function selection
Case: red gold, 48 x 39 mm, height 15.05 mm; sapphire crystal; transparent case back
Band: rubber, folding clasp
Price: $162,000
Variations: titanium ($158,000); white gold ($170,000); platinum ($205,000)

Despite the appearance of this model's movement finish—which is reminiscent of a very modern machine—traditional elements belonging to the art of fine watchmaking such as twin column wheels and a screw balance are alos in evidence in the design of Richard Mille's split-seconds chronograph.

Milus

At the beginning of Milus's history stands Paul William Junod (1896–1951). He founded the company in 1919 in Biel, and it remained in his family's possession until 2002. With the inauguration of the new enterprise Milus International SA, financially supported by the Peace Mark Group from Hong Kong, the brand has entered a new era. After a successful relaunch at Baselworld 2003, the new collections are in full production swing.

Playfulness and changeability are important concepts at Milus, something that was absolutely underscored two years ago with the advent of the Herios TriRetrograde Seconds Skeleton. This model conveys Milus's all-important concept of movement to the watch's heart—its movement—and now presents on the dial a fascinating interplay of triple retrograde hands—also available in a ladies' version called the Merea. "This watch isn't supposed to just look good, it is also supposed to embody continuous movement, which is so typical of Milus. This continuous movement on the dial is simply characteristic," explains Jan Edöcs, president of the ambitious watch brand. "This new timepiece not only looks good, it without a doubt also represents an excursion into the world of high watchmaking." The Zetios Chronograph from the men's line is, on the other hand, a distinct homage to the traditional past of the Milus brand: a modern classic that cleverly continues the design tradition of this Swiss concern.

Herios TriRetrograde Seconds Skeleton
Reference number: HERT 002
Movement: automatic, ETA Caliber 2892-A2 with special module developed exclusively for Milus; ø 30 mm; 37 jewels; 28,800 vph; three retrograde second hands with sectoral displays of 120° each; movement partially skeletonized; finely finished with côtes de Genève
Functions: hours, minutes, three retrograde second displays
Case: stainless steel, 41.7 x 42 mm, height 14.2 mm; sapphire crystal; transparent case back
Band: reptile skin, buckle
Price: $7,900
Variations: white gold; red gold; with diamonds; diverse band variations

Zetios Chronograph
Reference number: ZETC 400
Movement: automatic, ETA Caliber 2892-A2 with special module; 28,800 vph; skeletonized rotor
Functions: hours, minutes, subsidiary seconds; chronograph; large date
Case: red gold, ø 45 mm, height 14.5 mm; sapphire crystal; transparent case back
Band: reptile skin, buckle
Price: $16,900
Variations: white gold; stainless steel; diverse band variations

Merea TriRetrograde Seconds Skeleton
Reference number: MER 403
Movement: automatic, ETA Caliber 2892-A2 with special module developed exclusively for Milus; ø 30 mm; 37 jewels; 28,800 vph; three retrograde second hands with sectoral displays of 120° each; movement partially skeletonized; finely finished with côtes de Genève
Functions: hours, minutes, three retrograde seconds displays
Case: red gold, ø 37 mm, height 12.9 mm; bezel and strap lugs set with diamonds; sapphire crystal; transparent case back
Band: reptile skin, buckle
Price: $19,900
Variations: white gold; stainless steel

Apiana Chronograph
Reference number: APIC 013
Movement: automatic, ETA Caliber 2094; 28,800 vph; skeletonized rotor
Functions: hours, minutes, subsidiary seconds; chronograph
Case: stainless steel, 45 x 55 mm; bezel, case flanks, and crown set with diamonds; sapphire crystal; transparent case back
Band: stingray skin, buckle
Remarks: mother-of-pearl dial set with diamonds
Price: $17,900

H. Moser & Cie.

A brand ready to enter the hotly contested and correspondingly difficult market segment featuring expensive wristwatches can always choose the old-fashioned path of trying to speak to serious consumers with timeless quality, though this may be the more difficult way to go.
This, however, seems to be the way that the "new-old" brand H. Moser & Cie. from Schaffhausen is preparing to take. It was in this city, from 1820 until 1824, that Heinrich Moser learned the art of watchmaking from his father, a man who—like Heinrich's grandfather—fulfilled the role of "city watchmaker." After completing his apprenticeship, he went to Le Locle, a little city in the western part of Switzerland's Jura, which was the center of the watch industry at that time. Moser struck out on his own in 1825 at the age of twenty-one, and the following year moved to St. Petersburg, Russia, a city that offered competent watchmakers a good basis for business in that era. In 1828, upon founding H. Moser & Cie, the birth of his own watch brand was finally achieved, a brand that today has been resuscitated by a group of investors and watch experts together with Moser's great-grandson, Roger Nicholas Balsiger.

Very consciously, the refounders refer to Heinrich Moser's horological principles and demands on quality. Moser had established his own watch factory in Le Locle in order to be able to supply his Russian and other international customers with timekeepers corresponding to his ideas. He also managed his company on the basis of having to work with the best suppliers if one wanted to make good watches, as neither today nor at the beginning of the nineteenth century could any watch company get along without external partners.

Today's Moser Schaffhausen AG watch factory abstains from entering the general *manufacture* discussion and continues to work within the concept of classic Swiss division of labor: Individual components of the watches developed in Schaffhausen are purchased from the best supplier companies in the Swiss watch industry.

It's obvious that this does not detract from the timepieces' quality in any way. The finely decorated plates and bridges of the watches, regulated in six positions, are outfitted with a double-pull crown mechanism in order to place the different positions of the crown most precisely. These timekeepers are also outfitted with a "flash calendar" display, which sees to it that the date jumps directly to the beginning of the following month when the end of the current month has been reached—for example, at the end of February, either from the 28th or 29th the next number is a one.

The new movements contain a new type of escapement comprising a removable plate that bears the pallets, escape wheel, and balance. This complete subgroup is simply secured to the movement with two screws, very easy to remove and replace. When the watch goes in for revisions, this escapement is easily taken out and replaced with a new one from Schaffhausen.

Moser Perpetual 1
Reference number: 341.501-006
Movement: manually wound, Moser Caliber HMC 341.501; ø 34 mm, height 5.8 mm; 28 jewels; exchangeable escapement with gold pallet fork and gold escape wheel; twin spring barrels, seven days power reserve; calendar functions settable forward and backward; double pull crown mechanism; stop-seconds
Functions: hours, minutes, subsidiary seconds; perpetual calendar with large date, small month display in the middle, leap year display on the case back; power reserve display
Case: platinum, ø 40.9 mm, height 11.05 mm; sapphire crystal; transparent case back
Band: reptile skin, folding clasp
Price: $39,500

Monard
Reference number: 342.502-012
Movement: manually wound, Moser Caliber HMC 343.505; ø 34 mm, height 5.8 mm; 26 jewels; exchangeable escapement with gold pallet fork and gold escape wheel; twin spring barrels, seven days power reserve
Functions: hours, minutes, sweep seconds; power reserve display on the case back
Case: white gold, ø 40.9 mm, height 10.85 mm; sapphire crystal; transparent case back
Band: reptile skin, buckle
Price: $13,900
Variations: platinum; in rose gold; limited edition of 200 pieces in rose gold with black enamel dial

Mayu
Reference number: 321.503-007
Movement: manually wound, Moser Caliber HMC 321.503; ø 32 mm, height 4.8 mm; 27 jewels; exchangeable escapement with gold pallet fork and gold escape wheel; 80-hour power reserve
Functions: hours, minutes, subsidiary seconds
Case: rose gold, ø 38.8 mm, height 9.3 mm; sapphire crystal; transparent case back
Band: reptile skin, buckle
Price: $10,500
Variations: rose gold; white gold; limited edition of 50 pieces in white gold with enamel dial; platinum

HENRY Double Hairspring
Reference number: 324.607-004
Movement: manually wound, Moser Caliber HMC 321.503; 32.6 x 36.6 mm, height 4.8 mm; exchangeable escapement with Straumann double balance spring, gold pallet fork and gold escape wheel; four days power reserve
Functions: hours, minutes, subsidiary seconds; power reserve display on back
Case: rose gold, 38.9 mm x 44.1 mm, height 10.4 mm; sapphire crystal; transparent case back
Band: reptile skin, buckle
Price: $16,700
Variations: white gold; platinum

Montblanc

The air is truly thin at the top, especially if your name is Montblanc. This brand, which borrows the moniker of Switzerland's most famous snow-capped member of the Alps, has graced the pinnacle of the writing instrument industry since its founding in 1906. Scaling the peaks of the watch industry was not quite as easy for the brand. When its management decided to steer the marque into the watch segment after joining the world's biggest luxury watch group, Richemont, its first efforts were not exactly greeted with enthusiasm.

Ten years and several lines named for the brand's famous writing instrument series later, Montblanc has been hit by the equivalent of a horological lightning bolt. In early 2007 it was announced that the Richemont Group had purchased Minerva, a small, previously family-owned *manufacture* located in Villeret, Switzerland. When the owning family was ready to sell Minerva—a small company with a reputation that boomed like thunder, by the way—it was purchased by a group of Italian investors who were looking to upgrade the company's *manufacture* movements and small line of watches to sell them at much higher prices in the future. This concept didn't sit well with fans of the brand, however. The timing was just right, and Richemont stepped up. Richemont did not disclose what it planned to do with Minerva for a number of months; then all was revealed shortly before the S.I.H.H.

2007. Richemont had decided to turn Minerva into Montblanc's exclusive new movement maker. In recent years with the line's seriously improved design, this was exactly what had been missing for the brand: an element to attract real collectors and aficionados.

And with that the Collection Villeret 1858 was born. The line's name alludes to Minerva's location and founding year. This collection is so far based on Minerva Caliber 62-00 for the three-handed watches and Minerva Caliber 16-29 for the monopusher column wheel chronographs. Both movements are beautifully executed, finished, and engraved. They can be seen through the sapphire crystal case back that is only revealed when the hinged lid on the back is lifted. This is a nice touch that Montblanc's designers added to lend the line a slightly nostalgic feel.

Caliber 16-29 was originally a manually wound pocket watch movement as is still obvious today by its stately diameter of 38.4 mm. It contains the screw balance and swan-neck fine adjustment typical of Minerva's movements as well as German silver plates and bridges that have been rhodium-plated. The rather large 14.5 mm balance wheel beats at the slower frequency of 18,000 vph usual in movements of days gone by. Manually wound Caliber 62-00, somewhat smaller at 24 mm in diameter, displays all of the same characteristics with a 9.7 mm balance wheel.

The two chronographs and two three-handed watches featuring subsidiary seconds of the debut collection are all limited editions—and they are so detailed and attractive that it makes the serious connoisseur wonder just what Montblanc is going to come out with next year.

Montblanc

Star Lady Moon Phase Automatic
Reference number: 101625
Movement: automatic, Montblanc Caliber 4810/908 (base Dubois Dépraz 9231); ø 36 mm; 26 jewels; 28,800 vph
Functions: hours, minutes, sweep seconds; date; moon phase
Case: stainless steel, ø 36 mm, height 11.8 mm; sapphire crystal; transparent case back
Band: reptile skin, triple folding clasp
Price: $3,560

Sport Chronograph Automatic
Reference number: 101652
Movement: automatic, Montblanc Caliber 4810/501 (base ETA Valjoux 7750); ø 30 mm, height 7.9 mm; 25 jewels; 28,800 vph; C.O.S.C. officially certified chronometer
Functions: hours, minutes, subsidiary seconds; date; chronograph
Case: red gold, ø 41.5 mm, height 14.5 mm; unidirectionally rotating bezel with 60-minute divisions; sapphire crystal with magnifying lens over date; screw-in crown; water-resistant to 20 atm
Band: rubber, triple folding clasp
Price: $15,140

TimeWalker Chronograph Automatic
Reference number: 101565
Movement: automatic, Montblanc Caliber 4810/502 (base ETA Valjoux 7753); ø 30 mm, height 7.9 mm; 25 jewels; 28,800 vph
Functions: hours, minutes, subsidiary seconds; chronograph; date
Case: red gold, ø 43 mm, height 14.3 mm; sapphire crystal; transparent case back
Band: reptile skin, folding clasp
Price: $13,210
Variations: leather strap

TimeWalker Chronograph Automatic
Reference number: 101548
Movement: automatic, Montblanc Caliber 4810/502 (base ETA Valjoux 7753); ø 30 mm, height 7.9 mm; 25 jewels; 28,800 vph
Functions: hours, minutes, subsidiary seconds; chronograph; date
Case: stainless steel, ø 42 mm, height 11.6 mm; sapphire crystal
Band: reptile skin, buckle
Price: $2,150

Timewalker Large Automatic
Reference number: 101551
Movement: automatic, Montblanc Caliber 4810/401 (base ETA 2892-A2); ø 25.6 mm, height 3.6 mm; 21 jewels; 28,800 vph
Functions: hours, minutes, sweep seconds; date
Case: stainless steel, ø 42 mm, height 11.6 mm; sapphire crystal
Band: reptile skin, folding clasp
Price: $2,150

Sport Chronograph Automatic
Reference number: 35777
Movement: automatic, Montblanc Caliber 4810/501 (base ETA Valjoux 7750); ø 30 mm, height 7.9 mm; 25 jewels; 28,800 vph
Functions: hours, minutes, subsidiary seconds; chronograph; date
Case: stainless steel, ø 41.5 mm, height 14.5 mm; unidirectionally rotating bezel with 60-minute divisions; sapphire crystal with magnifying lens over date; screw-in crown; water-resistant to 20 at,
Band: reptile skin, triple folding clasp
Price: $2,450

Star XXL Chronograph GMT Automatic
Reference number: 36967
Movement: automatic, Montblanc Caliber 4810/503 (base ETA Valjoux 7750); ø 30 mm, height 7.9 mm; 25 jewels; 28,800 vph
Functions: hours, minutes, subsidiary seconds; date; chronograph; 24-hour indication (second time zone)
Case: stainless steel, ø 42 mm, height 14.5 mm; sapphire crystal; transparent case back
Band: reptile skin, triple folding clasp
Price: $2,750

Star Power Reserve Automatic
Reference number: 35871
Movement: automatic, Montblanc Caliber 4810/406 (base ETA 2897); ø 25.6 mm, height 4.85 mm; 21 jewels; 28,800 vph
Functions: hours, minutes, sweep seconds; date; power reserve display
Case: stainless steel, ø 40 mm, height 13 mm; sapphire crystal
Band: reptile skin, triple folding clasp
Price: $2,060

Mühle Glashütte

It has now been thirteen years that the company owned and operated by Hans-Jürgen and his son Thilo Mühle has been called Nautische Instrumente Mühle-Glashütte. Despite this, however, this company founded by Hans-Jürgen after the fall of the Berlin Wall located in the Müglitz Valley between Dresden and the Czech border can look back on almost 140 years of history.

When Robert Mühle founded the first company bearing the name Mühle in 1869, it was to manufacture measuring instruments for the watch industry and later tachometers, rpm displays, and clocks for automobile dashboards as well. After the end of World War II, Hans Mühle became the managing director of the company, which was then called Messtechnik Glashütte, founding his own firm in 1945. This grandson of the company founder banked on family tradition, and as one of the few independent entrepreneurs of the German Democratic Republic, produced components and motors for the photo and cinema industries and dial trains for pressure and temperature measuring instruments. His son Hans-Jürgen Mühle, who studied precision engineering and optics in Jena, took over the company in 1970 and managed it for another two years until it was expropriated and turned into a "people's company." During the remaining years before the opening of Eastern Europe, Hans-Jürgen Mühle was responsible for the distribution of VEB Glashütter Uhrenbetriebe's products, even becoming one of its managing directors until 1992.

Only two years later he founded Nautische Instrumente Mühle-Glashütte: like the family's previous generations, Mühle and his son Thilo took matters into their own hands and began producing ship's chronometers and electronic ship clock systems. In 1996, the entrepreneur also began making wristwatches, and today this genuine Glashütte family business has established itself in the industry with high-quality wristwatches and thirty-four employees. Last year, Mühle set up a new company in Glashütte in cooperation with the Swiss movement maker Sellita Watch Co. SA; GUROFA GmbH began operation the same year. Now in Glashütte, GUROFA manufactures additional precision products and components—among others for Nautische Instrumente Mühle-Glashütte.

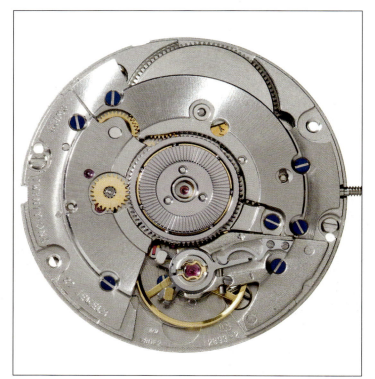

Mühle's base collection comprises business, technical, sports, and nautical lines with various high-quality watch models. Every year, the Saxon firm develops new models that feature the same characteristics all Mühle watches do: precision and purist design.

The success of these Glashütte watchmakers cannot only be ascribed to the great credibility of their products; this company also often works with select target audiences in developing and testing new products. For the S.A.R. Rescue-Timer, for example, it cooperated with the DGzRS (Deutsche Gesellschaft zur Rettung Schiffbrüchiger, or the German Sea Rescue Service). The captains of these rescue ships are outfitted with S.A.R. Rescue-Timers and continuously report their experiences to the Glashütte watchmakers.

This company's passionate ties to its Saxon home represent the continuity within its turbulent history. For this reason, it offers room for numerous internships for beginning watchmakers and those aspiring to be. Additionally, Thilo Mühle makes sure that via sports sponsoring the region remains attractive for vacationers and weekend warriors.

Mühle Glashütte

Business Dame
Reference number: M1-36-06-LB
Movement: automatic, ETA Caliber 2824-2; ø 25.6 mm, height 4.6 mm; 25 jewels; 28,800 vph; Mühle special finish
Functions: hours, minutes, sweep seconds; date
Case: stainless steel, ø 34.2 mm, height 9.2 mm; sapphire crystal; transparent case back; screw-in crown
Band: reptile skin, double folding clasp
Price: $1,499

Mercurius
Reference number: M1-24-25-LB
Movement: automatic, ETA Caliber 2824-2; ø 25.6 mm, height 4.6 mm; 25 jewels; 28,800 vph; Mühle special finish
Functions: hours, minutes, sweep seconds; date
Case: stainless steel, ø 38.5 mm, height 10.4 mm; sapphire crystal; transparent case back; screw-in crown; water-resistant to 10 atm
Band: reptile skin, double folding clasp
Price: $1,090
Variations: stainless steel bracelet; with blue or black dial

Teutonia II Chronograph
Reference number: M1-30-95-LB
Movement: automatic, ETA Valjoux Caliber 7750; ø 30 mm, height 7.9 mm; 25 jewels; 28,800 vph; Mühle special finish
Functions: hours, minutes, subsidiary seconds; chronograph; date, weekday
Case: stainless steel, ø 42 mm, height 15.5 mm; sapphire crystal; transparent case back; water-resistant to 10 atm
Band: reptile skin, double folding clasp
Price: $3,100
Variations: stainless steel bracelet

Quadrant
Reference number: M1-30-35-LB
Movement: automatic, ETA Caliber 2895; ø 25.6 mm, height 4.35 mm; 30 jewels; 28,800 vph; Mühle special finish; in-house woodpecker-neck regulation
Functions: hours, minutes, subsidiary seconds; date
Case: stainless steel, 38 x 38 mm, height 10.5 mm; sapphire crystal; transparent case back; water-resistant to 10 atm
Band: reptile skin, double folding clasp
Price: $2,690
Variations: black dial

S.A.R. Rescue-Timer
Reference number: M1-41-03-KB
Movement: automatic, ETA Caliber 2824-2; ø 25.6 mm, height 4.6 mm; 25 jewels; 28,800 vph; Mühle special finish
Functions: hours, minutes, sweep seconds; date
Case: stainless steel, ø 42 mm, height 13.5 mm; rubber-coated bezel; extra-thick sapphire crystal (extra-thick at 4 mm); screw-in crown; water-resistant to 100 atm
Band: rubber, spring buckle
Price: $1,795
Variations: stainless steel bracelet

Pilot 4
Reference number: M1-35-33-LB
Movement: automatic, ETA Caliber 2824-2; ø 25.6 mm, height 4.6 mm; 25 jewels; 28,800 vph; Mühle special finish
Functions: hours, minutes, sweep seconds; date
Case: stainless steel, ø 42 mm, height 11.1 mm; bezel with 60-minute divisions under crystal, bidirectionally rotating via crown; sapphire crystal; transparent case back; water-resistant to 10 atm
Band: leather, double buckle
Price: $2,195

Metior
Reference number: M1-26-51-MB
Movement: automatic, ETA Caliber 2824-2; ø 25.6 mm, height 4.6 mm; 25 jewels; 28,800 vph; Mühle special finish
Functions: hours, minutes, sweep seconds; date
Case: stainless steel, ø 37.6 mm, height 10.9 mm; sapphire crystal; transparent case back; screw-in crown; water-resistant to 10 atm
Band: stainless steel, folding clasp
Price: $899

Passagier II
Reference number: M1-36-27-LB
Movement: automatic, ETA Caliber 2824-2; ø 25.6 mm, height 4.6 mm; 25 jewels; 28,800 vph; Mühle special finish
Functions: hours, minutes, sweep seconds; date
Case: stainless steel, ø 42 mm, height 10.5 mm; sapphire crystal; transparent case back; screw-in crown
Band: reptile skin, double folding clasp
Price: $1,875

Franck Muller

Vartan Sirmakes

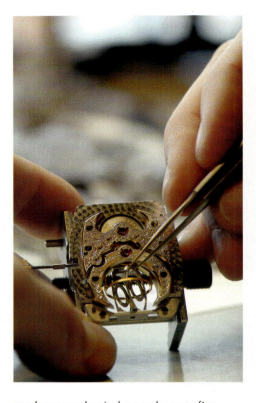

Franck Muller has been hailed since 1986 as one of the most creative minds of the wristwatch industry. It was in that year that the young master watchmaker sealed his legacy by being the first to add a tourbillon to a wristwatch—which he did for one of the industry's most reputable brands. Though that was a feat in itself, Muller has continued to astound the watch world in the ensuing years with complication upon complication—combining elements that no one had yet thought to unite in a wristwatch. Thanks to this, he has garnered a reputation as the "master of complications." Then Muller met Vartan Sirmakes, a man born into a jeweler's family who specialized in making watch cases. It wasn't long before Sirmakes and Muller put their heads together, creating what is now on the way to becoming one of the watch industry's supergroups. The Franck Muller brand's success has been without a doubt the result of clever model policies paired with a feel for shapes, colors, and surfaces—powered by Muller's legendary technical genius.

While the brand's namesake has retired from daily matters for the most part, the person who made it possible for the young watchmaker Franck Muller to find his way into big business in the first place has now stepped into the foreground: Vartan Sirmakes. Things that have not been widely communicated until now include the fact that the Franck Muller Group, founded in 1997, employs 880 people and owns outright or the majority of thirteen companies, including a total of six watch brands. Over the last five years, the Franck Muller group has created the Pierre Kunz brand, bought the European Company Watch (ECW), and purchased the majority in both the Parisian brand Barthelay and the Swiss design marque Rodolphe. In November 2005, the Franck Muller Group inaugurated a new watch brand combining the expertise of top diamond supplier Backes & Strauss with Watchland's horological know-how. And perhaps the most surprising news of 2007 has been the announcement of the Franck Muller Group's purchase of 51 percent of German master watchmaker Martin Braun. Technocase, Sirmakes's former main company, produces watch cases and sapphire crystals in Geneva's industrial suburb Plan-les-Ouates with 130 employees. GecoH in Meyrin manufactures crowns, small parts, and metal link bracelets with fifty employees and is now building a department for hand production. Dials come from Linder in Les Bois (more than fifty employees), and wheels, pinions, balances, and plates are supplied by Pignons Juracie SA in Lajoux with something like twenty employees. With all this combined expertise, it is no wonder that the Franck Muller brand produces mechanical marvels year after year. The group's 2007 spring exhibition, WPHH, was perhaps the best illustration of this yet. Alongside an array of tourbillons and other fun complications, Franck Muller presented the evolution of last year's Aeternitas. Raising the bar—and the size—for years to come, Aeternitas Mega will keep perfect track of the calendar for the next 1,000 years, chiming out the hours, quarter hours, and minutes along the way on its Westminster carillon.

Franck Muller

Aeternitas Mega 1
Reference number: 8888
Movement: automatic, FM Caliber; 33.8 x 40.8 mm; height 7 mm; one-minute tourbillon; modular movement design; micro rotor, twin spring barrels; power reserve 4 days
Functions: hours, minutes; minute repeater with grande and petite sonnerie (Westminster chime); power reserve indication for movement and repeater mechanism
Case: platinum; 42 x 59.9 mm, height 16 mm; sapphire crystal; transparent case back
Band: reptile skin, double folding clasp
Price: upon request

Aeternitas Mega 2
Reference number: 8888
Movement: automatic, FM Caliber; 33.8 x 40.8 mm; one-minute tourbillon; modular movement design; micro rotor, twin spring barrels; power reserve 4 days
Functions: hours, minutes; split-seconds chronograph; minute repeater with grande and petite sonnerie (Westminster chime); power reserve indication for movement and repeater mechanism
Case: platinum; 42 x 59.9 mm, height 16 mm; sapphire crystal; transparent case back
Band: reptile skin, double folding clasp
Price: upon request

Aeternitas Mega 3
Reference number: 8888
Movement: automatic, FM Caliber; 33.8 x 40.8 mm; one-minute tourbillon; micro rotor, twin spring barrels; power reserve 4 days
Functions: hours, minutes; split-seconds chronograph; perpetual secular calendar with date (retrograde), weekday, month (retrograde), moon phase, year, leap year; second and third time zones (24-hour display); equation of time; minute repeater with grande and petite sonnerie (Westminster chime); power reserve indication for movement and repeater mechanism
Case: platinum; 42 x 60.9 mm, height 18.8 mm; sapphire crystal; transparent case back
Band: reptile skin, double folding clasp
Price: upon request

Aeternitas Mega 4
Reference number: 8888
Movement: automatic, FM Caliber; 33.8 x 40.8 mm, height 13 mm; one-minute tourbillon; micro rotor, twin spring barrels; power reserve 4 days
Functions: hours, minutes; split-seconds chronograph; perpetual secular calendar with date (retrograde), weekday, month (retrograde), moon phase, year, leap year; second and third time zones (24-hour display); equation of time; minute repeater with grande and petite sonnerie (Westminster chime); power reserve indication for movement and repeater mechanism
Case: platinum; 42 x 61 mm, height 18.8 mm; sapphire crystal; transparent case back
Band: reptile skin, double folding clasp
Price: upon request

Secret Hours
Reference number: 7880 MT2
Movement: automatic; FM Caliber; ø 25.6 mm, height 5.6 mm; 34 jewels; 28,800 vph; when button is pushed, hour and minute hands jump to correct time then go back to resting position at 12 o'clock again when button is let go
Functions: hours, minutes (upon request)
Case: rose gold, 50.3 x 35.9 mm, height 11.5 mm; sapphire crystal
Band: reptile skin, buckle
Price: $27,500
Variations: yellow, white, or red gold

Conquistador Cortez
Reference number: 1000 SC Cortez
Movement: automatic, FM Caliber 2800; ø 25.6 mm, height 3.6 mm; 21 jewels; 28,800 vph
Functions: hours, minutes, sweep seconds; date
Case: rose gold, 41 x 41 mm, height 12.9 mm; sapphire crystal
Band: reptile skin, buckle
Price: $15,000
Variations: yellow gold ($15,000); white gold ($15,000); stainless steel ($8,300); platinum ($23,300)

Cintrée Curvex Quantième Perpétuel
Reference number: 7851 QPE
Movement: automatic, FM Caliber 2800 with module for perpetual calendar with retrograde displays
Functions: hours, minutes, sweep seconds; perpetual calendar with date, weekday, month (retrograde), moon phase, leap year; 24-hour display
Case: white gold, 48.7 x 35.3 mm, height 9.5 mm; sapphire crystal
Band: reptile skin, buckle
Price: $48,300
Variations: rose gold ($48,300); yellow gold ($48,300); platinum ($56,700); stainless steel ($41,700)

Cintrée Curvex Chrono QP Biretrograde
Reference number: 6850 CC QP B
Movement: automatic, FM Caliber 5888 BR; ø 30 mm, height 7.9 mm; 25 jewels (base movement); 28,800 vph; module for perpetual calendar with retrograde displays
Functions: hours, minutes; chronograph; perpetual calendar with date and day (retrograde), month, moon phase, leap year
Case: yellow gold, 47 x 34 mm, height 11.4 mm; sapphire crystal
Band: reptile skin, buckle
Price: $66,800
Variations: white or rose gold ($66,800); platinum ($75,200)

Franck Muller

Cintrée Curvex Master Banker
Reference number: 7880 MBL
Movement: automatic; ø 25.6 mm, height 5.6 mm; 31 jewels; 21,600 vph; finely finished, côtes de Genève
Functions: hours, minutes; second and third time zones, each with 24-hour indication; date; moon phase
Case: platinum, 50.4 x 36 mm, height 11.5 mm; sapphire crystal
Band: reptile skin, buckle
Price: $37,500
Variations: stainless steel ($22,500); yellow, rose, or white gold ($29,200)

Grande Date
Reference number: 8880 S6 GGDT
Movement: automatic; 34 x 30.5 mm, height 5.9 mm; 28,800 vph; finely finished, côtes de Genève
Functions: hours, minutes, subsidiary seconds; large date, weekday (retrograde), month
Case: white gold, 39.6 x 55.4 mm, height 11.8 mm; sapphire crystal
Band: reptile skin, buckle
Price: $29,800
Variations: yellow or rose gold ($29,800); stainless steel ($26,800); platinum ($38,200)

Long Island Tourbillon
Reference number: 1200 T
Movement: manually wound, FM Caliber 2001; 22.9 x 30.6 mm, height 5.3 mm; one-minute tourbillon
Functions: hours, minutes, subsidiary seconds (on tourbillon cage)
Case: white gold, 45 x 32.4 mm, height 11 mm; sapphire crystal
Band: reptile skin, buckle
Price: $100,000
Variations: yellow or rose gold ($100,000); platinum ($103,800)

Long Island Chronograph
Reference number: 1200 CC AT
Movement: automatic, FM Caliber 2094; ø 30 mm, height 7.9 mm; 25 jewels; 28,800 vph; platinum rotor
Functions: hours, minutes, subsidiary seconds; chronograph; date
Case: white gold, 45 x 32.4 mm; sapphire crystal
Band: reptile skin, buckle
Price: $25,000
Variations: yellow or rose gold

Long Island Master Calendar
Reference number: 1200 MCL
Movement: automatic; ø 25.6 mm, height 3.6 mm; 21 jewels (base movement); 28,800 vph; module for complete calendar and moon phase
Functions: hours, minutes; date, weekday, month, moon phase
Case: white gold, 45 x 32.4 mm, height 11 mm; sapphire crystal
Band: reptile skin, buckle
Price: $24,000
Variations: yellow or rose gold; platinum ($34,000)

Long Island
Reference number: 1000 SC
Movement: automatic, FM Caliber 2800; ø 25.6 mm, height 3.6 mm; 21 jewels; 28,800 vph; platinum rotor
Functions: hours, minutes
Case: white gold, 43 x 30.5 mm, height 8.15 mm; sapphire crystal
Band: reptile skin, buckle
Price: $14,000
Variations: rose or yellow gold; platinum ($22,300)

Art Déco
Reference number: 11000 H SC
Movement: automatic; ø 25.6 mm, height 4.4 mm; 26 jewels; 28,800 vph; finely finished with côtes de Genève
Functions: hours, minutes, sweep seconds
Case: white gold, 51.15 x 37.75 mm, height 12.95 mm; sapphire crystal
Band: reptile skin, buckle
Price: $13,500
Variations: rose or yellow gold ($13,500); platinum ($21,800)

Galet
Reference number: 3000 H SC
Movement: automatic; ø 26.2 mm, height 3.8 mm; 25 jewels; 28,800 vph; finely finished with côtes de Genève
Functions: hours, minutes, sweep seconds; date
Case: white gold, 47.15 x 37.7 mm, height 9.8 mm; sapphire crystal
Band: reptile skin, buckle
Price: $12,700
Variations: rose gold ($12,700)

Master Square Diamonds
Reference number: 6002 KSC DT DCD
Movement: automatic, FM Caliber 2800; ø 25.6 mm, height 3.6 mm; 21 jewels; 28,800 vph; platinum rotor
Functions: hours, minutes, sweep seconds; date
Case: white gold, 42.4 x 42.4 mm, height 10.35 mm; bezel and strap lugs set with brilliant-cut diamonds; sapphire crystal
Band: reptile skin, buckle
Price: $56,500

Master Square Color Dreams
Reference number: 6000 H SC
Movement: automatic, FM Caliber 2800; ø 25.6 mm, height 3.6 mm; 21 jewels; 28,800 vph; platinum rotor
Functions: hours, minutes, sweep seconds; date
Case: rose gold, 36.4 x 35.9 mm, height 11.5 mm; sapphire crystal
Band: reptile skin, buckle
Price: $11,700
Variations: white, rose, or yellow gold

Long Island
Reference number: 1000 SCD
Movement: automatic, FM Caliber 2800; ø 25.6 mm, height 3.6 mm; 21 jewels; 28,800 vph; with platinum rotor
Functions: hours, minutes
Case: white gold, 43 x 30.5 mm; bezel and lugs set with brilliant-cut diamonds; sapphire crystal
Band: reptile skin, buckle
Price: $35,700
Variations: stainless steel ($25,000); rose or yellow gold ($35,700); platinum ($44,000)

Long Island Black Magic
Reference number: 1000 SCD
Movement: automatic, FM Caliber 2800; ø 25.6 mm, height 3.6 mm; 21 jewels; 28,800 vph; platinum rotor
Functions: hours, minutes
Case: white gold, blackened, 43 x 30.5 mm, height 8.15 mm; bezel and lugs set with black diamonds; sapphire crystal
Band: reptile skin, buckle
Price: $38,300

Sweet Heart
Reference number: 5000 H SC
Movement: automatic, FM Caliber 0800SC; ø 26.2 mm, height 3.8 mm; 25 jewels; 28,800 vph; finely finished with côtes de Genève
Functions: hours, minutes
Case: white gold, 38.6 x 44.7 mm, height 9.1 mm; sapphire crystal
Band: reptile skin, buckle
Price: $12,700
Variations: platinum ($21,000)

Cintrée Curvex Totally Crazy
Reference number: 7851 CHDT
Movement: automatic, FM Caliber; ø 25.6 mm, height 5.6 mm; 27 jewels; 28,800 vph; special dial train for seemingly arbitrary jumps for hour and date displays
Functions: hours (jump), minutes; date
Case: white gold, 35.3 x 48.7 mm, height 9.4 mm; bezel set with brilliant-cut diamonds; sapphire crystal
Band: reptile skin, buckle
Price: $33,200

Conquistador Lady
Reference number: 8005 LSC O
Movement: automatic, FM Caliber 2600; ø 19.4 mm, height 3.6 mm; 20 jewels; 28,800 vph; platinum rotor
Functions: hours, minutes, sweep seconds; date
Case: stainless steel, 39 x 28 mm; sapphire crystal
Band: stainless steel, folding clasp
Price: $8,300
Variations: in rose, white, or yellow gold with leather strap

Conquistador King Chronograph
Reference number: 8005 CC KING
Movement: automatic, FM Caliber 7002; ø 30 mm, height 7.9 mm; 25 jewels; 28,800 vph
Functions: hours, minutes, subsidiary seconds; chronograph
Case: stainless steel, 56.45 x 40.35 mm; sapphire crystal
Band: stainless steel, folding clasp
Price: $20,700
Variations: yellow or white gold ($33,200); platinum ($44,800)

Ulysse Nardin

One might get the feeling from Ulysse Nardin that its whole concept isn't necessarily to manufacture watches according to ancient traditions. Overhauled, superfluous technology and components of questionable modern utilization such as gold chatons for bearings and swan-neck fine adjustments are elements one can search for forever at Ulysse Nardin without finding a single example.

Owner Rolf Schnyder and vice president Pierre Gygax tend more toward substantial progress in the movement technology used today—which may well be 250 years old. One of the most exceptional characteristics of the company's Freak concept watch is the Dual Direct Escapement it premiered, comprising two silicon wheels and an alternator, which transforms the rotation of the gear train into pendulum motion and passes it on to the balance.

After this escapement was reworked to the company's full satisfaction, it was recently introduced in automatic Caliber 160—a movement created for the company's 160th anniversary. After experiments with aluminum and a nickel-phosphorus alloy, Ulysse Nardin's technicians have returned to plasma silicon as the preferred material for escape wheels, also slightly modifying the shape of these wheels. Today, the Dual Direct Escapement achieves rate results that satisfy even Switzerland's official chronometer testing facility, the C.O.S.C. More than 200 movements outfitted with this exclusive escapement have already been certified by that organization.

The research and development department headed up by Gygax has experimented with materials in the last few years that would have been thought impossible for use in a watch movement before—in cooperation with universities and other research institutes.

With the InnoVision mechanism introduced in the fall of 2007, Ulysse Nardin has come very close to the ideal of a maintenance and lubrication-free mechanical movement. Its spring barrel revolves on a (nonlubricated) ball bearing with better performance both radially and axially, reducing friction at the same time. The Dual Ulysse Escapement is a subgroup component that Ulysse Nardin can manufacture in silicon, nickel-phosphorus, diamond, or diamond-coated silicon (DCS) according to what is needed.

Particularly strong bridges are crafted in a unique combination comprising a silicon core and nickel coating, and the balance's shock protection is even made of a single piece of silicon. This Silishock shock absorber takes on the functions of spring, bearing jewel, and endstone all in one. The ends of the balance staff revolve directly in a groove in the middle of the silicon disk. The outer part of this disk, shaped like a spring, is elastic and absorbs the shock.

Traditional jewel bearings have been taken completely out of the picture: the wheel axes revolve in precision drillings directly in the silicon bridge. This innovation is of great importance for the watch industry since this technology will certainly soon be used in conventional movement design. The precision of the bearing drillings' positioning is five times as exact on these silicon bridges as on traditional drilled brass bridges containing pressed bearing jewels. Additionally, the movement designer is no longer limited by the large diameter of a ruby and can position the bearing drillings much closer to the edge of a bridge if desired.

The future of the mechanical watch has now begun.

Ulysse Nardin

Freak DIAMonSIL
Reference number: 029-89
Movement: manually wound, Ulysse Nardin Caliber UN 200; ø 31 mm; 28 jewels; 28,800 vph; karussel tourbillon with patented escapement; escapement wheels made of new mixture of silicon and synthetic diamond, lubrication-free; escapement serves as hands; time setting via bezel; winding on case back; power reserve seven days
Functions: hours, minutes
Case: platinum, ø 44.5 mm, height 12.5 mm; sapphire crystal; transparent case back
Band: crocodile skin, double folding clasp
Remarks: limited edition of 28 pieces
Price: $95,000

Anniversary 160
Reference number: 1602-100
Movement: automatic, Ulysse Nardin Caliber UN 160; ø 30.2 mm, height 4.8 mm; 52 jewels; 28,800 vph; new escapement with escape wheels made of silicon; officially certified C.O.S.C. chronometer
Functions: hours, minutes, subsidiary seconds; large date
Case: red gold, 43 x 40.5 mm, height 12.7 mm; sapphire crystal; transparent case back
Band: crocodile skin, double folding clasp
Remarks: limited edition of 500 pieces; anniversary watch for 160 years of Ulysse Nardin
Price: $24,800

Macho
Reference number: 278-70/609
Movement: automatic, Ulysse Nardin Caliber UN 27 (base ETA 2892); ø 25.6 mm, height 5.1 mm; 28 jewels; 28,800 vph; officially certified C.O.S.C. chronometer
Functions: hours, minutes, subsidiary seconds; date; power reserve display
Case: palladium, 43 x 40.5 mm, height 13 mm; sapphire crystal; transparent case back; screw-in crown; water-resistant to 5 atm
Band: crocodile skin, double folding clasp
Remarks: power reserve designed as on a Ulysse Nardin pocket watch from 1912
Price: $19,800
Variations: diverse dial variations

Maxi Marine Diver Limited Edition
Reference number: 260-32-3A
Movement: automatic, Ulysse Nardin Caliber UN 26 (base ETA 2892); ø 25.6 mm, height 5.1 mm; 28 jewels; 28,800 vph; officially certified C.O.S.C. chronometer; white gold rotor
Functions: hours, minutes, subsidiary seconds; date; power reserve display
Case: white gold, ø 42.7 mm, height 11 mm; unidirectionally rotating bezel with 60-minute divisions; sapphire crystal; screw-in crown; water-resistant to 20 atm
Band: rubber/white gold, folding clasp
Remarks: limited edition of 500 pieces
Price: $24,800
Variations: white gold bracelet

Maxi Marine Diver Chronometer
Reference number: 263-33-3/97
Movement: automatic, Ulysse Nardin Caliber UN 26 (base ETA 2892); ø 25.6 mm, height 5.1 mm; 28 jewels; 28,800 vph; officially certified C.O.S.C. chronometer
Functions: hours, minutes, subsidiary seconds; date; power reserve display
Case: stainless steel, ø 42.7 mm, height 12 mm; unidirectionally rotating bezel with 60-minute divisions; sapphire crystal; screw-in crown; water-resistant to 30 atm
Band: rubber, double folding clasp
Price: $5,950
Variations: also available in 40 mm case size

Maxi Marine Chronometer
Reference number: 266-66/62
Movement: automatic, Ulysse Nardin Caliber UN 26 (base ETA 2892); ø 25.6 mm, height 5.1 mm; 28 jewels; 28,800 vph; officially certified C.O.S.C. chronometer
Functions: hours, minutes, subsidiary seconds; date; power reserve display
Case: red gold, ø 41 mm, height 12 mm; sapphire crystal; screw-in crown; water-resistant to 20 atm
Band: crocodile skin, folding clasp
Price: $15,900
Variations: rubber strap

Maxi Marine Chronometer 43 mm
Reference number: 263-67/43
Movement: automatic, Ulysse Nardin Caliber UN 26 (base ETA 2892); ø 25.6 mm, height 5.1 mm; 28 jewels; 28,800 vph; officially certified C.O.S.C. chronometer
Functions: hours, minutes, subsidiary seconds; date; power reserve display
Case: red gold, ø 43 mm, height 12 mm; sapphire crystal; screw-in crown; water-resistant to 20 atm
Band: reptile skin, folding clasp
Price: $19,800
Variations: rubber strap or gold bracelet

Maxi Marine Chronograph
Reference number: 353-66/323
Movement: automatic, Ulysse Nardin Caliber UN 26 (base ETA 2892 with module by Dubois Dépraz); ø 25.6 mm, height 5.1 mm; 28 jewels; 28,800 vph; exclusive 45-minute counter
Functions: hours, minutes, subsidiary seconds; chronograph; date
Case: stainless steel, ø 41 mm, height 12 mm; sapphire crystal; screw-in crown and buttons; water-resistant to 20 atm
Band: crocodile skin, folding clasp
Price: $6,260
Variations: rubber strap; red gold

Ulysse Nardin

Maxi Dual Time 42 mm
Reference number: 246-55/32
Movement: automatic, Ulysse Nardin Caliber UN 27 (base ETA 2892); ø 25.6 mm, height 5.35 mm; 23 jewels; 28,800 vph
Functions: hours, minutes, subsidiary seconds; large date; 24-hour display (second time zone)
Case: rose gold, ø 42 mm, height 11.8 mm; sapphire crystal; transparent case back; screw-in crown; water-resistant to 10 atm
Band: crocodile skin, double folding clasp
Price: $16,800
Variations: in various dial variations

Perpetual Calendar GMT+/-
Reference number: 322-66/91
Movement: automatic, Ulysse Nardin Caliber UN 32; ø 31 mm, height 6.95 mm; 34 jewels; 28,800 vph; perpetual calendar mechanism (settable forward and backward); patented large date and mechanism for quick-setting the hour hand; officially certified C.O.S.C. chronometer
Functions: hours, minutes, subsidiary seconds; perpetual calendar with large date, weekday, month, year; second time zone
Case: red gold, ø 42 mm, height 13 mm; sapphire crystal; transparent case back
Band: crocodile skin, double folding clasp
Price: $41,800

Sonata Cathedral
Reference number: 676-88
Movement: automatic, Ulysse Nardin Caliber UN 66; ø 34 mm, height 7.2 mm; 109 jewels; 28,800 vph; 24-hour mechanism that precludes mistaking 7:35 am for 7:35 pm; countdown display of alarm time, settable to the minute; large date settable backward and forward by crown
Functions: hours, minutes, subsidiary seconds; alarm with gong, second time zone, large date, countdown/alarm time
Case: red gold, ø 42 mm, height 13 mm; sapphire crystal
Band: crocodile skin, folding clasp
Price: $47,800

Royal Blue Tourbillon
Reference number: 799-80
Movement: manually wound, Ulysse Nardin Caliber UN 74; ø 31 mm, height 7.2 mm; 28 jewels; 28,800 vph; flying tourbillon with large sapphire endstone, circular winding mechanism, 130 hours power reserve, sapphire crystal plates
Functions: hours, minutes
Case: platinum, ø 41 mm, height 13.5 mm; sapphire crystal; transparent case back
Band: crocodile skin, folding clasp
Remarks: limited edition of 99 pieces
Price: $218,000

Triple Jack Jacquemarts Minute Repeater
Reference number: 736-61/E2
Movement: manually wound, Ulysse Nardin Caliber UN 73
Functions: hours, minutes; hour, quarter hour, and minute repeater
Case: red gold, ø 42 mm, height 11 mm; sapphire crystal; transparent case back
Band: crocodile skin, folding clasp
Remarks: onyx dial; limited edition of 50 pieces
Price: $275,000

San Marco Hour Strike
Reference number: 756-88/E2
Movement: manually wound, Ulysse Nardin Caliber UN 75; hour and half-hour strike
Functions: hours, minutes; function display
Case: red gold, ø 42 mm, height 11 mm; sapphire crystal; transparent case back
Band: crocodile skin, folding clasp
Remarks: onyx dial
Price: $78,000

Michelangelo UTC
Reference number: 223-68-7
Movement: automatic, Ulysse Nardin Caliber UN 22 (base ETA 2892); ø 25.6 mm, height 5.35 mm; 23 jewels; 28,800 vph
Functions: hours, minutes, sweep seconds; large date; 24-hour display (second time zone)
Case: stainless steel, 38 x 43 mm, height 15 mm; sapphire crystal; transparent case back; screw-in crown; water-resistant to 10 atm
Band: stainless steel, double folding clasp
Price: $6,400

Michelangelo Gigante Chronometer
Reference number: 273-68/421
Movement: automatic, Ulysse Nardin Caliber UN 27 (base ETA 2892); ø 25.6 mm, height 5.1 mm; 28 jewels; 28,800 vph; officially certified C.O.S.C. chronometer
Functions: hours, minutes, subsidiary seconds; date; power reserve display
Case: stainless steel, 38 x 43 mm, height 15 mm; sapphire crystal; screw-in crown; water-resistant to 5 atm
Band: reptile skin, folding clasp
Price: $5,950

Ulysse Nardin

Ulysse I
Reference number: 272-81
Movement: automatic, Ulysse Nardin Caliber UN 27 (base ETA 2892); ø 25.6 mm, height 5.1 mm; 28 jewels; 28,800 vph; officially certified C.O.S.C. chronometer
Functions: hours, minutes, subsidiary seconds; date; power reserve display
Case: stainless steel, ø 40 mm, height 13 mm; sapphire crystal; screw-in crown; water-resistant to 5 atm
Band: reptile skin, folding clasp
Price: $11,900

San Marco Chronometer
Reference number: 133-72-9-7/E3
Movement: automatic, Ulysse Nardin Caliber UN 13 (base ETA 2892); ø 25.6 mm, height 3.6 mm; 28 jewels; 28,800 vph; officially certified C.O.S.C. chronometer
Functions: hours, minutes, sweep seconds; date
Case: stainless steel, ø 37 mm, height 11 mm; sapphire crystal
Band: stainless steel, double folding clasp
Price: $5,600

San Marco Cloisonné
Reference number: 139-10/FLC
Movement: automatic, Ulysse Nardin Caliber UN 13 (base ETA 2892); ø 25.6 mm, height 3.6 mm; 28 jewels; 28,800 vph; officially certified C.O.S.C. chronometer
Functions: hours, minutes, sweep seconds
Case: platinum, ø 40 mm, height 11 mm; sapphire crystal
Band: reptile skin, buckle
Remarks: cloisonné enamel dial; limited edition of 30 pieces
Price: $36,900

Quadrato Dual Time
Reference number: 246-92/600
Movement: automatic, Ulysse Nardin Caliber UN 24 (base ETA 2892); ø 25.6 mm, height 5.35 mm; 23 jewels; 28,800 vph
Functions: hours, minutes, subsidiary seconds; large date; 24-hour display (second time zone)
Case: red gold, 42 x 42 mm, height 13 mm; sapphire crystal; transparent case back; water-resistant to 5 atm
Band: crocodile skin, folding clasp
Price: $22,800

Quadrato Dual Time Perpetual Calendar
Reference number: 320-90/69
Movement: automatic, Ulysse Nardin Caliber UN 32; ø 31.mm, height 6.95 mm; 34 jewels; 28,800 vph; perpetual calendar mechanism (settable forward and backward); patented large date and mechanism for quick-setting the hour hand; officially certified C.O.S.C. chronometer
Functions: hours, minutes, subsidiary seconds; perpetual calendar with large date, weekday, month, year; 24-hour display (second time zone)
Case: white gold, 42 x 42 mm, height 12.7 mm; sapphire crystal; transparent case back; water-resistant to 5 atm
Band: crocodile skin, double folding clasp
Price: $22,800

Caprice
Reference number: 136-91AC/695
Movement: automatic, Ulysse Nardin Caliber UN 13 (base ETA 2892); ø 25.6 mm, height 3.6 mm; 28 jewels; 28,800 vph; gold rotor set with diamonds
Functions: hours, minutes; date
Case: red gold, height 9 mm; bezel and strap lugs set with diamonds; sapphire crystal; transparent case back; water-resistant to 5 atm
Band: satin, folding clasp
Remarks: mother-of-pearl dial
Price: $24,300

Dual Time Lady
Reference number: 243-22B/391
Movement: automatic, Ulysse Nardin Caliber UN 24 (base ETA 2892); ø 25.6 mm, height 5.35 mm; 23 jewels; 28,800 vph
Functions: hours, minutes, sweep seconds; large date; 24-hour display (second time zone)
Case: stainless steel, ø 37 mm, height 13 mm; bezel set with diamonds; sapphire crystal; transparent case back; water-resistant to 10 atm
Band: crocodile skin, folding clasp
Remarks: mother-of-pearl dial
Price: $10,100

Lady Diver
Reference number: 8106-101E-3C/10
Movement: automatic, Ulysse Nardin Caliber UN 810; officially certified C.O.S.C. chronometer; rotor set with diamonds
Functions: hours, minutes, sweep seconds; date
Case: red gold, ø 40 mm, height 11.8 mm; bezel and strap lugs set with diamonds; sapphire crystal; transparent case back; water-resistant to 10 atm
Band: rubber with gold elements, folding clasp
Remarks: mother-of-pearl dial with diamond markers
Price: $20,800

Rainer Nienaber

Rainer Nienaber, born in 1955, learned the trade of toolmaker in a company that specialized in cameras and precision measuring technology. Since electronics had not yet become popular in all areas of this fine technology at that time, Nienaber experienced the world of precision production as a craftsman, and his favorite measurement was to become the thousandth of a millimeter.

Beginning with the repair of watches, he quickly developed into a designer of timepieces, thoroughly enjoying the construction and finishing of his ticking friends. From there, it was just a small step to becoming a producer himself, and it was only a matter of time before Nienaber began to design wristwatches. The handcrafted precision regulators he builds are known far beyond the borders of Germany and are very well received by collectors. Nienaber designed his King Size Regulator for the wrist to follow in the footsteps of his clocks, using dial visuals that are extremely loyal to those of the larger timepieces. Since there is no wristwatch movement in existence that features subsidiary seconds at 12 o'clock, however, he correspondingly rebuilt an old manually wound AS movement and can now proudly present the world's first and only wrist regulator with the "correct" dial divisions. Despite his love of traditional watch complications, Nienaber also experiments with uncommon displays. His RetroLator, for example, combines an unusual regulator display with a retrograde minute indicator—this mix making for a real eye-catcher.

To celebrate twenty years of watchmaking, Nienaber moved into a new workshop in 2004, that of a former carriage maker, completely renovated. Then the watchmaker, located in Bünde, Germany, celebrated his fiftieth birthday in 2005 with his most wonderful complication in a solid rose gold case.

After completing his retrograde trio with watches that display either the hours, minutes, or seconds in this manner, it seemed like a no-brainer to Nienaber to make a timepiece to include three retrograde hands. The result—the Tri-Retrograde—is exceptional in the world of horology.

Tri-Retrograde
Movement: manually wound, base ETA Unitas Caliber 6498; ø 36.8 mm, height 4.5 mm; 17 jewels; 21,600 vph; dial train modification for retrograde hours, minutes, and seconds; finely finished movements with côtes de Genève
Functions: hours, minutes, subsidiary seconds (all retrograde)
Case: yellow gold, ø 44 mm, height 13.5 mm; sapphire crystal; transparent case back
Band: reptile skin, buckle
Price: 27,000 euros
Variations: stainless steel (18,000 euros); stainless steel/gold (19,800 euros)

Golden Complication Retrograde Hours
Movement: manually wound, base AS Caliber 1130; ø 29 mm, height 4 mm; 17 jewels; 18,000 vph; dial train modification for retrograde hours, three additional jewels; finely finished movements with côtes de Genève
Functions: hours (retrograde), minutes, subsidiary seconds
Case: yellow gold, ø 43 mm, height 10 mm; strap lugs set with diamonds; sapphire crystal; transparent case back
Band: reptile skin, buckle
Price: 11,500 euros
Variations: without diamonds (10,000 euros); stainless steel (2,900 euros); stainless steel/gold (3,400 euros)

Golden Complication RetroLator
Movement: manually wound, base AS Caliber 1130; ø 29 mm, height 4 mm; 17 jewels; 18,000 vph; dial train modification for retrograde minute hand and precisely jumping hour hand, four additional jewels; finely finished movements with côtes de Genève
Functions: hours (retrograde), minutes (retrograde), subsidiary seconds
Case: yellow gold, ø 43 mm, height 10 mm; sapphire crystal; transparent case back
Band: reptile skin, buckle
Price: 12,000 euros
Variations: stainless steel (3,700 euros); stainless steel/gold (4,200 euros)

King Size Retrograde Seconds
Movement: manually wound, base AS Caliber 1130; ø 29 mm, height 4 mm; 17 jewels; 18,000 vph; dial train modification for retrograde minutes; finely finished movements with côtes de Genève
Functions: hours, minutes, subsidiary seconds (retrograde)
Case: stainless steel, ø 41 mm, height 10 mm; sapphire crystal; transparent case back
Band: reptile skin, double folding clasp
Price: 6,300 euros
Variations: in gold with 43 mm case size (13,300 euros); stainless steel/gold (6,800 euros)

Nivrel

Nivrel's owner, Gerd Hofer, who has added the tagline "since 1936" to his label, explains quite frankly how he called the Fédération de l'Industrie Horlogère Suisse ten years ago during his search for a "good" brand name for his newly founded watch business, Time Art GmbH. Stored there "temporarily" are countless names of Swiss watchmakers that have disappeared from the market until an interested party acquires and reactivates them. Hofer resurrected the name Nivrel, plain and simple, without any history, without any sort of background information on the firm—without even a logo.

Nivrel's watches themselves are also crafted with openness and honesty: Everything that looks like gold actually is gold, usually 18-karat. The crystals are always made of synthetic sapphire, and if the hour indicators are raised, then they are most certainly applied to the dial—never just stamped. The watch movements are beautifully finished, and the rings that secure them to the cases, as one would expect, are made of metal instead of plastic. Hofer's credo: "Attention to quality in the details shouldn't drive up the costs so high that one could justify poorer craftsmanship."

This is quite a remarkable statement, as there are simpler mechanical watches by Nivrel that can be easily acquired for a small amount of money. And extras, such as large date, moon phase, and various other calendar features, can be had for a very moderate price. This is made possible, on the one hand, by a modular system, in which a relatively modest number of movements and case types are varied to produce a wide range of very attractive models. On the other hand, Hofer consistently works with first-class suppliers as opposed to maintaining expensive internal development and production departments.

The ideas for his watches, however, come only from Hofer himself. "The idea is what counts," he says. And after looking over his current collection it becomes clear that he is not only a good businessman.

White Tiger
Reference number: N 950.001 RKS7K-NTT
Movement: automatic, Nivrel Caliber D87 (base ETA 2892-A2 with repeater module by Dubois Dépraz); ø 25.6 mm, height 3.6 mm (base movement); 21 jewels; 28,800 vph; completely skeletonized and hand-engraved; individual components galvanized black
Functions: hours, minutes; five-minute repeater
Case: rose gold, ø 42 mm, height 15 mm; sapphire crystal; transparent case back
Band: reptile skin, buckle
Remarks: unique silver dial with relief engraving of a tiger in the jungle and brilliant-cut diamonds as hour markers
Price: $43,200

Le Carré
Reference number: N 111.001 AAWFD
Movement: automatic, ETA Caliber 2892-A2; ø 25.6 mm, height 3.6 mm; 21 jewels; 28,800 vph
Functions: hours, minutes, sweep seconds; date
Case: stainless steel, 41 x 32 mm, height 9 mm; sapphire crystal; water-resistant to 5 atm
Band: stainless steel, folding clasp
Price: $900

Anniversary Watch
Reference number: N 125.020 AASDS
Movement: automatic, ETA Caliber 2824-2; ø 25.6 mm, height 4.6 mm; 25 jewels; 28,800 vph
Functions: hours, minutes, sweep seconds; date
Case: stainless steel, ø 40 mm, height 10.7 mm; sapphire crystal; transparent case back; water-resistant to 10 atm
Band: leather, buckle
Price: $600

Wild Sea
Reference number: N 541.001
Movement: automatic, ETA Valjoux Caliber 7750; ø 30 mm, height 7.9 mm; 25 jewels; 28,800 vph
Functions: hours, minutes, subsidiary seconds; date; chronograph
Case: stainless steel, ø 42 mm, height 16.8 mm; unidirectionally rotating bezel with 60-minute divisions; sapphire crystal; screw-in crown and buttons; water-resistant to 100 atm
Band: stainless steel, folding clasp with wetsuit extension
Price: $1,550

Nomos

There are very few companies who can successfully do what Nomos has achieved in the last eighteen months. This company set a course from *haute horlogerie* to a watch for the common man and back to a full collection of uncommon ladies watches—nothing short of awe-inspiring. This shouldn't be too surprising, however, for Nomos is one of the most uncommon companies to be found in the mid- to high-end watch segment. And to prove it, Nomos is currently opening a new nightclub in Glashütte. The "Club," as it is currently known, coincides with Nomos's first really new watch design since its inception in 1991.

The Club timepiece was created because Nomos's owner and creative head Roland Schwertner was interested in making a watch that younger people could afford and enjoy without it having to be battery-driven or plastic. "These are post-puberty, really adult-looking watches that will last one's whole life through. They can continue to be worn long after its wearer is out of college," Nomos's spokesperson Claudia Hoffmann explains. "But they aren't as staid or old-fashioned as some other timepieces available out there on the mechanical market."

These are not watches for people concerned with status symbols, but they are for people concerned with their appearance. And—not to be forgotten—they contain a *manufacture* caliber, something no other watch under $1,000 can boast. Additionally, try finding another watch outfitted with a Shell Cordovan strap, a domed sapphire crystal, and such a timeless design somewhere else at this price.

From the Club watch to *haute horlogerie*: let it not be forgotten that Nomos also masterminded the handmade Wempe masterpieces introduced in 2006. Nomos movement designer Thierry Albert conceived his series of twenty-five tourbillons literally as unique handmade pieces. It took him and master watchmaker Daniel Malchert fourteen weeks alone to manufacture the individual screws. They needed yet another thirty-two weeks to turn the pinions. Only four components in total were manufactured outside of Glashütte: the jewels, mainspring, balance spring, and the escape wheel.

Yet Nomos still had time to complete the final series of automatic movements in 2006's Tangomat and to decidedly redesign the Tetra for the feminine wrist. Sixteen new models of sixteen different colors grace the Tetra^2 collection. The reason is simple: by 1995 every fourth Nomos watch was being purchased by a woman, and by 2005 it was every third. These statistics indeed illustrate that women have a true interest in Nomos's Glashütte-made products. So why not offer them something custom-made? Something that isn't going to go out of style so quickly? Something that was manufactured with much love and passion? And something that will fit for a lifetime? The only trouble for these watches' new owners is going to be deciding which of the unusual colors to choose: liverwort, wild orchid, honeysuckle, daisy, marguerite, pheasant's eye, touch-me-not, speedwell, or possibly medlar?

Nomos

Tangente
Reference number: 101
Movement: manually wound, Nomos Caliber alpha; ø 23.3 mm, height 2.6 mm; 17 jewels; 21,600 vph; three-quarter plate, Glashütte click; movement surfaces rhodium-plated, Glashütte ribbing
Functions: hours, minutes, subsidiary seconds
Case: stainless steel, ø 35 mm, height 6.2 mm; sapphire crystal
Band: Shell Cordovan, buckle
Price: $1,420
Variations: with transparent case back ($1,620); with date display

Tangente Date Power Reserve
Reference number: 131
Movement: manually wound, Nomos Caliber delta; ø 32.15 mm, height 2.8 mm; 23 jewels; 21,600 vph; three-quarter plate, Glashütte click; movement surfaces rhodium-plated, Glashütte ribbing
Functions: hours, minutes, subsidiary seconds; date; power reserve display
Case: stainless steel, ø 35 mm, height 6.6 mm; sapphire crystal; transparent case back
Band: Shell Cordovan, buckle
Price: $2,840
Variations: without date display

Orion
Reference number: 301
Movement: manually wound, Nomos Caliber alpha; ø 23.3 mm, height 2.6 mm; 17 jewels; 21,600 vph; three-quarter plate, Glashütte click; movement surfaces rhodium-plated, Glashütte ribbing
Functions: hours, minutes, subsidiary seconds
Case: stainless steel, ø 35 mm, height 7.25 mm; sapphire crystal, domed
Band: Shell Cordovan, buckle
Price: $1,540
Variations: with domed sapphire crystal case back ($1,860)

Club
Reference number: 701
Movement: manually wound, Nomos Caliber alpha; ø 23.3 mm, height 2.6 mm; 17 jewels; 21,600 vph; three-quarter plate, Glashütte click; movement surfaces rhodium-plated, Glashütte ribbing
Functions: hours, minutes, subsidiary seconds
Case: stainless steel, ø 36 mm, height 8.2 mm; sapphire crystal
Band: Shell Cordovan, buckle
Price: $1,250
Variations: with dark dial

Tetra Gold
Reference number: 411
Movement: manually wound, Nomos Caliber alpha; ø 23.3 mm, height 2.6 mm; 17 jewels; 21,600 vph; three-quarter plate, Glashütte click; movement surfaces rhodium-plated, Glashütte ribbing
Functions: hours, minutes, subsidiary seconds
Case: yellow gold, 27.5 x 27.5 mm, height 6.05 mm; sapphire crystal
Band: Shell Cordovan, buckle
Price: $5,500
Variations: with mocha-colored dial

Tetra Large
Reference number: 408
Movement: manually wound, Nomos Caliber alpha; ø 23.3 mm, height 2.6 mm; 17 jewels; 21,600 vph; three-quarter plate, Glashütte click; movement surfaces rhodium-plated, Glashütte ribbing
Functions: hours, minutes, subsidiary seconds
Case: yellow gold, 29.5 x 29.5 mm, height 6.05 mm; sapphire crystal
Band: Shell Cordovan, buckle
Price: $1,620
Variations: with transparent case back ($1,820); with added power reserve display

Sport Index Date
Movement: manually wound, Nomos Caliber beta; ø 32.15 mm, height 2.8 mm; 23 jewels; 21,600 vph; three-quarter plate, Glashütte click; movement surfaces rhodium-plated, Glashütte ribbing
Functions: hours, minutes, subsidiary seconds; date
Case: stainless steel, ø 36.5 mm, height 7.5 mm; sapphire crystal
Band: Shell Cordovan, buckle
Price: $1,600
Variations: without date display; dial with Arabic numerals

Tangomat Date
Movement: automatic, Nomos Caliber zeta (base Nomos epsilon); ø 31 mm, height 4.3 mm; 26 jewels; 21,600 vph; bilaterally winding movement with rocking bar; three-quarter plate, Glashütte click
Functions: hours, minutes, subsidiary seconds; date
Case: stainless steel, ø 38.3 mm, height 8.2 mm; sapphire crystal; transparent case back
Band: Shell Cordovan, buckle
Price: $3,000
Variations: without date display

Omega

The first genuine new Omega caliber was long awaited with growing anticipation. Since 1999, Omega's watches have been outfitted with an interesting mixture of classic Swiss lever and traditional chronometer escapements. Though this fusion has only been used by Omega, a correspondingly reworked ETA base caliber has had to serve as the foundation technology. Since the serial development and industrial production of it took longer and became more difficult than originally thought, the manufacture of the brand-new coaxial caliber was delayed. This first Omega *manufacture* caliber of the modern era represents a milestone in the company's history. With a diameter of 29 mm (corresponding to 13 lines) and a height of 5.5 mm, Caliber 8500 enjoys rather stately dimensions for an everyday three-handed movement. The freely swinging balance is located under a charmingly curved bridge, shock-protected and not subject to much vibration. The black-colored balance swings at an unusual frequency of 25,200 vph (3.5 Hertz) after the industry standard of 28,800 vph (4 Hertz) turned out to be too fast for the complex motion of the coaxial escapement. Like all coaxial movements, Caliber 8500 is officially C.O.S.C. certified and comes with a chronometer certificate. Two serially operating spring barrels ensure enough energy and a power reserve of 60 hours, their performance enhanced by an inside coating of extra-hard, smooth DLC (diamond-like carbon).

The cutting-edge technology used everywhere in this movement contrasts with its classic, almost arabesque finishing with curved, ray-shaped *côtes de Genève* on the rotor and bridges. The simple red gold finish, which was utilized in the past for the exceptionally precise Omega chronometers, was in a way a trademark—just think of epoch-making Caliber 30 T2, for example.

With an uninterrupted series of more than 6,500 movements that have been successfully tested by the C.O.S.C. since last fall, Caliber 8500 also counts as one of these epochal Omega movements, even without the red gold plating.

The classically designed De Ville case that houses it is transparent on almost all sides thanks to a sapphire crystal ring around its circumference, held in place by two graceful case halves and some screws. There may not be much to see on the edge of a movement's base plate, but the airy nature of this case allows light into the depths of the movement, making the view through the sapphire crystal even more attractive.

Omega

Constellation Double Eagle Co-Axial Ladies Chronograph
Reference number: 121.57.35.50.13.001
Movement: automatic, Omega Caliber 3313 (base Omega 3303); ø 27 mm, height 6.85 mm; 37 jewels; 28,800 vph; co-axial escapement; officially certified chronometer (COSC)
Functions: hours, minutes, subsidiary seconds; date; chronograph
Case: rose gold, ø 35 mm, height 13.61 mm; bezel and case lugs set with diamonds; sapphire crystal; transparent case back; crown set with briolette diamond; water-resistant to 10 atm
Band: rubber, rose gold folding clasp
Price: $21,400
Variations: stainless steel without diamonds; titanium

Constellation Double Eagle Co-Axial Mission Hills Chronograph
Reference number: 121.92.41.50.01.001
Movement: automatic, Omega Caliber 3313 (base Omega 3303); ø 27 mm, height 6.85 mm; 37 jewels; 28,800 vph; co-axial escapement; officially certified chronometer (COSC)
Functions: hours, minutes, subsidiary seconds; date; chronograph
Case: titanium, ø 41 mm, height 13.9 mm; bezel with Roman hour markers; sapphire crystal; water-resistant to 10 atm
Band: rubber, titanium folding clasp
Remarks: carbon fiber dial; special series for Mission Hills World Cup
Price: $6,300

Constellation Double Eagle Co-Axial Chronograph
Reference number: 1619.51.91
Movement: automatic, Omega Caliber 3313 (base Omega 3303); ø 27 mm, height 6.85 mm; 37 jewels; 28,800 vph; co-axial escapement; officially certified chronometer (COSC)
Functions: hours, minutes, subsidiary seconds; date; chronograph
Case: rose gold, ø 41 mm, height 13.9 mm; bezel with Roman hour markers; sapphire crystal; water-resistant to 10 atm
Band: rubber, folding clasp
Price: $14,700
Variations: stainless steel

Constellation Quadro Chrono
Reference number: 113.57.28.70.63.001
Movement: quartz, Omega Caliber 520 (base ETA 251.971)
Functions: hours, minutes, subsidiary seconds; chronograph
Case: rose gold, 34 x 28 mm, height 9.8 mm; bezel set with 34 diamonds; sapphire crystal; sapphire crystal
Band: textile, rose gold folding clasp
Price: $13,200
Variations: stainless steel without diamonds

Seamaster NZL-32
Reference number: 2513.30.00
Movement: automatic, Omega Caliber 3602 C (base Omega 1120 with Dubois Dépraz module 2027); ø 30 mm, height 8 mm; 49 jewels; 28,800 vph; officially certified chronometer (COSC)
Functions: hours, minutes, subsidiary seconds; chronograph; regatta start display
Case: stainless steel, ø 42.2 mm, height 15.6 mm; sapphire crystal; screw-in crown; water-resistant to 15 atm
Band: stainless steel, double folding clasp
Price: $4,400
Variations: rubber strap

Seamaster Diver 300 M James Bond
Reference number: 2220.80.00
Movement: automatic, Omega Caliber 2500 (base Omega 1120); ø 25.6 mm, height 4.1 mm; 27 jewels; 25,200 vph; co-axial escapement; officially certified chronometer (COSC)
Functions: hours, minutes, sweep seconds; date
Case: stainless steel, ø 41 mm, height 12.7 mm; unidirectionally rotating bezel with 60-minute divisions; sapphire crystal; screw-in crown; water-resistant to 30 atm
Band: stainless steel, folding clasp
Remarks: case outfitted with helium valve
Price: $3,050
Variations: various case sizes, colors, and bands

Seamaster Planet Ocean Co-Axial Chronograph
Reference number: 222.62.46.50.01.001
Movement: automatic, Omega Caliber 3313 (base Omega 3303); ø 27 mm, height 6.85 mm; 37 jewels; 28,800 vph; co-axial escapement; column-wheel control of chronograph; officially certified C.O.S.C. chronometer
Functions: hours, minutes, subsidiary seconds; date; chronograph
Case: rose gold, ø 45.5 mm, height 17.3 mm; unidirectionally rotating rose gold bezel with 60-minute divisions; helium valve; sapphire crystal; screw-in crown; water-resistant to 60 atm
Band: rubber, rose gold folding clasp
Price: $16,000
Variations: rose gold link bracelet

Seamaster Planet Ocean Co-Axial Chronograph
Reference number: 22210.50.00
Movement: automatic, Omega Caliber 3313 (base Omega 3303); ø 27 mm, height 6.85 mm; 37 jewels; 28,800 vph; co-axial escapement; column-wheel control of chronograph; officially certified C.O.S.C. chronometer
Functions: hours, minutes, subsidiary seconds; date; chronograph
Case: stainless steel, ø 45.5 mm, height 17.9 mm; unidirectionally rotating bezel with 60-minute divisions; helium valve; sapphire crystal; screw-in crown; water-resistant to 60 atm
Band: stainless steel, folding clasp
Price: $5,560
Variations: orange-colored bezel

Omega

Seamaster Planet Ocean Co-Axial
Reference number: 2208.50.00
Movement: automatic, Omega Caliber 2500 (base Omega 1120); ø 25.6 mm, height 4.1 mm; 27 jewels; 25,200 vph; co-axial escapement; officially certified C.O.S.C. chronometer
Functions: hours, minutes, sweep seconds; date
Case: stainless steel, ø 45.5 mm, height 15 mm; unidirectionally rotating bezel with 60-minute divisions; sapphire crystal; screw-in crown; water-resistant to 60 atm
Band: stainless steel, folding clasp
Remarks: case outfitted with helium valve
Price: $3,400
Variations: black bezel; limited 007 edition with rubber strap

Speedmaster Ladies Diamonds Chronograph
Reference number: 3835.70.36
Movement: automatic, Omega Caliber 3220 (base ETA 2892-A2); ø 30 mm, height 6.5 mm; 47 jewels; 28,800 vph
Functions: hours, minutes, subsidiary seconds; chronograph
Case: stainless steel, ø 35.5 mm, height 12.55 mm; bezel set with 49 diamonds; sapphire crystal; water-resistant to 10 atm
Band: reptile skin, folding clasp
Price: $7,400
Variations: without diamonds; leather strap; various dial variations; stainless steel bracelet

Speedmaster Professional Moonwatch Chronograph Brown
Reference number: 311.30.42.30.13.001
Movement: manually wound, Omega Caliber 1863 (base Lémania 1873); ø 27 mm, height 6.87 mm; 18 jewels; 21,600 vph
Functions: hours, minutes, subsidiary seconds; chronograph
Case: stainless steel, ø 42 mm, height 13.7 mm; bezel with tachymeter scale; sapphire crystal; transparent case back; water-resistant to 5 atm
Band: stainless steel, folding clasp
Price: $4,300
Variations: leather strap

Speedmaster 50th Anniversary Patch
Reference number: 311.30.42.30.01.001
Movement: manually wound, Omega Caliber 1861 (base Lémania 1873); ø 27 mm, height 6.87 mm; 18 jewels; 21,600 vph
Functions: hours, minutes, subsidiary seconds; chronograph
Case: stainless steel, ø 42 mm, height 13.7 mm; bezel with tachymeter scale; sapphire crystal; water-resistant to 5 atm
Band: stainless steel, folding clasp
Remarks: limited edition of 5,957 pieces
Price: $4,000

Speedmaster Professional Moonwatch Co-Axial 50th Anniversary
Reference number: 311.33.42.50.01.001
Movement: manually wound, Omega Caliber 3201; ø 27 mm; 29 jewels; 28,800 vph; co-axial escapement; officially certified C.O.S.C. chronometer
Functions: hours, minutes, subsidiary seconds; chronograph
Case: stainless steel, ø 42 mm, height 12.9 mm; bezel with tachymeter scale; sapphire crystal; screw-in crown; transparent case back; water-resistant to 10 atm
Band: stainless steel, folding clasp
Remarks: limited edition of 1,957 pieces
Price: $9,800
Variations: rose gold; yellow gold; white gold

Speedmaster The Legend Collection Co-Axial
Reference number: 321.30.44.50.01.001
Movement: automatic, Omega Caliber 3313 (base Omega 3303); ø 27 mm, height 6.85 mm; 37 jewels; 28,800 vph; column wheel control of chronograph; certified COSC chronometer
Functions: hours, minutes, subsidiary seconds; chronograph; date
Case: stainless steel, ø 44.25 mm, height 13.55 mm; sapphire crystal; water-resistant to 10 atm
Band: stainless steel, double folding clasp
Price: $5,500
Variations: rubber strap

Speedmaster Co-Axial Broad Arrow Rattrapante
Reference number: 3582.51.00
Movement: automatic, Omega Caliber 3612 (base Omega 3313); ø 27 mm, height 8.45 mm; 38 jewels; 28,800 vph; co-axial escapement; officially certified C.O.S.C. chronometer
Functions: hours, minutes, subsidiary seconds; split-seconds chronograph; date
Case: stainless steel, ø 44.25 mm, height 15.2 mm; bezel with tachymeter scale; sapphire crystal; water-resistant to 10 atm
Band: stainless steel, folding clasp
Price: $11,750
Variations: leather strap; white dial

Speedmaster Co-Axial Broad Arrow 1957
Reference number: 321.93.42.50.13.001
Movement: automatic, Omega Caliber 3313 (base Omega 3303); ø 27 mm, height 6.85 mm; 37 jewels; 28,800 vph; co-axial escapement; officially certified C.O.S.C. chronometer
Functions: hours, minutes, subsidiary seconds; chronograph; date
Case: stainless steel, ø 42 mm, height 13.45 mm; rotating bezel with tachymeter scale; sapphire crystal; water-resistant to 10 atm
Band: reptile skin, folding clasp
Price: $6,900
Variations: rose or yellow gold

Omega

De Ville Hour Vision
Reference number: 431.63.41.21.02.001
Movement: automatic, Omega Caliber 8501 (base Omega 8500); ø 29 mm, height 5.6 mm; 39 jewels; 25,200 vph; co-axial escapement; officially certified chronometer (COSC)
Functions: hours, minutes, sweep seconds; date
Case: rose gold, sapphire crystal sides, ø 41 mm, height 12.2 mm; water-resistant to 10 atm
Band: reptile skin, rose gold folding clasp
Price: $13,600
Variations: rose gold link bracelet

De Ville Hour Vision
Reference number: 431.30.41.21.01.001
Movement: automatic, Omega Caliber 8500; ø 29 mm, height 5.5 mm; 39 jewels; 25,200 vph; co-axial escapement; officially certified chronometer (COSC)
Functions: hours, minutes, sweep seconds; date
Case: stainless steel, sapphire crystal sides, ø 41 mm, height 12.2 mm; water-resistant to 10 atm
Band: stainless steel, double folding clasp
Price: $6,380
Variations: leather strap; white dial

De Ville Co-Axial Chronograph Rattrapante
Reference number: 4847.50.31
Movement: automatic, Omega Caliber 3612 (base Omega 3303); ø 27 mm, height 6.85 mm; 33 jewels; 28,800 vph; co-axial escapement; column-wheel control of chronograph functions; officially certified chronometer (COSC)
Functions: hours, minutes, subsidiary seconds; split-seconds chronograph; date
Case: stainless steel, ø 41 mm, height 14.8 mm; sapphire crystal; transparent case back; screw-in crown; water-resistant to 10 atm
Band: reptile skin, folding clasp
Price: $10,650
Variations: grey or white dial

De Ville Co-Axial Chronoscope
Reference number: 4856.50.31
Movement: automatic, Omega Caliber 3313 (base Omega 3303); ø 27 mm, height 6.85 mm; 37 jewels; 28,800 vph; co-axial escapement; column-wheel control of chronograph functions; officially certified C.O.S.C. chronometer
Functions: hours, minutes, subsidiary seconds; chronograph; date
Case: rose gold, ø 41 mm, height 12.9 mm; sapphire crystal; transparent case back
Band: reptile skin, folding clasp
Price: $13,600
Variations: yellow gold; stainless steel

De Ville Co-Axial Chronoscope GMT
Reference number: 422.13.44.52.13.001
Movement: automatic, Omega Caliber 3603 (base Omega 3313); ø 27 mm, height 7.95 mm; 37 jewels; 28,800 vph; co-axial escapement; column-wheel control of chronograph functions; officially certified chronometer (COSC)
Functions: hours, minutes, subsidiary seconds; chronograph; date; 24-hour display (second time zone)
Case: stainless steel, ø 44 mm, height 15.11 mm; sapphire crystal; transparent case back; water-resistant to 10 atm
Band: reptile skin, folding clasp
Price: $7,300
Variations: rose gold

De Ville X2 Co-Axial Chronograph
Reference number: 423.53.37.50.01.001
Movement: automatic, Omega Caliber 3202; ø 27 mm, height 6.85 mm; 37 jewels; 28,800 vph; co-axial escapement; officially certified chronometer (COSC)
Functions: hours, minutes, subsidiary seconds; chronograph
Case: rose gold, 37 x 37 mm, height 14.05 mm; sapphire crystal; water-resistant to 5 atm
Band: reptile skin, folding clasp
Price: $16,200
Variations: stainless steel

De Ville Chronograph Ladies
Reference number: 4677.60.37
Movement: automatic, Omega Caliber 3313 (base Omega 3303); ø 27 mm, height 6.85 mm; 37 jewels; 28,800 vph; co-axial escapement; officially certified C.O.S.C. chronometer
Functions: hours, minutes, subsidiary seconds; chronograph; date
Case: rose gold, ø 35 mm, height 12.46 mm; bezel set with 42 diamonds; sapphire crystal; transparent case back; crown set with briolette-cut diamond; water-resistant to 10 atm
Band: leather, rose gold folding clasp
Price: $15,180

De Ville Tourbillon Co-Axial
Reference number: 513.53.39.21.99.001
Movement: automatic, Omega Caliber 2635; 52 jewels; 21,600 vph; co-axial escapement; central tourbillon with titanium carriage
Functions: hours, minutes (mystérieuse display without visible hand arbor), subsidiary seconds (on tourbillon)
Case: rose gold, ø 38.7 mm, height 12.98 mm; sapphire crystal
Band: reptile skin, folding clasp
Remarks: numbered edition
Price: $98,000

Omega

Caliber 8500
Mechanical with automatic winding, co-axial escapement; twin spring barrels, power reserve 60 hours; officially certified C.O.S.C. chronometer
Functions: hours, minutes, sweep seconds; date
Diameter: 29 mm
Height: 5.5 mm
Jewels: 39
Balance: without index, free-sprung balance spring
Frequency: 25,200 vph
Remarks: base plate with perlage, bridges and rotor with arabesque côtes de Genève, rhodium-plated; blackened balance and screws; 202 individual components

Caliber 8501
Mechanical with automatic winding, co-axial escapement; twin spring barrels, power reserve 60 hours; officially certified C.O.S.C. chronometer
Functions: hours, minutes, sweep seconds; date
Diameter: 29 mm
Height: 5.5 mm
Jewels: 39
Balance: without index, free-sprung balance spring
Frequency: 25,200 vph
Remarks: base plate with perlage, red gold rotor and balance bridge; blackened balance and screws; 201 individual components

Caliber 2500C
Mechanical with automatic winding, co-axial escapement; power reserve 44 hours; officially certified chronometer (COSC)
Functions: hours, minutes, sweep seconds; date
Diameter: 25.6 mm (11 1/2''')
Height: 3.9 mm
Jewels: 27
Balance: glucydur, with gold regulating screws
Frequency: 28,800 vph
Balance spring: free-sprung
Remarks: base plate with perlage, bridges and rotor with côtes de Genève, rhodium-plated

Caliber 3612
Base caliber: Omega 3313
Mechanical with automatic winding; co-axial escapement; power reserve 52 hours; officially certified chronometer (COSC)
Functions: hours, minutes, subsidiary seconds; date; split-seconds chronograph
Diameter: 27 mm (12''')
Height: 8.45 mm
Jewels: 38
Balance: glucydur
Frequency: 28,800 vph
Balance spring: free-sprung
Remarks: control of chronograph functions via two intermediate wheels

Caliber 1866
Base caliber: Nouvelle Lémania 1874
Mechanical with manual winding, power reserve 45 hours
Functions: hours, minutes, subsidiary seconds; date; moon phase; chronograph
Diameter: 27 mm (12''')
Height: 6.87 mm
Jewels: 18
Balance: glucydur, four-legged
Frequency: 21,600 vph
Balance spring: Nivarox I flat hairspring with fine adjustment
Remarks: base plate with perlage, beveled bridges with côtes de Genève; rhodium-plated; polished levers with beveled and polished edges

Caliber 2201
Base caliber: ETA Unitas 6498
Mechanical with manual winding, power reserve 60 hours; officially certified chronometer (COSC)
Functions: hours, minutes, subsidiary seconds
Diameter: 36.6 mm (16 3/4''')
Height: 4.5 mm
Jewels: 17
Balance: glucydur, three-legged
Frequency: 21,600 vph
Balance spring: Nivarox I flat hairspring
Shock protection: Incabloc
Remarks: base plate with perlage, bridges and cocks with côtes de Genève

Pronunciation Guide

What's in a Name?
A Pronunciation Guide by Elizabeth Doerr

The editors of *Wristwatch Annual* have often been asked to include a pronunciation guide for the names of the brands we list to aid those English speakers who do not have command of another language such as French or German, the most important languages in watchmaking. Along with the pronunciation guide, we also include a brief summary of the origin of the company's name.

Pronunciation Key:
ä = short a, as in the standard American pronunciation of father
ā = long a, as in day or date
ə = short French e, as in the u in the English word hurry
ē = long e, as in see
ī = long i, as in fine
ō = long o, as in bone
ö = French and German sound as found in French word *boeuf* or German *Söhne*
ū = long u, as in dune
ü = French or German pinched u sound, as in the French word *rue*, almost sounding like the English word you
n = nasal, French n as in the French word *bonjour*

Alpina   älpēnä
Name of watchmaker collective founded in 1890 in Glashütte.

Angular Momentum   pronounced as in English
Named for a concept taken from astrophysics that combines a moment of inertia with an angular velocity.

Anonimo   änōnīmō
Anonimo is the Italian word for anonymous, chosen by the brand's owners to depict the fact that good watchmaking is not contingent upon the names the watches bear.

Arnold & Sons   pronounced as in English
A brand named for famed British watchmaker John Arnold.

Askania   äskänēä
Name of Berlin-based instrument maker during the Weimar Republic.

Audemars Piguet   ōdəmär pēgā
Two French-language proper names taken from the Swiss founders watchmaker Jules Audemars and financial expert Jules Piguet.

Backes & Strauss   bäkəs & schtrows
Name of world's oldest diamond dealer, founded in Hanau, Germany, in 1789 by Georg Carl Backes. Max Strauss came along in 1856.

Ball   pronounced as in English
The last name of Ohio's Webb C. Ball.

Baume & Mercier   bōm ā mersēā
Two French-language proper names taken from the Swiss Baume family and Genevan jeweler Paul Mercier.

Bell & Ross   pronounced as in English
A play on founders' names Belamich and Rosillo to form a short English-sounding name for this French company.

Ernst Benz   ernst bents
Name of the company's Swiss-born founder.

Jochen Benzinger   yochən bentsinger
Name of this German engraver and guillocheur.

Blancpain   blänkpan
The French-language last name of founding Swiss businessman Jean Jacques Blancpain.

blu   blü
Fictional French word chosen for this Swiss company by its German founder, watchmaker Bernhard Lederer.

Rainer Brand   rīner bränt
This is German-born watchmaker Rainer Brand's name.

Martin Braun   martēn brown
This is German-born watchmaker Martin Braun's name.

Breguet   brəgā
The last name of Swiss-born watchmaker Abraham-Louis Breguet.

Breitling   brītling
The German-language last name of Swiss-born company founder Leon Breitling.

Brior   brēor
Fictional name for this German company composed of *bri* from "briar" and *or* from the French word for gold.

B.R.M.   pronounced as in English
Stands for Bernard Richards Manufacturing.

Carl F. Bucherer   kärl f būcherer
The name of the company's Swiss-born founder, jeweler Carl F. Bucherer.

Bulgari   bulgärē
The last name of the Italian Bulgari family.

Buti   būtē
Italian Tommaso Buti's last name.

Cartier   kärtēā
Last name of French-born Louis Cartier.

Chase-Durer   pronounced as in English
The name of this American company is a combination of the founding Chase family and Swiss watchmaker Stefan Durer.

Chopard   shōpär
This is the French-language last name of Swiss-born founder Louis-Ulysse Chopard.

Chronoswiss   krōnōswis
A fictional name chosen by German watchmaker Gerd-Rüdiger Lang for his Munich-based company.

Frédérique Constant   frederīk kōnstän
The names of owner and founder Peter Stas's great-grandmother Frédérique and great-grandfather Constant.

Corum   korūm
Swiss founding partners Gaston Ries & René Bannwart chose the Latin word *quorum* as the name of their company and simplified its spelling.

Cuervo y Sobrinos   kwervō ē sōbrēnōs
Last name of Cuban Ramón Rio y Cuervo, a jeweler who kept a watch shop in Havana with his nephews (Spanish: *sobrinos*).

Cyclos   pronounced as in English
The name Swiss countryman John C. Ermel gave his cyclical watches.

De Bethune   də bətün
Taken from a Swiss watchmaker known as Monsieur le Chevalier de Bethune.

De Grisogono   dā grisōgōnō
The maiden name of an associate's mother who worked with Italian-born founder Fawaz Gruosi when he opened his first boutique in Geneva.

Pierre DeRoche   pēər də roch
Swiss founder Pierre Dubois's first name and "of the rock" in French.

DeWitt   də vitt
Swiss founder Jérôme de Witt's last name.

Dornblüth & Sohn   dornblüt & zōn
Last name of German founder Dieter Dornblüth; *Sohn* means "son."

Doxa   pronounced as in English
Name chosen by Swiss-born company founder Georges Ducommun for his brand.

Dubey & Schaldenbrand   dübā ā shäldənbränt
The last names of founding Swiss watchmakers René Schaldenbrand and Georges Dubey.

Du Bois & Fils   dübwah ā fēs
Swiss founder Philippe Du Bois's last name and the French word for "son."

Roger Dubuis   rōjā dübwē
Swiss-born Roger Dubuis's French-language name.

Ebel   ābəl
Name taken from first letters of Eugene Blum et Levy, Levy being the maiden name of Swiss Eugene Blum's wife.

Eberhard   āberhärd
Last name of Swiss founder Georges-Emile Eberhard.

Epos   āpōs
Name chosen by Swiss company founder Peter Hofer.

Louis Erard   lūē ārärd
French-language name of Swiss founder Louis Erard.

Eterna   āternä
Name chosen by Swiss company founders Urs Schild and Dr. Josef Girard.

Jacques Etoile   jäk ätwäl
Francophone moniker taken from the names of master watchmaker and owner Klaus Jakob's last name and wife Yildiz Jakob's first name (*Yildiz* is Turkish for star, and *etoile* is French for star).

Fabergé   fäberjä
Last name of Huguenot Peter Carl Fabergé, born in St. Petersburg.

Fortis   fortis
Name chosen by Swiss founder Walter Vogt. It is Latin and means "strong."

Gérald Genta   jeräl jəntä
Name of Swiss-born watchmaker Gérald Genta, a man of Italian descent.

Girard-Perregaux   jirär perəgō
French proper names derived from the company that was eventually owned by Swiss countryman Constant Girard-Perregaux.

Glashütte Original   gläshütə originäl
Taken from Germany's historical watch city Glashütte.

Glycine   glicēn
A glycine is a type of climbing plant like wisteria. The founders of the Glycine watch brand, Switzerland's Charles Hertig and Sam Glur, named their brand for this plant that now graces the entire facade of the factory.

Graham   pronounced as in English
Named for British watchmaker George Graham.

Greubel Forsey   gröbəl forsē
Named for British watchmaker Steven Forsey and French watchmaker Robert Greubel.

Hanhart   hänhärt
Named for German founder Willy Hanhart.

Hautlence   ōtləns
An anagram of the city Neuchâtel.

Hermès   ermaz
Last name of founder Thierry Hermès, a man of French origin, though a German citizen.

continued on page 323...

Oris

For more than a century, the name Oris has stood for mechanical watches. And their characteristic design has helped this name gain recognition throughout the world.

With the founding of the Oris watch factory in Hölstein in 1904, the northwestern part of Switzerland—geographically distanced from the existing watch metropolises—successfully wrote a new chapter in the big book of Swiss watchmaking. Up to 1982, Oris was a genuine *manufacture* with a high degree of autonomy. All of the company's movements, their components, and their complete outfitting was done in-house, with the exception of the manufacture of balance springs, jewels, and mainsprings. With about 800 employees in the 1960s, Oris manufactured one to two million wristwatches and up to 100,000 alarm clocks each year. On today's market, Oris is one of the world's leading brands in its price class, reasonably offering mechanical watches and Swiss quality. Using original design ideas, clever model policies, and a consistent passion for the mechanical watch, Oris was able to make a real name for itself at the beginning of the mechanical renaissance—thanks in part to the catchy tagline: "It's high mech."

Oris has recently turned its attention to motor sports, with the brand becoming a partner of the Williams Formula 1 Team. Oris's commitment to Formula 1 has inspired the company's designers to a grand collection by the name of TT3. Capturing the look of modern, aerodynamic auto design, the dial of the newest chronograph is crafted in carbon fiber. Oris's crown system, which the company has christened Quick Lock, and the automatic winding system's red rotor, visible through the transparent case back, are just two of the technical innovations that remind one of the brand's ties to the high-speed, high-performance sport.

The Big Crown has definitively been the hallmark of a whole product line inspired by classic pilot's watches. Lending the model family its inimitable character, they are easily recognized at any distance thanks to the literally large crown. The Flight Timer model is even strikingly outfitted with an additional vertical crown at 2 o'clock with which the second time zone on the rotating flange underneath the sapphire crystal is set. The past and the future seem to be united in these classic models.

Thanks to this company's long history, Oris has the opportunity to reach back to classic models with that something special for modern inspiration. The Oris Artelier Handwinder dwells on the golden days of Art Deco: redesigned to make a modern classic, it is a real find for connoisseurs of manually wound timepieces with its 18-karat rose gold case in an elegantly slim design.

TT3 Chronograph 2nd Time Zone
Reference number: 677 7590 7764
Movement: automatic, Oris Caliber 677 (base ETA Valjoux 7754); ø 30 mm, height 7.9 mm; 25 jewels; 28,800 vph
Functions: hours, minutes; chronograph; date; 24-hour display (second time zone)
Case: black DLC-coated titanium, ø 42.5 mm, height 16 mm; rose gold-plated bezel; sapphire crystal; transparent case back; water-resistant to 10 atm
Band: rubber, folding clasp
Price: $3,495

TT3 Day Date
Reference number: 635 7589 7064
Movement: automatic, Oris Caliber 635 (base ETA 2836-2); ø 25.6 mm, height 5.05 mm; 25 jewels; 28,800 vph
Functions: hours, minutes, sweep seconds; date, weekday
Case: titanium, ø 43.5 mm, height 13 mm; sapphire crystal; transparent case back; water-resistant to 10 atm
Band: rubber, folding clasp
Price: $2,475
Variations: stainless steel bracelet; various dial variations

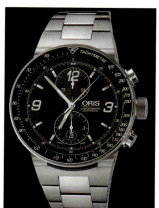

Williams F1 Chronograph
Reference number: 673 7563 41 84
Movement: automatic, Oris Caliber 673 (base ETA Valjoux 7750); ø 30 mm, height 7.9 mm; 25 jewels; 28,800 vph
Functions: hours, minutes; chronograph; date
Case: stainless steel, ø 45 mm, height 14 mm; bezel with tachymeter scale; sapphire crystal; transparent case back; water-resistant to 5 atm
Band: stainless steel, folding clasp
Remarks: carbon fiber dial
Price: $2,525
Variations: rubber strap; black coated case

Williams F1 Day Date
Reference number: 635 7595 41 94
Movement: automatic, Oris Caliber 635 (base ETA 2836-2); ø 25.6 mm, height 5.05 mm; 25 jewels; 28,800 vph
Functions: hours, minutes, sweep seconds; date, weekday
Case: stainless steel, ø 42 mm, height 11 mm; sapphire crystal; transparent case back; water-resistant to 5 atm
Band: rubber, folding clasp
Price: $1,125
Variations: stainless steel bracelet; various dial variations

Chronoris
Reference number: 672 7564 41 54
Movement: automatic, Oris Caliber 672 (base ETA Valjoux 7750); ø 30 mm, height 7.9 mm; 25 jewels; 28,800 vph
Functions: hours, minutes; chronograph; date
Case: stainless steel, 40 x 41.5 mm, height 14.8 mm; sapphire crystal; transparent case back; crown with Quick-Lock system; water-resistant to 50 m
Band: leather, folding clasp
Remarks: comes with additional stainless steel bracelet
Price: $2,795

Carlos Coste Chrono
Reference number: 678 7598 7184
Movement: automatic, Oris Caliber 678 (base ETA Valjoux 7750); ø 30 mm, height 7.9 mm; 25 jewels; 28,800 vph
Functions: hours, minutes; chronograph; date, weekday
Case: titanium, ø 47 mm, height 14.8 mm; unidirectionally rotating bezel with 60-minute divisions; helium valve on case; sapphire crystal; transparent case back; screw-in crown and buttons; water-resistant to 10 atm
Band: titanium, folding clasp with wetsuit extension
Remarks: limited edition of 2,000 pieces
Price: $3,195

Meistertaucher Regulator
Reference number: 649 7541 71 64
Movement: automatic, Oris Caliber 649 (base ETA 2836-2); ø 25.6 mm, height 5.05 mm; 27 jewels; 28,800 vph
Functions: hours (off-center), minutes, subsidiary seconds; date
Case: titanium, ø 44 mm, height 15.2 mm; unidirectionally rotating bezel with 60-minute divisions; sapphire crystal; helium valve on case; screw-in crown; water-resistant to 100 atm
Band: rubber, folding clasp with wetsuit extension
Remarks: comes with additional titanium bracelet and diver's equipment
Price: $2,125

Divers Date
Reference number: 733 7533 84 54
Movement: automatic, Oris Caliber 733 (base Sellita SW 200); ø 25.6 mm, height 4.6 mm; 26 jewels; 28,800 vph
Functions: hours, minutes, sweep seconds; date
Case: stainless steel, ø 44 mm, height 12.5 mm; unidirectionally rotating bezel with 60-minute divisions; sapphire crystal; transparent case back; water-resistant to 30 atm
Band: stainless steel, folding clasp with wetsuit extension
Price: $1,175
Variations: rubber strap; blue dial

Oris

Flight Timer R4118
Reference number: 674 7583 40 84
Movement: automatic, Oris Caliber 674 (base ETA Valjoux 7750); ø 30 mm, height 7.9 mm; 25 jewels; 28,800 vph
Functions: hours, minutes, subsidiary seconds; chronograph; date
Case: stainless steel, ø 44 mm, height 15 mm; ring under crystal with 12-hour scale, bidirectionally rotating via crown; sapphire crystal; transparent case back
Band: leather, snap clasp
Remarks: limited edition of 4,118 pieces commemorating World War II fighter jet Hurricane R4118
Price: $3,195

Big Crown Telemeter
Reference number: 674 7569 40 64
Movement: automatic, Oris Caliber 674 (base ETA Valjoux 7750); ø 30 mm, height 7.9 mm; 25 jewels; 28,800 vph
Functions: hours, minutes, subsidiary seconds; chronograph; date
Case: stainless steel, ø 43 mm, height 14.4 mm; bezel with telemeter scale; Plexiglas; transparent case back
Band: stainless steel, double folding clasp
Price: $2,195
Variations: leather strap ($2,150)

Big Crown Pointer Date
Reference number: 754 7543 40 61
Movement: automatic, Oris Caliber 654 (base Sellita SW 200); ø 25.6 mm, height 4.6 mm; 25 jewels; 28,800 vph
Functions: hours, minutes, sweep seconds; date
Case: stainless steel, ø 40 mm, height 11 mm; Plexiglas; transparent case back; water-resistant to 5 atm
Band: leather, buckle
Price: $925
Variations: stainless steel bracelet ($1,025); diverse dial variations

Dizzy Gillespie
Reference number: 733 7593 4089
Movement: automatic, Oris Caliber 733 (base Sellita SW 200); ø 25.6 mm, height 4.6 mm; 25 jewels; 28,800 vph
Functions: hours, minutes, sweep seconds; date
Case: stainless steel, 39 x 36.5 mm, height 10.7 mm; sapphire crystal; water-resistant to 5 atm
Band: reptile skin, buckle
Price: $1,495
Remarks: limited edition of 1,917 pieces

Artelier Handwinding
Reference number: 396 7580 6051
Movement: manually wound, Oris Caliber 396 (base ETA Peseux 7001); ø 23.3 mm, height 2.5 mm; 17 jewels; 21,600 vph
Functions: hours, minutes, subsidiary seconds
Case: rose gold, ø 40 mm, height 7.4 mm; sapphire crystal; transparent case back
Band: leather, buckle
Price: $4,995

Artelier Worldtimer
Reference number: 690 7581 40 51
Movement: automatic, Oris Caliber 690 (base ETA 2836-2); ø 25.6 mm, height 5.05 mm; 30 jewels; 28,800 vph; quick-setting of the second time zone via button, with date change
Functions: hours, minutes, subsidiary seconds; date; second time zone with day/night indication
Case: stainless steel, ø 42.5 mm, height 12.5 mm; sapphire crystal; transparent case back
Band: leather, double folding clasp
Price: $2,525
Variations: stainless steel bracelet ($2,625)

Artelier Complication
Reference number: 581 7592 40 51
Movement: automatic, Oris Caliber 581 (base ETA 2688/2671); ø 23.6 mm, height 5.6 mm; 17 jewels; 28,800 vph
Functions: hours, minutes, sweep seconds; date, weekday, moon phase; second time zone
Case: stainless steel, ø 40 mm, height 11.6 mm; sapphire crystal; transparent case back
Band: leather, folding clasp
Price: $1,550
Variations: stainless steel bracelet ($1,650); black dial

Artelier Pointer Day
Reference number: 645 7596 4051
Movement: automatic, Oris Caliber 645 (base ETA 2836-2); ø 25.6 mm, height 5.05 mm; 27 jewels; 28,800 vph
Functions: hours, minutes, subsidiary seconds; date, weekday
Case: stainless steel, ø 45 mm, height 11 mm; sapphire crystal; transparent case back
Band: leather, buckle
Price: $1,575
Variations: leather strap ($1,475)

Pronunciation Guide

... continued from page 319

Hublot — üblō
French word meaning "porthole" that Italian founder Carlo Crocco chose for his watches, as they reminded him of a ship's porthole.

IWC — pronounced as in English
Stands for International Watch Company, founded in Switzerland by American Florentine Ariosto Jones.

Jacob & Co. — jākəb
Russian-born American Jacob Arabo's first name, company founder and owner.

Jaeger-LeCoultre — yāgər ləkūltr
Taken from the last names of Swiss founders Pierre Jaeger and Charles-Antoine LeCoultre.

Jaquet Droz — jäkā drō
Taken from Swiss Pierre Jaquet Droz's last name.

JeanRichard — jänrichär
Taken from Swiss watchmaker Daniel JeanRichard's name.

F.P. Journe — jurn
French master watchmaker François-Paul Journe's name.

Kobold — kōbolt
Taken from American founder and president Michael Kobold's last name, a man of German descent.

Pierre Kunz — pēər kunts
The Swiss founder's name.

Maurice Lacroix — morēs läkwä
Fictional francophone name chosen for brand by Swiss parent company Desco von Schulthess.

Lang & Heyne — läng ūnt häynə
Taken from German founding watchmaker Ferdinand Adolph Lange's name.

A. Lange & Söhne — ä längə ūnt sönə
Taken from German founding watchmaker Ferdinand Adolph Lange's name.

Jacques Lemans — jäk ləmän
French-sounding name chosen by Austrian owner and founder Alfred Riedl.

Limes — lēməs
Brand name fabricated by the German Ickler family.

Longines — lonjēn
Swiss founder Ernest Francillon bought a property by the name of Longines, built a factory there, and named his brand after it.

Giuliano Mazzuoli — mätzūōlē
Italian designer Giuliano Mazzuoli's name.

MeisterSinger — mīstərzingər
Name chosen by German founder Manfred Brassler.

Richard Mille — rēschär mēl
French owner and founder Richard Mille's name.

Milus — mēlūs
Name chosen by Swiss founder Paul William Junod.

Montblanc — mōnblänk
Name of the German-based famed writing instrument company derived from the Swiss/French mountain Mont Blanc.

H. Moser & Cie. — mōzər & kōmpanyē
Name of Swiss founder Heinrich Moser.

Mühle — mülə
Last name of German founder Robert Mühle.

Franck Muller — fränk mülər
Name of Swiss-born watchmaker Franck Muller.

Ulysse Nardin — ūlis närdən
French-language name of Swiss founder Ulysse Nardin.

Rainer Nienaber — rīner nēnäber
This is German-born watchmaker Rainer Brand's name.

Nivrel — nēvrel
A registered Swiss name acquired by German Gerd Hofer for his company.

Nomos — nōmōs
The name of an historical Glashütte watch company. German owner and founder of the modern Nomos company, Roland Schwertner, acquired the name after the fall of the Berlin Wall.

Omega — ōmägä
Name chosen for the company by Swiss founder Louis Brandt's sons, Louis Paul and César.

Oris — oris
Named by Swiss founders Paul Cattin and Georges Christian for the small stream that runs near the factory.

Panerai — pänəri
The Italian word *officine* (sometimes included in the brand's name) means workshops, and Panerai is taken from the name of the Italian founder, Guido Panerai.

Parmigiani — pärmijänē
Last name of Swiss founder watchmaker Michel Parmigiani.

Patek Philippe — pätek filēp
Last names of founding Polish immigrant to Switzerland, entrepreneur Antoine Norbert de Patek, and French watchmaker Adrien Philippe.

Perrelet — perəlā
French-language last name of Swiss Abraham-Louis Perrelet.

Piaget — pēäjā
French-language last name of Swiss founder Georges Piaget.

Paul Picot — pōl pēkō
Name chosen by Italian entrepreneur Mario Boiocchi for his company.

Porsche Design — porshə dəsīn
Taken from German owner, and founder of the original licensing automobile brand, Ferdinand A. Porsche's last name.

Rado — rädō
Later director Paul Lüthi christened the Swiss company Schlup & Co. Rado in the mid 1950s.

RGM — pronounced as in English
Taken from American founder and owner Roland G. Murphy's initials.

Rolex — rōlex
German-born founder Hans Wildorf took the name from a combination of the Spanish words *relojes excelentes* (excellent watches) and modified it.

Daniel Roth — dänyel rōt
Taken from Swiss founding watchmaker Daniel Roth's name.

Scalfaro — skälfärō
Name invented by German founding brothers Kuhnle.

Jörg Schauer — yörg shauər
Taken from German-born goldsmith, founder, and owner Jörg Schauer's name.

Schaumburg — shaumburg
Region of northern Germany for which this company was named by owner and founder Frank Dilbakowski.

Alexander Shorokhoff — shorōkof
Named for Russian-born founder Alexander Shorkhov (the double f is the "fancy" French spelling of the original cyrillic.

Alain Silberstein — älən silbərstīn
Taken from French-born architect, founder, and owner Alain Silberstein's name.

Sinn — zin
Taken from German-born founder Helmut Sinn's last name.

Sothis — zōtis
German-born founder and owner Wolfgang Steinkrüger chose this name from Egyptian mythology for his brand.

Stowa — shtōvä
Derived from the name of German founder **Wa**lter **Sto**rz.

SWI — pronounced as in English
Brand name invented by the Ben-Schmuel family, standing for Swiss Watch International.

TAG Heuer — täg hoiər
Taken from Swiss founding watchmaker Edouard Heuer's last name and the TAG group, who had bought the brand in 1985.

Temption — temptsēōn
Name chosen by German founder and owner Klaus Ulbrich combining *temp*us and func*tion*.

Tissot — tisō
French-language last name of Swiss founders Charles-Félicien and Charles-Emile Tissot (father and son respectively).

Tutima — tūtēmä
Brand name derived from Latin word *tutus*, meaning certain or protected, by German-born founder Dr. Ernst Kurtz.

Urwerk — oorvərk
Name chosen by Swiss founders Felix Baumgartner and Martin Frei meaning "original movement."

Vacheron Constantin — väshərōn cōnstäntən
French-language last names of Swiss founders Jean-Marc Vacheron and Francois Constantin.

Ventura — pronounced as in English
Swiss-born founder and owner Pierre Nobs named his company after Ventura, California.

Wempe — vempə
Name of German jeweler family and the chain of stores.

Harry Winston — pronounced as in English
The name of prominent New Yorker jeweler Harry Winston, born in 1896.

Zenith — pronounced as in English
Swiss-born founder Georges Favre-Jacot gave this name to his company.

Panerai

In March of 1997 the Vendôme Group (now Richemont) took over Officine Panerai's division for watches, compasses, and optical precision instruments. With this, the watch brand Officine Panerai—formerly Panerai Sistemi—also received new owners. In the 1930s, Panerai was the official supplier to the Italian Navy for high-quality precision instruments. Alongside numerous ideas and instruments, Panerai developed a line of wristwatches especially for use in extreme and risky situations. These special models have been available to watch connoisseurs since 1993 in strictly limited editions under the original brand names Luminor and Mare Nostrum. With the 1997 takeover, Panerai began entering the international markets and the—second—success story of the company officially began.

Setting the scene for building the brand, a research and development center was created ten years ago. This was followed by the construction of an exceptionally selective distribution network with boutiques in five important international metropolises: Florence, Portofino, Hong Kong, Los Angeles, and Shanghai. In 2006, the *manifattura* was opened in Neuchâtel, employing highly specialized watchmakers occupied with production. Additionally, the brand opened a technical research center for the development of materials and movements using progressive technologies, moving along the development and production of movements that have now brought the company more than ten exclusive patents.

After the Florentine brand presented in-house manually wound Caliber P.2002, just prior to the S.I.H.H. 2007, it introduced another three new movements including an automatic mechanism and a long-awaited chronograph.

The automatic watch is outfitted with a power reserve of ten full days made possible by serially operating spring barrels, their reserve displayed by a linear indication with a small hand. Additionally, Caliber P.2003 is outfitted with an intelligent second hand reset system that gets activated simply by pulling the crown, as well as an hour hand that can be adjusted in increments of one hour—an extra very much appreciated by travelers.

The manually wound model is outfitted with the same functions, but also has a chronograph activated by a single button located at 7 o'clock. Start, stop, and reset are successively controlled by a column wheel, the only component along with the balance that can be seen under the expansive surface of Caliber P.2004's bridges. The energy flow of the chronograph takes place via a vertical clutch with two long levers.

A very special introduction is the tourbillon with an eight-day manually wound movement, the diameter of which was increased from 31.8 to 37.2 mm during development. This, however, hasn't got the least to do with what one might assume would be a usual tourbillon cage: not making revolutions around its own axis as conventional tourbillons do, its long axis and cage turn more "like a chicken on a spit," as head developer Eric Klein laughingly comments. In fact, its 30-second-tourbillon is not there to compensate for gravity but rather the error created by the "hanging" and "laying" positions of a wristwatch Naturally, this is a playful component that is also beautiful to look at—but strictly for the watch's owner, for it can only be seen from the back within its mirrored aperture.

Luminor Logo
Reference number: PAM 00005
Movement: manually wound, Panerai Caliber OP XI; ø 36.6 mm, height 4.5 mm; 17 jewels; 21,600 vph; officially certified C.O.S.C. chronometer
Functions: hours, minutes, subsidiary seconds
Case: stainless steel, ø 44 mm; sapphire crystal; crown with security brake lever lock; water-resistant to 30 atm
Band: leather, buckle
Price: $3,850

Luminor Marina Automatic
Reference number: PAM 00104
Movement: automatic, Panerai Caliber OP III; ø 30 mm, height 7.9 mm; 21 jewels; 28,800 vph; officially certified C.O.S.C. chronometer
Functions: hours, minutes, subsidiary seconds; date
Case: stainless steel, ø 44 mm; sapphire crystal; crown with security brake lever lock; water-resistant to 30 atm
Band: reptile skin, folding clasp
Price: $5,150

Radiomir Black Seal Automatic
Reference number: PAM 00287
Movement: automatic, Panerai Caliber OP III; ø 30 mm, height 7.9 mm; 21 jewels; 28,800 vph; officially certified C.O.S.C. chronometer
Functions: hours, minutes, subsidiary seconds; date
Case: stainless steel, ø 45 mm; sapphire crystal; screw-in crown; water-resistant to 10 atm
Band: reptile skin, folding clasp
Price: $5,400

Radiomir Black Seal Ceramic
Reference number: PAM 00292
Movement: automatic, Panerai Caliber OP XI; ø 36.6 mm, height 4.5 mm; 17 jewels; 21,600 vph; officially certified C.O.S.C. chronometer; swan-neck fine adjustment; "sandwich" dial with underlying luminous substance
Functions: hours, minutes, subsidiary seconds
Case: ceramic, ø 45 mm; sapphire crystal; screw-in crown; water-resistant to 10 atm
Band: reptile skin, folding clasp
Price: $6,500

Radiomir Chronograph
Reference number: PAM 00288
Movement: automatic, Panerai Caliber OP XII; ø 30 mm; height 7.9 mm; 27 jewels; 28,800 vph; officially certified C.O.S.C. chronometer
Functions: hours, minutes, subsidiary seconds; chronograph
Case: stainless steel, ø 45 mm, height 14.8 mm; sapphire crystal, screw-in crown; water-resistant to 10 atm
Band: reptile skin, folding clasp
Price: $7,000

Luminor Marina Automatic
Reference number: PAM 00279
Movement: automatic, Panerai Caliber OP III; ø 30 mm, height 7.9 mm; 21 jewels; 28,800 vph; officially certified C.O.S.C. chronometer
Functions: hours, minutes, subsidiary seconds; date
Case: titanium, ø 44 mm; sapphire crystal; crown with security brake lever lock; water-resistant to 30 atm
Band: stainless steel, folding clasp
Price: $8,100

Radiomir 8 Days
Reference number: PAM 00268
Movement: manually wound, Panerai Caliber P.2002/3; ø 31.8 mm, height 6.6 mm; 21 jewels; 28,800 vph; power reserve 8 days; triple spring barrels
Functions: hours, minutes, subsidiary seconds; power reserve display (linear)
Case: stainless steel, ø 45 mm; sapphire crystal; transparent case back; water-resistant to 10 atm
Band: reptile skin, buckle
Price: $10,000

Luminor 1950 10 Days GMT
Reference number: PAM 00270
Movement: automatic, Panerai Caliber P.2003; ø 31.8 mm, height 8 mm; 25 jewels; 28,800 vph; triple spring barrels, power reserve 10 days; reset for second hand
Functions: hours, minutes, subsidiary seconds; date; second time zone; power reserve display (linear)
Case: stainless steel, ø 45 mm; sapphire crystal; transparent case back; crown with security brake lever lock; water-resistant to 10 atm
Band: reptile skin, buckle
Price: $14,400

Panerai

Luminor 1950 8 Days Chrono Monopulsante
Reference number: PAM 00275
Movement: manually wound, Panerai Caliber P.2004/1; ø 31.8 mm, height 8.2 mm; 29 jewels; 28,800 vph; triple spring barrels, power reserve 8 days; one-button control of column-wheel chronograph
Functions: hours, minutes, subsidiary seconds; second time zone; day/night indication; power reserve display (linear)
Case: stainless steel, ø 45 mm; sapphire crystal; transparent case back; crown with security brake lever lock; water-resistant to 10 atm
Band: reptile skin, buckle
Price: $17,100

Luminor 1950 8 Days GMT
Reference number: PAM 00289
Movement: manually wound, Panerai Caliber P.2002; ø 31 mm, height 6.5 mm; 21 jewels; 21,600 vph; triple spring barrels, power reserve 8 days; reset for second hand
Functions: hours, minutes, subsidiary seconds; date; second time zone; day/night indication; power reserve display (linear)
Case: rose gold, ø 44 mm, height 15 mm; sapphire crystal; transparent case back; crown with security brake lever lock; water-resistant to 10 atm
Band: reptile skin, buckle
Price: $26,200

Luminor 1950 8 Days Chrono Monopulsante
Reference number: PAM 00277
Movement: manually wound, Panerai Caliber P.2004/1; ø 31.8 mm, height 8.2 mm; 29 jewels; 28,800 vph; triple spring barrels, power reserve 8 days; one-button control of column-wheel chronograph
Functions: hours, minutes, subsidiary seconds; second time zone; day/night indication; power reserve display (linear)
Case: rose gold, ø 45 mm; sapphire crystal; transparent case back; crown with security brake lever lock; water-resistant to 10 atm
Band: reptile skin, buckle
Price: $31,000

Radiomir 10 Days
Reference number: PAM 00274
Movement: automatic, Panerai Caliber P.2003; ø 31.8 mm, height 8 mm; 25 jewels; 28,800 vph; triple spring barrels; power reserve 10 days; reset for second hand
Functions: hours, minutes, subsidiary seconds; date; second time zone; power reserve display (linear)
Case: platinum, ø 45 mm; sapphire crystal; transparent case back; crown with security brake lever lock; water-resistant to 10 atm
Band: reptile skin, buckle
Remarks: limited edition of 50 pieces
Price: $51,400
Variations: limited edition of 250 pieces in rose gold; limited edition of 250 pieces in white gold

Luminor 1950 Submersible Depth Gauge
Reference number: PAM 00143
Movement: automatic, Panerai Caliber OP XV; ø 30 mm, height 7.9 mm; 21 jewels; 28,800 vph; officially certified chronometer (COSC); electronic depth gauge module with METAS certificate (official ministry of metrology)
Functions: hours, minutes, subsidiary seconds; depth gauge
Case: titanium, ø 47 mm; unidirectionally rotating bezel with applied steel markers; sapphire crystal; transparent case back; crown with security brake lever lock; water-resistant to 12 atm
Band: rubber, buckle
Price: $14,900

Luminor Marina Automatic
Reference number: PAM 00282
Movement: automatic, Panerai Caliber OP III; ø 30 mm, height 7.9 mm; 21 jewels; 28,800 vph; officially certified chronometer (COSC)
Functions: hours, minutes, subsidiary seconds; date
Case: titanium, ø 44 mm; sapphire crystal; crown with security brake lever lock; water-resistant to 30 atm
Band: reptile skin, double folding clasp
Price: $5,500

Luminor 1950 8 Days GMT
Reference number: PAM 00233
Movement: manually wound, Panerai Caliber P.2002; ø 31 mm, height 6.5 mm; 21 jewels; 21,600 vph; triple spring barrels, power reserve 8 days; reset for second hand
Functions: hours, minutes, subsidiary seconds; date; second time zone; day/night indication; power reserve display (linear)
Case: stainless steel, ø 44 mm, height 15 mm; sapphire crystal; transparent case back; crown with security brake lever lock; water-resistant to 10 atm
Band: leather, buckle
Price: $12,300

Luminor 1950 Tourbillon GMT
Reference number: PAM 00276
Movement: manually wound, Panerai Caliber P.2005; ø 37.2 mm, height 9.1 mm; 31 jewels; 28,800 vph; triple spring barrels, power reserve 6 days; 30-second tourbillon
Functions: hours, minutes, subsidiary seconds; tourbillon indication; second time zone; day/night indication; power reserve display (on back)
Case: stainless steel, ø 47 mm; sapphire crystal; transparent case back; crown with security brake lever lock; water-resistant to 10 atm
Band: reptile skin, buckle
Remarks: limited edition of 100 pieces
Price: $104,000

EXQUISITE
TIMEPIECES

1-800-595-5330 WWW.EXQUISITETIMEPIECES.COM
4380 GULFSHORE BOULEVARD NORTH, SUITE 800, NAPLES, FL 34103

Anonimo | Arnold & Son | Audemars Piguet | Azimuth | Bedat & Co | Bell & Ross
Blancpain | Breguet | BRM | Corum | Cvstos | Daniel Roth | DeWitt | Franck Muller
Gerald Genta | Glashutte Original | Graham | IWC | Jaeger LeCoultre | Jaquet Droz
Omega | Panerai | Parmigiani Fleurier | Pierre Kunz | Perrelet | Roger Dubuis
TB Buti | Urwerk | Vacheron Constantin

Parmigiani

What began as the undertaking of a single man—a gifted watchmaker and reputable restorer of complicated vintage timepieces—in a small town called Fleurier in Switzerland's Val de Travers, has now grown into an empire of sorts comprising several factories, about 400 employees, and a grand total of around 5,000 timepieces produced and delivered in 2007. And all of this within the last eleven years. It is obvious that growth is the order of the day at Parmigiani, a growth that is confirmed by the numbers in just two of the luxury brand's most important markets: the United States showed an increase of 43 percent from 2005 to 2006, while Germany was even able to cite growth of 300 percent over the same time period. Parmigiani's declared goal is 10,000 watches per year by 2010—and at this rate, there is no doubt the well-organized, goal-oriented concern, the majority of which is owned by the Sandoz Foundation, will be able to achieve it.

With the advent of Parmigiani's sponsoring commitment in the arena of hot-air ballooning, the brand has decided to make 2007 the year of the chronograph—the closest thing that Parmigiani gets to a real sports watch. This brand has concentrated on complications and elegant timepieces thus far in its development, though the new Kalpagraph is actually no less elegant than the rest of the collection. The chronograph collection is set to become the collection's entry point for a younger consumer. Hoping to aid the Kalpagraph in this goal, the company has also entered into a second marketing partnership, this time with Bernard Stamm, the Swiss sailor who has made three boat trips around the world in three years. The energetic Stamm is the brand's new ambassador.

The look of the Kalpagraph is obviously derived from the brand's established Kalpa line in its proportions, lug shapes, ergonomics, and curvaceous harmony. The chronograph's designers were after a certain sensuality, and Michel Parmigiani himself was looking to achieve a unisex feel for the watch, which is available in a variety of versions aimed at both men and women, despite the larger 53 x 39 mm case size.

The Kalpagraph's Caliber 334 is based on Parmigiani's existing automatic *manufacture* mechanism, with a new module providing the chronograph functions. Parmigiani already has his engineers hard at work on developing an integrated chronograph, which is expected to be ready for introduction in about four years. One Kalpagraph version currently available is crafted in the rare precious metal palladium. Certainly the first luxury manufacturer to tap into this metal's coming potential—Parmigiani initially introduced a palladium timepiece in 2005—the brand now offers its second serial timepiece clothed in the bright white element. A member of the platinum family, palladium contains all of platinum's precious advantages while being a little lighter, brighter, and currently less expensive. Parmigiani outfits all the brand's watches with exclusive Hermès straps.

Parmigiani

Kalpa Grande Automatic
Reference number: PF 011967.01
Movement: automatic, Parmigiani Caliber 331.02; ø 25.6 mm, height 3.5 mm; 32 jewels; 28,800 vph; twin spring barrels
Functions: hours, minutes, subsidiary seconds; date
Case: rose gold, 46.6 x 34 mm, height 9.25 mm; sapphire crystal; transparent case back
Band: Hermès alligator skin, buckle
Price: $14.600
Variations: various colored dials

Kalpa Grande Automatic Qualité Fleurier
Reference number: PF 012689.01
Movement: automatic, Parmigiani Caliber 331.01; ø 25.6 mm, height 3.5 mm; 32 jewels; 28,800 vph; twin spring barrels; officially certified C.O.S.C. chronometer
Functions: hours, minutes, sweep seconds; date
Case: rose gold, 46.6 x 34 mm, height 9.25 mm; sapphire crystal; transparent case back
Band: Hermès alligator skin, buckle
Remarks: tested and certified according to the Qualité Fleurier criteria; limited edition of 50 pieces
Price: $18,300
Variations: white gold

Kalpa XL Automatic Small Seconds
Reference number: PF 013466.01
Movement: automatic, Parmigiani Caliber 331.02; ø 25.6 mm, height 3.5 mm; 32 jewels; 28,800 vph; twin spring barrels
Functions: hours, minutes, subsidiary seconds; date
Case: stainless steel, 53 x 37.2 mm, height 10.7 mm; sapphire crystal; transparent case back
Band: Hermès alligator skin, double folding clasp
Price: $8,400
Variations: various colored dials; rose gold

Kalpa XL Hebdomadaire
Reference number: PF 011808.01
Movement: manually wound, Parmigiani Caliber 110.01; 29.3 x 23.6 mm, height 4.9 mm; 28 jewels; 21,600 vph; twin spring barrels, 8 days power reserve
Functions: hours, minutes, subsidiary seconds; date; power reserve display
Case: rose gold, 53 x 37.2 mm, height 11.2 mm; sapphire crystal; transparent case back
Band: Hermès alligator skin, buckle
Price: $26,200
Variations: various colored dials; palladium; in palladium with skeletonized movement Skeleton Chiaroscuro

Kalpa XL Hebdomadaire
Reference number: PF 003333.02
Movement: manually wound, Parmigiani Caliber 110.01; 29.3 x 23.6 mm, height 4.9 mm; 28 jewels; 21,600 vph; twin spring barrels, 8 days power reserve
Functions: hours, minutes, subsidiary seconds; date; power reserve display
Case: stainless steel, 53 x 37.2 mm, height 11.2 mm; sapphire crystal; transparent case back
Band: Hermès alligator skin, double folding clasp
Price: $18,300
Variations: various colored dials

Kalpa XL Tourbillon
Reference number: PF 013512.01
Movement: manually wound, Parmigiani Caliber 500.02; 29.3 x 23.6 mm, height 5.5 mm; 28 jewels; 21,600 vph; 30-second tourbillon; twin spring barrels, 7 days power reserve
Functions: hours, minutes, sweep seconds; power reserve display
Case: rose gold, 53 x 37.2 mm, height 11.5 mm; sapphire crystal; transparent case back
Band: Hermès alligator skin, buckle
Remarks: limited edition of 25 pieces
Price: $164,000
Variations: limited edition of 25 pieces in platinum

Kalpa XL Tourbillon
Reference number: PF 600317.01
Movement: manually wound, Parmigiani Caliber 500.02; 29.3 x 23.6 mm, height 5.5 mm; 28 jewels; 21,600 vph; 30-second tourbillon; twin spring barrels, 7 days power reserve
Functions: hours, minutes, sweep seconds; power reserve display
Case: platinum, 53 x 37.2 mm, height 11.5 mm; case and strap lugs set with 215 baguette-cut diamonds; sapphire crystal; transparent case back
Band: Hermès alligator skin, buckle
Price: $356,000

Kalpagraph
Reference number: PF 005162.01
Movement: automatic, Parmigiani Caliber 334.01; ø 30.3 mm, height 6.8 mm; 68 jewels; 28,800 vph
Functions: hours, minutes, subsidiary seconds; chronograph; date
Case: rose gold, 53.4 x 39.2 mm, height 12.8 mm; sapphire crystal; transparent case back
Band: Hermès alligator skin, buckle
Price: $23,500
Variations: with silver-colored or Havanna brown dial

Parmigiani

Kalpagraph
Reference number: PF 005162.01
Movement: automatic, Parmigiani Caliber 334.01; ø 30.3 mm, height 6.8 mm; 68 jewels; 28,800 vph
Functions: hours, minutes, subsidiary seconds; chronograph; date
Case: palladium, 53.4 x 39.2 mm, height 12.8 mm; sapphire crystal; transparent case back
Band: Hermès alligator skin, buckle
Price: $23,500
Variations: with silver-colored dial

Kalpagraph
Reference number: PF 005162.01
Movement: automatic, Parmigiani Caliber 334.01; ø 30.3 mm, height 6.8 mm; 68 jewels; 28,800 vph
Functions: hours, minutes, subsidiary seconds; chronograph; date
Case: stainless steel, 53.4 x 39.2 mm, height 12.8 mm; sapphire crystal; transparent case back
Band: stainless steel, double folding clasp
Price: $15,400
Variations: with black dial

Kalpa Tonda 42 Automatic
Reference number: PF 012506.01
Movement: automatic, Parmigiani Caliber 331.02; ø 25.6 mm, height 3.5 mm; 32 jewels; 28,800 vph; twin spring barrels
Functions: hours, minutes, subsidiary seconds; date
Case: rose gold, ø 42 mm, height 8.6 mm; sapphire crystal; transparent case back
Band: Hermès alligator skin, buckle
Price: $16,100
Variations: various colored dials; white gold

Kalpa Tonda 39 Skeleton
Reference number: PF 012704.01
Movement: automatic, Parmigiani Caliber 338.01; ø 25.6 mm, height 3.5 mm; 32 jewels; 28,800 vph; twin spring barrels; completely skeletonized
Functions: hours, minutes, subsidiary seconds; date
Case: rose gold, ø 39 mm, height 8.5 mm; sapphire crystal; transparent case back
Band: Hermès alligator skin, buckle
Price: $40,000
Remarks: limited edition of 50 pieces
Variations: white gold

Kalpa XL Minute Repeater
Reference number: PF 600399.01
Movement: automatic, Parmigiani Caliber 350.01; ø 24.85 mm, height 6.61 mm; 33 jewels; 21,600 vph
Functions: hours, minutes, subsidiary seconds; hour, quarter hour, and minute repeater on two gongs
Case: platinum, 53 x 37.2 mm, height 11 mm; sapphire crystal; case back with two exhibition windows for repeater
Band: Hermès alligator skin, buckle
Price: $268,000
Remarks: limited edition of 10 pieces
Variations: various colored dials; limited edition of 10 pieces in rose gold

Toric Quantième Perpétuel Rétrograde
Reference number: PF 002645.01
Movement: automatic, Parmigiani Caliber 333.01; ø 27 mm, height 5.5 mm; 32 jewels; 28,800 vph; autonomous module for retrograde perpetual calendar; twin spring barrels
Functions: hours, minutes, sweep seconds; perpetual calendar with retrograde date, weekday, month, year, leap year, precision moon phase
Case: rose gold, ø 40.5 mm, height 11.4 mm; sapphire crystal; transparent case back; crown with sapphire cabochon
Band: Hermès alligator skin, buckle
Price: $51,200
Variations: various colored dials; white gold

Toric Westminter
Reference number: PF 600516.01
Movement: manually wound, Parmigiani Caliber 255.01; ø 27.6 mm, height 7.7 mm; 42 jewels; 28,800 vph; one-minute tourbillon
Functions: hours, minutes; 24-hour display (second time zone); hour, quarter hour and minute repeater with 4 gongs (Westminster chime)
Case: platinum, ø 42 mm, height 14.25 mm; sapphire crystal; crown with sapphire cabochon
Band: Hermès alligator skin, buckle
Price: $476,000
Variations: white or rose gold

Bugatti 370 Type
Reference number: PF 008221.01
Movement: manually wound, Parmigiani Caliber 370.01; 21 x 16 x 27.4 mm; 37 jewels; 21,600 vph; movement with several plates and levels; twin serially operating spring barrels, 10 days power reserve
Functions: hours, minutes; power reserve display
Case: white gold, 32.4 x 52.5 mm, height 18.6 mm; sapphire crystal
Band: custom Hermès leather, double folding clasp
Remarks: starter instrument with electric motor to wind movement; limited edition of 50 pieces
Price: $200,000

Parmigiani

Caliber 331
Mechanical with automatic winding; twin spring barrels, 55 hours power reserve
Functions: hours, minutes, sweep seconds (Caliber 331.01) or subsidiary seconds (Caliber 331.02); date
Diameter: 25.6 mm
Height: 3.5 mm
Jewels: 32
Frequency: 28,800 vph
Remarks: as Caliber 331.03 tested and certified according to the Qualité Fleurier criteria as well as being an officially certified C.O.S.C. chronometer

Caliber 338
Mechanical with automatic winding; twin spring barrels, 55 hours power reserve; completely skeletonized
Functions: hours, minutes, sweep seconds (Caliber 338.01) or subsidiary seconds (Caliber 338.02); date
Diameter: 25.6 mm
Height: 3.5 mm
Jewels: 32
Frequency: 28,800 vph

Caliber 334.01
Mechanical with automatic winding; twin spring barrels, 50 hours power reserve
Functions: hours, minutes, subsidiary seconds; date; chronograph
Diameter: 30.3 mm
Height: 6.8 mm
Jewels: 68
Frequency: 28,800 vph

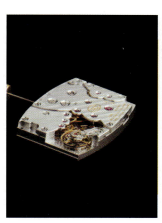

Caliber 110.01
Mechanical with manual winding; twin spring barrels, eight days power reserve
Functions: hours, minutes, subsidiary seconds; date; power reserve display
Dimensions: 29.3 x 23.6 mm
Height: 4.9 mm
Jewels: 28
Frequency: 21,600 vph

Caliber 333.01
Base caliber: 331 (module)
Mechanical with automatic winding; module for retrograde perpetual calendar; twin spring barrels, 55 hours power reserve
Functions: hours, minutes, sweep seconds; perpetual calendar with weekday, retrograde date, month, leap year, precision moon phase
Diameter: 27 mm
Height: 5.5 mm
Jewels: 32
Frequency: 28,800 vph

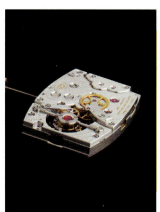

Caliber 500.02
Mechanical with manual winding; double bearing 30-second tourbillon; twin spring barrels, 7 days power reserve
Functions: hours, minutes, sweep seconds; power reserve display
Dimensions: 29.3 x 23.6 mm
Height: 5.5 mm
Jewels: 28
Frequency: 21,600 vph

Caliber 350.01
Mechanical with manual winding; 45 hours power reserve
Functions: hours, minutes, subsidiary seconds; hour, quarter hour, and minute repeater on two gongs
Diameter: 24.85 mm
Height: 6.61 mm
Jewels: 33
Frequency: 21,600 vph

Caliber 370.01
Mechanical with manual winding; movement designed on different "floors"; twin serially operating spring barrels, ten days power reserve
Functions: hours, minutes; power reserve display (drum display)
Dimensions: 21 x 16 x 27.4 mm
Jewels: 37
Frequency: 21,600 vph
Remarks: starter instrument with electric motor used to wind the movement since the long power reserve would demand more than 100 turns of the crown

Patek Philippe

Following two years of work and a complete restoration of its historical headquarters, the Patek Philippe *manufacture* inaugurated its fully new sales outlet on Geneva's Rue du Rhône this past winter. After the complete realization of the modern production center in Plan-les-Ouates in 1996 and putting together the Patek Philippe Museum, which opened in 2001, the renovation of this protected historical monument located between Rue du Rhône and General Guisan Quai represents the third large construction project the *manufacture* has undertaken in the last ten years. Here, customers can now find a clearly enlarged sales venue on two floors as well as the carefully renovated, historical Salon Napoleon III. On the upper floors, a number of modularly variable rooms for exhibitions and events with a view of Lake Geneva and its surroundings are also at the company's disposal.

Stylish aesthetics, tradition, and a well-cared-for company culture are Patek Philippe's most important values, and it is for good reason that this company is distanced from short-lived trends. The innovation that has become so important today takes place here in unseen ways—including the use of new materials so prevalent in the industry today, brought to bear solely for improvement in rate quality. Complicated things like tourbillons—presented by other brands with justifiable pride—are something that is rarely spoken of; they just exist here. The tourbillon cage completes its revolutions at the back of the watch, hidden. Understatement à la Patek Philippe.

This company places great value on its well-organized model palette, which basically rests upon the pillars of six model families. The typical Patek Philippe has for decades been the Calatrava model, manufactured as a simple timekeeper with two or three hands, which can even include an easy-to-read "small" complication. This watch can almost be said to be the epitome of the classic wristwatch.

The Gondolo model grew out of a business relationship with a jeweler in Rio de Janeiro. For more than thirty years, Patek Philippe manufactured a special watch collection for the Brazilian jewelers Gondolo & Labouriau. Finally, the Genevan *manufacture* named an existing model family comprising square, rectangular, tonneau, and cushion-shaped watches for its best customer. One of the new models Patek Philippe introduced at Baselworld 2007 was a Gondolo with a platinum case whose design was based on a watch housed in a tonneau-shaped case from 1925. At the same time, this case served as an occasion to make a new movement: the flat, beautifully shaped manually wound Caliber 25-21 REC.

Twenty-4 is a ladies' watch line exclusively comprising rectangular models—available in numerous variations of case, band, dial, and hands.

The Nautilus model was conceived in 1976 as an elegant sports watch for the younger customers of this old brand—it was, however, received just as well by older men in the prime of their lives. On the occasion of this model's thirtieth anniversary, which the Nautilus celebrated in 2006, it was carefully reworked to include an improved case design, which, however, was hardly noticeable. The Aquanaut is basically a modern relative of the Nautilus with an even sportier character.

An oval case is the main characteristic of the Ellipse d'Or, an elegant model timeless in shape and design, produced in a practically unchanged manner since 1968.

Finally, there is the wide spectrum of complicated watches, which extends from split-seconds chronographs and perpetual calendars to tourbillons, world time watches, and astronomical timepieces that confirm the unique reputation of the noble watch *manufacture* again and again.

Patek Philippe

Calatrava Travel Time
Reference number: 5134
Movement: manually wound, Patek Philippe Caliber 215 PS FUS 24 H; ø 21.9 mm, height 3.35 mm; 18 jewels; 28,800 vph; Seal of Geneva; hour hand settable forward and backward via button
Functions: hours, minutes, subsidiary seconds; second time zone; 24-hour display
Case: yellow gold, ø 37 mm, height 9.8 mm; sapphire crystal; transparent case back
Band: reptile skin, folding clasp
Price: $22,500
Variations: rose gold ($24,000); white gold ($24,000); platinum ($38,800)

Calatrava
Reference number: 5127
Movement: automatic, Patek Philippe Caliber 315 SC; ø 27 mm, height 3.22 mm; 29 jewels; 21,600 vph; Seal of Geneva
Functions: hours, minutes, sweep seconds; date
Case: yellow gold, ø 37 mm, height 8.5 mm; sapphire crystal; transparent case back; screw-in crown
Band: reptile skin, buckle
Price: $17,950
Variations: white or rose gold ($19,500); white gold on gold bracelet ($38,500); yellow gold bracelet ($35,700)

Calatrava
Reference number: 5119
Movement: manually wound, Patek Philippe Caliber 215 PS; ø 21.9 mm, height 2.55 mm; 18 jewels; 28,800 vph; Seal of Geneva
Functions: hours, minutes, subsidiary seconds
Case: rose gold, ø 36 mm, height 7.45 mm; bezel decorated with clous de Paris guilloché; sapphire crystal; transparent case back
Band: reptile skin, buckle
Price: $15,400
Variations: white gold ($15,400); yellow gold ($13,950)

Calatrava
Reference number: 5296
Movement: automatic, Patek Philippe Caliber 324 SC; ø 27 mm, height 3.3 mm; 29 jewels; 21,600 vph; Seal of Geneva
Functions: hours, minutes, sweep seconds; date
Case: rose gold, ø 38 mm, height 8.5 mm; sapphire crystal; transparent case back
Band: reptile skin, buckle
Price: $19,500
Variations: white gold ($19,500)

Calatrava
Reference number: 6000
Movement: automatic, Patek Philippe Caliber 240 PS C; ø 27.5 mm, height 2.53 mm; 27 jewels; 21,600 vph; micro rotor; Seal of Geneva
Functions: hours, minutes, subsidiary seconds; date
Case: white gold, ø 37 mm, height 10.15 mm; sapphire crystal; transparent case back
Band: reptile skin, folding clasp
Price: $19,900

Ellipse d'Or
Reference number: 3738
Movement: automatic, Patek Philippe Caliber 240; ø 27.5 mm, height 2.53 mm; 27 jewels; 21,600 vph; Seal of Geneva
Functions: hours, minutes
Case: white gold, 33.7 x 35.6 mm, height 5.65 mm; sapphire crystal
Band: reptile skin, buckle
Price: $18,900
Variations: rose gold ($18,900); yellow gold ($17,600)

Annual Calendar
Reference number: 5396
Movement: automatic, Patek Philippe Caliber 324 S QA LU 24 H; ø 33.3 mm, height 5.78 mm; 34 jewels; 28,800 vph; Seal of Geneva
Functions: hours, minutes, sweep seconds; date, day, month, moon phase (programmed for one year)
Case: rose gold, ø 38 mm, height 11 mm; sapphire crystal; transparent case back
Band: reptile skin, folding clasp
Price: $34,000

Annual Calendar
Reference number: 5146
Movement: automatic, Patek Philippe Caliber 315 S IRM QA LU; ø 30 mm, height 5.22 mm; 36 jewels; 21,600 vph; Seal of Geneva
Functions: hours, minutes, sweep seconds; date, day, month (programmed for one year); power reserve display
Case: white gold, ø 39 mm, height 11.2 mm; sapphire crystal; transparent case back
Band: reptile skin, folding clasp
Price: $29,700
Variations: yellow gold ($28,300); yellow gold bracelet ($44,500); platinum ($44,500); white gold bracelet ($47,500)

Patek Philippe

Annual Calendar
Reference number: 5135
Movement: automatic, Patek Philippe Caliber 324 S QA LU 24 H; ø 31.4 mm, height 5.78 mm; 34 jewels; 28,800 vph; Seal of Geneva; new Gyromax balance with four legs
Functions: hours, minutes, sweep seconds; annual calendar with date, day, month, moon phase; 24-hour display
Case: white gold, 51 x 40.33 mm, height 11.7 mm; sapphire crystal
Band: reptile skin, buckle
Price: $34,500
Variations: yellow gold ($32,900); rose gold ($34,500); platinum ($49,400)

Chronograph Perpetual Calendar
Reference number: 5970 R
Movement: manually wound, Patek Philippe Caliber CH 27-70 Q; ø 30 mm, height 7.2 mm; 24 jewels; 18,000 vph; Seal of Geneva
Functions: hours, minutes, subsidiary seconds; AM/PM display; chronograph; perpetual calendar with date, day, month, moon phase, leap year
Case: rose gold, ø 40 mm; height 13.8 mm; sapphire crystal; transparent case back
Band: reptile skin, folding clasp
Price: $103,200

Chronograph Annual Calendar
Reference number: 5960
Movement: automatic, Patek Philippe Caliber CH 28-520 IRM QA 24H (base CH 28-520); ø 33 mm, height 7.68 mm; 40 jewels; 28,800 vph; column-wheel control of chronograph functions; Seal of Geneva
Functions: hours, minutes, sweep seconds; chronograph with flyback function; annual calendar with date, day, month, moon phase; 24-hour indication; power reserve display
Case: platinum, ø 40.5 mm, height 13.55 mm; sapphire crystal; transparent case back
Band: reptile skin, folding clasp
Price: $63,500

Nautilus Chronograph
Reference number: 5980
Movement: automatic, Patek Philippe Caliber CH 28-520 C (base CH 28-520); ø 30 mm, height 6.63 mm; 35 jewels; 28,800 vph; column-wheel control of chronograph movement; rotor on zirconium oxide ball bearings; Seal of Geneva
Functions: hours, minutes, sweep seconds; chronograph; date
Case: stainless steel, ø 44 mm; height 12.16 mm; sapphire crystal; transparent case back; screw-in crown; water-resistant to 10 atm
Band: stainless steel, folding clasp
Price: $35,500

Perpetual Calendar
Reference number: 5980
Movement: automatic, Patek Philippe Caliber 28-520 C (base CH 28-520); ø 30 mm, height 6.63 mm; 35 jewels; 28,800 vph; Seal of Geneva
Functions: hours, minutes, sweep seconds; perpetual calendar with retrograde date, weekday, month, moon phase, leap year; power reserve display
Case: white gold, ø 38 mm, height 11.8 mm; sapphire crystal; hinged lid over transparent case back
Band: reptile skin, folding clasp
Price: $71,000
Variations: yellow gold ($69,500)

Sky Moon
Reference number: 5102
Movement: automatic, Patek Philippe Caliber 240 LU CL; ø 38 mm, height 6.26 mm; 45 jewels; 21,600 vph; Seal of Geneva
Functions: hours, minutes; moon phase and age of moon; map of starry sky
Case: white gold, ø 43.1 mm, height 9.78 mm; sapphire crystal; transparent case back
Band: reptile skin, buckle
Price: $194,200
Variations: yellow gold ($192,600)

World Time Watch
Reference number: 5130
Movement: automatic, Patek Philippe Caliber 240 HU; ø 27.5 mm, height 3.88 mm; 33 jewels; 21,600 vph; Seal of Geneva; dial disks with 24-hour display and world cities, synchronized via button; micro rotor in gold
Functions: hours, minutes; world time (24 hours/second time zone)
Case: platinum, ø 39.5 mm, height 9.4 mm; sapphire crystal; transparent case back
Band: reptile skin, folding clasp
Price: $44,800
Variations: white or rose gold ($31,500)

Chronometro Gondolo
Reference number: 5098
Movement: manually wound, Patek Philippe Caliber 25-21 REC; 21.5 x 24.6 mm, height 2.57 mm; 18 jewels; 28,800 vph; Seal of Geneva
Functions: hours, minutes
Case: platinum, 42 x 32 mm, height 8.9 mm; sapphire crystal; transparent case back
Band: reptile skin, buckle
Price: $34,500

An Internet-Based Market

Exhibit Buy Sell Trade

Pre-owned, antique and collectible wristwatches, pocket watches, art and sculpture clocks

ONE MARKET, MANY EXHIBITORS

We put the world of watches in the palm of your hand!

www.Net2Watches.com
Email: Net2Watches@Net2Watches.com
Tel: 877-777-9771 • Tel: 516-317-7741 • Fax: 516-773-4297

Patek Philippe

Nautilus
Reference number: 5712/1A
Movement: automatic, Patek Philippe Caliber 240 PS IRM C LU; ø 31 mm, height 3.98 mm; 29 jewels; 28,800 vph; micro rotor; Seal of Geneva
Functions: hours, minutes, subsidiary seconds; date, moon phase; power reserve display
Case: stainless steel, ø 43 mm; height 8.52 mm; sapphire crystal; transparent case back; screw-in crown; water-resistant to 6 atm
Band: stainless steel, folding clasp
Price: $23,750

Aquanaut
Reference number: 5167
Movement: automatic, Patek Philippe Caliber 315 SC; ø 27 mm, height 3.22 mm; 30 jewels; 21,600 vph; Seal of Geneva
Functions: hours, minutes, sweep seconds; date
Case: stainless steel, ø 40 mm, height 8.95 mm; sapphire crystal; screw-in crown; water-resistant to 12 atm
Band: Tropical rubber, folding clasp
Price: $13,900

Calatrava Travel Time
Reference number: 4934
Movement: manually wound, Patek Philippe Caliber 215 PS FUS 24 H; ø 21.9 mm, height 3.35 mm; 18 jewels; 28,800 vph; Seal of Geneva; hour hand settable forward and backward via button
Functions: hours, minutes, subsidiary seconds; second time zone; 24-hour display
Case: rose gold, ø 37 mm, height 9.8 mm; bezel set with 48 brilliant-cut diamonds; sapphire crystal; transparent case back
Band: reptile skin, buckle
Remarks: brown mother-of-pearl dial
Price: $27,200

Annual Calendar
Reference number: 4936
Movement: automatic, Patek Philippe Caliber 315 S QA LU; ø 30 mm, height 5.22 mm; 34 jewels; 21,600 vph; Seal of Geneva
Functions: hours, minutes, sweep seconds; date, day, month, moon phase (programmed for one year)
Case: rose gold, ø 37 mm, height 11.3 mm; bezel set with 78 diamonds; sapphire crystal; transparent case back
Band: reptile skin, buckle
Remarks: mother-of-pearl dial
Price: $32,900

Gemma
Reference number: 4991
Movement: manually wound, Patek Philippe Caliber 16-250; ø 16.3 mm, height 2.5 mm; 18 jewels; 21,600 vph; Seal of Geneva
Functions: hours, minutes
Case: rose gold, 37.2 x 22.4 mm, height 8.95 mm; bezel and lugs set with diamonds; faceted sapphire crystal
Band: reptile skin, buckle
Price: $23,000
Variations: white gold ($23,300)

Twenty-4
Reference number: 4910/10A
Movement: quartz, Patek Philippe Caliber E 15
Functions: hours, minutes
Case: stainless steel, 25.1 x 30 mm, height 6.8 mm; case sides set with diamonds; sapphire crystal
Band: stainless steel, folding clasp
Price: $9,250
Variations: rose gold; white gold

Calatrava
Reference number: 4896
Movement: manually wound, Patek Philippe Caliber 16-250; ø 16.3 mm, height 2.5 mm; 18 jewels; 28.800 vph; Seal of Geneva
Functions: hours, minutes
Case: white gold, ø 36 mm, height 6.35 mm; bezel set with 72 diamonds; sapphire crystal
Band: satin skin, buckle
Price: $19,250

Aquanaut Luce
Reference number: 5067
Movement: quartz, Patek Philippe Caliber E 23 SC
Functions: hours, minutes, sweep seconds; date
Case: stainless steel, 35 x 34 mm, height 7.9 mm; bezel set with 46 brilliant-cut diamonds; sapphire crystal; screw-in crown; water-resistant to 60 m
Band: Tropical rubber, folding clasp
Price: $11,950
Variations: in black, white, blue, and purple

Caliber 315/198
Mechanical with automatic winding, power reserve 46 hours, unidirectionally winding central ball-bearing rotor in 21-karat gold
Functions: hours, minutes, sweep seconds, annual calendar (date, day, month); 24-hour indication
Diameter: 30 mm (13 1/4'''); **Height:** 5.22 mm
Jewels: 35 (escape wheel with endstone)
Balance: Gyromax, with eight masselotte regulating weights
Frequency: 21,600 vph
Balance spring: flat hairspring
Shock protection: Kif
Remarks: base plate with perlage, beveled bridges with côtes de Genève, rotor with côtes circulaires, 316 individual parts

Caliber 324
Mechanical with automatic winding, power reserve 46 hours, unidirectionally winding central ball-bearing rotor in 21-karat gold
Functions: hours, minutes, sweep seconds, annual calendar with three windows (date, day, month) and moon phase; 24-hour indication
Diameter: 31.4 mm; **Height:** 5.78 mm; **Jewels:** 34
Balance: Gyromax, with four masselotte regulating weights
Frequency: 28,800 vph
Balance spring: flat hairspring
Shock protection: Kif
Remarks: Seal of Geneva; base plate with perlage, beveled bridges with côtes de Genève, rotor with côtes circulaires and an engraved cross of the Order of Calatrava

Caliber 16-250
Mechanical with manual winding, power reserve 36 hours
Functions: hours, minutes
Diameter: 16.3 mm (7''')
Height: 2.5 mm
Jewels: 18 (escape wheel with endstone)
Balance: monometallic ring
Frequency: 28,800 vph
Balance spring: flat hairspring with Triovis regulation and fine adjustment via micrometer screw
Shock protection: Incabloc
Remarks: base plate with perlage, beveled bridges with côtes de Genève, 99 individual parts

Caliber 25-21 REC
Mechanical with manual winding, power reserve 44 hours
Functions: hours, minutes
Dimensions: 24.6 x 21.5 mm
Height: 2.57 mm
Jewels: 18
Balance: Gyromax
Frequency: 28,800 vph
Balance spring: flat hairspring
Remarks: architecture inspired by shaped movements of the 1930s; base plate with perlage, beveled bridges with côtes de Genève, 142 individual parts; Seal of Geneva

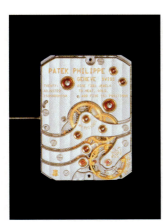

Caliber 28-20/220
Mechanical with manual winding, twin serially operating spring barrels, power reserve 10 days (240 hours)
Functions: hours, minutes, subsidiary seconds; power reserve display
Dimensions: 28 x 20 mm
Height: 5.05 mm
Jewels: 29 (escape wheel with endstone)
Balance: Gyromax in beryllium bronze with eight masselotte regulating weights
Frequency: 21,600 vph
Balance spring: flat hairspring
Shock protection: Kif
Remarks: base plate with perlage, beveled bridges with côtes de Genève, Seal of Geneva

Caliber 28-20/220
Caliber 28-20/220 as seen from the dial side. All steel parts such as springs, levers, and bars are beveled and polished according to the regulations for the Seal of Geneva, and their surfaces are brushed by hand. The holes for the screws in the steel parts are also polished. In addition, each and every tooth on the toothed wheels and pinions are polished by hand with a hard-wood disk. This is, by the way, the case for all Patek Philippe movements bearing the Seal of Geneva.

Patek Phillipe

Caliber 177
Mechanical with manual winding, power reserve 41 hours
Functions: hours, minutes
Diameter: 20.8 mm (9 ?''')
Height: ultra-flat, 1.77 mm
Jewels: 18 (escape wheel with endstone)
Balance: Gyromax, diameter 7.4 mm, in beryllium bronze with four Masselotte regulating weights
Frequency: 21,600 vph
Balance spring: flat hairspring
Shock protection: Kif
Remarks: base plate with perlage, beveled bridges with côtes de Genève, 112 individual parts; Seal of Geneva

Caliber 215
Mechanical with manual winding, power reserve 43 hours
Functions: hours, minutes, subsidiary seconds
Diameter: 21.9 mm (9 3/4''')
Height: 2.55 mm
Jewels: 18 (escape wheel with endstone)
Balance: Gyromax, with eight masselotte regulating weights
Frequency: 28,800 vph
Balance spring: flat hairspring
Shock protection: Kif
Remarks: base plate with perlage, beveled bridges with côtes de Genève, 130 individual parts; Seal of Geneva

Caliber 240 Q
Mechanical with automatic winding, power reserve 46 hours, unidirectionally winding off-center ball bearing micro-rotor in 22-karat gold, integrated into the movement
Functions: hours, minutes; perpetual calendar (date, weekday, month, leap year, moon phase) with 4 corrector buttons; 24-hour display
Diameter: 30 mm (13 1/2''')
Height: 3.75 mm
Jewels: 27 (escape wheel with endstone)
Balance: Gyromax, with eight masselotte regulating weights
Frequency: 21,600 vph
Balance spring: flat hairspring
Shock protection: Kif

Caliber 240 Q
Caliber 240 Q from the dial side.

Caliber 27-70 Q
Mechanical with manual winding, power reserve 58 hours
Functions: hours, minutes, subsidiary seconds, perpetual calendar (date, day, month, leap year, moon phase) with four corrector buttons; 24-hour display; chronograph with two counters (sweep seconds, minutes)
Diameter: 30 mm (13 1/2''')
Height: 7.2 mm
Jewels: 24 (escape wheel with endstone)
Balance: Gyromax, with eight masselotte regulating weights
Frequency: 18,000 vph
Balance spring: Breguet
Shock protection: Kif

Caliber CH 27-70 Q
Caliber CH 27-70 Q from the dial side. The stepped disk for the leap year display is visible next to the crown, divided into four cycles of twelve months each. Looking even more closely, one can even see the February with only 28 days in the leap year. The especially precise moon phase disk is visible at 6 o'clock; in the space of one year the moon phase's deviation is only 11 minutes and 47 seconds—in other words, only after 122 years will this display deviate by an entire day.
Remarks: base plate with perlage, beveled bridges with côtes de Genève, 350 individual parts; Seal of Geneva
Related calibers: 27-70/150 (CH 27-70 Q with split-seconds chronograph)

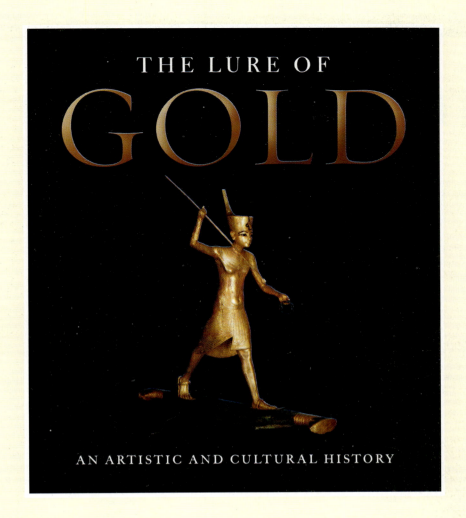

The Lure of Gold: An Artistic and Cultural History

The richly illustrated story of how gold, the world's most beautiful element, has influenced the art, economy, and society of every civilization, this beautiful volume explains how people throughout time have mined and refined gold (creating jewelry, religious objects, and diverse works of art) and used it for cultural and economic purposes.

By Hans-Gert Bachmann
285 full-color illustrations
280 pages · 10½ x 11¹³⁄₁₆ in.
Cloth · ISBN: 978-0-7892-0900-9
$75.00

Published by ABBEVILLE PRESS
137 Varick Street, New York, NY 10013
1-800-Artbook (in U.S. only)
Also available wherever fine books are sold
Visit us at www.abbeville.com

Perrelet

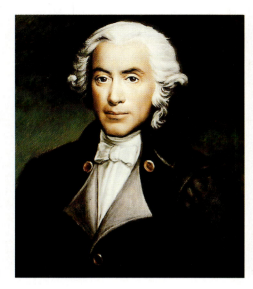

Abraham-Louis Perrelet (1729–1926) was the son of a middle-class farmer from Le Locle who developed an interest in watchmaking early on in his life. He was the first watchmaker in Le Locle to work on cylinder and duplex escapements, and it has been handed down that he made the first repeater to be heard echoing in the mountains.

Many watchmakers later to become famous were at one time Perrelet's apprentices, and some historians even include Abraham-Louis Breguet in this illustrious group. Although no conclusive proof for this has been uncovered over the years, one can at least assume that the two great watchmakers knew and respected each other.

Included among the numerous inventions that Perrelet contributed to the history of watchmaking was the "perpetual" watch from around the year 1770, a pocket watch that wound itself using the motion of the body. It was said that a constitutional lasting just eight minutes would be enough to keep said timepiece wound for a full twenty-four hours.

In light of this, it is not surprising that the newly refounded Perrelet brand (first refounded in 1993, then again in 2005) has given the automatic winding mechanism not only a technical but also a visual place of honor in its signature collection. These watches have not only two winding rotors coupled through the watch movement so as to improve winding performance, but the second rotor is also proudly displayed on the dial. This complicated mechanism, dubbed Caliber P-181, took a full five years to develop.

A decade after the first innovative double rotor timepiece was introduced, Perrelet launched the parallel double rotor in 2005, a mechanism that was developed in cooperation with famed Zurich master watchmaker Paul Gerber.

Today's incarnation of Perrelet is positioned in the "accessible luxury" segment. Its current goal is to interpret the brand's rich heritage while simultaneously finding modern and contemporary solutions, using automatic movements without exception. One new trademark of the brand is the special rotor that has been patented by Perrelet. This single rotor has been skeletonized and the missing metal has been replaced with a small pane of mineral crystal so that the finish and decoration of the high-quality movements can be admired. Almost all of Perrelet's modern watches are outfitted with this innovation.

Two-thousand seven saw the addition of a number of complicated new models to the growing palette of interesting timepieces in Perrelet's collection, mainly featuring modern reinterpretations of the contemporary brand's stable of timepieces featuring new materials and redesigned looks.

Big Size Central Lunar Phase
Reference number: A2034-5
Movement: automatic, Perrelet Caliber P.1030; ø 20 mm, height 6.5 mm; 28 jewels; 28,800 vph; exclusively developed for Perrelet
Functions: hours, minutes, sweep seconds; date; moon phase
Case: stainless steel, 30 x 40.3 mm, height 12.6 mm; bezel and strap lugs set with diamonds; sapphire crystal; transparent case back
Band: stingray skin, folding clasp
Price: $9,500
Variations: without diamonds

Double Rotor
Reference number: A5002/1
Movement: automatic, Perrelet Caliber P-181; ø 31.6 mm, height 4.6 mm; 21 jewels; 28,800 vph; second rotor located in center of dial
Functions: hours, minutes, sweep seconds; date
Case: titanium, ø 43.5 mm, height 13.6 mm; sapphire crystal; transparent case back
Band: rubber, folding clasp
Price: $5,800
Variations: stainless steel; rose gold

Regulator with Retrograde Hours
Reference number: A3014/2
Movement: automatic, Perrelet Caliber P-221; ø 26.2 mm, height 5.9 mm; 35 jewels; 28,800 vph
Functions: hours (retrograde), minutes (off-center); date
Case: rose gold, ø 42 mm, height 14.3 mm; sapphire crystal
Band: reptile skin, folding clasp
Price: $8,700
Variations: stainless steel; titanium; various dial variations

Skeleton Chronograph Dual Time
Reference number: A1010/1
Movement: automatic, Perrelet Caliber P-051 (base ETA Valjoux 7750); ø 30 mm, height 7.9 mm; 25 jewels; 28,800 vph; completely skeletonized; beveled edges, perlage
Functions: hours, minutes, subsidiary seconds; date; chronograph; 24-hour display (second time zone)
Case: stainless steel, ø 42 mm, height 14.7 mm; sapphire crystal
Band: reptile skin, folding clasp
Price: $9,950
Variations: rose gold; with diamonds; various dial variations

Poljot International

The roots of the Poljot International watch brand stretch back to Russia when the First Moscow Watch Factory was founded in the 1930s. In 1961, after Yuri Gagarin went into orbit as the first man in space, all watches manufactured by this factory were given the name Poljot (Russian for "flight").

In 1992, Poljot-V GmbH was established in Frankfurt, Germany. The managing director of this subsidiary, Alexander Shorokhov, called a new watch brand based on this company to life in 1995: Poljot International. Its goal was to continue the Russian traditions of the Poljot brand but in a slightly different way: utilizing high-quality materials in production, creating an individual and contemporary design, high-quality assembly, and a strict and systematic quality control.

The brand's manufacture, quality control, and service were then moved to Germany, which gave it the possibility to work completely independently and follow its own development strategy.

Poljot International's success made it possible for the company to take on a leading position among mid-priced watches. These products are sold today in thirty-five countries.

Among the most remarkable models are the Gorbatchov watches, created for the anniversary of the first president of the U.S.S.R., and the Gagarin model, which is dedicated to the first human flight in space. Poljot International continues to remain loyal to its tradition of paying homage to conquering space and remarkable personalities in Russian history.

Last year, Shorokhov met legendary Soviet cosmonaut Alexei Leonov in Moscow, the first person to take a space walk and later captain of the famed American-Soviet Soyuz-Apollo team.

The new model bearing the name Strela 2 ("arrow") is outfitted with a tourbillon movement conceived in the company's own workshop. The collection also contains regulator models developed at the company's Alzenau-based headquarters on the basis of the Molniya pocket watch movement, its Baikal watch with moon phase display, and the mechanical chronograph Moscow Nights.

Regulator
Reference number: 36031.8940441
Movement: manually wound, Caliber 36031 (base Molniya 3603); ø 36 mm, height 4.6 mm; 18 jewels; 18,000 vph; dial train modification; finely finished
Functions: hours (off-center), minutes, subsidiary seconds
Case: stainless steel, ø 43 mm, height 12.8 mm; mineral crystal; transparent case back
Band: leather, buckle
Price: $995
Variations: with sapphire crystal; with gold-plated case

Regulator
Reference number: 36033.9940552
Movement: manually wound, Caliber 36031 (base Molniya 3603); ø 36 mm, height 4.6 mm; 18 jewels; 18,000 vph; dial train modification; partial skeletonization under spring barrel; finely finished
Functions: hours (off-center), minutes, subsidiary seconds
Case: stainless steel, ø 43 mm, height 12.8 mm; mineral crystal; transparent case back
Band: leather, buckle
Price: $1,195
Variations: with sapphire crystal; with gold-plated case

Baikal Chronograph Moon Phase
Reference number: 31679.1940917
Movement: manually wound, Caliber 31679 (base Poljot 3133); ø 31 mm, height 7.35 mm; 23 jewels; 21,600 vph
Functions: hours, minutes, subsidiary seconds; chronograph; date, moon phase
Case: stainless steel, ø 43 mm, height 12 mm; mineral crystal; transparent case back
Band: leather, buckle
Price: $995
Variations: various dial variations

Gagarin Chronograph
Reference number: 31679.3081100
Movement: manually wound, Caliber 31679 (base Poljot 3133); ø 31 mm, height 7.35 mm; 23 jewels; 21,600 vph
Functions: hours, minutes, subsidiary seconds; chronograph; date, moon phase
Case: stainless steel, ø 44 mm, height 14 mm; bezel with tachymeter scale; mineral crystal; transparent case back
Band: leather, buckle
Remarks: limited edition of 500 pieces
Price: $1,395

Piaget

"When I look back to Piaget in early 2000," Piaget's CEO Philippe Léopold-Metzger remembers, "it was a very established watch brand. But when you ask people what Piaget is, most would say a European jewelry watch or jewelry brand. I think for me it was a very frustrating time because although it was nice to be recognized for something, I was very frustrated by the fact that Piaget got very little recognition for what it is today as a watchmaker. In a way I could understand it because the whole world was talking about very complicated watches. Okay, we did basic movements, but I thought it would be very important for Piaget to start going more complicated, and ultimately we launched the first tourbillon four years ago."

This first tourbillon—the Emperador Tourbillon—was a milestone in Piaget's history. Until that point, the empire that was founded in 1874 by Georges Edouard Piaget had been more interested in creating reliable base movements, both for itself and for other brands. It was only in 1940 under the second generation of Piagets that the company began signing its own movements and watches. Piaget, though now headquartered in Geneva's watch suburb Plan-les-Ouates, still maintains the original movement factory high in the Jura hills in La Côtes-aux-Fées. This is where all the brand's base and complicated movements are conceived and assembled.

From 2003's Emperador Tourbillon and its wondrously skeletonized evolution it was not really such a big jump to manufacture more of these ultra-high end beauties—like 2006's Tourbillon Relatif, which has its tourbillon placed literally on its sleeve for all to see. Looking like it perches directly upon the minute hand, this tourbillon makes a rotation all the way around the dial in a one-hour period—separated from any visible connection to its power source. Naturally, it is a clever planetary gear and set of disks that send the tourbillon on its orbit, but the illusion is phenomenal.

After several years occupied with the research and development of highly complicated pieces, Piaget declared 2007 a simpler year for itself, focusing on one of its staples from days gone by: ultra-thin movements. Precisely half a century ago, Piaget introduced Caliber 9P, the world's slimmest mechanical movement at the time, coming in at a mere two millimeters in height. This caliber was remarkable for its day, allowing wristwatches for the female to finally lay more elegantly flat on the wrist, but to become wider at the same time. It was far easier to read the time on the larger surfaces of these elegant timepieces' dials.

Piaget has now reissued Caliber 9P in honor of its fiftieth anniversary. Not only can it be admired in the classic white gold edition of the Altiplano, it also powers a unique rose gold square pocket watch on a chain. The Altiplano is limited to a total of fifty pieces, while the pocket watch will only find twenty-five new homes.

Piaget Altiplano from 1957 with Caliber 9P

Piaget

Altiplano
Reference number: G0A 32065
Movement: manually wound, Piaget Caliber 430P; ø 20.5 mm, height 2.15 mm; 19 jewels; 21,600 vph
Functions: hours, minutes
Case: rose gold, 33 x 33 mm, height 4.5 mm; sapphire crystal
Band: reptile skin, buckle
Price: $10,500
Variations: white gold

Altiplano
Reference number: G0A 32075
Movement: manually wound, Piaget Caliber 9P; ø 20.5 mm, height 2 mm; 18 jewels; 21,600 vph;
Functions: hours, minutes
Case: white gold, ø 38 mm, height 6.01 mm; sapphire crystal
Band: reptile skin, buckle
Remarks: new edition of historical Caliber 9P from 1957; genuine enamel dial; available exclusively in Piaget boutiques; limited edition of 50 pieces
Price: $14,500

Altiplano Double Jeu
Reference number: G0A 32153
Movement: two manually wound movements, Piaget Caliber 830P and 838P; each ø 26.8 mm, height 2.5 mm; 19 jewels; 21,600 vph
Functions: hours, minutes and hours, minutes, subsidiary seconds
Case: rose gold, ø 43 mm, height 11.7 mm; 3 sapphire crystals
Band: reptile skin, folding clasp
Remarks: two case parts joined by a hinge
Price: $24,900
Variations: white gold

Protocole XXL
Reference number: G0A 32004
Movement: manually wound, Piaget Caliber 830P; ø 26.8 mm, height 2.5 mm; 19 jewels; 21,600 vph; power reserve of 65 hours
Functions: hours, minutes
Case: white gold, 44 x 46 mm, height 7.97 mm; sapphire crystal; transparent case back
Band: reptile skin, folding clasp
Price: $18,900
Variations: rose gold

Polo Chronograph
Reference number: G0A 32039
Movement: automatic, Piaget Caliber 880P; ø 26.8, height 5.6 mm; 35 jewels; 28,800 vph; twin spring barrels; column-wheel control of chronograph functions; power reserve 52 hours
Functions: hours, minutes, subsidiary seconds; chronograph with flyback function; 24-hour display (second time zone); date
Case: rose gold, ø 43 mm, height 10.9 mm; sapphire crystal; transparent case back
Band: reptile skin, folding clasp
Price: $20,900
Variations: white gold

Polo Tourbillon Relatif
Reference number: G0A 31123
Movement: manually wound, Piaget Caliber 608P; ø 25.6, height 3.28 mm (without tourbillon); 27 jewels; 21,600 vph; power reserve 70 hours; flying one-minute tourbillon on the minute hand
Functions: hours, minutes
Case: white gold, ø 45 mm, height 13.3 mm; sapphire crystal
Band: reptile skin, folding clasp
Remarks: limited and numbered edition
Price: $235,000

Altiplano
Reference number: G0A 29112
Movement: manually wound, Piaget Caliber 430P; ø 20.5 mm, height 2.1 mm; 18 jewels; 21,600 vph
Functions: hours, minutes
Case: white gold, ø 38 mm, height 8 mm; sapphire crystal
Band: reptile skin, buckle
Price: $10,100
Variations: in yellow or rose gold

Altiplano
Reference number: G0A 29120
Movement: manually wound, Piaget Caliber 430P; ø 20.5 mm, height 2.1 mm; 18 jewels; 21,600 vph
Functions: hours, minutes
Case: yellow gold, ø 38 mm, height 8 mm; sapphire crystal
Band: reptile skin, buckle
Price: $9,500
Variations: in rose or white gold

Piaget

Altiplano
Reference number: G0A 29127
Movement: manually wound, Piaget Caliber 430P; ø 20.5 mm, height 2.1 mm; 18 jewels; 21,600 vph
Functions: hours, minutes
Case: white gold, ø 34 mm, height 9 mm; bezel set with 72 brilliant-cut diamonds; sapphire crystal
Band: reptile skin, folding clasp
Price: $14,500

Emperador XL
Reference number: G0A 32120
Movement: automatic, Piaget Caliber 524P; ø 24.6 mm, height 3.55 mm; 26 jewels; 21,600 vph
Functions: hours, minutes; date
Case: white gold, 36 x 46 mm, height 9.39 mm; sapphire crystal; transparent case back
Band: reptile skin, buckle
Remarks: limited edition of 200 pieces
Price: $16,900
Variations: rose gold

Emperador Coussin
Reference number: G0A 32017
Movement: automatic, Piaget Caliber 850P; ø 26.8 mm, height 4 mm; 30 jewels; 21,600 vph; twin spring barrels, power reserve 72 hours
Functions: hours, minutes, subsidiary seconds; date; second time zone with day/night indication
Case: rose gold, ø 42 mm, height 13.5 mm; sapphire crystal; transparent case back
Band: reptile skin, folding clasp
Remarks: limited edition of 200 pieces
Price: $17,900
Variations: white gold

Rectangle à l'Ancienne
Reference number: G0A 32062
Movement: automatic, Piaget Caliber 561P; ø 20.5 mm (base movement), height 5.1 mm; 31 jewels 21,600 vph
Functions: hours, minutes, subsidiary seconds (retrograde); date; power reserve display
Case: rose gold, 31 x 46 mm, height 9.5 mm; sapphire crystal
Band: reptile skin, buckle
Remarks: limited edition of 100 pieces
Price: $16,500

Altiplano
Reference number: G0A 31105
Movement: manually wound, Piaget Caliber 450P; ø 20.5 mm, height 2.1 mm; 18 jewels; 21,600 vph; finely finished; decorated with côtes circulaires
Functions: hours, minutes, subsidiary seconds
Case: white gold, ø 34 mm, height 9 mm; bezel set with 72 diamonds; sapphire crystal; transparent case back
Band: satin, buckle
Price: upon request
Variations: rose gold

Possession
Reference number: G0A 31091
Movement: quartz, Piaget Caliber 157P
Functions: hours, minutes
Case: rose gold, ø 28.7 mm, height 7 mm; rotating bezel set with one diamond; sapphire crystal
Band: satin, buckle
Price: $4,100
Variations: in white or yellow gold with black or brown dial; diverse strap variations

Polo
Reference number: G0A 26027
Movement: quartz, Piaget Caliber 690P
Functions: hours, minutes
Case: white gold, ø 28 mm, height 9 mm; sapphire crystal
Band: white gold, folding clasp
Price: $19,000
Variations: yellow gold; various case sizes

Miss Protocole
Reference number: G0A 24059
Movement: quartz, Piaget Caliber 57P
Functions: hours, minutes
Case: white gold, 24 x 39 mm, height 7.6 mm; movable upper strap lug with integrated clasp set with 30 brilliant-cut diamonds; sapphire crystal
Band: delivered with a set of two satin straps
Price: $9,000
Variations: in rose or yellow gold; various case sizes and strap variations

Piaget

Caliber 9P
Mechanical with manual winding, power reserve 36 hours
Functions: hours, minutes
Diameter: 20.3 mm
Height: 2.15 mm
Jewels: 18
Balance: with smooth three-legged balance wheel
Frequency: 19,800 vph
Balance spring: flat hairspring with fine adjustment via micrometer screw
Shock protection: Incabloc
Remarks: base plate with perlage, beveled bridges with côtes de Genève

Caliber 430P
Mechanical with manual winding, stop-seconds, power reserve 40 hours
Functions: hours, minutes, subsidiary seconds; date
Diameter: 20.5 mm
Height: 2.1 mm
Jewels: 18
Balance: glucydur
Frequency: 21,600 vph
Balance spring: flat hairspring with fine regulation via index
Shock protection: Incabloc

Caliber 504P
Mechanical with automatic winding, stop-seconds, power reserve 40 hours
Functions: hours, minutes, sweep seconds; date
Diameter: 24.6 mm
Height: 3.55 mm
Jewels: 26
Balance: glucydur
Frequency: 21,600 vph
Balance spring: flat hairspring with fine adjustment via index
Shock protection: Incabloc

Caliber 561P
Mechanical with automatic winding, stop-seconds, power reserve 40 hours
Functions: hours, minutes, subsidiary seconds (retrograde); date; power reserve display
Diameter: 20.5 mm
Height: 5.1 mm
Jewels: 31
Balance: glucydur
Frequency: 21,600 vph
Balance spring: flat hairspring with fine adjustment via index
Shock protection: Incabloc

Caliber 608P
Mechanical with manual winding, flying one-minute tourbillon on minute hand, power reserve 70 hours; twin spring barrels
Functions: hours, minutes
Diameter: 25.6 mm
Height: 3.28 mm (9.14 mm including tourbillon cage on minute hand)
Jewels: 27
Balance: glucydur, diameter 7.5 mm
Frequency: 21,600 vph

Caliber 850P
Mechanical with automatic winding, stop-seconds power reserve 72 hours
Functions: hours, minutes, subsidiary seconds; date; second time zone with day/night indication
Diameter: 26.8 mm
Height: 4 mm
Jewels: 30
Balance: glucydur
Frequency: 21,600 vph
Balance spring: flat hairspring with fine adjustment via index
Shock protection: Incabloc

Paul Picot

At Baselworld 2007 this Swiss brand with a predilection for Italian style surprised observers with its own tourbillon model, the development of which had been kept secret for two years. The model debuted in the Atelier line, which has contributed heavily to the brand's positioning and continues to be the center of Paul Picot's collection. The brand's leading line now seems cleverer, more technically demanding, and larger in size (42 mm) thanks to a fine lifting procedure. With this new model, Paul Picot also debuts a new decoration called *côtes visantes* to embellish the tourbillon's bridges. On the dial side, these are cleverly framed by the applied, brushed arcs of the retrograde calendar, power reserve display, and off-center seconds.

This new, exclusive complication reminds one of this brand's founding era, which is actually not that long ago, taking place in 1976 thanks to a large dose of pioneering spirit. In the middle of the toughest crisis the Swiss watch industry ever had to face, when many historic names went under, one of the newest companies in *haute horlogerie* was created. This firm was born of the will to save the rich tradition of the Swiss watch industry and let its true values once again come to light. The conventional customs of watchmaking were threatening to fall into disrepair; qualified masters of the craft were disappearing from the workplace, and the once-fascinating atmosphere of watchmakers' workshops had given way to the industrial hustle and bustle of anonymous trade names.

For company founder and president Mario Boiocchi, the only chance for the survival of European watch culture was to re-discover quality and precision. While Japanese and American competitors forced the Swiss watch industry to make compromises in order to meet the demands of mass consumption, Paul Picot chose to walk a different path.

Although the market was calling for futuristic design and electronic technology, Paul Picot entered it with fine gold cases and mechanical watch movements. In the years to follow, it was sporty, refined collections that opened the market for the brand. Diver's watches and chronographs sealed the deal, and the elegant collections with their shaped cases had already begun to write chapters of watch history all their own.

The diver's watch Le Plongeur has developed into an evergreen for Paul Picot. Featuring a unidirectionally rotating bezel outfitted with polished, angular numerals in relief on a granular background and an additional gripping edge, this powerful watch is just as elegant as it is practical, and just as attractive as it is robust—not every functional diver's watch needs to look like an iron lung. The middle ring made of hardened plastic that had originally served to reduce friction between the bezel and the case now also serves an aesthetic purpose with its yellow signal coloring. In this way the Plongeur C-Type has evolved into a yacht club classic. And for those who do not find the round C-Type a conspicuous enough timepiece, Paul Picot has just released a very striking square version called the Le Plongeur C-Type Carré. On this watch, it doesn't matter if the functional rotating bezel has been included or not—the envious stares of friends and acquaintances will more than make up for it.

A real cult watch has also developed out of Paul Picot's newest creation. The Technograph features a three-dimensional, highly unconventional dial visual for a chronograph. In the middle, above everything else, as a king on his throne, sits the hour and minute display. Underneath this raised main dial, the hands for the permanent subsidiary seconds and the chronograph's minute counter circulate. The ends of the hands are of differing lengths, thus sweeping two semicircular scales. Because, however, the hand arbors and the "unemployed" halves of the hands disappear under the main dial, the observer is left with the impression of two retrograde displays.

Paul Picot

Atelier 1100 Squelette
Reference number: 3090 SG
Movement: automatic, PP Caliber PP 1100 (base ETA 2892-2); ø 26.2 mm, height 4.95 mm; 30 jewels; 28,800 vph; officially certified C.O.S.C. chronometer; completely skeletonized
Functions: hours (off-center), minutes, subsidiary seconds; date; power reserve display
Case: stainless steel, ø 42 mm, height 11 mm; sapphire crystal; transparent case back; screw-in crown; water-resistant to 5 atm
Band: reptile skin, buckle
Price: $17,900

Atelier Classic 42 mm
Reference number: 3351 SG
Movement: automatic, PP Caliber PP 1400 (base ETA 2892-2); ø 25.6 mm, height 3.6 mm; 21 jewels; 28,800 vph; officially certified C.O.S.C. chronometer
Functions: hours, minutes, sweep seconds; date
Case: stainless steel, ø 42 mm, height 10 mm; sapphire crystal; transparent case back; screw-in crown; water-resistant to 5 atm
Band: reptile skin, buckle
Remarks: dial set with 5 diamond markers
Price: $8,500
Variations: various dial variations

Atelier Classic 42 mm
Reference number: 3351 RG
Movement: automatic, PP Caliber PP 1400 (base ETA 2892-2); ø 25.6 mm, height 3.6 mm; 21 jewels; 28,800 vph; officially certified C.O.S.C. chronometer
Functions: hours, minutes, sweep seconds; date
Case: rose gold, ø 42 mm, height 10 mm; sapphire crystal; transparent case back; screw-in crown; water-resistant to 5 atm
Band: reptile skin, buckle
Remarks: dial set with 5 diamond markers
Price: $19,300
Variations: various dial variations

Atelier 1100 Régulateur
Reference number: 3340 SG
Movement: automatic, PP Caliber PP 1100 (base ETA 2892-2); ø 26.2 mm, height 4.95 mm; 30 jewels; 28,800 vph; officially certified C.O.S.C. chronometer
Functions: hours (off-center), minutes, subsidiary seconds; date; power reserve display
Case: stainless steel, ø 42 mm, height 11 mm; sapphire crystal; transparent case back; screw-in crown; water-resistant to 5 atm
Band: reptile skin, buckle
Price: $10,900
Variations: various dial variations

Atelier 1200 42 mm
Reference number: 3058 SG
Movement: automatic, PP Caliber PP 1200 (base ETA 2892-2); ø 26.2 mm, height 4.95 mm; 24 jewels; 28,800 vph; officially certified C.O.S.C. chronometer
Functions: hours, minutes, sweep seconds; date; power reserve indication
Case: stainless steel, ø 42 mm, height 10.4 mm; sapphire crystal; transparent case back; screw-in crown
Band: reptile skin, buckle
Price: $9,700
Variations: various dial variations

Technograph
Reference number: 334 SG
Movement: automatic, Caliber PP 1350 (base ETA Valjoux 7750); ø 30 mm, height 8.4 mm; 28 jewels; 28,800 vph; reworked dial train
Functions: hours, minutes, subsidiary seconds; chronograph; date
Case: stainless steel, ø 44 mm, height 14.8 mm; sapphire crystal; transparent case back; screw-in crown; water-resistant to 10 atm
Band: leather, folding clasp
Price: $7,500
Variations: various dial variations

Technograph
Reference number: 334 QSG
Movement: automatic, Caliber PP 1350 (base ETA Valjoux 7750); ø 30 mm, height 8.4 mm; 28 jewels; 28,800 vph; reworked dial train
Functions: hours, minutes, subsidiary seconds; chronograph; date
Case: stainless steel, ø 44 mm, height 14.8 mm; sapphire crystal; transparent case back; screw-in crown; water-resistant to 10 atm
Band: leather, folding clasp
Price: $7,900
Variations: various dial variations

Technograph Wild Dial
Reference number: 334 SG
Movement: automatic, Caliber PP 1350 (base ETA Valjoux 7750); ø 30 mm, height 8.4 mm; 28 jewels; 28,800 vph; reworked dial train
Functions: hours, minutes, subsidiary seconds; chronograph; date
Case: stainless steel, ø 44 mm, height 14.8 mm; sapphire crystal; transparent case back; screw-in crown; water-resistant to 10 atm
Band: leather, folding clasp
Remarks: dial with leather inlay
Price: $8,400
Variations: various leather dial variations

Paul Picot

Technograph
Reference number: 334 RG
Movement: automatic, Caliber PP 1350 (base ETA Valjoux 7750); ø 30 mm, height 8.4 mm; 28 jewels; 28,800 vph; reworked dial train
Functions: hours, minutes, subsidiary seconds; chronograph; date
Case: rose gold, ø 44 mm, height 14.8 mm; sapphire crystal; transparent case back; screw-in crown; water-resistant to 10 atm
Band: reptile skin, folding clasp
Price: $21,900
Variations: various dial variations

Le Plongeur C-Type Chronograph Bicolor
Reference number: 3930 SRG
Movement: automatic, Caliber PP 1410 (base ETA Valjoux 7753); ø 30 mm, height 7.9 mm; 27 jewels; 28,800 vph; officially certified C.O.S.C. chronometer
Functions: hours, minutes, subsidiary seconds; chronograph; date
Case: stainless steel, PVD coated black, ø 43 mm, height 16.3 mm; unidirectionally rotating bezel with 60-minute scale and rose gold applied elements; sapphire crystal; screw-in crown and buttons; water-resistant to 30 atm
Band: rubber, folding clasp with extension
Price: $17,500

Le Plongeur C-Type Compass
Reference number: 851 TG
Movement: automatic, Caliber PP 1400 (base ETA 2824-2); ø 25.6 mm, height 3.6 mm; 21 jewels; 28,800 vph; officially certified C.O.S.C. chronometer
Functions: hours, minutes, sweep seconds; date; compass
Case: stainless steel, ø 43 mm, height 18.5 mm; unidirectionally rotating bezel with 60-minute divisions; sapphire crystal; screw-in crown; water-resistant to 30 atm
Band: rubber, folding clasp with wetsuit extension
Remarks: case can be opened, compass on case back
Price: $9,300

Le Plongeur C-Type Chronograph
Reference number: 4116GR
Movement: automatic, Caliber PP 1410 (base ETA 7753); ø 30 mm, height 7.9 mm; 27 jewels; 28,800 vph; officially certified C.O.S.C. chronometer
Functions: hours, minutes, subsidiary seconds; chronograph; date
Case: stainless steel, ø 43 mm, height 16.3 mm; unidirectionally rotating bezel with 60-minute scale; sapphire crystal; screw-in crown and buttons; water-resistant to 30 atm
Band: stainless steel, folding clasp with wetsuit extension
Remarks: limited edition of 500 pieces
Price: $6,600
Variations: rubber strap

Gentleman Chronodate
Reference number: 2034SG
Movement: automatic, PP Caliber 1320 (base ETA Valjoux 7750); ø 30 mm, height 7.9 mm; 28 jewels; 28,800 vph
Functions: hours, minutes, subsidiary seconds; chronograph; date
Case: stainless steel, ø 42 mm, height 14.65 mm; sapphire crystal; screw-down case back; screw-in crown; water-resistant to 5 atm
Band: reptile skin, buckle
Price: $4,700
Variations: stainless steel bracelet

Gentleman Régulateur
Reference number: 4114
Movement: automatic, PP Caliber 1000 (base ETA 2892 with module 3305); ø 25.6 mm, height 4.95 mm; 27 jewels; 28,800 vph
Functions: hours (off-center), minutes, subsidiary seconds
Case: stainless steel, ø 42 mm, height 9.7 mm; sapphire crystal; water-resistant to 5 atm
Band: reptile skin, buckle
Price: $4,100
Variations: stainless steel bracelet; various dial variations

Gentleman GMT
Reference number: 2031 SG
Movement: automatic, PP Caliber 1320 (base ETA Valjoux 7750); ø 30 mm, height 7.9 mm; 25 jewels; 28,800 vph
Functions: hours, minutes, subsidiary seconds; chronograph; date; 24-hour display (second time zone)
Case: stainless steel, ø 42 mm, height 14.65 mm; sapphire crystal; screw-in crown; water-resistant to 5 atm
Band: reptile skin, buckle
Price: $5,250
Variations: stainless steel bracelet

Gentleman GMT
Reference number: 2031 RG
Movement: automatic, PP Caliber 1320 (base ETA Valjoux 7750); ø 30 mm, height 7.9 mm; 25 jewels; 28,800 vph
Functions: hours, minutes, subsidiary seconds; chronograph; date; 24-hour display (second time zone)
Case: rose gold, ø 42 mm, height 14.65 mm; sapphire crystal; screw-in crown; water-resistant to 5 atm
Band: reptile skin, buckle
Price: $11,900
Variations: various dial variations

By Amanda Triossi and
Daniela Mascetti
600 full-color illustrations
320 pages · 9⅝ x 13³⁄₁₆ in.
ISBN: 978-0-7892-0945-0
$75.00 · Cloth

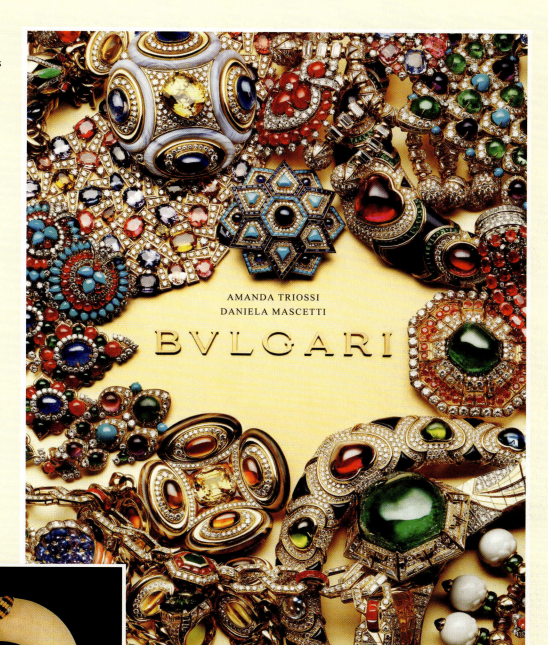

Bulgari

A dazzlingly illustrated history of Bulgari jewelry, this engaging book tells the story of the world's first family of jewelers, goldsmiths, and silversmiths, and the pieces that made their name.

Since its start in Rome in 1884, the Bulgari firm has succeeded in launching influential trends and revivals in jewelry design. In this captivating volume, new photography and archival pictures trace the development of the Bulgari style, a distinctive look that has enchanted royalty, movie stars, and others for more than a century.

Published by ABBEVILLE PRESS
137 Varick Street, New York, NY 10013
1-800-ARTBOOK (in U.S. only)
Also available wherever fine books are sold
Visit us at www.abbeville.com

Porsche Design

The quality of the products manufactured under the Porsche Design label speaks a lucid language. First-class and excellently worked materials, classic yet modern cases, and a clean design completely resisting superficial decoration constitute the characteristics of watches by Porsche Design. These are products that homogeneously fit into the line of other items created by F. A. Porsche's design studio: the company's style includes material combinations that may seem unusual at first glance, but are actually quite harmonious when the product is looked at more closely. The color black is nothing unusual for Porsche Design: in the late 1970s Porsche Design by Orfina was already presenting a simple chronograph whose case, dial, and even metal bracelet with folding clasp were kept to a simple matte black—a color that smacked of sportiness for automobile drivers back then.

Matte black accessories on cars have all but disappeared today, but in the watch industry this noncolor is experiencing a true comeback. Thus, Porsche Design introduced its sporty Dashboard chronograph last year in a black-coated aluminum case—and the brand's flagship model, Indicator, is also available in a black-coated titanium case. On the newest model, Worldtimer, the color black is not just an expression of the timepiece's sportiness—for this watch is not a short-term timer but rather a watch that displays a second time zone. What is more in the foreground here is underscoring the purist design of the timekeeper, concealing its stately shape.

Its curved case band with trapezoid-shaped strap lugs takes the force from this voluminous design. Despite this, the cylindrical basic shape of the case remains. However, the stately case size is not chosen without reason: a movement of 36 mm diameter and 10.1 mm height needs to find room within it. Eterna's technicians chose the Valgranges automatic caliber because of its sovereign torque; this watch's GMT function needs a great deal of reliable energy. Eterna's head technician Patrick Kury explains that this is not as simple to realize as it may seem, "The module is very complex and needs a great deal of room."

Perfection is not only demanded of movement technology and design. For this reason, the cases are not coated with powder or chrome-plated black like they previously were. The magic word today is PVD. These initials stand for physical vapor deposition, a somewhat awkward term for a process that serves to coat objects with thin layers of hard material. Put simply: hard coating material is made gaseous and then evenly applied to the case.

Porsche Design

Indicator P'6910
Reference number: 6910.10.40
Movement: automatic, Eterna Caliber 6036 (base ETA Valjoux 7750); ø 36 mm, height 14.3 mm; 28,800 vph; mechanical chronograph with digital display of stop functions; four spring barrels, power reserve display with two concentric disks
Functions: hours, minutes, subsidiary seconds; chronograph; power reserve display
Case: titanium, ø 49 mm, height 17.8 mm; bezel secured with four special screws; sapphire crystal; transparent case back; titanium and rubber crown; water-resistant to 50 m
Band: rubber, titanium clasp with two prongs
Price: $150,000
Variations: PVD-coated titanium case

Worldtimer P'6750
Reference number: 6750.13.44.1180
Movement: automatic, ETA Valgranges Caliber A07.111 with Eterna module; ø 36.6 mm, height 3.62 mm; 38 jewels; 28,800 vph
Functions: hours, minutes, sweep seconds; world time (24-hour display, second time zone)
Case: PVD-coated titanium, ø 45 mm, height 16.8 mm; sapphire crystal; screw-in crown; additional crown with integrated button; water-resistant to 10 atm
Band: rubber, folding clasp
Price: $18,000
Variations: matte titanium

Dashboard PGR P'6613
Reference number: 6613.69.50.1142
Movement: automatic, ETA Valjoux Caliber 7750 AR2; ø 30 mm, height 7.9 mm; 25 jewels; 28,800 vph
Functions: hours, minutes, subsidiary seconds; split-seconds chronograph; date; power reserve display
Case: red gold, ø 42 mm, height 16.3 mm; sapphire crystal; transparent case back; screw-in crown; water-resistant to 10 atm
Band: reptile skin, buckle
Price: $9,800
Variations: rubber strap; black dial

Dashboard PTR P'6613
Reference number: 6613.12.40.1145
Movement: automatic, ETA Valjoux Caliber 7750 AR2; ø 30 mm, height 7.9 mm; 25 jewels; 28,800 vph
Functions: hours, minutes, subsidiary seconds; date; split-seconds chronograph
Case: titanium, ø 42 mm, height 16.3 mm; sapphire crystal; transparent case back; screw-in crown; water-resistant to 10 atm
Band: rubber, folding clasp
Price: $9,800
Variations: titanium bracelet; reptile skin strap

Dashboard PTC Limited Edition 2007
Reference number: 6612.11.43.1179
Movement: automatic, ETA Caliber 2894-2; ø 28 mm, height 6.1 mm; 37 jewels; 28,800 vph
Functions: hours, minutes, subsidiary seconds; date; chronograph
Case: titanium, ø 42 mm, height 14.85 mm; sapphire crystal; transparent case back; screw-in crown; water-resistant to 10 atm
Band: lamb leather, buckle
Remarks: in set with cufflinks and keychain
Price: $6,300

Dashboard PAC P'6612
Reference number: 6612.17.46.0243
Movement: automatic, ETA Caliber 2894-2; ø 28 mm, height 6.1 mm; 37 jewels; 28,800 vph
Functions: hours, minutes, subsidiary seconds; chronograph; date
Case: aluminum with black PVD coating, ø 42 mm, height 14.8 mm; titanium bezel; sapphire crystal; transparent case back; screw-in crown; water-resistant to 10 atm
Band: titanium, folding clasp
Price: $5,400
Variations: rubber or crocodile skin strap

Flat Six P'6310 Automatic
Reference number: 6310.41.84.1167
Movement: automatic, ETA Caliber 2894-2; ø 28 mm, height 6.1 mm; 37 jewels; 28,800 vph
Functions: hours, minutes, sweep seconds; date; power reserve display
Case: stainless steel, ø 44 mm, height 10.5 mm; transparent case back; screw-in crown; water-resistant to 12 atm
Band: rubber, folding clasp
Price: $1,950
Variations: stainless steel bracelet; various dial colors

Flat Six P'6340 Chronograph
Reference number: 6340.41.44.0251
Movement: automatic, ETA Valjoux Caliber 7750; ø 30 mm, height 7.9 mm; 25 jewels; 28,800 vph
Functions: hours, minutes, subsidiary seconds; chronograph; date, day
Case: stainless steel, ø 44.5 mm, height 15 mm; bezel with tachymeter scale; sapphire crystal; screw-in crown; transparent case back; water-resistant to 12 atm
Band: stainless steel, folding clasp
Price: $3,500
Variations: rubber strap; various dial colors

Rado

With their unmistakable design, Rado watches have conquered a special place in the hearts of the watch-buying public. "Less is more" seems to be Rado's design motto these days, meaning that the brand is now leaving everything off its timepieces that could disturb their clean, expressive lines. This is perhaps why these watches carry a convincing aura of timelessness and a sovereign simplicity about them. They are more than just timekeepers—they are expressions of one's personality and style.

For a Swiss brand, Rado is relatively young, with a history that began in the year 1957 with the production of the first watches bearing this name. The cornerstone for its international success story was laid, however, in 1962. At that time, this company surprised the world with a revolutionary invention: the oval DiaStar, the first truly scratch-resistant watch ever, sporting a case made of scratchproof heavy metal. In 1985 its parent company, the Swatch Group, decided to utilize Rado's know-how and its extensive experience in developing materials. From then on the brand intensified its research activities at its home in Lengnau, Switzerland, and continued to produce only watches with extremely hard cases.

Within the Swatch Group, Rado was the most successful individual brand in the upper price segment for a long time, with consistent growth and appreciable turnover at a time that most brands would term "difficult." New creations kept the brand talked about and secured it a certain advantage over the competition. Nevertheless, numerous new model families in varying price categories watered down this brand's distinct image, and the splits Rado was performing between jeweled watches and high-tech icons threatened to tear the company apart.

It would seem that the pioneering spirit of the ceramic researchers has now won out. The company already holds more than thirty patents arising from the research and production of new case materials. Various powders, already mixed together with binding agents and additives to later create the desired color, are pressed into molds to make cases, which are then fired and finally polished with diamond powder.

"Rado watches are the perfect synthesis of special materials and exceptional design," says Rado's president Roland Streule. He could be specifically referring to two of the company's new introductions for 2007: Ceramica and Rado True, classic ceramic timepieces clothed in classic Rado minimalist design.

The Ceramica was originally introduced in 1989, at a time when its design was totally groundbreaking. This model made using ceramic a vehicle for color and created Rado's signature black look. Now reinterpreted and updated, the monochrome chronograph perfectly illustrates how Rado's cases and crystals merge to become an extension of each other.

The Rado True appears to be the exact opposite of the Ceramica. Also crafted in scratchproof ceramic, it is both round and white in sharp contrast to the usual square and black, containing fluid lines, perfect integration, and a brilliant purity. For sticklers for tradition, this model is also available in black ceramic.

Rado

Integral Automatic
Reference number: R 20 692 72 2
Movement: automatic, ETA Caliber 2681; ø 19.4 mm, height 4.8 mm; 25 jewels; 28,800 vph
Functions: hours, minutes, sweep seconds; date
Case: stainless steel, 36.2 x 30.3 mm, height 10.1 mm; sapphire crystal
Band: ceramic, double titanium folding clasp
Price: $2,400
Variations: in two case sizes; various dial variations

Integral Chronograph
Reference number: R 20 670 90 5
Movement: quartz, ETA Caliber 251.471
Functions: hours, minutes, subsidiary seconds; date; chronograph
Case: stainless steel, 36 x 30 mm, height 10 mm; sapphire crystal; set with 30 diamonds
Band: leather, folding clasp
Price: $3,900
Variations: red or blue leather strap; ceramic link bracelet

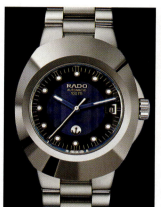

Original
Reference number: R 12 637 16 3
Movement: automatic, ETA Caliber 2824-2; ø 25.6 mm, height 4.6 mm; 25 jewels; 28,800 vph
Functions: hours, minutes, sweep seconds; date
Case: stainless steel, 30.6 x 46.2 mm, height 12 mm; hard metal bezel; sapphire crystal; screw-in crown
Band: stainless steel, folding clasp
Price: $995
Variations: in two case sizes; various dial variations

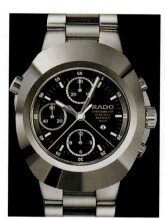

Original Split-Seconds Chronograph
Reference number: R 12 694 15 3
Movement: automatic, ETA Valjoux Caliber 7750; ø 30 mm, height 8.2 mm; 29 jewels; 28,800 vph; officially certified C.O.S.C. chronometer
Functions: hours, minutes, subsidiary seconds; split-seconds chronograph
Case: hard metal, 41 x 46 mm, height 13.5 mm; sapphire crystal; transparent case back; screw-in crown; water-resistant to 10 atm
Band: stainless steel, folding clasp
Price: $5,900
Variations: blue-black dial

Ceramica Chronograph
Reference number: R 21 715 15 2
Movement: quartz, ETA Caliber 251.471
Functions: hours, minutes, subsidiary seconds; date; chronograph
Case: stainless steel, 36 x 35 mm, height 11 mm; sapphire crystal
Band: matte ceramic, folding clasp
Price: $2,600
Variations: shiny ceramic bracelet; various dial variations

Ceramica
Reference number: R 21 712 70 2
Movement: quartz, ETA Caliber 280.002
Functions: hours, minutes
Case: stainless steel, 19.5 x 24.5 mm, height 7 mm; sapphire crystal
Band: ceramic, folding clasp
Remarks: dial set with four diamonds
Price: $1,690
Variations: two case sizes; dial with markers

Sintra Sport
Reference number: R 13 723 15 2
Movement: quartz, ETA Caliber 255.411
Functions: hours, minutes, sweep seconds; date
Case: ceramic, 35 x 44.5 mm, height 11 mm; sapphire crystal
Band: ceramic, folding clasp
Price: $2,200
Variations: various case sizes

Rado True
Reference number: R 27 696 71 2
Movement: quartz, ETA Caliber 980.106
Functions: hours, minutes, sweep seconds
Case: ceramic, ø 27 mm, height 7.6 mm; sapphire crystal
Band: ceramic, folding clasp
Price: $1,250
Variations: two case sizes; dial with markers

RGM

Roland Murphy is one courageous watchmaker. Originally hailing from Maryland, Murphy discovered at a fairly early age that he has a natural talent for working with his hands. After learning woodworking at a vocational school, he began to make cabinets at a clock company, where he discovered his love of the ticking treasures. It wasn't long before he was constructing his own clocks. His proclivity for watch and clock movements becoming apparent, he attended Lancaster, Pennsylvania's Bowman Technical School and then traveled to the mother country of watchmaking to graduate from the famed Wostep program in Neuchâtel, Switzerland. A few years with one of the industry's biggest names, the SMH (now the Swatch Group), taught him the rest of what he needed to know about the watch business. What seems like a lifetime later, Murphy introduced his Signature series, timepieces that are especially unique on the inside since they are powered by vintage Hamilton pocket watch movements—a company that incidentally, also hails from Lancaster, Pennsylvania—that Murphy chose thanks to their Swiss-style stem system, which is easier for him to convert for use in a wristwatch. Murphy uses Hamilton Calibers 921, 917, 923, and 945 in the timepieces and offers his customers a number of high-quality finishes to choose from: fully hand-engraved, skeletonized, or decorated with traditional Swiss finishing including *côtes de Genève*.

Murphy's latest project—perhaps the one that makes him proudest of all since it takes on a red, white, and blue tint for him—is called Caliber 801. "I designed this movement some time back," Murphy explains, "and now I have the resources to bring it to life. The bridge design is very much like an E. Howard movement from around 1917. It looks just like a traditional American movement."

Nineteen-jewel Caliber 801 has a jeweled spring barrel to prevent wear on the bridge and plate. Very traditional in design, a free-sprung version with regulation directly on the balance wheel can be special-ordered. "This is truly the first high-grade mechanical movement made in series in the U.S. since Hamilton stopped production of the 992B in 1969—of course, on a much smaller scale," Murphy grins.

Murphy's movement comprises some parts purchased in Switzerland and some of his own design that he produces or has produced regionally. Make no mistake, though, this movement is all American. "The CNC parts we order from local companies usually working for the medical industries are hand-finished here in our workshop," Murphy continues. "We tape threads, set jewels, hand-finish parts, basically building these movements one at a time. Any perlage, *côtes de Genève*, or guilloché is done by us."

Murphy expects to make about twenty-five pieces of Caliber 801 in 2007, though he hopes to increase this number in the following years. "As a strong, large mechanical movement, it will make a great base for complications we will add later. I am in the beginning stages of designing complications for this movement, which will also be made here in the U.S. And I am working on a tourbillon version to be called Caliber 801T."

RGM

801
Reference number: 150/801
Movement: manually wound, RGM Caliber 801, ø 37 mm (16 lines), 19 jewels, lever escapement, screw balance; caliber comprising U.S. and Swiss components; bridges, base plate, setting components, and winding click system made in Lancaster County, Pennsylvania
Functions: hours, minutes, subsidiary seconds
Case: stainless steel, ø 42 mm; sapphire crystal; sapphire crystal exhibition case back
Band: alligator skin, folding clasp
Remarks: limited edition of 25 pieces per year; can be custom-finished as customer wishes
Price: $7,950
Variations: gold case; movement finish, engraving, and guilloché can be individually customized

Left-Handed Chronograph
Reference number: 160/180
Movement: automatic, ETA Valjoux Caliber 7751, modified, ø 30 mm, height 7.9 mm; 26 jewels; 28,800 vph; côtes de Genève and perlage on bridges and plates
Functions: hours, minutes, subsidiary seconds; date, day, month, moon phase; chronograph; 24-hour indication
Case: stainless steel, ø 42 mm, height 15.2 mm; sapphire crystal; sapphire crystal exhibition case back
Band: alligator skin, folding clasp
Remarks: solid silver hand-guilloché dial with blued steel hands
Price: $8,500
Variations: 18-karat rose gold case

Seven Day
Reference number: 130
Movement: manually wound, RGM Caliber (base Jaquet 736); 19 jewels; côtes de Genève and perlage on bridges and plates; twin spring barrels; seven-day power reserve
Functions: hours, minutes, subsidiary seconds; power reserve display
Case: stainless steel, ø 42 mm, height 12.7 mm; domed sapphire crystal; sapphire crystal exhibition case back
Band: alligator skin, folding clasp
Remarks: limited edition of 30 pieces; solid silver hand-guilloché dial with blued steel hands
Price: $7,900

Big Date
Movement: automatic, ETA Caliber 2896, modified; ø 25.6 mm, height 4.85 mm; 22 jewels; 28,800 vph; côtes de Genève and perlage on bridges and plates
Functions: hours, minutes, sweep seconds; date
Case: stainless steel, ø 38.5 mm, height 10.5 mm; sapphire crystal; sapphire crystal exhibition case back
Band: alligator skin, folding clasp
Remarks: solid silver hand-guilloché dial with blued steel hands
Price: $5,200

Grand Guilloché
Reference number: 150E
Movement: manually wound, ETA Unitas Caliber 6498, modified; ø 36.6 mm, height 4.5 mm; 17 jewels; 18,000 vph; screw balance; three available finishes: côtes de Genève, guilloché, or skeletonized
Functions: hours, minutes, subsidiary seconds
Case: stainless steel, ø 42 mm, height 10.5 mm; sapphire crystal; exhibition case back; water-resistant to 50 m
Band: alligator skin, folding clasp
Price: $4,400
Variations: stainless steel bracelet; in rose gold

Victory
Reference number: 200
Movement: automatic, ETA Valgranges Caliber A01.111, modified, ø 36.6 mm, height 7.9 mm; 24 jewels; 28,000 vph; completely hand-engraved and hand-guilloché; hand-engraved 18-karat gold rotor
Functions: hours, minutes, sweep seconds
Case: rose gold, ø 42 mm, height 10.5 mm; sapphire crystal; exhibition case back; water-resistant to 50 m
Band: alligator skin, folding clasp
Remarks: limited edition of 6 pieces, each dial hand-engraved with different scene depicting the Battle of Trafalgar
Price: $19,500

Signature Series
Reference number: 222
Movement: manually wound, Hamilton Caliber 923, modified; 23 jewels, 18,000 vph; available hand-engraved or skeletonized
Functions: hours, minutes, subsidiary seconds
Case: stainless steel, ø 41 mm, height 12 mm; sapphire crystal; exhibition case back; water-resistant to 50 m
Band: alligator skin, folding clasp
Price: $5,800
Variations: optionally available with rare Hamilton calibers 921, 917, or 945

William Penn Collection
Reference number: 121
Movement: manually wound, RGM Caliber (base Jaquet 736); 22 jewels; shaped movement; côtes de Genève, perlage, hand-engraving
Functions: hours, minutes, subsidiary seconds; power reserve display; moon phase
Case: stainless steel, 40 x 28 mm; height 7.9 mm; sapphire crystal; exhibition case back; water-resistant to 50 m
Band: alligator skin, folding clasp
Price: $6,495
Variations: in 18-karat rose gold ($12,500); also available with date

Rolex

The brand featuring a crown in its logo is an icon of the Swiss watchmaking industry. If it wanted to, Rolex could celebrate a centennial in 2008—but that's not to say the famed marque will; looking back is not the mode of this company. Visitors to Baselworld 2007 were as surprised as they were delighted, for in the glass window of the brand's booth there were two interesting new interpretations of the legendary Milgauss to explore, a model that celebrated its fiftieth anniversary in 2007. The name itself awakens memories of the Oyster protected from magnetic fields in the 1960s, which—thanks to their rarity—today easily bring in many times their original retail price. Such a career is something the company also hopes its new Milgauss will achieve, a watch named for the word *mil*, or thousand in French, and the unit one measures magnetic fields by. Like the original, this timepiece is not particularly expensive, but rare—a very special Oyster with an extra core in the case made of "soft" iron and a dial crafted in the same material, protecting the movement from irritating magnetic fields from the outside. Showing that Rolex is ready to go down new paths in search of new clientele, the company introduced its Yacht-Master II at Baselworld as well. This may not be the first mechanical wristwatch with a programmable countdown function, but Rolex would not have dreamed of including such a display in one of its watches just a few years ago: complicated watches (except plain chronographs) just didn't exist.

The Yacht-Master II is outfitted with new Caliber 4160. The mere existence of its 360 components gives watch connoisseurs a taste of the complexity of this mechanism. Like Daytona chronograph Caliber 4130, this one is also outfitted with a column wheel and a vertical clutch. The heart of the movement beats at 28,800 vph and is outfitted with a blue Parachrom Breguet balance spring in order to be more than ten times as impervious to shocks and less sensitive to magnetic fields. Naturally, the movement has been tested by the independent Swiss authority C.O.S.C. (Contrôle Officiel Suisse des Chronomètres) for rate precision. The backward countdown function can be programmed in one-minute increments (to a maximum of ten minutes) and is activated by utilizing the two buttons and the bidirectionally rotating Ring Command bezel.

It can well be expected that Rolex's centennial won't become a nostalgic look to the brand's grand achievements (water-resistant screw-in crown and rotor winding, to name just two of the most important), but will more or less represent a starting block for the next hundred years.

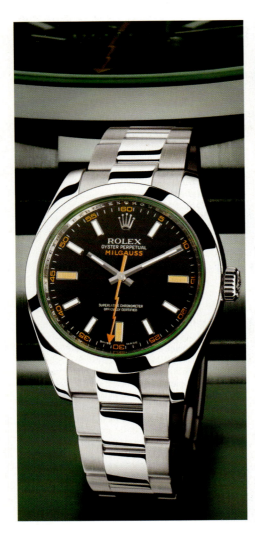

Rolex

Oyster Perpetual Air King
Reference number: 114200
Movement: automatic, Rolex Caliber 3130 (base Rolex 3135); ø 28.5 mm, height 5.85 mm; 31 jewels; Breguet balance spring, glucydur balance with microstella regulating screws
Functions: hours, minutes, sweep seconds
Case: stainless steel, ø 34 mm, height 11.1 mm; sapphire crystal; screw-in crown; water-resistant to 10 atm
Band: Oyster stainless steel, folding clasp
Price: $3,800
Variations: various dial variations

Oyster Perpetual Datejust
Reference number: 116200
Movement: automatic, Rolex Caliber 3135; ø 28.5 mm, height 6 mm; 31 jewels; Breguet balance spring, glucydur balance with microstella regulating screws; officially certified chronometer (COSC)
Functions: hours, minutes, sweep seconds; date
Case: stainless steel, ø 36 mm, height 11.8 mm; sapphire crystal with magnifying lens over the date display; screw-in crown; water-resistant to 10 atm
Band: Jubilé stainless steel, folding clasp
Price: $5,050
Variations: Oyster bracelet with extension element; various dial variations

Oyster Perpetual Datejust
Reference number: 116201
Movement: automatic, Rolex Caliber 3135; ø 28.5 mm, height 6 mm; 31 jewels; Breguet balance spring, glucydur balance with microstella regulating screws; officially certified chronometer (COSC)
Functions: hours, minutes, sweep seconds; date
Case: stainless steel, ø 36 mm, height 11.8 mm; rose gold bezel; sapphire crystal with magnifying lens over the date display; screw-in crown; water-resistant to 10 atm
Band: Oyster stainless steel/rose gold, folding clasp with extension element
Price: $7,750
Variations: with Jubilé bracelet; various dial variations

Oyster Perpetual Datejust
Reference number: 116234
Movement: automatic, Rolex Caliber 3135; ø 28.5 mm, height 6 mm; 31 jewels; Breguet balance spring, glucydur balance with microstella regulating screws; officially certified chronometer (COSC)
Functions: hours, minutes, sweep seconds; date
Case: stainless steel, ø 36 mm, height 11.8 mm; diamond-cut bezel in white gold; sapphire crystal with magnifying lens over the date display; screw-in crown; water-resistant to 10 atm
Band: Oyster stainless steel, folding clasp with extension
Price: $5,700
Variations: Jubilé bracelet; diverse dial variations

Oyster Perpetual Turn-O-Graph
Reference number: 116261
Movement: automatic, Rolex Caliber 3135; ø 28.5 mm, height 6 mm; 31 jewels; Breguet balance spring, glucydur balance with microstella regulating screws; officially certified chronometer (COSC)
Functions: hours, minutes, sweep seconds; date
Case: stainless steel, ø 36 mm, height 11.7 mm; bidirectionally rotating diamond-cut bezel in rose gold with 60-minute divisions; sapphire crystal with magnifying lens over the date display; screw-in crown; water-resistant to 10 atm
Band: Oyster steel/rose gold, folding clasp with extension
Price: $8,550

Oyster Perpetual Datejust
Reference number: 116138
Movement: automatic, Rolex Caliber 3135; ø 28.5 mm, height 6 mm; 31 jewels; Breguet balance spring, glucydur balance with microstella regulating screws; officially certified chronometer (COSC)
Functions: hours, minutes, sweep seconds; date
Case: yellow gold, ø 36 mm, height 11.8 mm; diamond-cut bezel; sapphire crystal with magnifying lens over the date display; screw-in crown; water-resistant to 10 atm
Band: reptile skin, folding clasp
Price: $14,700
Variations: various dial variations

Oyster Perpetual Day-Date
Reference number: 118205
Movement: automatic, Rolex Caliber 3155 (base Rolex 3135); ø 28.5 mm, height 6.45 mm; 31 jewels; Breguet balance spring, glucydur balance with microstella regulating screws; officially certified chronometer (COSC)
Functions: hours, minutes, sweep seconds; date, weekday
Case: rose gold, ø 36 mm, height 11.9 mm; sapphire crystal with magnifying lens over the date display; screw-in crown; water-resistant to 10 atm
Band: President rose gold, folding clasp
Price: $21,400
Variations: Oyster bracelet; various dial variations

Oyster Perpetual Datejust
Reference number: 178240
Movement: automatic, Rolex Caliber 2235 (base Rolex 2230); ø 28.5 mm, height 5.95 mm; 31 jewels; Breguet balance spring, glucydur balance with microstella regulating screws; officially certified chronometer (COSC)
Functions: hours, minutes, sweep seconds; date
Case: stainless steel, ø 31 mm, height 10.5 mm; sapphire crystal with magnifying lens over the date display; screw-in crown; water-resistant to 10 atm
Band: Oyster stainless steel, folding clasp with extension
Price: $4,700
Variations: Jubilé bracelet; various dial variations

Rolex

Oyster Perpetual Date
Reference number: 115234
Movement: automatic, Rolex Caliber 3135; ø 28.5 mm, height 6 mm; 31 jewels; Breguet balance spring, glucydur balance with microstella regulating screws; officially certified chronometer (COSC)
Functions: hours, minutes, sweep seconds; date
Case: stainless steel, ø 34 mm, height 11.2 mm; diamond-cut bezel; sapphire crystal with magnifying lens over the date display; screw-in crown; water-resistant to 10 atm
Band: Oyster stainless steel, folding clasp with extension
Price: $6,300
Variations: various dial variations

Oyster Perpetual Datejust
Reference number: 178245
Movement: automatic, Rolex Caliber 2235 (base Rolex 2230); ø 20 mm, height 5.95 mm; 31 jewels; Breguet balance spring, glucydur balance with microstella regulating screws; officially certified chronometer (COSC)
Functions: hours, minutes, sweep seconds; date
Case: rose gold, ø 31 mm, height 10.5 mm; sapphire crystal with magnifying lens over the date display; screw-in crown; water-resistant to 10 atm
Band: President rose gold, folding clasp
Price: $18,800
Variations: Oyster bracelet; various dial variations

Oyster Perpetual Lady Datejust
Reference number: 179161
Movement: automatic, Rolex Caliber 2235 (base Rolex 2230); ø 20 mm, height 5.95 mm; 31 jewels; Breguet balance spring, glucydur balance with microstella regulating screws; officially certified chronometer (COSC)
Functions: hours, minutes, sweep seconds; date
Case: stainless steel, ø 26 mm, height 10.3 mm; rose gold bezel; sapphire crystal with magnifying lens over the date display; screw-in crown; water-resistant to 10 atm
Band: Oyster stainless steel/rose gold, folding clasp with extension element
Price: $6,250
Variations: Jubilé bracelet; various dial variations

Oyster Perpetual Lady Datejust
Reference number: 179166
Movement: automatic, Rolex Caliber 2235 (base Rolex 2230); ø 20 mm, height 5.95 mm; 31 jewels; Breguet balance spring, glucydur balance with microstella regulating screws; officially certified chronometer (COSC)
Functions: hours, minutes, sweep seconds; date
Case: platinum, ø 26 mm, height 10.3 mm; sapphire crystal with magnifying lens over the date display; screw-in crown; water-resistant to 10 atm
Band: President platinum, folding clasp
Price: $29,350
Variations: various dial variations

Oyster Perpetual
Reference number: 177200
Movement: automatic, Rolex Caliber 2231 (base Rolex 2230); ø 20 mm, height 5.40 mm; 31 jewels; Breguet balance spring, glucydur balance with microstella regulating screws; officially certified chronometer (COSC)
Functions: hours, minutes, sweep seconds
Case: stainless steel, ø 31 mm, height 10.3 mm; sapphire crystal; screw-in crown; water-resistant to 10 atm
Band: Oyster stainless steel, folding clasp
Price: $3,725
Variations: various dial variations

Oyster Perpetual Datejust
Reference number: 116203
Movement: automatic, Rolex Caliber 2235 (base Rolex 2230); ø 20 mm, height 5.40 mm; 31 jewels; Breguet balance spring, glucydur balance with microstella regulating screws; officially certified chronometer (COSC)
Functions: hours, minutes, sweep seconds; date
Case: stainless steel, ø 36 mm, height 11.8 mm; yellow gold bezel; sapphire crystal with magnifying lens over the date display; screw-in crown; water-resistant to 10 atm
Band: Oyster yellow gold/stainless steel, folding clasp with extension
Price: $7,600
Variations: Jubilé bracelet; various dial variations

Prince
Reference number: 5443/9
Movement: automatic, Rolex Caliber 7040.1; 21 jewels, 28,800 vph; glucydur balance with microstella regulating screws; guilloché with Rayon Flamme de la Gloire like on dial; officially certified C.O.S.C. chronometer
Functions: hours, minutes, subsidiary seconds
Case: stainless steel, 46.8 x 27.6 mm, height 10 mm; sapphire crystal; water-resistant to 10 atm
Band: reptile skin, double folding clasp
Price: upon request

Oyster Perpetual Milgauss
Reference number: 116400GV
Movement: automatic, Rolex Caliber 3131 (base Rolex 3135); ø 28.5 mm, height 5.85 mm; 31 jewels; Parachrome Blue Breguet balance spring; special core inside case for protection from magnetic fields; officially certified C.O.S.C. chronometer
Functions: hours, minutes, sweep seconds
Case: stainless steel, ø 40 mm, height 13.2 mm; green-hued sapphire crystal; screw-in crown; water-resistant to 10 atm
Band: Oyster stainless steel, folding clasp with extension
Price: $6,250
Variations: with standard sapphire crystal; white or black dial

Rolex

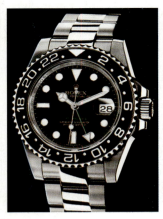

Oyster Perpetual GMT Master II
Reference number: 116710LN
Movement: automatic, Rolex Caliber 3186 (base Rolex 3135); ø 28.5 mm, height 6.4 mm; 31 jewels; Parachrome Blue Breguet balance spring, balance with microstella regulating screws; officially certified chronometer (COSC)
Functions: hours, minutes, sweep seconds; date; 24-hour display; second time zone via independently settable hour hand
Case: stainless steel, ø 40 mm, height 12.1 mm; bidirectionally rotating bezel with 24-hour scale; sapphire crystal; Triplock screw-in crown; water-resistant to 10 atm
Band: Oysterlock steel, folding clasp with extension element
Price: $5,950

Oyster Perpetual GMT Master II
Reference number: 116713LN
Movement: automatic, Rolex Caliber 3186 (base Rolex 3135); ø 28.5 mm, height 6.4 mm; 31 jewels; Parachrome Blue Breguet balance spring, balance with microstella regulating screws; officially certified chronometer (COSC)
Functions: hours, minutes, sweep seconds; date; 24-hour display; second time zone via independently settable hour hand
Case: white gold, ø 40 mm, height 12.1 mm; bidirectionally rotating yellow gold bezel with 24-hour scale; sapphire crystal; Triplock screw-in crown; water-resistant to 10 atm
Band: Oysterlock stainlss steel/yellow gold, folding clasp with extension element
Price: $31,500

Oyster Perpetual Yacht Master II Regatta Chronogrpah
Reference number: 116689
Movement: automatic, Rolex Caliber 4160 (base Rolex 4130); ø 30.5 mm, height 6.5 mm; 44 jewels; Parachrome Blue Breguet balance spring, glucydur balance with microstella regulating screws; officially certified chronometer (COSC); power reserve 72 hours
Functions: hours, minutes, subsidiary seconds; programmable countdown function with memory
Case: white gold, ø 42.6 mm, height 12.8 mm; Ring Command bezel with platinum numeral disk as control element for countdown; sapphire crystal; screw-in crown; water-resistant to 10 atm
Band: Oysterlock white gold, folding clasp
Price: $34,850

Oyster Perpetual Yacht Master II Regatta Chronogrpah
Reference number: 116688
Movement: automatic, Rolex Caliber 4160 (base Rolex 4130); ø 30.5 mm, height 6.5 mm; 44 jewels; Parachrome Blue Breguet balance spring, glucydur balance with microstella regulating screws; officially certified chronometer (COSC); power reserve 72 hours
Functions: hours, minutes, subsidiary seconds; programmable countdown function with memory
Case: yellow gold, ø 42.6 mm, height 12.8 mm; Ring Command bezel with ceramic numeral disk as control element for countdown; sapphire crystal; screw-in crown; water-resistant to 10 atm
Band: Oysterlock yellow gold, folding clasp
Price: upon request

Oyster Perpetual Cosmograph Daytona
Reference number: 116509
Movement: automatic, Rolex Caliber 4130; ø 30.5 mm, height 6.5 mm; 44 jewels; Parachrom Blue Breguet balance spring, glucydur balance with microstella regulating screws; power reserve appx. 72 hours; officially certified chronometer (COSC)
Functions: hours, minutes, subsidiary seconds; chronograph
Case: white gold, ø 40 mm, height 12.8 mm; bezel engraved with tachymeter scale; sapphire crystal; screw-in crown and buttons; water-resistant to 10 atm
Band: Oysterlock white gold, folding clasp with extension
Price: $27,000

Oyster Perpetual Cosmograph Daytona
Reference number: 116509
Movement: automatic, Rolex Caliber 4130; ø 30.5 mm, height 6.5 mm; 44 jewels; Parachrom Blue Breguet balance spring, glucydur balance with microstella regulating screws; power reserve appx. 72 hours; officially certified chronometer (COSC)
Functions: hours, minutes, subsidiary seconds; chronograph
Case: yellow gold, ø 40 mm, height 12.8 mm; bezel engraved with tachymeter scale; sapphire crystal; screw-in crown and buttons; water-resistant to 10 atm
Band: reptile skin, folding clasp
Price: $18,150

Cellinium
Reference number: 5241/6
Movement: manually wound, Rolex Caliber 1240; ø 23.8 mm, height 3.77 mm; 17 jewels; glucydur balance with microstella regulating screws
Functions: hours, minutes, subsidiary seconds
Case: platinum, ø 38 mm, height 6.3 mm; sapphire crystal
Band: reptile skin, folding clasp
Price: $15,400
Variations: with buckle ($12,850); various dial variations

Rolex Cellini Danaos
Reference number: 4243/9 BIC
Movement: manually wound, Rolex Caliber 1602; ø 20.8 mm; height 2.35 mm; 20 jewels; glucydur balance with microstella regulating screws
Functions: hours, minutes
Case: white gold, ø 38 mm, height 6.3 mm; rose gold bezel; sapphire crystal
Band: leather, folding clasp
Price: $7,350
Variations: various dial variations

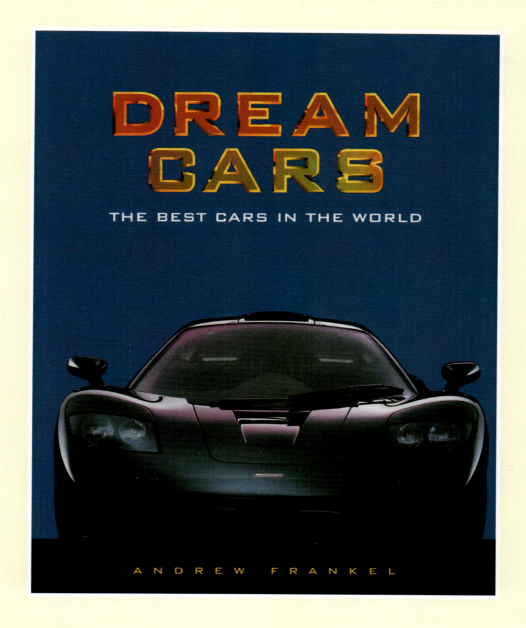

Dream Cars: The Best Cars in the World

This stunning celebration of the fifty most sought-after cars of all time, from the Rolls Royce Silver Ghost to the Ferrari F40, is now available in a newly revised and updated edition.

By Andrew Frankel
280 full-color illustrations
256 pages · 9 x 11 3/8 in. · Cloth
ISBN: 978-0-7892-0843-9
$39.95

Published by ABBEVILLE PRESS
137 Varick Street, New York, NY 10013
1-800-ARTBOOK (in U.S. only)
Also available wherever fine books are sold
Visit us at www.abbeville.com

Daniel Roth

There are products whose shapes are just so strikingly obvious at first glance that they don't even need a logo on them. Their silhouettes are enough for the consumer to be able to associate them directly with the brand. In the world of luxury watches there is a man who has also achieved this distinction of having his products directly recognized by their shape: Daniel Roth. The name was already well known in insider circles when this shy master watchmaker brought his first watch onto the market in 1990. Ever since, the Daniel Roth company has been one of the greats to grace the luxury industry.

Master watchmakers had been constructing complicated watches long before Roth decided to make his own timepieces. However, industry insiders were quickly impressed not only by the fact that Roth's watches contained movements of excellent quality with original complications and extra displays created especially by the master, but also by the fact that all cases emanating from his production bore an interesting standard shape, a shape with no equal up to that point, the creation of which took about two years. The effort was worth the trouble, for the Daniel Roth brand now plays an important role in the high-end watch industry.

Six years ago the Bulgari group bought the small *manufacture* and has since invested a great deal of money in the technical aspects and personnel of the brand. Today at Daniel Roth, it is possible to make completely proprietary watch movements. Two modern CNC machines utilizing forty-eight different tools produce the base plates, bridges, and cocks developed by two specialists in the company's design office. The necessary production software for the manufacture of the individual components is also developed in the old building located in Le Sentier. This know-how and these technical devices naturally benefit sister brands Gérald Genta and Bulgari as well—as their fast-growing collections filled with horological specialties can attest.

Company founder and namesake Daniel Roth has completely withdrawn from the day-to-day business for personal reasons. However, the brand that bears his name still embodies the spirit of this world-famous watchmaker. And that is surely not only due to the unique silhouette of the watches housed in the brand's signature Ellipsocurvex case, but also to the very clever developments that continue to be presented, such as those found at Baselworld 2007.

The most spectacular of these was surely the Tourbillon Lumière from the Masters Grandes Complications line. To achieve the light, airy look of this movement (*lumière* means "light" in French), the gifted developers at Daniel Roth created a new manually wound tourbillon movement expressly with the goal of skeletonization in mind—which means the watchmakers knew in advance how the skeletonized movement would look and created a movement just for this purpose. Its 200 components contain 18-karat gold barely-there bridges as well as plates and gear wheels plated in red gold, all of which have been hand-skeletonized, beveled, and engraved. Making for a wonderful contrast, the steel tourbillon bridge is tin-polished and left in its natural color.

Daniel Roth

Athys III
Reference number: 110.Y
Movement: automatic, Daniel Roth Caliber DR 1301 with GP module 3330; ø 28.8 mm, height 5 mm; 35 jewels; 28,800 vph; movement decorated by hand, côtes de Genève
Functions: hours, minutes, subsidiary seconds; large date, moon phase, power reserve indicator
Case: rose gold, 41 x 44 mm, height 9.2 mm; sapphire crystal; transparent case back
Band: reptile skin, buckle
Price: $19,400
Variations: white gold

Tourbillon 200 Hours Power Reserve
Reference number: 197.X.60.223.CC.BA
Movement: manually wound, Daniel Roth Caliber DR 197.X (base DR 720); 34.5 x 31.5 mm, height 6.3 mm; 25 jewels; 21,600 vph; one-minute tourbillon; twin spring barrels, power reserve 200 hours; movement beveled and decorated by hand
Functions: hours, minutes (off-center), subsidiary seconds; date; power reserve indication (case back)
Case: white gold, 40.35 x 43.35 mm, height 12.9 mm; sapphire crystal; case can be opened via hinge on upper strap lug
Band: reptile skin, buckle
Price: $133,750
Variations: rose gold; diamond-set bezel; platinum

Ellipsocurvex Perpetual Calendar Time Equation
Reference number: 121.Y
Movement: automatic, Daniel Roth Caliber DR 114; 26.5 x 29.5 mm, height 5.98 mm; 27 jewels; 28,800 vph; movement beveled and decorated by hand, côtes de Genève
Functions: hours, minutes; perpetual calendar with date, weekday, month, moon phase, leap year; length of month, and equation of time
Case: rose gold, 41 x 44 mm, height 13 mm; sapphire crystal; transparent case back
Band: reptile skin, folding clasp
Price: $91,800
Variations: white gold ($91,800); with diamonds; platinum ($117,150)

Ellipsocurvex Perpetual Calendar Tourbillon Retro Date
Reference number: 199.Y
Movement: automatic, Daniel Roth Caliber DR 740; 26.5 x 29.5, height 7.9 mm; 43 jewels, 21,600 vph; one-minute tourbillon; movement decorated by hand, côtes de Genève
Functions: hours, minutes; perpetual calendar with date (retrograde); weekday, month, leap year
Case: white gold, 41 x 44 mm, height 14.9 mm; sapphire crystal; transparent case back
Band: reptile skin, folding clasp
Price: $147,200
Variations: rose gold; platinum ($157,350); with diamonds

Automatic Chronograph
Reference number: 247.X
Movement: automatic, Daniel Roth Caliber DR 247.X (base Zenith El Primero); ø 30 mm, height 6.5 mm; 31 jewels; 36,000 vph; movement decorated by hand, côtes de Genève
Functions: hours, minutes, subsidiary seconds; chronograph; date
Case: white gold, 41 x 38 mm, height 11.3 mm; sapphire crystal; transparent case back
Band: reptile skin, folding clasp
Remarks: limited edition
Price: $26,400

Perpetual Calendar Time Equation
Reference number: 121.Y.60.168.CN.BD
Movement: automatic, Daniel Roth Caliber DR 114; 26.5 x 29.5 mm, height 5.98 mm; 27 jewels; 28,800 vph; hand-decorated; côtes de Genève
Functions: hours, minutes, perpetual calendar with date, weekday, month, moon phase, leap year; display of length of months, equation of time
Case: white gold, 44 x 41 mm, height 13 mm; sapphire crystal; transparent case back
Band: reptile skin, buckle
Price: $101,950
Variations: rose gold; platinum

Ellipsocurvex Papillon
Reference number: 318.Y.70.351.CM.BD
Movement: automatic, Daniel Roth Caliber DR 115; ø 25.6 mm, height 5.28 mm; 31 jewels; 28,800 vph; movement decorated by hand, côtes de Genève
Functions: hours (jump); minutes (two lateral, non-retrograde hands), subsidiary seconds in the center
Case: platinum, 41 x 44 mm, height 13.55 mm; sapphire crystal; transparent case back
Band: reptile skin, folding clasp
Remarks: limited edition of 500 pieces
Price: $44,150
Variations: red or white gold

Metropolitan Dual Time
Reference number: 858.Y.50.172.CC.BD
Movement: automatic, Daniel Roth Caliber DR 116; 31.4 x 34.8 mm, height 5.58 mm; 34 jewels; 21,600 vph; movement decorated by hand, côtes de Genève
Functions: hours, minutes; second time zone, world time reference city names; day/night indication for home time, AM/PM display for local time; indication of daylight savings time
Case: red gold, 41 x 44 mm, height 12.35 mm; sapphire crystal; transparent case back
Band: reptile skin, folding clasp
Price: $33,100
Variations: white gold; platinum

Scalfaro

Scalfaro is the result of the creative partnership of two brothers who let their Mediterranean feel for life and their ideas of luxury flow into a distinct form. Alexander and Dominik Kuhnle needed several years until they were finally able to formulate the dream of their own watch collection and translate it into wearable three-dimensionality.

"Contemporary luxury": the brothers' new interpretation stands for quality without compromise, passionate design, and high demands on composition and production. Scalfaro outfits its exclusive timekeepers, which are assembled in the workshops of experienced master watchmakers, wholly with highly refined Swiss automatic movements that have been decorated by hand. Every element of a Scalfaro is created with great attention to detail and bears the signature of the brand's two founders.

The quality of the workmanship on the cases, dials, and bracelets is obvious. Both of the large model families are available on link bracelets or leather straps. The striking center link element that extends from the upper and lower parts of the watch case is continued all the way around the bracelet, while at that same point on the leather strap there is a slim, padded track running the length of the material. The successful base design proves its versatility in exceptionally sporty variations of the Porto Cervo family: with a black bezel made of a special scratchproof alloy and a striking new dial design featuring Roman numerals, the Medium Sport model emanates a completely new charm.

Great care was taken in setting the proportions of the hands, the profile of the crown, and the design of the subsidiary seconds scale. The red 12, whether represented by a numeral or double marker, the solid crown protection, the screwed-in crown, and the screwed-on strap lugs are all wonderful details—but it is the screws that stand out most especially. These are special screws that were developed just for Scalfaro. The heads of these ScalfaScrews are reminiscent of Torx screws, but feature only five points.

The first exclusive complication watch including the brand's own registered caliber debuted at the beginning of 2006. Housed in the Porto Rotondo case, but most likely available later in other model families as well, Caliber ADK 152 comprises retrograde subsidiary seconds, a moon phase, a date display, and an off-center hour scale. It was created in close cooperation with a reputable Swiss specialist known for the development and production of complicated movements who was duly impressed by the ambition of the Kuhnle brothers.

This ambition is characteristic of the entire Scalfaro project, however, which the two young men have undertaken with amazing professionalism and vision. With the clear, harmoniously structured, and lavishly outfitted Scalfaro collection, they have immediately been able to position themselves well in the luxury watch markets of the world so dominated by conspicuous men's watches.

North Shore Chronograph TriCompax
Reference number: A04A.04.06A.1.12.L16.10
Movement: automatic, ADK Caliber 150 (base La Joux-Perret / ETA Valjoux 7750); ø 30 mm, height 8.85 mm; 28 jewels; 28,800 vph; côtes de Genève, perlage, blued screws, skeletonized rotor
Functions: hours, minutes, subsidiary seconds; chronograph; date
Case: stainless steel, ø 43.5 mm, height 16.9 mm; bidirectionally rotating ring with 60-minute divisions under crystal; sapphire crystal; transparent case back; screw-in crown; water-resistant to 10 atm
Band: leather, buckle
Price: $6,635

Porto Rotondo Chronograph Stealth
Reference number: A06A.04.61A.1.12.Q01.20
Movement: automatic, ADK Caliber 150 (base La Joux-Perret / ETA Valjoux 7750); ø 30 mm, height 8.85 mm; 28 jewels; 28,800 vph; côtes de Genève, perlage, blued screws, skeletonized rotor
Functions: hours, minutes, subsidiary seconds; chronograph; date
Case: blackened stainless steel, ø 44 mm, height 15.3 mm; sapphire crystal; transparent case back; screw-in crown; water-resistant to 5 atm
Band: reptile skin, folding clasp
Price: $7,735
Variations: diverse dial variations

Porto Rotondo RetroMoon
Reference number: A06A.06.06A.1.12.Q01.20
Movement: automatic, ADK Caliber 152; ø 29.2 mm, height 5.3 mm; 38 jewels; 28,800 vph; côtes de Genève, perlage, blued screws, skeletonized tungsten carbide rotor, ceramic ball bearings
Functions: hours, minutes (off-center), subsidiary seconds (retrograde); date; moon phase
Case: stainless steel, ø 44 mm, height 12.6 mm; sapphire crystal; transparent case back; screw-in crown; water-resistant to 5 atm
Band: reptile skin, double folding clasp
Remarks: multitiered dial with ScalfaScrews
Price: $11,990
Variations: diverse dial variations; stainless steel bracelet

Porto Cervo Chronograph
Reference number: A03B2.04.01A.1.12.Q01.10
Movement: automatic, ADK Caliber 150 (base La Joux-Perret / ETA Valjoux 7750); ø 30 mm, height 8.4 mm; 28 jewels; 28,800 vph; côtes de Genève, perlage, blued screws, skeletonized rotor
Functions: hours, minutes, subsidiary seconds; chronograph; date
Case: red gold, ø 42 mm, height 14.8 mm; sapphire crystal; transparent case back; screw-in crown; water-resistant to 10 atm
Band: reptile skin, buckle
Price: $25,450
Variations: diverse dial variations

Cap Ferrat Grand Tour Large Date Flyback
Reference number: A02A.05.61A.2.12.A00.31
Movement: automatic, ADK Caliber 151 (base La Joux-Perret / ETA Valjoux 7750); ø 30 mm, height 8.85 mm; 28 jewels; 28,800 vph; côtes de Genève, perlage, blued screws, skeletonized rotor
Functions: hours, minutes, subsidiary seconds; flyback chronograph; large date
Case: stainless steel, ø 43 mm, height 15.9 mm; bidirectionally rotating ring with 60-minute divisions under crystal, settable via crown; sapphire crystal; transparent case back; screw-in crown; water-resistant to 10 atm
Band: stainless steel, double folding clasp
Price: $8,870
Variations: reptile skin strap

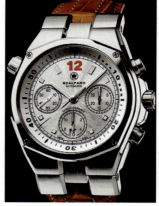

Cap Ferrat Grand Tour Chronograph TriCompax
Reference number: A02A.04.06A.2.12.Q16.20
Movement: automatic, ADK Caliber 150 (base La Joux-Perret / ETA Valjoux 7750); ø 30 mm, height 8.4 mm; 28 jewels; 28,800 vph; côtes de Genève, perlage, blued screws, skeletonized rotor
Functions: hours, minutes, subsidiary seconds; chronograph; date
Case: stainless steel, ø 43 mm, height 15.9 mm; bidirectionally rotating ring with 60-minute divisions under crystal, settable via crown; sapphire crystal; transparent case back; screw-in crown; water-resistant to 10 atm
Band: reptile skin, folding clasp
Price: $6,420
Variations: stainless steel bracelet

Porto Cervo Sport Chronograph
Reference number: A03A.04.61A.1.12.Q01.20
Movement: automatic, ADK Caliber 150 (base La Joux-Perret / ETA Valjoux 7750); ø 30 mm, height 8.4 mm; 28 jewels; 28,800 vph; côtes de Genève, perlage, blued screws, skeletonized rotor
Functions: hours, minutes, subsidiary seconds; chronograph; date
Case: stainless steel, ø 42 mm, height 14.8 mm; black-coated bezel; sapphire crystal; transparent case back; screw-in crown; water-resistant to 10 atm
Band: reptile skin, folding clasp
Price: $7,400
Variations: diverse dial variations; stainless steel bracelet

Porto Cervo Chronograph Large Date Flyback
Reference number: A03A.05.06A.1.12.A00.31
Movement: automatic, ADK Caliber 151 (base La Joux-Perret / ETA Valjoux 7750); ø 30 mm, height 8.85 mm; 28 jewels; 28,800 vph; côtes de Genève, perlage, blued screws, skeletonized rotor
Functions: hours, minutes, subsidiary seconds; chronograph with flyback function; large date
Case: stainless steel, ø 42 mm, height 15.7 mm; sapphire crystal; transparent case back; screw-in crown; water-resistant to 10 atm
Band: stainless steel, double folding clasp
Price: $9,175
Variations: diverse dial variations; reptile skin strap; set with diamonds

Jörg Schauer

The design of Schauer's watches does not exactly cater to mass consumer taste: Relinquishing obvious decoration, the sheer weight of the case and the working of its matte, unpolished surfaces lead one to believe that a "typical" watchmaker (if there is such a thing) is not at work here. Schauer has a different take on watches. For him, design, material, surface, and working of the details are most important. This is the goldsmith in him coming out.

He creates functional, edgy cases with a visibly screwed-on bezel, and sober dials in simple black or white characterize the strict design. There will never be models that follow fashion trends in Schauer's workshop, for he only makes watches that he himself likes.

And in the near future, there will be even fewer of these, for Schauer has decided to limit the number of collection watches he makes in one year to 500. Naturally, as the number of Schauer watches decreases, so will the range of different models that there are in his collection. Certainly, future emphasis will likely be placed on this unusual watchmaker's best-selling concepts, which include timepieces such as the Edition 10 and the Edition 12 chronograph.

Now, as ever, one of the main attractions of Schauer's watches is their cases, so machined in their appearance and so detailed in their execution. Schauer is a perfectionist, one who protects the hallmark of his brand with every ounce of his talent and energy. His blanks are produced by a leading German case maker, but Schauer touches each and every one of them up after they are delivered, polishing and working them, making sure that they receive his personal imprint and radiate his own brand of charm. This is a time-consuming process, one that no other watch company can boast, but one that Schauer deems necessary. "I do this because I place a great deal of value on the fact that my cases are absolutely perfect," he explains. "I can do it better than anyone, and I would never let anyone else do it for me."

This attitude naturally also has its consequences, and not only with regard to prices. For a while now, Schauer has hardly been able to satisfy the demand for his timepieces, and there is even a waiting list for some models. He has meanwhile decided to turn this situation into a better one for himself and his clientele by only manufacturing his chronographs on special order—naturally including even more opportunities for customer individualization.

Jörg Schauer

Chronograph Kulisse Edition 9
Reference number: Ed.9WL
Movement: automatic, ETA Valjoux Caliber 7751; ø 30 mm, height 7.9 mm; 28 jewels; 28,800 vph; decorated, blued screws, exclusive engraved Schauer rotor
Functions: hours, minutes, subsidiary seconds; chronograph; date, weekday, moon phase; 24-hour display
Case: stainless steel, ø 42 mm, height 15 mm; bezel secured with twelve screws; sapphire crystal; transparent case back; water-resistant to 5 atm
Band: leather, buckle
Price: $3,950
Variations: with Artus or Kubus metal bracelet ($4,350); black dial

Chronograph Kulisse Edition 10
Reference number: Ed.10L
Movement: automatic, ETA Valjoux Caliber 7753; ø 30 mm, height 7.9 mm; 28 jewels; 28,800 vph; decorated, blued screws, exclusive engraved Schauer rotor
Functions: hours, minutes, subsidiary seconds; chronograph
Case: stainless steel, ø 42 mm, height 15 mm; bezel secured with twelve screws; sapphire crystal; transparent case back; water-resistant to 5 atm
Band: leather, buckle
Price: $3,650
Variations: with Artus or Kubus metal bracelet ($4,050)

Chronograph Kulisse Edition 11
Reference number: Ed.11L
Movement: automatic, ETA Valjoux Caliber 7753; ø 30 mm, height 7.9 mm; 28 jewels; 28,800 vph; decorated, blued screws, exclusive engraved Schauer rotor
Functions: hours, minutes, subsidiary seconds; chronograph
Case: stainless steel, ø 42 mm, height 15 mm; bezel secured with twelve screws; sapphire crystal; transparent case back; water-resistant to 5 atm
Band: leather, buckle
Price: $3,650
Variations: with Artus or Kubus metal bracelet ($4,050)

Chronograph Kulisse Edition 12
Reference number: Ed.12L
Movement: automatic, ETA Valjoux Caliber 7753; ø 30 mm, height 7.9 mm; 28 jewels; 28,800 vph; decorated, blued screws, exclusive engraved Schauer rotor
Functions: hours, minutes, subsidiary seconds; chronograph
Case: stainless steel, ø 41 mm, height 15 mm; bezel secured with twelve screws; sapphire crystal; transparent case back; water-resistant to 5 atm
Band: leather, buckle
Price: $3,950
Variations: with Artus or Kubus metal bracelet ($4,350)

Quarada
Reference number: Quarada/S
Movement: automatic, ETA Valjoux Caliber 7750; ø 30 mm, height 7.9 mm; 28 jewels; 28,800 vph; decorated, blued screws, exclusive engraved Schauer rotor
Functions: hours, minutes, subsidiary seconds; chronograph
Case: stainless steel, 35 x 35 mm, height 14 mm; bezel secured with twelve screws; sapphire crystal; transparent case back; water-resistant to 5 atm
Band: Nappa leather, buckle
Price: $5,950
Variations: reptile skin strap

Day-Date Central
Reference number: DDZSL
Movement: automatic, ETA Caliber 2836; ø 26 mm, height 4.6 mm; 25 jewels; 28,800 vph; in-house rotor crafted in German silver; blued screws
Functions: hours, minutes, sweep seconds; date and weekday
Case: stainless steel, ø 41 mm, height 12.9 mm; bezel secured with twelve screws; sapphire crystal; transparent case back; water-resistant to 5 atm
Band: leather, buckle
Price: $2,550
Variations: with Artus or Kubus metal bracelet ($2,950)

Day-Date Central
Reference number: DDZSC
Movement: automatic, ETA Caliber 2836; ø 26 mm, height 4.6 mm; 25 jewels; 28,800 vph; in-house rotor crafted in German silver; blued screws
Functions: hours, minutes, sweep seconds; date and weekday
Case: stainless steel, ø 41 mm, height 12.9 mm; bezel secured with twelve screws; sapphire crystal; transparent case back; water-resistant to 5 atm
Band: leather, buckle
Price: $2,550
Variations: with Artus or Kubus metal bracelet ($2,950)

Day-Date 2836 GL42
Reference number: DD2836GL42L
Movement: automatic, ETA Caliber 2836; ø 26 mm, height 4.6 mm; 25 jewels; 28,800 vph; in-house rotor crafted in German silver; blued screws
Functions: hours, minutes, sweep seconds; date and weekday
Case: stainless steel, ø 42 mm, height 11 mm; bezel secured with twelve screws; sapphire crystal; transparent case back; water-resistant to 5 atm
Band: leather, buckle
Price: $2,150
Variations: with Artus or Kubus metal bracelet ($2,550); black dial

Schaumburg Watch

These mechanical watches are created—as their name already reveals—in Germany's Schaumburg region. There, company owner Frank Dilbakowski has designed individualistic and remarkable chronographs and chronometers since 1998. The brand's reputation cannot be measured in production numbers or the depth of its collection, however, for this little workshop doesn't subscribe to such quantitative categories when defending its demand for the highest quality: watches made by Schaumburg Watch are still a real insider tip. Realizing high-performance timepieces for rugged sports and professional use is especially important for this company. The chronometer line Aquamatic with water resistance to 1,000 meters and the Aquatitan models to 2,000 meters confirm the company's maxim that form, function, and performance are inseparable from one another. Schaumburg Watch is one of the few watch manufacturers in Europe to perform pressure testing up to 600 bar (6,000 meters of diving depth) in-house. For connoisseurs of traditional watchmaking, the watch seminars the company puts on allow participants to make their own "masterpiece" under the guidance of a master watchmaker.

Squarematic and Ellomatic with their unique, architecturally inspired designs embody a synthesis of careful craftsmanship and highly technical modern design. The Classoco line ideally joins function with elegance: the case in platinum, red gold, or white gold lends the watches not only a classic charm, but also an especially high material value.

Since 2006, the company has been working on its own movement modifications: the manually wound base movement containing a Schaumburg bridge premiered at Baselworld in 2007.

Aquamatic
Movement: automatic, Caliber SW 20A (base ETA 2824 or Sellita SW 200); ø 25.6 mm, height 4.6 mm; 25 jewels; 28,800 vph; officially certified C.O.S.C. chronometer
Functions: hours, minutes, sweep seconds; date
Case: stainless steel, ø 42 mm, height 16.9 mm; bidirectionally rotating bezel with 60-minute divisions; screw-in crown; helium valve; water-resistant to 100 atm
Band: buffalo leather, buckle
Price: $1,940
Variations: without chronometer certificate ($1,400); blackened stainless steel

Schaumburg Bridge Marine
Movement: automatic, Caliber SW 07.1HA (base ETA Unitas 6498); ø 36.6 mm, height 4.5 mm; 17 jewels; 21,600 vph; swan-neck fine adjustment; finely finished with côtes de Genève
Functions: hours, minutes, subsidiary seconds
Case: titanium, ø 44 mm, height 11.8 mm; screwed-down case back; transparent case back; water-resistant to 5 atm
Band: leather, buckle
Price: $1,800

Squarematic Art Nouveau
Movement: automatic, Caliber Dubois Dépraz 2040 (base ETA 2892); ø 30 mm, height 7.5 mm; 51 jewels; 28,800 vph; finely finished with côtes de Genève
Functions: hours, minutes, sweep seconds; date; chronograph
Case: stainless steel, 40 x 40 mm, height 11.8 mm; transparent case back
Band: buffalo leather, buckle
Price: $2,100
Variations: various case, band, and dial variations

Aquatitan 3D1
Movement: automatic, Caliber SW 20A (base ETA 2824 or Sellita SW 200); ø 25.6 mm, height 4.6 mm; 25 jewels; 28,800 vph
Functions: hours, minutes, sweep seconds; date
Case: titanium, ø 44 mm, height 16.8 mm; unidirectionally rotating bezel with 60-minute divisions and security system; screw-in crown; helium valve; water-resistant to 200 atm
Band: leather, buckle
Price: $1,500
Variations: with chronometer certificate ($2,050); with subsidiary seconds

Alexander Shorokhoff

These fine mechanical watches with a Russian soul are created in a small German city near Frankfurt: Alzenau. There, in a historical building in the city center, highly qualified and experienced engravers and watchmakers work together. And because these employees all originally come from the former empire of the czars or one of its satellite states, the goal of manufacturing aesthetically and technically exceptional watches must be achieved in a truly Russian manner and in genuine Russian tradition.

Though the base for these movements comes from established Russian movement makers, all engraving, guilloché, and skeletonizing are done with great care and talent by hand in Alzenau. The movements are then put together piece by piece and individually adjusted.

The 500-hour test that follows ensures high reliability for the watch, and thus each one has earned both its name and the predicate "made in Germany."
Company founder Alexander Shorokhov has dedicated the watches bearing a derivative of his own name to famous Russian compatriots like Tolstoy, Pushkin, Dostoevsky, and others he would like to pay homage to—according to him, mechanical watches are also a traditional handicraft constituting an honorable culture worth maintaining.

Tolstoy is a collection of skeletonized watches that look distinctly non-Swiss. The hand-wound models here are based on Russian Poljot movements, while the automatic versions run on Soprod/Valjoux 7750 calibers.

Tchaikovsky is a collection of alarm timepieces thus named because their ringing reminded Shorokhov of music. The cases of these models can be moved out of their frames to "sit up" on a desk or a night table, turning them into small travel clocks. All of the alarms are Poljot-based. An interesting line is Dostoevsky, which comprises crazy gambling-themed cases and dials in honor of this Russian writer and his passionate hobby. These interesting timepieces run on beautifully engraved Poljot (hand-wound) and ETA/Soprod (automatic) calibers.

Tolstoy Skeleton
Reference number: AS.LTS1 RGG
Movement: manually wound, Poljot Caliber 3133; ø 31 mm, height 7.35 mm; 23 jewels; 21,600 vph; completely skeletonized, hand-engraved, and gold-plated
Functions: hours, minutes, subsidiary seconds; chronograph
Case: red gold, ø 41 mm, height 12.5 mm; sapphire crystal; transparent case back
Band: reptile skin, buckle
Price: $6,495

Tolstoy Skeleton
Reference number: AS.LTS3 GL
Movement: manually wound, Poljot Caliber 3133; ø 31 mm, height 7.35 mm; 23 jewels; 21,600 vph; completely skeletonized, hand-engraved, and rhodium-plated
Functions: hours, minutes, subsidiary seconds; chronograph
Case: stainless steel, ø 41 mm, height 12.5 mm; red gold bezel; sapphire crystal; transparent case back
Band: reptile skin, buckle
Price: $2,995

Fedor Dostoevsky Manually Wound
Reference number: AS-FD1
Movement: manually wound, Poljot Caliber 3105; ø 31 mm, height 7.35 mm; 18 jewels; 21,600 vph; hand-engraved, finely finished
Functions: hours, minutes, subsidiary seconds; date
Case: stainless steel, 43.5 x 43.5 mm, height 11 mm; movable strap lug; sapphire crystal; transparent case back
Band: reptile skin, buckle
Price: $3,995

Fedor Dostoevsky Automatic
Reference number: AS-FD11
Movement: manually wound, Soprod Caliber 9060; ø 25.6 mm, height 5.1 mm; 21 jewels; 28,800 vph
Functions: hours, minutes, sweep seconds; date, weekday; power reserve display
Case: stainless steel, 43.5 x 43.5 mm, height 11 mm; movable strap lug; sapphire crystal; transparent case back
Band: reptile skin, buckle
Price: $4,495

Alain Silberstein

Besançon is a lovely midsized French city nestled in the hills of the Jura—but not on the side usually known for its watchmaking among today's connoisseurs. Although many watchmakers in this part of Switzerland tend to be French, or at least live in France for economic reasons, this particular area is no longer generally associated with watchmaking expertise.

It seems appropriate that when Parisian-born Alain Silberstein established his watchmaking business in 1985, he did so in Besançon. Like his company, Silberstein's designs go above and beyond modern watchmaking's traditional boundaries. A mustachioed industrial and interior designer turned watch designer, Silberstein has christened himself the "architect of time." It was his unorthodox ideas, however, that sealed his reputation. He combined high-grade diamonds with stainless steel long before it was fashionable to do so, and his fur- and leather-covered timepieces had watchmaking purists shaking their heads in disbelief during the 1990s. Some may think Silberstein's designs too avant-garde, but others recognize that they express a truly extraordinary *joie de vivre*. His are happy designs, full of resplendent color and geometric forms, so unusual among the staid conservative aesthetics of mainstream watchmaking.

In 2004, Silberstein introduced the latest of his funky collections, entitled Tourbillon d'Art, comprising sixteen flying tourbillon models limited to 500 pieces each. This was without a doubt the most striking embodiment of his watchmaking philosophy up to that point, blending high design with high horology. Such a feat was unprecedented, and the sheer volume of the high complications that needed to be manufactured would have been at the very least too daunting for most, but not for Silberstein.

The automatic and manually wound engines that power the watches in this collection feature visible flying tourbillons that were designed and signed by Silberstein and manufactured by Swiss craftsmen. A flying tourbillon is cantilevered, which means it is fixed to the base plate on one side only, allowing the observer an unimpeded view of the moving mechanism from the dial side. "These pieces are a wedding of high tech and color," was how Silberstein described them, being the first watchmaker to galvanize movement parts in ways that transform basic shades of silver and gold into hues of lilac, pink, black, blue, and brown.

Now celebrating twenty years in the watch industry, Silberstein has introduced two new fields of exploration. "In addition to color, I am now exploring finishings pertaining to grey metals—like titanium and ruthenium. This is like color for me, but more related to the material."

In honor of his company's anniversary, Silberstein is now inaugurating a new line called Basik in high-polished titanium and a commemorative model called Marine 20, which is reminiscent of his first chronograph. "This is a monster, but reminds me of a pebble. I'm trying to get back to the roots here, which is the shape, the form. Something neat and simple, searching for the elusively pure line."

Finally, Silberstein is also introducing a new tourbillon in honor of the jubilee year. This whirlwind contains a Technotime movement instead of a Progress caliber like the Tourbillon d'Art collection had, which means that the actual tourbillon is now located at 9 o'clock. Silberstein, ever the designer, is more interested in making a balanced collection than a new movement, however. "The movement is, of course, important for high watchmaking, but it would be a mistake to identify a timepiece only by that criterion."

Alain Silberstein

Tourbillon Black Arrow
Reference number: TT0301B
Movement: manually wound, TT Caliber 791.04; ø 30.4 mm, height 6.6 mm; 37 jewels; 28,800 vph; one-minute tourbillon; twin spring barrels; power reserve 120 hours
Functions: hours, minutes; date (retrograde)
Case: titanium, ø 39.8 mm, height 12.3 mm; sapphire crystal; transparent case back; water-resistant to 10 atm
Band: rubber, folding clasp
Remarks: limited edition of 20 numbered pieces; comes with alligator skin strap in set
Price: 113,000 euros

Marine 20 Krono
Reference number: MVK0301B
Movement: automatic, ETA Valjoux Caliber 7751; ø 30 mm, height 7.9 mm; 25 jewels; 28,800 vph
Functions: hours, minutes, subsidiary seconds; chronograph; date, day (Smileday), month, moon phase; 24-hour display
Case: titanium, ø 46 mm, height 17.1 mm; bidirectionally rotating bezel with reference marker; sapphire crystal; transparent case back; water-resistant to 20 atm
Band: rubber, folding clasp
Remarks: limited edition of 999 numbered pieces
Price: 8,000 euros
Variations: with grey bezel

Marine 20
Reference number: MVK0302B
Movement: automatic, ETA Caliber 2892-5; ø 26.2 mm, height 4.6 mm; 21 jewels; 28,800 vph
Functions: hours, minutes, sweep seconds; date; power reserve display
Case: titanium, ø 46 mm, height 16.4 mm; bidirectionally rotating bezel with reference marker; sapphire crystal; transparent case back; water-resistant to 20 atm
Band: rubber, folding clasp
Remarks: limited edition of 100 numbered pieces
Price: 7,400 euros
Variations: with yellow bezel

Krono Bauhaus Red Gold Black
Reference number: KT0801B
Movement: automatic, ETA Valjoux Caliber 7751; ø 30 mm, height 7.9 mm; 25 jewels; 28,800 vph
Functions: hours, minutes, subsidiary seconds; chronograph; date, day (Smileday), month, moon phase; 24-hour display
Case: red gold, ø 39.8 mm, height 14.2 mm; sapphire crystal; transparent case back; water-resistant to 10 atm
Band: reptile skin, buckle
Remarks: limited edition of 100 numbered pieces
Price: 27,700 euros

Krono Bauhaus Red Gold Red
Reference number: KT0802B
Movement: automatic, ETA Valjoux Caliber 7751; ø 30 mm, height 7.9 mm; 25 jewels; 28,800 vph
Functions: hours, minutes, subsidiary seconds; chronograph; date, day (Smileday), month, moon phase; 24-hour display
Case: red gold, ø 39.8 mm, height 14.2 mm; sapphire crystal; transparent case back; water-resistant to 10 atm
Band: reptile skin, buckle
Remarks: limited edition of 100 numbered pieces
Price: 27,700 euros

Krono Bauhaus Alligator Gold
Reference number: KT0608
Movement: automatic, ETA Valjoux Caliber 7751; ø 30 mm, height 7.9 mm; 25 jewels; 28,800 vph
Functions: hours, minutes, subsidiary seconds; chronograph; date, day (Smileday), month, moon phase; 24-hour display
Case: stainless steel covered with alligator skin, ø 40.5 mm, height 15 mm; sapphire crystal; transparent case back; water-resistant to 3 atm
Band: reptile skin, buckle
Remarks: limited edition of 999 numbered pieces
Price: 7,900 euros

Krono Bauhaus Alligator Silver
Reference number: KT0610
Movement: automatic, ETA Valjoux Caliber 7751; ø 30 mm, height 7.9 mm; 25 jewels; 28,800 vph
Functions: hours, minutes, subsidiary seconds; chronograph; date, day (Smileday), month, moon phase; 24-hour display
Case: stainless steel covered with alligator skin, ø 40.5 mm, height 15 mm; sapphire crystal; transparent case back; water-resistant to 3 atm
Band: reptile skin, buckle
Remarks: limited edition of 999 numbered pieces
Price: $9,800
Price: 7,900 euros

Krono Bauhaus 2 Flannel Grey
Reference number: KT0501
Movement: automatic, ETA Valjoux Caliber 7751; ø 30 mm, height 7.9 mm; 25 jewels; 28,800 vph
Functions: hours, minutes, subsidiary seconds; chronograph; date, day (Smileday), month, moon phase; 24-hour display
Case: stainless steel, cloisonné lacquered, ø 39.8 mm, height 14.2 mm; sapphire crystal; transparent case back; water-resistant to 10 atm
Band: rubber, folding clasp
Remarks: limited edition of 999 numbered pieces; comes with stainless steel bracelet and alligator skin strap in set
Price: 8,200 euros

Alain Silberstein

Krono Bauhaus 2 Titanium
Reference number: KT0301P
Movement: automatic, ETA Valjoux Caliber 7751; ø 30 mm, height 7.9 mm; 25 jewels; 28,800 vph
Functions: hours, minutes, subsidiary seconds; chronograph; date, day (Smileday), month, moon phase; 24-hour display
Case: polished titanium, ø 39.8 mm, height 14.2 mm; sapphire crystal; transparent case back; water-resistant to 10 atm
Band: rubber, folding clasp
Remarks: limited edition of 999 numbered pieces
Price: 7,400 euros
Variations: brushed titanium; various dial variations

Krono Bauhaus 2 White Night
Reference number: KT0504
Movement: automatic, ETA Valjoux Caliber 7751; ø 30 mm, height 7.9 mm; 25 jewels; 28,800 vph
Functions: hours, minutes, subsidiary seconds; chronograph; date, day (Smileday), month, moon phase; 24-hour display
Case: stainless steel, cloisonné lacquered, ø 39.8 mm, height 14.2 mm; sapphire crystal; transparent case back; water-resistant to 10 atm
Band: rubber, folding clasp
Remarks: limited edition of 999 numbered pieces; comes with stainless steel bracelet and alligator skin strap in set
Price: 8,200 euros

Le Reveil GMT
Reference number: LG0304B
Movement: automatic, La Joux-Perret Caliber 5900; ø 30.4 mm, height 7.75 mm; 31 jewels; 28.800 vph; automatic winding of movement and alarm mechanism
Functions: hours, minutes, sweep seconds; 24-hour display (second time zone); date; alarm
Case: brushed titanium, ø 39.8 mm, height 14.3 mm; sapphire crystal; transparent case back; water-resistant to 10 atm
Band: rubber, folding clasp
Remarks: limited edition of 999 numbered pieces
Price: 8,000 euros

Rondo Blue Dots
Reference number: OS501
Movement: automatic, ETA Caliber 2836-2; ø 26 mm, height 5.05 mm; 25 jewels; 28,800 vph
Functions: hours, minutes, sweep seconds; date and day ("Smileday")
Case: stainless steel with lacquer appliqué, ø 42.4 mm, height 10.5 mm; sapphire crystal; transparent case back; recessed crown; water-resistant to 10 atm
Band: rubber, folding clasp
Remarks: limited edition of 999 numbered pieces; comes with stainless steel bracelet and alligator skin strap in set
Price: 6,900 euros

Rondo Pink Dots
Reference number: OS503
Movement: automatic, ETA Caliber 2836-2; ø 26 mm, height 5.05 mm; 25 jewels; 28,800 vph
Functions: hours, minutes, sweep seconds; date and day ("Smileday")
Case: stainless steel with lacquer appliqué, ø 42.4 mm, height 10.5 mm; sapphire crystal; transparent case back; recessed crown; water-resistant to 10 atm
Band: rubber, folding clasp
Remarks: limited edition of 999 numbered pieces; comes with stainless steel bracelet and alligator skin strap in set
Price: 6,900 euros

Basik
Reference number: BA0301P
Movement: automatic, ETA Caliber 2836-2; ø 26 mm, height 5.05 mm; 25 jewels; 28,800 vph
Functions: hours, minutes, sweep seconds; date and day ("Smileday")
Case: titanium, ø 42.4 mm, height 10.5 mm; sapphire crystal; transparent case back; recessed crown; water-resistant to 10 atm
Band: rubber, folding clasp
Remarks: limited edition of 999 numbered pieces
Price: 4,000 euros

Basik
Reference number: BA0302P
Movement: automatic, ETA Caliber 2836-2; ø 26 mm, height 5.05 mm; 25 jewels; 28,800 vph
Functions: hours, minutes, sweep seconds; date and day ("Smileday")
Case: titanium, ø 42.4 mm, height 10.5 mm; sapphire crystal; transparent case back; recessed crown; water-resistant to 10 atm
Band: rubber, folding clasp
Remarks: limited edition of 999 numbered pieces
Price: 4,000 euros

Basik
Reference number: BA0303P
Movement: automatic, ETA Caliber 2836-2; ø 26 mm, height 5.05 mm; 25 jewels; 28,800 vph
Functions: hours, minutes, sweep seconds; date and day ("Smileday")
Case: titanium, ø 42.4 mm, height 10.5 mm; sapphire crystal; transparent case back; recessed crown; water-resistant to 10 atm
Band: rubber, folding clasp
Remarks: limited edition of 999 numbered pieces
Price: 4,000 euros

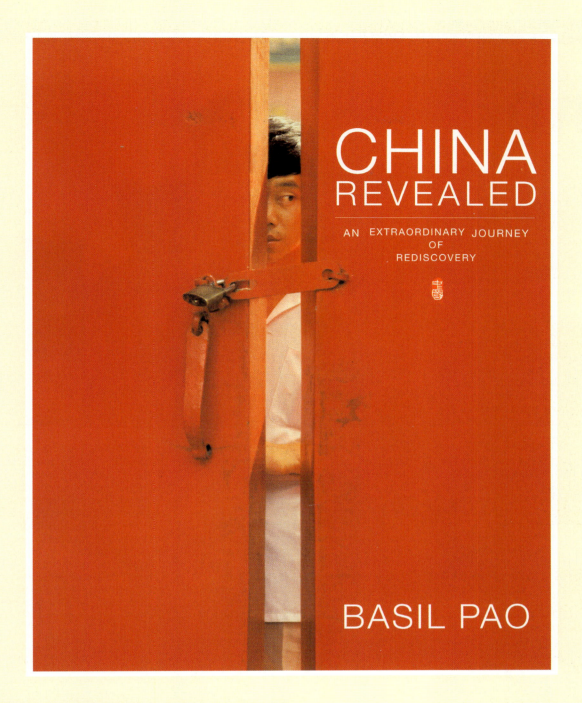

China Revealed

This richly illustrated travel guidebook portrays China's must-see places as well as regions visitors rarely discover. Basil Pao's spectacular photojourney highlights China's dramatic landscape and is accompanied by a personal and informative text, resulting in a fascinating volume that reveals China in the twenty-first century.

Text and photography by Basil Pao
381 full-color illustrations
384 pages · 11 $^{5}/_{8}$ x 9 $^{5}/_{8}$ · Cloth
ISBN: 978-0-7892-0947-4
$60.00

Published by ABBEVILLE PRESS
137 Varick Street, New York, NY 10013
1-800-Artbook (in U.S. only)
Also available wherever fine books are sold
Visit us at www.abbeville.com

Sinn

Sinn's clientele could well be described as fanatic: these are people who have a high affinity for technology and are enthusiastic about how the Frankfurt engineers seek and find solutions, such as protection from magnetic fields and scratch resistance. Sinn's clientele also contains people who need to rely on their watches 100 percent—like divers, pilots, and the GSG 9 special unit. They all swear by the performance, robustness, longevity, quality, and precision of these watches.

Functionality is Sinn's highest priority and in the end is what determines this brand's visuals. Searching for new technologies and materials, CEO Lothar Schmidt's product developers often find what they are looking for in other industries or the sciences. Consistent, Sinn makes sure its watches can withstand the hardest practical tests possible. The diver's watches U1, U2, and UX, one of the most successful model families thanks to their technical details, are impressive proof of this. The technical development of diver's watches is one of the greatest challenges: on every dive the factor of time plays an important role in survival. Therefore, diver's watches must be water-resistant, reliable, and robust as well as perfectly legible under all lighting conditions. The various models of the diver's watch line prove their suitability for everyday wear in many ways.

Thus, Sinn uses especially seawater-resistant submarine steel for these timepieces' cases. The rotating bezel, which cannot come off, is serially hardened to 1,500 Vickers while its sapphire crystal contains progressive reflective technology for perfect legibility. Since 2005, Hamburg's Germanischer Lloyd has tested and certified these diver's watches for water-resistance and pressure-proofing. The test confirms that the U1 model is pressure-proof to 100 bar, the U2 model to 200 bar, and the UX is even pressure-proof to 500 bar—while its case can withstand pressure to 1,200 bar.

In 2006, Sinn developed a testing procedure in conjunction with Germanischer Lloyd that has never been seen before in the watch industry: the certification of watches according to the European dive equipment norm. The result: testers confirmed the temperature stability and perfect functioning of the U1, U2, and EZM 3 models under extreme temperature differences.

Alongside diver's watches, all other models—such as the brand's reputable pilot's watches, the elegant Frankfurt Finance Watches, and the classic masterpieces—can be purchased directly from Sinn's official distributor in the United States. This is a system that allows the brand's excellent price/performance ratio to continue—an element along with the watches' performance that explains why Sinn's clientele loves it so.

Régulateur
Reference number: 6100 Klassik B
Movement: manually wound, Sinn Caliber SZ 04 (base ETA Unitas 6498-1); ø 36.6 mm, height 4.5 mm; 17 jewels; 18,000 vph; in-house dial train modification; finely finished with blued screws; shockproof and amagnetic according to DIN
Functions: hours (off-center), minutes, subsidiary seconds
Case: stainless steel, ø 44 mm, height 10.6 mm; sapphire crystal; transparent case back; crown with D3 sealing system; water- and pressure-resistant to 10 bar
Band: leather, buckle
Price: $2,600
Variations: gold-plated hands and applied elements

Régulateur
Reference number: 6100 Roségold
Movement: manually wound, Sinn Caliber SZ 04 (base ETA Unitas 6498-1); ø 36.6 mm, height 4.5 mm; 17 jewels; 18,000 vph; in-house dial train modification; finely finished with blued screws; shockproof and amagnetic according to DIN
Functions: hours (off-center), minutes, subsidiary seconds
Case: rose gold, ø 44 mm, height 10.6 mm; sapphire crystal; transparent case back; crown with D3 sealing system; water- and pressure-resistant to 10 bar
Band: leather, buckle
Price: $9,950
Variations: white gold

H4 Lémania Chronograph
Reference number: 903 H4
Movement: manually wound, Nouvelle Lémania Caliber 1883; ø 27 mm, height 6.87 mm; 18 jewels; 21,600 vph
Functions: hours, minutes, subsidiary seconds; chronograph; date; moon phase
Case: stainless steel, ø 41 mm, height 13.4 mm; bezel under crystal, unidirectionally rotating via crown with slide rule function; sapphire crystal; transparent case back; water- and pressure-resistant to 10 bar
Band: leather, buckle
Remarks: comes with additional stainless steel bracelet
Price: $4,100

The Skeletonized Gold Chronograph
Reference number: 2300
Movement: manually wound, Valjoux Caliber 23; ø 30 mm, height 6.25 mm; 17 jewels; 18,000 vph; historical movement, completely hand-skeletonized and engraved
Functions: hours, minutes, subsidiary seconds; chronograph
Case: yellow gold, ø 38 mm, height 11 mm; sapphire crystal; transparent case back; water- and pressure-resistant to 3 bar
Band: reptile skin, buckle
Price: $19,800

The Frankfurt Porcelain Watch
Reference number: 1746
Movement: automatic, ETA Caliber 2892-A2; ø 25.6 mm, height 3.6 mm; 21 jewels; 28,800 vph; finely finished, decorated
Functions: hours, minutes
Case: stainless steel, ø 42 mm, height 9.4 mm; sapphire crystal; transparent case back; water- and pressure-resistant to 10 bar
Band: leather, buckle
Remarks: hand-painted dial made of Höchst porcelain
Price: $5,200
Variations: diverse views of Frankfurt or Rhine countryside scenes as dial motifs; individual painting possible

1746 Frankfurt Classic
Reference number: 1746 Klassik
Movement: automatic, ETA Caliber 2892-A2; ø 25.6 mm, height 3.6 mm; 21 jewels; 28,800 vph; finely finished, decorated
Functions: hours, minutes; date
Case: stainless steel, ø 42 mm, height 9.4 mm; sapphire crystal; transparent case back; water- and pressure-resistant to 10 bar
Band: leather, buckle
Price: $2,100

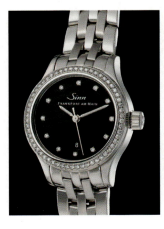

The Elegant Ladies' Watch with Diamonds
Reference number: 456 ST TW 70
Movement: automatic, ETA Caliber 2678; ø 17.2 mm, height 4.8 mm; 25 jewels; 28,800 vph
Functions: hours, minutes, sweep seconds; date
Case: stainless steel, ø 28 mm, height 11 mm; bezel set with 58 diamonds; sapphire crystal; transparent case back; water- and pressure-resistant to 20 bar
Band: stainless steel, double folding clasp
Remarks: dial set with 12 brilliant-cut diamond markers
Price: $4,900
Variations; on strap ($4,550); with yellow gold bezel

The Rallye Chronograph
Reference number: 956 KLASSIK
Movement: automatic, ETA Valjoux Caliber 7750; ø 30 mm, height 7.9 mm; 25 jewels; 28,800 vph; shockproof and amagnetic according to DIN
Functions: hours, minutes, subsidiary seconds; chronograph; date; power reserve display
Case: stainless steel, ø 41.5 mm, height 15 mm; sapphire crystal; transparent case back; screw-in crown; water- and pressure-resistant to 10 bar
Band: leather, buckle
Price: $3,400
Variations: stainless steel bracelet ($3,750); matte black dial

Sinn

U1 Divers
Reference number: U1
Movement: automatic, ETA Caliber 2824-2; ø 25.6 mm, height 4.6 mm; 25 jewels; 28,800 vph
Functions: hours, minutes, sweep seconds; date
Case: submarine steel, pearlblasted, ø 44 mm, height 14.35 mm; unidirectionally rotating bezel with 60-minute divisions; sapphire crystal; water- and pressure-resistant to 100 bar
Band: silicon, folding clasp with wetsuit extension
Remarks: non-losable diver's rotating ring
Price: $1,850
Variations: stainless steel bracelet ($2,050)

U2 EZM 5 Divers
Reference number: U2 (EZM 5)
Movement: automatic, ETA Caliber 2893-2; ø 25.6 mm, height 4.1 mm; 21 jewels; 28,800 vph
Functions: hours, minutes, sweep seconds; 24-hour display (second time zone); date
Case: submarine steel, pearlblasted, ø 44 mm, height 15.45 mm; unidirectionally rotating bezel with 60-minute divisions; sapphire crystal; screw-in crown; water- and pressure-resistant to 200 bar
Band: stainless steel (tegimented), folding clasp with wetsuit extension
Remarks: non-losable diver's rotating ring
Price: $3,050
Variations: silicon strap ($2,850)

UX GSG9 Divers
Reference number: UX (EZM 2B) GSG 9
Movement: quartz, ETA Caliber 955.652
Functions: hours, minutes, sweep seconds; date
Case: submarine steel, pearlblasted, ø 44 mm, height 13.2 mm; unidirectionally rotating tegimented bezel with 60-minute divisions; sapphire crystal; screw-in crown; unlimited water resistance; case completely filled with oil, thus pressure-proof to any reachable diving depth and legible under watch from every angle
Band: silicon, folding clasp with wetsuit extension
Remarks: non-losable diver's rotating ring
Price: $1,950
Variations: stainless steel bracelet ($2,150)

The Pilot's Chronograph with Magnetic Field Protection and Second Time Zone
Reference number: 856 S
Movement: automatic, ETA Caliber 2893-2; ø 25.6 mm, height 4.1 mm; 21 jewels; 28,800 vph; shockproof and amagnetic according to DIN
Functions: hours, minutes, sweep seconds; date; 24-hour display (second time zone)
Case: black tegimented stainless steel, ø 40 mm, height 10.7 mm; sapphire crystal; screw-in crown; water-resistant to 200 m
Band: black tegimented stainless steel; double folding clasp
Price: $2,100
Variations: leather strap ($1,750)

756 Diapal Oil Free Escapement
Reference number: 756 DIAPAL
Movement: automatic, ETA Valjoux Caliber 7750, modified; ø 30 mm, height 7.9 mm; 25 jewels; 28,800 vph; escapement with Diapal technology; magnetic field protection to 80,000 A/m; shockproof and amagnetic according to DIN
Functions: hours, minutes, chronograph; date; 12-hour hand (second time zone)
Case: tegimented stainless steel (1,200 Vickers), ø 40 mm, height 13.7 mm; sapphire crystal; screw-in crown; water- and pressure-resistant to 20 bar
Band: stainless steel, double folding clasp
Remarks: dehumidifying capsule
Price: $3,300
Variations: leather strap ($2,950)

757 Tegimented UTC Chronograph
Reference number: 757 UTC
Movement: automatic, modified ETA Valjoux Caliber 7750; ø 30 mm, height 7.9 mm; 25 jewels; 28,800 vph; shockproof and amagnetic to 80,000 A/m according to DIN
Functions: hours, minutes; chronograph; date, 12-hour hand (second time zone)
Case: tegimented stainless steel (1,299 Vickers), ø 435 mm, height 15.2 mm; unidirectionally rotating bezel with 60-minute divisions; dehumidifyng technology; sapphire crystal; screw-in crown; water- and pressure-resistant to 20 bar
Band: tegimented stainless steel; double folding clasp
Price: $3,100
Variations: leather strap ($2,800)

857 Tegimented Pilot's UTC
Reference number: 857
Movement: automatic, ETA Caliber 2893-2; ø 25.6 mm, height 4.1 mm; 21 jewels; 28,800 vph; magnetic field protection to 80,000 A/m
Functions: hours, minutes, sweep seconds; date; 24-hour display (second time zone)
Case: black tegimented stainless steel, ø 43 mm, height 12.17 mm; unidirectionally rotating bezel with 60-minute divisions; sapphire crystal; screw-in crown; water- and pressure-resistant to 20 bar
Band: leather, buckle
Price: $1,850
Variations: with tegimented stainless steel bracelet ($2,150)

The Anniversary Diver's Chronograph
Reference number: 203 Jubiläum
Movement: automatic, ETA Valjoux Caliber 7750; ø 30 mm, height 7.9 mm; 25 jewels; 28,800 vph; shockproof and amagnetic according to DIN
Functions: hours, minutes, subsidiary seconds; chronograph; date, weekday
Case: titanium, ø 41 mm, height 16 mm; unidirectionally rotating bezel with 60-minute divisions; sapphire crystal; screw-in crown and buttons; water- and pressure-resistant to 30 bar
Band: titanium, double folding clasp
Remarks: dehumidifying technology; comes with leather strap in set
Price: $2,700

Sinn

The Frankfurt Finance Watch
Reference number: 6000
Movement: automatic, ETA Valjoux Caliber 7750, modified; ø 30 mm, height 8.4 mm; 25 jewels; 28,800 vph; finely finished; shockproof and amagnetic according to DIN
Functions: hours, minutes, subsidiary seconds; chronograph; date; 12-hour hand (second time zone)
Case: stainless steel, ø 38.5 mm, height 16.5 mm; bezel under crystal with 12-hour scale (third time zone), unidirectionally rotating via crown; sapphire crystal; transparent case back
Band: stainless steel, double folding clasp
Remarks: comes with leather strap in set
Price: $4,250

The Frankfurt World Time Watch
Reference number: 6060
Movement: automatic, ETA Caliber 2893-2; ø 25.6 mm, height 4.1 mm; 21 jewels; 28,800 vph; finely finished; shockproof and amagnetic according to DIN
Functions: hours, minutes, sweep seconds; date; 24-hour display (second time zone)
Case: stainless steel, ø 38.5 mm, height 12 mm; bezel under crystal with 12-hour scale (third time zone), unidirectionally rotating via crown; sapphire crystal; transparent case back
Band: calfskin, buckle
Remarks: comes with stainless steel bracelet in set
Price: $2,950

The Frankfurt Finance Alarm
Reference number: 6066
Movement: automatic, ETA Caliber 5008 (base AS Kaliber 5008); ø 30.4 m, height 7.75 mm; 31 jewels; 28,800 vph
Functions: hours, minutes, sweep seconds; date; 24-hour display (second time zone); alarm
Case: stainless steel, ø 38.5 mm, height 15 mm; bezel under crystal with 12-hour scale (third time zone, unidirectionally rotating via crown; sapphire crystal; transparent case back
Band: stainless steel, double folding clasp
Remarks: comes with leather strap in set
Price: $4,950

The Frankfurt Finance Watch IV
Reference number: 6030
Movement: automatic, ETA Caliber 2094; ø 23.3 mm, height 5.5 mm; 33 jewels; 28,800 vph; finely finished
Functions: hours, minutes, subsidiary seconds; chronograph; date
Case: stainless steel, ø 34 mm, height 11.2 mm; bezel under crystal with 12-hour scale (second time zone), unidirectionally rotating via crown; sapphire crystal; transparent case back; water- and pressure-resistant to 10 bar
Band: stainless steel, double folding clasp
Remarks: comes with leather strap in set
Price: $3,850

The Frankfurt Finance Watch V
Reference number: 6033
Movement: automatic, ETA Caliber 2892-A2; ø 25.6 mm, height 3.6 mm; 21 jewels; 28,800 vph; finely finished; rotor engraved with financial bull and bear
Functions: hours, minutes, sweep seconds; date
Case: stainless steel, ø 34 mm, height 10.3 mm; bezel under crystal with 12-hour scale (second time zone), unidirectionally rotating via crown; sapphire crystal; transparent case back; water- and pressure-resistant to 10 bar
Band: stainless steel, double folding clasp
Remarks: comes with leather strap in set
Price: $2,350

The New Space Chronograph
Reference number: 142 St II
Movement: automatic, Dubois Dépraz Caliber 2070 (base ETA 2892-A2); ø 30.4 mm, height 7.5 mm; 33 jewels; 28,800 vph; sweep minute counter; shockproof and amagnetic according to DIN
Functions: hours, minutes, subsidiary seconds; chronograph; date; 24-hour display
Case: stainless steel, ø 44 mm, height 14.8 mm; bezel under crystal with 60-minute divisions, bidirectionally rotating via crown; sapphire crystal; transparent case back; screw-in crown; water- and pressure-resistant to 10 bar
Band: stainless steel, folding clasp with wetsuit extension
Price: $2,650

The Classic Pilot's Chronograph
Reference number: 103 A Sa
Movement: automatic, ETA Valjoux Caliber 7750; ø 30 mm, height 7.9 mm; 25 jewels; 28,800 vph; shockproof and amagnetic according to DIN
Functions: hours, minutes, subsidiary seconds; chronograph; date, weekday
Case: stainless steel, ø 41 mm, height 16.5 mm; bidirectionally rotating bezel with 60-minute divisions; sapphire crystal; transparent case back; screw-in crown and buttons; water- and pressure-resistant to 10 bar
Band: leather, buckle
Price: $1,950
Variations: stainless steel bracelet ($2,150)

The Pilot's Chronograph
Reference number: 356 Sa Flieger II
Movement: automatic, ETA Valjoux Caliber 7750; ø 30 mm, height 7.9 mm; 25 jewels; 28,800 vph; finely finished with blued screws; shockproof and amagnetic according to DIN
Functions: hours, minutes, subsidiary seconds; chronograph; date, weekday
Case: stainless steel, ø 38.5 mm, height 14.9 mm; sapphire crystal; screw-in crown; water- and pressure-resistant to 10 bar
Band: stainless steel, folding clasp
Price: $2,400
Variations: with Russian leather strap ($2,200); black dial

Sothis

This brand name originates in ancient Egyptian mythology, representing the personification of the Star of Sirius. For the Egyptians, the appearance of this star in the winter sky was a good omen meaning that the Nile would flood and that nothing could stand in the way of a good harvest. Sothis can now look back on eleven successful years of watchmaking in which this star was in its sky every year. The company's designer and founder Wolfgang Steinkrüger creates, develops, and produces new models every year that fit perfectly into Sothis's extensive collection. Today, it comprises a total of thirteen models that are each different, but which all mirror the unmistakable corporate identity of Sothis at a glance.

The unusual depiction of the moon phase featuring a revolving hand is as unique to the models Ikarus and Osiris as the date ring on the dials' flanges. On all watches in the Spirit of Moon line, the moon phase has been made by Sothis in-house, and the technology of the one-handed chronograph Horus is also exclusive.

This chronograph is completely different from the classicism of the rest of the collection: the new chronograph needs only a single hand to display the time. In a twelve-hour period, the two-legged hand featuring a stylized sun and star glides across the striking half-circle found in the upper half of the dial. The lone hand completes one revolution in 24 hours, still allowing it to display the time within two minutes. Every single one of these Sothis calibers based on Valjoux 7750/54 movements are rebuilt by hand as the model is strictly limited to 200 pieces per dial variation.

One special element of Sothis's cases is their screwed-on strap lugs: they guarantee great strength while the space between the case and the strap is almost nonexistent thanks to high manufacturing precision. A specially made screw with gasket elements guarantees absolute water-resistance to 10 atm. The case's ability to be dismantled allows the brand to simply replace individual parts should damage occur. Thus, the little Bielefeld-based factory can put any Sothis back into mint condition even years later.

Sothis

World Time Chrono 2
Reference number: 027001-B
Movement: automatic, ETA Valjoux Caliber 7754; ø 30 mm, height 7.9 mm; 25 jewels; 28,800 vph; finely finished with côtes de Gènève and perlage; blued screws
Functions: hours, minutes, subsidiary seconds; chronograph; date; world time display (second time zone)
Case: stainless steel, ø 44 mm, height 13.9 mm; bidirectionally rotating bezel with 24-hour divisions (third time zone); sapphire crystal; transparent case back
Band: leather, folding clasp
Price: $4,700
Variations: stainless steel bracelet ($5,400); white dial

Horus Single Hand Chronograph
Reference number: 026001-W
Movement: automatic, ETA Valjoux Caliber 7750, modified; ø 30 mm, height 7.9 mm; 25 jewels; 28,800 vph; finely finished with côtes de Genève and perlage; blued screws
Functions: hours, minutes, subsidiary seconds; chronograph; date
Case: stainless steel, ø 44 mm, height 14 mm; sapphire crystal; transparent case back
Band: reptile skin, folding clasp
Price: $5,100
Variations: stainless steel braclet ($5,800); black dial

Horus Single Hand Chronograph
Reference number: 026001-G
Movement: automatic, ETA Valjoux Caliber 7750, modified; ø 30 mm, height 7.9 mm; 25 jewels; 28,800 vph; finely finished with côtes de Genève and perlage; blued screws
Functions: hours, minutes, subsidiary seconds; chronograph; date
Case: stainless steel, ø 44 mm, height 14 mm; sapphire crystal; transparent case back
Band: reptile skin, folding clasp
Price: $ Price: $5,100
Variations: stainless steel bracelet ($5,800)

Spirit of Moon Osiris
Reference number: 025002-W
Movement: automatic, ETA Valjoux Caliber 7751, modified; ø 30 mm, height 7.9 mm; 25 jewels; 28,800 vph; finely finished with côtes de Genève and perlage; blued screws
Functions: hours, minutes, subsidiary seconds; chronograph; date, weekday, month, moon phase display
Case: stainless steel, ø 42.5 mm, height 13.9 mm; sapphire crystal; transparent case back
Band: leather, folding clasp
Price: $4,200
Variations: stainless steel bracelet ($4,900); black dial

Spirit of Moon Prestige
Reference number: 022002-GR
Movement: automatic, ETA Valjoux Caliber 7751, modified; ø 30 mm, height 7.9 mm; 25 jewels; 28,800 vph; finely finished with côtes de Genève and perlage; blued screws
Functions: hours, minutes, subsidiary seconds; chronograph; date, weekday, month, moon phase display
Case: stainless steel, ø 42.5 mm, height 13.9 mm; sapphire crystal; transparent case back; water-resistant to 5 atm
Band: leather, folding clasp
Price: $4,700
Variations: stainless steel bracelet ($5,400); black dial

Spirit of Moon
Reference number: 098003-B
Movement: automatic, ETA Valjoux Caliber 7751, modified; ø 30 mm, height 7.9 mm; 25 jewels; 28,800 vph; finely finished with côtes de Genève and perlage; blued screws
Functions: hours, minutes, subsidiary seconds; chronograph; date, weekday, month, moon phase display
Case: stainless steel, ø 42.5 mm, height 13.9 mm; sapphire crystal; transparent case back; water-resistant to 5 atm
Band: leather, folding clasp
Price: $4,200
Variations: stainless steel bracelet ($4,900); silver-colored or white dial

Big Bridge
Reference number: 098004-B
Movement: automatic, Dubois Dépraz Caliber 2025 (base ETA 2892-A2); ø 30 mm, height 6.9 mm, 47 jewels; 28,800 vph; finely finished with côtes de Genève and perlage; blued screws
Functions: hours, minutes, subsidiary seconds; chronograph; date
Case: stainless steel, 37 x 50 mm, height 12.7 mm; sapphire crystal; transparent case back
Band: leather, folding clasp
Price: $5,700
Variations: silver-colored, yellow, or carbon fiber dial

Janus
Reference number: 024003-B
Movement: automatic, ETA Valjoux Caliber 7750; ø 30 mm, height 7.9 mm; 25 jewels; 28,800 vph; finely finished with côtes de Genève and perlage; blued screws
Functions: hours, minutes, subsidiary seconds; chronograph; date and weekday
Case: stainless steel, ø 42.5 mm, height 13.9 mm; sapphire crystal; transparent case back; water-resistant to 5 atm
Band: leather, folding clasp
Price: $3,800
Variations: stainless steel bracelet ($4,500); white dial

Stowa

WIE DIE ZEIT VERGEHT.

Stowa—the German Quality Watch. This is how the traditional Pforzheim brand advertised eighty years ago. This elementary concept is being carried on in the current day and age: the watches continue to be as striking in their visuals as they are in their absolute functionality. In this way, the old pilot's watches, their designs unfailingly adapted, have today become luxury wristwatches, with their technical straightforwardness and uncomplicated clarity also maintained. Alongside the pilot's series, a maritime series—also historical in nature—is being reproduced. In keeping with the motto, "Characteristically original—the details of a Stowa," all Stowa watches are striking in their attention to detail. Nearly every piece of every serial watch undergoes its own individual revision and examination. That the watches are "made in Germany" and thus labeled is enough reason for the new owners of the name to deliver the highest-quality products. Also modern is also the way these watches are distributed in an online shop at www.stowa.de. Watch fans with shallower pockets will find mechanical watches of good quality here.

Stowa was founded in 1927 in Hornberg, Germany, by Walter Storz. In the 1930s and '40s, the company situated in the Black Forest produced especially high-quality, reliable watches. The degree of excellence achieved by their watches brought Stowa a good reputation, and their pilot's and observation watches were of special note. Alongside IWC, A. Lange & Söhne, Wempe, and Laco, this brand was also one of the German air force's official suppliers. These watches had to be completely precise and trustworthy, as they were used in ways that demanded 100 percent accuracy. The pilot in his cockpit had to be just as sure as the officer on the deck of his ship that his watch was correct.

Stowa is one of the few Pforzheim brands to be uninterruptedly active since the beginning of the twentieth century. Although the production rooms in Pforzheim were destroyed in the last days of World War II due to a devastating attack on the city, the Storz family didn't give up. Within just a few years, the clan was able to continue business as if the war had never happened. Werner Storz, son of the company's founder, became instrumental in the continued success of the firm. It was he who kept Stowa's head above water during the quartz crisis when cheap watches from the Far East flooded the European markets, structuring the company so that it was able to begin encasing reasonably priced quartz movements rather than being an assembler of mechanical mechanisms. Storz managed Stowa until it was purchased by Jörg Schauer in 1996.

Spurred on by the success of his own eponymous brand, Schauer once again steered Stowa to mechanical watches and took care to collect the remains of this rich inheritance in the form of a small museum. Thus, the Stowa Museum in Engelsbrand, the suburb of Pforzheim that is Schauer's home, contains old marine and pilot's watches as well as historical civilian models. Celebrating the eightieth anniversary of the Pforzheim brand, the museum's permanent collection has been extended with the addition of a few true specialties.

Stowa

Antea Small Seconds
Reference number: AnteaKSL
Movement: automatic, ETA Peseux Caliber 7001; ø 23.3 mm, height 2.5 mm; 17 jewels; 21,600 vph; côtes de Genève, blued screws
Functions: hours, minutes, subsidiary seconds
Case: stainless steel, ø 35.5 mm, height 6.8 mm; sapphire crystal; transparent case back
Band: Nappa leather, buckle
Price: appx. $540
Variations: reptile skin strap or stainless steel bracelet

Antea 365
Reference number: Antea365L
Movement: automatic, ETA Caliber 2824; ø 25.6 mm, height 4.6 mm; 25 jewels; 28,800 vph; in-house rotor in German silver, blued screws
Functions: hours, minutes, sweep seconds; date
Case: stainless steel, ø 36.5 mm, height 9.5 mm; sapphire crystal; transparent case back
Band: Nappa leather, buckle
Price: appx. $800
Variations: stainless steel bracelet

Antea Automatic
Reference number: AnteaSDL
Movement: automatic, ETA Caliber 2824; ø 25.6 mm, height 4.6 mm; 25 jewels; 28,800 vph; in-house rotor in German silver, blued screws
Functions: hours, minutes, sweep seconds; date
Case: stainless steel, ø 39 mm, height 9.5 mm; sapphire crystal; transparent case back; water-resistant to 5 atm
Band: leather, buckle
Price: appx. $400
Variations: stainless steel bracelet

Ikarus
Reference number: IkarusL
Movement: automatic, ETA Caliber 2824; ø 25.6 mm, height 4.6 mm; 25 jewels; 28,800 vph
Functions: hours, minutes, sweep seconds
Case: stainless steel, ø 40 mm, height 10.5 mm; sapphire crystal; transparent case back
Band: leather, buckle
Price: appx. $750
Variations: stainless steel bracelet

Marine Original
Reference number: Marine 6498L
Movement: manually wound, ETA Unitas Caliber 6498-2; ø 36.6 mm, height 4.5 mm; 17 jewels; 21,600 vph; côtes de Genève, screw balance, swan-neck fine adjustment, blued screws
Functions: hours, minutes, subsidiary seconds
Case: stainless steel, ø 41 mm, height 11 mm; sapphire crystal; transparent case back; water-resistant to 5 atm
Band: camel leather, buckle
Price: appx. $1,050
Variations: stainless steel bracelet

Airman
Reference number: Flieger40L
Movement: automatic, ETA Caliber 2824; ø 25.6 mm, height 4.6 mm; 25 jewels; 28,800 vph
Functions: hours, minutes, sweep seconds
Case: stainless steel, ø 40 mm, height 10.5 mm; sapphire crystal; transparent case back; water-resistant to 5 atm
Band: camel leather, buckle
Price: appx. $680
Variations: stainless steel bracelet

Seatime
Reference number: SeatimeSK
Movement: automatic, ETA Caliber 2824; ø 25.6 mm, height 4.6 mm; 25 jewels; 28,800 vph
Functions: hours, minutes, sweep seconds; date
Case: stainless steel, ø 42 mm, height 13 mm; unidirectionally rotating bezel with 60-minute divisions; sapphire crystal; screw-in crown; water-resistant to 30 atm
Band: rubber, folding clasp
Price: appx. $800
Variations: leather strap or stainless steel bracelet; various dial and bezel colors

Prodiver
Reference number: ProdiverS
Movement: automatic, ETA Caliber 2824; ø 25.6 mm, height 4.6 mm; 25 jewels; 28,800 vph
Functions: hours, minutes, sweep seconds; date
Case: stainless steel, ø 42 mm, height 15.5 mm; unidirectionally rotating bezel with 60-minute divisions; sapphire crystal; screw-in crown; water-resistant to 100 atm
Band: rubber, folding clasp
Price: appx. $1,350
Variations: orange-colored or rhodium-plated dial

Swiss Watch International

This brand was initiated four years ago by a family with a long heritage in the watchmaking industry. The Ben-Shmuel family has been distributing timepieces of all kinds in the United States for more than thirty years, and this type of experience shines through in the creation of their own brand.

The Ben-Shmuels' main objective with SWI was to create a new brand for the luxury segment, one that is not only luxurious and exclusive in its materials but also in its distribution and the number of pieces made of each style. This is well reflected in SWI's Limited Edition collection, in which there are at most 500 pieces of each model.

SWI's Limited Edition collection is completely classic in design, displaying few experiments, and manufactured in Switzerland using 100 percent Swiss parts. The lines feature a great array of timepieces for every taste and pocket depth, but it is the limited editions in particular that are a great value. The Limited Edition Diamond series comprises classic chronographs in Tricompax arrangement. The movement running this complication is a Dubois Dépraz 2025, which is based on the sturdy and reliable ETA 2824-A2, a high-quality 51-jewel movement. It can be seen working industriously underneath a sapphire crystal case back. In addition to hours, minutes, and the chronograph function, this timepiece also displays the date in a large window at 12 o'clock.

The 18-karat rose gold timepiece offered in the collection, available with either black or cream-colored dials, is limited to 100 pieces worldwide, with the black dial being particularly striking in conjunction with the classically warm rose gold tone of the case. This timepiece's bezel is set with forty-six top Wesselton diamonds for a total carat weight of 1.92. It is also available in yellow and white 18-karat gold.

Swiss Watch International's collection is very chameleon-like with its myriad of high-quality straps from which one may choose when purchasing one of these watches. The color of the strap really influences the appearance of the watch, and SWI takes full advantage of this fact by offering some unique hues. In the regular program, SWI offers ten matte alligator straps, ten shiny alligator straps, and three different ostrich straps in a rainbow of interesting colors. Depending on the strap chosen to complement the desired model, the look of the watch can completely change to perfectly suit its wearer.

Swiss Watch International

A9240
Reference number: A9240M.SS.B2
Movement: automatic, ETA Caliber 2834-2; ø 29 mm, height 5.05 mm; 25 jewels; 28,800 vph; power reserve 38 hours
Functions: hours, minutes, sweep seconds; date, day
Case: stainless steel, ø 42 mm, height 12 mm; sapphire crystal; exhibition screw-down case back; water-resistant to 10 atm
Band: stainless steel, folding clasp
Remarks: limited edition of 500 pieces; textured black mother-of-pearl dial with 10 diamonds; comes with SWI watch winder
Price: $2,995

A9240M
Reference number: A9240M.SS.W1
Movement: automatic, ETA Caliber 2834-2; ø 29 mm, height 5.05 mm; 25 jewels; 28,800 vph; power reserve 38 hours
Functions: hours, minutes, sweep seconds; date, day
Case: stainless steel, ø 42 mm, height 12 mm; sapphire crystal; exhibition screw-down case back; water-resistant to 10 atm
Band: stainless steel, folding clasp
Remarks: limited edition of 500 pieces; textured white mother-of-pearl dial with 10 diamonds; comes with SWI watch winder
Price: $2,995

A9243
Reference number: A9243M.SS.W1
Movement: automatic, ETA Caliber 2824-2; ø 25.6 mm, height 4.6 mm; 25 jewels; 28,800 vph; power reserve 38 hours
Functions: hours, minutes, sweep seconds; date
Case: stainless steel, ø 42 mm, height 12 mm; sapphire crystal; exhibition screw-down case back; screw-in crown; water-resistant to 10 atm
Band: stainless steel, folding clasp
Remarks: limited edition of 500 pieces; textured mother-of-pearl dial with 10 diamonds
Price: $2,795

A9240
Reference number: A92405.B.S.A.
Movement: automatic, ETA Caliber 2834-2; ø 29 mm, height 5.05 mm; 25 jewels; 28,800 vph; power reserve 38 hours
Functions: hours, minutes, sweep seconds; date, day
Case: stainless steel, ø 42 mm, height 12 mm; sapphire crystal; exhibition screw-down case back; screw-in crown; water-resistant to 10 atm
Band: stainless steel, folding clasp
Remarks: limited edition of 500 pieces
Price: $2,795

A9242
Reference number: A9242.SG.S1
Movement: automatic, Dubois-Dépraz Caliber 9000 (base ETA 2824-2); ø 25.6 mm (base movement), height 4.6 mm; 25 jewels; 28,800 vph; power reserve 38 hours
Functions: hours, minutes, sweep seconds; date, day, month, moon phase
Case: stainless steel, ø 42 mm, height 15 mm; 18-karat gold bezel; four hidden buttons for function correction; sapphire crystal; exhibition screw-down case back; water-resistant to 10 atm
Band: stainless steel and 18-karat gold, folding clasp
Remarks: limited edition of 500 pieces
Price: $6,995

A9258
Reference number: A9258.S.BR.S
Movement: automatic, ETA Valjoux Caliber 7750; ø 30 mm, height 7.9 mm; 25 jewels; 28,800 vph; power reserve 42 hours
Functions: hours, minutes, subsidiary seconds; date, day
Case: stainless steel, ø 46 mm, height 15 mm; unidirectionally rotating bezel with 60-minute scale and tachymeter scale; sapphire crystal; exhibition screw-down case back, screw-in crown; water-resistant to 20 atm
Band: stainless steel, folding clasp
Remarks: limited edition of 500 pieces
Price: $4,995

A9259
Reference number: A9259.S.S.S.
Movement: automatic, ETA Valjoux Caliber 7751; ø 30 mm, height 7.9 mm; 25 jewels; 28,800 vph
Functions: hours, minutes, subsidiary seconds; date, day, month, moon phase, chronograph
Case: stainless steel, ø 46 mm, height 15 mm; unidirectionally rotating bezel with 60-minute scale and tachymeter scale; sapphire crystal; exhibition screw-down case back; screw-in crown; water-resistant to 20 atm
Band: stainless steel, folding clasp
Remarks: limited edition of 500 pieces
Price: $5,995

A9240
Reference number: A9249.S.B.S.
Movement: automatic, ETA Caliber 2824-2; ø 25.6 mm, height 4.6 mm; 51 jewels; 28,800 vph; power reserve 38 hours
Functions: hours, minutes, subsidiary seconds; date
Case: stainless steel, ø 42 mm, height 15 mm; sapphire crystal, anti-reflective on front; exhibition screw-down case back; screw-in crown; water-resistant to 10 atm
Band: stainless steel, folding clasp
Remarks: limited edition of 500 pieces
Price: $4,795

TAG Heuer

Throughout its 146-year history, the fourth largest Swiss manufacturer of high-quality sports watches and chronographs has always fulfilled its self-set obligation of making sports' best performances measurable with absolute precision and in the smallest possible units of time: first tenths of a second, then hundredths, and finally thousandths and even ten-thousandths—both electronically and mechanically.

Mastering time has always driven the Heuer family. Thus, it is no accident that Heuer—and later TAG Heuer—created numerous technical milestones such as the first automatic chronograph caliber with micro rotor in 1969 (in cooperation with Hamilton-Büren, Breitling, and Dubois Dépraz), the incredible Calibre 360 with a mechanical chronograph able to measure hundredths of a second, and the fascinating mechanical movement V4 with belt-driven energy transmission.

Despite all its joy in innovation, TAG Heuer always returns to the sporty soul of the brand, which is tied above all to motor sports. The brand has been bound to automobile racing in every way, making for a long and authentic partnership. This began in 1964 when Jack W. Heuer, great-grandson of the company founder, created an homage to what was the most dangerous rally in the world at the time, the Carrera Panamericana Mexico, which launched the Carrera chronograph—a classic. In 1969, Heuer's logo could be found on the racing overalls of Swiss legend Jo Siffert as the first non-automobile sponsor in Formula 1's history.

An alliance with Scuderia Ferrari was added at a time when Heuer was the official timekeeper of all Formula 1 and long-haul races from 1971 to 1979 and also in a partnership with the team's drivers. During this cooperation, Heuer developed many innovations that were to play an important role in motor sports timekeeping for decades to come.

In 1985, TAG Heuer began a partnership with Team McLaren that has lasted until the present day. From 1992 to 2003, TAG Heuer was even official timekeeper for the FIA Formula 1 world championship and took over timekeeping for the super-fast Indy Racing League in 2004, where the cars are measured to the ten-thousandth of a second.

Along with many historical racers and legends of racing like Fangio, Siffert, Rindt, Ickx, Fittipaldi, Regazzoni, Andretti, Lauda, Villeneuve, Scheckter, Prost, Senna, and Schumacher, just to name a few, currently important drivers such as Fernando Alonso, Lewis Hamilton, Kimi Räikkönen, and Mark Webber (Formula 1); Jeff Gordon (NASCAR); Sébastien Bourdais (ChampCars); and Sarah Fisher (IRL) are ambassadors for the brand. Currently, and after a break of thirty-four years—earlier under the aegis of Scuderia Ferrari—TAG Heuer is once again a partner in the legendary 24-hour Le Mans race with two racing teams: Team Peugeot Sport and Team Barazi Epsilon.

TAG Heuer

Formula 1
Reference number: CAH1110.BA0850
Movement: quartz, ETA Caliber F06.111
Functions: hours, minutes, subsidiary seconds; chronograph; date
Case: stainless steel, ø 41 mm, height 13 mm; unidirectionally rotating bezel with 60-minute divisions coated with titanium carbide; sapphire crystal; screw-in crown; water-resistant to 20 atm
Band: stainless steel, folding clasp
Price: $995
Variations: various dial colors (white, red, orange); rubber strap

Aquaracer Calibre 5 Day-Date
Reference number: WAF2010.FT8010
Movement: automatic, TAG Heuer Caliber 5 (base ETA 2824-2); ø 25.6 mm, height 4.6 mm; 25 jewels; 28,800 vph
Functions: hours, minutes, sweep seconds; date, weekday
Case: stainless steel, ø 41 mm, height 12 mm; unidirectionally rotating bezel with 60-minute divisions; sapphire crystal; screw-in crown; water-resistant to 30 atm
Band: rubber, buckle
Price: $2,095
Variations: various dial colors; stainless steel bracelet

Aquaracer Calibre 16
Reference number: CAF2111.BA0809
Movement: automatic, TAG Heuer Caliber 16 (base ETA Valjoux 7750); ø 30 mm, height 7.9 mm; 25 jewels; 28,800 vph
Functions: hours, minutes, subsidiary seconds; date; chronograph
Case: stainless steel, ø 41 mm, height 15 mm; unidirectionally rotating bezel with 60-minute divisions; sapphire crystal; screw-in crown; water-resistant to 30 atm
Band: stainless steel, folding clasp with wetsuit extension
Price: $2,495
Variations: various dial colors (black, blue)

Aquaracer Calibre 16 Day-Date
Reference number: CAF2010.BA0815
Movement: automatic, TAG Heuer Caliber 16 (base ETA Valjoux 7750); ø 30 mm, height 7.9 mm; 25 jewels; 28,800 vph
Functions: hours, minutes, subsidiary seconds; date, day; chronograph
Case: stainless steel, ø 43 mm, height 15 mm; unidirectionally rotating bezel with 60-minute divisions; sapphire crystal; screw-in crown; water-resistant to 30 atm
Band: rubber, buckle
Price: $2,895
Variations: various dial colors (silver, blue); stainless steel bracelet

Aquaracer Calibre S Regatta
Reference number: CAF7110.BA0803
Movement: automatic, TAG Heuer Caliber S; patented electromechanical dial train; 230 individual components
Functions: hours, minutes; chronograph; date (retrograde) with perpetual calendar to 2099; regatta countdown function
Case: stainless steel, ø 41 mm, height 13 mm; unidirectionally rotating bezel with regatta countdown scale; sapphire crystal; water-resistant to 30 atm
Band: stainless steel, folding clasp with wetsuit extension
Price: $2,495
Variations: grey dial; CHINA TEAM limited edition of 2,000 pieces

Aquagraph
Reference number: CN211A.BA0353
Movement: automatic, TAG Heuer Caliber 60 (Dubois Dépraz 2073); ø 25.6 mm, height 7.4 mm; 46 jewels; 28,800 vph
Functions: hours, minutes, subsidiary seconds; chronograph; date
Case: stainless steel, ø 43 mm, height 16 mm; unidirectionally rotating bezel with 60-minute divisions and protection from accidental turning; sapphire crystal; screw-in crown with security indicator; water-resistant to 50 atm
Band: stainless steel, folding clasp with wetsuit extension
Remarks: automatic helium valve
Price: $3,195
Variations: rubber strap

Professional Golf Watch
Reference number: WAE1111.FT6008
Movement: quartz, Ronda Caliber 1005; exceptionally high shock-resistance to 5000 G
Functions: hours, minutes, sweep seconds; date
Case: stainless steel/titanium, 37.5 x 36.7, height 10.5 mm; sapphire crystal; screw-in crown positioned at 9 o'clock; water-resistant to 5 atm
Band: silicon, buckle integrated into case, two snaps
Remarks: developed in conjunction with Tiger Woods, first golf watch to orient itself on the ergonomic needs of a golfer; total weight only 55 grams
Price: $1,495
Variations: in white

Microtimer
Reference number: CS111C.FT6003
Movement: quartz, TAG Heuer Caliber HR 03 (base Valtronic HR03); multifunctional movement developed by TAG Heuer
Functions: hours, minutes, date; chronograph (1/1000 second); alarm; second time zone; perpetual calendar; F1 timekeeper with lap memory (80 laps) and best lap mode
Case: stainless steel, 38 x 42.73 mm, height 12 mm; sapphire crystal; water-resistant to 10 atm
Band: rubber, folding clasp
Price: $1,995

TAG Heuer

Link Calibre 5 Day-Date
Reference number: WJF2011.BA0592
Movement: automatic, TAG Heuer Caliber 5 (base ETA 2824-2); ø 25.6 mm, height 4.6 mm; 25 jewels; 28,800 vph
Functions: hours, minutes, sweep seconds; date, weekday
Case: stainless steel, ø 42 mm, height 13.5 mm; sapphire crystal; screw-in crown, transparent case back; water-resistant to 20 atm
Band: stainless steel, folding clasp
Price: $2,895
Variations: black dial; two-tone

Link Calibre 16
Reference number: CJF2110.BA0594
Movement: automatic, TAG Heuer Caliber 16 (base ETA Valjoux 7750; ø 30 mm, height 7.9 mm; 25 jewels; 28,800 vph
Functions: hours, minutes, subsidiary seconds; date; chronograph
Case: stainless steel, ø 42 mm, height 15.5 mm; bezel with engraved tachymeter scale; sapphire crystal; screw-in crown; water-resistant to 20 atm
Band: stainless steel, folding clasp
Price: $3,095
Variations: various dial variations (silver, blue, grey)

Link Calibre S
Reference number: CJF7110.BA0587
Movement: automatic, TAG Heuer Caliber S; patented electromechanical dial train; 230 individual components
Functions: hours, minutes; chronograph; date (retrograde) with perpetual calendar to 2099
Case: stainless steel, ø 42 mm, height 13.5 mm; bezel with engraved tachymeter scale; sapphire crystal; water-resistant to 20 atm
Band: stainless steel, folding clasp
Price: $2,895
Variations: silver-colored dial

Carrera Calibre 5
Reference number: WV211B.BA0787
Movement: automatic, TAG Heuer Caliber 5 (base ETA 2824-2); ø 25.6 mm, height 4.6 mm; 25 jewels; 28,800 vph
Functions: hours, minutes, sweep seconds; date
Case: stainless steel, ø 39 mm, height 12 mm; sapphire crystal; transparent case back; water-resistant to 5 atm
Band: stainless steel, folding clasp
Price: $1,795
Variations: silver-colored dial; leather strap

Carrera Calibre 5
Reference number: WV2110.BA0790
Movement: automatic, TAG Heuer Caliber 5 (base ETA 2824-2); ø 25.6 mm, height 4.6 mm; 25 jewels; 28,800 vph
Functions: hours, minutes, sweep seconds; date
Case: stainless steel, ø 36 mm, height 12 mm; sapphire crystal; transparent case back; water-resistant to 5 atm
Band: stainless steel, folding clasp
Price: $1,795
Variations: black dial; two-tone

Carrera Calibre 16 Tachymeter Racing
Reference number: CV2014.FT6007
Movement: automatic, TAG Heuer Caliber 16 (base ETA Valjoux 7750); ø 30 mm, height 7.9 mm; 25 jewels; 28,800 vph
Functions: hours, minutes, subsidiary seconds; chronograph; date
Case: stainless steel, ø 41 mm, height 16 mm; bezel with tachymeter scale; sapphire crystal; transparent case back; water-resistant to 5 atm
Band: rubber, folding clasp
Price: $2,895
Variations: stainless steel bracelet

Carrera Calibre 16 Tachymeter
Reference number: CV2010.BA0786
Movement: automatic, TAG Heuer Caliber 16 (base ETA Valjoux 7750); ø 30 mm, height 7.9 mm; 25 jewels; 28,800 vph
Functions: hours, minutes, subsidiary seconds; chronograph; date
Case: stainless steel, ø 41 mm, height 16 mm; bezel with tachymeter scale; sapphire crystal; transparent case back; water-resistant to 5 atm
Band: stainless steel, folding clasp
Price: $2,995
Variations: calfskin strap with holes; silver-colored dial

Carrera Chronograph Calibre 360 LE
Reference number: CV5041.FC8164
Movement: automatic, TAG Heuer Caliber 360; high-frequency chronograph movement (360,000 vph) precise to 1/100th second, 100 minutes power reserve; sandwiched with Caliber 7 (ETA 2892-2)
Functions: hours, minutes, subsidiary seconds, chronograph; date
Case: rose gold, ø 41 mm, height 15.8 mm; sapphire crystal; transparent case back; water-resistant to 5 atm
Band: reptile skin, buckle
Remarks: limited edition of 500 pieces
Price: $18,000
Variations: limited to 100 pieces in white gold; limited to 360 pieces in stainless steel

TAG Heuer

Monaco Calibre 6 Lady Diamonds
Reference number: WW2114.FC6215
Movement: automatic, TAG Heuer Caliber 6 (base ETA 2895-1); ø 25.6 mm, height 4.35 mm; 30 jewels; 28,800 vph
Functions: hours, minutes, subsidiary seconds; date
Case: stainless steel, 37 x 37 mm, height 13.5 mm; case set with 26 diamonds; sapphire crystal; transparent case back; water-resistant to 5 atm
Band: reptile skin, folding clasp
Remarks: dial set with 13 diamonds
Price: $4,995
Variations: black or brown python skin strap with matching dial

Monaco Calibre 17 Steve McQueen Edition
Reference number: CW2113.BA0780
Movement: automatic, TAG Heuer Caliber 17 (base ETA 2894-2); ø 28.6 mm, height 6.1 mm; 37 jewels; 28,800 vph
Functions: hours, minutes, subsidiary seconds; chronograph; date
Case: stainless steel, 40 x 40 mm, height 13.5 mm; Plexiglas
Band: stainless steel, folding clasp
Remarks: limited edition of 4,000 pieces
Price: $3,295
Variations: blue reptile skin strap

New Monaco Vintage Limited Edition
Reference number: CW211A.FC6228
Movement: automatic, TAG Heuer Caliber 17 (base ETA 2894-2); ø 28.6 mm, height 6.1 mm; 37 jewels; 28,800 vph
Functions: hours, minutes, subsidiary seconds; chronograph; date
Case: stainless steel, 40 x 40 mm, height 13.5 mm; Plexiglas
Band: reptile skin, folding clasp
Remarks: limited edition of 4,000 pieces; dial displays colors and logo of Porsche 917K that Steve McQueen drove in the film *24 Hours of Le Mans* (1970)
Price: $3,295

Monaco Sixty Nine
Reference number: CW9110.FC6177
Movement: manually wound, TAG Heuer Caliber 2 (base ETA Peseux 7001); additional chronograph Caliber HR 03 (quartz)
Functions: hours, minutes, subsidiary seconds (front); chronograph (1/1000 second); alarm; second time zone; perpetual calendar; F1 timekeeping with lap memory (80 laps) and best lap mode (back)
Case: stainless steel, 40 x 41 mm, height 18 mm; 180° rotating case; sapphire crystal; water-resistant to 5 atm
Band: reptile skin, folding clasp
Price: $6,900

Monza Calibre 36
Reference number: CR5111.FC6175
Movement: automatic, TAG Heuer Caliber 36 (base Zenith El Primero 400); ø 30 mm, height 6.5 mm; 31 jewels; 36,000 vph; officially certified chronometer (COSC)
Functions: hours, minutes, subsidiary seconds; chronograph; date
Case: stainless steel, ø 39.5 mm, height 14 mm; sapphire crystal; transparent case back; water-resistant to 5 atm
Band: reptile skin, folding clasp
Price: $4,495
Variations: black dial; brown crocodile skin strap

New TAG Heuer SLR for Mercedes-Benz Limited Edition
Reference number: CAG2111.FC6009
Movement: automatic, TAG Heuer Caliber 17 (base ETA 2894-2); ø 28.6 mm, height 6.1 mm; 37 jewels; 28,800 vph
Functions: hours, minutes, subsidiary seconds; chronograph; date
Case: stainless steel, ø 45 mm, height 13 mm; unidirectionally rotating bezel with 60-minute divisions under crystal, settable via crown; screw-in crown; sapphire crystal; water-resistant to 10 atm
Band: rubber, folding clasp
Remarks: limited edition of 3,500 pieces
Price: $3,995
Variations: stainless steel bracelet

Grand Carrera Calibre 8 RS Grande Date GMT
Reference number: WAV5113.FC6231
Movement: automatic, TAG Heuer Caliber 8 (base ETA 2824 with module); GMT rotating system disk display; officially certified C.O.S.C. chronometer
Functions: hours, minutes, sweep seconds; large date; 24-hour display (second time zone)
Case: stainless steel, ø 42.5 mm, height 13 mm; screw-in crown; sapphire crystal; case back with two exhibition windows; water-resistant to 10 atm
Band: reptile skin, folding clasp
Remarks: limited edition of 3,500 pieces
Price: $3,695
Variations: stainless steel bracelet

Grand Carrera Calibre 17 RS
Reference number: CAV511A.BA0902
Movement: automatic, TAG Heuer Caliber 17 (base ETA 2894-2); ø 28.6 mm, height 6.1 mm; 37 jewels; 28,800 vph; GMT rotating system disk display; officially certified C.O.S.C. chronometer
Functions: hours, minutes, subsidiary seconds; chronograph; date
Case: stainless steel, ø 43 mm, height 14.5 mm; bezel with engraved tachymeter scale; screw-in crown and buttons; case back with two exhibition windows; sapphire crystal; water-resistant to 10 atm
Band: stainless steel, folding clasp
Price: $4,695
Variations: black or brown alligator skin strap

Temption

Temption is a design-oriented company focused on the manufacture of functional watches. Founder and owner Klaus Ulbrich has long occupied himself with the question of why some things created by humans easily last for decades, even centuries, and remain contemporary, while other creations hardly make it a season. Ancient cave drawings, for example, represent animals with a stylistic elegance and grace that are still fascinating today. They radiate an incomparable dignity, not influenced by trends and short-term showmanship. Some buildings also survive the times, while others are rightly torn down after a short while. Surely there must be a law to it, one which Temption could harness and transfer to its watch designs. From the Moderns come components such as a general simplicity in appearance, from wabi sabi the attention to materials and easy warmth, and from both philosophical schools the reduction to only that which is necessary. Less really is often more.

Thus watches are created that are absolute, refusing anything superfluous or anything that has even a whiff of nostalgia. These are watches that are so alive in their functionality that they contain the base platform for timelessness. This does not mean, however, that there is no room for beauty here—or even luxury. In the fourteenth century, the founder of wabi sabi still decorated his basic daily necessities with peripheral ornaments in order to relieve some of their strictness and to give them a little warmth despite their simplicity.

The focal point of Temption's design character is a paradigm that Ulbrich likes to call the "information pyramid." At the top of this pyramid are located the central hour and minute indicators; other functions follow below these in order to give these main functions visual priority. For this reason, the most contrast within the dial visuals can be found between the dial and hands. The date window is the same color as the dial and not framed (so the dial remains calm); the totalizers and stop functions are not encircled, and the stop hands are not outfitted with arbors for the same reason. At the low end of this information pyramid is situated the brand's logo, most unimportant to reading the time, and for this reason it is printed in shiny black on a matte black background, where it may only be seen—and then quite clearly—when light shines on it from the side.

The new models of the Classic and CGK204 families are called Curare. South American Indians increase the effect of their blowpipe arrows with a poison that is made from tiny rainforest frogs of this

name. Along with the color, Temption derives this name from the brand's attempt to also use "natural" methods to achieve even better legibility and ergonomics for its watches.

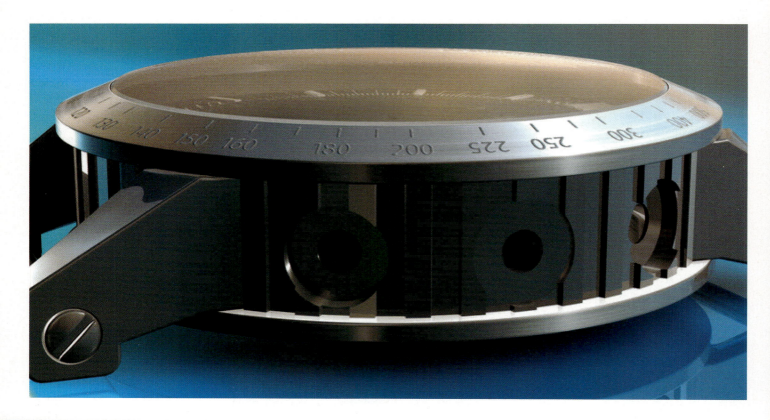

Temption

Chronograph Classic Curare
Movement: automatic, ETA Valjoux Caliber 7750; ø 30 mm, height 7.8 mm; 25 jewels; 28,800 vph; decorated
Functions: hours, minutes, subsidiary seconds; chronograph; date, weekday
Case: stainless steel, ø 43 mm, height 14.8 mm; bezel engraved with tachymeter scale; sapphire crystal; transparent case back; screw-in crown and buttons; amber cabochons
Band: leather, folding clasp
Price: $3,450

Chronograph CGK204 Curare
Movement: automatic, Temption Caliber T18.1 (base ETA Valjoux 7750); ø 30 mm, height 7.8 mm; 25 jewels; 28,800 vph; decorated
Functions: hours, minutes, subsidiary seconds; chronograph; date, weekday, month, moon phase
Case: stainless steel, ø 43 mm, height 14.8 mm; bezel engraved with tachymeter scale; sapphire crystal; transparent case back; screw-in crown and buttons; amber cabochons
Band: leather, folding clasp
Price: $4,200

CM03 GMT
Movement: automatic, Temption Caliber T16.1 (base ETA 2893-2); ø 25.6 mm, height 4.1 mm; 21 jewels; 28,800 vph; rhodium-plated, perlage, blued screws
Functions: hours, minutes, sweep seconds; date; 24-hour hand (second time zone)
Case: stainless steel, ø 42 mm, height 10.7 mm; unidirectionally rotating bezel with 60-minute divisions; sapphire crystal; transparent case back; screw-in crown; water-resistant to 10 atm
Band: stainless steel, double folding clasp
Price: $2,100
Variations: black dial

Chronograph CGK204 Coral
Movement: automatic, Temption Caliber T18.1 (base ETA Valjoux 7751); ø 30 mm, height 7.8 mm; 25 jewels; 28,800 vph; decorated
Functions: hours, minutes, subsidiary seconds; chronograph; date, weekday, month, moon phase
Case: stainless steel, ø 43 mm, height 14.8 mm; bezel engraved with tachymeter scale; sapphire crystal; transparent case back; screw-in crown and buttons; coral cabochons
Band: leather, folding clasp
Price: $3,750

Chronograph CGK204 Black
Movement: automatic, Temption Caliber T18.1 (base ETA Valjoux 7751); ø 30 mm, height 7.8 mm; 25 jewels; 28,800 vph; decorated
Functions: hours, minutes, subsidiary seconds; chronograph; date, weekday, month, moon phase
Case: stainless steel, ø 43 mm, height 14.8 mm; bezel engraved with tachymeter scale; sapphire crystal; transparent case back; screw-in crown and buttons; onyx cabochons
Band: leather, folding clasp
Price: $3,750

Chronograph Classic
Movement: automatic, Temption Caliber T17.1 (base ETA Valjoux 7750); ø 30 mm, height 7.8 mm; 25 jewels; 28,800 vph; rhodium-plated, perlage, blued screws
Functions: hours, minutes, subsidiary seconds; chronograph; date, weekday
Case: stainless steel, ø 43 mm, height 14.8 mm; bezel engraved with tachymeter scale; sapphire crystal; transparent case back; screw-in crown and buttons; water-resistant to 10 atm
Band: leather, folding clasp
Price: $3,200

Chronograph Cora
Movement: automatic, Temption Caliber T22.1 (base ETA 2094); ø 23.9 mm, height 5.5 mm; 33 jewels; 28,800 vph; decorated
Functions: hours, minutes; chronograph; date
Case: stainless steel, ø 29.2 mm, height 10.8 mm; sapphire crystal; transparent case back; screw-in crown and buttons
Band: leather, folding clasp
Price: $4,200
Variations: rose gold; various dial variations

GMT Curie
Movement: automatic, Temption Caliber T16.1 (base ETA 2893-2); ø 25.4 mm, height 5.2 mm; 21 jewels; 28,800 vph; decorated
Functions: hours, minutes, sweep seconds; date; second time zone
Case: stainless steel, ø 35 mm, height 9.8 mm; sapphire crystal; transparent case back; screw-in crown
Band: stainless steel, double folding clasp
Price: $1,950
Variations: leather strap ($1,850)

Tissot

Tissot was founded in 1853 by Charles-Félicien Tissot and his son Charles-Emile in the Jura region of Switzerland. With their sense of innovation and great passion for high-quality products, these two men laid the cornerstone for a strong company culture that continues to be tangible today in the Le Locle headquarters.

During the course of its history, Tissot has introduced a great number of products that were enthusiastically received by the industry. Whether it was the movements' technology, the use of new materials, or the actual functions of the watch, this company's engineers and watchmakers have always presented true novelties—including the first antimagnetic watch (1930), the Astrolon with a movement made of plastic (1971), the Rock Watch whose case was created from natural stone (1985), the Wood Watch with a case made of wood (1987), and in more recent history the T-Touch, outfitted with a crystal featuring tactile functions (2000).

Tissot has belonged to the Swatch Group since 1983, and thanks to a network of select retailers, it is available in more than 150 countries. Its know-how and decisiveness have helped the brand become a dynamic presence among the grand names of the watch industry.

Sports have been an important and irrefutable point of communication for the brand for many, many years, conveying emotion and excitement and reaching a multitiered audience. Every sport that Tissot sponsors has its own fans enthusiastic about the special discipline, following its ups and downs. Thus, the brand has been a staple of certain sports since the Swiss Skiing World Cup of 1938. It was the official timekeeper of tennis's Davis Cup in 1957, and motorcycle racing would literally no longer be the same without it: the reigning world champion of MotoGP, Nicky Hayden, is one of the brand's most popular ambassadors.

In 1973, Tissot sponsored a Renault Alpine in the Rallye Monte Carlo, and in 1974 its logo blazed from a Porsche in the legendary 24-hour Le Mans race. In 1976, Tissot joined the Formula 1 circus as a sponsor of the British Ensign team, becoming a full partner for the successful team in 1979.

In the new millennium, Tissot is both official timekeeper and a true international partner to four basic sports: cycling, motorcycling, ice hockey, and fencing. At a regional level, the brand supports events in the 150 countries where it is available. Additionally, Tissot was an official partner of the Olympic Games in Athens in 2004, dedicating a whole collection to this event. In 2002, Tissot was represented at the Asian Games, and repeated this association in 2006.

PRC 100 Automatic Chronograph
Reference number: T008.414.11.201.00
Movement: automatic, ETA Valjoux Caliber 7750; ø 30 mm, height 7.9 mm; 25 jewels; 28,800 vph
Functions: hours, minutes, subsidiary seconds; chronograph; date, weekday
Case: stainless steel, ø 39.8 mm, height 14.3 mm; sapphire crystal; transparent case back; screw-in crown; water-resistant to 10 atm
Band: stainless steel, folding security clasp
Price: $1,295
Variations: silver-plated dial; leather strap

PRS 516 Automatic Chronograph
Reference number: T021.414.26.051.00
Movement: automatic, ETA Valjoux Caliber 7750; ø 30 mm, height 7.9 mm; 25 jewels; 28,800 vph
Functions: hours, minutes, subsidiary seconds; chronograph; date, weekday
Case: stainless steel, ø 42 mm, height 14.7 mm; black PVD-coated bezel with tachymeter scale; sapphire crystal; transparent case back; screw-in crown; water-resistant to 10 atm
Band: leather, folding clasp
Price: $995
Variations: silver-plated dial; stainless steel bracelet

Le Locle Automatic Power Reserve
Reference number: T006.424.16.053.00
Movement: automatic, ETA Caliber 2897; ø 25.6 mm, height 4.85 mm; 21 jewels; 28,800 vph
Functions: hours, minutes, sweep seconds; date; power reserve display
Case: stainless steel, ø 39.3 mm, height 10.2 mm; sapphire crystal; transparent case back
Band: leather, folding clasp
Price: $995
Variations: diverse dial variations; stainless steel bracelet

T-Touch
Reference number: T33.7.888.92
Movement: quartz, ETA Caliber E40.305; ø 35 mm, height 9.8 mm; multifunctional electronic module with LCD display integrated into the dial
Functions: hours, minutes; chronograph, altimeter, thermometer, barometer, alarm and compass in the LCD display, activated by touch-sensitive sensors in the crystal
Case: titanium, ø 42 mm, height 12 mm; bezel engraved with 360° divisions and compass directions; sapphire crystal with sensors
Band: titanium, folding clasp
Price: $795
Variations: rubber strap; diverse dial variations

Bar and Beverage Books from Abbeville Press

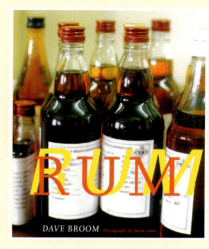

Rum

This handsome volume, the first full-color guide to the history and appreciation of one of the world's favorite spirits, includes an island-by-island survey of the greatest pure rums.

Winner of the Drink Book prize at the 2004 Glenfiddich Food and Drink Awards

Text by Dave Broom
Photography by Jason Lowe
80 full-color illustrations
176 pages · 9½ x 11 in. · Cloth
ISBN: 978-0-7892-0802-6 · $35.00

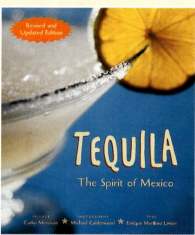

Tequila: The Spirit of Mexico
Revised and Updated Edition

A comprehensive guide to the culture and connoisseurship of tequila, this vibrantly illustrated volume features ratings of more than 100 brands.

"... captures the romance and spirit of Mexico." —*Playboy*

By Enrique F. Martínez Limón
155 full-color illustrations
184 pages · 9½ x 11¼ in. · Cloth
ISBN: 978-0-7892-0837-8 · $39.95

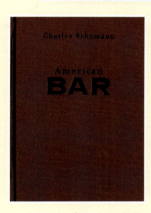

American Bar: The Artistry of Mixing Drinks

This "bar bible" provides recipes for mixing more than 500 drinks, classic and exotic, as well as tips for serving them correctly.

Over 200,000 copies sold!

"The drink mixer's bible." —*The New York Times*

By Charles Schumann
Over 100 two-color illustrations
392 pages · 5 x 6¾ in. · Hardcover
ISBN: 978-1-55859-853-9 · $24.95

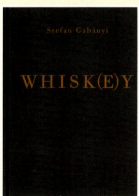

Whisk(e)y

Featuring more than 1,000 impressively detailed, alphabetized entries and hundreds of illustrations, this is the ultimate handbook for whisk(e)y lovers.

A selection of the Book-of-the-Month Club

Text by Stefan Gabányi
Illustrations by Günter Mattei
560 two-color illustrations
368 pages · 5 x 6¾ in. · Hardcover
ISBN: 978-0-7892-0383-0 · $24.95

Published by ABBEVILLE PRESS
137 Varick Street, New York, NY 10013
1-800-Artbook (in U.S. only)
Also available wherever fine books are sold
Visit us at www.abbeville.com

Tutima

Pilot's watches have been Tutima's specialty since the early 1940s. It was then that this brand, which was based at the time in Germany's legendary watchmaking city Glashütte, created timepieces for the German air force that became a sought-after collector's classic. Dieter Delecate, Tutima's owner since 1960, recreated this classic pilot's chronograph at the beginning of the 1990s. "Thanks to the collector's boom of the 1980s, prices for the original pilot's chronograph, which some pilots still had after the end of the war, soared upward like a rocket. They are meanwhile bought and sold for no less than between $5,000 and $10,000 for well-preserved pieces—and these prices are paid, no questions asked."

The reissue, simply called 1941, is still one of the brand's bestsellers even after more than fifteen years. In honor of the company's eightieth anniversary, Tutima decided to introduce a variation on the theme in a larger case and a more contemporary dial, but one that still retains the fluted case with its telltale red reference marker.

The Grand Classic Havanna UTC Limited Edition, restricted to 800 pieces in honor of the brand's anniversary, and its unlimited sibling are housed in a contemporary 43 mm case. The Grand Classic's black dial and white chronograph subdials lend the theme a refreshingly updated quality.

Obviously spreading its wings since the great success the brand has enjoyed in the era of the mechanical renaissance, Tutima is now branching out: focusing on aviation to this point, the Ganderkesee-based company has recently begun committing a great deal of energy to sailing and yachting.

Not only is Tutima the official timekeeper of sailing's biggest event—the Kiel Week—but the brand has now embarked upon a very special regatta that sees boats sailing 3,600 sea miles across the Atlantic from Newport, Rhode Island, to Hamburg, Germany: the HSH Nordbank Blue Race 2007.

This adventurous race kicked off in Newport on June 16, 2007. With the Tutima Academy's aerobatic plane zooming around upside down overhead, the Tutima Yacht and its crew prepared to undertake the journey, expected to last fourteen to eighteen days. In honor of these active sailors, Tutima has also introduced a yachting chronograph featuring a regatta countdown function crafted in pure titanium.

And this is not all that is going on at Tutima. The year 2007 has obviously been an exciting one for the family-owned brand, especially since it has decided to honor its roots in a special way. At the end of World War II, Dr. Ernst Kurtz—the manager in charge of the companies manufacturing the Tutima brand—fled Glashütte and settled in what soon became West Germany.

With the fall of the Berlin Wall, Glashütte has once again become Germany's premier venue for luxury watchmaking. And what better place for Tutima to also be located? Currently building a new factory in the fabled town, Tutima plans to open a subsidiary there in late 2007 and will thus continue to manufacture part of its products in the factory in Ganderkesee that the brand has occupied for more than forty years. Given the brand's growth and roots, the second factory in Glashütte will be an interesting addition.

Tutima

Chronograph F2 UTC Eurofighter Typhoon
Reference number: 780-59
Movement: automatic, ETA Valjoux Caliber 7754, modified; ø 30.4 mm, height 7.9 mm; 25 jewels; 28,800 vph
Functions: hours, minutes, subsidiary seconds; chronograph; date; 24-hour display (second time zone)
Case: stainless steel, ø 38.7 mm, height 15.8 mm; bidirectionally rotating bezel with reference marker; sapphire crystal; sapphire crystal case back with Eurofighter outline; screw-in crown; water-resistant to 100 m
Band: reptile skin, folding clasp
Price: $4,100
Variations: stainless steel bracelet

Chronograph F2 PR
Reference number: 780-83
Movement: automatic, ETA Valjoux Caliber 7750, modified; ø 30.4 mm, height 7.9 mm; 25 jewels; 28,800 vph
Functions: hours, minutes, subsidiary seconds; chronograph; date; power reserve display
Case: stainless steel, ø 38.7 mm, height 15.8 mm; bidirectionally rotating bezel with reference marker; sapphire crystal; sapphire crystal case back; screw-in crown; water-resistant to 100 m
Band: reptile skin, folding clasp
Price: $4,300
Variations: stainless steel bracelet; white dial

Yachting Chronograph
Reference number: 751-01
Movement: automatic, Lémania Caliber 5100; ø 31 mm, height 8.2 mm; 17 jewels; 28,800 vph; sweep minute counter
Functions: hours, minutes, subsidiary seconds; chronograph; date
Case: titanium, ø 43 mm, height 14.6 mm; bidirectionally rotating bezel with compass markings; sapphire crystal; screw-in crown; water-resistant to 20 atm
Band: reptile skin, folding clasp
Price: $4,350
Variations: titanium bracelet

DI 300
Reference number: 629-16
Movement: automatic, ETA Caliber 2836-2; ø 25.6 mm, height 5.05 mm; 25 jewels; 28,800 vph
Functions: hours, minutes, sweep seconds; date and day
Case: titanium, ø 43.8 mm, height 12.5 mm; unidirectionally rotating bezel with 60-minute divisions; sapphire crystal; screw-in crown; water-resistant to 30 atm
Band: titanium, folding clasp with wetsuit extension
Price: $1,750
Variations: rubber strap

Grand Classic Havanna UTC Limited Edition
Reference number: 781-01
Movement: automatic, ETA Valjoux Caliber 7754; ø 30.4 mm, height 7.9 mm; 25 jewels; 28,800 vph
Functions: hours, minutes, subsidiary seconds; chronograph; date; 24-hour display (second time zone)
Case: stainless steel, ø 43.1 mm, height 15.9 mm; bidirectionally rotating bezel with reference marker; sapphire crystal; sapphire crystal case back; screw-in crown; water-resistant to 10 atm
Band: leather, buckle
Remarks: limited to 800 pieces; case back decorated with large T and year 1927
Price: $4,200
Variations: stainless steel bracelet

Grand Classic UTC
Reference number: 781-04
Movement: automatic, ETA Valjoux Caliber 7754; ø 30.4 mm, height 7.9 mm; 25 jewels; 28,800 vph
Functions: hours, minutes, subsidiary seconds; chronograph; date; 24-hour display (second time zone)
Case: stainless steel, ø 43.1 mm, height 15.9 mm; bidirectionally rotating bezel with reference marker; sapphire crystal; sapphire crystal case back; screw-in crown; water-resistant to 10 atm
Band: stainless steel, folding clasp
Remarks: case back decorated with large T and year 1927
Price: $4,400
Variations: leather strap

Grand Classic
Reference number: 781-05
Movement: automatic, ETA Valjoux Caliber 7750; ø 30.4 mm, height 7.9 mm; 25 jewels; 28,800 vph
Functions: hours, minutes; chronograph
Case: stainless steel, ø 43.1 mm, height 15.9 mm; bidirectionally rotating bezel with reference marker; sapphire crystal; sapphire crystal case back; screw-in crown; water-resistant to 10 atm
Band: leather, buckle
Remarks: case back decorated with large T and year 1927
Price: $2,990
Variations: stainless steel bracelet

Flieger Chronograph F2 G
Reference number: 754-02
Movement: automatic, ETA Valjoux Caliber 7750; ø 30 mm, height 7.9 mm; 25 jewels; 28,800 vph
Functions: hours, minutes, subsidiary seconds; chronograph; date
Case: yellow gold, ø 38.2 mm, height 15.7 mm; bidirectionally rotating bezel with reference marker; sapphire crystal; sapphire crystal case back; screw-in crown; water-resistant to 10 atm
Band: yellow gold, folding clasp
Price: $26,650
Variations: reptile skin strap

Tutima

Flieger Chronograph Classic
Reference number: 783-02
Movement: manually wound, ETA Valjoux Caliber 7760, modified; ø 30.4 mm, height 7 mm; 21 jewels; 28,800 vph
Functions: hours, minutes, subsidiary seconds; chronograph
Case: stainless steel, ø 38.7 mm, height 14.8 mm; bidirectionally rotating bezel with reference marker; sapphire crystal; water-resistant to 10 atm
Band: stainless steel, folding clasp
Price: $3,550
Variations: leather strap

Valeo Reserve
Reference number: 640-02
Movement: automatic, ETA Caliber 2892-A2 modified; ø 25.6 mm, height 5.1 mm; 28 jewels; 28,800 vph
Functions: hours, minutes, sweep seconds; large date; power reserve display
Case: red gold, ø 38.5 mm, height 14.1 mm; sapphire crystal; sapphire crystal case back; water-resistant to 100 m
Band: reptile skin, red gold folding clasp
Price: $11,900
Variations: silver or anthracite-colored dial

FX Chronograph UTC
Reference number: 740-84
Movement: automatic, ETA Valjoux Caliber 7754, modified; ø 30.4 mm, height 7.9 mm; 25 jewels; 28,800 vph
Functions: hours, minutes, subsidiary seconds; chronograph; date; 24-hour display (second time zone)
Case: stainless steel, ø 38.5 mm, height 16.4 mm; bidirectionally rotating bezel with 24-hour divisions; sapphire crystal; sapphire crystal case back; screw-in crown; water-resistant to 10 atm
Band: stainless steel, folding clasp
Price: $4,090
Variations: stainless steel bracelet

FX Chronograph
Reference number: 788-31
Movement: automatic, ETA Valjoux Caliber 7750; ø 30.4 mm, height 7.9 mm; 25 jewels; 28,800 vph
Functions: hours, minutes, subsidiary seconds; chronograph; date
Case: stainless steel, ø 38.5 mm, height 15.5 mm; sapphire crystal; transparent case back; screw-in crown; water-resistant to 100 m
Band: leather, buckle
Price: $2,450
Variations: stainless steel bracelet; rotating bezel with 60-minute divisions

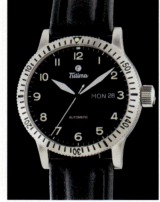

Automatic FX
Reference number: 631-31
Movement: automatic, ETA Caliber 2836-2; ø 25.6 mm, height 5.05 mm; 25 jewels; 28,800 vph
Functions: hours, minutes, sweep seconds; date and day
Case: stainless steel, ø 38.5 mm, height 12.4 mm; bidirectionally rotating bezel with 60-minute divisions; sapphire crystal; sapphire crystal case back; screw-in crown; water-resistant to 10 atm
Band: leather, buckle
Price: $1,300
Variations: stainless steel bracelet

Military Flieger Chronograph TL
Reference number: 750-02
Movement: automatic, Nouvelle Lémania Caliber 5100; ø 31 mm, height 8.20 mm; 17 jewels; 28,800 vph
Functions: hours, minutes, subsidiary seconds; chronograph; date and day; 24-hour display
Case: titanium, ø 43 mm, height 14.6 mm; bidirectionally rotating bezel with 60-minute divisions; sapphire crystal; screw-in crown; water-resistant to 20 atm
Band: titanium, folding clasp with wetsuit extension
Price: $4,250
Variations: leather strap

Military Flieger Chronograph TLG
Reference number: 738-02
Movement: automatic, Nouvelle Lémania Caliber 5100; ø 31 mm, height 8.20 mm; 17 jewels; 28,800 vph
Functions: hours, minutes, subsidiary seconds; chronograph; date and day; 24-hour display
Case: titanium, ø 43 mm, height 14.6 mm; bidirectionally rotating yellow gold bezel with 60-minute divisions; sapphire crystal; screw-in crown; water-resistant to 20 atm
Band: titanium/gold, folding clasp with wetsuit extension
Price: $11,500
Variations: leather strap

Commando II
Reference number: 760-42
Movement: automatic, Nouvelle Lémania Caliber 5100; ø 31 mm, height 8.20 mm; 17 jewels; 28,800 vph
Functions: hours, minutes; chronograph; date
Case: titanium, ø 43.2 mm, height 14.5 mm; sapphire crystal; screw-in crown; water-resistant to 20 atm
Band: titanium, folding clasp with wetsuit extension
Price: $3,950
Variations: with tachymeter scale; leather strap

Exceptional Destinations books from Abbeville Press:
A perfect combination of beautiful photography and useful travel information

Bicycling
Along the World's Most Exceptional Routes
An outstanding guide to twenty-five scenic bicycling vacations around the world for riders of all abilities.

"Bicycling is an international inspiration for dedicated cyclists and ideal for armchair travelers..."
—*Midwest Book Review*

By Rob Penn
100 full-color illustrations
160 pages · 8¼ x 9½ in. · Cloth
ISBN: 978-0-7892-0846-0
$29.95

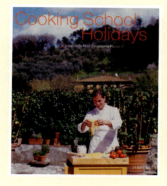

Cooking School Holidays
In the World's Most Exceptional Places
An appetizing guide to learning vacations for food lovers at the world's most prestigious and scenically situated cooking schools.

"Just the cover of *Cooking School Holidays* makes you want to run to the computer and book a flight to one of the cooking schools featured in this beautifully illustrated guide."
—*Trump World Magazine*

By Jenni Muir
150 full-color illustrations
160 pages · 8¼ x 9½ in. · Cloth
ISBN: 978-0-7892-0836-1
$29.95

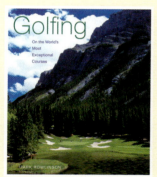

Golfing
On the World's Most Exceptional Courses
A magnificent guide to twenty-five of the world's top golfing vacations, selected for their breathtaking locations, venerable traditions, notable course design, and first-rate accommodations.

"This is a keeper."—*USA Today*

By Mark Rowlinson
100 full-color illustrations
160 pages · 8¼ x 9½ in. · Cloth
ISBN: 978-0-7892-0866-8
$29.95

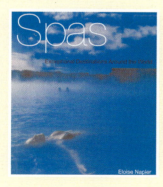

Spas
Exceptional Destinations
Around the World
A dream book of places to be pampered and unwind that unveils the world's twenty-five best vacation spas.

"From its cool blue cover to the inside photos of sand-dune joggers and massage recipients, this is a volume that fuels daydreams."
—Christopher Reynolds, *Los Angeles Times*

By Eloise Napier
240 full-color illustrations
160 pages · 8¼ x 9½ in. · Cloth
ISBN: 978-0-7892-0798-2
$29.95

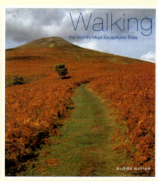

Walking
The World's Most Exceptional Trails
The ultimate guide to the world's top walking vacations, selected for their unusual locations, spectacular scenery, and awesome wildlife.

Selected as one of independent booksellers' top gift recommendations in *USA Today*!

By Eloise Napier
240 full-color illustrations
160 pages · 8¼ x 9½ in. · Cloth
ISBN: 978-0-7892-0801-9
$29.95

Published by ABBEVILLE PRESS
137 Varick Street, New York, NY 10013
1-800-Artbook (in U.S. only)
Also available wherever fine books are sold
Visit us at www.abbeville.com

Vacheron Constantin

When Jean-Marc Vacheron founded his manufacture in 1755, things were much different. A master watchmaker had to find a location for his workshop that could house both family and apprentices. Genevan watchmakers tended to settle in what is now the old city center, with their workshops on the top floor to take advantage of every minute of sunlight.

Back then, customers visited the workshops directly to order watches and check on their progress, which took a certain amount of time. Eventually, client reception areas were created on ground floors to avoid watchmakers having to drag their clientele through the whole house.

Vacheron Constantin's Geneva boutique is now really much more than just a shop—when it was renovated in 2004, it was set up as a modern take on this tradition. The 1875 purpose-built premises just a stone's throw from the Tour-de-L'Ile—a thirteenth-century landmark—continues to be the home of Vacheron Constantin's face to the public (the factory section moved out to Plan-les-Ouates in 2004). The ground floor does indeed house the "boutique," where customers can peruse the current collection and have consultations. The second floor contains the Vacheron Constantin Heritage Center, an intensely interesting venue where the visitor can view exhibitions, look at tools and watches dating from 1755 to the present day, and observe master craftsmen at work restoring vintage timepieces and constructing new bespoke ones now made possible by the company's Atelier Cabinotiers Special Order program, which also follows the *manufacture's* long traditions.

The history of the *manufacture's* serial offerings is perhaps best exemplified today by its Patrimony collection, which was created as a new interpretation of tradition in a contemporary spirit, though corresponding to contemporary values and tastes. The line's simple, elegant, round cases and timelessly classic style are divided into two lines: Patrimony Traditionelle and Patrimony Contemporaine, which contains timepieces of larger diameters as in tune with the more current trend.

One may not forget the great and grand complications that this brand has also been known for throughout its long career, which are perfectly exemplified by Patrimony Traditionelle Caliber 2755, originally launched for the company's 250th anniversary celebration. The evolution of this fabulously complicated caliber is outfitted with three of the highest complications known to *haute horlogerie*: the minute repeater, the tourbillon, and the perpetual calendar. Caliber 2755 comprises 602 individual components as well as some new technology. The company's master watchmakers have built a unique centripetal speed regulator into the strike movement of the repeater, which ensures that the repeater chimes the time in an otherwise completely noiseless manner: all you hear are the chimes, no reverberations and no vibrations.

Vacheron Constantin

Patrimony Traditionelle Automatic
Reference number: X87G9194
Movement: automatic, Vacheron Constantin Caliber 2455 VC; ø 25.6 mm, height 3.6 mm; 27 jewels; 28,800 vph; Seal of Geneva
Functions: hours, minutes, subsidiary seconds
Case: white gold, ø 38 mm, height 7.97 mm; sapphire crystal; transparent case back
Band: reptile skin, buckle
Price: $19,600
Variations: rose gold

Patrimony Contemporaine Automatic
Reference number: X85R9006
Movement: automatic, Vacheron Constantin Caliber 2450 VC; ø 25.6 mm, height 3.6 mm; 27 jewels; 28,800 vph; Seal of Geneva
Functions: hours, minutes, sweep seconds
Case: rose gold, ø 40 mm, height 8.31 mm; sapphire crystal; transparent case back
Band: reptile skin, buckle
Price: $17,200
Variations: yellow or white gold

Patrimony Traditionelle Calibre 2755
Reference number: X80R9193
Movement: manually wound, Vacheron Constantin Caliber 2755 VC; ø 33.3 mm, height 7.9 mm; 40 jewels; 18,800 vph; one-minute tourbillon; Seal of Geneva
Functions: hours, minutes, perpetual calendar with date, weekday, month, leap year; minute repeater
Case: rose gold, ø 44 mm, height 13.65 mm; sapphire crystal; transparent case back
Band: reptile skin, double folding clasp
Price: $559,000

Patrimony Bi-Retro Day-Date
Reference number: X86R8463
Movement: automatic, Vacheron Constantin Caliber 2460 R31 R7; ø 25.6 mm, height 5.4 mm; 27 jewels; 28,800 vph; Seal of Geneva
Functions: hours, minutes; date and weekday (retrograde)
Case: rose gold, ø 42.5 mm, height 10.07 mm; sapphire crystal; transparent case back
Band: reptile skin, double folding clasp
Price: $29,600

Patrimony Traditionelle Skeletonized Perpetual Calendar
Reference number: X43P9108
Movement: automatic, Vacheron Constantin Caliber 1120 QPSQ; ø 28 mm, height 4.05 mm; 36 jewels; 19,800 vph; Seal of Geneva; completely skeletonized movement
Functions: hours, minutes, perpetual calendar with date, weekday, month, moon phase, leap year
Case: platinum, ø 39 mm, height 8.67 mm; sapphire crystal; transparent case back
Band: reptile skin, buckle
Price: $130,000
Variations: rose gold

Patrimony Contemporaine 40 mm
Reference number: X81G6987
Movement: manually wound, Vacheron Constantin Caliber 1400 VC; ø 20.35 mm, height 2.6 mm; 20 jewels; 28,800 vph; Seal of Geneva
Functions: hours, minutes
Case: white gold, ø 40 mm, height 6.7 mm; sapphire crystal
Band: reptile skin, buckle
Price: $13,300
Variations: in yellow or rose gold

Patrimony Power Reserve Automatic
Reference number: X47G5350
Movement: automatic, Vacheron Constantin Caliber 1127; ø 24.75 mm, height 4.85 mm; 45 jewels; 28,800 vph
Functions: hours, minutes, subsidiary seconds; date; power reserve display
Case: white gold, ø 36 mm, height 11.8; sapphire crystal; transparent case back
Band: reptile skin, buckle
Price: $16,600
Variations: yellow gold

Overseas Automatic
Reference number: X47A6953
Movement: automatic, Vacheron Constantin Caliber 1226 VC; ø 26 mm, height 3.25 mm; 28,800 vph; soft iron core magnetic field protection
Functions: hours, minutes, sweep seconds; date
Case: stainless steel, ø 42 mm, height 9.7 mm; sapphire crystal; water-resistant to 15 atm
Band: stainless steel, double folding clasp
Price: $10,400

Vacheron Constantin

Overseas Chronograph
Reference number: X496954
Movement: automatic, Vacheron Constantin Caliber 1137 VC; ø 26 mm, height 6.6 mm; 21,600 vph
Functions: hours, minutes, subsidiary seconds; chronograph; large date
Case: stainless steel, ø 42 mm, height 12.45 mm; sapphire crystal; transparent case back; screw-in crown and buttons; water-resistant to 15 atm
Band: stainless steel, double folding clasp
Price: $15,600
Variations: yellow gold

Overseas Dual Time
Reference number: X47R8530
Movement: automatic, Vacheron Constantin Caliber 1222VC; ø 26 mm, height 4.95 mm; 28,800 vph; soft iron core magnetic field protection
Functions: hours, minutes, sweep seconds; second time zone, day/night indication; date; power reserve display
Case: yellow gold, ø 42 mm, height 10 mm; sapphire crystal; transparent case back; water-resistant to 15 atm
Band: yellow gold, double folding clasp
Price: $33,700
Variations: rose gold (sold out); stainless steel

Toledo 1952
Reference number: X47R8293
Movement: automatic, Vacheron Constantin Caliber 1125; ø 26.6 mm, height 5.53 mm; 36 jewels; 28,800 vph; finely finished with côtes de Genève
Functions: hours, minutes, subsidiary seconds; date, weekday, month, moon phase display
Case: rose gold, 35.7 x 41 mm, height 12.7 mm; sapphire crystal; transparent case back
Band: reptile skin, buckle
Price: $24,400
Variations: in yellow or white gold

Malte Perpetual Calendar Open Face
Reference number: X47P8439
Movement: automatic, Vacheron Constantin Caliber 1226 QPRD; ø 26 mm, height 5.05 mm; 36 jewels; 28,800 vph; red gold base plate; visible calendar module
Functions: hours, minutes; date (retrograde), weekday, month, year (four-digit, digital), leap year
Case: platinum, ø 38.5 mm, height 13 mm; sapphire crystal; transparent case back
Band: reptile skin, buckle
Remarks: sapphire crystal dial
Price: $84,400

Malte Tourbillon Tonneau
Reference number: X30P4979
Movement: manually wound, Vacheron Constantin Caliber 1790 VC; 27.37 x 29.3 mm, tonneau-shaped, height 6.1 mm; 27 jewels; 18,000 vph; one-minute tourbillon
Functions: hours, off-center minutes, subsidiary seconds (on tourbillon cage); date; power reserve display
Case: platinum, ø 36 mm, height 12 mm; sapphire crystal; transparent case back
Band: reptile skin, buckle
Price: $135,000
Variations: red gold

Malte Tonneau Chronograph
Reference number: X49R5715
Movement: manually wound, Vacheron Constantin Caliber 1137 VC; ø 25.6 mm, height 6.6 mm; 21,600 vph
Functions: hours, minutes, subsidiary seconds; chronograph; large date
Case: rose gold, ø 36 mm, height 14 mm; sapphire crystal; transparent case back
Band: reptile skin, folding clasp
Price: $28,700
Variations: in stainless steel with stainless steel bracelet or leather strap

Malte Tonneau Dual Time
Reference number: X47G6962
Movement: automatic, Vacheron Constantin Caliber 1222 VC; ø 26 mm, height 4.95 mm; 28,800 vph; finely finished with côtes de Genève
Functions: hours, minutes; second time zone, day/night indication; date; power reserve display
Case: white gold, ø 36 mm, height 11.2 mm; sapphire crystal; transparent case back
Band: reptile skin, folding clasp
Price: $25,600
Variations: rose gold

Malte Power Reserve and Date
Reference number: X83G9195
Movement: manually wound, Vacheron Constantin Caliber 1420; ø 20.35 mm, height 4.2 mm; 20 jewels; 28,800 vph; Seal of Geneva
Functions: hours, minutes, subsidiary seconds; date; power reserve display
Case: rose gold, ø 38 mm, height 11.8 mm; sapphire crystal; transparent case back
Band: reptile skin, buckle
Price: $21,200
Variations: white gold ($23,200)

Vacheron Constantin

Patrimony Contemporaine Limited Edition
Reference number: X81G9486
Movement: manually wound, Vacheron Constantin Caliber 1400 SS; ø 20.35 mm, height 2.6 mm; 20 jewels; 28,800 vph; Seal of Geneva
Functions: hours, minutes, sweep seconds
Case: platinum, ø 40 mm, height 6.7 mm; sapphire crystal
Band: reptile skin, buckle
Remarks: sold out
Price: $26,000

Malte Minute Repeater with Perpetual Calendar
Reference number: X30R6978
Movement: manually wound, Vacheron Constantin Caliber 1755 QP; ø 30.8 mm, height 4.9 mm; 30 jewels; 18,000 vph
Functions: hours, minutes; perpetual calendar with date, weekday, month, moon phase, leap year; minute repeater
Case: rose gold, ø 41 mm, height 10.45 mm; sapphire crystal; transparent case back
Band: reptile skin, folding clasp
Remarks: limited edition of 30 pieces
Price: $386,000

Malte Regulateur Dual Time
Reference number: X42G4960
Movement: automatic, Vacheron Constantin Caliber 1206 RDT; ø 26.2 mm, height 4.92 mm; 31 jewels; 28,800 vph; finely finished with côtes de Genève; officially certified C.O.S.C. chronometer
Functions: off-center hours, minutes, subsidiary seconds; date; 24-hour display (second time zone)
Case: white gold, ø 38.5 mm, height 11 mm; sapphire crystal; transparent hinged case back
Band: reptile skin, buckle
Price: $24,300
Variations: rose or yellow gold

Patrimony Small Seconds
Reference number: X81G5707
Movement: manually wound, Vacheron Constantin Caliber 1400 VC; ø 20.35 mm, height 2.6 mm; 20 jewels; 28,800 vph; Seal of Geneva
Functions: hours, minutes, subsidiary seconds
Case: white gold, ø 38.5 mm, height 8.2; sapphire crystal; transparent case back
Band: reptile skin, buckle
Price: $11,700
Variations: yellow or rose gold

Malte Chronograph Platinum Collection Excellence Platine
Reference number: X47P8237
Movement: manually wound, Vacheron Constantin Caliber 1141; ø 27 mm, height 5.57 mm; 21 jewels; 18,000 vph; swan-neck fine adjustment, finely finished with côtes de Genève
Functions: hours, minutes, subsidiary seconds; chronograph
Case: platinum, ø 41.5 mm, height 10.9 mm; sapphire crystal; transparent case back
Band: reptile skin, buckle
Price: $50,300

Patrimony Extra Plate
Reference number: X33G0411
Movement: manually wound, Vacheron Constantin Caliber 1003; ø 20.8 mm, height 1.64 mm; 18 jewels; 18,000 vph; thinnest mechanical movement; Seal of Geneva
Functions: hours, minutes
Case: white gold, ø 31.5 mm, height 5.25 mm; sapphire crystal
Band: reptile skin, buckle
Price: $12,500
Variations: rose gold

Egérie
Reference number: X25R9120
Movement: quartz, Vacheron Constantin Caliber 1202
Functions: hours, minutes
Case: rose gold, 27.5 x 36 mm, height 9.53 mm; sapphire crystal
Band: reptile skin, buckle
Price: $10,400
Variations: yellow or white gold

1972
Reference number: X25G9173
Movement: quartz, Vacheron Constantin Caliber 1202
Functions: hours, minutes
Case: white gold, 21 x 34 mm, height 6.7 mm; bezel, dial, and buckle set with 177 diamonds; sapphire crystal
Band: reptile skin, buckle
Price: $20,300
Variations: rose gold

Vacheron Constantin

Caliber 1410
Mechanical with manual winding, power reserve approximately 40 hours
Functions: hours, minutes; moon phase; power reserve display
Diameter: 20.35 mm (9''')
Height: 4.2 mm
Jewels: 20
Balance: glucydur
Frequency: 28,800 vph
Balance spring: flat hairspring with fine adjustment via index
Shock protection: Kif
Remarks: base plate with perlage, edges beveled, bridges with côtes de Genève; polished steel parts; Seal of Geneva

Caliber 1141
Mechanical with manual winding, power reserve appx. 48 hours, column-wheel control of chronograph functions
Functions: hours, minutes, subsidiary seconds; chronograph with 30-minute counter
Diameter: 27 mm (12''')
Height: 5.6 mm
Jewels: 21
Balance: screw balance
Frequency: 18,000 vph
Balance spring: flat hairspring with swan-neck fine adjustment
Shock protection: Kif
Remarks: base plate with perlage, edges beveled, bridges with côtes de Genève; polished steel parts; Seal of Geneva

Caliber 1400
Mechanical with manual winding, power reserve approximately 40 hours
Functions: hours, minutes, subsidiary seconds
Diameter: 20.3 mm (9''')
Height: 2.6 mm
Jewels: 20
Balance: glucydur
Frequency: 28,800 vph
Balance spring: flat hairspring with fine adjustment via index
Shock protection: Kif
Remarks: base plate with perlage, edges beveled, bridges with côtes de Genève; polished steel parts; Seal of Geneva

Caliber 1790
Mechanical with manual winding, one-minute tourbillon; power reserve approximately 45 hours
Functions: hours, minutes, subsidiary seconds (on tourbillon cage); date; power reserve display
Dimensions: 28.5 x 26.9 mm
Height: 6.1 mm
Jewels: 27
Balance: screw balance in tourbillon cage
Frequency: 18,000 vph
Remarks: base plate with perlage, edges beveled, bridges with côtes de Genève; polished steel parts; Seal of Geneva

Caliber 2455
Mechanical with automatic winding, power reserve approximately 43 hours
Functions: hours, minutes, subsidiary seconds
Diameter: 25.6 mm
Height: 3.6 mm
Jewels: 27
Balance: glucydur
Frequency: 28,800 vph
Remarks: base plate with perlage, edges beveled, bridges with côtes de Genève; polished steel parts; Seal of Geneva

Caliber 246 R31 R7
Mechanical with automatic winding, power reserve approximately 43 hours
Functions: hours, minutes, date, day (retrograde)
Diameter: 25.6 mm
Height: 5.4 mm
Jewels: 27
Balance: glucydur
Frequency: 28,800 vph
Remarks: base plate with perlage, edges beveled, bridges with côtes de Genève; polished steel parts; Seal of Geneva

Caliber 2475
Mechanical with automatic winding, power reserve approximately 55 hours
Functions: hours, minutes, sweep seconds; date, day, power reserve indication
Diameter: 26.2 mm
Height: 5.5 mm
Jewels: 27
Balance: glucydur
Frequency: 28,800 vph
Remarks: base plate with perlage, edges beveled, bridges with côtes de Genève; polished steel parts

Villemont

Want to hear an incredible story about global warming? Jorgen Amundsen, relative of famed Norwegian explorer Roald Amundsen, founded the first and only watch company in that Scandinavian country in 2002. To prove that his timepieces would withstand temperatures to -50°C, he buried number 1 of his limited edition Polar Timepiece at the North Pole in honor of Roald, who had met his demise there. The timepiece was placed in a box with a note handwritten by Jorgen asking the finder to contact him. He viewed the chances of this happening in his lifetime as nonexistent.

Three years later, he received an e-mail from the Faroe Islands. Anna Jacobsen's eleven-year-old son had found the box on the beach near their home. With regard to global warming and prevailing conditions in the Arctic Ocean, this story provides some important information: it took just under three years for the timepiece in its box to journey from the geographic North Pole to the open seas. Thus, Jorgen Amundsen completely unintentionally carried out polar exploration in the spirit of his ancestor.

What does this have to do with Villemont, a Swiss luxury watch company? Everything, actually, for Amundsen Oslo and Villemont SA merged this past year, now becoming the Villemont Group SA under the direction of Villemont's founder, Olivier Müller.

Located in the heart of Geneva's old city, Villemont has benefited from the great flexibility of being in Switzerland's unofficial capital of watchmaking: both in the proximity to artisans ensconced there as well as in Müller's extreme experience with case making and metals helping to shape the face of the brand.

Müller's goal was to create timepieces with strong, modern personalities, each detail in perfect harmony—timepieces that are original while remaining traditional. This will be even easier for him in the future since Villemont now offers the Amundsen Collection in addition to the brand's already established Aston T, Aston R, Lady V, and Ultime lines. The Amundsen line features professional instruments based on the history of Roald Amundsen in polar exploration, sailing, and aviation. Needless to say, these timepieces are now manufactured in Villemont's exceptional quality with emphasis on unique cases and materials. Complex, with distinctive beveled edges, generous volumes, and contrasts such as polishing and satin-finishing, Villemont's tripartite cases are a distinct technical feat. One element that sets them apart from all others is the use of *clou de Villemont*, a special guilloché pattern Müller has created that is visible around the circumference of the crown as it intertwines with the initials V and M.

The Ultime is so named in honor of the metal its case is made of: ultimum is an alloy created just for Villemont, comprising only the precious metals palladium, ruthenium, and platinum—a first for the watch industry, where alloys until now have all contained at least 5 percent of other metals. This case features a distinctive engraved bezel mirroring the guilloché found on the grey meteorite dial, both a reinterpretation of the *clou de Villemont* pattern. It is available only in a limited edition of twenty-eight pieces.

Villemont

7 Seas
Reference number: 1405.03002
Movement: automatic, Caliber VM 107 (base ETA Valjoux 7750); ø 30 mm, height 7.9 mm; 25 jewels; 28,800 vph; rotor bridge and rotor decorated with Clou de Villemont
Functions: hours, minutes, subsidiary seconds; date, day; chronograph
Case: red gold/titanium, ø 44.5 mm, height 12 mm; unidirectionally rotating bezel; sapphire crystal; exhibition case back; water-resistant to 120 m
Band: reptile skin, triple folding clasp
Remarks: 18-karat gold dial, center decorated with clou de Villemont guilloché pattern
Price: $15,300

Solar Navigator
Reference number: 1302.03702
Movement: automatic, Caliber VM 108 (base AS 5008); 13 lines; 31 jewels; 28,800 vph; bridges with perlage; rotor with côtes de Genève; blued screws
Functions: hours, minutes, subsidiary seconds; date; alarm; Solar Navigator system
Case: red gold, ø 43 mm; sapphire crystal; water-resistant to 200 m
Band: reptile skin, red gold triple folding clasp
Remarks: center of dial decorated with clou de Villemont guilloché pattern
Price: $21,000

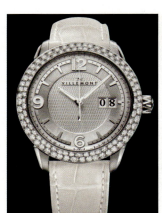

Big Date
Reference number: 1206.21302
Movement: automatic, Caliber VM 103 (base ETA 2896); ø 25.6 mm, height 4.85 mm; 22 jewels; 28,800 vph; bridges with perlage; 22-karat gold rotor set with 42 diamonds
Functions: hours, minutes, subsidiary seconds; date; alarm; Solar Navigator system
Case: stainless steel, ø 39 mm; bezel and case set with 160 diamonds; sapphire crystal; water-resistant to 30 m
Band: reptile skin, triple folding clasp
Remarks: center of dial decorated with clou de Villemont guilloché pattern
Price: $11,800

Aston R GMT Alarm
Reference number: 1302.02301
Movement: automatic, Caliber VM 105 (base AS 5008); 13 lines; 31 jewels; 28,800 vph; bridges with perlage; rotor with côtes de Genève; blued screws
Functions: hours, minutes, subsidiary seconds; date; alarm; second time zone
Case: red gold, ø 43 mm; sapphire crystal; water-resistant to 30 m
Band: reptile skin, red gold triple folding clasp
Remarks: center of dial decorated with clou de Villemont guilloché pattern
Price: $18,350

Aston T Night Hawk
Reference number: 2306.01582
Movement: automatic, Caliber VM 101 (base ETA Valjoux 7750); ø 30 mm, height 7.9 mm; 26 jewels; 28,800 vph; bridges with perlage; rotor with côtes de Genève; blued screws
Functions: hours, minutes, subsidiary seconds; date; chronograph
Case: stainless steel with black DLC coating, 53 x 39 mm; sapphire crystal; exhibition case back; water-resistant to 30 m
Band: reptile skin, triple folding clasp
Remarks: dial center decorated with clou de Villemont guilloché pattern
Price: $8,300

Aston T Dual Time Chronograph
Reference number: 2301.01002
Movement: automatic, Caliber VM 101 (base ETA Valjoux 7750); ø 30 mm, height 7.9 mm; 26 jewels; 28,800 vph; bridges with perlage; rotor with côtes de Genève; blued screws
Functions: hours, minutes, subsidiary seconds; date, weekday; chronograph
Case: yellow gold, 53 x 39 mm; sapphire crystal; exhibition case back; water-resistant to 30 m
Band: reptile skin, triple folding clasp
Remarks: dial center decorated with clou de Villemont guilloché pattern
Price: $21,900

Aston R Dual Time Chronograph
Reference number: 1303.03002
Movement: automatic, Caliber VM 101 (base ETA Valjoux 7750); ø 30 mm, height 7.9 mm; 26 jewels; 28,800 vph; bridges with perlage; rotor with côtes de Genève; blued screws
Functions: hours, minutes, subsidiary seconds; date; chronograph
Case: white gold, ø 43 mm; sapphire crystal; water-resistant to 30 m
Band: reptile skin, triple folding clasp
Remarks: dial center decorated with clou de Villemont guilloché pattern
Price: $23,000

Aston R Dual Time Chronograph
Reference number: 1303.33202
Movement: automatic, Caliber VM 101 (base ETA Valjoux 7750); ø 30 mm, height 7.9 mm; 26 jewels; 28,800 vph; bridges with perlage; rotor with côtes de Genève; blued screws
Functions: hours, minutes, subsidiary seconds; date; chronograph
Case: white gold, ø 43 mm; case set with 57 baguette-cut diamonds (3.9 ct); sapphire crystal; water-resistant to 30 m
Band: reptile skin, triple folding clasp
Remarks: gold dial center decorated with clou de Villemont guilloché pattern; flange set with 96 baguette-cut diamonds (2 ct)
Price: $90,900

Urwerk

The German word *Urwerk* is a play on words, but one that fits the outlook of this company very well. *Werk* is easy to describe; it means a watch movement. *Ur*, however, is tricky. *Ur* as a prefix denotes something like the source, the beginning, or the essential. The word Uhr, however, is pronounced exactly the same way and means a watch or clock—and is usually the word to precede Werk. Urwerk—the company—is not about its name; this is only the starting point for a certain design philosophy, one embodied by watchmaker Felix Baumgartner and designer Martin Frei, the two creative heads who make up Urwerk.

"We started with a blank piece of paper, dropped all our preconceptions, and decided to create a time machine. Our philosophy was to take ideas from the past and reshape them for contemporary living. Allow these ideas to arouse emotions that would not just look good, but also bring a bit of the stargazer and adventurer back into our interior consciousness," the duo says of their ideals. Baumgartner's calibers have so far included the premise of a "control board" on the back: here the duo's latest timepiece, called the 201, displays an oil change indicator (maintenance interval), a 100-year plus indicator (similar to an odometer), and a fine-tuning index, which gives the wearer the opportunity to reg-ulate his or her own watch forward or backward to a maximum of 30 seconds in a 24-hour period.

To display the time on the front, satellite modules rotate so that the number currently in use moves along the minute scale located along the bottom of the "dial."

201 Platine Noir Hammerhead
Movement: manually wound, Urwerk Caliber 7.01; 21,600 vph; power reserve 50 hours; digital transporters coated with Movic surface lubrication
Functions: hours (digital satellite), minutes; day/night indicator; power reserve display
Case: platinum with black PE-CVD coating, 45.6 mm x 43.5 mm, height 15 mm; control board on back with oil change indicator, 100-year plus indicator, and fine tuning screw; sapphire crystal
Band: alligator skin, buckle
Remarks: limited edition of 10 pieces; dial crafted in black ARCAP P40
Price: $178,000
Variations: white gold ($128,000); rose gold ($125,000); limited edition of 10 pieces in platinum ($158,000)

201 Rose Gold Hammerhead
Movement: manually wound, Urwerk Caliber 7.01; 21,600 vph; power reserve 50 hours; digital transporters coated with Movic surface lubrication
Functions: hours (digital satellite), minutes; day/night indicator; power reserve display
Case: rose gold, 45.6 mm x 43.5 mm, height 15 mm; control board on back with oil change indicator, 100-year plus indicator, and fine tuning screw; sapphire crystal
Band: alligator skin, buckle
Remarks: dial crafted in black ARCAP P40
Price: $125,000
Variations: white gold ($128,000); limited edition of 10 pieces in platinum ($158,000); limited edition of 10 pieces in black platinum ($178,000)

103.03 White Gold
Movement: manually wound, Urwerk Caliber 3.03; 21,600 vph; power reserve 43 hours; triple base plate in ARCAP P40 black PVD; hour satellites and orbital cross in Grade 2 titanium with black PVD coating
Functions: hours (digital satellite), minutes
Case: white gold, 43.5 x 45.6 mm, height 15 mm; titanium control board on back with chrono meter (15-minute and 60-second dials) and fine tuning screw for adjusting up to 30 seconds per 24-hour period; sapphire crystal
Band: alligator skin, buckle
Price: $58,000
Variations: red gold ($55,000)

103.05
Movement: manually wound; 21,600 vph; power reserve 43 hours; triple base plate in ARCAP P40 black PVD; hour satellites and orbital cross in Grade 2 titanium with black PVD coating
Functions: hours (digital satellite), minutes; day/night indicator; power reserve display
Case: platinum, 43.5 x 45.6 mm, height 15 mm; titanium control board on back with chrono meter (15-minute and 60-second dials) and fine tuning screw for adjusting up to 30 seconds per 24-hour period; sapphire crystal
Band: alligator skin, buckle
Remarks: limited edition of 50 pieces
Price: $88,000

Ventura

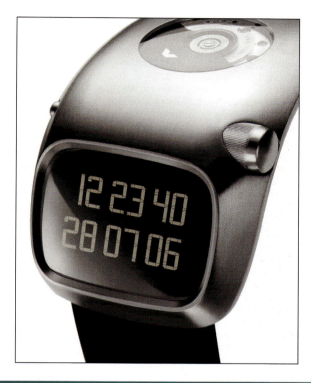

Founded in 1990 by Pierre Nobs, Ventura Design on Time has decided to follow a different path beginning in 2006. This decision came from the desire "to remain authentic, individual, full of character for strong personalities, without conforming," according to Nobs. "Rather than just dressing ETA movements in different clothes, we would prefer to carve out our own niche."

Ventura now focuses on digital displays of time powered by *manufacture* quartz movements that the company has developed and produced itself. Now dubbing itself the *manufacture electronique*, the company promotes sleek watch designs still partially created by Hannes Wettstein, though Paolo Fancelli, a Swiss industrial designer who had already worked with the company on its Sparc rx model, has also contributed an evolution of the v-tec. These new timepieces are called v-tec Sigma, and although the v-tec DNA is still recognizable as such, these ergonomic pieces are certainly individualistic. Retaining the same practical EasySkroll control for selecting functions, Fancelli has now framed the appearance of these timepieces as contemporary and futuristic at the same time, also adding a user-conscious and discreet element in having the display on the side of the wrist.

v-tec Alpha
Reference number: W15 S
Movement: quartz, Ventura Caliber VEN_03; multifunctional quartz movement with EasySkroll wheel
Functions: hours, minutes, seconds; chronograph; perpetual calendar with date, day, month, year; second time zone; alarm and countdown
Case: stainless steel (Durinox), 33.5 x 39 mm, height 8.5 mm; sapphire crystal
Band: stainless steel (Durinox), folding clasp
Price: $1,800
Variations: rubber strap

v-tec Delta
Reference number: W20.01. S
Movement: quartz, Ventura Caliber VEN_04; multifunctional quartz movement with EasySkroll wheel
Functions: hours, minutes, seconds; chronograph; perpetual calendar with date, day, month, year; second time zone; alarm and countdown
Case: stainless steel (Durinox), 35 x 40.6 mm, height 8.5 mm; sapphire crystal
Band: stainless steel (Durinox), folding clasp
Price: $1,500
Variations: leather strap

SPARC fx
Reference number: W10 R
Movement: quartz, Ventura Caliber 99; autonomous energy creation via rotor and micro generator; automatically turns off
Functions: hours, minutes; date, month
Case: titanox, ⌀ 35 mm, height 10.9 mm; sapphire crystal; transparent case back
Band: rubber, double folding clasp
Price: $2,300
Variations: with titanox bracelet

SPARC px
Reference number: W11 S
Movement: quartz, Ventura Caliber 99; autonomous energy creation via rotor and micro generator; automatically turns off
Functions: hours, minutes; date, month
Case: stainless steel, 42.4 x 32.5 mm, height 8.4/11.7 mm; sapphire crystal; transparent case back
Band: stainless steel, double folding clasp
Price: $2,150
Variations: with leather strap; with white diamonds; with black diamonds

George J von Burg

Sixty years ago, George J. von Burg (1914–1986) was already initiating developments in the Swiss watch industry that were far ahead of their time, setting numerous new standards. As the son of a watchmaker, von Burg learned about the manufacture of watches at a rather young age, acquiring all the necessary knowledge and skills. When he was barely twenty years old, he had already manufactured and sold his first timekeepers under the registered name of Geo Automatic. In the 1950s, von Burg immigrated with his family to the United States, where he founded a company for watch accessories. During this time, he purchased a watch factory in Switzerland, which he directed under the name Semag after returning from the United States. His company expanded, and von Burg opened another branch of the factory in Claro (in the Swiss canton Tessin) where he—one of the first of his guild to do so—manufactured mechanical watch movements for reputable watch brands on modern production machines. Claro Watch SA was established in 1961 for the manufacturing of mechanical pallet escapement movements.

Semag and Claro developed into two of the largest manufacturers of mechanical movements and wristwatches sold under various brand names all over the world. These companies are still owned by the von Burg family today and are managed by George J. von Burg II and George J. von Burg III.

The individual components of the chronographs come from various suppliers. They are, however, of the best quality, from the carefully polished cases and valuable leather straps to the finely finished Valjoux chronograph movements and cleanly structured dials. At first glance, the sweep chronograph hands inlaid with luminous substance seem a bit surprising, but they are an important style element that is incorporated into all four of the model families.

Modern Collection
Reference number: 10021 B
Movement: automatic, ETA Valjoux Caliber 7750; ø 30 mm, height 7.9 mm; 28 jewels; 28,800 vph
Functions: hours, minutes, subsidiary seconds; chronograph; date, day
Case: stainless steel, ø 40 mm, height 15 mm; sapphire crystal; screw-in crown; water-resistant to 10 m
Band: stainless steel, double folding clasp
Price: $ 2,600
Variations: reptile skin strap

Classic Collection
Reference number: 20012 C
Movement: automatic, ETA Valjoux Caliber 7750; ø 30 mm, height 7.9 mm; 28 jewels; 28,800 vph
Functions: hours, minutes, subsidiary seconds, chronograph; date, day
Case: gold-plated stainless steel, ø 40 mm, height 15 mm; sapphire crystal; screw-in crown; water-resistant to 10 m
Band: reptile skin, buckle
Price: $ 3,200
Variations: stainless steel bracelet

Sport Collection
Reference number: 30021 C
Movement: automatic, ETA Valjoux Caliber 7750; ø 30 mm, height 7.9 mm; 28 jewels; 28,800 vph
Functions: hours, minutes, subsidiary seconds, chronograph; date, day
Case: stainless steel, ø 40 mm, height 15 mm; sapphire crystal; screw-in crown; water-resistant to 10 m
Band: reptile skin, buckle
Price: $ 2,600
Variations: stainless steel bracelet

Roman Rattrapante
Reference number: 70021 C
Movement: automatic, GJVB Caliber 8721 (base ETA Valjoux 7750); ø 30 mm, height 8.4 mm; 27 jewels; 28,800 vph; finely finished with côtes de Genève
Functions: hours, minutes, subsidiary seconds; split-seconds chronograph; date
Case: stainless steel, ø 42 mm, height 16 mm; sapphire crystal; transparent case back; screw-in crown
Band: reptile skin, buckle
Remarks: limited edition of 50 pieces
Price: $13,600
Variations: in yellow, rose, or white gold; jeweled

Vogard

Michael Vogt has been active in the Swiss watch industry since 1992. In the decade to follow, he was able to gain wide business experience in senior marketing positions at TAG Heuer, Ebel, and Gucci. By 1999, the mechanical watch industry was in high gear, and Vogt left the established path to join an Internet start-up as a partner. A couple of years later, he sold his shares, using the profit to start a new business that had been maturing in his head for a while: Vogard, the company that would turn his vision of the "best traveler's watch ever" into a reality.

This native of Grenchen, Switzerland, had been around long enough to know that quality is key, so he enlisted the aid of independent master watchmaker Thomas Prescher to engineer this unusual watch's unique movement.

What emerged was the Timezoner system, a horological development that seems so meticulous and simple it could only be the product of Prescher's perfectionist mind. Consisting of three basic components added to its ETA base, a patent is currently pending. This mechanical system integrates the bezel, the case, and the movement to achieve its goal of being an easy-to-use worldtimer. And the practical Vogard Timezoner system is the first traveler's watch ever to allow for the indication of Daylight Savings Time at a given location.

The bezel is marked with twenty-four reference destinations, one for each of the time zones that our world is currently divided into. The wearer no longer needs to know the difference between home time and local time to set his or her watch: it's enough just to know the desired reference destination on the bezel. The watch automatically sets the correct local time at the selected reference destination when the wearer moves the bezel thanks to a set of sophisticated transmission wheels connecting the bezel with the movement.

Now on the market for four years, these super travelers enjoy a solid reputation for practical, innovative technology. And what may have seemed a bit like a one-hit wonder at the beginning is now evolving nicely into a full collection of attractive travel companions.

Business Officer
Reference number: BU 2133
Movement: automatic, Caliber Timezoner 01 (base ETA 2892-A2 Soprod); 28,800 vph; time zone mechanism coupled to the rotating bezel via the crown wheel
Functions: hours, minutes, sweep seconds; 24-hour display (world time) taking daylight savings time into account
Case: stainless steel, ø 43 mm, height 14 mm; bidirectionally rotating bezel with 24 reference city names; activating and security lever on side of case; sapphire crystal; transparent case back; water-resistant to 10 atm
Band: reptile skin, folding clasp
Price: $6,500
Variations: city names can be personalized

Formula 1 Limited Edition
Reference number: Black F1/38
Movement: automatic, Caliber Timezoner 01 (base ETA 2892-A2 Soprod); 28,800 vph; time zone mechanism coupled to the rotating bezel via the crown wheel
Functions: hours, minutes, sweep seconds; 24-hour display accounts for daylight savings
Case: black titanium carbide-coated stainless steel, ø 43 mm, height 14 mm; bidirectionally rotating bezel with 24 reference city names; activating and security lever on side; sapphire crystal; transparent case back
Band: reptile skin, folding clasp
Remarks: motor sport race tracks as reference names for time zones; limited edition of 100 pieces
Price: $6,700

18-Karat Gold Edition
Reference number: OR 9931
Movement: automatic, Caliber Timezoner 01 (base ETA 2892-A2 Soprod); 28,800 vph; time zone mechanism coupled to the rotating bezel via the crown wheel
Functions: hours, minutes, sweep seconds; 24-hour display (world time) taking daylight savings time into account
Case: rose gold, ø 43 mm, height 104 mm; bidirectionally rotating bezel with 24 reference city names; activating and security lever on side of case; sapphire crystal; transparent case back; water-resistant to 10 atm
Band: reptile skin, folding clasp
Price: $24,000
Variations: city names can be personalized

Super Traveler
Reference number: ST2137
Movement: automatic, Caliber Timezoner 01 (base ETA 2892-A2 Soprod); 28,800 vph; time zone mechanism coupled to the rotating bezel via the crown wheel
Functions: hours, minutes, sweep seconds; 24-hour display (world time) taking daylight savings time into account
Case: stainless steel, ø 43 mm, height 104 mm; bidirectionally rotating bezel with 36 reference city names for setting the time zones; activating and security lever on side of case; sapphire crystal; transparent case back; water-resistant to 10 atm
Band: reptile skin, folding clasp
Price: $6,700

Vostok-Europe

Before 1930, when the First Moscow Watch Factory was founded, Imperial Russia was home to only small watch workshops, usually kept by Swiss watchmakers following Catherine II's call for quality watch- and clockmakers. Naturally they used Swiss parts in their creations, and even sold entirely Swiss-made timepieces, which they imported from their Jura-based factories. After the October Revolution of 1917, the whole of this little industry was absorbed into a precision mechanics combine, and individual business entities ceased to exist.

Watch parts and components were, however, in sore demand, as the Soviet Union realized that it still needed portable timekeepers. The country's council for labor and defense passed a resolution regarding watch production in 1927, and a committee was sent to Western Europe to purchase machinery. Fearful of losing a large export market, the Swiss weren't of much help, so the delegation moved farther west, to the United States. There they were able to purchase Dueber Hampton Watch & Co. and Ansonia Clock Company, both of which were dismantled and rebuilt in Russia. In May 1930, it is reported that thirty American watchmakers and fifty wagons full of equipment reached Moscow, where the First Moscow Watch Factory was put into action and the Russian watch industry founded. The first Russian caliber, Type 1, was actually a rebuilt Dueber. Modified and varied, it continued to be produced for years: between 1935 and 1941 alone, the First Moscow Watch Factory manufactured about 2.7 million pocket and wristwatches using this caliber.

In 1975, Swiss-made production machines finally made it to the Soviet Union, and Swiss-style calibers were introduced at the factory. The design of chronograph Caliber 3133, first issued in 1983, is based on the Swiss Valjoux Caliber 7734, with a diameter of 31 mm, 23 jewels, and 42 hours of power reserve. This is Russia's premier movement and the particular one that makes the watches manufactured today by Volmax Watch Company competitive on the world market.

By the 1990s, the First Moscow Watch Factory, known as Poljot (Russian for "flight") since 1961, was exporting 80 percent of its watches to seventy different countries, including the United States, Western Europe, Asia, and, of course, Germany, where they have always been immensely popular. In the wake of the collapse of the Soviet Union, Volmax Watch Company was born, taking its name from a brand the First Moscow Watch Factory created in the '60s.

Against a backdrop of resuscitated interest in Russian watches caused by the opening of the Russian markets, Vostok-Europe premiered in 2003. Cost-effectiveness, quality, and a pedigree from the oldest and largest Russian watchmaking company established the brand. Each piece in the Vostok-Europe model line is inspired by and christened with a Soviet technological, architectural, or cultural achievement.

The N1 is the world's largest rocket, and the case of the model that took its name is reminiscent of its first stage.

The Expedition Trophy is the world's longest winter off-road race, with the coming edition literally running all the way around the world. Vostok-Europe supplies the official watches for this event.

Vostok Europe

Mriya
Reference number: 2432/5515036B
Movement: automatic, Vostok Caliber 2432; ø 24 mm, height 6.3 mm; 32 jewels; 19,800 vph; power reserve 38 hours; blued screws; côtes de Genève on rotor
Functions: hours, minutes, sweep seconds; date; day/night indicator; digital GMT display
Case: stainless steel, ø 43 mm, height 14.5 mm; unidirectionally rotating bezel; screw-in crown; mineral crystal; exhibition case back; water-resistant to 100 m
Band: stainless steel; folding clasp
Remarks: named for world's largest aircraft, the AN-225 Mriya; means "dream" in Ukrainian
Price: $335
Variations: black dial; yellow or rose gold; leather

Red Square
Reference number: 2432/6105056B
Movement: automatic, Vostok Caliber 2432; ø 24 mm, height 6.3 mm; 32 jewels; 19,800 vph; power reserve 38 hours; blued screws; côtes de Genève on rotor
Functions: hours, minutes, sweep seconds; date; day/night indicator
Case: stainless steel, 35 x 46 mm, height 13 mm; mineral crystal; screwed-down case back; water-resistant to 50 m
Band: stainless steel; double folding clasp
Remarks: unique square-shaped animated day/night indicator for namesake
Price: $359
Variations: rose gold with black or silver dial; mid-sized edition with two-tone bracelet

Red Square
Reference number: 2432/6169065
Movement: automatic, Vostok Caliber 2432; ø 24 mm, height 6.3 mm; 32 jewels; 19,800 vph; power reserve 38 hours; blued screws; côtes de Genève on rotor
Functions: hours, minutes, sweep seconds; date; day/night indicator
Case: rose gold-plated stainless steel, 32 x 41.5 mm, height 13 mm; mineral crystal; screwed-down case back engraved with Savior Tower; water-resistant to 50 m
Band: stingray, buckle
Remarks: unique square-shaped animated day/night indicator for namesake; mother-of-pearl dial
Price: $319

Metro
Reference number: 2432/0526031
Movement: automatic, Vostok Caliber 2432; ø 24 mm, height 6.3 mm; 32 jewels; 19,800 vph; power reserve 38 hours; blued screws; côtes de Genève on rotor
Functions: hours, minutes, sweep seconds; date; day/night indicator
Case: yellow gold-plated stainless steel, 48 x 38.5 mm, height 12.5 mm; mineral crystal; screwed-down exhibition case back; water-resistant to 50 m
Band: leather, buckle
Remarks: named for "underground palaces" of Moscow, the city's famed subway system
Price: $299
Variations: rose gold plate with silver dial

Arktika
Reference number: 2432/0325032B
Movement: automatic, Vostok Caliber 2432; ø 24 mm, height 6.3 mm; 32 jewels; 19,800 vph; power reserve 38 hours; blued screws; côtes de Genève on rotor
Functions: hours, minutes, sweep seconds; date; day/night indicator
Case: PVD-rose gold plated stainless steel, ø 41 mm, height 13 mm; mineral crystal; screwed-down mineral crystal exhibition case back; water-resistant to 30 m
Band: leather, buckle
Remarks: named for Arktika Icebreaker, first surface ship to ever reach North Pole; rivets on case reminiscent of ship's hull
Price: $299

Expedition Trophy
Reference number: 2426/5405052
Movement: automatic, Vostok Caliber 2426; ø 24 mm, height 6.3 mm; 32 jewels; 19,800 vph; power reserve 38 hours; blued screws; côtes de Genève on rotor
Functions: hours, minutes, sweep seconds; date; second time zone
Case: stainless steel, ø 42 mm, height 14.5 mm; bidirectionally rotating bezel with names of Russian cities the Expedition Trophy Race passes through; mineral crystal; screwed-down case back; screw-in crown; water-resistant to 100 m
Band: leather, double buckle
Remarks: official watch of the world's longest winter off-road race, held in Siberia
Price: $299

Expedition Trophy Around the World
Reference number: 2426/5905084
Movement: automatic, Vostok Caliber 2426; ø 24 mm, height 6.3 mm; 32 jewels; 19,800 vph; power reserve 38 hours; blued screws; côtes de Genève on rotor
Functions: hours, minutes, sweep seconds; date; second time zone
Case: stainless steel, ø 43 mm, height 14 mm; mineral crystal; screwed-down case back; water-resistant to 100 m
Band: leather, double tang buckle
Remarks: named for and official watch of a unique race that sees vehicles racing around the globe
Price: $299
Variations: also available with black dial

N1 Rocket
Reference number: 2426/2204048B
Movement: automatic, Vostok Caliber 2426; ø 24 mm, height 6.3 mm; 32 jewels; 19,800 vph; power reserve 38 hours; blued screws; côtes de Genève on rotor
Functions: hours, minutes, sweep seconds; date; second time zone
Case: black stainless steel, ø 42 mm, height 13.5 mm; unidirectionally rotating bezel; mineral crystal; screwed-down exhibition case back; screw-in crown; water-resistant to 100 m
Band: black stainless steel, folding clasp
Remarks: named for the world's largest rocket
Price: $419
Variations: blue charcoal grey dial; stainless steel model; leather strap

Wempe Chronometerwerke

Glashütte is once again the epitome of German watchmaking—as it was a century ago. The products from the little city located in this remote valley of the east Erzgebirge mountains, a good twenty miles from Saxony's capital city Dresden, pay homage to the cult of quality, aesthetics, and precision based on the tradition of reputable Glashütte pocket watch *manufactures*.

The watchmaker dynasty Wempe, at home in Hamburg, has maintained long business and personal ties to the Saxon region, and when the decision was finally made for Wempe to produce its own wristwatches, it was soon clear that such a fabrication could only take place in Glashütte. Thus, Wempe turned the city's former observatory, Urania, located high above the Müglitz Valley, into a watchmaking workshop.

The production of watches under the Wempe Chronometerwerke logo is the result of a partnership conceived at the highest expert level: both models were developed, designed, and manufactured on the basis of an exclusive agreement with the Nomos watch *manufacture* in Glashütte. These timekeepers in tonneau-shaped cases are powered by a new shaped *manufacture* movement, with the tonneau shape consistently determining the visuals. Its toric, domed shape allows the case to fit the movement precisely. Even the dial is clean in its design. A look through the sapphire crystal case back to the well-finished caliber reveals the Saxon origins of this watch. This talking piece is outfitted with a (certified chronometer) tourbillon movement, which was developed by Nomos movement designer Thierry Albert. And he made all twenty-five of this model's movements, too.

Manual Winding Tourbillon
Reference number: WG740001
Movement: manually wound, Wempe Caliber CW 2; 32.6 x 22.6 mm, height 6.5 mm; 19 jewels; 21,600 vph; one-minute tourbillon; Breguet hairspring; bridges with sunburst pattern, rhodium-plated; officially certified chronometer according to DIN 8319
Functions: hours, minutes, subsidiary seconds
Case: platinum, 51 x 40.9 mm, height 13.7 mm; sapphire crystal; transparent case back water-resistant to 5 atm
Band: reptile skin, buckle
Remarks: limited edition of 25 pieces
Price: $110,500

Manual Winding Wempe Chronometerwerke
Reference number: WG740006
Movement: manually wound, Wempe Caliber CW 1; 32.6 x 22.6 mm, height 3.6 mm; 23 jewels; 21,600 vph; twin spring barrels; swan-neck fine adjustment; three-quarter plate with sunburst pattern, hand-engraved balance cock; officially certified chronometer according to DIN 8319
Functions: hours, minutes, subsidiary seconds
Case: yellow gold, 45.6 x 37 mm, height 10.2 mm; sapphire crystal; transparent case back; water-resistant to 5 atm
Band: reptile skin, buckle
Price: $9,950

Manual Winding Wempe Chronometerwerke
Reference number: WG040001
Movement: manually wound, Wempe Caliber CW 1; 32.6 x 22.6 mm, height 3.6 mm; 23 jewels; 21,600 vph; twin spring barrels; swan-neck fine adjustment; three-quarter plate with sunburst pattern, hand-engraved balance cock; officially certified chronometer according to DIN 8319
Functions: hours, minutes, subsidiary seconds
Case: stainless steel, 45.6 x 37 mm, height 10.2 mm; sapphire crystal; transparent case back; water-resistant to 5 atm
Band: reptile skin, buckle
Price: $5,500

Manual Winding Wempe Chronometerwerke
Reference number: WG040004
Movement: manually wound, Wempe Caliber CW 1; 32.6 x 22.6 mm, height 3.6 mm; 23 jewels; 21,600 vph; twin spring barrels; swan-neck fine adjustment; three-quarter plate with sunburst pattern, hand-engraved balance cock; officially certified chronometer according to DIN 8319
Functions: hours, minutes, subsidiary seconds
Case: stainless steel, 45.6 x 37 mm, height 10.2 mm; sapphire crystal; transparent case back; water-resistant to 5 atm
Band: reptile skin, buckle
Price: $5,500

Wempe Zeitmeister

Wempe's second watch line is exciting for both connoisseurs of chronometer movements and also for budding fans of precise watchmaking. The reissue of the Zeitmeister line, originally manufactured in the 1950s and '60s, not only fulfills the highest horological demands, but also allows beginners an entry into the art of mechanical watchmaking.

All watches of this line are located in the mid-priced segment, one that the luxury watch industry has distanced itself from more and more with its products. The highlight of this model family is the Zeitmeister Chronograph, which is outfitted with a mechanical stopwatch function. "Proof" of the uncompromising quality of this wristwatch chronometer collection made in Glashütte: a lavish relief engraving of the observatory embellishes the back of every watch.

German chronometry remains closely related to the name of this family business, the origins of which lie in the founding of the Hamburg Chronometerwerke, which Herbert Wempe purchased in 1939. He had recognized its potential as a work and educational facility for the production of precision watches, soon manufacturing ship's chronometers that gained worldwide reputations.

Since the sought-after Swiss C.O.S.C. certificate cannot be obtained in Germany, Wempe has created not only a workshop for watch production, but also one for testing chronometers, which are then certified by the German Chronometer Calibrating Service according to the German industrial norm (DIN) 8319.

The Glashütte chronometer testing workshop will at first only certify wristwatches. The basic difference between this and the Swiss chronometer norm is that DIN 8319 sees complete watches tested, and not just movements as in Switzerland. Another difference for the German norm is that the watch must be settable to the second.

Automatic Chronometer-Chronograph
Reference number: WM540004
Movement: automatic, ETA Valjoux Caliber 7753; ø 30 mm, height 7.9 mm; 27 jewels; 28,800 vph; officially certified chronometer according to DIN 8319
Functions: hours, minutes, subsidiary seconds; date; chronograph
Case: stainless steel, ø 42 mm, height 15 mm; sapphire crystal; water-resistant to 5 atm
Band: stainless steel, double folding clasp
Price: $2,765

World Time Watch
Reference number: WM340001
Movement: automatic, ETA Caliber 2893-2; ø 25.6 mm, height 4.1 mm; 21 jewels; 28,800 vph; officially certified chronometer according to DIN 8319
Functions: hours, minutes, sweep seconds; date; 24-hour display (world time, second time zone)
Case: stainless steel, ø 42 mm, height 11 mm; sapphire crystal; water-resistant to 5 atm
Band: reptile skin, buckle
Price: $2,350

Grand Automatic Power Reserve
Reference number: WM440002
Movement: automatic, ETA Caliber A07.161; ø 36.6 mm, height 7.9 mm; 24 jewels; 28,800 vph; officially certified chronometer according to DIN 8319
Functions: hours, minutes, sweep seconds; date; power reserve display
Case: stainless steel, ø 45 mm, height 11 mm; sapphire crystal; water-resistant to 5 atm
Band: reptile skin, buckle
Price: $2,650

Quartz Chronometer
Reference number: WM050003
Movement: quartz, ETA Caliber 255.111; officially certified chronometer according to DIN 8319
Functions: hours, minutes, sweep seconds; date
Case: gold-plated stainless steel, ø 38 mm, height 9.6 mm; sapphire crystal; water-resistant to 5 atm
Band: reptile skin, buckle
Price: $1,250

Harry Winston Rare Timepieces

It would not be unusual if, on seeing this section, you exclaimed in surprise, "But I thought Harry Winston was a jeweler!" You wouldn't be wrong at all, in fact. The Harry Winston company is one of the world's finest jewelers. Alongside selling large, famous sparklers such as the Star of Sierra Leone and the Taylor-Burton, Harry Winston's fame probably also originated in the fact that he invented a new platinum setting that allowed his dazzling jewels to shine in a three-dimensionality unknown to that point.

Harry Winston passed away in 1978, and his son Ronald took over the company's reins. Like his father, Ronald has shown talent in his chosen profession and even received several patents for his work with precious metals. His goal in this was to create a collection of precious, rare watches.

His only worry lay in whether he would be able to develop watch movements and designs to match the company's diamonds. Taking his father's motto—"only the exceptional"—to heart, in 1990 he created two watch lines: one showcasing the finest precious gems as the company's focus and one containing clever, complicated timepieces.

With the start of a new millennium and an energetic, young new managing director in the driver's seat of the recently founded Harry Winston Rare Timepieces in Geneva, it was time for something truly exceptional in the overall scope of the Swiss watchmaking industry: the Opus project.

The very limited, very exclusive Opus timepieces are created in conjunction with one exceptional independent watchmaker per year. A very small series of these timepieces

without example are produced, each of which contains a *manufacture* movement especially created for the project. The first Opus timepiece was introduced in 2001 in conjunction with François-Paul Journe. Opus 2 followed the ensuing year with twenty-four tourbillons made by Genevan master watchmaker Antoine Preziuso. Twelve of them featured a perpetual calendar on the back. At Baselworld 2003, Harry Winston Rare Timepieces introduced its work with Vianney Halter in form of Opus 3. A.H.C.I. member Halter created fifty-five spectacular pieces according to the unusual look also found in his own line. Opus 4 was created by repeater specialist Christophe Claret, who has meanwhile developed a number of interesting and complicated timepieces for the small Genevan company. Opus 5 originated in the mind of Felix Baumgartner of Urwerk fame, whose satellite vision translated well to Winston's project. Last year saw the tourbillon team Greubel Forsey take its deep whirlwind research to the Opus 6 project. This past Baselworld was Andreas Strehler's chance to come forth with an exceptional piece—as if any of the aforementioned weren't exceptional. His is a wondrously beautiful movement with the grace of a butterfly: Strehler has made it possible to see the oversized gear wheels, but not by skeletonizing them. The ingenious idea is that these gear wheels operate an alternating display: when the button on the case is pushed, the single display will show the hours, minutes, or remaining power reserve, technically achieved by using a disk, not conventional hands.

Harry Winston Rare Timepieces

Avenue
Reference number: 310/LQWW.D01/D3.2/D3.2
Movement: manually wound, Frédéric Piguet Caliber 610; 21,600 vph
Functions: hours, minutes
Case: white gold, 21 x 36 mm; case, bezel, and strap lugs set with diamonds; sapphire crystal; exhibition case back
Band: white gold set with diamonds, folding clasp
Remarks: dial paved with diamonds
Price: $67,100

Excenter Perpetual Calendar
Reference number: 200/MAPC41WL.A
Movement: automatic, Girard-Perregaux Caliber 3306 with Harry Winston module 111; 28,800 vph
Functions: hours, minutes (off-center); second time zone (12-hour hand); date (retrograde); month (retrograde); moon phase, leap year
Case: white gold, ø 41 mm; sapphire crystal; exhibition case back
Band: reptile skin, buckle
Price: $54,000
Variations: with silver-plated dial

New Avenue
Reference number: 310/LQWL.MDO/00
Movement: quartz, ETA Caliber 980.163/H3
Functions: hours, minutes, subsidiary seconds
Case: white gold 21 x 36 mm; case, bezel, and strap lugs set with diamonds; sapphire crystal; water-resistant to 3 atm
Band: satin, buckle
Remarks: mother-of-pearl dial paved with diamonds
Price: $35,900
Variations: black dial

Avenue C
Reference number: 330/LQWW31.M/D3.1/D2.1
Movement: quartz, Energizer Caliber 315
Functions: hours, minutes
Case: white gold 19.5 x 38.5 mm; case, bezel, and strap lugs set with 43 diamonds; sapphire crystal
Band: white gold bangle set with diamonds
Price: $47,700

Ocean Chrono
Reference number: 400/MCRA44RL.W
Movement: automatic, Frédéric Piguet Caliber 1185 with module HW 2831; ø 32 mm, height 7.2 mm; 49 jewels; 28,800 vph
Functions: hours, minutes (off-center), subsidiary seconds (retrograde); chronograph with retrograde counters
Case: red gold, ø 44 mm; screw-in crown; sapphire crystal; transparent case back
Band: reptile skin, folding clasp
Remarks: mother-of-pearl dial
Price: $31,500
Variations: white gold; anthracite-colored dial

Ocean Diver
Reference number: 410/MCA44WZL.K
Movement: automatic, Girard-Perregaux Caliber 31 C6; 28,800 vph
Functions: hours, minutes, subsidiary seconds; chronograph; date
Case: white gold, ø 44 mm, height 14 mm; screw-in crown; sapphire crystal; water-resistant to 20 atm
Band: rubber, buckle
Price: $35,900
Variations: rose gold; grey dial

Premier Midsize Chrono
Reference number: 200/UCQ32RRC.KD/D3.1/D2.1
Movement: quartz, Frédéric Piguet Caliber 1270; mechanical chronograph dial train
Functions: hours, minutes, subsidiary seconds; chronograph
Case: red gold, ø 32 mm; case, bezel, lugs set with diamonds; sapphire crystal
Band: rose gold/rubber with diamonds, folding clasp
Remarks: chronograph counters set with diamonds
Price: $61,000

Ultimate Duchesse
Reference number: 517/LQPPD/01
Movement: quartz, ETA Caliber E01.701/H4
Functions: hours, minutes
Case: platinum, set with 114 baguette-cut diamonds; sapphire crystal
Band: platinum, set with 255 brilliant-cut and 217 baguette-cut diamonds, folding clasp
Remarks: dial set with 81 brilliant-cut diamonds
Price: upon request

Dino Zei

The man actually behind Panerai's meteoric rise to the forefront of the watch world is not an employee of the Richemont Group. Nor is he Swiss. In fact, Dino Zei, a native Italian with a background in naval engineering, is about as far removed from all that as they come. Zei spent many years in the service of his country's navy. However, in 1972 when Giuseppe Panerai passed away, Zei finally left his governmental employer to manage Guido Panerai e Figlio, a company that was involved in important and delicate work for the navy's special units.

Zei literally shaped the face of the Panerai watch brand, kicking off the massive oversized trend that has since gone down in watch history and thereby shaping the face of modern Florentine watchmaking. Difficulties in Panerai's other division caused the sale of the watch brand and trademark to Cartier in 1997. But it wasn't long before the rest of the company was also sold, at which point Zei retired. That was in 1999. This retirement was not to last, and Zei is back once again at the occupation he loves so much. Teaming with Anonimo's Federico Massacesi, Zei is embarking upon a very special—and familial—collaboration. Anonimo's very Florentine watch style was instantly recognized as such by the former Panerai executive, and it seemed a natural for him to turn to this "anonymous" brand upon feeling the desire to return to the horological arena. He now applies his considerable skills to research and development, as well as in an advisory role.

"Anonimo has a special way of manufacturing," says Zei in his typically understated manner. "I am very proud to be associated with it."

The collaboration has thus far produced a number of collection timepieces, including limited edition sets which Scott Moskovitz, U.S. distributor and part owner of Anonimo, terms "a merging of the two brands' styles." He continues, "These models are true to Panerai form, but with original cases, different from Anonimo's, and certainly pre-Richemont in style."

Like Anonimo, the timepieces in Dino Zei's line are housed in special cases that were milled from one entire piece of metal to avoid changing their molecular structure. The Dino Zei models also employ Kodiak straps, a process under patent at Anonimo giving calfskin the ability to be immersed in any type of water for extended periods of time without damage.

After introducing bronze cases in 2006, the brand is currently presenting Dino Zei's newest member of the family. Collaborating with both Zei and Franco Zavattaro, commander of the combat frogmen force of the Italian Navy between 1968 and 1971 and the San Marco Battalion between 1972 and 1975, this watch was conceived with military operations in mind. It owes its name to the battalion that valiantly defended Venice during World War II, a name that has become synonymous with the Italian Lagunari. Careful studying of the demands of landing forces led to the design of a one-piece steel case structure to guarantee strength and higher resistance, a broader strap connection to reduce wear, easier access to the crown, and a dial legible even under adverse light conditions.

Dino Zei

Argonauta Bronze
Reference number: 11005
Movement: automatic, ETA Caliber 2893-1; ø 26.2 mm, height 4.25 mm; 21 jewels, 28,800 vph; power reserve 40 hours; colimaçon finish on rotor and movement
Functions: hours, minutes, sweep seconds; date; world time
Case: marine bronze UNI5275, ø 46 mm, height 14 mm; screw-locked marine bronze bezel; sapphire crystal; screw-down stainless steel case back with off-center exhibition window; bayonet quick-tightening crown with screw-locked tube; water-resistant to 200 m
Band: Kodiak calfskin leather, buckle
Price: $6,100

Argonauta Steel
Reference number: 11005
Movement: automatic, ETA Caliber 2893-1; ø 26.2 mm, height 4.25 mm; 21 jewels, 28,800 vph; power reserve 40 hours; colimaçon finish on rotor and movement
Functions: hours, minutes, sweep seconds; date; world time
Case: stainless steel, ø 46 mm, height 14 mm; sapphire crystal; screw-down case back with off-center exhibition window; bayonet quick-tightening crown with screw-locked tube; water-resistant to 200 m
Band: Kodiak calfskin leather, buckle
Price: $5,700

Nemo
Reference number: 11001
Movement: automatic, ETA Valjoux Caliber 7750, modified; ø 30.4 mm, height 7.9 mm; 25 jewels; 28,800 vph
Functions: hours, minutes, sweep seconds; date, day; chronograph
Case: stainless steel, ø 46.7 mm, height 15.35 mm; sapphire crystal; screw-down case back with off-center exhibition window; screw-in crown and buttons; water-resistant to 120 m
Band: Kodiak calfskin leather, buckle
Price: $5,450

Glauco Bronze
Reference number: 11006
Movement: automatic, ETA Caliber 2895-2; ø 26.2 mm, height 4.25 mm; 30 jewels, 28,800 vph; power reserve 40 hours; colimaçon finish on rotor and movement
Functions: hours, minutes, subsidiary seconds; date; power reserve display
Case: marine bronze UNI5275, ø 46 mm, height 14 mm; screw-locked marine bronze bezel; sapphire crystal; screw-down stainless steel case back with off-center exhibition window; water-resistant to 200 m
Band: Kodiak calfskin leather, buckle
Price: $5,200

Glauco Steel
Reference number: 11006
Movement: automatic, ETA Caliber 2895-2; ø 26.2 mm, height 4.25 mm; 30 jewels, 28,800 vph; power reserve 40 hours; colimaçon finish on rotor and movement
Functions: hours, minutes, subsidiary seconds; date
Case: stainless steel, ø 46 mm, height 14 mm; screw-locked bezel; sapphire crystal; screw-down case back with off-center exhibition window; bayonet quick-tightening crown with screw-locked tube; water-resistance to 200 m
Band: Kodiak calfskin leather, buckle
Price: $4,800

Nautilo Steel
Reference number: 11007
Movement: automatic, Soprod Caliber 9040 (base ETA 2892-A2); ø 25.6 mm, height 5.10 mm; 24 jewels, 28,800 vph; power reserve 40 hours; colimaçon finish, personalized rotor
Functions: hours, minutes, sweep seconds; date; power reserve indication
Case: stainless steel, 44 x 54 mm, height 14.8 mm; screw-locked bezel; sapphire crystal; screw-down case back with off-center exhibition window; bayonet quick-tightening crown with screw-locked tube; water-resistance to 20 atm
Band: Kodiak calfskin leather, buckle
Price: $5,200

Nautilo Bronze
Reference number: 11007
Movement: automatic, Soprod Caliber 9040 (base ETA 2892-A2); ø 25.6 mm, height 5.10 mm; 24 jewels, 28,800 vph; power reserve 40 hours; colimaçon finish, personalized rotor
Functions: hours, minutes, sweep seconds; date; power reserve indication
Case: marine bronze alloy, 44 x 54 mm, height 14.8 mm; screw-locked bezel; sapphire crystal; screw-down case back with off-center exhibition window; bayonet quick-tightening crown with screw-locked tube; water-resistance to 20 atm
Band: Kodiak calfskin leather, buckle
Price: $5,600

San Marco
Reference number: 12000
Movement: automatic, Soprod Caliber 9055 (base ETA 2892-A2); ø 25.6 mm, height 5.10 mm; 30 jewels, 28,800 vph; power reserve 40 hours; colimaçon finish, personalized rotor
Functions: hours, minutes, sweep seconds; date; second time zone; countdown function
Case: stainless steel, 46.5 x 55.5 mm, height 15.5 mm; screw-locked bezel; sapphire crystal; monocoque case construction with no separate case back; bayonet quick-tightening crown with screw-locked tube; water-resistance to 20 atm
Band: Kodiak calfskin leather, buckle
Price: $6,950

Zenith

Thierry Nataf has been the head of the more than 150-year-old watch *manufacture* Zenith for three years now. At the beginning, Nataf gave himself the task of "leading Zenith back to the zenith." The center of the brand and its entire collection were reconceived, and today tradition, modernity, technology, and emotion all play equal roles.

When "refounding" the *manufacture*, Nataf used its existing, legendary, historical movements as his support pillars: the El Primero and the Elite. "My vision comprises building on the long, successful tradition of the Zenith *manufacture*, but parallel to that, keeping the future clearly in view," the effusive Frenchman explains. "Contrary to many other traditional *manufactures*, we can still dream at Zenith, take risks. We took on a design and technology challenge to create timepieces that do more than just measure the time. We are developing a new, unmistakable Zenith style." Thus, the critically acclaimed Defy line continues to be complemented with new models. Defy Classic received matte rose gold elements that, along with the line's characteristic guilloché pattern, make it even more stunning. The Defy Xtreme models are now also available in rose gold, though it was admittedly pretty hard to top this audacious piece of technology first introduced in 2006.

As on a Formula 1 racing car, the design of the Defy Xtreme was created to complement its functionality. The dial comprises several different layers of carbon fiber, hesalite, and aluminum, while its honeycomb design lends it a resistant texture. The propeller-shaped chronograph hands and second hand guarantee robustness in addition to providing interesting design elements.

The movement of the Defy Xtreme also contains an exclusive alloy: zenithium. Three times as hard as steel, this innovative material combines titanium for robustness, aluminum for lightness, and nobium for flexibility. The company has used balance cocks, chronograph bridges, and escape bridges made of the material for its Open and Chrono movements, which primarily strengthen the escapement, even 1,000 meters under water—which is the depth the Xtreme line can hold up under.

Emotions play a very large part in Nataf's work. This becomes obvious as he explained his decision to create the Defy Xtreme sports watch line: "I thought I should introduce a sports watch. I realize that everything has been done in this sector; certainly you see fantastic watches by my competitors all over. So I said, if I do sport, I would reinvent it in a way that is very, very new. It was like I was defying myself to find the best name for it, as well as the best design, so I called it Defy. My work is a mix of tradition and modernity, but this time I came up with the idea to go even faster, stronger, higher. Defy is a way of life, a way of being, a style."

Nataf seems to be able to do it all: at Zenith he is creative director, head of development, and president of sales all in one. His creativity mirrors his passion for the brand, presenting an excellent example for his 250 employees in the Le Locle factory.

Grande ChronoMaster XXT Tourbillon
Reference number: 18.1260.4005/01.C505
Movement: automatic, Zenith Caliber 4005 El Primero; ø 35 mm, height 7.55 mm; 35 jewels; 36,000 vph; one-minute tourbillon; contra-rotating date ring between bridge and cage
Functions: hours, minutes; chronograph; date
Case: rose gold, ø 45 mm, height 14.1 mm; sapphire crystal; transparent case back
Band: reptile skin, triple folding clasp
Price: $130,000
Variations: yellow or white gold; platinum

ChronoMaster Open Retrograde T
Reference number: 40.0240.4023/01.C495
Movement: automatic, Zenith Caliber 4023 El Primero; ø 30 mm, height 7.75 mm; 39 jewels; 36,000 vph; movement partially skeletonized underneath cutaway in dial
Functions: hours, minutes, subsidiary seconds; chronograph; date; power reserve display
Case: platinum, ø 40 mm, height 14.5 mm; sapphire crystal; transparent case back
Band: reptile skin, triple folding clasp
Price: $39,000
Variations: XXT version in 45 mm case size; rose gold

ChronoMaster Open XXT
Reference number: 03.1260.4010/01.C505
Movement: automatic, Zenith Caliber 4010 El Primero; ø 30 mm, height 7.75 mm; 39 jewels; 36,000 vph; movement partially skeletonized underneath cutaway in dial
Functions: hours, minutes, subsidiary seconds; chronograph; power reserve display
Case: stainless steel, ø 45 mm, height 14.1 mm; sapphire crystal; transparent case back
Band: reptile skin, triple folding clasp
Price: $8,300
Variations: steel bracelet or rubber strap; 40 mm case size

Grande ChronoMaster Grande Date XXT
Reference number: 03.1260.4010/01.C505
Movement: automatic, Zenith Caliber 4010 El Primero; ø 30 mm, height 7.65 mm; 31 jewels; 36,000 vph
Functions: hours, minutes, subsidiary seconds; chronograph; large date
Case: stainless steel, ø 45 mm, height 14.1 mm; sapphire crystal; transparent case back
Band: reptile skin, triple folding clasp
Price: $8,000
Variations: rose gold; 40 mm case size

Port Royal Open Concept
Reference number: 95.0550.4021/77.C550
Movement: automatic, Zenith Caliber 4021 C El Primero; ø 30 mm, height 7.75 mm; 39 jewels; 36,000 vph; movement partially skeletonized underneath cutaway in dial; transparent dial crafted in TR90
Functions: hours, minutes, subsidiary seconds; chronograph; power reserve display
Case: titanium, 36 x 51 mm, height 13 mm; sapphire crystal; transparent case back
Band: carbon fiber, triple folding clasp
Price: $15,600
Variations: in case size 34 x 48 mm

Port Royal Open
Reference number: 03.0550.4021/01.R512
Movement: automatic, Zenith Caliber 4021 El Primero; ø 30 mm, height 7.75 mm; 39 jewels; 36,000 vph; movement partially skeletonized underneath cutaway in dial
Functions: hours, minutes, subsidiary seconds; chronograph; power reserve display
Case: stainless steel, 36 x 51 mm, height 13 mm; sapphire crystal; transparent case back
Band: rubber, triple folding clasp
Price: $8,300
Variations: in case size 34 x 48 mm; leather strap

Grande Class Tourbillon
Reference number: 65.0520.4035/21.C492
Movement: automatic, Zenith Caliber 4035 El Primero; ø 37.5 mm, height 7.55 mm; 35 jewels; 36,000 vph; one-minute tourbillon
Functions: hours, minutes; chronograph; date
Case: white gold, ø 45 mm, height 14.8 mm; sapphire crystal; transparent case back; water-resistant to 5 atm
Band: reptile skin, triple folding clasp
Remarks: limited edition of 25 pieces
Price: $140,000
Variations: limited edition of 25 pieces in rose gold

Grande Class Traveller Open Multicity
Reference number: 18.0520.4037/71.C491
Movement: automatic, Zenith Caliber 4037 El Primero; ø 30.5 mm, height 9.05 mm; 43 jewels; 36,000 vph; movement partially skeletonized underneath cutaway in dial
Functions: hours, minutes, subsidiary seconds; chronograph; large date; 24-hour display (world time); power reserve display
Case: rose gold, ø 46 mm, height 14.8 mm; ring under bezel with reference city names of world time zones, settable via crown; sapphire crystal; transparent case back
Band: reptile skin, triple folding clasp
Remarks: limited edition of 25 pieces
Price: $30,000
Variations: stainless steel

Zenith

Grande Class Rattrapante Grande Date
Reference number: 65.0520.4026/21.C492
Movement: automatic, Zenith Caliber 4026 El Primero; ø 30 mm, height 9.35 mm; 32 jewels; 36,000 vph; officially certified C.O.S.C. chronometer
Functions: hours, minutes, subsidiary seconds; split-seconds chronograph; large date
Case: white gold, ø 44 mm, height 14.8 mm; sapphire crystal; transparent case back
Band: reptile skin, triple folding clasp
Price: $37,700

Class Open
Reference number: 03.0520.4021/01.C492
Movement: automatic, Zenith Caliber 4021H El Primero; ø 30 mm, height 7.75 mm; 39 jewels; 36,000 vph; movement partially skeletonized underneath dial cutaway
Functions: hours, minutes, subsidiary seconds; chronograph; power reserve display
Case: stainless steel, ø 44 mm, height 14.5 mm; sapphire crystal; transparent case back
Band: reptile skin, triple folding clasp
Price: $8,300
Variations: rose gold; in 40 mm case size

Class Automatique RDM
Reference number: 03.1125.685/01.C490
Movement: automatic, Zenith Caliber 685 Elite; ø 25.6 mm, height 4.48 mm; 38 jewels; 28,800 vph
Functions: hours, minutes, subsidiary seconds; date; power reserve display
Case: stainless steel, ø 37 mm, height 10 mm; sapphire crystal; transparent case back
Band: reptile skin, triple folding clasp
Price: $5,000
Variations: yellow gold; rose or white gold

Defy Classic Open
Reference number: 86.0526.4021/01.M527
Movement: automatic, Zenith Caliber 4021 SC El Primero; ø 30 mm, height 7.75 mm; 39 jewels; 36,000 vph; movement partially skeletonized underneath dial cutaway; rotor with tungsten carbide oscillating weight
Functions: hours, minutes, subsidiary seconds; chronograph; power reserve display
Case: stainless steel, ø 46.5 mm, height 17.1 mm; unidirectionally rotating rose gold bezel with 60-minute divisions; sapphire crystal; transparent case back; screw-in crown and buttons; water-resistant to 30 atm
Band: steel/rose gold, triple folding clasp
Price: $20,500
Variations: rubber or leather strap; 43 mm case

Defy Classic Chrono Aero T
Reference number: 86.0516.4000/21.R642
Movement: automatic, Zenith Caliber 4000 SC El Primero; ø 30 mm, height 6.5 mm; 31 jewels; 36,000 vph; rotor with tungsten carbide oscillating weight
Functions: hours, minutes, subsidiary seconds; chronograph; date
Case: stainless steel, ø 43 mm, height 15.1 mm; unidirectionally rotating rose gold bezel with 60-minute divisions; sapphire crystal; transparent case back; screw-in crown and buttons; water-resistant to 30 atm
Band: rubber, buckle
Price: $11,900
Variations: leather strap; stainless steel/rose gold bracelet; in 46.5 mm case; stainless steel

Defy Classic Open Steel
Reference number: 03.0516.4021/01.R642
Movement: automatic, Zenith Caliber 4021 SC El Primero; ø 30 mm, height 7.75 mm; 39 jewels; 36,000 vph; movement partially skeletonized underneath dial cutaway; rotor with tungsten carbide oscillating weight
Functions: hours, minutes, subsidiary seconds; chronograph; power reserve display
Case: stainless steel, ø 43 mm, height 15.1 mm; unidirectionally rotating bezel with 60-minute divisions; sapphire crystal; transparent case back; screw-in crown and buttons; water-resistant to 30 atm
Band: rubber, buckle
Price: $10,200
Variations: leather strap; 46.5 mm case

Defy Classic Chrono Aero
Reference number: 03.0526.4000/21.M526
Movement: automatic, Zenith Caliber 4000 SC El Primero; ø 30 mm, height 6.5 mm; 31 jewels; 36,000 vph; bridges and cocks made of shock-absorbing special alloy
Functions: hours, minutes, subsidiary seconds; chronograph; date
Case: stainless steel, ø 46.5 mm, height 17.1 mm; unidirectionally rotating bezel with 60-minute divisions; sapphire crystal; transparent case back; water-resistant to 30 atm
Band: stainless steel, triple folding clasp
Price: $8,900
Variations: leather or rubber strap; silver-colored dial

Defy Classic Power Reserve
Reference number: 03.516.685/01.R666
Movement: automatic, Zenith Caliber 685 SC Elite; ø 25.6 mm, height 4.48 mm; 38 jewels; 28,800 vph; balance cock, automatic and gear train bridge crafted in shock-absorbing special alloy (Zenithium)
Functions: hours, minutes, subsidiary seconds; date; power reserve display
Case: stainless steel, ø 43 mm, height 15.1 mm; unidirectionally rotating bezel with 60-minute divisions; sapphire crystal; transparent case back; water-resistant to 30 atm
Band: stainless steel, triple folding clasp
Price: $6,300
Variations: black dial; stainless steel and leather bracelet

Zenith

Defy Xtreme Open
Reference number: 96.0528.4021/21.R642
Movement: automatic, Zenith Caliber 4021 SX El Primero; ø 30 mm, height 7.75 mm; 39 jewels; 36,000 vph; chronograph bridge and balance cock in shock-absorbing alloy (Zenithium)
Functions: hours, minutes, subsidiary seconds; chronograph; power reserve display
Case: titanium, ø 46.5 mm, height 21.1 mm; unidirectionally rotating bezel with 60-minute divisions and rose gold applied elements; sapphire crystal; screw-in crown with protective bridge; water-resistant to 100 atm
Band: rubber, buckle
Price: $29,700
Variations: leather strap; titanium/rose gold link bracelet; stainless steel

Defy Xtreme Chronograph
Reference number: 96.0528.4000/21.M528
Movement: automatic, Zenith Caliber 4000 SX El Primero; ø 30 mm, height 6.5 mm; 31 jewels; 36,600 vph; chronograph bridge and balance cock in shock-absorbing alloy (Zenithium)
Functions: hours, minutes, subsidiary seconds; chronograph; date
Case: titanium, ø 46.5 mm, height 21.1 mm; unidirectionally rotating bezel with 60-minute divisions and applied rose gold elements; sapphire crystal; screw-in crown with protective bridge; water-resistant to 100 atm
Band: titanium/rose gold, triple folding clasp
Remarks: dial partially skeletonized, carbon fiber appliqués
Price: $25,900

Defy Xtreme Open
Reference number: 96.0525.4021/21.M525
Movement: automatic, Zenith Caliber 4021 SX El Primero; ø 30 mm, height 7.75 mm; 39 jewels; 36,000 vph; chronograph bridge and balance cock in shock-absorbing alloy (Zenithium)
Functions: hours, minutes, subsidiary seconds; chronograph; power reserve display
Case: titanium, ø 46.5 mm, height 21.1 mm; unidirectionally rotating bezel with 60-minute divisions and applied elements; sapphire crystal; screw-in crown with protective bridge; water-resistant to 100 atm
Band: stainless steel, Kevlar, and carbon fiber; triple folding clasp
Remarks: Hesalite and carbon fiber dial appliqués
Price: $22,300

Defy Xtreme Chronograph
Reference number: 96.0525.4000/21.M525
Movement: automatic, Zenith Caliber 4000 SX El Primero; ø 30 mm, height 6.5 mm; 31 jewels; 36,600 vph; chronograph bridge and balance cock in shock-absorbing alloy (Zenithium)
Functions: hours, minutes, subsidiary seconds; chronograph; date
Case: titanium, ø 46.5 mm, height 21.1 mm; unidirectionally rotating bezel with 60-minute divisions; sapphire crystal; screw-in crown with protective bridge; water-resistant to 100 atm
Band: stainless steel, Kevlar, and carbon fiber; triple folding clasp
Remarks: dial with carbon fiber appliqués
Price: $17,100
Variations: rubber or leather strap

Star Open Heart
Reference number: 18.1230.4021/01.C588
Movement: automatic, Zenith Caliber 4021 El Primero; ø 30 mm, height 7.75 mm; 39 jewels; 36,000 vph; movement partially skeletonized underneath heart-shaped dial cutaway
Functions: hours, minutes, subsidiary seconds; chronograph; power reserve display
Case: rose gold, ø 37.5 mm, height 14 mm; sapphire crystal; transparent case back
Band: satin, triple folding clasp
Price: $13,600
Variations: with diamond-set bezel; yellow gold; stainless steel

Star Open Sea
Reference number: 03.1233.4021/83.C598
Movement: automatic, Zenith Caliber 4021 El Primero; ø 30 mm, height 7.75 mm; 39 jewels; 36,000 vph; movement partially skeletonized underneath star-shaped dial cutaway
Functions: hours, minutes, subsidiary seconds (on Sea Star); chronograph; power reserve display
Case: stainless steel, ø 37.5 mm, height 14 mm; sapphire crystal; transparent case back; water-resistant to 10 atm
Band: stingray skin, triple folding clasp
Remarks: mother-of-pearl dial
Price: $7,700
Variations: yellow or rose gold

Star El Primero
Reference number: 22.1230.4002./21.C528
Movement: automatic, Zenith Caliber 4002 El Primero; ø 30 mm, height 6.5 mm; 31 jewels; 36,000 vph; officially certified C.O.S.C. chronometer
Functions: hours, minutes, subsidiary seconds; chronograph; date
Case: stainless steel, ø 37.5 mm, height 14 mm; bezel set with brilliant-cut diamonds; sapphire crystal; transparent case back
Band: stingray skin, buckle
Price: $7,300
Variations: without diamonds; yellow gold; stainless steel

Star El Primero
Reference number: 03.1230.4002./31.C577
Movement: automatic, Zenith Caliber 4002 El Primero; ø 30 mm, height 6.5 mm; 31 jewels; 36,000 vph; officially certified C.O.S.C. chronometer
Functions: hours, minutes, subsidiary seconds; chronograph; date
Case: stainless steel, ø 37.5 mm, height 14 mm; bezel set with brilliant-cut diamonds; sapphire crystal; transparent case back
Band: reptile skin, triple folding clasp
Price: $5,600
Variations: with diamonds; with colorful dials and matching rubber and leather straps

Zenith

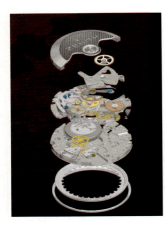

El Primero 4000 SC
Mechanical with automatic winding, power reserve more than 50 hours, ball-bearing rotor with tungsten carbide oscillating weight; column-wheel control of chronograph functions
Functions: hours, minutes, subsidiary seconds; chronograph; date
Diameter: 30 mm (13''')
Height: 6.5 mm
Jewels: 31
Balance: glucydur
Frequency: 36,000 vph
Balance spring: self-compensating flat hairspring with fine adjustment
Shock protection: Kif

El Primero 4001
Base caliber: El Primero 410
Mechanical with automatic winding, power reserve more than 50 hours, ball-bearing rotor; column-wheel control of chronograph functions
Functions: hours, minutes, subsidiary seconds; date, weekday, month, moon phase; chronograph with flyback function
Diameter: 30 mm (13'''); **Height:** 7.55 mm
Jewels: 31
Balance: glucydur
Frequency: 36,000 vph
Balance spring: self-compensating flat hairspring with fine adjustment
Shock protection: Kif
Remarks: 355 components; quick-set date and moon phase

El Primero 4002
Base caliber: El Primero 400
Mechanical with automatic winding, power reserve more than 50 hours, ball-bearing rotor; column-wheel control of chronograph functions
Functions: hours, minutes, subsidiary seconds; date; chronograph
Diameter: 30 mm (13''')
Height: 6.5 mm
Jewels: 31
Balance: glucydur
Frequency: 36,000 vph
Balance spring: self-compensating flat hairspring with fine adjustment
Shock protection: Kif
Remarks: 266 components; quick-set date

El Primero 4003
Base caliber: El Primero 410
Mechanical with automatic winding, power reserve more than 50 hours, ball-bearing rotor; column-wheel control of chronograph functions
Functions: hours, minutes, subsidiary seconds; perpetual calendar (date, weekday, month, moon phase); chronograph with flyback function
Diameter: 30 mm (13'''); **Height:** 8.1 mm
Jewels: 31
Balance: glucydur
Frequency: 36,000 vph
Balance spring: self-compensating flat hairspring with fine adjustment
Shock protection: Kif
Remarks: moon phase with disk display; quick-set date and moon phase

El Primero 4021 Open
Mechanical with automatic winding, power reserve more than 50 hours; ball-bearing rotor; column-wheel control of chronograph functions
Functions: hours, minutes, subsidiary seconds; chronograph; power reserve display
Diameter: 30 mm (13''')
Height: 6.5 mm
Jewels: 39
Balance: glucydur
Frequency: 36,000 vph
Balance spring: self-compensating flat hairspring with fine adjustment
Shock protection: Kif
Remarks: base plate in the area of the escapement is open (image is dial side) and the flat parts are skeletonized

El Primero 4010
Mechanical with automatic winding, power reserve more than 50 hours; ball-bearing rotor; column-wheel control of chronograph functions
Functions: hours, minutes, subsidiary seconds; chronograph; large date
Diameter: 30 mm (13''')
Height: 7.65 mm
Jewels: 31
Balance: glucydur
Frequency: 36,000 vph
Balance spring: self-compensating flat hairspring with fine adjustment
Shock protection: Kif

Caliber 4021 SX Defy
The El Primero version found in the extreme chronograph Defy contains special components, such as the chronograph bridge, balance cock, and support bridges, crafted in a new light metal alloy called Zenithium. This new alloy, whose function is to protect the sensitive components of the winding mechanism and regulating organ against strong blows, possesses shock-absorbing characteristics.

El Primero 4026
Mechanical with automatic winding, power reserve more than 50 hours; ball-bearing rotor; column-wheel control of chronograph functions; officially certified C.O.S.C. chronometer
Functions: hours, minutes, subsidiary seconds; split-seconds chronograph; large date
Diameter: 30 mm (13''')
Height: 9.35 mm
Jewels: 32
Balance: glucydur
Frequency: 36,000 vph
Balance spring: self-compensating flat hairspring with fine adjustment
Shock protection: Kif

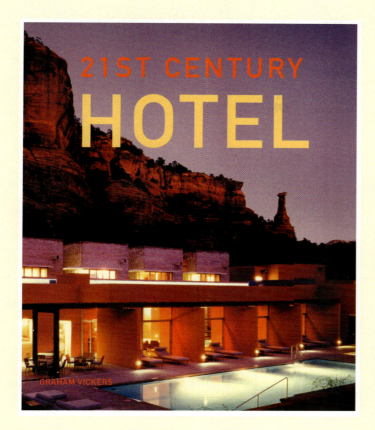

21st Century Hotel

Newly built hotels are being admired throughout the world by travelers and architects, and this strikingly illustrated survey features the best new designs, from the lavishly appointed Ritz-Carlton Miami to a Quebec hotel constructed entirely of snow and ice.

By Graham Vickers
230 illustrations, 210 in full color
240 pages · 9¼ x 11¼ in. · Cloth
ISBN: 978-0-7892-0859-0
$65.00

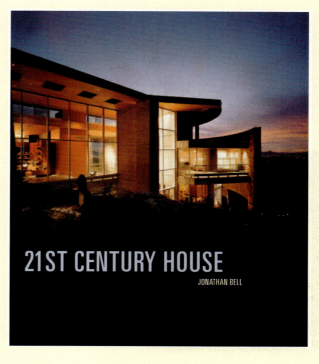

21st Century House

"Outstanding... offers up a focus on the home as a symbol of change and innovation."
—*Library Bookwatch*

This elegant illustrated survey profiles the most architecturally distinguished new houses from around the globe. The diversity of the fifty-five houses featured in this photo-packed volume, by architects like Alvaro Siza and Tony Fretton, demonstrates that the single-family home continues to play a pivotal role as a means of architectural expression and experimentation in the new millennium.

By Jonathan Bell
300 color photos and 150 black-and-white architectural drawings
256 pages · 7½ x 8½ · Hardcover
ISBN: 978-0-7892-0885-9
$29.95

Published by ABBEVILLE PRESS
137 Varick Street, New York, NY 10013
1-800-Artbook (in U.S. only)
Also available wherever fine books are sold
Visit us at www.abbeville.com

ETA

This Swatch Group movement manufacturer produces more than five million movements a year. And after the withdrawal of Richemont's Jaeger-LeCoultre as well as Swatch Group sisters Nouvelle Lémania and Frédéric Piguet from the business of selling movements on the free market, most watch brands can hardly help but beat down the door of this full service manufacturer. ETA offers a broad spectrum of automatic movements in various dimensions with different functions, chronograph movements in varying configurations, as well as pocket watch classics (Calibers 6497 and 98) and manually wound calibers of days gone by (Calibers 1727 and 7001)—this company offers everything that a manufacturer's heart could desire. That's not to mention the sheer variety of quartz technology: from inexpensive three-hand mechanisms to highly complicated multifunctional movements and futuristic Etaquartz featuring autonomous energy creation using a rotor and generator. The almost stereotypical accusation of ETA being "mass goods," however, might just sound like praise in the ears of new ETA director Thomas Meier: he knows only too well how difficult it is to consistently manufacture high-quality filigreed micromechanical technology. This is certainly one of the reasons why there are no (longer) any other movement factories today in Europe that can compete with ETA, or that would want to. Since the success of Swatch—a pure ETA product—millions of Swiss francs have been invested in new development and manufacturing technologies. ETA today owns more than twenty production locales in Switzerland, France, Germany, Malaysia, and Thailand.

ETA, which was created from an amalgamation of several independent *ébauche* manufacturers called Ebauches SA, still delivers some of its movements as half-done "kits" to be re-assembled, rebuilt, and/or decorated. These go to specialized workshops such as Soprod, Sellita, La Joux-Perret, and Dubois Dépraz as Swiss watch tradition has dictated for decades. This practice is supposed to come to an end soon: the Swatch Group's concern management is no longer interested in leaving the lion's share of movement upscaling to others, but will only deliver complete movements in the future, ready for encasing, with personalization and individualization already done as the client wishes.

Caliber 2660
Mechanical with manual winding, power reserve 42 hours
Functions: hours, minutes, sweep seconds
Diameter: 17.2 mm (7 3/4''')
Height: 3.5 mm
Jewels: 17
Frequency: 28,800 vph
Fine adjustment system: ETACHRON

Caliber 1727
Mechanical with manual winding, power reserve 50 hours
Functions: hours, minutes, subsidiary seconds at 6 o'clock
Diameter: 19.4 mm (8 3/4''')
Height: 3.5 mm
Jewels: 19
Frequency: 21,600 vph
Fine adjustment system: ETACHRON
Remark: Movement based on prototype AS 1727

Caliber 7001
Mechanical with manual winding, ultraflat, power reserve 42 hours
Functions: hours, minutes, subsidiary seconds at 6 o'clock
Diameter: 23.3 mm (10 1/2''')
Height: 2.5 mm
Jewels: 17
Frequency: 21,600 vph
Fine adjustment system: ETACHRON

Caliber 2801-2
Mechanical with manual winding, power reserve 42 hours
Functions: hours, minutes, sweep seconds
Diameter: 25.6 mm (11 1/2''')
Height: 3.35 mm
Jewels: 17
Frequency: 28,800 vph
Fine adjustment system: ETACHRON
Related caliber: 2804-2
(with date window and quick-set)

Caliber 2671
Mechanical with automatic winding, ball-bearing rotor, stop-seconds, power reserve 38 hours
Functions: hours, minutes, sweep seconds; date window with quick-set at 3 o'clock
Diameter: 17.2 mm (7 3/4''')
Height: 4.8 mm
Jewels: 25
Frequency: 28,800 vph
Fine adjustment system: ETACHRON with index
Related calibers: 2678 (additional day window at 3 o'clock, height 5.35 mm)

Caliber 2681
Mechanical with automatic winding, ball-bearing rotor, stop-seconds, power reserve 38 hours
Functions: hours, minutes, sweep seconds; day/date window with quick-set at 3 o'clock
Diameter: 19.4 mm (8 3/4''')
Height: 4.8 mm
Jewels: 25
Frequency: 28,800 vph
Fine adjustment system: ETACHRON with index
Related calibers: 2685
(sweep date hand and moon phase at 6 o'clock)

ETA

Caliber 2000
Mechanical with automatic winding, ball-bearing rotor, stop-seconds, power reserve 40 hours
Functions: hours, minutes, sweep seconds; date window with quick-set at 3 o'clock
Diameter: 19.4 mm (8 3/4''')
Height: 3.6 mm
Jewels: 20
Frequency: 28,800 vph
Fine adjustment system: ETACHRON with index

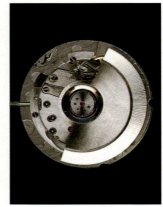

Caliber 2004
Mechanical with automatic winding, ball-bearing rotor, stop-seconds, power reserve 40 hours
Functions: hours, minutes, sweep seconds; date window with quick-set at 3 o'clock
Diameter: 23.3 mm (10 1/2''')
Height: 3.6 mm
Jewels: 20
Frequency: 28,800 vph
Fine adjustment system: ETACHRON with index

Caliber 2824-2
Mechanical with automatic winding, ball-bearing rotor, stop-seconds, power reserve 38 hours
Functions: hours, minutes, sweep seconds; date window with quick-set at 3 o'clock
Diameter: 25.6 mm (11 1/2''')
Height: 4.6 mm
Jewels: 25
Frequency: 28,800 vph
Fine adjustment system: ETACHRON with index
Related Calibers: 2836-2 (additional day window at 3 o'clock, height 5.05 mm)

Caliber 2834-2
Mechanical with automatic winding, ball-bearing rotor, stop-seconds, power reserve 38 hours
Functions: hours, minutes, sweep seconds; date window with quick-set at 3 o'clock and day display with quick-set at 12 o'clock
Diameter: 29 mm (13''')
Height: 5.05 mm
Jewels: 25
Frequency: 28,800 vph
Fine adjustment system: ETACHRON with index

Caliber 2891-A9
Mechanical with automatic winding (base caliber 2892-A2), ball-bearing rotor, stop-seconds, power reserve 42 hours
Functions: hours, minutes, sweep seconds; perpetual calendar (date, day, month hands), moon phase disk, leap year indication
Diameter: 25.6 mm (11 1/2 ''')
Height: 5.2 mm
Jewels: 21
Frequency: 28,800 vph
Fine adjustment system: ETACHRON with index
Related Calibers: 2890-A9 (without second hand and stop-seconds)

Caliber 2892-A2
Mechanical with automatic winding, ball-bearing rotor, stop-seconds, power reserve 42 hours
Functions: hours, minutes, sweep seconds; date window with quick-set at 3 o'clock
Diameter: 25.6 mm (11 1/2''')
Height: 3.6 mm
Jewels: 21
Frequency: 28,800 vph
Fine adjustment system: ETACHRON with index

Caliber 2893-1
Mechanical with automatic winding, ball-bearing rotor, stop-seconds, power reserve 42 hours
Functions: hours, minutes, sweep seconds; date window with quick-set at 3 o'clock; world time with central disk
Diameter: 25.6 mm (11 1/2''')
Height: 4.1 mm
Jewels: 21
Frequency: 28,800 vph
Fine adjustment system: ETACHRON with index
Related Calibers: 2893-2 (24-hour hand/second time zone instead of world time disk); 2893-3 (only world time disk without date window)

Caliber 2895-1
Mechanical with automatic winding, ball-bearing rotor, stop-seconds, power reserve 42 hours
Functions: hours, minutes, subsidiary seconds at 6 o'clock; date window with quick-set at 3 o'clock
Diameter: 25.6 mm (11 1/2''')
Height: 4.35 mm
Jewels: 30
Frequency: 28,800 vph
Fine adjustment system: ETACHRON with index

Caliber 2896
Mechanical with automatic winding, ball-bearing rotor, stop-seconds, power reserve 42 hours
Functions: hours, minutes, sweep seconds; large date window (double digits) at 3 o'clock
Diameter: 25.6 mm (11 1/2''')
Height: 4.85 mm
Jewels: 22
Frequency: 28,800 vph
Fine adjustment system: ETACHRON with index

Caliber 2897
Mechanical with automatic winding, ball-bearing rotor, stop-seconds, power reserve 42 hours
Functions: hours, minutes, sweep seconds; power reserve display at 7 o'clock
Diameter: 25.6 mm (11 1/2''')
Height: 4.85 mm
Jewels: 21
Frequency: 28,800 vph
Fine adjustment system: ETACHRON with index

Caliber 2894-2
Mechanical with automatic winding, ball-bearing rotor, stop-seconds, power reserve 42 hours
Functions: hours, minutes, subsidiary seconds at 3 o'clock; chronograph (30-minute counter at 9 o'clock, 12-hour counter at 6 o'clock, sweep stop second hand); date window with quick-set at 4 o'clock
Diameter: 28.6 mm (12 1/2''')
Height: 6.1 mm
Jewels: 37
Frequency: 28,800 vph
Fine adjustment system: ETACHRON with index
Remarks: Module construction

Caliber 2094
Mechanical with automatic winding, ball-bearing rotor, stop-seconds, power reserve 40 hours
Functions: hours, minutes, subsidiary seconds at 9 o'clock; chronograph (30-minute counter at 3 o'clock, 12-hour counter at 6 o'clock, sweep stop second hand); date window with quick-set at 3 o'clock
Diameter: 23.3 mm (10 1/2''')
Height: 5.5 mm
Jewels: 33
Frequency: 28,800 vph
Fine adjustment system: ETACHRON with index

ETA

Caliber 7750
Mechanical with automatic winding, ball-bearing rotor, stop-seconds, power reserve 42 hours
Functions: hours, minutes, subsidiary seconds at 9 o'clock; chronograph (30-minute counter at 12 o'clock, 12-hour counter at 6 o'clock, sweep stop second hand); day/date window with quick-set at 3 o'clock
Diameter: 30 mm (13 1/4'''); **Height:** 7.9 mm
Jewels: 25
Frequency: 28,800 vph
Fine adjustment system: ETACHRON with index
Related calibers: 7751 (with sweep date hand, windows for day and month below the 12, moon phase at 6 o'clock, 24-hour hand at 9 o'clock); 7765 and 7760 (manually wound versions)

Caliber 7751 (dial side)
Based on chronograph Caliber 7750, Caliber 7751 differs in having 24-hour hand, moon phase indication, sweep date hand, and windows for day and month placed prominently below the 12. All calendar functions, including moon phase, can be quick-set.

Caliber 7754
Mechanical with automatic winding, ball-bearing rotor, stop-seconds, power reserve 42 hours
Functions: hours, minutes, subsidiary seconds at 9 o'clock; chronograph (30-minute counter at 12 o'clock, 12-hour counter at 6 o'clock, sweep stop second hand); date window with quick-set at 3 o'clock; settable sweep 24-hour hand (second time zone)
Diameter: 30 mm (13 1/4''')
Height: 7.9 mm
Jewels: 25
Frequency: 28,800 vph
Fine adjustment system: ETACHRON with index

Caliber A07.111
Mechanical with automatic winding, ball-bearing rotor, stop-seconds, power reserve 42 hours
Functions: hours, minutes, subsidiary seconds at 9 o'clock; chronograph (30-minute counter at 12 o'clock, 12-hour counter at 6 o'clock, sweep stop second hand); date window with quick-set at 3 o'clock
Diameter: 36.6 mm (16 3/4''')
Height: 7.9 mm
Jewels: 24
Frequency: 28,800 vph
Fine adjustment system: ETACHRON with index
Remarks: Based on Caliber 7750, this movement is also available in a manually wound version

Hanhart
PIONEER'S TIMING
SINCE 1882

Hanhart watches can look back on a proud tradition reaching twelve decades through history.

Hanhart's new Attaché is reminiscent of the great classic style of the 1960s. A railroad track minute scale and foille-shaped hands speak the language of the era, while power reserve and large date displays respond to the demands of watch connoisseurs. The Attaché aims to please classic chronograph aficionados and watch lovers by delivering both modern design interpretation and state of the art technology.

For further information, please contact your nearest Hanhart authorized retailer or the address below.

Eric Armin, Inc.
Fine Watch Division
118 Bauer Drive - P.O.Box 7046
Oakland, NJ 07436-7046
Phone: 800-272-0272
www.hanhartusa.com

EAI *Fine Watch Division*

Caliber 7765
Mechanical with manual winding, stop-seconds, power reserve 42 hours
Functions: hours, minutes, subsidiary seconds at 9 o'clock; chronograph (30-minute counter at 12 o'clock, sweep stop second hand); date window with quick-set at 3 o'clock
Diameter: 30 mm (13 1/4''')
Height: 6.35 mm
Jewels: 17
Frequency: 28,800 vph
Fine adjustment system: ETACHRON with index
Related calibers: 7760 (with additional 12-hour counter at 6 o'clock and day window at 3 o'clock; height 7 mm); 7750 and 7751

Caliber 6497/6498
Only a few watch fans know that ETA still manufactures two pure pocket watch movements. Caliber 6497 and 6498 are available in two qualities: as 6497-1 and 6498-1 (rather sober, undecorated version); and 6497-2 and 6498-2 (with off-center striped decoration on bridges and cocks as well as beveled and striped crown and ratchet wheels). The photograph shows Lépine Caliber 6497-2.
Functions: hours, minutes, subsidiary seconds
Diameter: 36.6 mm (16 1/2 ''')
Height: 4.5 mm
Jewels: 17
Frequency: 21,600 vph
Fine adjustment system: ETACHRON with index

Addresses

Alpina
Bellport Time Group, LLC
112 South Country Road, Suite 101
Bellport, NY 11713
Tel.: 631-776-1135
Fax: 631-776-1136
www.alpina-watches.com

Angular Momentum USA
Münstergasse 20
3011 Bern, Switzerland
Tel: 011-41-31-311 83 00
Fax: 011-41-31-311 22 00
www.angularmomentum.com

Anonimo Firenze USA
4501 Beacon Drive
Nashville, TN 37215
Tel.: 615-665-8331
Fax: 615-665-8347
anonimofirenzeus@aol.com
www.anonimousa.com

Arnold & Sons
British Masters, LLC
444 Madison Avenue, Suite 601
New York, NY 10022
Tel.: 212-688-4500
Fax: 212-888-5025
www.thebritishmasters.biz

Askania
Détente Distribution Group
48 Main Street, 2nd Floor
Colchester, CT 06415
Tel.: 1-877-4VOSTOK
info@detentewatches.com
www.detentewatches.com

Audemars Piguet (North America) Inc.
40 East 57th Street
New York, NY 10022
Tel.: 212-758-8400
Fax: 212-758-8538
www.audemarspiguet.com

Aviator
Détente Distribution Group
48 Main Street, 2nd Floor
Colchester, CT 06415
Tel.: 1-877-4VOSTOK
info@detentewatches.com
www.detentewatches.com

Azimuth
Coast Time
800 S. Pacific Coast Highway, Suite 8-446
Redondo Beach, CA 90277
Tel.: 888-609-1010
Fax: 801-459-6438
www.azimuthwatchusa.com

Backes & Strauss
Montres Franck Muller USA, Inc.
207 W. 25th Street, 8th Floor
New York, NY 10001
Tel.: 212-463-8898
Fax: 212-463-7082
www.backesandstrauss.com

Ball Watch Company, Inc.
1131 4th Street North
St. Petersburg, FL 33701
Tel.: 800-922-HESS
www.ballwatch.com

Baume & Mercier
Richemont North America
Fifth Avenue and 52nd Street
New York, NY 10022
Tel.: 212-753-0111
Fax: 212-753-7250
www.baume-et-mercier.com

Bell & Ross, Inc.
1688 Meridian Ave., Suite 504
Miami Beach, FL 33139
Tel.: 305-674-9464
Fax: 305-672-3840
information@bellrossusa.com
www.bellross.com

Ernst Benz USA
555 South Old Woodward Avenue
Birmingham, MI 48009
Tel.: 248-203-2323
Fax: 248-203-6633
info@ernstbenz.com
www.ernstbenz.com

Jochen Benzinger
WatchBuys
Tel.: 888-333-4895
info@watchbuys.com
www.watchbuys.com

Blancpain
The Swatch Group (U.S.), Inc.
1200 Harbor Boulevard
Weehawken, NJ 07087
Tel.: 201-271-1400
Fax: 201-271-4633
www.blancpain.com

blu – source du temps SA
1, avenue de Longueville
2013 Colombier, Switzerland
Tel.: 011-41-32-843 41 26
Fax: 011-41-32-843 41 12
info@blu.ch
www.blu.ch

Bozeman Watch Company
11 East Main Street
Bozeman, MT 59715
Tel.: 406-585-0062
Fax: 406-585-0064
www.bozemanwatch.com

Rainer Brand
Friedensstrasse 9
63872 Heimbuchenthal, Germany
Tel. 011-49-6092–5372
Fax. 011-49-6092–6903
info@rainerbrand.de
www.rainerbrand.com

Martin Braun USA
6602 Wolf Creek Pass
Austin, TX 78749
Tel.: 512-499-0123
Fax: 512-499-8112
info@time-central.com
www.martinbraunusa.com

Breguet
The Swatch Group (U.S.), Inc.
1200 Harbor Boulevard
Weehawken, NJ 07087
Tel.: 201-271-1400
Fax: 201-271-4633
www.breguet.com

Breitling U.S.A. Inc.
206 Danbury Road
Stamford, CT 06897
Tel.: 800-641-7343
Fax: 203-327-2537
www.breitling.com

Brior
WatchBuys
Tel.: 888-333-4895
info@watchbuys.com
www.watchbuys.com

B.R.M. Manufacture North America
1415 Slocum Street, Suite 102
Dallas, TX 75207
Tel.: 214-231-0144
Fax: 214-231-0145
fgasser@brm-manufacture.com
www.brm-manufacture.com

Carl F Bucherer
1805 South Metro Parkway
Dayton, OH 45459
Tel.: 800-395-4300
info@cfbnorthamerica.com
www.carl-f-bucherer.com

Bulgari Corporation of America
730 Fifth Avenue
New York, NY 10019
Tel.: 212-315-9700

Buti
DOMUSHora
1784 West Avenue Bay 3
Miami Beach, FL 33139
Tel.: 305-538-9300
Fax: 305-534-1952
info@domushora.com
www.tbbuti.it

Cartier Inc.
Fifth Avenue and 52nd Street
New York, NY 10022
Tel.: 1-800-CARTIER
Fax: 212-753-7250
www.cartier.com

Cellini Jewelers
509 Madison Avenue at 53rd Street
New York, NY 10022
Tel.: 1-800-CELLINI
www.CelliniJewelers.com

Addresses

Chase-Durer
9601 Wilshire Boulevard, Suite 1118
Beverly Hills, CA 90210
Tel.: 310-550-7280
Fax: 310-550-0830
www.chase-durer.com

Chopard
630 Fifth Avenue
Suite 3410
New York, NY 10111
Tel.: 1-800-CHOPARD
Fax: 212-397-0197
www.chopard.com

Chronoswiss
Bellport Time Group, LLC
112 South Country Road, Suite 101
Bellport, NY 11713
Tel.: 631-776-1135
Fax: 631-776-1136
www.chronoswiss.com

Frédérique Constant
Bellport Time Group, LLC
112 South Country Road, Suite 101
Bellport, NY 11713
Tel.: 631-776-1135
Fax: 631-776-1136
www.frederique-constant.com

Corum USA, LLC
3 Mason
Irvine, CA 92618
Tel.: 949-458-4200
Fax: 949-458-1258
www.corum.ch

Cuervo y Sobrinos
CyS Distributing, LLC
220 Congress Park Drive, Suite 100
Delray Beach, FL 33445
Tel.: 561-330-0088
Fax: 561-283-7869
www.cuervoysobrinos.com

Cvstos
Montres Franck Muller USA, Inc.
207 W. 25th Street, 8th Floor
New York, NY 10001
Tel.: 212-463-8898
Fax: 212-463-7082
www.cvstos.com

Cyclos International LLC
1350 Old Skokie Road
Highland Park, IL 60035
Tel.: 847-400-5010
Fax: 847-400-5011
www.cyclos-watch.ch

De Bethune America
580 Fifth Avenue LL0103
New York, NY 10019
Tel.: 212-729-7152
america@debethune.ch
www.debethune.ch

De Grisogono, Inc.
824 Madison Avenue, 3rd Floor
New York, NY 10021
Tel.: 1-866-DEGRISO
www.degrisogono.com

Pierre deRoche
6602 Wolf Creek Pass
Austin, TX 78749
Tel.: 512-499-0123
Fax: 512-499-8112
info@time-central.com
www.pierrederoche.com

DeWitt
Wings of Time
4330 N.E. 2nd Avenue
Miami Beach, FL 33137
Tel.: 305-572-9802
Fax: 305-572-9810
www.dewitt.ch

Dornblüth
WatchBuys
Tel.: 888-333-4895
info@watchbuys.com
www.watchbuys.com

Doxa Watches USA
5847 San Felipe, 17th Floor
Houston, TX 77057
Tel.: 877-255-5017
Fax: 866-230-2922
www.doxawatches.com

Du Bois & Fils
6602 Wolf Creek Pass
Austin, TX 78749
Tel.: 512-499-0123
Fax: 512-499-8112
info@time-central.com
www.dubois.de

Dubey & Schaldenbrand
PK Time Group LLC
30 West 57th Street, 2nd Floor
New York, NY 10019
Tel.: 888-919-TIME
Fax: 212-397-0960
info@pktime.com
www.pktime.com

Roger Dubuis
2, rue André de Garrini
1217 Meyrin-Geneva, Switzerland
Tel.: 011-41-22-783 28 28
Fax: 011-41-22-783 28 82
info@rogerdubuis.com
www.rogerdubuis.com

Ebel U.S.A. Inc.
750 Lexington Avenue
New York, NY 10022
Tel.: 212-888-3235
Fax: 212-888-6719
www.ebel.ch

Eberhard & Co.
DOMUSHora
1784 West Avenue Bay 3
Miami Beach, FL 33139
Tel.: 305-538-9300
Fax: 305-534-1952
info@domushora.com
www.eberhard-co-watches.ch

Edox
Swiss Watch International
101 South State Road 7, Suite 201
Hollywood, FL 33023
Tel: 866-SHOP-SWI
Fax: 954-985-1828
www.theswigroup.com

Epos
GNT Incorporated
P.O. Box 6724
Providence, RI 02940
Tel.: 1-800-689-2225
www.gntwatches.com

Louis Erard
Wolf Designs
22761 Pacific Coast Highway, Suite 107
Malibu, CA 90265
Tel.: 310-456-7072
Fax: 310-456-8393
www.louiserard.ch

Jacques Etoile
WatchBuys
Tel.: 888-333-4895
info@watchbuys.com
www.watchbuys.com

Fabergé
17764 Preston Road # 250
Dallas, TX 75252
Tel.: 877-863-2234
Fax: 972-713-9928
victor.mayer@faberge.de
www.faberge-jewelry.com

Ferrari: Engineered by Panerai
645 Fifth Avenue
New York, NY 10022
Tel.: 1-877-PANERAI
Fax: 212-891-2315
www.panerai.com

Fortis
LWR Time Ltd.
15 South Franklin Street, Suite 214
Wilkes-Barre, PA 18711
Tel.: 570-408-1640
Fax: 570-408-1657
www.fortis-watch.com

Gérald Genta
730 Fifth Avenue
New York, NY 10019
Tel.: 1-866-DRandGG

Addresses

Girard-Perregaux
Tradema of America, Inc.
201 Route 17 North
Rutherford, NJ 07070
Tel.: 1-877-846-3447
Fax: 201-507-1553
gpwebmaster@girard-perregaux-usa.com
www.girard-perregaux-usa.com

Glashütte Original
The Swatch Group (U.S.), Inc.
1200 Harbor Boulevard
Weehawken, NJ 07087
Tel.: 201-271-1400
Fax: 201-271-4633
www.glashuette-original.com

Glycine, LLC
444 Madison Avenue, Suite 601
New York, NY 10022
Tel.: 212-688-4500
Fax: 212-888-5025
www.glycine-watch.ch

Graham
British Masters, LLC
444 Madison Avenue, Suite 601
New York, NY 10022
Tel.: 212-688-4500
Fax: 212-888-5025
www.thebritishmasters.biz

Greubel Forsey
9595 Wilshire Boulevard, Suite 511
Beverly Hills, CA 90212
Tel.: 310-205-5555
Fax: 310-279-1000
www.greubelforsey.com

Hamilton
The Swatch Group (U.S.), Inc.
1200 Harbor Boulevard
Weehawken, NJ 07087
Tel.: 201-271-1400
Fax: 201-271-4633
www.hamilton-watch.com

Hanhart
Eric Armin, Inc.
Fine Watch Division
118 Bauer Drive, P.O. Box 7046
Oakland, NJ 07436-7046
Tel.: 800-272-0272
www.hanhartusa.com

Hautlence
9595 Wilshire Boulevard, Suite 511
Beverly Hills, CA 90212
Tel.: 310-205-5555
Fax: 310-279-1000
www.hautlence.com

HD3
9595 Wilshire Boulevard, Suite 511
Beverly Hills, CA 90212
Tel.: 310-205-5555
Fax: 310-279-1000
www.HD3complication.com

Hermès of Paris, Inc.
55 East 59th Street
New York, NY 10022
Tel.: 800-441-4488
Fax: 212-835-6460
www.hermes.com

Hublot of America, Inc.
The International Bldg, ST-4
2451 East Sunrise Blvd
Fort Lauderdale, FL 33304
Tel.: 800-536-0636
Fax: 954-568-6337
www.hublot.ch

IWC North America
645 Fifth Avenue, 6th Floor
New York, NY 10022
Tel.: 1-800-432-9330
Fax: 212-872-1312
www.iwc.ch

Jacob & Co. Watches
48 East 57th Street
New York, NY 10022
Tel.: 212-888-2330
Fax: 212-719-0074
contact@jacobandco.com
www.jacobandco.com

Jaeger-LeCoultre
645 Fifth Avenue
New York, NY 10022
Tel.: 800-JLC-TIME
www.jaeger-lecoultre.com

Montres Jaquet Droz SA
Rue Jaquet Droz 5
2300 La Chaux-de-Fonds, Switzerland
Tel.: 011-41-32-911 28 88
Fax: 011-41-32-911 28 85
jd@jaquet-droz.com
www.jaquet-droz.com

JeanRichard
Tradema of America, Inc.
201 Route 17 North, 8th Floor
Rutherford, NJ 07070
Tel.: 1-877-357-8463
Fax: 201-507-1553
webmaster@djr-usa.com
www.djr-usa.com

Michel Jordi
9595 Wilshire Boulevard, Suite 511
Beverly Hills, CA 90212
Tel.: 310-205-5555
Fax: 310-279-1000
www.micheljordi.com

F.P. Journe – Invenit et Fecit
Wings of Time
4330 N.E. 2nd Avenue
Miami Beach, FL 33137
Tel: 305-572-9802
Fax: 305-572-9810
www.fpjourne.com

Kiber
Détente Distribution Group
48 Main Street, 2nd Floor
Colchester, CT 06415
Tel.: 1-877-4VOSTOK
info@detentewatches.com
www.detentewatches.com

Kobold Watch Co.
1801 Parkway View Drive
Pittsburgh, PA 15205
Tel.: 1-877-SOARWAY
Fax: 412-788-2885
info@koboldwatch.com
www.koboldwatch.com

Pierre Kunz
Montres Franck Muller USA, Inc.
207 W. 25th Street, 8th Floor
New York, NY 10001
Tel.: 212-463-8898
Fax: 212-463-7082
www.pierrekunz.com

Maurice Lacroix USA
401 Hackensack Avenue
Hackensack, NJ 07601
Tel.: 1-800-794-7736
www.mauricelacroix.com

Lang & Heyne Uhren
Plattleite 35
01324 Dresden, Germany
Tel.: 011-49-351-810 73 32
Fax: 011-49-351-802 34 41
manufaktur@langundheyne.de
www.langundheyne.de

Lange Uhren GmbH
Altenberger Str. 15
01768 Glashütte, Germany
Tel.: 011-49-35053-44 0
Fax: 011-49-35053-44 100
info@lange-soehne.com
www.lange-soehne.com

Jacques Lemans
Swiss Watch International
101 South State Road 7, Suite 201
Hollywood, FL 33023
Tel: 866-SHOP-SWI
Fax: 954-985-1828
www.theswigroup.com

Limes
WatchBuys
Tel.: 888-333-4895
info@watchbuys.com
www.watchbuys.com

Longines
The Swatch Group (U.S.), Inc.
1200 Harbor Boulevard
Weehawken, NJ 07087
Tel.: 201-271-1400
Fax: 201-271-4633
www.longines.com

Addresses

Giuliano Mazzuoli
Fifth Avenue Luxury Group
306 West Somerdale Road
Vorhees, NJ 08043
Tel.: 800-988-3254
Fax: 859-673-5979

MB&F Max Büsser & Friends
9595 Wilshire Boulevard, Suite 511
Beverly Hills, CA 90212
Tel.: 310-205-5555
Fax: 310-279-1000
www.mbandf.com

MeisterSinger
WatchBuys
Tel.: 888-333-4895
info@watchbuys.com
www.watchbuys.com

Richard Mille
9595 Wilshire Boulevard, Suite 511
Beverly Hills, CA 90212
Tel.: 310-205-5555
Fax: 310-279-1000
www.richardmilleusa.com

MILUS USA, Inc.
342 North Rodeo Drive, Suite 202
Beverly Hills, CA. 90210
Tel.: 866-726-4587
Fax: 310-424-5526
info.usa@milus.com

Montblanc International
26 Main Street
Chatham, NJ 07928
Tel.: 908-508-2301
www.montblanc.com

H. Moser & Cie.
CyS Distributing, LLC
220 Congress Park Drive, Suite 100
Delray Beach, FL 33445
Tel.: 561-330-0088
Fax: 561-283-7869
www.h-moser.com

Mühle
Zeitwinkel GmbH
Am Wäldchen 29
66424 Homburg, Germany
Tel.: 011-49-6841-75 92 11
Fax.: 011-49-6841-792 07
peter.nikolaus@zeitwinkel.de
www.mühle-glashütte.de

Montres Franck Muller USA, Inc.
207 W. 25th Street, 8th Floor
New York, NY 10001
Tel.: 212-463-8898
Fax: 212-463-7082
www.franckmullerusa.com

Ulysse Nardin Inc.
2101 NW Corporate Boulevard, Suite 101
Boca Raton, FL 33431
Tel.: 561-988-6400
Fax: 561-988-0123
usa@ulysse-nardin.com
www.ulysse-nardin.com

Rainer Nienaber
Bahnhofstr. 33a
32257 Bünde, Germany
Tel.: 011-49-5223-122 92
Fax: 011-49-5223-57 47 97
www.nienaber-uhren.de

Nivrel
WatchBuys
Tel.: 888-333-4895
www.watchbuys.com
Right Time International Watch Center
Tel.: 888-846-3388
www.RightTime.com

Nomos USA
AMEICO
1 Church Street
New Milford, CT 06776
Tel.: 860-354-8765
Fax: 860-354-8620
info@ameico.com
www.glashuette.com

Omega
The Swatch Group (U.S.), Inc.
1200 Harbor Boulevard
Weehawken, NJ 07087
Tel.: 201-271-1400
Fax: 201-271-4633
www.omegawatches.com

Orbita Corporation
1205 Culbreth Drive
Wilmington, NC 28405
Tel.: 910-256-5300
Fax: 910-256-5356
info@orbita.net
www.orbita.net

Oris USA, Inc.
2 Skyline Drive
Hawthorne, NY 10532
Tel.: 914-347-6747
Fax: 914-347-4782
sales@orisusa.com
www.oris-watch.com

Panerai
645 Fifth Avenue
New York, NY 10022
Tel.: 1-877-PANERAI
Fax: 212-891-2315
www.panerai.com

Parmigiani Fleurier USA
33552 Valle Road
San Juan Capistrano, CA 92675
Tel.: 949-489-2885
Fax: 949-488-0116
www.parmigiani.ch

Patek Philippe
1 Rockefeller Plaza, #930
New York, NY 10020
Tel.: 212-581-0870
Fax: 212-956-6399
info@patek.com
www.patek.com

Perrelet
H5 Groupe
10 East 53rd Street, 31st Floor
New York, NY 10022
Tel.: 888-596-9483
info@perreletusa.com
www.perrelet.com

Piaget
663 Fifth Avenue, 7th Floor
New York, NY 10022
Tel.: 212-355-6444
Fax: 212-909-4332
www.piaget.com

Paul Picot
International Time Group
7700 Congress Avenue, Suite 1115
Boca Raton, FL 33487
Tel.: 561-241-3509
Fax: 561-241-3574
www.paulpicot.ch

Poljot International
Greenwich Distribution Ltd
8306 Mills Drive No. 222
Miami, FL 33183-4838
Tel.: 815-572-8890
Fax: 815-550-8908
as@greenwichdistribution.com
www.greenwichdistribution.com

Porsche Design
540 Madison Avenue, 34th Floor
New York, NY 10022
Tel.: 212 904-0408
Fax: 212 904-0409
www.porsche-design.com

Thomas Prescher Uhren GmbH
Im Moos 6
2513 Twann, Switzerland
Tel.: 011-41-32-315 28 66
Fax: 011-41-32-315 28 11
www.prescher.ch

Rado
The Swatch Group (U.S.), Inc.
1200 Harbor Boulevard
Weehawken, NJ 07087
Tel.: 201-271-1400
Fax: 201-271-4633
www.rado.com

RGM Watch Company
801 West Main Street
Mount Joy, PA 17552
Tel.: 717-653-9799
Fax: 717-653-9770
rgmwatches@aol.com

Rodolphe
Montres Franck Muller USA, Inc.
207 W. 25th Street, 8th Floor
New York, NY 10001
Tel.: 212-463-8898
Fax: 212-463-7082
www.rodolphe.ch